AMERICAN
POLITICS

Policies, Power, and Change

AMERICAN POLITICS

Policies, Power, and Change

KENNETH M. DOLBEARE
University of Washington

MURRAY J. EDELMAN
University of Wisconsin

D. C. HEATH AND COMPANY
Lexington, Massachusetts

Photographs by Sue Walker.

Copyright © 1971 by D.C. Heath and Company.

Published simultaneously in Canada.

Printed in the United States of America.

Library of Congress Catalog Card Number: 72-135426

Preface

This book is a different kind of text. No doubt every author believes this about his book; otherwise it would be impossible to sustain himself amidst the drudgery involved in writing it. But we have little doubt that our colleagues will concur that this book *is* different, even if they disagree with its conceptual framework and its conclusions. For one thing, it is not an encyclopedia of facts nor a comprehensive survey of the last ten years of political science research. It is grounded in such material, but it has a central theme: power in the United States is concentrated in such a way that large numbers of people have relatively little concrete effect on public policies.

We first undertake to describe what public policies have been enacted in four major areas, and then to explain how and why such decisions are made in the economic, social and institutional context of American politics. This approach aims at revealing who benefits, where power is located, and how change can and does come about in the political process. Our principal purpose is to help citizens acquire the skills of analysis and evaluation that will enable them to make themselves felt in the political system, and not incidentally to show them that the concepts and techniques of political science are relevant to such goals.

There is probably more economics and political sociology in this book than in most others which are available for the introductory college course. There is certainly more emphasis on contemporary value conflict, on the sources and character of contemporary political ideologies, and on the meaning of various ideas and processes for the prospect of political change. Not least, there is more of the authors' own perspectives and value judgments than in most beginning books. We expect citizens to disagree with us, and we are confident that they will be capable of selecting and rejecting from among the judgments that we express.

We welcome comments from teachers and students. We have had much advice from both in the process of preparing the book, and it has been invaluable. Each should be confident of our close attention to any comments offered in the future.

K.M.D.
M.J.E.

Contents

I. INTRODUCTION 1

1. Politics: An Introduction 5
2. Contrasting Images of Power and Purpose in the 1970's 22
3. A Framework for Analysis and Evaluation 51

II. PUBLIC POLICIES 77

4. National Security through Military Superiority 81
5. Poverty and Racism 111
6. Economic Growth and Stability 145
7. U.S. Foreign Policy and the Third World 169

III. INSTITUTIONS AND PROCESSES 201

8. Elites and Masses: Who Governs? 205
9. The Constitution: Structure, Symbol, and
   Resultant Political Style 242
10. Power and Decisionmaking in National Institutions 267
11. Relationships Between "Public" and "Private"
    Centers of Power 298
12. Linkage: Elites and Masses 321
13. Nonelites: Political Context and Basic Attitudes 352
14. Political Participation by Nonelites 376
15. The Impact of Nonelites on Public Policy 401

IV. POLITICAL CHANGE IN THE UNITED STATES 427

16. Patterns of Power 431
17. Political Change 454

APPENDIXES 477

The Declaration of Independence 477
The Constitution 480
Bibliography 492

INDEX 501

INTRODUCTION I

As the two hundredth anniversary of American independence approaches, the United States is rent by the most serious value conflicts in four decades, perhaps since the Civil War. Nearly all the combatants identify themselves with the principles of the Declaration of Independence, some preparing widespread repression in the name of liberty and others insisting upon the citizen's right of revolution. In this Part, we shall briefly note the wide differences in political perceptions and values that separate Americans today. Rigorous analysis begins, however, with a clear sense of purpose, inclusive definitions, and carefully designed approaches. Thus, we shall also map out a strategy for understanding American politics today.

Politics: 1
An Introduction

The American economic, social, and political systems are currently undergoing great — in some ways unprecedented — pressures. Technological changes, world upheavals, and deep internal social problems (to cite only the foremost examples) are placing drastic and perhaps unanswerable demands upon our eighteenth-century political ideas and machinery. Substantial transformation of these systems seems inevitable.

But the character and direction of current change are not yet clear. Neither revolution nor the emergence of a full-fledged police state is beyond possibility, though there are many, and more likely, possibilities between these two extremes. For example, change may take the form of new policies which increase the social and economic status of lower class whites and blacks. Progress of this kind may be rapid or slow, sustained or erratic, far-reaching or narrow. It may or may not be accompanied by broader sharing of political power at home and new standards in formulating policies toward other nations. Or change may go in the opposite direction toward more rigid and forceful defense of established values and practices. In this case, repression may escalate according to the number and character of clashes generated by continued insistence upon the political status quo in spite of vast changes occurring in other spheres of life.

What does seem clear after the cauldron of the 1960's is that much of the conventional wisdom about American politics is no longer true. Traditional and still dominant assumptions about a harmonious society and a democratic political process in which all citizens are able to secure their legitimate goals are no longer accepted by some groups of Americans. No amount of self-congratulatory rhetoric upon the two hundredth anniversary of the Declaration of Independence can lull some citizens into ceasing their efforts to make a living reality of the rights and goals so eloquently expressed in that document. Nor will it cause others to lessen their resistance to the progress of the "have-nots."

In short, despite patriotic rhetoric and appeals to unity, concrete issues and problems make the United States a deeply divided, conflict-ridden society. Crucial choices having the most fundamental consequences for both the immediate and long-range future must be made in the next several years. Individual citizens will influence the nature of these choices in a wide variety of ways, from undertaking violent revolution to voting in elections to deliberately withdrawing from all contact with public affairs.

The question is not *whether* they will influence these choices, but *in what manner* and *in what direction* they will do so. Those who seek revolution may succeed only in politicizing vast majorities against themselves; or aided by inept government actions and excessive countermeasures, they may build a successful movement. Those who practice the conventional politics may produce, or more accurately endorse, any number of consequences according to their preferences, power, numbers, skills, and the circumstances of the times. Those who seek to withdraw are not only choosing to become the passive objects of others' determinations but are also in effect casting their support to the status quo. If the myth that "you can't fight city hall" were not authored by the occupants of city halls around the nation, it has surely served very well to reduce opposition to their policies. The fact that to not oppose government action is to support it is implicit in the term "the silent majority."

Taking action of some kind in politics, even if it is only withdrawal and acquiescence in the decisions of others, implies that the citizen has a judgment about what should be done in public affairs. But not all judgments are equally sound. *Some* judgments are better than others because they are more firmly rooted in an accurate understanding of the present and a clear sense of the probable consequences of alternatives for the future. By asking the right questions about the distribution and usage of power in the United States, by employing evidence carefully, and by using the other skills and concepts of political analysis, the citizen can make sound judgments about whether his government should be improved, and if so, how. Our goal in this book is to place these skills and approaches at the service of the citizen. Ideally, he should emerge with a new capacity to analyze more critically, evaluate more soundly, and act more effectively in the political world to which he is subject.

In this chapter, we shall first take a closer look at some of the preliminary facts about politics to which we have already alluded in these opening paragraphs. Although these are truisms about politics which may be unnecessary in one sense, they nevertheless seem a valuable introduction to the fuller statement of our purposes and approach which follows in the subsequent section. Since our approach differs considerably from that in most American government textbooks, we have thought it necessary to be explicit about our perspectives and purposes at the outset, even at the risk of stating some very basic and probably obvious truths.

THE SCOPE AND CHARACTER OF POLITICS

Politics is natural and unavoidable. Its impact on every citizen ranges from the very trivial to the routine structuring of daily living to matters of literally life-or-death importance. It presents enduring, apparently insoluble dilemmas to which men must nevertheless seek to find answers; in the course of doing so, much may be learned about power, conflict, and cooperation — in short, about man himself. Let us consider each of these aspects of politics in turn.

The Natural and Unavoidable Nature of Politics

In order to live together on some continuing basis and to achieve their various goals in life, men seek and employ power in ways that affect the lives of their fellows. In other words, they engage in politics.[1] They erect governments to maintain order, further mutual goals, and promote general well-being. Around and through the framework of that government, they continue to seek their individual and group goals. People can no more live without politics in this sense than they can dispense with food, love, or other basic human needs and wants. Politics is the activity by which they seek their goals, maintain the kind of context which is conducive to pursuing those goals, or defend what they have already gained through their previous efforts. For many people, of course, politics serves all three purposes.

Those men who have more of the resources of power — such as wealth, prestige, strength, or oratorical talent — are better able to persuade or compel others to alter their intended patterns of behavior. Others, by combining their lesser resources, may influence or even reverse the decisions of the more powerful. In the broadest definition of the term, political activity occurs whenever a group of people bring their cumulative resources of power to bear, not only on government, but on any other individual or group whose behavior they desire to change. If tenants withhold the payment of rent in order to induce a landlord to make needed improvements on a

[1] For refinement and qualification of this definition, see p. 10 and Chapter 3.

building, they can, in a general sense, be considered as engaging in political activity.

But regardless of how little involved an individual may be in employing his own political resources to influence the actions of others, he cannot escape the *consequences* of political decisions in the modern society. If only as the consumer of the political products generated by the actions of others, everyone is involved. Thus, we are all in politics, whether we like it or not, inevitably and permanently.

The Scope and Importance of Politics

Because war has been a continuing fact of history, politics has always held life or death importance for at least some people. With the coming of nuclear weapons, politics has come to mean the same for practically everybody. But it is not only in relation to other countries that politics holds life or death significance. In domestic politics, the more powerful elements in a society prescribe behavior which is in their eyes consistent with the established order of things and fix punishments for those who break their rules. Further, thousands of men are hired and equipped with weapons to enforce such codes of behavior. For those willing to accept the rules and able to avoid conflict with them, the political preferences they reflect and the power applied to enforce them do not raise crucial issues. For those not satisfied with the status quo, however, the same rules may serve as an apparently unjust obstacle to desired change. But violation of the rules, or even talk of the justice of doing so, often brings swift retribution in the form of death, jail, or physical injury. Members of the Black Panther Party, for example, would not fail to recognize that domestic politics may well have life or death importance. Nor, on a lesser scale, would the participants in many of today's other radical movements.

Perhaps more important in the daily lives of most people, however, are the frequency and intimacy with which the consequences of politics affect them. A few examples should suffice. An individual's life chances are shaped by the quality and amount of education which governments have made available to him. The nature and even the fact of his income may depend on governmental policies. Political choices to spend more on military supplies mean employment for some, but reduced social services to many others. Fair employment laws frequently mean better chances for employment for blacks, but anti-inflation measures cause unemployment on the part of less skilled workers, including blacks, who are laid off as businesses seek to cut costs. Government reaches into the most intimate aspects of personal lives as well, through controls over the availability of birth control materials, supervision of what is shown on television, and prescription of what books and movies can be offered to the public. Some people are constantly seeking to use government to impose upon others their own views of what is moral or desirable personal conduct. Paradoxically, other areas of broader public concern, such as pollution of our natural environment, are left unregulated.

At every hour of his day, throughout practically every activity in which he engages, the individual is affected by the consequences of politics. Consider so prosaic an act as driving to a drugstore to buy a pack of cigarettes. The driver (licensed by the state) gets into his car (licensed and registered with the state; fitted with safety devices according to federal specifications; sold at prices reflecting manufacturers' success with federal antitrust laws, labor-management relations practices, and interstate commerce rate controls; and taxed by federal, state, and local governments.) He drives (according to local and state ordinances, and subject to local traffic officers) to the drugstore (where the state-licensed pharmacist is closely regulated as to the hours he may be open and the prescriptions he may sell to customers.) He buys (with federal government currency) the cigarettes (which have been the subject of extensive federal testing for danger to health, carry a required warning to users, and are taxed by both federal and state governments.) Mercifully, we shall terminate the account at this stage. But the point is that this relationship of the individual to politics *never* ends. And every instance of contact with politics implies that there has been a prior history of conflict and choices made by governments according to the preferences of those with the greatest amount of power at a particular time or over a particular issue. Thus, the individual exists in a world shaped by the many decisions of others, and not even the most determined effort to extract oneself from such effects can be successful.

The Dilemmas of Politics and the Insights They Provide

Politics is an endlessly changing human activity in which many of the same dilemmas continue to arise in different forms during different eras. Can a government be constructed so that it will have all necessary power to do the things that are *good*, but no power to do things that are *bad*? Can large numbers of people actually take part in politics and yet enjoy a government which does what is objectively the right thing in particular situations? How can people who are wealthy, powerful, or in positions of leadership be prevented from shaping government actions in their personal interest instead of in the public interest? When two valid principles are in conflict (as when the liberty of some limits the equality of others), which should take precedence? How should such questions of priority be decided within the society?

Centuries of experience have contributed to the recognition that these and other problems are enduring dilemmas to which different generations (indeed, different people within the same generation) offer different answers. We shall explore the various alternative solutions to such problems suggested by actors in the American political system today. And it is also important to note that the attempts to grapple with these questions force analysts to think more clearly and precisely about them. For example, in seeking to understand the phenomenon of power, we would quickly realize that familiar slogans are useless. What appears to be "bad" may be neither objectively good nor bad in itself, but merely neutral. And, conversely, what seems "neutral" may be nothing but a reflection of dominant preferences, and hence good, bad, or neutral depending on a variety of factors, including the perspective of the observer. "Absolute power corrupts absolutely" is about as true (and as false) as "absolute *lack* of power corrupts absolutely," and neither is useful as a guide to thought or action. Power is the capacity to influence the actions of others, and as such it is neutral; it may be used for good, or for evil, depending on the interests of the powerholder in relation to those people over whom he wields power. Once power has been exercised, of course, the resulting behavior reflects the preferences of those who induced it. This is why laws only rarely are truly neutral. In the ordinary course of events, they bear more heavily on some than on others for the obvious reason that the social context in which they are formulated is not one in which all men are equal or similarly situated. This is summarized aptly in the wry observation, "The law is the same for the rich man as for the poor man: each will be shot for stealing a loaf of bread." A law expressing group or class interests is not neutral, but rather it is a fit subject for evaluation as good or bad depending on its origin and nature and on the value preferences of the observer.

Even this brief discussion of some of the aspects of politics should indicate the need for a careful, systematic approach to the subject. Politics is of crucial importance to every citizen. It is worth taking some time at the outset of an investigation to be clear about the purposes involved and the methods to be used. We begin this effort in the next section.

POLITICS: PRELIMINARY DEFINITIONS AND PURPOSES

Politics is a process (a) in which power is employed to gain rewards, and (b) through which the interests of broad segments of the population are affected. We like the shorthand phrasing of a leading political scientist who characterized politics as "who gets what, when, and how." [2] This is a wide-ranging definition (which we shall have to refine shortly), for it takes us well outside of "government" or "the state" to a focus on the other holders of power in the society and the way they use it to achieve their goals and create effects on people.

Equally important to shaping our approach is a consideration of the purposes for which one undertakes the study of politics. We think that citizens must learn to think independently and critically about the political processes that shape their lives. This means not only analysis of the workings of the established political system, but explicit evaluation of its performance and understanding of the need for, and prospects of, various forms of change. In the remainder of

[2] Harold Lasswell, *Politics: Who Gets What, When, How* (New York: McGraw-Hill, 1936).

this section, we shall specify in a general way how these purposes may be served.

One may approach politics from two quite different perspectives: *analysis* and *evaluation*. As political scientists, we are primarily (though not exclusively) analysts. Our primary task will be to present evidence, within a conceptual framework, so as to build a comprehensive *description* of the activities of individuals, groups, corporations, and other powerholders as they seek to achieve their goals in the society. As far as possible, we shall ground our presentation on evidence, objectivity, logic, comprehensiveness, and other social science standards. Secondarily, however, we shall seek to raise crucial questions and focus on issues about the uses of power which we describe. Our purpose in this case will be to encourage evaluations and judgments on the part of the citizen. The question of whether an action is good or bad, right or wrong, is not one that can be answered exclusively by collecting facts and explaining who did what with what results. But nevertheless, it *must* be asked and answered. We shall help to frame the questions, assemble the components of answers, and consider their implications. We shall try to preserve the act of value judgment, however, for the citizen. Our task is to convey approaches and techniques which show *how* to think, not *what* to think.

But, although we shall try to avoid gratuitous interpretations and unsupported value judgments, it should be clear that our conclusions and preferences are involved in this presentation. Text authors cannot avoid projecting their own views into their work, for they must select conceptual frameworks, make choices about what to present and how, and employ only selected evidence. Inevitably, they are likely to structure readers' conclusions. The most encyclopedic and exclusively "factual" text fails to be neutral, for it either helps to perpetuate benevolent assumptions or discourages critical judgment entirely. Readers must be alert to our choices and selections, and they must challenge the basis of our concepts and interpretations — just as they would any other authors' work. Because one of our primary purposes is to aid in the development of readers' independent critical capacities, we have taken a broadly iconoclastic approach to American politics. We intend that our presentation be equally subject to skeptical challenge, particularly Part IV of this book, where we reach conclusions about the implications of the main body of analysis and speculate about the future.

(1) The Analytical Perspective: Politics as Power, Process, and Rewards

Men frequently have different, and often conflicting, values and goals. They usually seek their ends through and around institutions and processes ("government") which have been shaped by the values and goals which were dominant in the past. Some men are more powerful than others because they have more of the resources that induce or compel others to alter their behavior. Their chances for success in the political arena, where many participants seek varied goals in a context of changing circumstances, are considerably better than those of other men. Nor can "government," however neutral and mechanistic the term may sound, be an impartial arbiter. Government, after all, consists of men who are pushed and pulled by contending forces but who also have their own values and goals. Officeholders, moreover, are well situated to seek the ends they believe are right. Out of this unceasing and utterly natural process of human interaction — sometimes savage, frequently tragic, occasionally humorous or uplifting — emerge the public policies which structure our lives. And year after year, the increasing needs (and vulnerability) of our complex society mean that governmental policies structure our lives more and more closely.

How should analysts approach the problem of understanding this process? What are the central, organizing *questions* and *concepts* that will lead most directly and efficiently to understanding? Some suggestions are implicit in our shorthand definition of politics as who gets what, when, and how.

(a) The ultimate question for the analyst is, quite simply: Who rules? Who can say *whether* and *how* government shall be employed on any matter? Several subsidiary questions immediately follow: What difference does it make? What are the rulers' goals and priorities? Who benefits from their actions and in what ways? And finally, how did such patterns come about, and what sustains them now? Of course, these questions must be subdivided still further for purposes of investigation, but as framed here, they indicate one ultimate goal of our inquiry. If comprehensively answered, they would provide a thorough description of politics at any level. Finding the evidence on which to base such an answer, however, may be very difficult. Rulers may find it preferable or more efficient to remain unidentified, and thus they may assume a shadowy role behind a facade of prominent institutions and processes. Or there may be many "rulers" competing for control of various government actions with varying degrees of success at different times and under different circumstances. Perhaps there are *no* rulers, and politics and economics evolve through accumulated momentum and casual happenstance. Or perhaps "the people" are somehow manifested in the institutions of government and their wishes routinely and infallibly translated into law — as some democratic mythologists would have us believe.

(b) Faced with such a wide range of possibilities, the analyst must select two or three *concepts* which seem capable of imposing order and coherence upon a large body of elusive and potentially confusing evidence. As we have already intimated above, we see *power* as a useful basic concept when employed in conjunction with the two supplementary concepts of *resources* and *consequences*. By power, we mean the possession of political *resources* (such as money, fame, social position, time, or skills) sufficient to cause other political participants to conform their behavior to what they perceive the holder of the resources prefers. Again, there are problems of evidence in identifying those occasions where power was actually at work in influencing behavior, for it is difficult to distinguish between instances in which people were induced or compelled to act in a certain way and those in which they did so of their own volition. But this problem may be solved in large part by focusing on the *consequences* of government action or conscious inaction. We may fairly infer that repeated patterns of governmental distribution of the *rewards* of politics (tax benefits, contracts, subsidies, price supports, or freedom from regulation) or its *burdens* (tax obligations, prohibitions on political activity, or denial of services) are more likely to reflect the relative power of various political actors than to be the product of coincidence or deliberate generosity on the part of others. Thus, in seeking to answer the question of who rules, we shall look for *power* and its *consequences*.

One of the major resources of power, of course, is *legitimacy*. Legitimacy is a status conferred by people generally upon the institutions, acts, and officials of their government. When people believe that their government is the right one — that it works properly and for desirable ends — they place their trust in it and grant it obedience. Elected officials, bureaucrats, and law enforcement personnel all acquire some of this special status by virtue of their institutional positions in that government. This enables higher officials at least to exert considerable influence over what people believe, to draw support for their actions, and (under normal circumstances) to shape the agenda of politics so as to gain their ends more easily. But legitimacy is a fluid and intangible attribute. It can be diluted by frequent requests for uncritical support, by actions inconsistent with expectations or traditions, and by extreme misconduct. It may be withdrawn by some segment, or even most, of the people. Under such circumstances, voluntary compliance with the acts of government and normal cooperative routines may cease. If this occurs among large proportions of the population, men in government may have to fall back on outright coercion to achieve their ends. The shift to this form of power, of course, means that the political system is close to breakdown.

Our approach to political analysis thus stresses the question of who rules, how they rule, and what difference it makes to people and problems in the society. It does so through a focus on power, which is located by exploring the resources that contribute to it and tracing the consequences of government actions. With solid grounding in the realities of power and its usage, the citizen should be able to evaluate the performance of his political system effectively. The major strengths which we see in the definition of politics as "who gets what, when, and how" are the emphases this places on (a) the consequences of government activity (or deliberate inactivity), and (b) the role of power, its distribution and usage. It forces us to pay attention to behavior outside of government, because power comes in so many forms and is used in so many ways to influence first whether, and then how, government will be employed. Many of the really significant political decisions in the United States (i.e., most of the determinative uses of power shaping who rules, who benefits, and how such patterns are sustained) may be made outside of the formal institutions of government. If all we analyzed were intra-governmental activities, we might overlook most of our subject and thus surely reach erroneous conclusions. By focusing on recurring patterns of what government does and does not do, and who benefits thereby, and by then proceeding to an investigation of power and its usage, we should be led to a more comprehensive and revealing understanding of American politics.

(2) The Evaluative Perspective: Politics as a Set of Questions for Ethical Judgment

Explanation of how and why government policies have the form they do, and of what difference that form makes to people and problems in the society, is an interesting and important task. But it is only a preliminary for the citizen who wishes to be more than a helpless consumer of the products generated by the power and activity of others. The citizen must decide whether a particular policy is good or bad, whether the political system is working satisfactorily or not, and both whether and how to seek improvement in either policy or system. The citizen's needs may sound great, and perhaps they appear to exceed his capacity to absorb knowledge and reach responsible judgments.

But his problem can be rendered manageable. A variety of simplifying approaches opens the way to informed, decisive judgment and timely, effective action. The citizen need not try to duplicate the scholarly analyst; his requirements are met by solid evidence, and he need not necessarily await scientific comprehensiveness which is most often unattainable. The citizen can specialize in certain policy areas or problems that are crucial to him; he need not become informed about all the nuances of the political process. Further, he can eliminate much, often immobilizing, analytical effort by emphasizing his basic role — that of a consumer of the products of politics. By taking the actual performance of government in a particular area as a measuring standard, he can make judgments about how well a policy or the political system is working without undertaking a full-scale exploration of all the details of how the system operated to produce those results.

Finally, the citizen can derive maximum return from his investment in the study of politics by clarifying his approach to action within the political system and to evaluation of the outputs of that system. For example, the citizen should clarify for himself what *standards* are appropriate to his evaluation, and the implications of each. A standard which emphasizes maintaining established procedures or the traditional way of doing things, for example, is likely to lead to an essentially status quo judgment. So is a standard which emphasizes what is "practical" or "pragmatic" under the circumstances of today's power distribution. Today's procedures, of course, promote the interests and preferences of those who hold the balance of power now. What is "realistic" is what they can permit to take place without serious danger to their own predominance. In both cases, therefore, use of such standards inevitably directs judgments toward very incremental changes which have the effect of supporting the basic outlines of today's power distribution. On the other hand, standards which emphasize efficiency or economy in the solution of problems are likely to lead to severe judgments about the need for drastic change, in many cases at the cost of some important human values. Useful standards require explicit specification of the relative priorities to be accorded to each of several desired results. In the case of "equality" as a standard, it must be clear whether one means equality in the formal, legalistic sense or in terms of the actual social and economic conditions of individuals. In the case of "democracy," it must be clear whether one means merely participation and civil rights, or also the nature of the relationship between popular needs and desires and the product of government action. The tie between the standard of judgment employed, and its implication for who gets what, when, and how, is a very close one.

The citizen should also consider how change in political relationships comes about in the United States — both through and outside the established processes — and he must then make his commitments to action in the light of that understanding. A determination that a policy or a characteristic of the system is wrong and requires improvement, and a commitment to act toward that end, may still be totally unproductive (or even counter-productive) if the citizen has no idea of how to bring about his goals. Some efforts toward change may produce results (or unanticipated consequences) that are on balance worse than the unsatisfactory present situation. In short, evaluation is not complete without careful selection of routes toward change, and consequent maximization of the chances that policies based on the citizen's evaluation will be put into effect.

In seeking to provide the citizen with the tools necessary to analysis, evaluation, and effective action in politics, political scientists again must observe certain boundaries. Our strengths lie in data collection and interpretation, systematic linking of causes and effects, and comprehensive identification of crucial questions, alternatives, and implications about the distribution and usage of power. We can bring the citizen to the point of judgment, but we are obligated to leave him truly free to apply his own values en route to a conclusion. The citizen, of course, has no restraints. He will ultimately range from analyst to judge to actor in his own right. At first, we expect, he will profit from our demonstration of the tools of analysis and our suggestions about the elements to be considered in the process of evaluation. As he acquires the skills of analysis and critical evaluation, however, he should become more and more independent. This is the division of labor that will be assumed in the chapters that follow. But before we go further, let us explicitly take up some of the major barriers to clear thinking about politics.

PROBLEMS OF OBJECTIVITY AND ACCURACY

It is time to become more rigorous about how one seeks to achieve an understanding of a subject like politics, so embedded in emotions, patriotic loyalties, threats, and symbolic diversions. How can we assure ourselves that the understanding we acquire consists of valid interpretations, and not merely uncritical projections of our assumptions, hopes, or fears about American politics? We shall consider some of the technical problems of data collection and interpretation as they arise in later chapters. The more serious problems of nonobjectivity and misinterpretations, however, are conceptual in character. Let us try to identify some of them now, in hope that we may reduce or avoid their effects throughout our analysis.

(1) Culture-Bound or Ideological Premises and Assumptions

The primary cause of nonobjectivity is the set of values, assumptions, and myths about how our government works and should work ("ideology") which we all have acquired in our early years. We learn in school and through patriotic literature to have strong emotional attachments for the United States, its policies and processes, and to see government in this country in particular ways. In part this "socialization"[3] provides accurate enough cues as to what government is and how it reflects public interests. Much of it, however, consists of lore and myth which can be misleading. Political education — or "socialization" — has goals other than objective analysis and understanding: it is intended to build loyal citizens, to instill patriotism, and to encourage people to comply with the main directions of established policy. At the most impressionable ages, therefore, children are likely to learn, both from direct teaching and from more subtle cues, a simplistic and distorted model of government and policymaking. They learn, for example, that elections give people the leaders and policies they want. No attention is paid to the many necessary qualifications of that assertion, and no hint is given that what people get, and even what they want, may be decided largely by political leaders and the actions they take.

We are all more or less captives of our culture and the products of years of inculcation in its values and assumptions about what is right and good. What is, is right. And what exists in the United States is necessary, desirable, or at least the best that is practical under all the circumstances. These beginning (and often subconscious) premises, to say nothing of the social or official pressures to adhere to them, or the economic self-interest we may have in endorsing the status quo, cause even sophisticated observers to introduce approving evaluations into their supposedly objective "descriptions." Everyone who would be an objective analyst must go through a process of wrenching himself loose from such premises, assump-

---

[3] Political socialization is the process through which individuals learn the accepted attitudes and beliefs about politics and political institutions. It occurs not only through formal education but through informal communication and interaction with others, especially one's own family.

tions, and conceptual blinders. The process is a lengthy and difficult one, for ideology reaches deep into the culture — into stereotypes (or "pictures in the mind" about the world), symbols, even into the language that we use. Benevolent images are conjured up in most of us by such words as "Constitution," "free enterprise," "the rule of law," "free speech," and the use of such terms to describe what exists may lead us to believe that reality fits into such "good" patterns. Sometimes reality may indeed be as the words implicitly declare, but reality is not controlled by the words or assumptions which are used to describe it. Reality has its own independent set of characteristics and causes, and it may be the opposite of what the familiar words urge us to believe. If that reality happens to serve the interests of a political actor, however, he may describe it with the familiar words which induce automatic approval. To him, reality may appear to fit those terms; he need not be deliberately seeking to deceive us. But in objective terms, reality might be quite distinct from the usual meanings of the words. If we are diverted from objective perception by such symbols, stereotypes, and loaded words, we may never come to know reality as it is.

How can we avoid or reduce the effects of ideology in our analyses? Becoming alert to its pervasive influence is a sound start. We can ask ourselves whether the descriptive words we use have been carefully defined, so that their use is not merely another way of saying that something is good or bad. We can try to avoid making any advance assumptions about what our evidence will show and design evidence collection broadly so that all possible sets of facts and interpretations would be included within our reach. We can purge ourselves of culture-bound definitions and assumptions by asking whether our use of a term is applicable only to the United States, or whether it is conceptually neutral enough to be applicable generally. Other important ways of avoiding the biases of ideology are an emphasis upon demonstrable facts and actual behavior rather than formal powers and rules of procedure, avoidance of an exclusive focus on the words and acts of leaders, and deliberate expansion of the frame of reference in which interpretation occurs. Each of these routes toward objectivity deserves further discussion.

(2) The Nature of Evidence

What do we need to know in order to say that a political institution or process works in a particular way? We cannot accept assumptions or speculations, exhortations about how they *should* work, or the self-serving assurances of their sponsors about how they operate. No matter how hallowed and revered the authority which prescribes or declares how things work, we cannot accept such characterizations as truth. Instead, we must demand precise specification of who actually did what, when, and with what effects. Facts about actual behavior must be the building blocks of our analyses. Indeed, there may be occasions when we shall appear neurotically fixed upon statistics or other tabular presentation of data. But the vital principles of objectivity and accuracy can only be served in this way.

We *must* be able to say with confidence that thus-and-so is the way the Congress works, or that voters respond to factors X, Y, and Z in deciding which candidates to support. To be able to do so, we must have enough facts and data on hand for a comprehensive characterization — one which leaves no gaps to be filled by ideology-affected assumptions.

When we have achieved exhaustive and accurate description, we are ready to attempt explanation: *why* do men do what they do in politics? Again, we rest primarily on factual evidence — on cause and effect relationships which are demonstrable to us or at least strongly inferable from the evidence — rather than on what men offer as explanations or what other sources declare *should be* their basis for action. In seeking explanation for empirically identified patterns of behavior, analysis must be aided by theory. In this sense, theory means hypotheses (informed guesses about causes, which can be tested against available evidence) reflecting experience and sophistication about politics. In order to arrive at hypotheses, we must employ our sense of the wide range of possible causes, the many forces at work within a context, and the structure of power relationships in the area.

It is tempting, once one adapts to exclusively data-based analysis, to assume that the gathering of empirical data is all that is important and that we can accurately come to know and understand politics and the political process simply by building up larger amounts of more concrete and rigorous data. The fact is, however, that observation or experiment that is not based upon a body of theory is not only useless, but also likely to be quite misleading. For example, we can observe, read, and count many volumes of rules and regulations issued by the Interstate Commerce Commission to govern the behavior of American railroads. The obvious conclusion to be drawn from this kind of empirical observation is that the ICC regulates the rates and conduct of railroad carriers in minute detail to protect passengers and shippers, and a simple listing or counting of the regulations implies that conclusion and seems to verify it persuasively. The social scientist who knows something about the social psychology of governmental regulation will want to ask and answer some other questions, however, the answers to which might suggest the opposite conclusion from the simple one that first seemed obvious. He will want to ask to what degree the ICC regulations reflect the interests of the railroad carriers rather than those of the railroad users, and what their results are. He will want to ask how the ambiguous or unclear regulations are applied in concrete cases and whose interests these particular applications serve. Theory generates questions of this type that might otherwise not occur to the researcher; and the questions in turn generate new forms of empirical observations which often give quite new or modified meanings to early observations.

(3) The Focus of Analysis

We must look comprehensively at the acts of all (or at least most) of the powerholders who are active in any given area, and not direct our analyses exclusively at either the acts or words of leaders or the official decisions, laws, or regulations of organs of government. The easiest way to observe and analyze politics is to look at the public acts and words of political leaders on the assumption that they make the key decisions and set the goals their followers accept. The political leader acts in public. One of his chief functions is to make a strong and widespread impression. Because he has a stake in being dramatic, he makes good copy for journalists; and journalistic accounts of politics consist very largely of descriptions of the statements, actions, and interactions of political leaders.

Only a little observation and analysis makes it clear, however, that such absorption in the performances of leaders yields a highly superficial and misleading picture of the political process. It fails, for one thing, to tell us why officials' instructions are often ignored or sabotaged. After serving in the most powerful political office in the world, former President Harry Truman observed that the President often says he wants this or that done and then finds that nothing happens. Other political leaders similarly learn that the range of their discretion is rather narrowly limited by what other powerholders and their potential followers will accept. Limiting of political observation to leadership also fails to tell us by what processes particular aspirants are chosen for high posts and for what reasons they sometimes lose their followings. Modern leadership theory, as we will learn in more detail later, places a heavy emphasis upon the interests of potential followers and upon their willingness to be moved in particular directions.

The political analyst who confines his attention to leaders is likely to be led astray at every turn. If there is a riot, he assumes that ringleaders or outside agitators must have "caused" it. The social scientist looks deeper: at the social, economic, and political conditions that explain the willingness of rioters to engage in violence, to follow leaders who advocate it, and to ignore potential leaders who counsel patience or peaceful courses of action.

Another pitfall political analysts should try to avoid is the assumption that everything important in politics and policy formation takes place in the formal institutions and organs of government. A high proportion of the decisions about resource allocations take place through economic and social transactions that are outside the corridors of government buildings and the formal governmental structure, though their outcomes are closely tied to people's assumptions about how great the political power of the actors is. Even the actions that can be observed taking place inside governmental institutions often convey a very superficial or misleading notion of what is going on. For example, for many years the unemployment compensation laws passed by the Illinois legislature have been compromises which were bargained collectively by the labor and management organizations of the state through private meetings and then rubber stamped by the legislature.[4] This procedure is only one clear example of the very

---

[4] *Cf.* Gilbert Y. Steiner, *Legislation by Collective Bargaining* (Institution of Labor and Industrial Relations, 1951).

common occurrence that laws made in legislative bodies reflect bargains agreed to by interested parties outside its halls. Similarly, the formal actions of administrative agencies of government can often be understood only if the interests and tactics of groups affected by their rulings are carefully examined.

Still another reason formal governmental acts can be misleading is that they are frequently not put into practice. Almost twenty years after the United States Supreme Court had declared segregation by color in public schools unconstitutional, racial segregation still existed in a very high proportion of American school classrooms. What goes on in courts, legislatures, bureaus, and United Nations meetings certainly has to be observed; but merely observing it usually tells little about its meaning. To understand the significance of formal governmental actions, the political analyst has to observe many other activities as well. And he has to have in mind a theoretical framework that tells him how the activities he observes are related to each other.

(4) The Frame of Reference of Analysis

A final barrier in the way of objective and accurate analysis is that of the breadth of the frame of reference within which, or the level at which, the analysis is conducted. Every effort at research and analysis must accept some premises or givens about the world from which to begin. But the act of making such beginning assumptions (an act which is frequently unconscious) may sharply confine the kinds of conclusions which can be reached. For example, if we assume the validity (or perpetuity) of existing American values, *and* if we assume that the present structure of power in government is fixed, then the only object upon which we would focus analysis or evaluation would be the specific details of the policies and the way in which they related to the problems involved. This could be a relatively superficial analysis, because it might not reach to the real causes of the character of the policy, or to the roots of the problem. When applied to the Vietnam War, for example, such an approach might conclude that its failure was due merely to some tactical mistakes or errors of judgment on the part of particular policymakers. The whole matter could thus be rectified by replacing those men with better informed individuals.

But perhaps a more deep-probing analysis would suggest that more fundamental causes were involved. Analysis might go one step beyond *policies* to look at the *political system* itself: perhaps the relative freedom of the President to commit the country, or the over-reliance on military assurance of capability, or the impotence of the Congress in foreign policy, or the influence of economic interests with investments in the Third World nations are more significant causes of the Vietnam situation. None of these, of course, would have been reached by an analysis which was limited in its scope to policy alone. Or analysis could go further still and look at the *underlying values* which give rise to both the political system *and* the policy. Using the same example, perhaps causal origins of the Vietnam War lie in fears of communism, cultural or racial arrogance, or the needs of the American economic system. The point is that exploration of such possibilities would have been unlikely unless the analyst's frame of reference extended below the policies to the political system and then to the underlying values which sustain both. Only then, with such a deliberately broadened and deepened frame, could he be sure of including all possible sources of explanation and of avoiding building in ideological endorsement for whatever he found to exist. In some cases, clearly, causes of problems lie at the more fundamental levels, and failure to realize this may result in omitting from analysis the very characteristics or values which gave rise to the problem in the first place. A wide frame of reference which probes all three levels of analysis must be part of our approach.

2 Contrasting Images of Power and Purpose in the 1970's

Not long ago, challenges to the complacent image of the United States as an affluent society with freedom and justice for all were readily dismissed or ignored. In the 1970's, however, they have become the principal dynamic of political life. The roots of current conflicts lie deep in our evolving cultural heritage, economic order, social class structure, and the present patterns of burdens and benefits within the society which result. Closer to the surface, specific technological and environmental problems and particular government policies (such as the Vietnam War) help to focus these conflicts sharply. As a consequence, and for the first time in decades, millions of Americans have come to openly deny the legitimacy of the economic, social, and political structures of their country.

In very gross terms, the new dynamic of American politics pits those who see the United States as a responsive, democratic political system (perhaps with a few minor failures) against those who view it as an inflexible oligarchy whose policies bring unnecessary deprivation to much of the world and many of its own citizens. The orthodox (and dominant) view holds that affluence, freedom, and justice are, for practical purposes, facts. Although acknowledging room for improvement, it maintains that progress is steadily being made — and that the legitimate interests of a majority of the society preclude more drastic efforts. The challengers deny the reality of affluence, freedom, and justice, except as it is extended to the favored few, and then only at the cost of suffering on the part of deprived Americans and helpless Third World peoples. They see the causes of injustice in the nature of the values of American society, the imperatives of its economic system, and the corruption of its political institutions — all of which require change of the most fundamental kind.

These contrasting viewpoints call into question many standard interpretations and much conventional wisdom about American politics. To understand the matters that divide people and generate such conflict today, we must briefly analyze each set of beliefs. But before doing so, we shall establish some benchmarks by examining the basic political values which have structured American political thought and practice over the years.

AMERICAN POLITICAL VALUES

Political values are the most fundamental commitments which people hold about what is right and wrong in politics. They justify dogged defense of the status quo, or violent efforts toward drastic change. They are the building blocks for thinking about how political systems should be organized, and why. As such, they underlie more elaborate ideologies, or systems of belief about what is and should be in politics. We shall touch upon three political values that have had major impact on American political thought and practice.

Individualism

The focal point of political thought in the United States is the individual. From this beginning, all other relationships and values follow. The individual is the basic unit of politics, for whose benefit the political system is erected. Individuals are viewed as naturally competitive, and their competition makes for personal fulfillment and social progress. The principal goals of political life have to do with providing a suitable context for the individual's satisfaction and happiness. His self-fulfillment is sought, and principles of government are deduced, from assumptions about what is needed to serve that individual's needs. In the mid-eighteenth century, for example, the chief impediment to individual self-attainment seemed (with good historical reason) to be the inhibiting effects of governmental power wielded by royal or aristocratic authorities. The principal means of assuring individual opportunity, therefore, was a firm set of limitations on the power of government and an equally determined *laissez faire* (hands off) approach to the role of government in the society and economy.

Under these assumptions, the individual is taken to be basically rational, in the sense that he can relate evidence to a concept of the public interest and make a sound decision. And because every individual is thought to possess such capacity, popular participation in decisionmaking and majority rule are proper means of policymaking. Men are not perfect, but they are improvable through such efforts as education. The result of continued emphasis on education and participation is expected to be continued improvement both in the nature of the policies produced and in the individual members of the society themselves — or, in short, progress. Through steady application of his intelligence to the conditions of the environment, man can reasonably expect to steadily better his lot in the world, and one can look forward to greater and greater fulfillment of the satisfactions and goals of the individual.

The "Natural Rights" of the Individual

As part of his entitlement on earth, and due him solely by virtue of his existence, the individual has certain rights. These consist of the right to property — to be secure in the possession of goods and land, to be able to rely upon the value of money, and to be able to collect debts owed; of the right to life and liberty, in the sense of not being deprived of either without being granted the due processes of the law of the land (hearing, trial, fair procedures, etc.); and the right to participate to some degree at least in the decisions of government.

Although almost all American thinkers have strongly subscribed to the first two of these components of individual rights, two issues have long endured concerning the last. One surrounds the extent to which participation and sharing of power should be *equal* among all individuals. Although equality is a value of long-standing and great symbolic strength, definitions of what is required in practice to fulfill that standard have never been finally established. One standard analysis is that the operational definition has been in an irregular process of expansion throughout American history. Property-based limitations on the right to vote have given way over the years, as have sex and racial restrictions. In some respects, however, these have been formal changes only. Until very recently, urban voters were not equal in voting strength to rural voters, even though they each had only one vote to cast on election day. This was because constitutionally-validated districting arrangements placed many more voters in urban legislative districts than in rural ones. Black voters are still discouraged from voting by the threat of economic retaliation and social harassment, or by the cultural heritage of these informal but effective pressures. Literacy tests based on relatively restrictive views of a proper education were eliminated only in 1965. Thus, "equality" in political participation is more goal than fact — and even as a goal, it has controversial dimensions.

The second issue concerning equality is the extent to which it should take on extrapolitical meaning. Should it, for example, be generalized into a minimum level of "human rights" and lead to support for various forms of social welfare action by government? Or, in other words, should equality be given an economic or social dimension? Can there be true political equality without the prerequisites of social and economic equality? In the early years of this country, it was assumed that the individual could attain his economic and social ends through his own efforts. The chief threat to this goal appeared to be the single major source of power then known — government. But government was sufficiently prevented from interfering with this natural process of individual self-realization. The result would be a rough equality of opportunity. Jefferson, for example, strongly defended the principle of *laissez faire* on behalf of this equalitarian purpose. In later years, however, it appeared that other sources of power besides government, or other socially-produced limitations, prevented the individual from attaining his ends. Some thinkers, therefore, sought to expand the implications of equality to include government action to preserve opportunity or to provide a floor of educational and social status so that individuals could compete more equally. Once again, there was strong resistance on the part of others who held to more restrictive definitions of equality. Thus, though equality is symbolically potent, its practical effectuation in both political and socioeconomic dimensions has been tentative and controversial.

By contrast, attachment to property as a legitimate and paramount value has been widely shared and rarely challenged. No major American thinker, including Jefferson (supposed by some in his time to have been unsympathetic to the wealthy and propertied), has failed to strongly support the individual's right to be secure in whatever land, goods, and money he could amass. Hamilton and some other Federalists took these purposes to be the central goals of man's motivations and sought to construct a government to serve these ends. To men like Adams and Jefferson, property gave men political independence, a stake in the society, and judgmental capacity and entitlement — from which wiser public decision-making might be anticipated. To be sure, there have been disagreements surrounding the nature of property rights, but they are qualitatively different, and much less fundamental, than the debates over equality. Questions concerning property rights have centered on tensions between *types* of property, or at times on whether property should be granted *exclusive* entitlement (not just *primacy*) on the priority ranking of values to be served through the political system. Jefferson's long struggle with Hamilton and the Federalists illustrates the former type of issue. Jefferson opposed the creation of the national bank and the Federalist program of fostering manufacturing through import tariffs because he felt that these measures were creating an artificial form of property — interest on stocks and investments — which did not reflect labor and merit in the same way as did the cultivation of land. In part, Jefferson also saw an accumulation of wealth, governmentally fostered for a few, which might threaten political equality, but his challenge and that of his followers was couched in behalf of an alternative form of property.

Although property rights are only one of several natural rights, both political thinkers and practical politicians have frequently tended to elevate them to first place on the priority scale and sometimes to exclusive entitlement. Alexander Hamilton, an eminently practical thinker, was very blunt about his priorities: "Money is the vital principle of the body politic." Vital as his efforts toward nation-building must be acknowledged to be, his writings concede little comparative importance to equality or other "human rights" among the natural rights. The problem is, of course, that property rights often come into conflict with other natural rights, particularly equality, and thus the issue of which is to receive priority over the other is crucial. The deep and bitter conflict over slavery may serve to illustrate this point and demonstrate the powerful and usually ascendant grip of property as an American political value. None of the Framers of the Constitution seriously doubted that slaves were property, to be provided for as such. The early debates concerning limited slavery or emancipation foundered on the sums involved for the uncontroverted need to compensate for the taking of property. The Abolitionists were bitterly resisted by most Northerners, at least partly because of the antiproperty implication of their position. And when emancipation came, it was as a limited expediency in the course of a difficult war. In this sequence of events, there were relatively few voices raised on behalf of granting equality primacy over property, and it was only the commitment to preserve the Union which finally mobilized the use of force, the by-product of which was emancipation.

This conflict between property and other natural rights is real and repeated — in the progressive income tax, in social security, in the poverty program, and in the regulation of the economy generally. But such conflict is anticipated and feared by those who hold property far more than actual inroads upon their possessions would seem to justify. The Framers and the early Federalists feared depredations upon property and radical redistribution in the event that majorities were able to work their will through the political system; consequently, they built in a series of restraints upon the power of government.[1] In justifying this principle, they developed and promulgated the idea of "majority rule *and* minority rights." By minority rights, of course, they intended property rights. But the two are logically inconsistent: no political system can provide *both* majority rule *and* minority rights in the absolute sense. An effective limit upon majority rule on behalf of minority rights means that the system does not really have majority rule. Conversely, if majority rule succeeds in working its will in all cases, the system *cannot* always be providing minority rights. Nevertheless, most Americans subscribe to both and acknowledge such limitations on the power of majorities — perhaps a testimony to the success of the Federalists in establishing their view as an integral component of American polit-

[1] For a full presentation of the Framers' ideas, one should not fail to examine the *Federalist Papers,* available in many inexpensive editions.

ical ideology. Or possibly *all* Americans — not just the propertied but nervous Federalists and their successors — have accepted property as a primary value, therefore imposing limitations upon themselves and not seeking any of the redistributions that were anticipated. The other possibility, of course, is that men of property and their supporters have always been sufficiently dominant in practice to use government exclusively to further their own interests, celebrating their achievements in rhetoric and in the writing of history as they operate to divert, deflect, or repress the redistributive aspirations of the lower classes. We shall consider this hypothesis more fully in a later chapter.

Limited Government

At least as far as eighteenth-century thinkers were concerned, the necessary corollary of the basic commitments to individualism and natural rights (in which property rights hold primacy) is the principle of limited government. If the individual is anterior to government, possessed of rights flowing from the law of nature, then government is his creation. It can have only those powers consistent with his natural rights and which have been conferred upon it by the collectivity of individuals who together possess all powers. Its sphere of action is constrained both by the limited scope of the powers granted to it and by the inviolacy of the rights of individuals.

In this view, government becomes a marginal and semi-illegitimate instrument. Regardless of the fact that the society (or collectivity of individuals) has no other agent capable of acting on behalf of the whole, each effort to employ government for particular purposes is viewed with suspicion and challenged as to its necessity and propriety. To justify their proposed use of government as an instrument to accomplish (presumably) majoritarian purposes, supporters of the contemplated action must show a special need, which is not being (or capable of being) served in other ways. They must show cause, in other words, why circumstances are so unusual as to legitimate the use of government on this specific occasion and in this particular manner. Such action is an exception to the general principle of private solutions to problems, and adoption of the program or policy by government does not change its status very much, nor does it set much of a precedent for the future. Any further extension of the same program, or proposal to initiate a similar program, would probably experience the same kind of resistance on exactly the same bases. The principle of limited government lingers on, despite recurring (and ever more frequent) pragmatically justified exceptions. Not being challenged frontally, the principle itself therefore endures, and it continues — at least if one can accept the rhetoric of officeholders and other political thinkers — to act as an effective inhibitor of comprehensive or large-scale use of government for societal purposes.

This is not to suggest that the principle of limited government has always been scrupulously followed, even by those in and out of office who most often declare their commitment to it. From the days of Hamilton to the present, government has been used by particular industries and interests to further their needs. The early tariff, internal improvements, and banking controversies were the first in a series of measures which is today represented by subsidies to aircraft manufacturers, price supports for growers of particular crops, and import limitations on certain inexpensive foreign-made goods. But relatively few objections have been raised to such specific actions, except by *laissez faire* purists such as William Graham Sumner[2] or Milton Friedman.[3] The limited government principle appears to be more of a general inhibition, perhaps felt most strongly by the general public and/or its leaders, which is particularly operative in regard to the social welfare activities of government. In this respect, it may have sloganistic utility as a traditional basis for opposition to contemplated national government action.

These three core values — individualism, natural rights (with property contending with and usually ascendant over equality and other human rights), and limited government — represent the basic political values of the American tradition. Their preeminence in the early years set the framework within which development would occur, and they are evident today in only marginally evolved form. But there are also two basic values which, although not principally political in the sense that they determine the character of the governmental system, are nevertheless important as forces which have animated politics and the uses of government over the past two centuries.

Materialism and the Business Ethic

From the earliest days of this nation, observers have repeatedly commented upon the special disposition of Americans to seek private economic gain. Acquisitiveness and profit-seeking are sometimes related to a so-called "Protestant ethic," according to which ultimate salvation depends upon striving and attainment in this world. National celebration of such motivations reached its height at the end of the nineteenth century, in the days of Horatio Alger and the Robber Barons. Although it would be little more than caricature to attribute such motivations to most Americans today, it is clear that the United States is a business-oriented society. The underlying value system (and particularly the core values just discussed) strongly supports such capitalist principles as the value of consumption by individuals, the equation of the propriety and desirability of new ventures with their profitability, and the measurement of individual achievement by the accumulation of wealth.

These values and motivations, broadly shared, affect the criteria employed to determine the priorities and programs of government.

[2] William Graham Sumner, *What Social Classes Owe to Each Other* (Caldwell, Idaho: Caxton Printers, 1947).

[3] Milton Friedman, *Capitalism and Freedom* (Chicago: University of Chicago Press, 1962).

Because private profit and consumption are valued so highly, public expenditure is suspect. Government outlays for such public purposes as schools, hospitals, and welfare may be seen as "spending" and therefore undesirable, while corporate expenditures for new and perhaps unnecessary consumer products are "investments" and therefore good. Government action may be assessed with a kind of tradesman's approach, in which short-range questions of profitability dominate: Can the Post Office be run as a business and bring in enough income to balance its costs? Will the proposed bridge earn enough income to pay off the cost of building it in a fixed period of years? The unasked question in each of these cases, of course, is whether income-production or profitability is either a necessary or a sufficient standard by which to decide upon government action. Perhaps other values besides profitability would be served — and should be served — by taking the contemplated action. Hospitals, bridges, and postal services provide vital returns to people, and if their desirability were measured by the nature and importance of these returns, a whole new set of governmental priorities might emerge. But the tangible and familiar criteria, with their analogies in the world of private business, tend to predominate in decisionmaking about government as well. Success is measured more easily from the size of the Gross National Product than by the state of mind of the urban poor. Government revenue-expenditure ratios are understood more readily by analogy to the family budget than by the complicated process of envisioning essentially paper transfers from some members of the "family" (taxpayers) to other members of the "family" (bondholders, who are also taxpayers). The net result is that government action which cannot be justified by the criteria of private business is minimized, and goals and purposes which depend on acceptance of social, humanitarian, or other intangible values are less likely to be served.

Racism

Almost equally long-lived and pervasive in American society is the value of white supremacy. Perhaps originating in Western culture centuries ago, the sense of superiority of the white race has been an animating feature of Americans and their governmental policies throughout our history. Neither the American Indian nor the Afro-American were thought fit for full citizenship until very recently, if then. Recent scholarship indicates that nearly all of the major leaders at the time the Constitution was framed, as well as in subsequent periods, held white supremacy assumptions.[4] However unconscious such notions may have been, they were instrumental in shaping policies which removed Indians, repressed slaves, and built a sometimes unrecognized racist strain into the American value system. After centuries of official action in accordance with these premises, it is not surprising that those who are of a mind to seek evidence

[4] Thomas F. Gossett, *Race: The History of an Idea in America* (New York: Schocken Books, 1963).

of the degradation of the nonwhite races are readily able to do so. Efforts to remedy the work of centuries, however, run up against denial of personal responsibility and failure to perceive the racist bases of existing policies, as well as the normal resistance to change. Nor is it easy for most Americans to understand the extent to which the subtle and not-so-subtle racial barriers have enclosed the non-white poor within artificial constrictions which prevent them from rising via the routes taken by the immigrant poor of the nineteenth and early twentieth centuries. Given such widespread and deep-seated racism, it is not difficult to understand why the limited governmental steps taken have nevertheless been highly controversial, and why the tangible indications of change are so few.

There are many important factual questions to be asked about all of these values, of course. We do not know which groups or strata within the society actually held or hold them, how widely shared or intensely felt they are, or whether people who assert them actually act in such terms. To some extent, these are questions we shall attempt to answer later. For the moment, however, it is important to see the part played by these values in the two sets of political beliefs which we are about to examine. Dominant American political thinking finds the traditional values basically acceptable and operational, and it denies that racism is currently one of them. The challengers take one of two positions. Some perceive failures to put certain values into effect (e.g., equality, due process) or they see faulty priorities among them (e.g., property is given primacy over equality, racism endures). Others see these as being the wrong values entirely, and insist that the values of community, humanistic justice, and equality must completely replace property rights, materialism, and racism.

THE AMERICAN POLITICAL SYSTEM: THE DOMINANT VIEW

The dominant political belief system holds that the basic political values just described are realized on a day-to-day basis in American politics. In part, this is the natural function of a nation's political ideology, and it is that orthodox ideology which we shall be exploring in this section. We defined ideology earlier as the set of operative myths (true *or* false) actually held by numbers of people about how their political system does and should work. As such, it provides the link between the basic political values and the routine observations and beliefs of citizens about politics. For most people, the core political values are acquired early in life and remain unquestioned; they are the fundamental building blocks for all subsequent political thinking. At a much more superficial level of consciousness, people also become aware of many political events, such as speeches, the enactment of laws, characteristics of the U.S. Congress, demonstrations, and so on. Ideology fills the mental gap between daily events and the basic values. It prepares people to perceive (or misperceive) events in terms of their values; it provides them with a simplifying interpretive screen that promotes "understanding" of events; and it reassures them that all is well. In effect, ideology is a kind of map in the mind, telling people how to harmonize what they see with their strongly-held convictions about what is good.

Ideology develops over time, as the acceptance of the basic political values spreads and they become commonplace — and as the daily operations of government continue to be rationalized within that frame of reference. After nearly two hundred years, we should anticipate that, even if the described political values were held only by the Framers, they have by now permeated widely in some form through at least the dominant classes in the society. The public school system and the principle of compulsory education are major means of effectively transmitting values to other groups, including newly arrived immigrant populations. Contemporary mass media are another means whereby the political standards of leaders may be extended to become general criteria for the political behavior of all. Over time, as people not only accept the political values but come to believe that government acts along these lines, a political ideology linking values and "reality" emerges and acquires an independent existence. Because it is simplifying and reassuring, it is also seductive and frequently unconscious. It tends to be strongest among those who have had the most formal education, possibly because their economic interests and social positions act to reinforce what they have heard so often and in so many different forms in the educational process. Others, particularly those who experience more contrast between the ideology and the realities of daily existence, may be less prone to uncritical adoption of it.

The functions of ideology are as important as they are numerous. All nations develop a dominant ideology which serves to unify and rationalize the political activity of people and leaders. During the 1950's in the United States, it became fashionable to speak of the "end of ideology" — meaning the elimination of clashes between groups of people with contrasting views of how things did and should work. It probably would have been more accurate to have said that a single ideology was so dominant during that period — so widely held among leaders at least, and so strongly promulgated — that all others were of very little significance. As long as one ideology dominates, it performs the function of providing a benevolent gloss on conditions and events. If people are poor, it must be because they did not work hard enough or save their money; if others are wealthy, they must have talent and determination. Ideology blurs inequality: the United States is a country without social classes, in which such measures as the progressive income tax have served to redistribute wealth.

Ideology functions, in short, to make social control easier, more effective, and less physically coercive. Smoothly explaining, rationalizing, and persuading, it structures understanding and induces behavior so that challenges and discord are minimized. Men in government trust, support, and defend each other; citizens are urged to trust their government — its Constitution, the Office of the President, and the integrity and sincerity of officials. With such ideology-induced confidence, those few who (however accurately) believe a given policy to have disastrous implications will have great difficulty in gaining support from a majority of their fellow citizens. Or ideology may serve to divert or frighten people so completely as to distort consideration of various problems. American anticommunism in the post-World War II decades was apparently strong enough to reduce concern for standards of due process and to prevent rational consideration of priorities and alternatives in policymaking. We shall illustrate two components of dominant American political ideology (in terms of both content and consequence) in the paragraphs that follow.

(1) *The ideology holds that the basic political values of the United States are reflected in the structure of the American government, and that the resulting political system is democratic in character.* American ideology teaches that the core political values are so formative of the machinery of American government that one may understand government as the manifestation and reification of those values. To a great extent, the Framers did indeed seek to operationalize those primary values, although it is at least questionable (a) whether they did so in such a way that the benefits were to be realized in some automatic way by the entire population, or chiefly by the Framers and others like them; and (b) whether, regardless of their purposes, their product can fairly be termed democratic in character. Each type of question raises some potentially revealing issues.

The core political values of individualism, limited government, natural rights (with property rights ascendant over equality and other human rights), and procedural regularity, are patently manifest within the Constitution and the government it creates. The theory of the Constitution holds that individuals, possessed of the familiar natural rights and acting by mutual agreement, delegated certain powers to the new federal government and prohibited it from exercising certain other powers. This is a legal fiction, of course, but every organization rests on some similar basis. Ideology goes beyond such basic assumptions, however. It holds first that the particular forms of American government (i.e., a two-house legislature, separation of the legislative, executive, and judicial powers among the three major institutions of government, distribution of powers and areas of responsibility between national and state governments, the Supreme Court's power of "judicial review," or power to declare statutes unconstitutional and void) somehow embody the basic values or will inevitably result in their promotion and defense. The connection, of course, is far from inevitable: the same values might be served through other types of institutional structure, or other forms of government might more fully serve such purposes.

Next, ideology holds that the institutional forms will operate as if controlled by an unseen hand and will deliver the results assumed by those who subcribe to that set of values. The interplay of presidential and congressional power yields a mechanistic (and there-fore appropriate) product; the decision of the Supreme Court repre-sents a higher law's mandate, not the preferences of five judges. In short, ideology suggests that the translation of the values into institutions and powers has achieved a nonpartisan, depoliticized apparatus which works to the benefit of all.

Finally, the ideology says that what this structure creates is a situation allowing full play to the "natural" workings of human ca-pacities, wants, and the economic market, which will result in the greatest good for the greatest number of people. Thus, the estab-lished political values are seen as manifested in a particular set of institutions; these institutions interact in a mechanical manner; and the result is the furtherance of a natural order in which talent and effort are rewarded and the incompetent and slothful are carried along by the successful.

Not only do the institutions of government themselves, with all their unique features, promote the policies deemed good by the basic political values, but the principles on which the American govern-ment operates also have the same purpose and effect. "Laissez faire," or "hands off" with reference to the economy, is a sound principle in that it assures maximum opportunity for individuals to seek their own ends. The view that regulation of the economy is illegitimate in principle is given force and effect by the principle of individual capacity to challenge the acts of the national govern-ment. In 1934, for example, billions of dollars in public and private financial obligations, and perhaps the future of the economy itself, hung on a lawsuit involving $34. One individual had sued the gov-ernment for full value on a World War I debt certificate, despite subsequent devaluation of the currency. Contracts, after all, ought to be adhered to and enforced, regardless of the economic con-sequences. The Supreme Court found a way to avoid enforcing this contract, however, though not without serious controversy.

The teachings of ideology with respect to the structure and op-erations of government are that all will benefit equally, or at least substantially, from such procedures. But it seems clear that the character of the institutional setup, and the principles on which they frequently operate, neither benefit all equally nor leave results to chance. They advantage those who are situated so as to be able to seize opportunities for gaining power and influence. Separation of powers, distribution of powers between nation and states, and the protections provided for property rights, for example, mean that it is very difficult to enact laws which change the status quo. The principle of laissez faire means that people with private economic power are left free to use that power as they see fit, and it is difficult (and perhaps wrong in any event) for others to try to use government to control such activities. If government works mechan-ically, of course, nobody should be aggrieved about these results, because they are inherent in the (good) design of the American governmental structure itself. Thus, it turns out that nothing is responsible for the advantages secured by those with economic or social power except their own talents in the free and open struggle for individual achievement.

Perhaps even more important than the manner in which the basic political values are related to the structure and operations of government, however, is the way in which the ideology equates the values *and* the nature of American government with democracy. Democracy is good; the United States is good; the United States is a democracy; democracy is what we experience in the United States. Circularity and poor logic are no obstacles for a powerful ideology, and it may be fruitless — perhaps unpatriotic — to try to unravel the relationships here. What has apparently happened is that the ideology has adapted to the powerful appeal generated by democracy in the last two centuries and interpreted American values and institutions in this light. Thus, the commitment to private property and individualism becomes a characteristic of democratic man, and community and egalitarianism (properly) trail behind. Or, the power of judicial review, designed to frustrate popular will expressed through the elected legislature, becomes a vehicle for expression of the democratic values of civil liberties. A statute outlawing political participation by people of a particular viewpoint becomes democratic because it preserves the "freedom" of the "democratic" electoral process. A natural tendency to believe that what we have is good, if not the best possible, leads to favorable (democratic) interpretations of whatever we have.

We are not arguing that what exists in the United States is necessarily *un*democratic, though by this time we may appear to be taking a harsh view of some much-revered things. But we are saying that both the act of *assuming* that American institutions are democratic, and that of *defining* "democracy" in terms of what exists in the United States, are essentially *ideological* in character. In both cases, American and democratic become synonymous — testimony to the power of ideology to suggest conclusions rather than the rational judgmental capacity of the observer. A careful definition of democracy in terms of civil liberties, due process, political participation, and so forth, would in our view give the United States relatively high marks among the nations of the world. How high, and whether or not the level of democracy was sufficient, would depend on the values of the observer. But it is probably safe to say that almost any empirical assessment of American institutions in the light of a precise standard of democracy would conclude that democracy in the United States in many respects existed *in spite of and not because of* the character of American political institutions. As we shall show in a later chapter, the antidemocratic bias of the Constitution is clear, and the Framers' preference for an elite-centered regime is reflected in their construction of every institution. The real characteristics of politics, however, are less significant to the content of ideology than what leaders expound, and people accept, in the way of beliefs.

The desire to think well of what we have works — at least to some extent — in both ways. In other words, the ideology's presentation of the American system as benevolent and democratic helps to move it in that direction. Officeholders and other elites are among those most powerfully affected by dominant ideology, and they may on occasion take it so seriously as to construe their responsibilities in that light. Further, in rationalizing government in terms of the basic political values, the benevolent and democratic glow surrounding institutions and actions may rub off on the values themselves. For example, the harshness and competitiveness of individualism and self-striving may be moderated by the ideology's soothing assurance that all works democratically, and consequently they become less of a source of conflict. These effects probably require extended time to come about and are probably of much less immediate impact than the other consequences we have been discussing. It is the social control thrust of American ideology — its capacity to disarm analysis and provide benevolent interpretations — that is so significant to contemporary American politics. Few if any Americans are fully captured by all the characteristics of ideology which we have touched upon, but practically everyone is influenced by at least some of them. In the next section, we shall discuss aspects of ideology held even by some scholars and students of American politics, social life, and economic activity.

(2) *The ideology holds that the process of political decisionmaking in the United States consists of negotiation and compromise among many factions and groups, and the product is a reasonable approximation of both democracy and the public interest.* In the next five paragraphs, we shall characterize the generally accepted view of the American political process, sometimes termed "democratic pluralism."

To begin with, the system is considered to be open to all those who wish to take the time and trouble to participate. For the most part, Americans actually do participate through the vehicle of voluntary associations, organized around the interests that are real to people: ethnic, religious, occupational, social, economic, political, or other bases of shared concern. A single citizen may belong to several different groups. These groups articulate the needs and desires of the people at all levels throughout the society, but particularly with reference to government.

In organizing support among the population and presenting their claims upon the government, groups come into conflict with other groups. Each group's efforts to achieve its goals is likely to call into play another group with different or opposed goals in the same subject area. This is sometimes termed the principle of "countervailing powers." The various groups with interests in this field then engage in an elaborate process of negotiation, bargaining, appeals to principle and popular support, pressures on decisionmakers, and finally compromise. Because each group represents a significant segment of opinion and probably has access to some power position within the governmental structure, it can usually delay if not completely frustrate an extreme demand made by another group. This means that each group is induced to compromise and agree to a solution that falls short of achieving its full goals because if it does not, it may end up with nothing.

A further spur to harmonious handling of conflict through compromise is the influence of the informal rules for group goal-seeking. Each group is assumed to be sufficiently concerned with the fairness and openness of the process (because the attainment of each group's goals depends on getting a fair hearing from the others) so that all share a strong commitment to defend the procedures for decision-making. Above all, parties to the goal-seeking process should be willing to see the other side's problems, and also be willing to compromise at a point not only short of their own goals but also short of absolute disaster for the other side. This becomes particularly sound strategy when it is realized that those who happen to win today may be on the losing side tomorrow, in which case they can expect the same consideration from their new opponents. Thus, the informal rules promote compromise and help to build a shared feeling of mutual approval for the decisionmaking system itself. An opponent, after all, is a man who plays the game by the rules and is entitled to respect for his views and the demands placed on him by his constituency. Those who do not accept the rules are not playing the right game, or are cheating, and are properly opposed by all the regular players. When the regular groups do find themselves in disagreement, or at other moments when major decisions must be made, the basic directions for national policy are set through popular elections. In this way, the day-to-day activities of group goal-seeking are channeled; they become the specific working out of the details of policies decided upon by the mass electorate.

Groups perform many functions within the social and political order. They serve as major means of representation, providing people with a sense that their voices are heard in the halls of government in other ways than through the familiar geographical or party systems of representation. Thus, if a citizen belongs to the minority political party in his state or congressional district, he can nevertheless feel represented in his government by the efforts of one or more interest groups which seek to further his goals. In discharging this representative function, groups also root the citizen more thoroughly in the society — giving him a sense of place, status, and fulfillment. Further, in a reciprocal manner, groups give public officials a means of knowing what the people want and need, and a way of communicating back and forth which makes for more responsive government.

There are also other democratic consequences from the pattern of group activity in politics. People who participate in groups acquire the skills of tolerance for others and fair procedures that help to support a democratic system. They also probably belong to two or more groups, which means that on some occasions their interests are in conflict. For example, one citizen may belong to both the League of Women Voters and the Catholic Church. If the League seeks to take a position contrary to the Church on birth control issues, the citizen may be "cross-pressured" and take a much less extreme position on the issue than she otherwise would have. At the same time, her influence within each organization helps to hold *it* to a less extreme position. This "cross-cutting cleavages" effect, multiplied many times over for many issues, helps to keep the political system on an even keel by reducing the extremity of pressures on it. The process is both democratic and creative of results which are in the public interest. It is democratic because everybody has a chance to be heard, the procedures for "playing the game" are known and followed, and a general consensus based on compromise and tolerance for the other side emerges before the decision is cast into final form. It is in the public interest chiefly because it *does* represent a consensus of all the relevant groups. It is something which everybody can accept, and therefore very likely to be something which is both in harmony with the experience and capacity of the system and responsive to the policy problem involved.

THE AMERICAN POLITICAL SYSTEM: THE CHALLENGERS' VIEWS

Adherents of the dominant set of beliefs about the American political process have in effect translated their commitment to the basic values into convictions about American politics by means of ideology. (Later analysis will shed some light on how much of their assumptions and beliefs is accurate, and how much false.) Their challengers, however, less persuaded of the reality or propriety of the basic values, reject benevolent images of American politics and develop alternative ideologies of their own. Experience, observation, and interpretation lead them out of the orthodox images and assumptions to another set of beliefs and aspirations. This road was followed by several groups and movements in the 1960's, frequently as a result of vainly trying to gain their goals through the political channels which they saw as available to them. In many cases, their goals were incompatible with long-established values and procedures, and would have required sweeping changes in many basic features of the economic, social, and political systems. Thus, they were either brusquely dismissed by men in power or delayed and finally absorbed by the ponderous procedures of the established system. In response, the new movements rejected procedures and system alike, steadily escalating their tactics from confrontation to (in some cases) deliberate violence. Nor were some officials reluctant to defend orthodox beliefs and practices with violence and other forms of repression on their part. Thus, the conflict deepened and polarized.

In the following analysis, we shall focus briefly on what made the beliefs and aspirations of the new movements so distinctive and so incompatible with established thought and policies. Then, because there are many different strands of thought involved in the contemporary challenge to American orthodoxy, we shall have to examine two representative belief systems in somewhat greater detail — the black liberation movement and the SDS-originated white radical movement.

Shared Features of the New Political Values and Ideologies

Many aspects of the new approach to politics help to carry it outside the mainstream. For one thing, the new movements took a contextual and comprehensive approach to issues and goals. They did not seek only one or two tangible results from politics, nor did they focus on one problem at a time. Instead, they aimed at several problems simultaneously, looking for the common cause of all of them. They began to look behind the apparent sources of problems at the assumptions and power distribution that were even more basic causes, and this tends to lead to queries about the nature of political values and the character of the economy as ultimate sources of power.

But perhaps the most distinctive difference about the approach to politics characteristic of the various new movements of the 1960's was the shift from primary concern for the procedural side of political decisionmaking to priority for the substantive side — the content of the public policies which the government produced, and their sufficiency in the light of the problems that existed. Previous generations had been caught up in the intricacies of procedures, such as the manner of holding elections, the nature of decisionmaking in the Congress and the proper rules for considering legislation, or the requirements of due process. They saw democracy as chiefly the manner in which people went about making their decisions, and assumed that if everything was done according to the rules, the result would be appropriate or at least the best possible under the circumstances. This may have been brought about first by the trauma of the Civil War, in reaction to which some people came to believe that Americans cared too much for the substance of what government did in those days, and the nation suffered tragically because of it. Whatever the reason, the nearly exclusive focus on *how* things were done led to greatly reduced regard for *what* was being done. But the new groups took just the opposite tack; they insisted that the *only* thing that mattered was the results of government action. Judged by this standard the American claim to equality and freedom was a fraud. They disdained procedural complexities as status quo-supporting rationalizations, asking in effect: If the system is so good, why is its product so bad? Segregation was unconstitutional, according to the Supreme Court, but the fact of segregation and discrimination was brought home to blacks in North and South in dozens of ways every day. Some of these were lawful, according to courts; others could not be remedied because the due procedures had not been followed. The same pattern existed elsewhere. In Vietnam, the United States talked peace and waged bloody war; consequences that appeared morally wrong could not be altered because established procedures had not been followed. When the procedures were followed, it appeared that the result was perpetuation of the status quo. When protests were made, the procedures turned out to be effective means of prosecution and punishment. Soon the procedures themselves were lumped together with the rejected policies and denounced as synonymous with immorality and wrongdoing. To follow the established procedures was often simply to invite rejection of one's claim, and so the procedures too were condemned. This oversimplified account nevertheless highlights the essence of the shift from a politics of means to a moralistic politics of ends. No more fundamental difference could separate approaches to politics in the American context.

Nor were the demands being made capable of being readily deflected. For example, they were not economic in character. They could not be resolved by providing more money or more goods and services because the demanders either already had high levels of affluence, did not care about material rewards, or (in the case of blacks) held fast to status claims which transcended economic attainments. Tensions over the war in Vietnam, for example, could not be solved by increasing the total economic product and distributing more to the protestors. Instead, the prizes under contention were indivisible: if one side won, the other side had to lose. As such, the level of conflict had to be higher than normal. The same held true in the case of the blacks' demand for equality in the full sense; such a demand could not be met entirely by economic solutions but only by whites yielding of some of their prerogatives and sense of superiority — which of course they were likely to resist bitterly. The non-economic character of the new demands, and the refusal of their advocates to be caught up in procedural complexities, meant that some of the flexibility in the system was short-circuited and the level of conflict remained abnormally high.

The central part played by race conflicts in the new politics would practically by itself lift them into an unprecedented status — at least since the Civil War. No issue cuts so deeply into the American consciousness, arousing in both blacks and whites mixed fear, guilt, hatred, sympathy, and helplessness. And yet the issue of race arises again and again today in every arena and in every subject area of American politics. It can neither be avoided, nor (apparently) resolved, within the confines of the established values and ideology of the American system, and therefore it must be a constant source of threat to that system. When raised as the chief theme of the black movement and as a major focus for white radicals, and, from an opposite perspective, by some of their reactionary counterparts, race relations cannot fail to continue to make for a new and potentially much more explosive kind of politics in the United States.

Thus, in taking a deep-probing, contextual approach which sees underlying values and other basic sources of power as prime causes, in viewing power as concentrated in a few hands and not broadly diffused among people, in judging American politics not by its procedures but by its products, in asserting demands not readily converted, diverted, or absorbed by the flexibility of the system, and in centering on the inflammable subject of race relations, the new movements have taken themselves outside the range of what the established American system can find digestible. The label "new politics" is not an overstatement; it is an accurate characterization of at least some major new elements which seek significant change. The dynamics which these movements impart to American politics today cannot yet be fully evaluated, but it seems clear that they presage change of a substantial kind. American politics will not be the same after it emerges from this period. For a full analysis of the scope and substance of these thrusts toward change, however, we must have a somewhat more detailed insight into some representative examples. We shall examine two major movements and their ideologies, emphasizing what sets them apart from traditional movements rather than attempting a comprehensive characterization. What effect they may have depends, of course, at least initially on what they believe and what they seek. We shall examine the black liberation movement and the SDS-originated white radical movement, because they present perhaps the greatest challenge to the established system. This is partly because their ideologies introduce class analyses into American politics, accompanying all the other features just described, and partly because their tactics include some which can result in widespread violence and the most fundamental changes in the system. Though their adherents are comparatively few, their significance is not correspondingly slight.

The Black Liberation Ideology

We cannot hope to do justice to the scope and character of the black struggle for freedom in the United States; indeed, we attempt only a characterization of the ideology of one segment (perhaps an emerging vanguard) of that movement, and then only in terms of what factors take it out of the mainstream of traditional American politics. The first post-World War II efforts by blacks were an attempt to use the system's own values and procedures to raise their legal and social status. Taking the American endorsement of the natural rights of equality, freedom, and justice at face value, the NAACP used the legal process to secure substantial victories in the Supreme Court. But they soon found that these "victories" had little or no effect on the daily lives of ordinary blacks; neither the legal process nor appeals to the treasured values succeeded in integrating schools, lunchrooms, or other public facilities in the South. Nonviolent protest marches, sit-ins, and other tactics dramatized the nation's failure to adhere to its oft-stated principles, and they eventually resulted in a succession of civil rights statutes prohibiting discrimination in voting, housing, and employment. Once again, however, the consequences for the average black citizen were minimal: subtler discrimination, economic handicaps, training and educational deficiencies, insistence upon following the time-consuming established processes, and other factors combined to hold blacks in the same position as before. Blacks were useful to white society in Vietnam, but otherwise they filled no significant role in America.

Black Power grew out of these frustrations and sank its roots in the fundamental conviction that the United States was a racist society.[5]

---

[5] The first major book, and perhaps still the most comprehensive articulation of the black power argument, is Stokely Carmichael and Charles V. Hamilton, *Black Power: The Politics of Liberation in America* (New York: Vintage, 1967).

Martin Luther King had come to the same conclusion in his last year,[6] though (chiefly on tactical grounds) he remained aloof from the Black Power leaders. The premise of basic societal racism in the United States both explains the failure of the earlier efforts at achieving equality through the established system and points to directions for the future. It says, for example, that it is no accident that the procedures of the American legal system were slow, cumbersome, and ineffective in achieving integration, and not really remarkable that no substantial economic assistance was forthcoming for blacks' education and training. White society did not sincerely *want* to help the black man, and never had. The only solution was to build such self-pride and sense of identity among blacks that they could achieve their goals by themselves, or, in other words, *Black Power*. The task would be a staggeringly difficult one, of course; centuries of deprivation and exploitation had left Afro-Americans at the lowest levels of the economic order, and many held associated self-images of their worth. Without resources, constituting only 10 percent of the nation's population, enclosed in urban ghettos, and surrounded by both subtle and blatant proofs of white society's attitudes, the situation of American blacks was indeed desperate.

To the Black Power leaders, however, this meant only that they had nothing to lose. There was no hope of real help from white society, and any effort on the part of whites would be destructive in any event: whites would only invite blacks into their society on their own terms — terms which defined the black man as inferior. Thus, any integration or accommodation with whites would inevitably mean surrender and perpetuation of blacks' second-class status. Accordingly, they set about to create a black consciousness that was independent of white influences and capable of standing firmly on a distinct set of (black) values. Among other things, this meant elimination of whites from their organizations and causes, rejection of many of the values and practices of the dominant society, disavowal of nonviolence as a technique, and preparation for self-defense when the inevitable white repression began to occur. Other black leaders, believing white support necessary for a 10 percent minority and seeing their only hope in eventual integration, began to draw away from Black Power. Their removal left the new and younger leadership with both the opportunity and the necessity to develop their own analysis and ideology as to how black liberation could be attained.

Two important movements, each with its own ideology, have emerged from the early ambiguities of the call for Black Power. Both seek to instill black identity and pride among their own people, both use the Third World as a model for Afro-Americans, and both seek eventually to fundamentally alter white society in the United States. One, perhaps best represented for a time by Stokely Carmichael,[7]

---

[6] Martin Luther King, "Letter From A Birmingham Jail," in *Why We Can't Wait* (New York: Harper and Row, 1964).

[7] Carmichael and Hamilton, *op. cit.*

called for a kind of cultural nationalism among blacks with the ultimate goal of changing the white racist value system. Racism was the key, and their primary target. By awakening their own people to their independent traditions and heritage, blacks would steadily build self-reliance and personal independence from white values. The route by which blacks were to acquire their sense of identification, mutual loyalty, and independent value system was through emphasizing the achievements of black people in the past and reconstructing a distinct black culture. For these purposes, the success of the Third World independence movements was a paramount example. Black and brown men had rid their lands of white invaders, dramatically established their own validity, reasserted their past heritages, and now regularly stood up to the powerful white states in the United Nations and elsewhere.

By "thinking black," and helping to build viable economic bases for their own communities, American blacks similarly could *lift* themselves out of their deprived state. Once they had developed real pride and capacity to accomplish their ends on their own — and not until then — it would be possible to reestablish contact with the white world. Whites, seeing blacks doing as well as or better than they, and becoming aware that blacks neither were nor considered themselves inferior, might be forced to reexamine their own values. This process would probably not occur without some serious clashes as blacks asserted their rights, but Carmichael alleged at one point that it was the only alternative to full-scale guerrilla warfare in the United States. Carmichael himself ultimately despaired of developing the necessary power to achieve these goals in the face of continued white opposition and harassment. He concluded that the active assistance of Africans and Asians would be necessary, and left the country. But others have and no doubt will continue to pursue this essentially nationalist route toward black liberation within the United States.[8]

The second position generated by the black liberation movement is associated with Eldridge Cleaver and the Black Panther Party.[9] Equally determined to achieve black identity and pride, and to create a new set of values that would acknowledge black independence and worth, they nevertheless mapped out a somewhat different route to follow. Racism was a major target, but not the only one; behind racism, creating and maintaining racist attitudes and systematically exploiting both blacks and whites, was the capitalist economic system. They saw blacks as specially deprived victims at the very bottom of the social and economic order, requiring concentrated self-help efforts to create the capacity to resist and eventually triumph over the established system. But the lowest echelons of whites were also exploited by the capitalist system, and their true class interests if recognized would lead to joint

[8] See, for example, LeRoi Jones, *Home: Social Essays* (New York: William Morrow, 1966).

[9] This version is drawn from Robert Scheer, ed., *Eldridge Cleaver: Post-Prison Writings and Speeches* (New York: Random House, 1969).

efforts to break free. Those (few) whites who were in one way or another able to extricate themselves from the capitalist-encouraged racist syndrome could become allies — though in practice this was both tenuous and difficult because so many whites were not really free and blacks were naturally suspicious of open-armed whites. The Third World was again a model, but this time both for its triumphs of black and brown over white *and* for its triumphs over capitalist imperialism. Further, the Third World might now provide tangible assistance in a world-wide struggle by undermining the U.S. economy and hastening its breakup.

These divergences of emphasis within the militant black liberation movement should not obscure their broadly shared rejection of the basic outlines of the American system. They both see its procedures as facades for white manipulation of blacks; police are the military power sent to crush legitimate disobedience to exploitative actions by "respected" white businessmen; and the only recourse of blacks is to resist by any means necessary. The consequences of action in accordance with such principles by even a relatively small number of blacks are not limited to those which they envision, of course. Far more likely is drastic change in the operating principles of the American political system toward greater repression and more or less constant use of force in isolated ghettos.

SDS-Originated, White Radical Ideologies

The origins of the Students for a Democratic Society, like those of black liberation, lie in efforts to actually bring about the rhetorically familiar values of equality, freedom, and justice.[10] The last years of the 1950's and the early 1960's saw numbers of Northern college students taking part in freedom rides, sit-ins, and voter registration drives in the South. The inability or the unwillingness of those who were dominant in the American political system to make equality a reality for blacks led many of them to look more closely at other claims on behalf of the system. Contrasting the affluence of some with the poverty of others, or marginal government actions with the depth and breadth of problems, they concluded that the familiar values were not only unrealized but that the really operative priorities were all wrong. Private comfort and advantage clearly took precedence over public needs. The escalation of the Vietnam War was one tragic example of outmoded priorities at work.

At first, the roots of the problem seemed to lie in an implacable technology, operating largely on its own momentum and using the media and other teaching vehicles to create values and wants in the image of what it found possible to produce.[11] Thus, conformity with materialistic values and a commitment to seek ever-increasing personal comforts, were gently but completely accomplished either

[10] Comprehensive description of the early stages of this movement may be found in Jack Newfield, *A Prophetic Minority* (New York: New American Library, 1966), from which this is drawn.

[11] This stage of analysis is well represented by Herbert Marcuse, *One Dimensional Man* (Boston: Beacon Press, 1964).

through inducement or coercion or both — making the nation into an example of smooth, plastic unfreedom. Much of the originating thrust of SDS in 1962 flowed from efforts to find ways to break free of the materialist priorities and self-seeking that seemed to accompany the technological society, to bring meaningful choices back into the lives of ordinary citizens, and to accomplish in reality the accepted goals of equality, freedom, and justice first for all members of the American society, and then for others in the world. The principle of decentralization or "participatory democracy" was first conceived as a means of providing citizens with power to control the things that were affecting their lives. Community organizing, "student power" movements on campuses, and other participatory activities were first based on the same democratic aspiration.

Again like the black movement, the first efforts to achieve these essentially orthodox goals were unsuccessful. Participatory groups were able to secure control only over matters that were insignificant, or on which their antagonists were others no better off than themselves. When they attempted to obtain new leverage over matters that seemed important, they were met with a barrage of procedural limitations or other restrictions. Racism in both North and South continued undiminished. The capacity of the established order to promise change, and then to delay or frustrate it, seemed unlimited. In the eyes of many, the Vietnam War was the classic example of official hypocrisy. Escalating steadily throughout the mid-1960's and bringing with it the threat of conscription, the Vietnam War seemed to show the American government as callously pursuing an immoral policy under the outmoded banner of anticommunism. Instances of officials' overoptimism, concealment, and insistence upon the citizenry's patriotic obligation to support such policies only made the war a greater violation of supposed American commitments to democracy, freedom, and peace.

The enormity of American deviance from professed goals, and the complacence of both the establishment and much of the population in the face of it, seemed to mandate a more profound analysis of causation than the deterministic technological-society-gone-wrong on which the earlier movement had been based. By the late 1960's, SDS and its supporters and sympathizers had more or less arrived at the conclusion that the answers were to be found in the nature of the American capitalist economic system.[12] They began to see Vietnam and other Third World adventures in terms of imperialist efforts to acquire control over raw materials and markets. Black repression was not just the product of idiosyncratic racism, but of a racism partially created and thoroughly encouraged by capitalist values. Upper classes were profiting from the exploitation of the black and other working classes, and thus they were quick to defend establishment policies in all essential respects.

For at least some members of this loose coalition, the only solution

[12] A full statement, based on the Vietnam experience, may be found in Carl Oglesby and Richard Shaull, *Containment and Change* (New York: Vintage, 1967).

seemed to lie in eliminating the basic causes of racism and injustice at home, and of wars against Third World peoples abroad — in short, in putting an end to capitalism and introducing some form of socialism. Some saw it as essential to build alliances with the working classes, despite the difficulties in reaching a group which seemed in large part both satisfied and unsympathetic to middle class college students, and then seek to use electoral and other routes to power. Others believed, again like some black militants who served as models, that conditions were so bad that they had nothing to lose from engaging in destructive or revolutionary acts immediately. Still others saw the prospective revolution more in terms of a complete change in life style and values, and sought to live out their lives in illustrations of those better values.[13] By creating in time a "counter culture," they hoped to recruit others and ultimately to affect the dominant values of the nation. At the end of the 1960's, the number of young whites who considered the ending or drastic transformation of the capitalist economic order to be essential — and by means which included revolutionary violence if necessary — seemed to be still growing. A much larger number, however, dismissed such aspirations as hopeless romanticism; but nevertheless, they shared many of their hopes for equality and democracy and saw these as unattainable without substantial change in the American system.

The Political Impact of the New Ideologies

These two illustrations of nontraditional, change-oriented ideologies are not an exhaustive listing. They are important because of what they *stand for* (alliances among the lowest classes to bring about the end of capitalism through revolution in some form), and for the kind of reaction which their beliefs and tactics may *provoke* (rigid policies, repression, police state). Their reactionary counterparts, increasingly visible and certainly both more numerous and more powerful, seemed likely to act in essentially similar ways if and when the radical groups approached success. All of these groups play a different game of politics — an ends-oriented, play-for-keeps kind of game — which neither accepts the traditional standards known and treasured by the "establishment," nor is prepared to abide by them. The extent to which the new groups are indeed engaged in a new and different game may be quickly grasped from some of their tactics. In many cases, these tactics appear — from the perspective of the establishment and the old rules of American politics — to be irrational, counterproductive, or simply the senseless self-indulgence of spoiled children. But even if an objective analysis would occasionally agree, these tactics uniformly reflect the ideological premises and goals of the movements and usually are entirely rational and effective in those terms.

Such tactics as deliberate disruption of public speeches, public defiance of laws concerning parades and demonstrations, destruction of Selective Service records, physical blockades of government or

[13] This argument is made by Theodore Roszak, *The Making of a Counter Culture* (New York: Doubleday Anchor, 1969).

university buildings, and violent resistance to attempts at law enforcement, became familiar occurrences in the late 1960's. At subsequent trials of members of the various movements, the legal system
was mocked and defied. The charge of Communist influence or infiltration was met with derision or welcome acknowledgment.

Each of these apparently self-defeating challenges to strongly-held
American values of procedural regularity, law and order, and anticommunism, however, carries its own rationale. It can surely be
argued that resistance is the only moral course for a man who believes
the government to be immoral. On more tactical grounds, it is true
that such public displays gain attention for the causes involved and
perhaps recruit some new members to the movement. They also have
a radicalizing effect on people who participate: few emerge from
violent confrontations or a night in jail with the same benevolent
view of the American political system. Moreover, confrontations of
this kind are thought to reveal the true nature of the system — that is,
its determination to repress any serious effort to accomplish change.
In cases where violent or unlawful tactics have been employed in
behalf of black or poor peoples' demands, one of the real purposes
has frequently been to mobilize new support from among people
previously inert and hopeless, and only secondarily to achieve specific
results from the original demands upon official decisionmakers.

Broader rationalizations also support such tactics. For one thing,
the ultimate success of any revolutionary movement depends in part
on withdrawing legitimacy from the established political order, at
least in the eyes of a substantial segment of the population. If the
government can be shown to act arbitrarily, vindictively, and in violation of its own expressed standards of due process, it will be seen as
being no better than other contending forces. The voluntarily extended acquiescence and cooperation which makes government possible then begins to break down, and the prospects for drastic change
are much greater. Further, a larger perspective would not see violence
as being initiated by the protestors. Where the state is viewed as exploitative and the police force as the agents of its necessary physical
coercion, violence by ordinary citizens may be seen as counterviolence — or, in effect, as legitimate resistance by any means necessary.[14] There is no obligation to submit nonviolently to police power
and a legal system which are deliberately set up to work injustice
upon citizens; nothing is owed to such a system, and nothing is an
unfair or improper tactic to be used against it, if it appears likely to
contribute to overthrow of that system. The charge of Communist
influence, of course, appears merely archaic. The New Left has little
respect for the Soviet brand, which it sees as repressive, bureaucratic,
and as technologically dominated as the United States. Communists
are conservatives, however, in their tactics and in their timetables; to
charge these new groups with Communist leanings or influences is so

---

[14] For a full statement of the "counterviolence" rationale, see Marcuse, *op. cit.*,
and Marcuse, *An Essay on Liberation* (Boston: Beacon Press, 1968).

hopelessly irrelevant to their real goals and purposes as to provoke laughter.

The reactions of the vast majority of still-uninvolved Americans, so far as they can yet be understood, show both the strengths and weaknesses of such tactics. Serious attention has been gained on the part of intellectuals, college youth, and many blacks, but support for generalized goals is much more readily forthcoming than agreement with ultimate purposes or with many of the specific tactics. The deepest thrusts into the defenses which standard American values and ideology provide for the established order have occurred when liberals have been mobilized around such comparatively orthodox issues as police brutality or denial of due process. For the most part, however, it appears that the white majority has simply not understood either the demands or the tactics, and when they have, they have been repelled. Some lower middle class elements, perceiving themselves threatened, have apparently hardened in resistance. The long-heralded "backlash" of lower class whites appears to be a stronger possibility than the hoped-for alliance of workers, students, and blacks.

It is even more precipitate to speculate about the future effects of these movements than it is to attempt to assess their current political impact. The nature of the demands that are now being made, however, and the tactics by which these demands are being pressed, seem to assure that change of some kind in the nature of American politics is inevitable. Three differing directions seem possible. (1) If stability-producing factors are still strong enough, the result may be another triumph for flexibility and continued incremental change. One variant might have continuing incremental change taking place over a sustained period of time, so that the total amount of change would be somewhat greater than in other periods of change in the past. (2) Another possible result is a rigidification around the defense of the status quo, perhaps accompanied by strong measures to put down the actions of the new revolutionary movements. The risk here of course is that an insecure establishment will drop all concern for procedural regularity and due process, thereby confirming the American political system in the image that its critics now create for it. A domestic "garrison state" is one possible variant of this type of change. (3) Successful revolution is of course theoretically possible too, although most observers would either dismiss the prospect or hold that, if it came to that, right-wing forces would be much more likely to succeed than their black and white radical counterparts. It seems certain that, whatever the directions of the change impelled by the emergence of the new political forces, the establishment will be hard-pressed to defend its position and its version of the American system against challenges from both sides. Indeed, it could be argued that the most promising strategy for the left could be to so provoke reaction from the right as to force the beleaguered establishment to choose between the two sides — and hope that the choice would be in their favor.

THE DISPUTED QUESTIONS OF POWER AND PURPOSE

These two sets of beliefs not only give rise to sharp conflicts in American politics, but also pose some substantial issues for the political analyst and the citizen. The dominant belief system sees the basic American political values as desirable and in operation in an essentially sound system which must be preserved. The challenging beliefs see instead an indefensible system which acts on the wrong values and must be drastically changed. Clearly, they cannot both be correct in their contrasting images of how power is distributed and used in the United States. The political analyst must find some evidential basis for accurately describing how the system does in fact operate, and for whose benefit. Nor can the citizen avoid making the most portentous choices between the contrasting views as to how much change is desirable, and how it should be achieved.

The "pluralist" image of how American politics works is a basic part of American political ideology. It conveys an image of power as diffused among many groups, all of which are ultimately subject to the general control of the people through elections. Many facts support such an image, but the gaps among them and the assumptions that must be made to relate them all to each other make pluralism at least partly an ideological, rather than a factual, interpretation. The inclusiveness and representativeness of groups are often challenged, for example, as are the assertions that elites disagree about important matters and carry such key issues to the electorate for resolution. It is charged that pluralism's characterization of the American political process as democratic is made from the perspective of governing elites, and that when one views it from the ground up — from the perspective of the masses — very different conclusions ensue.

In pointing up the probable role of ideology in shaping the pluralist image of power, we do not mean to suggest that there is not a potentially analogous element of ideology at work in contrasting images of power. There may well be more, or less, depending on the particular image. Our purpose is simply to show that *any* image of power (including pluralism) probably rests in part on ideological assumptions. All the important contrasting images proceed from the not very unique insight that a few people hold much more power — whether the source is wealth, status, talent, or institutional position — than most others, and that the interests of these people are not the same as that of the general public. But they differ as to the degree of conscious cooperation which they assert takes place among such elites, and as to the source of the shared interest that holds the elites together. The economic ruling class view sees a tightly concentrated elite of very wealthy businessmen acting coherently to advance their selfish economic goals. Another image of power sees a somewhat looser association of businessmen, socially prominent families, and public officials who hold most of the power positions in the society and act together because of their shared class origins, expectations, and preferences. Drawing on many of the same facts as pluralism, they reach different conclusions.

FIGURE 1
Selection of Power Distribution Models by Years of Education

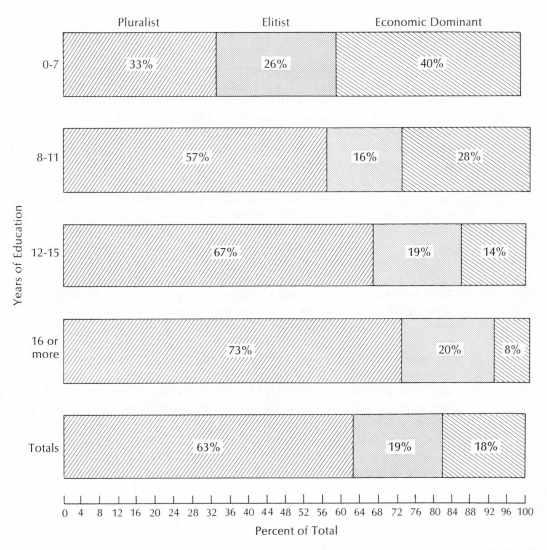

Source: William H. Form and Joan Rytina, "Ideological Beliefs on the Distribution of Power in the United States," *American Sociological Review,* vol. 34 (January, 1969), pp. 19–31 (Table 2, p. 23).

Nor are contrasting images of power necessarily limited to holders of well-elaborated political belief systems. People of differing class levels apparently sometimes hold quite different images, a fact which (if true generally) would lend support to the argument that the dominant pluralist ideology is *not* widely shared. In one survey study using samples drawn from various strata of the population of a Midwestern city, it was found that images of power distribution varied sharply with education. The alternatives presented were in the form of brief paragraphs describing pluralist, "economic dominance," and "elitist" forms of power distribution, the latter two being equivalent to those we described in the last paragraph. The researchers found that 63 percent accepted the pluralist characterization, 19 percent the elitist, and 18 percent the economic dominance (or "ruling class"). When separated according to years of schooling, however, the results were very distinctive, as Figure 1 indicates. The longer a respondent had been in school, the more likely he was to believe in the pluralist model. Was this because he saw the world more clearly and accurately? Or because he was more fully ideologized? Or because his class level was such as to insulate him against the kind of reality which would contrast with the pluralist model generally taught? It is certainly worth noting that a total of two-thirds of the least-educated (and presumably lowest-class) respondents in the survey chose one or the other of the more elitist images of power. The authors could provide no clear answers on the basis of this single study, nor can we. But it is clear that the issue of the "real" structure of power in the United States is both vital and highly controversial.

The essence of the conflict of the 1970's is captured by the two focal questions of power and change. The first is a chiefly empirical one: What is the nature of power distribution — the structure of power — in the United States? What maintains such patterns, and how is that power used? The second is chiefly a question of value preference: How much change is desirable? It does, however, have a considerable empirical component: How does change come about, and what actions are most likely to bring about desired results? In the rest of this book, we shall be seeking evidence to construct a sound image of the structure of power in the United States, to clarify the choices the citizen faces in seeking change, and to assess the prospects of various forms of change. In the next chapter, we shall set forth a strategy to accomplish these ends.

A Framework for 3
Analysis and Evaluation

We have just seen that two key disputes underlying today's political dynamics are (a) the nature of power distribution and usage, and (b) how much change is both desirable and possible to achieve, and how it may best be brought about. Because it is chiefly an empirical question, the first will serve as the central organizing question of the analytical sections (Parts II and III) of this book. The second is more of an evaluative problem. It will be the focus of the last two chapters (Part IV), although throughout the intervening analytical sections we shall devote some attention to the empirical aspect of the question — how change comes about. But it should be clear that we can say little about whether (and, if so, how) the American political system should be improved until we have a clear sense of how it works and for whom.

In this chapter, we shall first set forth our basic conceptual framework and analytical strategy to answer the key questions of how power is distributed and used, and to shed some light on the process of change. Next, we shall show explicitly what our definition of politics implies for the scope and character of our inquiry. Then we shall shift to the problem of evaluation, and suggest some ways of avoiding confusion and developing independent evaluative capacities concerning the policies and processes we shall be analyzing. Finally, because our approach is not the only possible one to use (indeed, it is different from all other texts we know), we describe some alternative conceptual frameworks which political scientists often use. This last section is not integral to the development of our approach and readers are welcome to defer or ignore it. We include it because we have no desire to entrap unwary readers in our iconoclastic approach without offering more familiar alternatives.

POLITICAL ANALYSIS: A STRATEGY

Establishing the purposes, describing the tools, and identifying the central, organizing questions for our inquiry — as we have already done in the first two chapters — is a significant part of our task. We now have merely to map out an effective way of putting these tools (solid evidence, clear concepts, etc.) to work to answer the questions (power distribution and change) that serve our purposes (comprehensive understanding, evaluation, development of independent critical capacities.) We shall follow a two-stage approach. First, we shall describe both the policies actually followed by the United States government in regard to some major problems and the consequences which these policies have brought about. Each of the four chapters of Part II deals with a separate policy area and undertakes such an analysis. Second, we shall seek to explain how and why these policies came about. The eight chapters of Part III examine distinct aspects of the general problem of who decides upon what policies are to be followed, who influences their decisions, and how political institutions and processes interact with underlying values and the attitudes of the people to generate such policies. *In effect, we shall use the policies of government and their consequences as a kind of prism through which to look at power, conflict, decisionmaking, and elite-mass relationships in the American political system.*

The description of policies and their consequences is necessary to provide us with a concrete basis for knowing what it is that our government is actually doing. It avoids much of the confusion, diversion, and potential ideological myopia of a focus on hallowed institutions and procedures. It forces us to confront the realities of problems and the actual rather than the rhetorical role of government in dealing with those problems. And it provides a solid foundation of fact and the criteria of relevance necessary for sifting through the many characteristics of institutions and processes in search of those that are most crucial for the outcome of politics.

With this grounding, we can proceed to an analysis of elites in American politics — their composition, role in decisionmaking, and relationships with the general mass of the people. Here we shall examine the total context of power that leads to government action, looking at the various sources of power, governmental and nongovernmental, and at the ways in which the latter move through or interact with government to cause policies to emerge as they do. Our ultimate goal, of course, is to trace policy consequences through government to their original causes in the uses of power wherever it exists in the society. Power is a complex and elusive target which is difficult to pursue and characterize, but we attempt to synthesize the entire analysis into a description of the structure of power in the United States in Chapter 16.

Our discussion of change will constitute a continuing thread running throughout the analytical sections of this book. The implications of these findings will be drawn together in Part IV, *after* we reach some tentative conclusions about the structure of power in the United States. But we must be alert throughout the analysis to the issues of the scope, character, and direction of change that are so important to our ultimate purposes. What can we extract from our analysis of the "is" of American politics today that will help us to understand how change does and may come about? We can hardly do more at this point than begin to identify some necessary analytical tasks and some areas for concentrated inquiry. First, let us define change as shifts in the structure of authority which operates the political system (the elites which together hold the decisive preponderance of power) and/or in the tangible results of public policies. Next, let us distinguish types of change by *degree or scope* (marginal vs. fundamental), by *direction* (broader distribution of power, status, or economic rewards vs. either status quo or narrower distributions), and by the origins and processes which are associated with each. Change may come from the top down, with elites taking action and securing popular acceptance in some way. Or it may come from the bottom up, with masses mobilizing, asserting themselves, and installing new elites in power to replace the old ones. If change is instituted from the top down through the management of established elites, the degree of change is likely to be quite modest. This is because established elites rose through, and are generally committed to, the basic outlines (and sometimes many specific details) of the present system. In the context of the United States today, the direction could be either incremental movement toward wider distributions (increased welfare-type services, for example), or toward sterner measures to defend the status quo. If change occurs from the bottom up, the degree of change is likely to be much more drastic. A mass-based movement which succeeds in reconstituting the governing elites is almost by definition likely to arise only when the goals sought involve substantial change. In the context of the United States today, such fundamental change is sought chiefly by groups oriented toward broader distributions of power and economic rewards.

In the real world, change would probably involve some combination of the two contrasting models (top-down, bottom-up) just posed. Elites might act first, perhaps because of their perceptions about mass desires or for other reasons of their own. Mass response might then confirm elites in or divert them from their intended path, or conceivably even cause them to lose control of the movement they set in motion. Again in the context of the United States today, initiative seems (at least at the outset of the process, and on the basis of what we have been describing in this chapter) to lie with established elites. But we have no way of knowing in advance how much effect on their actions can be generated from below, or in what directions the resulting equation of forces will carry the course of change. Our problem is to ascertain *to what extent* the ongoing process of change is top-down, *how much* initiative is coming up from below, and what the *directions* of such pressures are. Four principal areas for concentration appear likely to provide evidence and insight to answer this need. Each involves successively wider scope to the analysis required and poses increasingly difficult problems of evidence collection.

First, we might concentrate on elites. At least in the past, the American establishment has enjoyed broad discretion over the policies it institutes. The easiest, likeliest, and least disruptive kind of change is elite-accomplished. We should try to understand the present characteristics of, as well as the kinds of change that are occurring in, the composition of elites, their attitudes, their actual behavior, and their economic and other interests. What changes are occurring (if any) in the kinds of people who come to positions of power? What are the ways in which people succeed in rising to such positions, and what kinds of people seem to be next in line for succession to power? What affects who actually does wield power?

Second, we might focus on the sources of power. What resources are employed by those who affect the outcome of the political process? Do the resources which lead to power change from time to time? If so, we would want to know in what ways, and whether any such motion was identifiable at the present time. If not, perhaps it is possible for those who are currently powerless to develop power through certain activities, such as by demonstrations or riots, and we would then seek to clarify the extent to which such new power was being acquired on a permanent rather than a transitory basis. We need, in short, a kind of map that traces the flow of power through the society. Without significant transfer of power from those who are currently dominant to some new grouping, there is little likelihood of change which is more than incremental in nature. In effect, this inquiry would take us behind the first line of analysis, to ask what power bases were likely to give rise to elites in the near future.

Third, we might shift to a longer time span and ask what changes are underway in the political values and ideology that underlie the system. We would need to be clear on the extent to which such values and ideology shape and direct elite behavior, but it seems likely at least that they provide some basic channels within which elites must choose their policy alternatives. What changes in societal values are occurring, and what implications do these carry for shifting to new boundaries of the "main stream" of politics? For example, how widespread is the "counter-culture" of values being generated by some of the young New Left groups? What political consequences can be projected from the dissemination of such values?

Finally, we should focus major efforts on the masses or nonelites who are in theory the objects for which the system functions. The

tasks of data collection are very large, but we should try to understand the political role of the mass public, its effects on elites, and the
currents of dissatisfaction, aspiration, and willingness to take action
that flow through the population. What new goals are gaining adherents, how ready are people to act to bring them about, and what
forms of action are attractive to them? What part is played by the
electoral process? Despite the strong grip of the two-party system,
what types of momentum toward change are being provided by the
education, provocation, and psychological releases accompanying
recent elections? In short, what do the various strata of the population *want* through politics, and what are they prepared to do to get it?

These are, of course, not the only ways to move into an analysis of
change. But in the context of American politics today, they offer some
focused points of entry into the problem that may increase understanding. The process itself has nothing predetermined about it.
Nothing is inevitable, and the United States of the 1980's may be much
the same as it was in the 1960's — or it may be drastically restructured.
Unfamiliar forces are at work, and in such circumstances we can only
attempt to keep abreast of what is actually happening. But this will
be achievement enough in the years to come in the United States. To
identify the points of leverage within the system at which the directions of change are determined is a crucial intellectual achievement
for those who would understand or effectively participate in shaping
those directions. These are the kinds of questions that we shall be
trying to answer in the remainder of this book.

THE IMPLICATIONS OF A DEFINITION

Nothing is more tedious, nor more important, than the precise definition of what it is that we are talking about. This is particularly true
of the emotion-encrusted subject of politics. We have deliberately
adopted a distinctive definition of politics in order to employ the
widest possible, and least ideologically-shaped, frame of reference
for our inquiry. But, even at the risk of tedium, we feel that we must
spell out in detail what is implied in our definition, and how it differs
from the more familiar and more limited (and more self-congratulatory) definitions usually employed.

A definition of politics is the link between the goals of inquiry, the
concepts employed, the evidence gathered, and the implications that
may be drawn from them. It sets boundaries for the evidence that
will be considered and shapes the nature of the interpretations that
are drawn from that evidence. It is instrumental in determining
whether our analysis will be both *manageable* and *communicable* —
one which can be applied by the authors in a manner intelligible to
the readers in a single short book — and (more important, and more
difficult) *significant* — one which contributes to answering our ultimate questions. We have been approaching politics as a process (a)
in which power is employed to gain rewards, and (b) through which
the interests of broad segments of the population are affected. The
vagueness and comprehensiveness of the concept of power, however,

is both a strength and a weakness for political analysis. It is a strength because it forces us to deal inclusively with nongovernmental activity — the often highly significant conflicts, decisions, and other actions which precede, shape, prevent, or anticipate government action. But the pursuit of "power" and its usage threatens to lead us astray from immediate political consequences and into areas where evidence is speculative or nonexistent. We must try to refine our definition so that it retains those elements which should have our highest priority and yet is sufficiently concrete and manageable that we can conduct revealing analyses of events and behavior in American politics.

We have shown our conviction that we must preserve sensitivity to extragovernmental activity which bears on who rules, who benefits, and how change comes about. The basic reason is that government is only one of several channels through which vital goals are obtained. Its use therefore implies change or confirmation of pre-existing patterns of benefits — either of which is of vital concern to political actors. More fundamentally revealing uses of power may occur over the question of *whether* government should act in a given area than over *the way in which* government is to act. Some will gain, and some will lose, in either event. The consequences for ordinary people, who inevitably receive the impact of this struggle in one form or another, may be very great — and eminently a product of *politics*.

Further, a concern for the nature of problems and the character of extragovernmental activity will alert us to the processes by which an issue enters the arena where it becomes recognized as a possible subject for political debate or government action. Some subjects are routinely understood as appropriate for government action, some (such as poverty or racial discrimination) are seen as problems for government only at very late stages, and some (nationalization of major industries, compensation for victims of crime) not at all. Sometimes a subject at first appears quite outside the range of "practical" political consideration, but after a period of years it moves into the field of political debate and finally takes a place among the policies of government. This was the case, for example, first with medical care for the aged and more recently the guaranteed annual wage or "negative income tax." Throughout the period when some political actors are trying to move a subject from the unthinkable stage to the stage of debate and perhaps action, many forces are at work to shape understanding of the issue, whether it should be a subject for government, and if so what should be done about it. These shaping forces reach deep into the underpinnings of our politics. Our understanding of what is proper for government action, for example, is strongly affected by the cultural values and assumptions which we have acquired during the process of growing up. But these values and assumptions are not coincidental: somebody or something has taught them to us. The result is that some participants in politics are better able to gain their ends — usually those who do not need government or might be hindered by it in some way. Nevertheless, *some* issues and problems *do* rise to public attention and *are* acted upon by government. Which ones can do this, and why, and under what conditions? And when they do, who acts in what ways to shape our understanding of the nature of these issues and what is at stake in such areas?

The temptation is strong to try to understand too much, to treat almost every event and pattern of social and economic activity as if it had political implications. The fact is, of course, that almost everything does. But we must exclude much of this activity in order to be able to cope concretely with some of it. We shall limit ourselves to matters which have a *direct and proximate relation to the present character or future prospect of government action*. Our definition of politics then becomes: *the process by which power is employed to affect whether and how government will be used in any given area*. Power means the possession of those resources, ranging from money and prestige to official authority, which cause other political actors to modify their behavior and conform to what they perceive the possessor of the resources prefers. The resources need not be tangible, for what counts is what others perceive as one's resources. They need not actually be mobilized and employed in any particular situation, because others may act in anticipation or expectation. Indeed, much politically significant behavior occurs because of one's own "voluntary" conformance with what one takes to be the expectations of others. Thus, politics is a vast interactive process of power applications which, although some are unintended, nearly always have consequences for others. From the beginning stage of acquiring ideology to the proximate acts of defining what is a "problem" for government, we are subject to the effects of past and present power. Fortunately, our definitional limitation to those uses of power which bear directly on *whether* and *how* government will be employed makes it unnecessary for us to trace the entire web of power transactions in society. The line marking the boundaries of what bears "directly" or "proximately" on the use of government will not always be a clear-cut one; but we shall try to hold to what is tangible and demonstrable, and thereby serve our need for manageability.

Limiting our definition in this way should also clarify the conceptual relationship between the components of our inquiry. Our premise is that government is one important channel through which powerholders work to gain their ends. By focusing on the consequences of government action and deliberate inaction, and reaching back from such evidence to analyze the uses of power which created them, we shall be led to identification of who or what interests hold decisive power with regard to government — or, in short, to a significant part of the "who rules?" question. Our definition, as just refined (the uses of power which directly affect whether and how government will be employed), is the connecting link between the patterns of consequences of government action or inaction and who holds decisive power, or "who rules."

We shall not see *all* of "who rules?" in this way, but we shall see important parts of the picture. And we shall clearly see who benefits and who loses from government action, provided that we view the policies of government with a comprehensive perspective which includes the total context of the problem in its focus. In looking at public policies in regard to racial discrimination, for example, we must proceed from a characterization of the overall circumstances of blacks in the United States today — including the symbiotic relationship of fear, guilt, hatred, and aggressiveness between whites and blacks, and the historical, social, economic, political, and cultural factors which gave rise to them. It is the consequences of government action *in this context* which will show us who holds power and what difference it makes. At the same time, changes in the character of government action, or in holders or users of power, can be made the focus of special analyses which aim at the ultimate question of how change comes about. In summary, we shall conduct a relatively limited inquiry centering on government policies in a context of national problems and emphasizing control of government as one of several uses of power. Though limited, however, this approach can be revealing — because it leads directly toward answers to significant questions about power, purposes, and change.

PROBLEMS IN EVALUATION

Developing one's own view of what *should be* is even more difficult and frustrating than understanding the *is* of politics. Most people can acquire facts about their political system, although sometimes they do so in the fashion of spectators at a game or as passive memorizers in the classroom rather than as analytical and purposeful, independent citizens. Relatively few people make the effort to self-consciously and comprehensively survey alternative ends and means in politics and arrive at their own set of standards and goals for political action. But not to do so is to commit oneself in advance to a passive role in the processes which determine the shape of the future, and in effect to acquiesce in whatever those now in power decide is best for themselves and perhaps for others. The citizen without an independent basis for analysis and evaluation in politics *must* be somebody's pawn, and the only remaining question is whose. That is the reason for this section: we shall consider the kinds of decisions that have to be faced by people who seek to develop their own political positions and to have a basis for evaluating the actions of their government. It is an intricate intellectual process, ultimately the work of a lifetime. But it must be begun sometime, and, while nobody can provide standards for another, we can at least explore the nature of the intellectual acts involved and indicate the issues about which decisions must be made. We shall first consider what is involved in setting up personal judgmental standards, and then discuss a variety of approaches to evaluating government performance.

Developing a Personal Political Perspective

Centuries of reflection and writing by the great political theorists have not produced agreement among them or even consensus among their respective followers, for reasons which are by now obvious to readers. But analysis of their work reveals remarkable consistency in the kinds of problems which they found it essential to face. Because these problems accord also with our view of the intellectual issues involved, we shall use some classic categories to indicate the central questions which must be faced by a student of politics who seeks to establish his own independent judgmental framework. Each individual must answer three basic questions, however temporary those answers may be, in order to evolve an independent political stance.

(1) What is the nature of man, and of his relationship to his society and environment? To some extent these are empirical questions, but for the most part we must simply assume or speculate, in which case our answers are more or less frank expressions of our value preferences. Some assume that man's nature is fundamentally good — that he is essentially a cooperative, rational being. If so, then governing processes can be designed to maximize openness and participation, in the confidence that the right things will be done. Others assume that man in general is selfish, emotional, and likely to follow short-range interests and demagogues, but that there are some who possess superior talents. Under these assumptions, a strong government run by the talented few would seem requisite to civilizing men and maintaining order and a modicum of justice in the society. In other words, a whole series of conclusions and preferences is built upon or related to one's assumptions about the nature of man.

Assumptions must also be made about the character of society and the extent to which both man and his society are incapable of or resistant to change. For some, "society" is a term with real meaning — an independent entity with a life of its own, apart from the men who happen to make it up at any given time. In such cases, the "needs of the society" are likely to be placed paramount to any particular member's preferences, and some device for ascertaining what those needs are must be found. The net result is likely to be a form of government by a relatively few, better qualified persons in the society. A less mystical use of the term "society" is as a synonym for all or a majority of individuals who happen to be present at any moment within its geographical confines. In such uses, needs of the society and majority preference are one and the same, and an entirely different decisionmaking process seems proper. Another set of assumptions concerns the extent to which man is irretrievably the product of something innate within himself, or, alternatively, the product of his environment. If the latter is true, he can be improved (at least to some extent, although with the threat of some accompanying risks) through manipulation of the environment. If the former is true, of course, such efforts are both hopeless and potentially very dangerous.

Which of these sets of alternative assumptions is better or more soundly based? At the moment, there seems to be no way in which a case for one or another can be conclusively established or "proved." There are scraps of evidence regarding aspects of these issues, but they often support equally plausible and contrasting interpretations. Each citizen is therefore forced to adopt what seems to him to be the most reasonable set of assumptions. Because this is just about the same as expressing one's preferences, such position-taking tells the listener or reader little about the nature of man but much about the originator's political values.

(2) What are the proper goals of social and political life, and with what order of priorities and at what cost should they be sought? This is the area in which evidence is of least assistance; men must answer these questions in response to their own preferences and with only their personal values for guidance. The questions are rarely put so bluntly, of course: they arise in the context of defining familiar concepts or establishing priorities among familiar and generally shared goals. For example, the concept of "freedom" carries several alternative meanings. To some, it may mean freedom from government interference, and lead them to seek severe limitations on the activities of government. To others, it may mean freedom to do the things that one would want if only the handicaps of poverty and ignorance could be removed; this would lead them to seek broad expansion of the social welfare activities of government. The concept of "equality" is equally malleable according to one's preferences. It may mean equality in the sense of the right to use whatever talents one happens to have in the pursuit of one's goals; or it can be expanded slightly to include the right to at least a minimum of education and a minimum standard of living; or it can be broadened still further to signify that all men are entitled to full social and economic parity with one another. Economic equality is a much more ambitious goal than mere political equality, but even within the latter concept there is room for considerable difference of viewpoint. In the eighteenth century, some defined political equality in terms of suffrage which was limited to males who owned a certain amount of property. More recently, sharp controversy has developed over the question of whether this generally agreed upon goal required "one man, one vote" arrangements at all levels of government. The fact that men who strongly subscribe to the goal of political equality can sincerely argue that some kinds of people should have more votes than others indicates that there is wide room for disagreement even when the basic goal is shared "in principle." Thus, it is the determination of the specific content to be attached to familiar terms which is critical in setting up one's own independent framework. No definition is necessarily "correct" or better than another, for no man is the ultimate arbiter of the meaning of words; they mean for each citizen what he says they mean, and that is why there is bound to be disagreement in politics.

These differences in meaning may become apparent only when an issue arises in which the concept must be put into practice (or "operationalized"). At other times, generalized agreement on the propriety of the undefined concept of "freedom" or "equality" or "justice" may create the illusion of consensus. This illusion may be similarly fostered by the widespread acknowledgment of these goals on the part of all despite sharply differing views as to which should be given first priority. Once again, the illusion is dispelled only when it is sought to actually *do* one or the other. Consider the dilemma of the man who subscribes strongly to both "liberty" and "equality": at some point, he will have to decide which is paramount for him, because they are frequently conflicting goals. In order to provide equality for some, it may be necessary to limit the liberty of others to do what they want to with their property or their talents. If equality is defined as rough parity of opportunity to compete for the goals of life, and as such is a paramount goal, then one reluctantly concludes that in this instance liberty must be limited. But if one holds to a more restrictive view of equality, or considers liberty to be the goal deserving of first priority, then this would be an utterly wrong way for government to act. The same type of problem is involved in recent controversies over the rightful priority rankings of "justice" and "order," two goals readily acknowledged as vital by all. To some, nothing is more important than order and tranquility, while to others the obtaining of the rights and privileges which are component elements of justice deserves precedence.

When neither specific meaning nor priority rankings have been established for either of these concepts, they are not much more than glittering generalities in citizens' minds. As such, they are aspects of ideology, and we may tend to believe that since all right-thinking men share the same views, all that needs to be done to resolve conflicts is for men to sit down and "reason together"; or we may believe that our leaders are acting for us and hold the same views as we do because they use thes words in their explanations or exhortations. Clearly, these concepts offer us nothing but symbolic satisfactions and complacency until we undertake to set up specific content and relative valuations for them.

(3) What means — institutions and processes — offer the best prospects of reaching the goals established in (2), given the assumptions of (1)? In other words, how can we get from the specific assumptions about the nature of man to the characteristics of the good life? What logically consistent and empirically practicable means are there for reaching the goals desired? This is the area where we should be able to get the most assistance from factual knowledge about the workings of political institutions and processes. In seeking to establish some coherent linkage between the nature of man and the realization of his goals in life, we have for guidance considerable evidence as to how particular institutions work and why. We know, for example, that all congressmen in the House of Representatives are not equally influential in determining the provisions of new statutes, and we would not rest our hopes for goal attainment on the prospects of their being so. Thus, one of the first necessities in this area is familiarization with some of the basic facts and explanations of how the political system presently works, and use of this understanding to establish certain landmarks around which value preferences are to be exercised.

A second requirement in this area, as suggested above, is that of logical consistency. If man is irrational and selfish, for example, one can hardly expect to achieve equality for all through political mechanisms which are highly responsive to individual preferences. The character of each set of institutions and processes depends upon the particular characteristics of the men who design and operate them, and in turn shapes the kinds of goals that can be attained through them. This is a crucial point: the nature of men, the character of institutions and processes, and the goals that can be realized, are interdependent matters in politics. When we study institutions and processes we do so with the realization that they have been structured by the values and natures of the men who created and animate them, and also with the realization that their character determines in major ways the nature of the goals that can be achieved through them. Because this is so, we must organize our personal political positions to take this interdependence into account.

This is not to say that we must proceed consecutively from a determination about what man's nature is, to what ought to be in an ideal world, and finally to the institutional tinkering necessary to link the two together. Most political thinkers probably start with certain highly valued goals and some convictions about what does and does not work in the real world of institutions and processes, and then seek to fill in the rest more or less consistently and adequately. Nor do all the possible questions and problems in these three areas have to be resolved before the personal framework becomes functional. It is enough to be aware of the interdependencies between the areas and, therefore, to perceive what is at stake when considering one area in what might otherwise appear to be isolation and to see the implications that findings or assumptions in one carry for the others. What *is* important is to begin to build a map in one's mind of what is, can be, and ought to be in politics. This, in turn, will make it possible to respond rationally and selectively to the urgings and pleadings of others and to shape one's own independent course in politics.

Approaches to Evaluation of Governmental Performance

The act of evaluating either particular institutions or policies of government, or even whole areas of the political process, is considerably less demanding than the construction of one's own basic political position. It is a "middle-range" act, in the sense that it does not require the evaluator to have answers to or even to confront the great questions of politics; it requires only that the evaluator have at hand some relevant and clearly defined criteria with which to measure and exercise judgment upon the policy, institution, or process involved. But there are problems in the selection, clarification, and application of the criteria employed for this purpose. In an effort to avoid some of those problems, we shall consider two types of criteria.

(1) "Democracy" as an evaluative standard

As may be anticipated after the last section, the great difficulty in using "democracy" as a standard lies in the fact that its meaning has never been agreed upon. Instead, and particularly because the basic idea of democracy is so attractive to so many people and nations, it is probably used in more different ways to describe more disparate political systems than any other concept in the world of politics. Nevertheless, it is almost impossible for any political analyst, especially Americans, to think or act without some "democratic" measuring criteria in mind. We might, therefore, try to impose some kind of order upon the incipient chaos which is threatened by widespread use of this standard.

Uses of the concept of "democracy" may be distinguished according to the *nature* and the *objects* of its application. By the *nature* of its use, we mean that it may be used descriptively or prescriptively, either as a term applied to characterize a state of facts alleged or shown to exist, usually in the United States, or as an ideal to which present practice should aspire but currently fails to achieve. The former usage is the familiar one in which authors speak of "the politics of American democracy" or "the problems of American democracy." In doing so, of course, they have declared in effect that democracy is a term which is descriptive of politics in the United States; this usage deprives the term of any evaluative content because it can mean only whatever exists in the United States. No one can object if authors or publicists choose to use "democracy" and "the United States" as interchangeable words, for that is their business (and it sells books). But we can note that no evaluation has occurred, because "democracy" has been given content exactly equivalent to the "is" of American politics. Before evaluative usage of the concept can take place, it must have some meaning independent and apart from the object which it is used to measure. Thus, a definition must be constructed from other elements and then applied to the political system under examination.

The last imperative leads to use of the term in a prescriptive manner. In the effort to maximize evaluative capacity in the word (or simply because one prefers to think in ideal forms), "democracy" may be used, for example, in the sense of the New England Town Meeting model. All citizens would then be thought to have decided in open meeting what policies their government should follow on all matters, with full knowledge of the relevant facts and available alternatives; thereafter, officials in government faithfully act to execute those decisions. Insertion of such content in the term assures that the political system under evaluation will be found wanting, because no large society can actually operate this way in the modern world. Indeed, it is questionable whether, given what we now think we know from Marx, Freud, and experimental psychology alone, such a polity ever really existed. In any event, use of the New England town meeting model to measure how "democratic" the national government is today yields a negative judgment. But we may question whether use of the term in this manner makes much sense. It might be more useful to our evaluative purposes to design a definition of democracy which contained both evaluative capacity and the potential for discrimination among attainable political realities. In other words, we might seek an accommodation between mere celebration of the "is" and wholly unattainable idealized versions. Many observers have done this, of course, and there are many definitions of "democracy," with varied proportions of descriptive and prescriptive components, from which we might select to suit our individual preferences. We shall return to these alternatives in a moment.

Uses of the concept of "democracy" are also distinguishable according to the *objects* to which it is being applied. To some, the term means the familiar political characteristics of free speech, voting rights, majority rule, political parties with alternative programs, regular elections, fair procedures and due process, tolerance of the rights of others, etc. Reasonable men may differ as to the exact nature and quality of these political rights which are requisite to the accolade "democracy," but they would all be necessary at least to some extent. But this is an exclusively *political process*-oriented approach to the definition. It does not include consideration of the underlying conditions in the social structure or the economy which might be requisite to the real existence of the political forms just described. Nor does it include consideration of the relationship between the policy produced by the government and the desires of all the people or at least the majority of them. Neither of these would be satisfactory replacements for the process-oriented definition, but they may be important and revealing supplements. It is certainly true that if sharp differentials in social status among individuals, or acute economic disparities, could lead to such preponderance of social and economic influence on the part of a few people over all others, the political manifestations of "democracy" would be nothing more than a facade. And the fullest observance of the procedural features of "democracy" would count for little if in fact the policy produced by the government through these processes was seriously distinct from what the majority of the people wanted, or from minimal standards of justice in the eyes of a significant minority. For these reasons, we should be wary of any definition cast solely in terms of the presence or absence of the standard civil liberties and electoral opportunities; these are necessary, but not sufficient, conditions for the existence of "democracy."

What we have done so far is to establish some parameters, or outside boundaries, within which the definition of "democracy" may be located. We think it is useless and misleading to define "democracy" as whatever "is" in the United States. It is just as unprofitable in our eyes to impose an unrealizable ideal such as the New England Town Meeting model on a modern industrialized society. We must therefore find our operational definition (if we *must* employ "democracy" as a measuring standard) in some accommodation which mixes reality with ideals. The precise mix which is to be taken as "democracy" must be determined by the individual reader for himself; the only requirements which intellectual rigor and responsibility impose is that he formulate the definition independently of his analysis of an operating system and that he state his criteria clearly and unambiguously. It goes without saying that he should not ignore the social and economic roots which give real meaning to the political forms of "democracy," though the exact extent to which he will require their presence is again a matter for individual determination. And our commitment to a substantive dimension to "democracy" — attention to the policies produced by the political system and comparison of them with the desires of substantial segments of the people — should be clear from the emphasis in this book on the facts of what government is actually doing to people and which people it is having an effect upon. Within these boundaries, however, let those who feel compelled to employ "democracy" as a standard suffer the uncomfortable consequences of having to spell out their own definitions and then search for agreement.

(2) Alternative criteria for evaluation of the political system's performance

Our unenthusiastic attitude toward the use of "democracy" as an evaluative criterion is due not only to the foregoing problems inherent in its use, but also to the traces of cultural arrogance associated with it. Why should we assume that "democracy" is the only or even the most important basis on which an institution, policy, or political system should be evaluated? Americans frequently *have* done so (and have at times gratuitously included a capitalist economic system as a necessary aspect of democracy), but there is no compelling logical reason for it. Furthermore, there are other, certainly less culturebound and probably more objective, criteria which might be used instead. We might simply seek to measure the extent to which a given object of analysis (an institution, policy, or process) is of service to a demonstrated or posited need, goal, or value. It might be demonstrated that a given political system faced a particular need, such as the necessity of raising revenue, and analysis could then be directed at the success of the system in doing so. Or we might simply posit the need to maintain some kind of consent for the policies of the government and then analyze the extent to which the system actually did so. Similarly, goals such as rapid industrialization, or increased standard of living, or stability might be the basis for evaluation. Or values such as equality, justice, or freedom (suitably defined) might serve as means of reaching judgments.

Of course the evaluator would bear the burden of demonstrating to the satisfaction of his audience that his standard was a reasonable one for the political system under the current circumstances of its existence, and that his definitions and sense of priorities among various possible needs, goals, or values were defensible. But this is no different from the obligation to do the same in regard to *any* standard — including democracy, justification for the use of which is so often assumed. The analysis would probably lead to a judgment that the needs, goals, or values had been *more or less* achieved, rather than *either* realized *or* not. Gradations of achievement would be suggested by the nature of the evaluative tool, and this is in accord with the reality of politics. Appropriate use of the term "democracy" would also make it possible to rate all countries on a scale of greater or lesser amounts, because all systems differ only relatively marginally in degree of one characteristic or another. But the concept is only infrequently formulated or employed with such precision.

This alternative approach thus involves no problems not inherent in the use of "democracy," and offers several advantages. It avoids many of the confusions of definition, not because there is no obligation to be precise in specifying the criteria or definitions to be employed, but because there are no pre-existing assumptions or stereotypes surrounding the words and concepts to be used. The symbolic associations and assumptions accumulated over centuries tend to attach themselves to every use of the term "democracy," regardless of how careful we may seek to be. This is perhaps less true of "efficiency" or "responsiveness to problems," for which we provide a specific operational meaning suited to the circumstances of its use. These latter concepts are still somewhat ambiguous, of course. Readers may disagree with our use, but they should at least know in advance and with clarity what it is that they disagree with. Further, occasional use of such alternative criteria enable us to avoid the culture-bound assumption that all systems do or should place "democracy" high on their priority ranking, or that if a system has separation of powers and two-party politics it must be a "democracy."

This excursion in search of generally applicable and objective standards for evaluation should provide some guidance for our study of the American political system. Whatever we can do to purge ourselves of prior assumptions about the utility or "democraticness" of politics in the United States — and particularly of the tendency to define "democracy" in terms of what exists in this country — will be helpful in enabling us to see the real characteristics of American politics more clearly. This is not to say that the United States *is not* a democracy, of course, but simply to point out that the judgment as to whether it is or not is a partly definitional, partly empirical question which each individual reader must decide for himself.

Devising evaluative standards, and working with different standards under different circumstances, are thus part of the intellectual techniques which one seeks to develop in order to make rational judgments and actions in politics.

Throughout our analysis, we shall raise alternatives, ask what difference findings and interpretations make, and suggest possible implications. When we analyze policies, for example, we shall ask who benefits. In studying institutions, we shall ask who controls them. In exploring values and ideology, we will want to know which social classes hold what beliefs, how such beliefs are shaped, and who benefits thereby. In considering relationships between elites and masses, we shall look for where initiative lies, what constraints are observed by elites or can be imposed on them by masses, and to what extent leaders shape (or follow) popular preferences. At every juncture, the citizen should supplement our questions with queries of his own: is this good, right, consistent with the values of equality or justice? Is it democratic and how is this term defined? Is it appropriate to the problems of the 1970's? Should I seek improvement in this or that feature of policy, or do my goals require more far-reaching change in the political system itself or the underlying values which sustain it? In either case, what are the ways in which my goals can be realized most effectively? As analysts, we shall make every effort to do our part in this division of labor; and we assume the citizen will do the same in his multiple roles of analyst, evaluator, and actor.

THREE OTHER STRATEGIES OF POLITICAL ANALYSIS

We have completed our presentation of our approach. But readers may wish to employ other, more orthodox — and possibly as useful — schemes; three major conceptual frameworks are described below. We remind the reader that, if he is content to proceed within the authors' design, he may well prefer to defer or ignore this section entirely.

To create strategies for political analysis that provide a useful union of theory and observation is difficult and often complex, but it is essential, and its very complexity makes it challenging and intriguing. Political scientists do not agree fully as to which strategies are most useful or upon how well they work. The approaches to be outlined here, however, are the most widely used and are increasingly seen as helping students of politics to avoid serious errors and to produce a body of knowledge that is more than lore or myth.

(1) Group Theory

The set of ideas known as group theory was first systematically suggested by Arthur F. Bentley in 1908 in a landmark book, *The Process of Government.*[1] It has come to have a particularly strong influence upon political science theory and research since the end of World War II. Group theory reflected and reinforced the interest during the postwar years in looking beyond descriptions of formal governmental institutions and actions to find a way to explain and predict political occurrences.

The basic tenet of group theory holds that all public policy results from the interplay of group interests. This proposition is probably best understood if we are clear about what it denies or refuses to accept. It denies, for one thing, that one can usefully understand public policy formation by assuming that it is individual wants, needs, or feelings that explain how policy becomes what it is — that the individual is the independent variable.

What we perceive to be individual values cannot be the starting point of the political process because these values do not arise in and of themselves; instead, they come from the groups with which a person associates. Each human being acquires some of his values and wants very early in life from his family. Later he is influenced by other face-to-face groups such as clubs, churches, social gatherings, and unions. He is also a product of "categoric groups," all members of which never meet face-to-face but do have something important in common: age level, religion, work skill, income level, or skin color. He is further influenced by "reference groups": those people whose values or ideas an individual takes as his benchmark and which help him decide what he likes and dislikes. In making up his mind, he may ask himself what "true liberals" would think, and follow their lead; or he may ask himself how a right-wing extremist would play it and

[1] Arthur F. Bentley, *The Process of Government,* ed. Peter H. Odegard (Cambridge, Mass: Harvard University Press, 1967).

then move in the opposite direction. In this case right-wing extremists constitute a negative reference group for him.

More generally, an individual's personality is in large measure (some social psychologists would say entirely) a product of his social interactions. He is constantly examining his own intended actions and values to see whether they conform to the expectations of other persons or groups who are important to him; and in this way he learns who he is from his social contacts and his choice of particular "others" as his benchmarks. As different individuals are sure to vary somewhat in their choices of a range of significant others, people develop somewhat different personalities, and there is the possibility of striking out in new patterns of behavior and thinking. But because there is also bound to be a large measure of overlap in the choice of significant others, and because some reference groups are taken as significant by almost everybody, there is also a large measure of agreement, conformity, and uniformity among the members of a single society.[2]

There is of course no question that individuals are separate from each other as masses of flesh, bone, blood, and tissue; but it is equally certain, though less obvious, that in their beliefs, emotions, attitudes and choices about ways of behaving they are the products of their group attachments and therefore not separate from one another. Because politics deals with interests and with decisions about satisfying interests rather than with physiological organisms, advocates of group theory believe it is more useful to take the group than the individual as the unit of analysis. Group theorists do not believe they leave the individual out of account; they argue rather that they see him realistically for what he is — composed of many group interests.

For many of the same reasons, the "state," the "public interest," or the "general welfare" are not accepted in group theory as useful explanations of how public policy is determined. All these terms, and others like them, always stand for different things whenever a specific controversial public policy is under consideration. Those who want to spend more money for manned space flights and those who would prefer to use the money to help the poor both think they are promoting the public interest, as do both proponents and opponents of a stronger missile defense system, an increase in the minimum wage, and the abolition of capital punishment. The fact is that on most controversial issues there is a wide range of groups of people who define the problem differently, whose feelings about it vary in intensity, and who differ in their evaluation of what should be done about a particular issue and how much money and effort should go into its solution. Terms like the "state" and the "national welfare" create a fictitious image of a unified political organism and of clarity as to what is right. For group theorists, therefore, these terms are seen as useful only in propaganda — in creating the false impression that the speaker's position represents the true interests of everybody. They

[2] See George Herbert Mead, *Mind, Self, and Society* (Chicago: University of Chicago Press, 1934).

are regarded as useless, and indeed highly misleading, in serious political observation and analysis.

Every individual, then, shares group interests with others; but the total pattern of interests he holds is not completely like anybody else's pattern. He may support broadening civil rights for minorities and have an interest in keeping trade unions from gaining economic power; but others who stand with him on one of these interests may be against him on the other one. In this way, the society includes a crisscrossing of many group interests which both unite men and divide them. It may seem paradoxical at first, but the crisscrossing and the overlapping in group interest patterns is probably the most effective social cement that exists. So long as there is widespread overlapping, serious civil conflict is unlikely. A country is in real danger when there is a high measure of coincidence in people's group interest patterns: when those who agree on civil rights also stand together on economic policy, foreign policy, educational policy, and the other issues that excite men most. Society then comes to be polarized into two hostile camps with intense aversions toward each other, little in common, and continuous reinforcement of conflicting attitudes on both sides. It is easy to perceive the other camp as a threat to the good life, and attempts at suppression, intimidation, and physical conflict are likely. Where people who disagree on one significant issue are in agreement on others, the conflict is obviously minimized, and it becomes harder to build coalitions that oppose each other in a continuing and intense way.

Group theory also makes use of the notion of "potential" groups, and this concept can also be an aid in promoting a sophisticated understanding of policy formation and in avoiding some simplistic pitfalls. In their political interests, people are certainly concerned with possibilities that may arise as well as with problems that are currently serious; and so policymakers have to be responsive to these potential interests as well. Even at a time when almost everybody who wants a job has one, it is clear that a severe increase in unemployment will give rise to strong and widespread demands for governmental action to help the jobless. In the planning of economic policy, such potential interests have to be taken into account, for the politician or administrator who neglects them may be reminded by a severe loss of votes or strong public protest that he is out of touch with his constituency base and is paying a penalty for it.

Group theory, then, like any useful theory, helps an observer of the political scene to ask some searching questions, to avoid some pseudo-issues, and to make sense of the answers he gets. He looks at an administrative agency setting private electric power rates and sees its staff members reflecting the interests of stockholders in the companies, the management of the companies, and the sympathizers and supporters of private enterprise generally who will predictably support the management if it is threatened. But he also sees staff members reflecting the interests of the utility's customers and of people who identify with the interests of consumers even though they are not served by regulated companies in this instance. He notices further that individual staff members differ in the degree to which they support one or another of these groups' interests, but that most of them are ambivalent in some measure, reflecting in their reports, recommendations, and draft proposals some degree of compromise concerning these conflicting interests. In arriving at a particular kind of compromise, he recognizes that staff members are influenced by their own values, which amount to identifications with one or another of the concerned groups. He also recognizes that these identifications are based broadly upon each staff member's upbringing and education, the pattern of other groups with which he comes into contact, and his future aspirations, including perhaps his ambition to join the staff of a regulated utility some day. Sometimes he recognizes that identifications are based upon bribes. The group theorist, therefore, looks at much the same kinds of data as others; but he makes distinctions in a particular way, avoids certain non-empirical assumptions (such as the assumption that values are self-generating in the individual rather than derived from group ties), and has a ready scheme for fitting his observations into a meaningful pattern.

Clearly, the same kinds of observations and analysis can be made in studying a court, a legislative body, an international organization like the United Nations or the International Labor Organization, or the decisions of a high-ranking executive. All of them reflect a pattern of group interests with different sanctions or forms of pressure available to each. In every case, the range of group interests includes an interest in survival and in achieving some measure of status for the court, legislature, or other government agency itself.

(2) Systems Theory

Since about the middle of the decade of the 1950's, political scientists have relied more and more heavily upon another strategy for guiding political observation and analysis — systems theory. To think of sets of related political behaviors as "systems" forces political analysts to ask themselves exactly how different political activities affect each other and what contribution each activity makes to the total pattern. It therefore helps analysts avoid drawing incorrect conclusions about the meaning of particular political activities, which often take on quite a different meaning when viewed as part of a larger picture.

Any "system" is made up of different component parts which together can do something the separate parts cannot accomplish by themselves. An electric battery, some bell wire, a bell, an electric switch, and a person who sometimes wants a bell to ring compose the components of a system; but as individual parts they ring no bells, achieve no end, and therefore do not comprise a system. Yet when properly connected to each other, they do become a system capable of creating a ringing sound. To study each of the component parts of this system as an independent object would tell an observer little or nothing about the system; it would very likely lead him to false guesses about the uses of the individual parts. Once he sees them hooked together and learns something about the ties among them, he quickly recognizes what their separate functions are within the system: providing energy, transmitting it, converting it from an electrical flow to a hammer striking a bell, starting and stopping the energy flow, and deciding when to start and when to stop. The system is something quite different from the sum of its unconnected parts; and each of the parts becomes something different when it is connected to the rest of the system.

In the same way, a political activity becomes a different phenomenon and acquires a different value when it is part of a system. To see an administrative agency ask for a large boost in its budget for the next fiscal year might lead an observer to conclude that its officers are politically unrealistic or that it expects to face a drastic increase in its workload or that it is terribly imperialistic or greedy. Once the observer recognizes that the operating agency is one part of a long-established system whose parts have different functions, however, he is likely to revise these initial impressions. He will learn that in the federal system of appropriating money, operating agencies are expected to ask for substantial increases and that other units of the system (the Bureau of the Budget and the Appropriations Committee of the House of Representatives) are expected to cut these down. An agency that fails to play its expected role creates uncertainty as to how the whole system will function; it runs the danger of having its budget cut and of antagonizing all the groups that rely upon it to play its part. In this light, then, a large increase request does not mean lack of realism or greed, or even a workload increase, but rather the willingness of the agency to accept the established procedures of the system in which it operates.[3]

This example also illustrates some of the other uses of systems theory for political scientists. In this instance our concern was with how decisions about federal appropriations are made. For this purpose one can define a system by (1) identifying all the people, groups, and government units which play some part in appropriating federal money and (2) determining just what the function of each component of this system is. To do this forces an analyst to notice that the observations do not always conform to the conventional assumptions about how government works or to the formal definitions of what an administrative agency, legislative body, or other unit does. The administrative agency, for example, is not simply "carrying out" a law, but rather is trying to expand its operations or at least protect them from diminution or disruption. A major committee of the Congress is not simply reflecting the "will" of its constituents but consistently wielding an axe on requests from operating agencies. Each of these observations, and others that would have to be made if the whole system were examined further, has to be interpreted in the light of the functions they serve for the system. The use of systems theory is likely, therefore, to challenge conventional and formal

[3] Aaron Wildavsky, *The Politics of the Budgetary Process* (Boston: Little, Brown, 1964).

assumptions about how things work and what they mean, and to encourage and guide empirical observation.

The same example illustrates still another use of systems theory: that it defines the system in the light of a practical purpose of the observer and not on the basis of conventional organizational lines or geographic boundaries. The system for appropriating includes part, but not all, of Congress as an organization and sees this component as interacting with other organizations or parts of them. The systems analyst is thus forced by his problem to carry on his observations wherever there is pertinent activity, regardless of prior assumptions about what is pertinent. In this way, the "boundaries" of the system can only be learned pragmatically — by finding out what the inputs, conversion processes, and outputs[4] of the particular system are. It becomes very difficult, and probably impossible in principle, to define "boundaries" in the abstract; but it is especially important to avoid defining them in advance along conventional or formal lines because political activity seldom takes this neat form. It is true that a particular organization like Congress can be thought of as a system in itself and that some political scientists now treat it in this way. But this is probably not an especially useful application of systems theory or the systems metaphor. Such usage can lead simply to translating conventional observations about Congress as an organization into the language of systems theory without forcing new kinds of observations or insights about the meaning of particular activities inside Congress.

Although it is common in systems theory to speak of "inputs" and "outputs," these terms do not imply that any system is isolated from other political systems or that it comes to an end after it produces outputs. The outputs of the system in reference to federal appropriations are, of course, money appropriations to federal agencies; and these monies, in turn, become inputs for many other political systems. An appropriation to the Department of State is part of the input for the political system that determines foreign policy. Similarly, an output affects the inputs of the very system that produced it, through what is known as "feedback." A large appropriation for space research, for example, establishes an expectation that space research will start with a larger base the following year.

It should be clear from this discussion that there is nothing right or wrong about treating sets of political activities as systems. As in the case of group theory, the question for the analyst has to be, "Is this kind of theory useful in suggesting questions, forms of observation, or new interpretations?" If so, he is justified in using it, always remembering that it is a tool for analysis and not a description of the world.

---

[4] The classification of systems variables into inputs, conversion processes, and outputs is suggested in David Easton, *A Framework for Political Analysis* (Englewood Cliffs, N. J.: Prentice-Hall, 1964), probably the most influential application of systems theory to the political process. In Easton's formulation, demands and support constitute inputs which are "converted" into outputs, including but not limited to public policies.

(3) Functional Theory

A third widely used strategy for political research is called functional theory. It builds upon the ideas used in systems theory, but is concerned less with finding the range and boundaries of a system than with carefully examining the contribution made by each component part of the system to its survival or successful functioning. As in the cases of the other theories discussed, it is at least as important to recognize the mistakes the strategy helps us avoid as to list its benefits.

A key advantage of functional theory is that it concentrates upon examination of the *consequences* activities have for the systems of which they are a part. It thus prevents the political scientist from focusing only upon the *causes* of these activities, which may not be part of the political system at all. How a particular set of rules for conducting elections developed in a country is an important part of the history of that country; but in itself it tells the political analyst nothing about the *function* of the election laws. It may appear upon careful study that the election laws consistently keep certain elites in positions of power; or that they consistently keep certain minorities from exercising proportionate influence or holding public office; or that they encourage widespread participation in elections and therefore reassure the population that it has a significant voice in governing itself. These are all politically important consequences of the election laws and they tell us what part these laws play in maintaining a particular kind of political system. If attention is focused only upon how the laws developed historically or upon why individual voters behave as they do in the voting booth, the functions the voting act serves for the system as a whole are not learned.

Functional theory also encourages the political analyst to be as rigorous as possible in determining the nature and value of the contribution of a particular component to the entire system. What function, for example, does the drafting of a national political party platform serve for the American party system? The platform professes to tell the voters what policies the party candidates will support if they are elected; but it takes relatively little observation to notice that candidates often ignore the platform once they are in office. It is therefore easy to reach the conclusion that American party platforms are sheer hypocrisy whose function it is to mislead the voters. To some extent they do of course serve this function; but they do more. They serve as a barometer of the sensitivity of the party activists to contending interest groups and of the willingness of the party to make concessions to particular groups. In this way, the platform helps pressure groups and individuals decide upon their strategies with respect to such matters as campaign contributions and what kinds of pressures have some chance of succeeding at particular times. They also become a tactic through which the party organization puts together a coalition of groups supporting its candidates. These are all more specific functions, and rather different ones, than the forecasting of individual candidates' policy positions once they are in office.

If the precise function of an activity is known, it becomes possible to recognize which activities serve the same function and therefore which can be substituted for each other. In every political system, for example, there has to be some device for ascertaining how intense and how widespread opinions are on controversial issues. Is it functionally equivalent for factions within catch-all political parties to represent opposing positions and for ideologically homogeneous parties to compete with each other? Do these alternative devices for interest "aggregation" have the same results for the system or different results? Functional theory forces the political analyst to raise this kind of question and to try to answer it. The example also underlines another key use of theory: to suggest types of questions and types of observations that might otherwise not occur to an observer of the political scene.

If functional theory helps students to recognize in what respects political activities serve comparable or different political functions, it ought to be especially useful in comparing the political institutions of different countries and different cultures. This is, in fact, the field in which it first achieved prominence in political science and the field in which it has been most conspicuously applied. It seemed to offer students of comparative government a systematic way of doing something more searching and more rigorous than describing the political institutions of different countries, one at a time.

Its use as a conceptual framework in comparative government is associated with the name of Gabriel Almond, who has tried to develop a workable scheme for applying it cross-nationally and cross-culturally.[5] Almond suggests that in every political system there are four "input" functions and three "output" functions. The first input is political socialization and recruitment: "induction into the political culture" through teaching people a set of attitudes that define the culture. The second is interest articulation or the expression of political opinions and attitudes. The third is interest aggregation or the formation of public policies that are based upon the articulated interests. The fourth is political communication, the exchange of information which makes the performance of the other functions possible. The three "output" functions are rule making, rule application, and rule adjudication. By examining the devices for accomplishing each of these functions in different countries and cultures it is hoped that the student of comparative government will learn which differences in political institutions and behaviors are basic and which are superficial, and that he will also learn something about the alternative ways of maintaining political systems, of changing them, and perhaps of destroying them.

All three of the theoretical strategies for political observation and analysis discussed here have been extensively criticized as well as praised. Certainly they are all incomplete and gloss over many un-

---

[5] Gabriel A. Almond, "A Functional Approach to Comparative Politics," in *The Politics of the Developing Areas,* eds. Gabriel A. Almond and James S. Coleman (Princeton, N. J.: Princeton University Press, 1960).

certainties and unclear definitions. While they suggest some important hypotheses and lines of inquiry, they may deflect attention from other possible approaches. It may be that they are all more useful in helping political scientists to avoid some common pitfalls than in positive guidance. It may also be that they all have a conservative bias: for they usually focus attention upon existing systems of action rather than upon change or imaginable but untried systems of action. Doubtless they will be replaced eventually by other strategies designed to deal with some of the shortcomings just listed. Still, they have made the study of politics more careful, more self-conscious about its methods and assumptions, more empirical, and more rigorous than it was before they appeared.

These are the issues and approaches with which students of politics deal. It is important now to consider more carefully what it is that makes knowledge of political institutions and processes important, for the methodological and conceptual questions with which this section of this chapter has dealt are not a reason for studying politics. These are tools for acquiring accurate knowledge, but they are worth using only because politics itself is a vital human activity. Like religion, love, and the arts, people are always involved in it, moved by it, responsive to it. This is true because, like these other classic concerns of man, politics is a basic channel for realizing human values. It is through politics that men get or are denied many of the things they seek.

Lending further challenge and subtlety to political analysis is the circumstance that the payoffs are not all tangible and not always in money or power. These are the obvious kinds of benefits that flow from political activity, but people sometimes come to feel even more strongly about psychological, emotional, or symbolic political payoffs whose character they do not always recognize themselves. The ratification of a constitutional amendment prohibiting the manufacture, sale, and use of intoxicating liquor confers status and a national endorsement upon a group of rural southern and midwestern fundamentalist Protestants and denies status to urban Catholics whose subculture condones or encourages drinking; and the later repeal of the same amendment reverses this distribution of status symbols.[6] An antitrust law reassures anxious consumers that their state will protect them against price rigging by business monopolies — whether or not it actually does so.[7]

Courtroom procedures, rituals, and rules of evidence amount to a continuing proclamation that the law is fair and justice blind. Such payoffs of the political system are fundamental, for they maintain confidence, assure wide public support, and so make possible the tangible payoffs, usually to much smaller groups, that might otherwise be met with widespread resistance and protest.

To learn about the fundamental processes through which values

---

[6] Cf. Joseph R. Gusfield, *Symbolic Crusade* (Urbana, Ill.: University of Illinois Press, 1963).

[7] Thurman Arnold, *The Folklore of Capitalism* (New Haven, Conn.: Yale University Press, 1937).

are achieved or denied is, therefore, to try to understand a fundamental and classic mode of behavior; and it should be clear from
what has already been said about the complexities of its study that
simple common sense is often a very inadequate and misleading
guide to understanding in this field.

While human beings feel elation and excitement at acquiring any
kind of knowledge that is not self-evident, some forms of knowledge
also bring the ability to influence events and decisions. Indeed, John
Dewey defined knowledge in terms of the power to control. Knowledge about politics is clearly of this kind, for it is not simply an
intellectual exercise, but a resource for influencing the course of
affairs: for getting what you want and for helping other people get
what they want.

Every conflict that becomes a political issue involves a clash of
values. In most cases, the clash is resolved in some kind of compromise. The sophisticated student of politics is clear-eyed about what
is at stake, what tactics and strategies may influence payoffs, and who
wins or loses how much. To be clear-eyed, however, he must be able
to understand political interplay in all its complexity. He must have a
sophisticated appreciation of the subtle ways in which values, organizations, procedures for policymaking, and personalities interweave
with each other to make up the political process.

If he is both imaginative and rigorous in the study of political
interplay, he can also be creative: both as a contributor of fresh
insights into the process and as a tactician for groups with something
at stake in politics.

PUBLIC POLICIES II

The four chapters in this Part describe United States government policies and their consequences in four major problem areas: national security, poverty and racism, economic growth and stability, and foreign policy toward the Third World. These subjects were selected because of their contemporary importance, and because they appear to be disconnected areas in which different interests and different configurations of power and purposes might be involved. In each case, we shall explore both the problem itself and the policies employed to cope with that problem.

The first chapter in this Part undertakes some special tasks. It seeks to illustrate the approach of the book in comprehensive fashion. It not only describes certain national security policies and their consequences, but also explicitly indicates what may be implied by such patterns in regard to our central questions of power and change.

It also shows how the analytical techniques and concepts of political science may contribute to understanding complex issues. In the three subsequent chapters, we shall concentrate on government policies and their consequences, relying on the reader to see the implications in such patterns for our central questions.

National Security Through 4
Military Superiority

Since the end of World War II, the policy of the United States government has been to seek national security by maintaining military power superior to that of the major communist nations. In recent years, however, at least some aspects of this basic policy have been challenged. Concern over mounting military expenditures, reports of the wasting of billions of dollars in military procurement practices, and allegations about a "military-industrial complex" have become familiar features of American politics. Some have argued that the military is no longer under effective civilian control, either overseas or at home. Others insist that only the awesome might of American weaponry, alertly managed and constantly poised, has prevented nuclear war and maintained the "free world" against communist expansion.

Because this is our first policy-focused chapter, we shall undertake a more comprehensive presentation than in later chapters. We want to show specifically how an exploration of government policies and their consequences raises important questions and suggests implications about where power lies and how it is wielded within the American political system. We shall also self-consciously demonstrate some of the analytical and conceptual principles discussed earlier. The subject of national security, of course, or even that of the current role of the military in American policymaking, clearly is much too broad to be covered adequately in a single chapter. Instead of attempting such a task, we are in effect using this relatively familiar subject area to show the distinctive nature of our approach and how it can be employed to yield insightful hypotheses about power and change. Starting with a description of the basic policy of military superiority, we shall move first to a survey of some of its consequences, and then to specifying some of the questions and implications that emerge from this analysis.

MILITARY SUPERIORITY: THE BASIC ASSUMPTIONS

Conventional wisdom holds that German aggression prior to World War II occurred because of the military weakness of potential opponents; military preparedness, it is therefore assumed, is the key to peace and stability in an uncertain and amoral world. Applied to the major communist nations, which were perceived as expansionist and implacably hostile to the United States, this assumption led to the conclusion that the security of the United States required maintenance at all times of military strength superior to that of the communists. In order to provide the security sought, this military superiority would have to be sufficient to assure unacceptable (if not total) destruction of the Soviet Union, and recently China as well, even if such nations should first launch a surprise attack on the United States. Instituted in 1946 in the aftermath of World War II, the policy of security through military superiority still rests on these basic assumptions.

Security is an elusive and frustrating goal. For several reasons, it can never be finally assured; and, paradoxically, the more it is sought, the more it may recede. At any moment, an enemy may achieve a scientific breakthrough enabling him to achieve military supremacy through technology. Or he may drastically alter the strategic situation through a sudden diplomatic success, subversion, or other means. The more a nation seeks assurance of security by military means, the more it must commit its resources to weapons, research and development, procurement of multiple attack and defense systems, alliances with the governments of other nations, economic and military support for such governments if necessary, and anticipatory intelligence and subversion activities throughout the world. Every such act, of course, provokes the potential enemy to undertake or expand similar activities, and these in turn reduce the first nation's security and require countering moves. Nearly three decades of "Cold War" amidst the continuing threat of nuclear annihilation, combined with a special fear of communism, have made such commitments almost unquestionable among American policymakers.

In order to maintain military superiority at the level considered necessary, the United States invested more than $550 billion in direct military expenditures during the decade from 1959 through 1968. Even before the peak reached during the Vietnam War, the military share of the national budget was approaching $80 billion per year, or nearly 50 percent of the federal government's annual expenditures. One critic of military expenditures summarizes the amounts expended in this way:

Each year the federal government spends more than 70 cents of every budget dollar on past, present, and future wars. The American people are devoting more resources to the war machine than is spent by all federal, state, and local governments on health and hospitals, education, old-age and retirement benefits, public assistance and relief, unemployment and social security, housing and community development, and the support of agriculture.[1]

Although this stark comparison suggests some serious questions of priorities in government expenditures, we must first translate the meaning of these sums in terms of the military superiority and security they have provided, and then examine their consequences.

The military establishment consisted in 1969 of 3,400,000 men and women in the armed forces; 1,300,000 civilians working directly for the Defense Department; and about 100,000 companies working on defense orders and employing about 3,800,000 more civilians.[2] The active duty forces included 18 divisions and over 10,000 aircraft in the Army, 932 ships and over 8,000 aircraft in the Navy, and more than 15,000 aircraft in the Air Force. Department of Defense holdings of land and buildings in the United States, valued at their acquisition cost of many years ago, totalled over $40 billion; personal property such as plant and equipment, at current costs, add another $162 billion. Overseas, the Defense Department leases additional bases in more than thirty countries; 429 of these are classed as major, and 2,972 as minor. Their total operating cost exceeds $4.5 billion per year, and they house more than a million men and half as many dependents.

The key criterion of military power in the nuclear age, however, is the nuclear striking force which one nation can effectively deliver upon another. As of 1969, the United States had 1,054 land-based intercontinental ballistic missiles (ICBMs), mostly in protected sites in the U.S., 41 Polaris submarines with 656 submarine-launched ballistic missiles (SLBMs), 646 nuclear-armed strategic bombers, plus many medium-range missiles and bombers deployed around the borders of China and the Soviet Union. The intercontinental strike force alone was capable of delivering more than 4,000 nuclear warheads, and the medium-range force approximately another 2,500. Although intelligence estimates concerning Soviet strength tend to fluctuate according to domestic political factors, the best authorities appear to

[1] Richard J. Barnet, *The Economy of Death* (New York: Atheneum, 1969), p. 5.
[2] William Proxmire, *Report From Wasteland* (New York: Praeger, 1970). The data in the next two paragraphs are drawn from page 11 following.

agree that the American striking force is significantly more powerful than the Soviets'. Figure 1 shows the Defense Department figures for 1967 and 1968. The American total has been roughly stable, in part because of the need for funds in the Vietnam War since 1967, the point at which the buildup of the early 1960's reached its peak. The Soviets, drastically outdistanced in the mid-1960's, have begun to narrow the gap. The Chinese, of course, have just begun to develop the capability of short-range delivery of nuclear weapons, and their entry into active superpower status is still many years away.

Far more important than absolute or comparative numbers of nuclear weapons is the number of warheads that can under various circumstances be reasonably expected to strike their targets, and the number necessary to wreak unacceptable destruction upon an enemy. According to Defense Department estimates, 200 nuclear warheads landing on major Soviet targets would kill 52 million people (21 percent of the population) and destroy 72 percent of the Soviet industrial capacity.[3] In addition, millions of others would be injured or homeless, the physical environment contaminated, and social organization thoroughly disrupted. We may take this as representing "unacceptable" levels of destruction, sufficient to deter Soviet policymakers from launching a surprise attack on the United States. Assuming that five times the required number of missiles must be launched from protected land sites and from under the sea in order to assure that 200 of these penetrate Soviet air defenses and reach their targets, it still appears that the United States possesses enough nuclear armament to destroy the Soviet Union several times over. The reverse is true also, of course. No matter how large the U.S. strategic forces grow, not even an American surprise attack could prevent the Soviet Union from launching a prohibitively destructive second strike from its protected sites and submarines.

Thus, superiority in terms of numbers of nuclear warheads no longer means assurance of security, if it ever did. The relative destructive capabilities of each side can still be affected by perfecting, building, and installing defense systems that will reduce the effectiveness of incoming ICBMs — or by developing new weapons systems that will multiply destructiveness per ICBM — but each side remains fully capable of inflicting intolerable destruction upon the other. Only major scientific breakthroughs permitting instantaneous mass annihilation can seriously alter this balance. But this does not mean either that the world is becoming more stable or that the arms race has ended. The prospect of nuclear war through miscalculation or irrationality remains, and both sides continue to seek to maximize their relative security by developing new attack and defense systems and pressing forward their research and development of potential new weapons.

In 1969 and 1970, the United States initiated a new cycle in this

---

[3] Barnet, *op. cit.*, pp. 24-25.

FIGURE 1
U.S. vs Soviet Intercontinental Nuclear Force, 1967/68

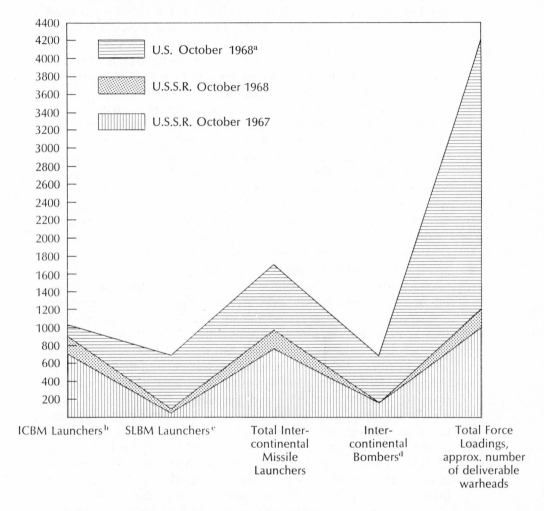

Source: George W. Rathjens, *The Future of The Strategic Arms Race: Options for the 1970s* (New York: The Carnegie Endowment for International Peace, 1969), p. 6.

[a] The size of the U.S. strategic force has not changed significantly since mid-1967.

[b] Excludes ICBM test range launchers which could have some operational capability against the United States. The Soviets also have Medium Range Ballistic Missiles (MRBMs) and Intermediate Range Ballistic Missiles (IRBMs) which are capable of striking Eurasian targets.

[c] In addition to the SLBMs on nuclear-powered submarines, the Soviets also have SLBMs on diesel-powered submarines, whose primary targets are believed to be strategic land targets in Eurasia. The Soviets also have submarine-launched cruise missiles, whose primary targets are believed to be naval and merchant vessels.

[d] In addition to the intercontinental bombers, the Soviets also have a force of medium bomber/tankers capable of striking Eurasian targets.

Source: Department of Defense, Secretary of Defense Robert S. McNamara, "Approach to the Fiscal Year 1969–73," Program and Fiscal Year 1969 Budget, in U.S. House of Representatives (90th Cong., 2d Sess.). *Department of Defense Appropriations for 1969. Hearings before a Subcommittee on Appropriations, Part I* (14 Feb., 1968), p. 147; some of the figures are based on a statement by Secretary of Defense Clark M. Clifford, 25 Oct., 1968; see *New York Times*, 26 Oct., 1968.

process.[4] Although Secretary of Defense Clifford characterized Soviet capabilities as being seven years behind the United States in land-based ICBMs, 10 years behind in submarine missiles, and inferior in number and quality of bombers and missiles, the military proposed two new systems for immediate deployment and several others for development. Still operating on the principle of military superiority, the Nixon administration proceeded with the multiple independently-targeted re-entry vehicle (MIRV), which permits each ICBM to deliver several warheads and thereby multiplies their capability many times. Funds were also sought for the anti-ballistic missile (ABM) defense system, which if perfected, a goal doubted by many scientific authorities, would somewhat reduce the number of Soviet missiles which might penetrate American defenses. These were termed necessary to hedge against the possibility that the Soviets might exceed all expectations and apparent economic capabilities and deploy similar weapons in the immediate future. Feeling that U.S. "overkill" capacity was already high enough, and that the Soviet Union had no capacity to suddenly make up for ten years' production of weapons, several senators questioned the value of the new programs more strongly than at any time since before World War II. The result was a narrow victory for the ABM system and continued expansion of MIRV capabilities. But budget analysts foresaw even greater military needs in the future; either approved, under development, or strongly endorsed were several new aircraft and missile systems, ships, carriers, manned bombers, and other weaponry sufficient to send the military budget up instead of down after the end of the war in Southeast Asia.

For nearly three decades, the same basic assumptions about the utility of military superiority and the danger of communism have dominated American thinking about national security and have resulted in granting military needs highest priority among federal expenditures. What was unique about the 1970's was the first stirring of public challenge to the desirability of these priorities. Congressional disclosures of vast waste totalling billions of dollars in military procurement activities were one source of this concern, but there were more fundamental developments in the world context that also led to the new questioning. The concept of security itself, at least as it had been understood in the past, appeared to be undermined by these changes.

The emergence of many newly independent nations, the rise of some secondary powers to nuclear or near-nuclear status, and the development of serious tensions among the communist nations, all contributed to a much more volatile and uncertain world situation. With power widely diffused and multiple conflicts likely, some of which were quite unrelated to competition between the superpowers,

[4] Proxmire, *op. cit.*, pp. 202-205. For a full presentation of the contending arguments here, together with their scientific bases, see (pro-ABM) Johan J. Hoist and William Schneider, Jr., eds., *Why ABM? Policy Issues in the Missile Defense Controversy* (Elmsford, N. Y.: Pergamon Press, 1969); and (anti-ABM) Abram Chayes and Jerome B. Weisner, eds., *ABM: An Evaluation of the Decision to Deploy an Anti-Ballistic Missile System* (New York: Harper and Row, 1969).

"security" would require preparation for many more contingencies, and it would be far more difficult to assure. Also, the advance of technology created two contrasting forms of pressure on established definitions and policy. On one hand, highly sophisticated but vastly expensive new attack and defense systems appeared possible. Their efficacy was not clear, but if they worked, both sides would be tempted to develop them, and thereby greatly increase their armaments expenditures. On the other hand, highly destructive nuclear weapons were becoming cheaper and easier to manufacture; in fact, they were so readily available that private groups or individuals might be able to acquire them. The only distinction remaining to the established superpowers, therefore, was the capacity to deliver thousands of tons of nuclear destructiveness by intercontinental rockets. Finally, and perhaps most important, serious domestic needs became visible. Rebuilding the cities, restoring the environment, repairing worsening race relations, and generally reconstructing the American social order appeared to demand high priority. But none of these goals would be attainable within reasonable time limits, unless they could receive a priority rivalling that of military expenditures. Moreover, "security" could not be merely an externally-oriented concept; it seemed in many peoples' eyes to be applicable to domestic problems as well, and to justify placing such needs alongside military demands.

TWO DECADES OF MILITARY PRIORITIES: A SURVEY OF CONSEQUENCES

We must observe immediately that there has been no nuclear war. Whether this is *because of* or *in spite of* the American policy of strategic superiority is not so clear. We have approached the brink of mutual annihilation with some frequency, in Berlin, in Vietnam, in Cuba, and in the Middle East. Whether, under different strategic conditions, American policies would have been less intransigently anticommunist, or Soviet policies more or less provocative in response, is a question which if answerable at all would require much deeper analysis than is possible here. But we can say with assurance that the *domestic* consequences of assigning the highest budgetary priority to military expenditures have become readily identifiable. And increasingly, they have appeared to many to outrank international consequences in importance. Let us explore some of these domestic consequences before returning to the strategic scene.

Since World War II, a large new industry has been created.[5] During the war years, the bulk of federal war expenditures went to long-established companies which simply sold their usual products to the government for the duration of the emergency. At most, companies would develop closely related products to meet defense needs or

---

[5] The most comprehensive analysis of the economic impact of defense expenditures is found in the work of Murray Weidenbaum of the Economics Department at Washington University, St. Louis. The next paragraphs draw particularly from his "Defense Expenditures and the Domestic Economy" in Edwin Mansfield, ed., *Defense, Science, and Public Policy* (New York: W. W. Norton, 1968).

adapt an existing model for military purposes. Automobile manufacturers diverted production to tanks, aircraft manufacturers shifted
to military aircraft. Many firms expanded production facilities, but
few new industries were created. Even for those, such as automobile
and aircraft companies, which modified their productive processes,
postwar conversion to civilian production was practical, anticipated,
and consistent with prior management experience and expertise.

Developments in electronics, nuclear power, and rocket propul-
sion, however, have changed the character of military needs. Since the
mid-1950's, the technological complexity of military requirements has
spurred the rise of new companies (or substantially independent
subsidiaries of established corporations) which specialize in such
work — sometimes to the exclusion of all other products. Thus, in
time there has developed a segment of the economy with an exclusively military focus, in which there is no background experience of
production for civilian needs or competitive consumer sales. For
example, in 1964, 52 percent of all defense-space expenditures went
to the aircraft industry, 25 percent to electronics, and between two
percent and five percent each to automobiles, oil, rubber, construction, chemicals, and educational institutions. The remaining 5.8 percent was shared among all other industries.[6] The pressing need for
scientific research and testing of the new products has also drawn a
significant segment of the creative scientific manpower of the nation
into this work. And the high cost of developing new weapons at a rate
faster than the Soviet Union has meant that the federal government
either shared or paid all of the cost of this scientific research. Thus, a
link of mutual dependency and shared interest between particular
types of industries and the military services was initially forged out of
technical and economic necessity.

The rise of these new companies and the development of independent military-oriented components of established corporations
also involved new geographic mobility and a high concentration of
such firms in certain areas of the country. For the most part, the new
industries selected locations in the Southwest and West, and this had
a kind of reinforcing effect on the location choices of other manufacturers. Eventually, defense expenditures became heavily concentrated in relatively few regions. The economies of these states and
localities in turn came to depend intimately on the continuation of
such expenditures; one estimate holds, for example, that 43 percent
of the economy of the Los Angeles area depends on direct defense
expenditures and the jobs and other services they generate.[7] Neither
the states and localities which extended tax benefits to lure these
industries, nor the congressmen who are tuned to the economic well-
being of their districts, can fail to be concerned about the continued
investment of federal funds in such military production.

Because of the high research and development costs as well as the
specialized and exclusively military value of the products, the Defense

[6] *Ibid.,* p. 20.
[7] *Ibid.,* p. 25.

Department buys much of its equipment on a "cost-plus" basis. In other words, suppliers are permitted to simply add up all their costs, add on their margin of profit, and bill the government for the total. Competitive bidding may be impractical because only one company has the research and scientific skills to produce a certain product. (In 1968, for example, 58 percent of all contracts awarded by the Defense Department were by negotiation with a single supplier.[8]) Or it may be ignored because the Defense Department wishes to spread its expenditures to several different companies or regions for technical or political reasons. In such cases, the basis of obtaining contracts may be an informal rapport or sense of confidence between responsible officials in the Defense Department and their counterparts in industry. Former military officers are frequently employed by major defense contractors, many of them moving from the military procurement side to executive positions with supplying firms where they do business with their former subordinates.

Another domestic consequence of the high priority given to military expenditures is the fact that the costs of the new weaponry have sent the federal budget spiraling upward. From a post-Korean War low of just over $40 billion, the military budget has risen to more than $80 billion. Each succeeding generation of new weapons and defense systems is substantially more expensive than the last. And in addition, there has been a consistent tendency of suppliers and military services to underestimate the ultimate costs of major units, thus making their initial adoption more palatable politically. The average actual unit cost of missiles in the 1950's and 1960's was three times the original estimated cost; for fighter aircraft the ratio was between 2.2 and 2.3 times the original estimate. The Manned Orbiting Laboratory announced in the early 1960's had doubled its cost estimates by late 1968 and was still far from operational; the Safeguard ABM system, originally estimated at $4 billion, was unofficially estimated at nearly twice that sum before it was even authorized.[9]

Substantial sums have been simply wasted, or invested in unnecessary stockpiles of unuseable materials, or consumed by pyramiding profits in transactions between contractors and subcontractors. Documentation of such instances has recently occupied congressmen and publicists alike.[10] But such inefficiencies and profiteering are not of primary concern to our analysis, and they may be proportionally no more widespread in defense industries than in any of the smaller-scale transactions of government or business. What is of crucial significance is the absolute magnitude of military expenditures, the proportion of

[8] John Kenneth Galbraith, *How to Control the Military* (New York: New American Library, 1965).

[9] These data are drawn from a major review of budget alternatives for the 1970's by Charles L. Schultze, former Director of the Bureau of the Budget. See Charles L. Schultze, "Budget Alternatives After Vietnam," in *Agenda for the Nation*, ed. Kermit Gordon (Washington, D. C.: Brookings Institution, 1968).

[10] Documentation may be found in U.S. Senate, Committee on Governmental Operations, Report of the Permanent Subcommittee on Investigations, *Pyramiding of Profits and Costs in the Missile Procurement Program* (1964); see also Julius Duscha, *Arms, Money, and Politics* (New York: Ives Washburn, 1964).

federal financial resources which they represent, and their anticipated sharp upward trend in the immediate future. Although the Vietnam War expenditures are expected to decrease in the early 1970's, it is estimated that new weapons systems already approved, pay increases, cost escalations, and new weapons systems proposed but not yet funded (ABM, MIRV, various new types of ships and aircraft) will mean military budgets of $100 billion or more by the mid-1970's.[11]

A third domestic consequence of directing enormous sums — roughly half the federal budget each year — toward military defense is that an irreversible momentum may be generated and an unhealthy predominance of military and supplier influence may be developed. This prospect usually bears the label of "the military-industrial complex," after a famous passage in President Eisenhower's Farewell Address of 1961. The full text of that section of his speech is as follows:

The conjunction of an immense military establishment and a large arms industry is new in American experience. The total influence is felt in every city, every state house, every office of the federal government. We recognize the imperative need for this development. Yet we must not fail to comprehend its grave implications. Our toil, resources, and livelihood are all involved; so is the very structure of our society.

In the councils of government, we must guard against the acquisition of unwarranted influence, whether sought or unsought, by the military-industrial complex. The potential for the disastrous rise of misplaced power exists and will persist. We must never let the weight of this combination endanger our liberties or democratic processes. We should take nothing for granted. Only an alert and knowledgeable citizenry can compel the proper meshing of the huge industrial and military machinery of defense with our peaceful methods and goals, so that security and liberty may prosper together.[12]

At the very least, such expenditures warp the economy in visible and significant ways. About 10 percent of the working population of the United States is directly involved in defense production.[13] In six states (Utah, Alaska, Hawaii, Washington, Virginia, and California), defense expenditures account for more than 10 percent of all personal income. The implication, of course, is one of dependency and its reciprocal consequence, pressure for continued or higher spending of this nature. In the eyes of one student of the economic impact of defense expenditures, however, it is the "catalytic" effect that is most significant.[14] The pre-emption of scientific talent, the concentration of fast-growth industries in a few localities, and the independence of defense industry from all market forces are among the effects cited.

Fourth, the space program supplements and deepens this same pattern of federal expenditure and intensifies its domestic impact. Although the space program is conducted by the National Aeronautics and Space Agency rather than the Defense Department, its

[11] Based on Schultze, op. cit., updated by the authors.

[12] Eisenhower's speech may be found in full in Vital Speeches of the Day (1961) (City News Publishing Company), p. 229.

[13] Weidenbaum, op. cit., p. 24.

[14] Ibid., p. 13-14.

relationship with the national defense program is very close. The technology developed by NASA and the information and experience gathered in the course of space exploration all have important military uses. Satellites, for example, are now a prime means of securing intelligence concerning other nations' military activities. The largest NASA contractors and suppliers are essentially the same ones serving the Defense Department's needs. Thus, the more than $5 billion per year (soon to approach $10 billion) invested in space exploration could well be included within the military proportion of the federal budget. Together, these programs absorb ten percent of the entire annual gross national product (the total of all goods and services produced) of the United States. Perhaps even more important is the fact that they occupy three-fifths of the scientific and engineering talent of the country, knotting the scientific community and the universities to the military-industrial alliance.

Finally, a less tangibly demonstrated but perhaps equally important consequence is to be found in the probable effect of military expenditures of the current magnitude upon the sense of priorities which animates the government and presumably the nation. To date, funds allocated to domestic needs, however pressing, have been limited to the federal revenue which remains after all military needs are met. Congress regularly appropriates all that the military requests, and frequently more for some programs, with only the most perfunctory examination. Domestic appropriations, on the other hand, particularly for social programs, receive much more detailed and challenging investigation and usually suffer sharp reductions. After more than 20 years of such experience, military priorities may have become so institutionalized as to forestall a serious questioning of their value or necessity; and the general public may have been led to view military needs as inviolate. Any effort to reorder priorities is thus blunted.

What emerges from this brief survey is heightened realization of the domestic implications of an ostensibly external policy. Through choice or oversight or some combination of the two, an engine has been created and set underway; whether that engine is still under control or not is currently the subject of heated debate, but the characteristics of the problem seem clear enough. The trend of these domestic consequences is likely to be more of the same in the future, but at an accelerating rate. Major post-Vietnam War investments in new weaponry of various kinds, together with rising costs, will absorb most of the revenue to be released by the end of the war and most of the growth of the economy. If the Soviet Union responds to American development of new weapons with new developments or deployments of its own, our subsequent expenditure curves may rise even more steeply.

But the sudden recognition of significant domestic consequences of military priorities should not prevent awareness of some of the international effects of the American strategic superiority policy. As we noted earlier, we cannot say that this posture was causally related to the absence of massive nuclear war. But neither should we dismiss the possibility that the balance of terror of the past decades was a major contributor to the relative peace of those years. "Small" wars have been kept relatively small, even though superpower tensions have occasionally been very high. The mutual deterrence of the superpowers has permitted many smaller nations to gain their independence and attract assistance for their own purposes, which they might otherwise not have been able to do. Essentially, *time* has been purchased, during which change could (and did) take place in world conditions and the capability of military technology.

The contemporary implications of these international consequences (if such they be) of American military policies and priorities, however, are what are most crucial for our present purposes. The core of America's strategic problem today is still the definition of what constitutes "security." But the contextual conditions — international, technological, and domestic — are so different as to totally change some of the factors to be weighed and to introduce quite new alternatives. We may be at a point where *less* security, rather than *more,* is produced by the development of new weaponry, because several nations will possess the power to destroy each other without the certainty of suffering retaliatory destruction in turn. The same result may occur because the domestic society, its problems unattended to, either erupts in civil conflict or degenerates into a police state. What is "security"? Must it include the kind of domestic order and tranquility which is attainable only through general acquiescence in some version of justice? If so, then perhaps national security itself demands a reordering of national priorities away from military "strategic superiority" and an accelerated arms race toward providing for domestic needs. But if so, would the accumulated momentum of the Cold War and the influence of the "military-industrial complex" permit such a change in priorities? Or is it really unwise and dangerous to do *anything* that would alter the policy of "erring on the side of American superiority" that characterized the previous decades — even though the sums involved might require a slighting of domestic needs and problems?

These were the issues that were raised in the first years of the Nixon administration, as ABM, MIRV, and other vastly expensive new weapons were proposed amidst claims for federal action to cope with problems in race relations, the cities, and the environment. As the debate wore on, the Congress continued to steadily appropriate military funds with the same paramount priority as before (though with somewhat more headline-attracting inquiry). Analysts and participants alike sought explanations and urged solutions for this apparent disinclination to consider the consequences of escalating military expenditures. Did the international situation require it? Or was the nation in the grip of a military-industrial complex so powerful that it could not be denied? The continuation of the policy of military superiority, and the consequences of that policy, raise questions about the possession and use of power within the American system that the rest of this book seeks to answer. But we can suggest some kinds of explanations here by way of illustration.

SUPPORT FOR MILITARY SUPERIORITY: THE DECISIONMAKING PROCESS

The policy of maintaining military superiority rests on some basic features of the distribution and usage of power in the United States, on some characteristics of American political values and practices, and on the specific interests and actions of major political actors. In other words, it was not inevitable, but neither is it uncharacteristic of the American social order, broadly conceived. In the brief analysis of the process of decisionmaking that follows, we shall see how institutions, traditions, values, and the interplay of both government and private power combine to produce this policy.

Each year, the President submits to the Congress a budget which reflects his judgments and preferences about national priorities for the coming fiscal year. The Congress then reviews the proposed funding for each department and activity of the government, and modifies allocations in accordance with its own priorities before appropriating the money. Underlying this formal description, of course, are some hard realities: each year a bitter contest takes place, first within the executive branch and then in the Congress, among the armed services themselves and also between the military together with their supporters and those seeking other priorities for government action. Each service naturally believes that its needs are paramount and that with new weaponry it can make an even greater contribution to national security. The cumulative effect of sincere and persuasive arguments for the pressing needs of Air Force, Army, Navy, and Marine Corps is to force other governmental departments and functions to defend themselves or be content with what is left over. In this competitive process, three factors contribute to the advantage of the military services.

(1) As large and complex organizations, the military services constantly need increased funds merely for self-maintenance. Over the years, they have perfected tactics for effectively influencing the Congress and the public; in this, they have been advantaged by a general aura of patriotic necessity and selfless sacrifice in the struggle against communism. Not surprisingly, generals and admirals in testimony before Congress, in speeches, and in books consistently endorse the doctrine that only superior military power can keep the peace and assure the security of the United States and the Free World. When budget-cutting pressures begin to appear, they are likely to report new advances by Soviet military forces and to project dire consequences unless our own appropriations are increased. In all of this, we may be sure that they are sincere in reporting conditions as they perceive them; they even believe that it is part of their job, if not their duty, to proceed in such fashion. At some point, however, a natural enthusiasm and confidence in the importance of one's life work is likely to produce claims which are, from the broader perspective of *all* national needs and resources, out of proportion. But it is not easy for either a citizen or a congressman to resist when confronted by a high-ranking military officer's expert testimony that

national security will be endangered unless another $5 billion is provided for a new defense system. Nor do congressmen relish hearing their opponents at the next election attack their records on the ground that they have been "penny-pinching with the nation's security" or "advocating unilateral disarmament."

Below the level of patriotic publicity and exhortation, the military services operate effectively with the pressure tactics familiar to American politics.[15] They lobby regularly with supporters and potential supporters in the Congress, showing in detail the economic benefits to districts and regions resulting from new defense contracts and rewarding their friends with free air transportation or round-the-world trips that are not much more than vacations. Because the Armed Services Committees and the related members of the Appropriations Committees of the two houses are so crucial to approval of new spending programs, the military services pay special attention to them. They lobby in behalf of their friends for appointment to these cherished positions, and they build new bases in, and direct defense contracts toward, the districts represented by such members.

The services are also able to call on some powerful allies in their efforts to influence decisionmakers. Each service has one or more private associations closely aligned with it which carries much of the burden of lobbying, particularly in ways that might seem improper for military officers on active duty. These associations are made up of former military officers and reservists, plus the contractors and suppliers who do business with that service and some interested citizens. By holding conventions, issuing statements, visiting congressmen, and otherwise engaging in pressure tactics, these associations serve as nongovernmental extensions of the various services. A second and growing body of allies has also recently been found in that segment of the scientific community which is engaged in research and development work for the military services and NASA. Some scientists have left the universities to set up businesses which provide skills and products for the services, while others retain their university bases; in both cases, their prestige and seeming independence lend useful support to the military argument.

(2) The military services can count on powerful and closely co-ordinated support from major defense suppliers who stand to gain or lose large sums as a result of budget decisions. As we have noted, defense contracts are primarily issued to a few companies. In 1968, the 100 largest defense contractors had just over two-thirds of all the defense business; the top twelve such firms had one-third of all military business. Many of these companies depend on such spending for the major share of their income. Of the 35 largest contractors in 1964, defense and space sales represented more than 75 percent of all sales in nine companies, 50 percent to 74 percent in seven, and

[15] There are many accounts of military pressure tactics, as there are of other efforts to influence the Congress. One extended and generally reliable one is that of Julius Duscha, a widely-published freelance journalist. See Duscha, *op. cit.*, note 10 above.

less than 50 percent in the rest.[16] The profits from such work are frequently very high. The proportions of sales stemming from military contracts for the 38 corporations who did more than a billion dollars worth of defense business in the period from 1961-1967 are shown in Table 1. These data indicate at the very least that a few large companies depend very heavily upon defense expenditures, and we may assume that they as well as their subcontractors and other service-providing businesses are highly concerned about the continuation of such spending.

Computation of the profitability of defense contracting is made difficult by unavailability of data on contractor-subcontractor transactions and uncertainty as to the accuracy of costs assigned to materials used by both levels of contractors. Congressional and private inquiries have documented instances where particular contractors have compounded profits among subsidiaries and subcontractors to the point where total profits on some items approached 100 percent.[17] Looking at the nation's 25 largest businesses, another study analyzed the proportion of total profits which were attributable to military contracts. It found that eight of these giant corporations received more than 20 percent of their profits from such business, and that the average for all of them was between 11 percent and 12 percent.

It seems fair to conclude that these companies have a vital interest in the outcome of military appropriations controversies, some because of near-complete dependency and others because of the profitability of this portion of their business. Nor are these companies reluctant to press their efforts to acquire contracts: frank statements of determination to secure shares of this business lie behind extensive lobbying, contributions to the services' associations, and institutional advertising in national magazines and scientific and engineering journals. Coordination in developing an integrated lobbying campaign, as well as close contacts for the purpose of securing contracts and administering them smoothly, are achieved through the contractors' well-established pattern of employing high-ranking retired military officers with procurement experience. Senator Proxmire of Wisconsin released figures in 1970 showing that, as of February 1969, 2,124 former high-ranking officers were employed by the 100 largest military contractors.[18] The ten largest suppliers employed 1,065 of these retired officers; Lockheed had 210, Boeing, 169, General Dynamics, 113, North American Rockwell, 104, and General Electric, 89. As a group, the top ten suppliers employed about three times as many ex-high-ranking officers in 1969 as they had a decade earlier in 1959. The same rate of increase applies to the top 100 defense contractors.

(3) The key members of Congress are strong supporters of the military services, and most others are vulnerable to the economic opportunities for their districts represented by military contracts. The Armed Services Committees of the two houses, and their counterparts

---

[16] Widenbaum, op. cit., p. 21.
[17] Duscha, op. cit., p. 78.
[18] Proxmire, op cit., pp. 153-154.

TABLE 1
Total Business from Defense Contracts

The following table lists the 38 U.S. companies that were awarded prime military contracts totaling in excess of $1 billion during the fiscal years 1961-1967. Amounts are in millions of dollars. In the column at far right, the cumulative totals for the seven-year period are expressed as percentages of the companies' total business. The companies listed gained between two percent and 96 percent of total business from defense contracts.

FISCAL YEAR	1961	1962	1963
1. Lockheed Aircraft	$1,175	$1,419	$1,517
2. General Dynamics	1,460	1,197	1,033
3. McDonnell Douglas	527	779	863
4. Boeing Co.	920	1,133	1,356
5. General Electric	875	976	1,021
6. North American-Rockwell	1,197	1,032	1,062
7. United Aircraft	625	663	530
8. American Tel. & Tel.	551	468	579
9. Martin-Marietta	692	803	767
10. Sperry-Rand	408	466	446
11. General Motors	282	449	444
12. Grumman Aircraft	238	304	390
13. General Tire	290	366	425
14. Raytheon	305	407	295
15. AVCO	251	323	253
16. Hughes	331	234	312
17. Westinghouse Electric	308	246	323
18. Ford (Philco)	200	269	228
19. RCA	392	340	329
20. Bendix	269	286	290
21. Textron	66	117	151
22. Ling-Temco-Vought	47	133	206
23. Internat. Tel. & Tel.	202	244	266
24. I.B.M.	330	155	203
25. Raymond International*	46	61	84
26. Newport News Shipbuilding	290	185	221
27. Northrop	156	152	223
28. Thiokol	210	178	239
29. Standard Oil of N.J.	168	180	155
30. Kaiser Industries	—	87	49
31. Honeywell	86	127	170
32. General Tel.	61	116	162
33. Collins Radio	94	150	144
34. Chrysler	158	181	186
35. Litton	—	88	198
36. Pan. Am. World Air.	127	147	155
37. F.M.C.	88	160	199
38. Hercules	117	182	183

u-unavailable
*Includes Morrison-Knudsen, Brown & Root, and J. A. Jones Construction Co.

Source: Ralph E. Lapp, *The Weapons Culture* (1968), p. 186-187.

1964	1965	1966	1967	7-Year Total	% of To-tal Sales
$1,455	$1,715	$1,531	$1,807	$10,619	88%
987	1,179	1,136	1,832	8,824	67
1,360	1,026	1,001	2,125	7,681	75
1,365	583	914	912	7,183	54
893	824	1,187	1,290	7,066	19
1,019	746	520	689	6,265	57
625	632	1,139	1,097	5,311	57
636	588	627	673	4,167	9
476	316	338	290	3,682	62
374	318	427	484	2,923	35
256	254	508	625	2,818	2
396	353	323	488	2,492	67
364	302	327	273	2,347	37
253	293	368	403	2,324	55
279	234	506	449	2,295	75
289	278	337	419	2,200	u
237	261	349	453	2,177	13
211	312	440	404	2,064	3
234	214	242	268	2,019	16
257	235	282	296	1,915	42
216	196	555	497	1,798	36
247	265	311	535	1,744	70
256	207	220	255	1,650	19
332	186	182	195	1,583	7
196	71	548	462	1,568	u
400	185	51	188	1,520	90
165	256	276	306	1,434	61
254	136	111	173	1,301	96
161	164	214	235	1,277	2
152	219	441	306	1,255	45
107	82	251	306	1,129	24
229	232	196	138	1,124	25
129	141	245	202	1,105	65
170	81	150	165	1,091	4
210	190	219	180	1,085	25
164	158	170	115	1,046	44
141	124	163	170	1,045	21
137	101	120	195	1,035	31

on the Appropriations Committees, enjoy a virtual monopoly of influence over the substance of military authorizations and appropriations. They have the time and opportunity to become informed about the details of military activities and expenditures. In the past decades, they have usually been willing to appropriate *more* than the services requested. The ordinary congressman is habituated to take the word of his colleagues who are specialists in a subject area, unable to acquire the inside knowledge that permits informed challenge or preparation of sensible alternatives, and vulnerable to the economic needs of his district. This dependence on the evaluations and recommendations of others carries several implications. The geographic concentration of defense business creates both strong defensiveness on the part of congressmen who want to hold business for their districts, and strong acquisitiveness on the part of others who want to share it more widely. Three states (California, New York, and Texas) split one-third of all defense business in 1967, and ten states accounted for two-thirds. Others, chiefly in the Midwest, were especially low in defense business. Although the lack of any real opposition to military budget appropriations makes analysis of congressional voting patterns on this issue meaningless, it is clear that such opposition as exists comes quite disproportionately from the Midwest and some urban areas where the level of defense business is particularly low.

To many congressmen, defense contracts have come to be another (and larger) "pork barrel," much like public works. A politician's constant need to be able to show his constituents that he is working effectively in their behalf finds fulfillment in announcing new defense contracts, even where he had little or nothing to do with securing them. The military and the White House have contributed to the gamesmanship and spoils system aspects of defense contracting by helping to make congressmen "look good" in this respect — through arranging for them to make public announcements of contract awards, for example. The question of who has, or who can, do most for the district in the way of obtaining contracts is regularly an issue in many congressional campaigns. California, which has enjoyed the lion's share of defense business in recent years, may serve as an example.[19]

In 1964, President Johnson opened the discussion by reminding Californians that they had received $21 billion in defense contracts between 1961 and 1964, and that they were responsible for more than 23 percent of the entire defense effort — with the payrolls that were implied in that total. Senatorial candidate Murphy later complained that defense appropriations were actually down from the previous year and that unemployment threatened. Congressman Wilson of Los Angeles, however, hastened to reassure Californians with figures showing that NASA had placed more than 50 percent of its 1963 contracts with California companies, and it was made evident in a campaign elsewhere that California (even with its large population) was in effect receiving $143 per person in defense contracts as

---

[19] This story is told in detail in Duscha, *op. cit.,* Chap. 3.

compared to pennies in some states. This style of campaign argumentation, of course, reinforces the self-interest of congressmen in securing defense business and indirectly creates pressure for increasing the overall total of such appropriations.

POLICY ANALYSIS: THE FIRST STEPS

Let us pause for a moment to review the progress of our analysis of the policy of military superiority and of its roots in the decisionmaking process. What should we have learned from the analysis so far? What tools have been illustrated? We began with the premise that we could not ask *why* things happened until we knew *what* had happened in response to *what problems*. The problem of national security has its origins in the history of past decades, of course, and we had space for only the briefest review. Nevertheless, it should be clear how much foreign policy is a product of a nation's domestic politics and ideology, and not just an inevitable or automatic response to contemporary events or the actions of other nations. Ideology played a large part in preparing American policymakers and public to interpret the war-devastated Soviet Union of 1945-1946 as posing a day-to-day threat to engulf Europe, and, no doubt, in promoting fears on the part of the Soviets that the Western nations would resume their prewar hostility toward communism in Russia.

We should note also that highly significant reversals of basic government policies can occur in American politics without any real popular involvement at all. The shift from cooperation with the Soviet Union to full-scale Cold War, including the Truman Doctrine, the Marshall Plan, and the revival of the draft, all took place between the presidential elections of 1944 and 1948. The congressional election of 1946 was contested chiefly on the issue of war-weariness, characterized by such slogans as "had enough?" or "Back to Normalcy." By the time of the presidential campaign of 1948, the Cold War was an established fact, endorsed by both major parties, and the splinter party which sought to raise the issue was effectively discredited as procommunist. This is not to say that the people would necessarily have decided differently than the decisionmakers in power, but only that they were not participants in this major policy commitment.

Defining the consequences of the policy of military superiority suggested several questions. Knowing whose interests were affected and in what ways led us to additional implications about the problem of security itself. The connection between foreign policy and domestic effects was very clear, for example. Indeed, some might well ask: Given the extent of economic benefits realized by one segment of the economy, for whose primary benefit does the policy of strategic superiority actually work? The costs of military weaponry, further, are very high — not only in dollars and proportions of the federal budget, but also in terms of the other possible programs displaced by them. These consequences were not the ones set forth in policymakers' statements of intention when they instituted the policies, nor were they part of the rationale for continued appropriations. But they are, nevertheless, inextricably related to the policies; they must be seen as part of the total context, and perhaps as part of the problem itself.

It should also be obvious that we have sought to avoid ideologically-based or chauvinistic assumptions about the propriety or inevitability of American actions. Analysis must proceed on a detached basis, not a we/they or good/bad frame of reference. Our goal is understanding, not celebration of things American. Thus, we should try to seek the evidence needed to test characterizations, neither balancing allegations in a pseudo-"objective" fashion nor avoiding statements of fact where they are supported by the evidence.

In this case, for example, the comparison of Soviet and American missile forces (Figure 1) shows that the Soviets are probably about to forge ahead in one category (ICBM), but not in others. They are apparently moved as much by their concern about China as by American advance. Further, we know that the supply of missiles stored in attack-proof missile sites in the United States is more than enough to destroy the Soviet Union and China several times over. We have the word of two Secretaries of Defense that American research and development in the ABM field is well ahead of the Soviet Union's, and we know that MIRVs are already being prepared for American missiles. These facts lead us to view any fears that the United States is about to fall behind in the arms race and suffer serious danger to its security as primarily based on ideology, self-interest, or some less rational ground. Having presented the evidence, we are obligated to proceed on the basis of our conclusion.

The importance of a detached perspective on the part of one who would analyze political activity can hardly be overemphasized. To take another illustration, is there danger that the Soviets will break any treaty agreements regarding arms control which might be reached in the future? Of course there is; all nations, certainly including the United States, either break or redefine their treaty "obligations" when they perceive that their national interest mandates it. But the Soviets do not do so more than other nations, nor might they break a treaty if and when it is in their interest to abide by it. Those who are most strongly imbued with anticommunist ideology, however, are likely to believe that there is no prospect of Soviet performance of any treaty obligation, even if this meant that Soviet behavior in breaking a treaty would be completely irrational or opposed to its national interest. To take another issue with such overtones, are China's leaders irrational and therefore a new and drastic danger in international politics? Careful analysis of the occasions when China has actually used force in its foreign policy would show that they have been quite rational, i.e., acting in carefully calculated ways and in response to provocation or opportunity. But standard American ideology would have it otherwise, and once again we see reason to demand evidence in place of assumption.

A detached, evidence-demanding perspective may also help avoid hasty and ideology-influenced conclusions. For example, one should exercise caution in attributing causal relationships to facts or events that occur simultaneously. The growth of new industry and the proportions of total sales gained by certain geographically concentrated businesses, for instance, are demonstrably caused by defense contracts. But the link is not so clear in the case of strategic superiority causing the absence of nuclear war. The reader might try proposing such a relationship and then carefully testing the "facts" he has marshalled by two questions: How much of what he lists as "facts" are really assumptions or expectations which he holds because he is an American? Have the relationships between facts been demonstrated so thoroughly as to eliminate all other possible causes?

When we reach the point of searching for explanations of *why* such patterns of policy and consequences exist, we encounter the problems of combining several different types of analysis. Both the formal structure of government and the realities of power distribution and self-interest motivations are inescapably part of the explanation for the success of the military in securing their appropriations. In the Congress, authorizations and appropriations are almost completely controlled by relatively small groups of members to whom the military and their supporters can make an assortment of appeals. Presidential desires to control military expenditures, or harmonize them with domestic priorities, when and if pressed, may still be defeated by the capacity of congressmen to bring high-ranking officers to testify in committee sessions about their acute need for more appropriations. The self-interest of congressmen and defense suppliers is too obvious to require comment, as is the supportive role of the political values of patriotism and anticommunism among the general public. Thus, what is evidenced here is the mobilization of power based on a combination of basic values, self-interest, and economic benefit, and then the flow of that power through the governmental decision structure to culminate in the policy of military appropriations and strategic superiority. The explanation does not lie exclusively in the configuration of power and the structure of decisionmaking, of course; our case study shows clearly that world conditions and changing technology introduce problems or opportunities which induce or permit such actions on the part of men of power. The context makes possible, in other words, an intricate interplay of power which leads to the particular results under analysis.

Our analysis in this section followed the priority of first describing the formal structure and then inserting facts about the actual behavior of men within that structure. Neither of these aspects of description is very meaningful unless supplemented by the other, and they will go hand in hand throughout our study. But perhaps most worthy of comment in this section are the uses to which data are put to establish factual assertions. In the second section, for example, we have made three separate points about the impact of defense contracts on the economy — that they are concentrated among a few companies, that these same companies depend to a great extent on such contracts, and that, in general, the profits from defense business for all companies engaged in it are high enough to be valuable to them (and thus the work is not undertaken merely as a patriotic duty).

Each assertion was followed by supporting evidence on a step-by-step basis, and each bit of evidence was designed and presented in such a way that it seemed to us to confirm the point. The same is true of the Proxmire data on the number of military officers employed by defense suppliers in 1969. Many assertions have been made about "the military-industrial complex" and its characteristics, but only hard data can ground such discussions in fact. Of course, there is still only inference to support the conclusion that the interlock between suppliers and military is not entirely in the public interest. The apparently large number of ex-military officers employed by suppliers might be an entirely benign way of speeding up the preparation of bids on vitally needed missiles. But at least — until further evidence is produced — we have a better basis for inference and are less likely to make patently wrong assertions.

Although facts tell us much, they do not necessarily tell the whole story. We have seen that military expenditures are shaped by the convergence of public and private power, economic interests, anti-communist ideology, and the general context of American institutions and practices. But our explanation to this point is still preliminary and superficial. It has dealt only with the actions of men in government and those immediately in contact with them. It has not sought to develop a comprehensive interpretation of what this continuing pattern of policy and consequences may imply for the structure of power in the United States. In other words, the facts presented constitute a description, but they have not yet acquired much meaning. Deeper levels of analysis are required before these facts will provide insight into the structure of power or, subsequently, the prospects for change. We shall next examine some representative interpretations involving deeper levels of analysis, as a means of seeing how different levels of inquiry suggest different explanations of power and, consequently, different prescriptions about change.

THE IMPLICATIONS OF THE POLICY OF MILITARY SUPERIORITY: THREE LEVELS OF ANALYSIS

In undertaking this illustration of different levels of analysis concerning military policy, we should first note that the dominant view among American policymakers holds that there is no serious problem to be examined. Some may feel that a problem may exist, but they also believe that current policy is essential under contemporary world conditions and that military expenditures should therefore not be queried or made the subject of political analysis. Challenged about a "military-industrial complex," Secretary of Defense Laird gave a speech in September 1969 before the National Security Industrial Association, a group he described as "leaders of the military-industrial-labor-academic-scientific complex." He declared that the United States would have to invent such a complex if it did not have one and that it was the much-criticized complex that had put American astronauts on the moon. In conclusion, he added:

Nothing would delight me more than to live in a world in which the international climate would permit drastic reduction in defense spending.

But the time has not yet come when we can drastically slash the military budget without exposing the American people to inordinate risks.[20]

The Nixon administration clearly saw no alternative but to continue with the status quo of military over domestic priorities, at least until the end of the Vietnam War released some "fiscal dividend" for other purposes. Marginal reductions in military force levels were made, but the sums saved thereby were much smaller than the cost increases estimated for the new systems. (The "status quo" of military priorities, it should be noted, means continuity of the same primacy for military needs and not continuity of expenditure levels. There is no "leveling off" or "holding the line" in *dollar amounts* devoted to military purposes under the technological conditions of the 1970's — only expansion, and at accelerating rates.)

The critics of military expenditure policies, however, were increasingly numerous at the start of the 1970's. Their analyses and prescriptions were many and varied, but they fall into three broad levels of analysis. One set of criticisms is directed at the level of *men and their decisions;* a second at *institutional powers and procedures;* and the third at the *underlying values of American society and imperatives of the economic order.* We shall look briefly at some examples of each in turn.

(1) Analysis at the level of men and their decisions

This type of analysis holds that the policy is faulty or mistaken, and that better information or more wisdom on the part of decisionmakers could produce improved policies. If men of power are persuaded by rational means, they will then change their ways. The argument for arms control illustrates this level of analysis; we shall use as an example a document published in 1969 by The Carnegie Endowment for International Peace entitled "The Future of the Strategic Arms Race." [21] Written by a former Assistant to the Director of the United States Arms Control and Disarmament Agency, it argues that the availability of the new weapons systems, with their potential of drastically altering the present strategic balance, places the United States and the Soviet Union at a fundamental crossroads.

The author dismisses the recent growth of Soviet offensive capability as strategically insignificant, noting that both nations have long had the capacity to destroy each other several times over. He sees little value to the ABM, for even if perfected it can be overwhelmed by MIRVs. Moreover, the development of both of these systems, he argues, would greatly increase the possibility of preemptive attack. This would be so because MIRVs would destroy the confidence of each side in its capacity to deter the other with the threat of an overwhelming second strike. In a time of tension, therefore, the only sure

[20] *San Francisco Chronicle,* September 19, 1969, p. 11.
[21] George W. Rathjens, *The Future of the Strategic Arms Race: Options for the 1970s* (New York: Carnegie Endowment for International Peace, 1969).

defense might be to strike first. The problem is infinitely complicated by the advent of other nuclear powers, particularly China, which is less vulnerable to second strike deterrence and perhaps more likely to mount a first strike in response to provocations. If the new strategic systems and their associated systems are decided upon, the author points out, the economic commitment will be in the neighborhood of $25 billion per year by the mid-1970's (and even more later).

In this context of probable instability and danger, to say nothing of the expenditures involved, the author proposes negotiations with the Soviet Union aimed at arms limitation. His first step would be to reach some understanding with the Soviet Union which would break the "action-reaction sequence which propels the arms race." For practical purposes, he would concentrate on limiting ABM deployment. This is more verifiable than MIRV controls, more expense-limiting because of its far greater costs, and more effective in that it reduces the need for enough MIRVs to overwhelm defenses — cutting back strategic needs in the latter category to those necessary to assure second strike deterrence capability. Thus, ABM is, or was, the key to avoidance of another cycle. And China is, or will be, a major factor in any arms limitation negotiation, because both superpowers believe that they must deter and defend not only against each other but also against China.

This argument for arms control negotiations is "realistic" in the sense that it envisions no rapid change in the tensions or mutual hostilities of the Cold War, it asks for no dramatic unilateral act on the part of the United States, and it accepts practically all of the established strategic assumptions of American policy. It is highly rational in its calculation of the relative prospects of annihilation from the two courses presented at this crossroads, and as such, it is directed at a rather narrow spectrum of specialists in this policy area. It bears little relation to simplistic calls for total disarmament, instant brotherhood, or world peace through law. *But it meets the same fate as if it did.* To most policymakers in this field, arms control exposes the United States to intolerable dangers, and its advocates are something less than realistic in their assessment of the determinants of Soviet behavior. In part, this perception exists because such policymakers are men with lifetime commitments to present policies who are not likely to be affected by rational argument to the contrary. But this is just the point, and it reveals the major weakness of the arms-limitation alternative as it has been presented in recent years: rational argument is not likely to be successful if it is directed at a relatively small group of men whose careers and whole strategic posture have been built on contrary premises. The arms-limitation advocates have never sought to identify the sources of power that have established current commitments, nor have they looked at the problem of how counter-forces might be mobilized to change these commitments. By failing to do so, and perhaps by accepting a role as advocates who work "inside" the structure of decisionmaking assumptions and processes, they have contributed to their own ineffectiveness. It seems much more likely that the question of arms limitation has never been effectively presented for judgment to the society than that it has been presented and rejected.

(2) Analysis at the Level of Institutions

Reaching somewhat deeper, this type of analysis focuses on the relationships between men and the social and organizational settings in which they operate, rather than on their judgments as individuals. It is a more comprehensive approach; not satisfied with the fact that decisions are made by certain individuals, it goes on to ask what factors in addition to the supposed merits of the issue led them to make such decisions. There are many illustrations of this level of analysis in the current debates about the "military-industrial complex" and its power. Some see an interlock between military officers, their friends in Congress, and the managers of the major military contractors and suppliers. Others add the strong support of militarized civilian leaders drawn from business and the legal profession to this interlocking relationship. Analysts differ as to whether the initiative rests chiefly with the military or chiefly with the industrial managers, but the principal thrust of their arguments is that it is the relationship between these holders of power in interdependent institutions that is the real cause of military ascendancy.

One illustration of this type of analysis is put forth in John Kenneth Galbraith's *How to Control the Military*.[22] As suggested by the title, the well-known Harvard economist sees the self-maintenance needs of the military as providing the impetus for this nonconspiratorial but shared-interest aggregation of power. He is convinced that military leaders are sometimes carried away by their anticommunism, that they seek excessive levels of security, and that they are often wrong in their assessments of both American capability and foreign nations' intentions and capacities. Their ascendancy in Washington is such that, with their allies in industry, they exert a nearly independent discretion over major aspects of American foreign and domestic policy. Galbraith goes on to argue that this unhealthy influence gives the military a kind of sovereignty over the American people, which should be broken by restoring their power to the Congress.

After reviewing the sources of the military's strength, he argues that conditions now make the military-industrial complex vulnerable. Essentially, this is because the communist world has fragmented, and the American people are no longer as tense about the communist threat as they once were, the American population is alerted to military indiscretion because of the Vietnam War, domestic problems are visible, and there are divisions of interest which make some businessmen opposed to military expenditures. Galbraith's solutions follow from his analysis and his political experience: electoral action at the presidential and congressional levels, pressure tactics (particularly with regard to placing new members on the Congressional Armed Services Committees), a target goal of eliminating $5 billion per year

[22] Galbraith, *op. cit.*, note 8 above.

in the production of weapons that encourage an arms race but leaving the space program intact, and an independent body of scientists to audit military needs.

Galbraith's argument has the merit of grounding itself in an analysis of the sources of military-industrial ascendancy, and of seeking to take such factors into account in developing counter-measures to bring about change. As he admits, however, his view of the extent of change in circumstances that is likely, and of the probable efficacy of his proposals, is highly optimistic. All of his proposals require substantial popular mobilization and involve electoral action — which would demand that millions of people become informed and learn to see this issue as more crucial than any other. They also assume that other forces (such as military persuasiveness or economic well-being of particular areas) will not intervene and lead decisionmakers back to the established priorities. Modest and traditional as his proposals are, they appear to depend on forces and events not now in the area of probable accomplishment. And there is an element of self-contradiction in them: if the military-industrial complex is as powerful as he says it is, it must have deep roots in the values of the society and in the economy. But if so, can it then be controlled through an electorally-based attack focusing chiefly on the military?

Another type of institutional analysis sees the causes of military policy lying in the ideology of major civilian decisionmakers in various institutions of government, or in the developing "military socialism" inherent in the close and continuing relationship between the Defense Department, its holdings of land and equipment, and its major suppliers. In *The Economy of Death*,[23] for example, Richard Barnet — formerly an official of the U.S. Arms Control and Disarmament Agency — makes both of these points. Much like Galbraith, he argues that, regardless of the individuals who actually hold office and make the decisions, the existence of the "national security ideology" and the fact that institutions are dependent upon help from one another would make the emerging military policy the same. The remedies that he would add to those urged by Galbraith have to do with reallocation of powers and responsibilities among the institutions of government, placing more initiative in the hands of Congress.

Similar arguments are made by Senator William Proxmire in his *Report From Wasteland*.[24] He argues that the United States has developed much more than a military-industrial complex — that universities rank among the top 100 defense contractors and are heavily involved in military work, for example, as are other nonprofit institutions. Thus, the institutional interlock extends well beyond the manufacturers of defense supplies into many other areas of social life. What has been achieved is an integrated power system, involving both "public" and "private" institutions. One telling illustration offered in Proxmire's book concerns the blue-ribbon panel of "private" citizens appointed by President Nixon to review Pentagon policies and prac-

---

[23] Barnet, *op. cit.*
[24] Proxmire, *op. cit.*

tices.[25] Composed of 16 members, the Commission included nine members who held official positions with 13 different companies doing business with the Pentagon; many of these men had held high positions in the Department of Defense or in the military before attaining their present positions. The chairman of the panel was chairman of the board of directors of an insurance company which had more than a billion dollars worth of loans outstanding to 24 defense contractors and which owned more than $30 million worth of stock in defense contracting companies. The other members of the commission included a labor leader, a close friend of President Nixon who was president of *The Reader's Digest,* a former professional football halfback now a beer company public relations man, and four other persons with no background in military affairs. The chief of staff for the commission, and several other staff members, were Pentagon assistants loaned to the commission for its study. The prescriptions that Proxmire offers, however, are aimed chiefly at greater economy in procurement practices.

(3) Analysis at the Level of Underlying Values and Economic Imperatives

This type of analysis locates causes at a still deeper level. It says in effect that regardless of the men in positions of official responsibility, and regardless of institutional changes, the policy of military superiority would go on until there were changes in the kinds of values that Americans hold and/or in the nature of the capitalist economic system.[26] One example of this type of analysis is found in an essay by Marc Pilisuk and Tom Hayden, the former an academic and the latter an activist, entitled "Is There a Military-Industrial Complex Which Prevents Peace?" [27] The authors first deny that available evidence can support the idea of a conspiracy, or even of a closely coordinated elite, at the apex of military and industrial leadership ranks. They then argue that the convergence of opinion and behavior evident at these levels is shared throughout government, and indeed widely diffused among the society as a whole. They see certain "core beliefs" as continuously unquestioned ("by any potent locus of institutionalized power"), widely shared among the entire population, and therefore animating decisionmakers and supporters alike. These shared premises, according to the authors, are convictions that (a) efficacy is preferable to principle in foreign affairs (thus military means are chosen over nonviolent means); (b) private property is preferable to

---

[25] *Ibid.,* pp. 141-150.

[26] See, for example, Victor Perlo, *Militarism and Industry: Arms Profiteering in the Missile Age* (New York: International Publishers, 1963), which argues that a full analysis must include the profits which American corporations make from foreign investments protected by the American military shield; and Carl Oglesby, *Containment and Change* (New York: Macmillan, 1967). Perhaps the best concise argument concerning business-dominated military and foreign policy, and the manner in which this leads to apparent society-wide "consensus" (thus obviating conspiracies) is Gabriel Kolko's *The Roots of American Foreign Policy* (Boston: Beacon Press, 1969).

[27] Marc Pilisuk and Thomas Hayden, "Is There a Military Industrial Complex Which Prevents Peace?" *The Journal of Social Issues,* vol. 21 (July, 1969), pp. 67-117.

public property; and (c) government patterned roughly according to the American model is preferable to any other system of government. The problem of world order and security, they go on to argue, is that the United States seeks to protect these premises or assumptions at any cost. It does not devote resources to finding routes toward change, nor to establishing the conditions of world peace, but to the preservation and effectuation of these values. The authors conclude their analysis by noting that they do not visualize American society as containing a military-industrial complex, but as *being* a military-industrial complex.

This analysis can hardly be faulted for failure to probe deeply enough into the origins of present power distribution, nor for lack of comprehensiveness. But Pilisuk and Hayden do not carry it to the point of prescription. Although they quite properly note that proposed solutions must rest on a basis of sound analysis and careful planning, like many other academics they then declare that the necessary research has not yet been done, and instead of prescriptions, they next offer suggestions for accomplishing this research. This is not to denigrate the potential insight of their analysis, but merely to note that the absence of prescription leaves the argument open to a wide range of possible interpretations. Most damaging of all, perhaps, is the thought that the argument proves too much — either that the roots of militarism lie so deep that nothing short of miraculous or cataclysmic change will suffice to redirect American priorities, or that the American military posture is a democratic product of the will of the American people.

THE BRIDGE FROM ANALYSIS TO EVALUATION AND ACTION

The level at which one undertakes to find explanations shapes the type of evaluation, and may control the approach toward change, that one will undertake. Mere description is only a preliminary to reaching overall judgments about the meaning of events, or their implications, in regard to specified standards of right and wrong. Nor is it very helpful for the citizen to have reached such a conclusion but to have no idea of how to take action to change things to fit his preferences. Although we think we have stopped short of suggesting conclusions, we have deliberately tried to show the range of judgments and prescriptions that have been put forward in the policy area of military expenditures. (The official view of the necessity for strategic superiority has no additional spokesman in this final section, in view of the fact that it was presented and analyzed as established policy throughout. This also reflects our view of our task in this book — to develop understanding of why policies emerge the way they do and to provide opportunities for citizens to develop skills of critical analysis and evaluation; we do not want merely to describe current policies in a manner which may suggest that we consider them all equally inevitable, right, or proper.)

In each of the three arguments presented in some detail in this section, the authors were drawing (even if only implicitly) on their premises about the American political process and their analysis of why military policy has its present form; the aim of each was to arrive at a prescription about how things should be done. The reasons which they assigned for the arms race were very different and were responsive to their differing assumptions and frame of reference about politics. The arms control argument apparently assumes that ideology, power distribution, and self-interest are less important to the outcome of public policymaking than rational assessment of probable consequences. Galbraith sees the strategic position of the wrong-headed military as usurping the proper role of the Congress within the policymaking process. Pilisuk and Hayden deny that either of these analysts points to the real cause. They see the roots of militarism deep in the basic values of the American society, so that altering the rational calculations of policymakers or shifting power from the military to the Congress would be meaningless in bringing about a change in policy. With such differing analyses of the causes of present circumstances, it is no wonder that they espouse different goals and prescribe different ways to achieve them.

Notice that such evaluative differences are closely related to the scope of the questions these authors asked about politics at the outset of their work. In arranging these three illustrative arguments, we began with the one that accepts the most "givens" about American politics. The arms control argument did not challenge the power held by major decisionmakers, nor did it suggest that anything in the way of change in *how* we make decisions was necessary — only that the decisions should be different ones, though apparently made by the same people. Galbraith's broader search for causes of present circumstances led him to focus on what he saw as an apparently isolated flaw in an essentially well-designed system. In its basic outline, according to him, the system is workable and proper. Thus, mobilization of the people and action at the polls is the way to put down the military and restore the apparently well-intentioned Congress to its rightful ascendancy. The final argument challenges much more fundamentally, finding the failure to lie not in wrong decisions, nor even in the wrong men making those decisions, but in the society's wrong values and motivations. What is implied is that the society holds such values because some group or class has inculcated them for its own benefit, and further that only a major reversal of these values can change the essential direction of policy at this point. How that reversal is to be achieved is unspecified, but it is clearly a vast undertaking.

Thus, readers should be alert not only to the premises and uses of evidence employed in contending prescriptions, but also to the scope of questions asked and how much of the present is accepted as fixed or given. The citizen's task is then to decide which analysis of the present, and which assessment of its causes, is best supported by the available evidence. Next, he must decide which goals are most desirable in the light of his understanding of the problem and his personal preferences. Finally, he must decide what tactics for reaching such a goal make sense, given the contemporary characteristics of

American politics. When he has arrived at this point, he has his own political position and should be ready to act on it.

In the chapters which follow, we shall examine in more detail three other problems in American society — poverty and racism, economic stability and growth, and U.S. relations with the Third World. Our aim is to explore the applicable American public policies and their consequences. Our efforts to comprehensively explain all of these policies will begin in Part III. There we shall explore decisionmaking, power distribution and usage, and prospects for change, in detail, searching for the explanations at various levels of analysis much as we did here. The questions and implications raised by the analysis of policies and consequences in the next three chapters will, we hope, be answered by these subsequent analyses.

Poverty and Racism 5

Poverty has been a continuing fact of life throughout American history. That it became a subject of government activity in the 1960's, during a period of relative affluence for most of the population, is probably due primarily to two major factors. One is the intimate link between poverty and the status of black people in the United States. Amid "affluence," blacks as a group experienced four times as much poverty as whites, and had on the average half as much income and twice the unemployment rate of whites; as many as one in three black youths were unemployed, more than four times the rate for whites. By 1964, the civil rights movement had been underway for a decade, was developing political power, and, therefore gave higher priority to alleviating the economic deprivations of blacks. The other reason that poverty became a political concern of the sixties is the background and aspirations of then-President Lyndon Johnson. Seeking a means of establishing an independent place in history and revitalizing the Democratic Party, Johnson drew upon his New Deal experience and set about to emulate Franklin D. Roosevelt's accomplishments.

The impetus given to the War on Poverty of the 1960's by the new militancy of blacks is a fitting illustration of the intricate linkage of poverty and racism in the United States. Many whites are poor, for a variety of reasons which we shall analyze shortly. But a much larger proportion of blacks are poor because the weight of enduring American racism has supplemented and enforced the other barriers to economic and social mobility across the decades. Thus, it makes sense for us to analyze government policies concerning poverty and race relations together; indeed, it would be very difficult to talk about one without the other. Our discussion must necessarily be selective, but it nevertheless raises some important questions. We shall begin by surveying the historical background of government posture toward poverty and racism, and then examine the conditions that gave rise to the policies of the 1960's. After reviewing the character and impact of the War on Poverty, we shall consider some of the questions that are raised by the pattern of policies in this area.

THE HERITAGE: PAST POLICIES TOWARD POVERTY AND RACISM

Prior to the twentieth century, the main thrust of government policy was to either affirmatively support inequality or to consciously refrain from acting to change the effects wrought by the "natural" workings of the economic order. Blacks were not just poor but legally held as slaves until the Emancipation Proclamation of 1863. Subsequently, custom, tradition, and force maintained a caste or peonage system with much the same practical effect. The existence of slavery and its maintenance through legal and political institutions both reflected and nurtured a widely believed myth that blacks were biologically inferior to whites and were ordained by God or by natural law to serve as slaves. It was thus perceived as a noble act to support slavery.

Without a myth of this kind no public policy supporting the maintenance of wide status differences between sectors of the population or encouraging the harassment or killing of large groups of people can long survive. Only in comic books and bad fiction do people recognize themselves as doing evil and yet consciously and willfully choose to persist in it. Real human beings act in a persistent way only when they have convinced themselves that at worst they are not harming others in doing so, or perhaps that they are even serving noble ends — furthering the public interest or the national interest or the general welfare; the phrasing varies. The writings and speeches of the time leave no doubt at all that belief in the divinely and biologically ordained basis of slavery was strong and widespread in the pre-Civil War period, and an acceptance of these ideas still persists in many people. If today most whites concede that they are not biologically superior to blacks, they have replaced this more traditional basis for racial discrimination with equally strong beliefs in the social, economic, or cultural inferiority of the black man. A myth of this type underlies all caste and rigid status systems, and it is often accepted by the low caste and low status participants in the system even more fervently than by those who benefit from it. For many centuries, untouchables in India accepted their status as divinely ordained, as, apparently, did at least some American slaves. The same basic myth underlies the acceptance among low status people of the view that they should "keep their place" and that they are mentally or biologically incapable of doing what their "betters" do. The laws of pre-Civil War America which authorized slavery and gave public officials and slave owners the means to maintain it reflected and perpetuated popular belief in such a myth.

The myth was challenged, of course, and slavery became an increasingly bitter political issue in the decades before emancipation. It is important, however, for the student of poverty to recognize that for a long period of our history the American government supported and helped to spread an extreme form of poverty and political impotence both by morally sanctioning and legitimizing slavery and by employing force to maintain it. The very fact, moreover, that the issue was not defined as "poverty," but as the proper hierarchical relationship between blacks and whites helped legitimize both slavery and poverty.

It has been suggested that the growing opposition to slavery was not only on moral grounds, but also on economic grounds: the recognition that in the age of factory production ushered in by the industrial revolution it was cheaper to employ wage laborers who could be laid off in slack times or replaced by machines. Slaves, by contrast, had to be supported at all times, including their years of childhood and old age. Although this rationale was not a conscious and deliberate one among all employers, it was certainly reflected both in industrial practices and in public policy during the years following the Civil War.

Despite the clear evidence that poverty was a major social problem, one must conclude that in this period of industrialization as well, government did more to create and perpetuate it than to eliminate it. As the slavery example demonstrates, public policies ostensibly dealing with quite different issues may have a more telling impact upon poverty than those policies specifically labeled as dealing with the problems of the poor. So it was in the last half of the nineteenth century and through the early twentieth century. To find the relationship of government to the incidence and treatment of the poor in the last 100 years, one must look chiefly at the kinds of leeway the legal system allowed industry in dealing with its employees and allowed bankers in manipulating securities and thereby contributing to cycles of business activity — to frequent periods of serious depression, unemployment, and widespread destitution. This is not the place to present a detailed or technical description of these public policies; the next chapter analyzes some of them. The chief point here is that for the most part the American government allowed both employers and banking groups wide leeway to engage in practices that exposed a large part of the population to the risk of poverty while leaving them impotent either to prevent it or to ameliorate it — or even to effectively challenge the structures which supported it.

The common law, for example, provided powerful legal defenses that shielded employers from having to support or recompense workers injured or killed in industrial accidents. And even after the states passed workmen's compensation laws in the twentieth century, wide loopholes for employers remained, and the compensation rates soon became obsolete.[1] Not until the mid-1930's were employees insured against involuntary unemployment. But even then many remained outside the coverage of the laws, and compensation rates became less and less adequate as the price level rose. Until the 1930's, moreover, positive governmental intervention into the labor-management relationship was almost entirely limited to the outlawing of efforts by workers to organize into unions on the ground that such efforts amounted to unlawful conspiracies which restrained trade or constituted offenses against the common law or, later, the antitrust laws.

It is hard not to conclude from this chapter in American economic and legal history that the major impact of public policy toward labor was to insure the persistence of a considerable amount of poverty in the United States while justifying the legal measures that contributed to it on quite other grounds: the value of laissez-faire for business, the long-run benefits everyone would derive from allowing competition among employers unobstructed by governmental interference, and the importance of freedom of contract for the individual worker. All this added up to a practice, if not a conscious policy, of dealing with poverty merely in a token fashion, while ignoring the fact that some of its major causes derived from public policy itself.

Beginning late in the nineteenth century, some state legislation to *protect* workers did begin to appear: laws banning child labor, prescribing minimal safety and health standards in hazardous industries and compensation for workers injured in industrial accidents, and authorizing the setting of maximum hours and minimum wages for women and juvenile employees. Such laws, however, dealt only marginally and indirectly with poverty, for they carried no benefits at all for the great mass of the population that did not have jobs in covered industries and states, or that otherwise failed to meet the eligibility requirements. The benefits provided were typically highly inadequate, and administration and enforcement were lax and harassed by hostile court actions.[2] In this period, moreover, governments continued to promote, rather than to mitigate, a major underlying cause of deprivation for the black population: discrimination in education, employment, and housing. These generalizations continued to hold true in all but a few states until after World War II.

---

[1] See Herman M. Somers and Ann R. Somers, *Workmen's Compensation* (New York: John Wiley, 1954).

[2] The most thorough account of this chapter in American economic history can be found in John R. Commons and Associates, *History of Labor in the United States*, vol. 3 (New York: Macmillan, 1935).

More directly bearing on poverty in this period than such "protective" measures were provisions by local governments for the destitute, provisions whose nineteenth-century history helps us understand their character, their limitations, and the assumptions upon which they were based. As one writer put it, "The aim of public relief in the nineteenth century was to prevent starvation and death from exposure as economically as possible."[3] In the early 1800's, adults found to be idle or vagrant were frequently "indentured": legally required to work for particular individuals who supported them, a relationship not far short of slavery. Orphans and other poor children were indentured as late as the 1870's. Sometimes local public officials auctioned the services of poor people to the person willing to accept the smallest amount of money for their care; the low bidders in human stock then usually profited by skimping on the food, clothing, fuel, and housing they furnished to their destitute charges.

Before the Civil War, almshouses supported by the city, county, or township were filled indiscriminately with all who could not support themselves: the aged, blind, insane, feeble-minded, sick, alcoholics, and foundlings. The degrading setting typically so demoralized the inhabitants of these almshouses that it turned temporary problems into permanent poverty. After the Civil War, the more progressive states established state commissions with power to suggest or require improvements in the almshouses and also established separate hospitals, orphanages, asylums, and reformatories. Private charity supplemented this trend and became increasingly important.

THE NEW DEAL PROGRAMS

With the Great Depression of the 1930's, poverty could no longer be looked on as an unfortunate but marginal and minor concomitant of industrial progress. Poverty was so pervasive and seemed to be crippling the economic system in such a fundamental way that even the chief beneficiaries of that system recognized the need for systematic governmental provisions to alleviate it. The New Deal measures to bring relief to the needy and the enactment of social security and other economic protections for the employed were implemented because they drew broad support from a middle class grown fearful that the whole system from which it benefited would collapse without such programs. The poor alone lacked the political power to sponsor such programs successfully. We see here a pattern generally applicable to public policies aimed at alleviating poverty. The poor gain power when the more affluent support them; and the more affluent support them chiefly when they fear that failure to do so will destroy or weaken the basis of their own affluence.[4]

[3] Robert H. Bremner, *From the Depths: The Discovery of Poverty in the United States* (New York: New York University Press, 1964), p. 47. The description here of nineteenth-century institutions for relief of the poor is based upon Bremner's book.

[4] *Cf.* Murray Edelman, "New Deal Sensitivity to Labor Interests," in *Labor and the New Deal,* eds. Milton Derber and Edwin Young (Madison, Wis.: University of Wisconsin Press, 1957), pp. 157-193; Michael Lipsky, "Protest as a Political Resource," *American Political Science Review,* vol. 62 (December, 1968), pp. 1144-1158.

The assumptions with which the New Deal programs were structured are crucial. Not only do they still shape the pattern of government action in regard to poverty, but they also help to explain the
present character of poverty and the nature of American attitudes
toward ameliorative action. The basic purpose of the New Deal social
legislation was to protect individuals against hazards beyond their
control — both natural or biological hazards (aging, blindness) and
economic hazards (unemployment, disability through accident on the
job). The assumption was that if individuals were given certain minimum assurances of economic security, a revived and prosperous
economy would do the rest. The basic approach thus was a series of
social insurance programs (a federal system of old-age, survivors,
disability, and health insurance, and a federal-state system of unemployment insurance) which working people (and their employers)
would pay for throughout their working lives. Men and women in
covered occupations were entitled to benefits, the amounts of which
were based chiefly on their earnings while employed. Supplementing
these systems on what was assumed to be a temporary basis were
public assistance or "welfare" programs, such as those assisting the
blind, disabled, elderly, and families with dependent children, which
were distributed through the states but which utilized federal funds
to a great extent. These programs were expected to "wither away" as
an expanding economy drew more and more people back to work
and social insurance programs were expanded. A strictly temporary
program of government employment was instituted, in which many
new public works were built — bridges, highways, public buildings,
etc. The rights to form unions and to engage in collective bargaining
were also protected by new laws. The final major component of this
package of policies was minimum wage legislation, which required
that employers in covered fields must pay at least the specified
minimum hourly wage to all employees.

Throughout, the assumption was that the minimum needs of people
could be met adequately by the workings of a reasonably prosperous
economy, provided only that certain minimum assurances were
legally established. There was no provision for assistance to those who
did not work, except under stringent conditions. Fearing that the
incentive to work might otherwise be lost, or that moral damage
might be inflicted, public assistance programs required that disability
or destitution be shown as conditions for receiving aid.

The social insurance programs, chief among which is social security,
have for the most part fulfilled expectations.[5] About 90 million people
now contribute to social security, and 90 percent of the population
age 65 and over are eligible for monthly social security benefits. In
1967, a monthly average of 23 million people received benefits of
$25.7 billion. A very large proportion of employed people now have

---

[5] Department of Health, Education, and Welfare, *Toward A Social Report* (Washington, D. C.: U.S. Government Printing Office, 1969), p. 49. The data in this and the
next three paragraphs are drawn from this source. See also Gilbert Y. Steiner, *Social
Insecurity* (Chicago: Rand McNally, 1965), pp. 18-47.

protection against loss of income from several important causes. In 1967, five million people received $2.2 billion in unemployment compensation. Levels of benefits are not high enough to enable most people to support themselves without further income, and they are paid only to those who have previously paid into these funds, but basic sums are available to such people under the specified conditions.

Public assistance programs, however, have not lived up to original assumptions and expectations. No "withering away" has occurred; instead, total amounts expended for assistance have continued to rise, with most of the increase coming in the category of aid to families with dependent children. Nevertheless, federal agencies responsible for public assistance programs as well as many students of welfare policy have continued to talk and plan in terms of the "withering away" assumption. Like the previous capacity to ignore poverty, this phenomenon is further evidence of man's ability to hold self-serving or insulating beliefs without empirical support, and even to spread such beliefs to others. Figure 1 shows the actual trends in number of recipients in major categories. The continued need for public assistance of this kind, and particularly in the category of families with dependent children, points to some important flaws in the assumptions, design, or effects of the New Deal programs.

To begin with, these programs aimed almost exclusively at economic security for those who were already working or who (it was assumed) would soon again be employed in an expanding economy. The economy eventually did expand to unprecedented levels of activity, as a result of World War II; but poverty and the need for public assistance nevertheless endured — as Figure 1 shows. The New Deal policies did not take into account those who lacked education or training for employment, those who could not work for reasons of health or because of their responsibility for children, or the fact that racial discrimination prevented many people from working in any but the lowest-paid and most exploited positions. Moreover, they took no consideration of those who worked but remained very poor as a result of low income, size of family, frequent illnesses in the family, and so forth. As a result, large numbers of poor people receive little or no assistance from these programs. In 1965, for example, only 20 percent of poor persons received public assistance payments and, of these, 82 percent remained poor in spite of such payments. Moreover, payment levels vary sharply with state policies; in New York, monthly payments for a family of four under aid to dependent children was about $250, while it was $115 in Ohio and $35 in Mississippi. Legal restrictions on eligibility for assistance, in addition to demeaning and stigmatizing recipients and potential recipients, deny aid to 73 percent of the population below the official poverty line. One expert summarizes the situation this way:

The programs aimed at the aged exclude three poor households out of every five. Those aimed at fatherless families fail to reach one out of three poor households headed by nonaged women. And for households in poverty headed by a nonaged male, 92 percent received no form of public assis-

FIGURE 1
Trends Among Types of Public Assistance

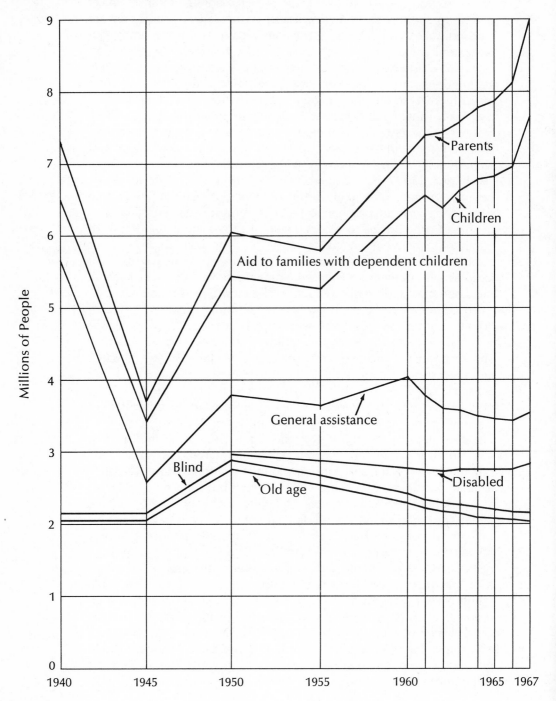

tance in 1966. The bulk of the excluded poor are in this nonaged male head category of household.[6]

Minimum wage requirements rarely affect this situation, because of family size, intermittent employment, or unemployability. Indeed, minimum wage legislation has come to be as much a device for protecting industries in one region against competition from similar industries in lower-wage regions as for raising the income of the lowest paid workers. Protections for the stature of unions are as much hindrance as help for the poor, in part because of the poor's lack of skills and in part because of many unions' rules regarding apprenticeship and seniority and their discrimination against racial minorities. In short, the New Deal programs, assuming that all would be equally benefited by an expanding economy, simply ignored a substantial segment of the really poor people of the country. But other factors were also working to perpetuate or increase both poverty and its imperviousness to the New Deal programs. Let us consider these as part of a larger analysis of the scope and nature of poverty in the United States.

POVERTY IN THE 1960'S: THE CONSEQUENCES OF 100 YEARS

The extent of poverty depends on the definition used to mark the boundary between poor and nonpoor. The first definition, used by the President's Council of Economic Advisers in the Economic Report of 1964, held simply that all families below a cash income of $3000 and all individuals with a cash income below $1,500 were "poor." By this definition, one-fifth of the people of the United States were "poor" in 1963. One third of all poor families were headed by a person over age 65; one fourth were headed by a woman; and over eleven million children were included among the poor. Twenty-two percent of the poor were nonwhite, and nearly half of *all* nonwhites were below the poverty line. Such numbers may be less meaningful than comparisons. One observer points out that the "Other America," with its roughly 35,000,000 poor people, could be viewed as an underdeveloped nation within the United States. As such, it would be exceeded in population (among the "underdeveloped" nations of the world) by only six nations. He continues:

Of 19 Latin-American republics, only Brazil and Mexico were larger than our own "nation" of the poor. In Africa, only Nigeria had more people. All the rest of some 35 underdeveloped African countries had far fewer. There was no country in the Middle East as large; Egypt with 28 million came closest of the thirteen countries in that area. Our own internal "nation of the poor" has twice as many people as Canada. As a matter of fact, a separate nation of American poor would constitute the fifteenth largest nation of the world.[7]

[6] Statement of Harold W. Watts, Director of the Institute for Research on Poverty, University of Wisconsin, Hearings Before the Joint Economic Committee, U.S. Congress, June, 1968.

[7] John C. Donovan, *The Politics of Poverty* (New York: Western Publishing Company, 1967), p. 96.

Since 1964, new definitions with greater sensitivity to family size and composition, as well as to living costs in urban and rural areas, have come into use. The basic numbers of poor persons, however, remain essentially unchanged.

Who Are the Poor, and Where Do They Live?

In terms of absolute numbers, the poor are white (69 percent) and urban (57 percent) and in families headed by a man (75 percent). But the poor are *disproportionately* drawn from the reverse of each of these: black, rural, and families headed by women. Table 1 summarizes the totals for the years 1966 and 1967. It shows that between three and four times as many blacks are poor as whites — although there are more than twice as many whites as blacks among the poor. This is due, of course, to the fact that blacks make up only about 12 percent of the population. Blacks are more heavily concentrated in the central cities, however; the white poor are located in rural areas and to some extent in smaller urban settings. It is estimated

TABLE 1
Selected Statistics on the Prevalence and Distribution of Poverty

	Persons in poor households				
	As percentage of all persons		Number (millions)		Percentage of poor persons living in
Race	1966	1967	1966	1967	central cities (1964)
White	11.5	10.2	19.5	17.6	23.8
Nonwhite	40.0	35.3	9.3	8.3	41.7

Sources: Persons in poor households — Bureau of the Census, *Current Population Reports*, Series P-60, No. 55, Aug. 5, 1968; percentage of poor in central cities — *Report of the National Advisory Commission on Civil Disorders*, Mar. 1, 1968, p. 127.
Reprinted from James Tobin, "Raising the Incomes of the Poor," in *Agenda for the Nation*, ed. Kermit Gordon (Washington, D. C.: Brookings Institution, 1968), p 78.

that, in 1965, 25 percent of rural residents, 13.8 million persons, were poor.[8] Only a quarter of these poor persons live on farms, and the rest live in small towns and villages.

Behind these initial statistics lie some dramatic facts concerning population migration in recent decades. First, the mechanization of agriculture has forced people from the farm to the cities. The percentage of the labor force in agriculture has been dropping steadily, from 53 percent in 1870 to 27 percent in 1920 and five percent in 1967. Between 1959 and 1966, the number of farms fell again — by

[8] James Tobin, "Raising the Incomes of the Poor," in *Agenda For the Nation*, ed Kermit Gordon (Washington, D. C.: Brookings Institution, 1968), p. 81 and ff. Data in the next paragraph are drawn from this source also.

20 percent. And the process is still continuing; there are still more than a million and a half "subsistence" farms (those with annual sales under $5,000), and emigration is running at the rate of almost a million persons a year. Second, this pressure to leave the land and seek employment in the industrial cities has focused most heavily on the most vulnerable members of the agricultural work force — blacks. Of course, black migration from the South was spurred by other factors also. But the result has been a dramatic shift to the major cities of the North and West. Coupled with a simultaneous exodus of whites and a relatively higher birth rate, the black proportions of central cities populations have risen sharply across the country. Figure 2 shows this net migration from the South by time periods. It makes clear that this process too is still underway, though at a declining rate. Black proportions of central city populations in many major cities more than doubled between 1950 and 1965, and in many cases this proportion is expected to rise to the point where many such cities will be well over half black by 1980. Because of lack of education and training, and as a result of racial discrimination, these migration patterns have meant a sharp focusing of poor people within these same central cities.

But the category of poor is not limited to those who are unable to work, unqualified for work, or otherwise prevented from finding gainful employment. More than half of the households classified as "poor" include working people.[9] Fifty-four percent of the poor families in 1966 were headed by persons in the labor force, including 39 percent of families headed by females. Only very small proportions reported themselves unemployed; even among those over 65, substantial proportions were employed. The incomes they were able to earn, however, or the size and circumstances of their families, caused them to remain among the ranks of the poor. We shall look more carefully at some of the reasons for this phenomenon.

Why Are They Poor?

Two leading causes of poverty are unemployment/subemployment and racial discrimination. Unemployment/subemployment for the poor normally runs well above the average for the nation as a whole; lacking skills, they are usually the last hired and the first laid off as the economy expands and contracts. For blacks, unemployment rates average about twice those of whites. Unemployment remained substantial for the poor, and particularly for blacks, throughout the slack period of the late 1950's and early 1960's. Despite the Kennedy administration's efforts, it succeeded in lowering the overall unemployment rate from its initial nearly seven percent level in 1961 to no lower than 5.5 percent in 1963. Figure 3 shows, however, that blacks' unemployment held at roughly twice the rate of whites. For black teenagers, the rate was 27 percent in June 1965 and 32 percent in June 1966. The special difficulties experienced by blacks and by young people apparently are built into the character of the economic system;

---

[9] *Ibid.*, p. 86. Data in this paragraph are all drawn from this source.

FIGURE 2
Black Migration from the South

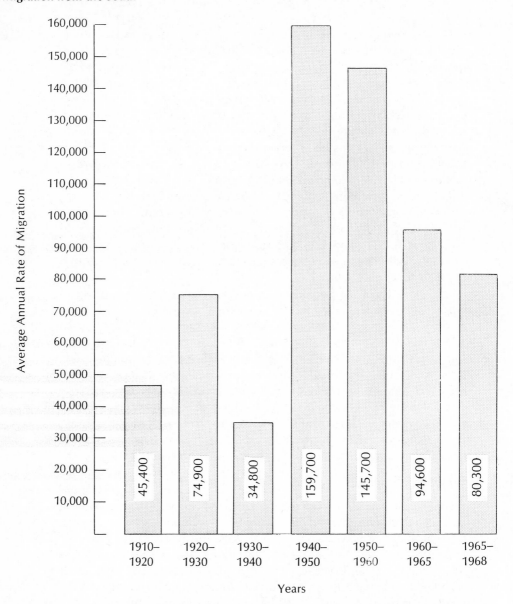

Years

Sources: Data for 1910–1960, *Report of the National Advisory Commission on Civil Disorders* (Washington, D.C.: U.S. Government Printing Office, 1968), p. 117; data for 1960–1968, U.S. Bureau of the Census, unpublished. Figure adapted from table appearing in James L. Sundquist, "Jobs, Training, and Welfare for the Underclass," in *Agenda for the Nation*, ed. Kermit Gordon (Washington, D.C.: Brookings Institution, 1968), p. 64.

not even "full employment" levels of less than four percent unemployment succeed in reducing the unemployment of these groups to anything approaching such figures.

But not all those who are actually employed are earning at full capacity. The Labor Department uses the term "subemployment" to describe those persons who are employed but who earn less than $3,000 per year and those who are unemployed for more than 15 weeks in any given year. In 1966, 9.1 million persons were subemployed, 10 percent of the working population.[10] The rate for white men, however, was only eight percent, while it was 22 percent for nonwhites. *In ten major urban slums, the rate rose to 34 percent.*

Racial discrimination, the second major factor, operates both through cumulative disadvantages (lower levels of education and opportunity over decades) and contemporaneously (nonwhites are denied entry into specific positions for which they are qualified). The results are visible in many ways. Figure 4 compares white and nonwhite proportions by occupational levels, and Table 2 by income categories. It shows that nonwhites hold the lesser-status positions, and earn less income than whites; moreover, the gap between the median income of whites and nonwhites actually widened between 1960 and 1966. Although nonwhites improved their real income by slightly more than $1,000 per year, whites' incomes rose in the same period by more than $1,300.

TABLE 2
Income Trends, 1947-1966

	Nonwhite			White		
	1947	1960	1966	1947	1960	1966
Number of families (in millions)	3.1	4.3	4.9	34.2	41.1	44.0
Median income	$2,284	$3,441	$4,481	$4,458	$6,244	$7,517
Change, 1947-1966:						
Dollar			2,197			3,059
Percent			96.2			68.6

Source: Bureau of Labor Statistics, *The Social and Economic Conditions of Negroes,* 1966, pp. 41-42.

Thus, the general structure of nonwhite occupational status and income lags well behind that of whites. Accordingly, nonwhites experience exaggerated degrees of poverty. The National Advisory Commission on Civil Disorders reported in 1968 that two-thirds of

[10] James Sundquist, "Jobs, Training, and Welfare for the Underclass," in Kermit Gordon, *op. cit.,* p. 50. Data in this paragraph are drawn from this source.

FIGURE 3
Average Annual Unemployment Rates

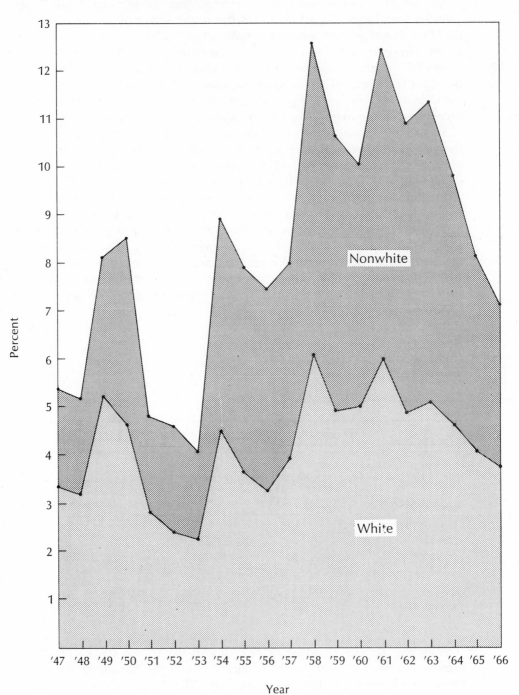

FIGURE 4
Unemployment by Occupation and Sex, 1966

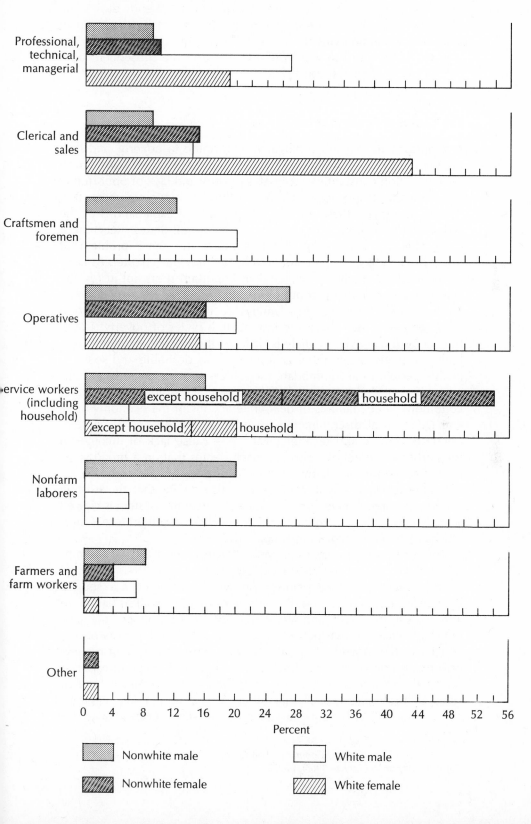

those blacks in the under-$3,000 income group, or 20 percent of *all* blacks in the country, were making no progress at all out of poverty.[11] The data on which this report was based reflected trends during the period of speed-up in the economy brought about by the Vietnam War, when unemployment was at its lowest level in a decade. We may therefore estimate with confidence that in the subsequent periods of recession and rising unemployment the figures would be much higher.

The Causes of Poverty: Levels of Analysis

Unemployment and subemployment contribute to poverty, and they endure for the poor even under "full employment" conditions. Racial discrimination constantly exacerbates poverty and lack of opportunity for nonwhite groups, particularly for their younger members. But, though important, these are not comprehensive explanations of the scope and permanence of poverty in the United States. Reaching a comprehensive explanation involves much the same problem of levels of analysis as we encountered in the previous chapter. At issue is the question of whether poverty has important roots not just in the availability of employment but eventually in the values, expectations, and psychological makeup of families, so that over time, generation after generation remain locked in repeating cycles of poverty. This is the "culture of poverty" analysis; it takes the existing economic system and its evolution either as a given or as desirable and seeks to enable people to accommodate themselves to the demands and opportunities of that system. A different approach holds that structural conditions — i.e., failures or deliberate actions of the economy or its managers, racial discrimination, or other characteristics of contemporary economic and technological life — cause lack of income on the part of some people. This approach denies that, in a broad view, lack of education or apathy on the part of poor people are really responsible for their plight. Moreover, it also denies that the existing economic system is given or is desirable; instead that system is viewed as the very source of inequality and deprivation, and therefore it must be changed in order to eliminate poverty.

Both of these approaches are more far-reaching than the assumptions which shaped the New Deal programs. The analysis made, of course, determines the premises on which remedies are sought. Perhaps for obvious reasons, the culture of poverty analysis had more adherents in the 1960's and was dominant in the shaping of the anti-poverty policies of that period. As usually articulated, it rests on the conviction that poverty is not as simple as merely the lack of money; poverty also has subjective effects on people. It involves an expectation that one will continue to be deprived of the comforts, and of some of the "necessities," that others enjoy; and it involves perceiving oneself as having the status of the poor. Oscar Lewis, for

---

[11] *Report of the National Commission on Civil Disorders* (Washington, D. C.: U.S. Government Printing Office, 1968), p. 252.

example, has written of the "culture of poverty" that is created by such expectations and perceptions among the poor. In a culture of poverty, such as can be found in most urban black ghettos, among the destitute whites of the Appalachia region of eastern Kentucky, and in parts of the Barrio (the Puerto Rican community of New York City), attitudes, beliefs, and some forms of behavior are markedly different from those of the middle class. The few material goods available are seen as things to be used immediately and not saved. Saving is not likely to be perceived as a virtue, for there is no reason to believe that saving can bring escape from poverty. The government and its representatives, whether social workers, policemen, or the President of the United States, are likely to be viewed with suspicion, hostility, and fear, not as benevolent servants of the people.[12] The individual in this culture is likely to feel inferior, dependent, helpless, and unable to shape his own life or future career. Though there is a good deal of informal socializing, there is little organization beyond the family and little sense of community or *esprit de corps*.

Probably most important of all, a culture of poverty is self-perpetuating. Because it brings into the open and stands as a constant reminder of the unlikelihood or impossibility that things will change, it inures people to the expectation that their children will live in the same culture; not incidentally, it teaches children the same lesson. All too often, of course, this is a wholly realistic expectation — more realistic than the belief common among many of the middle class that individual ambition and initiative can raise the poor from their poverty or the blacks from their demeaning status. Assuming there indeed is such a "culture of poverty," it may be basically a response to systematic deprivations created by the functioning of the economy.

Thus, under these assumptions, the principal goal of policies intended to alleviate poverty would be preparation of the poor to compete more successfully within the existing economic order — in short, to integrate the poor into middle-class "affluence." By focusing particularly on youth and providing concentrated education and training, the cycle might be broken and the children of poor families enabled to take their places in the stable, productive labor force. As we shall see, this approach met with considerable difficulty and resistance; in all probability, efforts to modify economic or social structures so as to distribute income more equitably towards the poor would have met with even less success.

CONTEMPORARY POLICIES: ORIGINS, CHARACTER, IMPACT

Origins

The significance of poverty as both an economic and a social problem was highlighted for some Americans with the publication in the early 1960's of a number of widely publicized books and articles. The most

[12] See Dean Jaros, Herbert Hirsch, and Frederic J. Fleron, Jr., "The Malevolent Leader: Political Socialization in an American Sub-Culture," *American Political Science Review*, vol. 62 (June, 1968), pp. 564-575.

influential of these in awakening Americans to an issue that had long been relatively ignored was Michael Harrington's *The Other America.*[13] The title of the book called attention to the fact that the middle class and the affluent in America were isolated from the poor and found it easy to forget and ignore their existence. Harrington's book eloquently described the plight of groups who were poor for different reasons: their color, their age, their lack of education and skills, their unconventional way of life. Other studies that received wide publicity in the early sixties were an essay by Dwight MacDonald,[14] and studies by Robert Lampman about disparities in the distribution of wealth and income in American society.[15] Though these writings helped make poverty a live political issue, their popularity and influence were also in part a result of the rising public assistance rolls and the rising volatility of blacks and civil rights advocates.

Because the poor tend to become segregated in urban or rural ghettos and because their culture amounts to a formula for resignation and adaptation to their poverty, the nonpoor are remarkably insulated from contact with them. There is, moreover, a strong inclination among people who are not poor themselves to ignore poverty as a social problem, remain unaware of its dimensions, and soothe themselves with the belief that poverty can be attributed to the laziness or moral unworthiness of those who suffer from it. Those who explain it to themselves in this way need feel no incentive to do anything about it. To recognize poverty as a social and political problem, due less to the inadequacies of individuals than to the inadequacies of economic, political, and social institutions, is to recognize a need for governmental action to cope with it. Some change from the first view to the second occurred among a sector of the American public in the early and mid-1960's.

Understanding some of the major reasons for this particular change can tell us something about the dynamics of social change in general. The high unemployment levels of the fifties and sixties already mentioned were certainly part of the reason that poverty became more visible. Unlike the unemployment of the thirties, this development occurred and continued in the midst of affluence and unprecedented prosperity for most Americans, and layoffs struck in large part at people who had themselves grown accustomed to hearing about the affluence of the American economy.

Other reasons for the change in viewpoint revolved around developments in race relations. Not only did the poverty of blacks and the reinforcing patterns of poverty to which ghetto life gives rise become startlingly visible to whites, but the black race itself began to make powerful demands for greater equality. An important contributing factor to the restiveness of the black poor was the celebrated Supreme Court decision in the case of *Brown* v. *Board of*

[13] Michael Harrington, *The Other America* (New York: Macmillan, 1962).
[14] Dwight MacDonald, "Our Invisible Poor," *The New Yorker* (January 19, 1963).
[15] Robert Lampman, *The Share of Top Wealth-Holders in National Wealth* (Princeton, N. J.: Princeton University Press, 1962).

Education,[16] declaring that segregation of black children in the public schools is a violation of the equal protection clause of the United States Constitution. The decision made it impossible for blacks to continue to believe their second class citizenship was either legal or morally ordained, became a compelling symbol of the right of blacks to equal treatment, and so encouraged efforts by both black people and white civil libertarians to break down remaining social and political restrictions. Rarely has there been a clearer instance of a public policy catalyzing a change in the perceptions of a large part of the mass public.

Such developments, which began in the fifties and escalated in the sixties, unequivocally called the attention of many Americans to poverty and racism as related social problems, and fostered the belief that these had originated and were perpetuated due chiefly to institutional inequities. Blacks became increasingly impatient with the persistence of the old patterns of segregation and deprivation. Figure 5 shows the change of attitude within both groups between 1942 and 1963. Young blacks, less impressed than their elders with the tenacity of obstacles to change, more energetic, and more willing to take risks, initiated a series of actions in the early 1960's that brought wider national attention to race problems than any development since the Civil War and its legal aftermath. These took the form at first of nonviolent resistance to segregation: sit-ins at segregated lunch counters and swimming beaches, a long but ultimately successful boycott of the Jim Crow Montgomery buses under the leadership of Dr. Martin Luther King, boycotts of the downtown stores in Montgomery, Alabama, street demonstrations by blacks and white sympathizers in many Southern cities, and voter registration drives among Southern blacks.

Although the demonstrators, led chiefly by such civil rights organizations as SNCC, CORE, and the Southern Christian Leadership Conference, did not deviate from their nonviolent philosophy in this period, their actions repeatedly brought violent responses from some whites and especially from Southern policemen and sheriffs. Beatings of demonstrators, before and after they were arrested, were routine; some demonstrators were beaten, shot, or bombed to death.

All these actions received national publicity, which was a critical factor in making a large part of the public aware to an unprecedented degree of the political, economic, and social problems posed by the related phenomena of poverty and racism. Though such news events to some extent polarize the population, leading the previously apathetic to support one or the other side, there is little question that they were especially helpful to the pro-civil rights group. The spectacle of beatings and murder by white supremacists helped marshal support for their opponents. There is little doubt, on the other hand, that most of the new civil libertarian support came from Northern whites and Southern liberal whites, neither of whom were in a position to effect far-reaching immediate change in the economic and

---

[16] 374 U.S. 483 (1954).

FIGURE 5
Percent of Whites Approving Residential and Public Transportation Integration

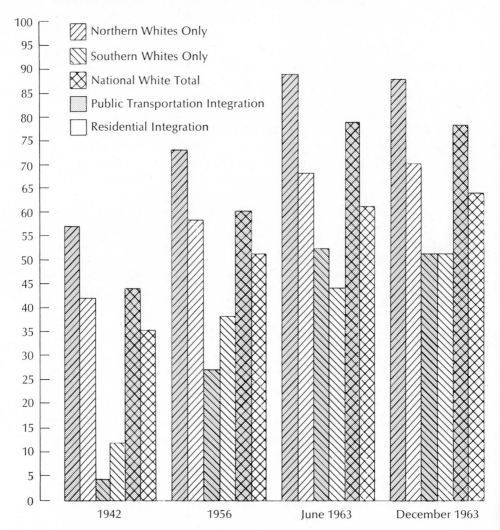

Source: Paul B. Sheatsley, "White Attitudes Toward the North,"*Daedalus*, vol. 95 (1966), pp. 217-38 (p. 222).

political position of Southern blacks, for they did not have influence in Southern local and state governments. The demonstrations of the late fifties and early sixties, therefore, primarily served chiefly to bring about the enactment of some new *federal* civil rights laws, dealing with the right of blacks to vote, and to make civil rights a more visible and potent public issue than it had been.

The major policy impact of these developments, however, was still greater polarization, in the North even more than in the South. To many Northern whites the passage of the civil rights laws and the widely publicized egalitarian court decisions were evidence of substantial black progress toward equality.[17] But to blacks living in the urban ghettos or forced off Southern plantations by labor-saving agricultural machinery the civil rights laws were much less meaningful as signals of progress than the daily evidence of their own demeaning living conditions, destitution, harassment by police, and political weakness.

At the same time, the civil rights laws and decisions as well as increased talk of a civil rights "revolution" symbolized to blacks the new support which the idea of equality had gained. For them, the gap between the deprivation they suffered in their daily lives and the idea of equality with whites, to which the law said they were entitled, seemed even wider than it had been. In a relative sense, therefore, the deprivation of the black man increased as a result of civil rights demonstrations and policies because it made him more acutely aware of the enormous disparity between the standards of living of white and black America.

This growing relative deprivation, moreover, brought major changes in some of the major civil rights organizations and in the behavior of Northern blacks. Because results were slow in being achieved, and seemed to depend on white charity instead of acknowledgement of their prerogatives, black groups began to shift their tactics. SNCC and CORE now moved to rid themselves of the white liberals who favored integration, conventional civil rights laws, and nonviolence. Both organizations began to adopt the attitudes and actions of those blacks who insisted with a new militancy upon "black power," who lauded their African heritage, black culture, and contributions to American culture, and who in general emphasized the special worth and distinct identity of blacks and disparaged the desirability of integration with whites and white culture.

Character

The new concern with poverty and race relations had to have dramatic political expression; it took the form of passage of The Economic Opportunity Act of 1964 and a great deal of subsequent publicity and debate over the "War on Poverty," as the Administration and the newspapers labeled it. The "opportunity" to be provided under the statute was an increased chance for the individual to compete for jobs under the established economic system. The strategy of the Economic Opportunity Act of 1964 is well summarized by one of its framers as follows:

The war on poverty had a radical objective — "to eliminate the paradox of poverty in the midst of plenty," the Economic Opportunity Act declaimed — but the means to that end were essentially conservative. The legislation built for the most part upon the methods and administrative structures of the past. The underclass would be given its new opportunities through more and better services of the kind traditionally provided — better education,

---

[17] William Brink and Louis Harris, *Black and White* (New York: Simon and Schuster, 1966), p. 230, Appendix D, Table 1(c); *Newsweek*, August 22, 1966.

better health services, better training and counseling, and so on, all improved through better community organization.[18]

The programs aimed particularly at the young and the black, and sought to prepare them for jobs that were assumed to exist in the private economy.

By 1970, six years after the "war" began, it was apparent to careful students that it had generated a great deal of talk and political controversy, a widespread impression that the Johnson and the Nixon administrations were working to help the poor, several concrete programs that had an impact upon a small fragment of the poor, and a relatively small investment of money and other resources — an investment that represented experimentation in attacking poverty rather than an effort to eliminate it or reduce it substantially. To put it another way, the Economic Opportunity Act of 1964 had some important political consequences, but its economic and social impact in helping the poor has been relatively small and the exact nature of that impact is difficult to pinpoint.

One evidence of the disparity between the War on Poverty as a symbol and its real impact on the poor of America is the fact that the Economic Opportunity Act contributed only a very small increment to the federal budget of the 1960's. Appropriations for programs under the act never exceeded $2 billion; they totalled $1.8 in 1968, and $1.9 in 1969. It is possible, and sometimes tempting, to portray the federal budget as containing tens of billions of dollars in social welfare expenditures. The fact is, however, that nearly all of these sums are either long-authorized assistance to the states for specific social programs or sums which were originally paid in by workers during their employed careers. Very small amounts, comparatively speaking, have been made available for the poor, as distinguished from the steadily employed and middle-income worker. At the same time as the Office of Economic Opportunity was struggling to preserve its chances for $2 billion in appropriations, the space program was receiving almost three times as much and the military was receiving more than 35 times that amount — $20 billion for the war in Vietnam alone.

The most experimental and innovative of the antipoverty programs under the OEO has been the Community Action Program. Intended as a way of organizing the poor in cities and rural communities and enabling them to help themselves and to bring pressures for further services, community action has taken many forms in the approximately 1000 communities in which programs have been established. In each community, a community action agency (CAA) is established locally and supported by the OEO. While their emphases have varied, most CAA's have given greatest attention to education, employment, health, legal, and other social welfare services. As a result some of the poor in these communities have benefited from new or additional services.

But in most communities the CAA's have done little to plan and

[18] Sundquist, *op. cit.*, p. 53.

coordinate federal, state, private, and local resources to help the poor, another emphasis of the Economic Opportunity Act. In large part this has been due to insufficient funds, inexperienced staff, and the number of extremely difficult choices that had to be made.

Several of the specific programs carried on under the aegis of the community action program deserve special mention, for they are imaginative efforts to cope with some noneconomic aspects of the culture of poverty. About 40 percent of all CAP expenditures have gone into Headstart, which provides educational, health, social, and other services for preschool children from poor families. The strategy of the program is to overcome the disadvantages of the child's background by giving him special attention and help before he enters school. It involves parents of the Headstart children as well as college and high school student volunteers, thereby strengthening family relations, community ties, and black-white cooperation and understanding. The chief benefits of such a program, in the form of the improved mental and physical health of the children, are bound to be long-term in character; but it is still too early to evaluate them. In its early stages, the program was more successful in initially improving the alertness, motivation, and skills of the children than in maintaining these gains as they grew older. Cutbacks in funds helped reduce the chance to follow through with such programs once the children entered the public school system.

Headstart, Upward Bound (a remedial program to permit high school students from poor neighborhoods to increase their chances for success in college), comprehensive health services, legal services, and some other programs have been given national emphasis by OEO, with some effort to introduce them into every community with a community action program. Together they account for about half of all CAP expenditures, most of this being allocated to Headstart. The other half have gone into a wide range of programs based upon local initiative and local needs, and into the costs of administration and research.

The most ambitious of a number of OEO programs for manpower development and training has been the Job Corps, intended to provide low-income and disadvantaged young men and women between 14 and 21 years of age with the education, vocational training, or work experience to make them more employable and productive. Job Corps has been carried out at men's urban centers, women's urban centers, and men's rural or conservation centers. Public and private organizations under contract with OEO have recruited and screened applicants and in some cases have operated the centers.

Job Corps trainees have shown increased employment and earning power, but after only a few years experience with the program it is hard to evaluate its success. One careful "cost-benefit" study concluded that the program had demonstrated its worth;[19] another was

[19] Glenn G. Cain, *Benefit/Cost Estimates for Job Corps* (Institute for Research on Poverty, Discussion Paper, mimeo, 1968).

dubious.[20] Among the problems this experimental effort confronted was the short length-of-stay of many corps members, the inexperience of the contracting agencies, and the apparent inclination of some of the private contractors to pay less attention to the quality and adequacy of educational and training facilities than to the profitability of the operation. In 1969, the new Nixon Administration announced that it would close most of the rural centers, expand the urban ones somewhat, and transfer administration of the Job Corps program from OEO to the Department of Labor.

Any evaluation of Job Corps or similar programs to improve the employability and the chances for promotion of the poor and the underpaid must take account of the fact that statistical measures of their success are bound to be inadequate. Apart from the difficulty of assembling accurate data, there is a more fundamental problem. Those people with the fewest skills and the lowest physical and mental ability obviously need the most help; yet they are also least likely to show dramatic progress in the course of their training. Administrators of such programs who are eager to show a statistically impressive record of job placements and of retention of trainees on their jobs are tempted to engage in what has been called "creaming": recruiting the most qualified trainees, most of whom would probably cope successfully in the job market without any additional training. While it may be statistically and politically successful, such a policy clearly defeats the purpose of a war on poverty. The student of government might consider how such programs can be planned and administered so as to achieve their goals as completely as possible, yet not incur the concomitant risks that can defeat them politically.

In the fiscal year 1968, about $100 million was spent by OEO for health services. The Bureau of the Budget claimed that the federal government spent a total of $4.1 billion that year on health care for the poor, but by far the largest single component of this expenditure was for medicare programs, which are very largely an aid to the middle class rather than the poor and are more reasonably classified as insurance paid for by the recipients than as governmental assistance.

The largest OEO program in the health field has been the Comprehensive Health Services Program, designed to devise and test new methods of delivering health care to the poor. Health centers for this purpose have been established in a number of cities, none of them yet offering really comprehensive services. Mental health care and dental care, for example, have been difficult to include in the early years. The centers have, however, provided free or low-cost care in some areas, and there has been some effort to involve the poor themselves in planning and carrying out the work.

A number of experimental projects of various kinds round out the package of OEO programs undertaken in the late 1960's. From what evidence is available, many of these were unsuccessful. Whether the

---

[20] *Review of Economic Opportunity Programs* By the Comptroller General of the United States Made Pursuant to Title II of the 1967 Amendments to the Economic Opportunity Act of 1964, 91st Congress, 1st Session, 1969, pp. 50-66.

conditions of city life and poverty would have been amenable to any other kind of marginal social intervention is at least debatable. It seems clear that the level of need and of social disorganization in city ghettos is such as to be unresponsive to most limited efforts at assistance. In this case, there were two additional obstacles of formidable stature. These were the Vietnam War, which resulted after 1966 in practical elimination of funding for many projects that had been planned and anticipated, and the dogged opposition of many local governments and established elites, who were disturbed by the prospects of change in the local status quo.

Impact

It is very difficult to be certain about the extent to which the War on Poverty programs of 1965 through 1968 assisted people in rising out of poverty. There was very little money spent; after only a short time, most program funds were cut back sharply or eliminated. Moreover, meaningful improvements take time, and visible effects might well be attributable to other causes. The number of people below the poverty line did drop between 1964 and 1967, but most of the evidence suggests that this was due to the Vietnam-provoked speed-up of the economy. The unemployment rate, for example, dropped below the usual "full employment" figure of four percent. But by 1968, the economic danger was seen as inflation and possible recession; and by 1969, the trend of unemployment rates had reversed itself and seemed heading for recessionary levels. Thus, the apparent gains of poverty-level people achieved in 1965-1968 were substantially eliminated by the economic downturn of the post-1968 months. Although there had been undeniable progress, particularly for blacks, there was serious question as to its permanence, its long-term effects, and the extent to which blacks were really catching up with whites.

The living conditions of some of the rural poor have been even worse so far as immediate suffering is concerned, though the causes of their poverty and the outlines of a solution for it may be less complicated. Among migrant farm workers and among Southern farm workers displaced from their jobs by machinery in the last two decades, there has been actual hunger, severe malnutrition, and a consequent high incidence of nutritional and related diseases: goiter, rickets, tuberculosis, and infant mortality rates higher than in many countries with far lower gross national products and per capita income than the United States. In April, 1969, members of the House Education and Labor Committee were told of a New Mexico family so poor that it regularly ate chipmunks and wild birds, and of an Arkansas family with children so undernourished they could not walk, talk, or eat. Based on an estimate by the United States Department of Agriculture that it required about $1200 annually simply to feed a family of four in early 1969, it appeared that as many as ten million Americans did not have enough money to eat adequately, many of them suffering enough to be sick with hunger.

In 1962, the federal government established a food stamp program to make surplus foods accumulated under the farm subsidy program available to the poor. Although it has alleviated hunger somewhat, the food stamp program has been highly inadequate in its first eight years of operation. This inadequacy stems partly from the fact that it is administered by the Department of Agriculture, which is more sensitive to the interests of farmers than to the needs of the poor. As a result, a series of procedural requirements have amounted to a guarantee that the program would not go very far to eliminate hunger and malnutrition. Until 1968, counties could not participate in the program at all unless their officials chose to do so, and many, especially in the South, did not so choose because wealthy white farmers on county supervisory boards were not concerned with the problems of the black poor or, worse, they believed that if the poor were fed they would not be willing to work when low-wage farm laborers were needed. In 1968, the Department was authorized to establish the food stamp program in counties in which the local authorities had not applied for it, but the Department's need to satisfy its farmer clientele made it reluctant o carry out this policy aggressively.

A more serious and widespread reason for the inadequacy of the food stamp program was the fact that the poor frequently did not have enough cash on hand to permit them to participate. To receive the stamps participants had to pay for a portion — usually more than half — of their value. Frequently there is simply no cash in the house on the date stamps must be bought once the rent is paid or an emergency requires that a doctor be called. The very poorest, who most needed help, were therefore the people who could not afford to receive it.

Finally, the stamps will buy only the commodities American farmers grow in surplus, and these are not necessarily the things people need or the items that will give them anything like a balanced diet. Such commodities as coffee, cocoa, soap, cleaning supplies, and toilet paper are not available.

One of the most concentrated and serious foci of rural poverty is the "Appalachian Region," extending from southern New York to central Alabama. Victims of the swift decline of the coal mining industry, the steep drop in demand for farm labor, lack of industrial development and public services in some areas, and a culture of poverty, millions of people within this region are close to hopelessness. In the southern part of the region close to 50 percent of the population is unemployed and probably unemployable, living on a surplus commodity diet and public assistance.

After several years of overtures, talks, and plans between the states of the region and the federal government, Congress passed the Appalachian Regional Development Act of 1965. It created an Appalachian Regional Commission, consisting of representatives from each of the states in the area and from the federal government, to develop plans for and to coordinate federal, state, and local efforts to deal with the region's most urgent problems.

The Appalachia program has received considerable publicity. A total of $1,092,400,000 in federal funds was appropriated for it for the six-year period 1965 to 1971: an average of $182,065,000 a year. Of this sum, almost 80 percent was earmarked for highway construction. In consequence, new highways now run past the dilapidated shanties in which the region's poor exist, but few of the unemployed ex-miners and ex-farmers could find jobs in their construction or can afford to enjoy them. The benefits of the federal contracts to the construction companies and their skilled employees are clearer than the benefits to the poor who are the ostensible beneficiaries of the Appalachia program. The relatively small sums not used for developing a highway system have been allocated to a variety of projects including demonstration health facilities, supplements to earlier federal grant-in-aid programs, and vocational education.

In addition to the strictly limited effects of the War on Poverty, racial discrimination appeared by the end of the 1960's to have thwarted the goal of integration in many areas. The public schools of many major cities, for example, were becoming *more,* instead of *less,* segregated as the years went by. This was superficially due to the shifting housing and residential patterns in which whites moved out to the suburbs as blacks moved into the cities, but the underlying motivation and explanation seemed to be racial attitudes on the part of whites. And the effect was to leave the poorer schools with lower funding and segregated classrooms.

Overall, it seems fair to say that the War on Poverty never really got off the ground. It was never well-funded, even in the early burst of enthusiasm. By the time that administrative organizations and projects were ready for real funding, the needs of the Vietnam War and the accumulated disenchantment of congressmen and their local constituents combined to eliminate all but a skeleton program. Thus, this modest effort had little chance to produce visible consequences. Much more powerful forces were at work in the economy, and it would be very difficult to be confident that any particular result was owed to this program.

By the close of the 1960's, the entire concept of assistance from the federal government to the poor as a group seemed open to challenge. Resentments against demonstrations and an apparent general trend toward conservatism seemed to spell the end of active poverty programs. One alternative, however, seemed to attract support from many sides of the political spectrum, despite its departure from the familiar "work ethic." This was the principle of eliminating welfare programs and substituting some form of automatic "income maintenance" program, which would assure a minimum level of income for American families even though they may not qualify for benefits under a welfare or antipoverty program. Some advocates favor accomplishing this through allowances to families for the support of children; the United States is one of the few industrialized countries without such a scheme. Another approach winning support from some conservatives as well as many liberals would establish a "negative income tax" — an arrangement under which families with incomes under the "poverty line" would receive money from the government in amounts sufficient to maintain a subsistence standard of living but not so large as to cut off their incentive to work. A third kind of income maintenance proposal would make the government the "employer of last resort." This is a plan to assure government jobs to those unable to find work in the private sector.

In the summer of 1969, the Nixon administration recommended the most thorough revision of the American welfare program since the Social Security Act of 1935. Even though Congress may alter these recommendations, they are worth attention as indications of what the administration saw as solutions to two major political problems: growing restiveness with the inadequacies of existing welfare provisions and pressure from conservatives and from Southern white elites to give local and state governments greater influence in manpower programs.

Under the Nixon proposals, the existing aid to dependent children program would be abolished. In its place, every family would be guaranteed a minimum income by the federal government. For a family of four with no outside income, this payment would be $1600 a year, and the states might augment it if they wished. This same family could earn up to $720 a year with no loss of benefits; but above that amount its benefits would be reduced 50 cents for each dollar earned, until its income reached $3920. This part of the plan constitutes a modest negative income tax program.

To encourage welfare recipients to work, the administration proposed that all recipients other than mothers with dependent children be required either to accept a job deemed "suitable" by a state employment agency or else undergo job training. The state employment agency would direct applicants for job training into what it considered the proper program, rather than leaving applicants free, as before, to choose among Job Corps, neighborhood youth corps, or the many other training programs previously established. The manpower features of the Nixon proposals amounted to a large-scale change to state administration of training programs.

The program thus represented both an effort to modify some of the most inadequate and inequitable features of ongoing welfare programs and to respond to political pressures from the conservatives and the Southerners who had offered Nixon the most political support. Under the minimum federal payment provisions, the assistance rolls would expand substantially, probably covering about 23 million people rather than four million; and many proponents of welfare thought it a major gain that the principle of a negative tax should be officially advocated, even though a family of four would still be in deep poverty if it received only $1600 a year.

At the same time, the work requirement provisions, combined with state and local administration, might easily permit local public officials and employers to require welfare recipients to accept work at very low wages or to accept jobs they found highly distasteful. Some found this possibility appealing and others thought it appalling. The additional appropriations required by the Nixon proposals would go disproportionately to the Southern states. The 1969 plan, in short, reflected both the need to keep the poor and their sympathizers from violent protest action and the values of the administration's chief political backers.

QUESTIONS AND IMPLICATIONS

In its impact and consequences, the current range of public policies to deal with poverty in America must be recognized as a very mixed bag, serving some functions for the poor but serving important functions as well for other political groups. A review of these functions tells us a great deal about some of the key ways in which the American political system is responsive to demands upon it as well as some of the instances in which it is either unresponsive or responsive in only a special and often misleading sense.

In comparison with the massive publicity it has received, or in comparison with expenditures for defense and war, the money channeled into the War on Poverty of the sixties and into public assistance programs has been a small amount indeed. No doubt this money has served to help some Americans avoid the worst effects of poverty. But it may not have done much more in that respect than the almshouses and private charity of the nineteenth and early twentieth centuries. And if it has usually done it in a somewhat less humiliating way, even this has not always been the case. The experience gained in such programs as the Job Corps and Headstart may serve as precedents for larger future efforts. As yet, however, it seems clear that the major institutions of the economic and political systems remain essentially unchanged, and that the basic outlines of the status quo regarding the poor remain as they were before the War on Poverty began.

One of the lessons emerging from this experience seems to be that the nature of government fiscal policy, together with the state of the private economy, have a greater influence on levels of income and on patterns of income distribution than do poverty and public assistance programs. Massive expenditures for military and space purposes have spurred the expansion of the economy to the point of creating both jobs and inflation. Some of this expansion affected the poor and did far more to aid them than the specifically-aimed policies of the poverty program. The same effects, of course, could be created by similar levels of spending for domestic purposes; and most economists would argue that domestic spending would do even more, because it would create public improvements and add to the gross national product in ways that soon-obsolete, expendable, and unproductive military supplies do not. But the choices are complex, and certainly not politically easy to make.

The Policy Dilemma

Black militancy was apparently the catalyst that inspired policymakers to act with respect to the conditions of the poor. Although the poor made up a substantial segment of the entire American population, and nearly half of all nonwhite Americans were poor, government policies had not previously addressed this group as a distinct unit. Once the problem was forced onto the political agenda, however, the question became one of the premises and assumptions under which it was to be acted upon. The dilemma inherent in this choice was fundamental to the outcome of the poverty program.

The New Deal programs, as we have seen, did not take the poor as a focus. Instead, they saw long-range economic security needs as a basis for planning welfare measures; and these were viewed as necessary only until the economy could be put back into a more productive working order. Thus the chief concern was to establish a floor for individuals and then to allow the expansion of the economy to do the rest. The War on Poverty of the 1960's did identify the poor as a distinct group which had been by-passed under the New Deal social insurance programs and which constituted an enduring (and increasingly prohibitive) drain on the existing New Deal-originated public assistance programs. But the remedies devised again relied on the private economy as the principal means of enabling poor individuals to share more fully in middle-class "affluence." Education and training, concentrated on youth, were its chief tactics. The community action programs did seek to mobilize the poor and to enable them to claim their rightful share of social services, which, though generally available to all, had been in practice utilized principally by the more active and effective middle classes. But by 1967, all of these efforts ended for practical purposes in the Vietnam War-induced shift in federal funding priorities. The more conservative Congress elected in 1966, together with complaints from many local governments and an apparent popular disenchantment, confirmed the Johnson administration in its own commitment to give the Vietnam War primacy and to sharply reduce such "nonessential" expenditures as the War on Poverty. Although OEO itself lingered during the Nixon administration, many specific programs and projects were transferred to other departments or reduced to "research and development" or pilot project status. The principle of citizen participation in community action agencies was clouded by severe criticism, much of it directed at the idea that federal government financing was supporting the poor's militant efforts toward change in their local communities.

The War on Poverty, therefore, raised the expectations of the poor far more than it delivered on such hopes. In part, this may have been due to the Vietnam War, failures of implementation, and excessive innocence about the prospect of resistance from various sources. But in part, the problem was one of premises and assumptions. If the private economy is to be the principal means of uplift, government policies must be aimed at driving unemployment well below the four percent "full employment" figure. Otherwise, the poor, and particularly the black poor, will experience widespread unemployment and remain in poverty. The very best that could occur under existing circumstances would be that today's poor might gain and hold jobs, but that a new poor would be created from among those whom they replaced. Yet it is apparently impossible to keep the unemployment rate at low levels without generating serious inflation. Granted, only

war-related spending has actually been effective in substantially reducing unemployment, so experience in this respect is limited. Nevertheless, the policy dilemma appears to force a choice between reducing poverty and creating inflation, or accepting current or rising
poverty (and unemployment) in order to prevent inflation. One
analyst frames the issue this way:

> Reduction of unemployment below 4% has been accompanied by
> acceleration of the increase in the consumer price index from less than
> 1½% per year, 1960-1965, to more than 3% per year, 1965-1968. Reducing
> the unemployment rate from 3½% to 3% would further increase the speed
> of inflation, perhaps to 4 or 5% per year. On the other hand, it would at
> the same time raise real GNP about $4 billion or $5 billion. More important
> in this context, it could be expected to lower the prevalence of poverty
> in the population by four-tenths of a percentage point . . . .[21]

This dilemma between inflation and reducing poverty exists, of course,
only when the private economy in its present form is taken to be the
principal means of assisting the poor. If government acted as an
"employer of last resort" instead of relying on the private economy to
employ the poor, different results might ensue. Or if other means of
income redistribution were considered practical, the equation would
again be different. The point is that the assumptions by which policies
are shaped lie at the heart of the question of whether their ostensible
goals will be achieved.

Political Functions of the War on Poverty

These realizations bring us to a speculative exploration of some of the
other (non-poverty-reducing) functions which may have been served
by the War on Poverty. It appears that, although they have had relatively little concrete impact on the lives of poor people, they have
had considerably more effect on polarizing people politically. Some
programs have been largely tokens, which is to say that they have
helped people concerned about the existence of poverty to believe
that significant strides toward eliminating it have been taken, even
when they have not. The Community Action Program has been little
more than tokenistic in most cities so far. Nor has enough money
been spent on Appalachia or on model cities to make a substantial
difference in socio-economic conditions in these areas. Many widely
publicized civil rights programs, notably those requiring school desegregation, have similarly been more effective in creating an impression of change than in actually creating change itself. This effect must
be recognized as a rather common kind of impact that public policy
has and one which can lessen demand for change and therefore
lessen stress in the political system. For reasons noted earlier and
summarized below, it has not had that effect in this case.

   Another political function some of the poverty programs have
served is to provide benefits to the affluent, either directly or indirectly. Assistance to families of dependent children is directly

---

[21] Tobin, *op. cit.*, p. 88.

beneficial to the children and to their impoverished mothers, and it indirectly benefits the landlords in the ghettos where many of these AFDC recipients live. Without AFDC the landlords would often not be paid and their rents would have to be lower. For this reason, landlords have, in fact, been a source of support for AFDC programs in state legislatures. More directly benefiting the affluent have been those programs which employ large corporations to carry out part of the work. The benefits the Appalachia program confers upon highway contractors is one example.

Job Corps represents a somewhat less extreme case of the same thing. The operation of many of the Job Corps camps has been sub-contracted to private corporations and in some cases to universities. The camp at Camp Kilmer, New Jersey, for example, was operated until its closing in July, 1969, by the Federal Electric Corporation; that at Paducah, Kentucky, by Southern Illinois University. In both instances, the camps represented important sources of income to the contractors, and in some cases there were complaints by the trainees and some congressmen that the contractors were tempted to increase the profitability of these operations by subordinating their educational goals to simplistic notions of economy and efficiency. At both Kilmer and Paducah there were several incidents of protest, riot, or vandalism by trainees which could be attributed in part at least to their resentment of this situation.

Similarly, the schemes for federal grants to corporations for the purpose of providing jobs for the unemployed amount to an important source of income or of insurance against loss for these businesses. The same is true of the plans for "black capitalism," involving governmental encouragement of black-owned businesses in the ghettos. Whether this effect is inevitable in our society is a question not easily answered, and whether it is desirable every citizen must decide for himself. These programs may be more accurately viewed as payments to private organizations which can perform services more efficiently than government can perform them; or they may be seen as subsidies to the affluent involving subordination of the goal of helping the poor to the goal of maximizing profits.

The major political function served by the poverty policies of the 1960's, however, may have been the impact they had on the expectations and demands of numbers of people. In this regard, they must be seen together with the civil rights legislation of the same period. The impetus given to the concept of equality by court decisions and new civil rights laws has encouraged new expectations, beliefs, and behavior. Although upper middle class whites may have perceived some progress by blacks and been led to complacency, lower middle class whites have apparently perceived so rapid a black advance as to constitute an economic and social threat. Blacks, on the other hand, have seen little material progress, although they have been encouraged to believe that some would be forthcoming and that they might reasonably expect more in the future. Thus, while the upper middle class assumes progress, there is also lower middle class white resentment and readiness for forceful suppression of blacks, and black demands, verbal and violent, for material improvements corresponding to legal promises. Together, these beliefs and behaviors add up to an explosive mixture which increasingly dominated American domestic politics in the late sixties.

In effect, these various federal programs seem to have contributed a wedge into the social coalition that the New Deal programs, engineered by Franklin D. Roosevelt, had built. Taking advantage of the shock of the Great Depression, Roosevelt had conceded the need for protection against the worst economic problems that individuals faced, possibly thereby saving the established economic system from complete collapse or mass rejection. The coalition that rallied to the Democratic Party in response included high proportions of the nation's workers, farmers, intellectuals, blacks, and European ethnic minorities.

In the late sixties, this coalition had come apart; the new social problems (and, to an extent, the new public policies reviewed here) had done much to create new alignments. A substantial proportion of the working class whites, now above the poverty line and aspiring to affluence but perceiving a threat from black geographical and occupational mobility, supported the established status relationships and favored suppression of all who threatened them, especially blacks and students. The European ethnic minorities were frequently in the forefront of this group. The more affluent whites were splitting — some supporting social and economic change to help the poor and the blacks, some favoring suppression of black social and political movements. The young, the academic, and part of the intellectual upper middle class were especially conspicuous in the former group. In short, the issue of how to alleviate the problems of the disadvantaged and the relatively powerless was becoming the decisive one around which new coalitions, more polarized and more willing to resort to militant action than their predecessors, were forming. In a sense, that had also been the decisive issue in the thirties, but at that time a different group, the industrial workers, were the disadvantaged.

Both in the thirties and in the sixties it was conspicuously true that the disadvantaged groups which gained the most political weight were those that enjoyed the support of other groups with more status and money. What is involved is a perception by the more powerful that their own interests can be served in large measure by administering to some of the needs of the disadvantaged. In the middle sixties, for example, the formerly ignored and "invisible" poor, the "Other America," became visible and began to acquire some political influence when a substantial part of the affluent middle class came to believe that the related problems of poverty and racism threatened the whole social fabric and the very continuation of our society. These problems seemed to threaten not only the material well-being of the affluent but their self-conception as democratic, liberal, and compassionate people. Demonstrations, riots, and some eloquent writings all helped bring about this critical change in the perceptions and beliefs of part of the white middle class.

Because only a part of the middle class saw its own interests and its future in this new light, however, the change also served to create a new bitterness in political alignments — a polarization that expressed itself in a greater willingness to resort to violence and physical repression. Despite the small sums actually appropriated for their furtherance, poverty and civil rights policies seem to have had striking effects on the perceptions, beliefs, and expectations of major parts of the population. With all the demonstrable results of the entire range of social insurance, public assistance, and other social welfare programs of more recent vintage, they remain in concrete terms marginal — alongside the powerful effects of government fiscal and monetary policies and the state of the private economy. But in symbolic terms, few acts of government are more consequential than its posture with regard to the status of the poor and the black.

Economic Growth and Stability 6

The major influence upon how affluently or how poorly Americans live is the general state of the economy. Crucial to this is the character of government economic policies, the sum total of which affects the economy's productivity, employment and price levels, and distribution patterns in fundamental ways. Far more significant in these respects than policies designed to help particular groups, such as the poverty programs just discussed, are the broader policies that help determine employment levels, how fast prices will rise, whether wages lag behind the cost of living, and what volume of goods and services will be produced. These interrelated economic trends may sound technical and abstract, but in human terms they are neither. They decide in large measure what the quality of life will be, and who will receive how much of what rewards there are to be divided. No area of public policy is more critical for the human condition, and therefore economic growth and stability must be one of the areas on which our examination of policy focuses. After a brief review of the character of economic problems, we shall examine one area (price and wage stability) in depth, and then explore the policies adopted and the impact generated by government in recent decades.

Before the 1930's the government undertook little or no economic planning to improve future standards of living for citizens or to influence the distribution of income among different groups of the population over the long run. Some kinds of public policies did, of course, help or hurt specific groups economically: subsidies to businesses and to farmers, doles and pensions to the very poor (chiefly by local units of government), minimum wage and maximum hour laws for women and children, regressive or progressive taxes, etc. These policies were responses to particular and immediate political needs, problems, and influence. They did not add up to a plan for increasing economic well-being in the future or for preventing the wild fluctuations in prices and wages that mean gross inequality of sacrifice and of benefits.

A basic reason for the increased interest in planning for economic growth and stability in the postwar period is the quite recent advances in economic theory that make the success of such planning more likely. Until we believed we could devise economic policy that would encourage high levels of employment and continuing growth in the quantity and quality of goods and services we produce each year without steep price increases, there could be little political pressure to plan for economic growth. The macroeconomic theory stemming from the seminal work of John Maynard Keynes in the 1930's was influential in fostering such a belief. That work had itself been stimulated by the social problems flowing from the worldwide great depression. The work of Keynes, and of his successors and critics, led in turn to the development of empirical indicators of economic activity far more complete and sensitive than had been available earlier. Economists could therefore work with fairly reliable data on such matters as investment and savings trends, production, productivity, and price fluctuations. Even if these advances in economic theory and data collection were not a necessary condition for economic planning, they certainly provided convenient political rationalizations on both sides of the question. A useful and probably necessary complement to these technical and scientific advances was the invention after World War II of electronic computers that could help in formulating complex models of how the economy works and could handle the complicated mathematical computations quickly and accurately.

Once it was deemed practical to make deliberate decisions to forego certain kinds of economic benefits in the present in order to assure larger benefits in the future, it was inevitable that the issue would become a political one. It clearly involved conflicts of interest over who should do how much foregoing and who should benefit to what extent. Once it is technically feasible for governments to influence rates of economic growth by deliberate planning and also to exert influence over which groups benefit how much through changes in price and wage levels, public policy regarding economic growth and economic stability can be expected to remain a major area of political controversy for the indefinite future. These policies directly affect how well people live and how evenly the output of the economy is distributed.

ECONOMIC GROWTH AND STABILITY: A POLITICO-ECONOMIC PROBLEM

It might seem at first blush that economic growth, like happiness and motherhood, is something that everybody favors — that it should involve no political conflict. If growth meant simply that more goods and services were produced and that everybody's share of these benefits were increased, then perhaps it would not be a serious political issue. The fact is, however, that the governmental decisions that foster growth always hurt some groups of the population. Specific proposals intended to encourage economic growth, therefore, do become controversial political issues. Let us see how.

Growth means the production of a larger volume of goods and services than was previously produced. To accomplish this the country either has to employ its productive resources (manpower and machinery chiefly) more fully than it had previously done; or it has to increase the quantity or the quality of manpower and other resources used in production. To do either one of these things involves sacrifices, absolute or relative, for some people. In the long run, growth *may* mean benefits for everyone, but it can do so only by requiring the foregoing of some benefits in the present to make larger future benefits possible; and the sacrifices in the present are far from equal, just as the benefits in the future are certain to be unequal.

Suppose the strategy is to promote economic growth by employing some of the presently available men and machines that are lying idle or that are employed only occasionally. Unemployed men constitute an obvious economic and social problem and unemployed machines are a financial burden to those who own them; to employ either more fully might seem a clear gain. Yet it would not be a benefit for everybody.

For one thing, a higher level of employment is very likely to mean that prices will rise. More people earning money will be bidding for the supply of consumer goods and services, enabling sellers to charge more. Higher prices have a very unequal impact. Those living on pensions and other fixed incomes and those who lack the bargaining power to charge more for their services will bear the brunt of the price rises, while some people's earnings will increase even faster than prices do. The federal, state, and local governments, as major buyers of goods and services, will experience rising costs, and these will have to be paid through taxes or borrowing, which themselves fall quite unequally on different groups of people.

Employers who have been able to find workers easily because the unemployed were eagerly looking for work may now find that full employment means labor shortages and forces them to pay higher wages. The burden this imposes on different employers is unequal, however, for in some highly automated industries (such as oil refining) labor costs are such a small proportion of total costs that higher wages are a negligible factor, while in other industries (such as building construction), labor is the major cost, and even a slight wage rise sends total costs soaring.

These are only a few of the ways in which a policy of full employment means unequal burdens for different groups of people; but they illustrate the reasons why a full employment policy is bound to cause political controversy.

There is certain to be heated political infighting over every specific means of achieving it: over proposals that government itself provide jobs for the unemployed, for example; over proposals to make credit easier in order to encourage more private spending, which, in turn, should foster more production and fuller use of productive resources; over proposals to retrain the unemployed for new kinds of jobs; over increased spending by governments themselves.

Economic growth poses an even more fundamental political and ethical issue than these. How well people live depends far less on the total quantity or the monetary value of the goods and services produced than upon *what* is produced. When part of the country's productive means are devoted to producing worthless or harmful patent medicines, cancer-producing cigarettes, armaments, and poison gas, these add to economic growth statistics exactly as do the production of milk, the building of schools, or the establishment of a symphony orchestra. They may indirectly contribute even more, because people injured by the patent medicines, cigarettes, and armaments will require the services of physicians, which constitute another component of economic growth statistics. The point is, of course, that growth in itself, as that term is defined by economists, does not necessarily improve the general quality of people's lives; it may only improve the quality of life for a very few, and it may even cheapen and degrade life for many others. Nor is growth in the gross national product (GNP) ever free; it entails costs. For that reason, some economists have suggested that it would be just as accurate to describe the total value of goods and services produced in a year as "Gross National Costs" as to use the term "Gross National Product."

The political conflict that affects growth policy will normally not be presented, publicized, or generally perceived as a conflict over economic growth at all, but rather over more immediate values and goals. The provision of jobs by government is perceived as a welfare policy or as a step toward socialism — a source of competition with private industry. And further controversy is likely to arise over the value of the work performed on government projects. Some see the adoption of measures to loosen credit as a step toward inflation of prices and others see it as a means to encourage more spending and more jobs. Retraining of the unemployed is often perceived as a new tax burden. Increased governmental spending on specific projects, such as space exploration, defense, public health, public education, highways, or welfare, inevitably involves controversy over the value of these activities, over who benefits and who bears the major tax burdens.

A list of political conflicts of this sort is bound to look neater, simpler, and more clear-cut than the actual engagement in them which people experience in their daily lives. A worker who likes the idea of learning a new skill in a retraining program may at the same time oppose tax increases and not see the two as related to each other. (The tax increase, of course, may be principally for other purposes.) A person who is thrilled by the idea of sending a man to the moon may at the same time criticize the growth of a large federal bureaucracy and governmental spending of billions of dollars a year. People are ambivalent in various degrees; the political outcomes of conflicts like these, therefore, depend not only upon objective economic interests, but also upon *which* among several conflicting interests and values come to be perceived as those which are involved in a particular policy. As suggested elsewhere, one function public policy and political rhetoric serve is to influence the perceptions of large groups of people. They may cause people to see the allocation of a great deal of money to space research as a way to achieve national greatness or, alternatively, as a federal subsidy to large corporations at the expense of antipoverty and welfare policies, for example.

Besides measures to employ available men and machinery more fully, economic growth is promoted by increasing the quantity or the quality of available men, machinery, and other productive resources. Indeed, this second strategy is clearly the more effective and more durable one, and some economists maintain that it is the only true road to economic growth.[1] It can be accomplished by measures to encourage the invention and use of more efficient machinery in productive processes (i.e., in factories, mines, farms, and service industries) and by measures to increase the supply of labor having useful skills. While such changes obviously involve decisions by private individuals and corporations as well as by governments, it is clear that deliberate public policy plays a crucial part, and very likely *the most* crucial part.

A little analysis shows why this is true. Private corporations have an interest in augmenting their profits, and one way to accomplish this is to become more efficient and increase their output and their sales, though it is not the only way. They also have a strong interest in expanding their share in the market for whatever they produce, so as better to control the economic environment in which they operate and influence their competitors' decisions. Thus, General Motors can very largely shape its three competitors' decisions on the pricing of automobiles, and United States Steel exerts a similar in-

---

[1] Strictly speaking, economic growth can only occur over the long run by increases in productivity i.e., increases in the efficiency of capital and labor employed in production.

fluence over other firms in the steel industry. Yet studies of private business decisions make it clear that corporations do not forego profits in the present or the near future simply to contribute to national economic growth in the long run; they do so only when it presents an opportunity for the corporation itself to profit; and that opportunity is basically created by public policies.

In what ways? There are a great many, all of them involving benefits for some people and deprivations for others, and all of them therefore controversial. One of the most direct ways government encourages increased productivity is through provision for "fast tax write-offs" for new plant and equipment. This amounts in effect to a drastic cut in the federal income tax a corporation has to pay relative to the degree that it invests in new plant and equipment; it is therefore a form of governmental subsidy, which encourages such investment. The taxes not paid by the corporation must of course come from other people, most of them with lower incomes than the corporation stockholders who benefit from the subsidy.

Another way government encourages increased productivity and economic growth is through federal financing of research and development projects. The invention and development both of more efficient methods of producing goods and services and of new types of goods and services (whether they help people or hurt them) is obviously a basic strategy for promoting economic growth. Through research contracts to develop particular kinds of products, through grants to scientists and graduate students to upgrade the quality and quantity of basic and applied research, and through research carried on directly by such government agencies as the National Bureau of Standards and the National Institute of Health, government is by far the largest patron of efforts to find more effective products and more efficient productive processes. At the beginning of the decade of the seventies the federal government curtailed its research expenditures sharply, but remained the major source of research funds.

In other, less direct ways, government makes further substantial contributions to the research and development of new products. For example, corporations may deduct their research expenses from their earnings in computing their income taxes. And under "cost-plus" contracts, some corporations are able to add all or most of their research costs to their charges against the government. Each of these public policies promotes growth, but each imposes immediate costs upon very large numbers of taxpayers while conferring immediate benefits upon smaller numbers of managers, stockholders, and employees of the businesses carrying on research.

Still other public policies foster economic growth by increasing the productive effectiveness of people rather than machines and products. This is accomplished by retraining workers and by attracting into the labor force people who would otherwise not use their skills — members of a minority group who suffer from discrimination and women with spare time, for example. Such measures increase the size of the productive labor force and may increase its quality and productive efficiency.

PRICE AND WAGE STABILITY: THE PROBLEM IN DEPTH

Closely related to the political controversies over policies to promote economic growth is another kind of economic policy issue: price stability, or rates of increase in wages and prices. Prices are a major influence upon people's incomes and expenses, and therefore upon how well they live. But although they are enormously important to everyone, prices have different impacts upon different groups of people. Increases in wages (an important kind of price) are avidly sought by workers, but represent a cost to their employers. Increases in food prices represent income to farmers and food processors but raise the cost of living for everyone. Increases in the prices of industrial products usually benefit those who hold stock in the companies that manufacture them and may confer added prestige upon the management of these companies, but they represent higher costs to those who buy the products, including farmers. Public policies that have an influence upon any or all of these kinds of prices can therefore be expected to be controversial whenever people are aware of their effects.

These policies, moreover, affect people's economic welfare in other ways that make them still more important and controversial. Quickly rising prices are likely to occur when the economy is booming and there is little unemployment. Policies to slow down price rises tend to slow down the economy generally and to throw some people out of work, usually those with the fewest skills and the lowest incomes. Given a capitalist economy and Keynesian principles of management, policymakers often have to choose between the disadvantages of higher prices and the disadvantages of more unemployment. Which horn of this dilemma seems less harsh depends, of course, upon one's economic situation. In 1969, as occasionally before and since, many businessmen concerned about rising wages and other costs favored slowing down the economy to prevent further price increases, while workers opposed such action for fear it would mean layoffs for themselves. Both sides tried, naturally enough, to win wide public support for their positions. The President's Business Advisory Council, consisting of top officers of large corporations who advise the Commerce Department and the President, suggested that an increase in unemployment from about 3.5 percent to 4.5 percent of the labor force would have a "healthy" effect on prices. But labor spokesmen pointed out that this would mean serious hardship to almost a million workers and their families, and some professional economists expressed serious doubt that it was possible to "fine tune" the economy with enough sensitivity to stop rising unemployment at the 4.5 percent figure once a slowdown was under way. Unemployment might well go to six or seven percent of the labor force and a serious economic depression could be created. Such a result, even if intended by no one, would not only seriously impede long-range economic growth but would also cause intense suffering among the unemployed and those whose incomes would be severely curtailed.

A recent study demonstrates, contrary to widely held beliefs, that general price rises hurt the poor less than the nonpoor. The higher demand for labor that accompanies rising prices not only provides more employment for the poor but also provides greater gains for them, as compared to other groups, in increased hours worked and by increased wages. Because the assets of the poor are small in total value, inflation can do little to lower their value still more.[2] The evils of inflation are a middle class perception, and they often serve to justify measures that increase unemployment and poverty.

Sometimes the case for slowing down the economy is far stronger than it was in 1969 and enjoys widespread support, even among labor groups. This was clearly the case during both World War II and the Korean War, when production of war materials cut unemployment to a minimum, gave people more money to spend, gave jobs to many who had previously not chosen to work or could not find work, and at the same time reduced production of the peacetime consumer goods on which money could be spent. A great deal of money bidding for a relatively small supply of goods naturally boosted price levels rather fast; and it was apparent to everyone that the government had somehow to restrict price rises in order to prevent runaway inflation.

What kinds of public policies *can* be adopted to restrict price rises? When the government is under strong pressure to curb inflation, as it is in wartime, the most direct and conspicuous response is to set "ceilings" or maximum levels on prices and wages, with penalties for those who violate them. In both World War II and the Korean War, such direct price and wage controls were imposed.

"Ceilings" is not a wholly accurate description of this strategy, for it is never possible simply to fix maximum prices. Both the economic and the political resistance to such a simple policy would quickly destroy it. Direct price control programs are, therefore, always somewhat flexible, responding to current economic and political pressures by allowing exceptions or raising the ceilings. The wages of a particular group of workers may be allowed to rise above what the general rule would allow because their existing pay scales are far below the average or yield less than a decent standard of living, or because other workers doing the same job in the same plant or in the same area are already being paid substantially more. Remember that in wartime, with labor scarce, employers as well as workers frequently are eager to increase wages so as to be able to attract the workers they need to fulfill their production contracts. Employers are therefore cross-pressured in their support for anti-inflation programs, as is everybody else to a greater or lesser degree. Workers of course want higher wages, but they are also consumers who want to keep the prices of the goods they buy low enough so that they can afford them. Businessmen might like to charge more for the goods they sell, but they know that if everybody else can do that, costs will increase so fast that their profits may disappear.

[2] Robinson G. Hollister and John L. Palmer, *The Impact of Inflation on the Poor* (Institute for Research on Poverty, University of Wisconsin, 1969, mimeo).

The government officials responsible for administering direct price and wage control programs are subject to exactly these same kinds of cross-pressures, and their policies reflect the conflicting interests of which they are a part and which have access to them, formally or informally. As a result, every governmental program to place direct controls on prices and wages is effective only insofar as there is basic public support for it, rather than resentment, opposition, and resort to opportunistic or illegal efforts to defeat it. The mechanisms through which both support and opposition are conveyed to policy-makers are analyzed in the chapters on political processes; but their results and effectiveness can only be known definitively by observing policy outcomes and impacts.

The Effects of Controls: Two Contrasting Situations

The two fairly recent periods in which the United States has resorted to direct controls[3] provide examples of quite different mixes of popular support and opposition, and the differences in outcome are revealing. During World War II, the war dominated people's attention and activities, effecting major changes in living patterns, employment patterns, and even in the availability of food and other consumer goods. The sense of crisis and of urgency was strong and widespread. Unemployment was virtually erased, and many new people were attracted into the labor force. By 1945, 18.61 percent of the labor force were serving in the armed forces, and a large proportion of the national product was going into war materials rather than consumer goods.

The psychological effect of the drastic changes in normal ways of living was naturally substantial, and one form it took was general concern about the danger of runaway inflation and consequent support for the price control program. As already noted, that support was always modified by the efforts of particular groups to achieve relaxed controls over whatever it was they sold (whether their own labor or goods), but recognition of the need for an effective program was quite general. Consequently, the control program was effective.

Politically, however, its success must be examined in rather different terms. The controls over prices imposed by the Office of Price Administration and those over wages administered by the War Labor Board caused constant strains, demands for exceptions, resentments, and occasional strikes, as well as generalized support. These strains resulted both in official relaxation of particular controls and in illegal evasions of the official policies.

The wage control program was continuously subject to some revision and softening, both through new general policies and through decisions to accept particular applications requesting permission to raise wages for certain groups of workers. In May, 1942, for example, the War Labor Board adopted the "Little Steel Formula," permitting an increase in straight-time hourly earnings of 15 percent over the

[3] A wage control program was in effect for a short period during World War I as well.

January, 1941, levels. Most workers had already received such an increase, and the Formula was intended to permit the laggards to catch up to them.

Another kind of general policy that helped make the controls palatable for workers was the willingness of the Board to permit increases in fringe benefits which would not have an immediate impact upon production costs and therefore upon prices. In consequence, the years 1943 through 1945 saw a rash of new industrial contracts providing for retirement plans, welfare and health plans, and vacations. This wartime expedient in turn gave a strong incentive to fringe benefit demands and concessions after the war.

The demands of a particular group of workers for increases beyond the ceilings often had to be granted at least in part, either by making exceptions for them or, what amounted to the same thing, by inventing a new rationalization for the particular increases. Thus, the United Mine Workers Union engaged in several wartime strikes that placed great pressure upon the War Labor Board to meet their wage demands.

It is revealing to examine the range and types of diverse pressures upon the Board in cases like these. Because the Board was officially responsible not only for keeping a lid on wages but also for settling disputes that might hurt the war effort, and because most disputes were about wages, there was always a strong temptation to make some concessions on the wage issues in order to insure continued production of war goods. Indeed, the very fact that jurisdiction over both disputes and wage controls was vested in the same agency insured that some compromise between the two goals would have to be made. In choosing the exact form of the compromise the Board was bound to reflect conflicting values and pressures in the larger society. Many people felt strongly that it was unpatriotic for workers to strike in wartime; just after America's involvement in the war, moreover, there had been a "no-strike pledge" by the unions in return for formal union representation on the War Labor Board. At the same time the miners' bargaining position was an unusually strong one. Mining is highly skilled and extremely hazardous work, and miners were in short supply. The demand for coal was high, and as John L. Lewis, President of the United Mine Workers, reminded his critics who wanted troops to take over the mines or the miners drafted into the army, "You can't mine coal with bayonets." The work of the miners was, moreover, contributing to the profits of the mine owners even during the occasional periods of federal government "seizure" of struck mines. The issues, therefore, were heated and evoked widespread and strong reaction, including not only "seizures," but occasional fines against the Union and its officers. In order to insure continued production, however, the Board did several times find reasons to grant a large part of the workers' demands; and the same general pattern of pressures and of concessions occurred in some other key industries.

Unquestionably, there were some "under the counter" sales of scarce goods above the legal prices and some black markets; but the general record of compliance with the direct controls of World War II was good.

Direct wage and price controls during the Korean War from 1949 to 1953 were, on the other hand, relatively ineffective. At that time there was far less fear that inflation was a major threat to the civilian economy and to the war effort. This uncertainty about the economic and military need for controls was reflected in far greater willingness by the wage board (now called the National Wage Stabilization Board) to find justifications for granting permission to pay higher wages and by the price agency (Office of Price Stabilization) to do the same thing for prices. The result was, on the wage side, that the Board's primary function was that of generating rationalizations for permitting wage increases in a period of labor scarcity. Intraplant inequities, interplant inequities, seasonal work inequities, substandard of living inequities, tandem situations (a finding that permission for wage increases for a group of workers justified similar permission for others in similar situations) — all these reasons and others were officially recognized by the Board as bases for accepting joint applications by particular companies and the unions representing their workers to pay wages above the general ceiling. The result of these policies was that wages rose rapidly during the period of "controls." Several eminent labor economists who later studied this record, one of them himself a former member of the National Wage Stabilization Board, concluded that the "controls" had not controlled; that, indeed, they had probably contributed to a faster rise in wage levels than would have occurred without any control program at all.

A realistic political analyst must recognize that direct controls always serve political functions whether or not they accomplish the economic functions for which they are ostensibly established. Every time a government imposes direct wage or price controls it is proclaiming in a very dramatic way that it is doing something significant to counter the threat of inflation which is occasioning public concern. The control program, and the continuing news reports about new rules and other changes in it, thus reassure anxious people, softpedal suspicions that businessmen and workers are selfishly profiting from a national emergency, provide opportunities for politically powerful corporations and unions to get what they want with government blessings, and win support for the administration in power. For these reasons, direct controls are sometimes a *political* necessity even when economists are not sure they will be effective in holding down prices or that they are required for economic reasons. Direct controls, moreover, have still another kind of political effect useful to the administration in office. They continuously remind people that there *is* a national crisis or emergency and so increase their willingness to make sacrifices they would otherwise resent and possibly resist. These political and psychological consequences of direct control programs may or may not be consciously recognized or deliberately sought by those in power. But during World War II, there is evidence that officials did in fact seek public acquiescence in the sacrifices which such programs foster.[4] Belief that the country faces a national crisis makes it easier to secure public acceptance of military drafts, food shortages, price increases, wage freezes, longer hours, harder work, austerity budgets, and other deprivations. This kind of influence upon the state of mind of a people, and therefore upon their acquiescence in leadership they might otherwise resist, must be recognized as a major outcome of certain forms of public policy — policy of which direct price and wage controls are a prime example. It should also be realized that most of the forms of deprivation that such measures make psychologically easier to accept, do contribute to faster economic growth, for they involve more labor and greater willingness to forego immediate consumption of what is produced.

It should now be possible to recognize the aspect of direct control programs that explains the two key functions we have noticed: their relative economic ineffectiveness unless there is strong popular support for the program and their political and psychological function of emphasizing the existence of a crisis and of bolstering public support for governmentally sanctioned deprivations. In both cases the fact that direct control programs require active public involvement and cooperation is the critical factor. Even if part of the population withholds its economic cooperation and evades the rules, the political effect can be substantial. This conclusion is evident from foreign as well as domestic experience with direct wage and price control programs.[5]

The conclusion becomes even clearer when we compare these programs with *indirect* controls, the alternative strategy open to governments faced with an inflationary threat. Indirect controls do not require the voluntary cooperation of the general public. People have little choice about cooperating; buyers and sellers cannot agree to charge and pay more than the legal price.

What happens, rather, is that governmental agencies make the decision to affect the supply or demand for money or for goods in such a way that prices are inevitably raised or lowered. The economic technicalities are somewhat complicated, but the basic mechanisms are easy enough to understand, even without extensive training in economics. Indirect controls involve either monetary policy or fiscal policy. Monetary policy refers to governmental manipulation of the supply of money or credit available for use in the country. In the United States such manipulation is chiefly exercised by the Board of Governors of the Federal Reserve System, an agency established in 1914 to regulate and help the nation's banks in various ways. If the Federal Reserve Board believes that price increases need to be curbed, it can increase the rates of interest charged for borrowing money and

[4] *Cf.* Victor A. Thompson, *The Regulatory Process in OPA Rationing* (New York: 1950).

[5] Murray Edelman and R. W. Fleming, *The Politics of Wage-Price Decisions: A Four Country Analysis* (Urbana, Ill.: University of Illinois Press, 1965).

otherwise make it harder for banks to obtain the money and credit they need to make loans. A smaller supply of money and credit helps to keep prices going down, and it also makes it harder for business corporations and individuals to obtain funds to expand their businesses, undertake new enterprises, and in other ways expand production and employment. Indirect monetary controls of this kind therefore curb both inflation and economic growth and do it in such a way that the public's active cooperation is not necessary to make the curbs effective. In contrast to direct price controls, then, monetary policy can be counted on to have significant economic effects whether or not there is wide public concern about inflation. Its political effects, on the other hand, are likely to be delayed and uncertain, for it involves decisionmaking of a highly technical, complex kind conducted by a small group of people whose operations, and even whose existence, are not widely known or appreciated by the general public.

The other major form of indirect control over prices, employment, and growth available to the federal government is through fiscal policy — that is, taxing and spending policies. These influence the pace of the economy and its effects on different groups in a number of ways. Probably the most telling influence over the long run is the balance between the federal government's income and its expenditures. When the government spends more than it receives in taxes, it uses credit. Such "deficit spending" has a stimulating effect upon the economy, for it expands the amount of money and credit available to buy goods. Indeed, economists have found that deficit spending has a "multiplier effect"; i.e., each dollar of public spending beyond government income stimulates the private spending of three or four dollars. For the same reason, a surplus of public revenue over expenditures has a depressing or deflationary effect on the economy; it reduces the amount of money and credit available to buy goods and services and so puts a brake upon the ability of private individuals and corporations to produce goods and services, employ workers, or raise prices.

The governmental budget, therefore, has come to be recognized as performing a basically different function from the budget of private families; it is probably misleading to use the same word for both of them. The public budget does not serve chiefly as a guide to how much money is available for expenditures, for the government can continue to expand the amount of money and credit available to it as long as it retains public confidence that it will meet its obligations; and we have learned from experience that that confidence can be retained in spite of very large deficits.[6]

The more significant point is that the governmental budget is a powerful instrument for controlling both the rate of economic growth and the degree of price stabilization. Tax cuts and increases in public spending tend to stimulate growth, employment, and price levels. Tax

[6] It is true that in creating deficits the government shifts somewhat the burden of financing public functions, though the nature of the shift depends upon the tax structure and the devices relied upon to finance and pay off the public debt.

increases and cuts in spending tend to put a brake upon the rate of growth and upon price increases and to increase the proportion of the labor force that is unemployed.[7] In the 1960's, the United States government for the first time in its history began deliberately to use fiscal policy to control the pace of economic growth in this fashion. In 1964, there was a tax cut for the avowed purpose of stimulating the economy and avoiding recession; in 1968, a 10 percent tax surcharge was imposed for the explicit purpose of "cooling off" the economy and slowing down the rate of price increases attributable chiefly to the enormous costs of the Vietnam War. It seems inevitable that the federal budget will continue to be used in the future as an instrument for economic control and not only as a device for recording the balance of revenues and expenditures. This is true even though the budget is a gross rather than a sensitive regulator. We can predict in what direction a deficit or a surplus will push the economy, but we cannot be sure how fast it will be pushed. Perhaps future advances in economic theory will permit more accurate "fine tuning" of the economy than is now possible.

Even though the overall balance between revenues and expenditures influences economic growth and stabilization, it is of course also true that the details of both tax laws and appropriation bills influence the distribution of benefits and deprivations among particular groups of people. As already noted, a provision of the income tax laws permitting corporations to depreciate their new plants rapidly encourages a high level of investment in the building of new plants. Tax benefits to the wealthy usually go into savings. They flow in part into new productive facilities, which may or may not be used to capacity; generally, these benefits make no contribution to economic growth, depending of course upon the demand for whatever they can produce. Tax benefits to low income groups are likely to be spent on consumer goods, and such expenditures indirectly stimulate investment and employment. Similarly, *subsidies* from the public treasury to high income groups (as is the case with subsidies for the construction of airports, ships, supersonic aircraft and for many other industries) and to low income groups (as in welfare benefits and unemployment compensation) have a different impact upon growth.

And even more clear-cut is the differential impact they have upon current well-being. A major pitfall in analyzing the growth or stabilization effects of public economic policies is the danger of overlooking the obvious fact that public money spent on the poor helps meet the most basic immediate needs for food, clothing, and shelter, while money to finance various corporate activities is justified in terms of more remote benefits such as national security, space research, or "parity" for farmers. Even if the aggregate growth and stabilization effects of the two forms of expenditures are fairly similar, the values they promote are very different.

[7] Walter H. Heller, ed., *Perspectives on Economic Growth* (New York: John Wiley, 1968), pp. 73-74.

Even a cursory examination of where federal money comes from and how it is distributed makes it clear that in practice if not always in rhetoric the forms of spending that benefit high income groups consume most of the budget. About 70 cents of every federal dollar, for example, pays for past, present, or future wars. On the income side, the income tax is the major source of revenue, but the exemptions and evasions available to high income groups make it far less progressive than is generally assumed.

Figure 1 pictures the sources of federal revenues and the uses of appropriations, and Table 1 shows trends for expenditures. We have already seen the amount, uses, and beneficiaries of the small proportion of the budget devoted to welfare and antipoverty activities in Chapter 5. As noted there, even the slice of expenditures for social security (listed in Table 1 as "income maintenance") largely represents benefits to the middle class rather than to people below the poverty line. Arms and defense expenditures, moreover, are far more difficult to cut when a strong push for "economy" develops. Long-term commitments to weapons systems, the lobbying of military contractors, and obligations to veterans mean that these parts of the budget are largely immune to reductions, while foreign economic aid and domestic antipoverty programs are readily available for economizing.

Widely held opinions about the effect upon growth of taxation of high and low incomes are sometimes strikingly inaccurate. It is commonly believed that high rates of taxation on large incomes reduce investment and therefore curb growth. The most careful studies, however, suggest that the reverse is closer to the truth. A rich man who feels no tax pressure upon his income is likely to save a large part of it rather than invest it in ventures contributing most effectively to growth, for these are the ventures carrying the highest risks. But high tax rates on large incomes virtually force the wealthy into venturesome investment, the income from which will be treated as "capital gains" and therefore taxed at much lower rates. Thus, high tax rates on larger incomes may actually *promote* growth.

Since 1946, both the executive branch and Congress have established specialized agencies to keep in touch with economic trends affecting growth and price stabilization and to recommend courses of action in this complex field. The Employment Act of 1946 provided for a three-man Council of Economic Advisers in the Executive Office of the President and for a Congressional Joint Committee on the Economic Report consisting of congressmen from both houses. Economists appointed to the three-man Council and to its small professional staff have been eminent and competent people under all presidents since 1946. They have served chiefly, however, not as initiators of basic policy directions, but as technicians recommending the best means to realize the various values and goals that each President has favored. Their reports have also become foci of discussion and debate among professional economists regarding theoretical approaches on issues about which the profession does not have a consensus.

FIGURE 1
The Federal Government Dollar, 1968
(For year ending June 30. Based on estimated federal administrative budget and trust fund receipts and expenditures.)

Where it comes from . . .

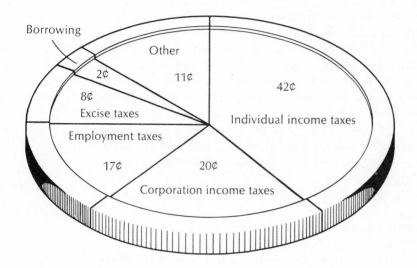

Where it goes . . .

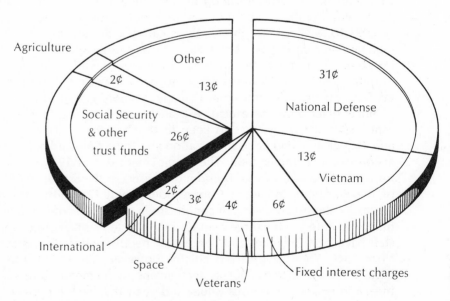

Source: Chart prepared by Dept. of Commerce, Bureau of the Census. Data from Executive Office of the President, Bureau of the Budget.

TABLE 1

Trends in Budget Outlays by Major Category, Fiscal Years 1970-71ᵃ (billions of dollars)

Category	Outlays					Average annual change in outlays			
	1960	1965	1967	1969	1971	1960-1965	1965-1967	1967-1969	1969-1971
National defense	46.0	49.9	70.6	81.4	75.3	0.8	10.3	5.4	−3.0
Space	0.4	5.1	5.4	4.2	3.4	0.9	0.1	−0.6	−0.4
Income maintenanceᵇ	24.5	34.2	43.9	56.8	72.7	1.9	4.9	6.5	7.9
Education, health, manpower	2.5	4.1	8.6	10.3	12.8	0.3	2.3	0.8	1.2
Housing and community developmentᶜ	0.7	1.5	2.6	3.3	6.8	0.2	0.6	0.4	1.7
Physical resources	6.4	10.2	10.3	10.8	13.3	0.8	0.0	0.2	1.2
Interest	6.9	8.6	10.3	12.7	13.5	0.3	0.8	1.2	0.4
Other outlays (net)	4.9	5.9	7.8	6.2	8.3	0.2	1.0	−0.8	1.0
Sale of assets	−0.1	−1.1	−1.2	−1.1	−5.2ᵈ	−0.2	0	0	−2.0
Total	92.2	118.4	158.3	184.6	200.8	5.2	20.0	13.2	8.1
Total, nondefense, adjusted for asset sales	46.3	69.6	88.9	104.3	130.7	4.7	9.6	7.7	13.2
Annual percentage increase	. . .	. . .	. . .	. . .	. . .	8.5	13.0	8.3	11.9

Source: Authors' reclassification of data from *The Budget of the United States Government* for Fiscal Years 1962, 1967, 1969, and 1971. Figures are rounded and may not add to totals.

ᵃ Individual categories are "grossed up" to exclude the effect of asset sales. Asset sales include: direct sales of mortgages and loans, stockpile sales, and (in 1971 only) realization of royalties from continental shelf oil escrow account. The 1971 pay raise has been allocated to each category.

ᵇ Income maintenance is broadly defined to include the budget category "income security" *plus* Medicare, Medicaid, farm income supports, and veterans' compensation and pensions.

ᶜ Includes rural housing and veterans' housing; excludes outlays for "maintenance of the mortgage market."

ᵈ Includes $0.8 billion transferred from continental shelf oil escrow account.

Reprinted from Charles L. Schultze, with Edward K. Hamilton and Allen Schick, *Setting National Priorities: The 1971 Budget* (Washington, D.C.: Brookings Institution, 1970), p. 12.

THE IMPACT OF MACROECONOMIC POLICIES AFTER WORLD WAR II

A review of some of the major American public policies affecting growth and stability in the postwar years should illustrate and clarify these observations about the general impact of economic policies on the welfare of various groups in the population. They illustrate: (1) the influence of private business decisions upon the pace of the economy; and (2) the ways in which public monetary and fiscal actions or inactions condition what these private decisions are, and how profitable they will be.

Over the twenty-five-year period between the end of World War II in 1945 and 1970, the American economy has gone through three quite distinct phases: (1) a "high phase" of boom, low unemployment, and rising prices between 1947 and 1955; (2) a "low phase" of decline in consumer spending and investment and of high unemployment between 1956 and 1964; and (3) a renewed boom period, followed by the decline of 1969 and 1970. It is instructive to examine the reasons for each of these stages, their effects on specific groups of people, the political pressures to which they gave rise, and the degree of governmental success in attempting to alter the trends.

At the end of the second World War, the fundamental economic fact was an unusually high, pent-up demand for goods. During the war, high employment levels and rising wages and profits had provided people with a lot of money but relatively few consumer goods and services available to buy, for almost 40 percent of the gross national product was absorbed by the federal government, largely in war materials. After the war, both business organizations and consumers were anxious to spend their wartime savings on the things they had been unable to buy previously. From 1947 to 1955, automobile sales, investment in plant and equipment in the durable goods manufacturing industries, and investment in housing increased at rates between six and 12 percent each year. In these same years, the gross national product rose at an annual rate of 4.2 percent. In an important sense, of course, it was the prior war that explained the private and business decisions to invest and to spend during these years. Public and private policies are bound to be dependent upon each other.

The indicators of the pace of economic activity and growth (the investment and sales of various industries, the level of employment, and prices) never change direction at exactly the same time; but all these indicators reached peaks at various times between 1955 and 1957, marking the start of a new pattern of economic behavior. A fundamental reason for the change was the satisfaction of the pent-up demand for consumer goods and a buildup of inventories to their normal levels. From 1955 to 1962, the gross national product rose by only a little over 20 percent, an average annual increase of only 2.7 percent. Beginning in 1964, a new phase of the growth trend cycle started, with annual increases averaging about four percent for several years.

To speak of "trends" of these kinds suggests, quite misleadingly, that there is something impersonal or inevitable about changes in the level of economic activity. The fact is, of course, that all economic "trends" reflect the decisions of private individuals and public officials to do particular things, though it is also true that they rarely foresee or intend all the consequences to which their decisions contribute. Let us look a bit more closely now at some of the major reasons growth and price trends took the form they did at two key junctures of the postwar years. We will consider as examples the years 1953-54 and the years 1967-69.

As already noted, the 1953-54 biennium occurred near the end of a period of relatively fast growth in the gross national product, during which time there was no severe reversal in the economic indicators of stability and growth. There was, however, a marked drop in government defense spending due to the end of the Korean War. This was followed by a marked rise in unemployment, from a low of about 2.1 percent of the civilian labor force in the third quarter of 1953 to 5.5 percent of the labor force in the first quarter of 1954. Because the sharply increased unemployment (an addition of about 2.2 million people unable to find work) was heavily concentrated in industrial areas rather than evenly distributed throughout the country, its visibility and psychological and political impact was all the greater.

We can fairly easily identify the governmental policies that brought on this recession, though they were not intended to do so. And we can also identify the governmental policies that helped bring a recovery from the recession and that *were* so intended. The rapid drop in government spending in 1953 was largely due to the end of the Korean War; but the adverse effects it had on the people thrown out of work were not any less serious because the cut was not a deliberate tactic to slow down the economy. Another public policy contributing to the recession was intended to slow down price rises, for these had been extremely rapid during the Korean War years in spite of the imposition of direct price and wage controls. The Federal Reserve Board and the Treasury Department both took action early in 1953 to make credit harder to obtain. The combination of these restraining fiscal and monetary policies slowed down the economy more rapidly than had been anticipated, as the steep unemployment increase already mentioned indicates.

More than most economic developments, unemployment places pressure on governmental officials to take ameliorative action, for it raises fears that the unemployed and a wider public that shares their concerns will vote against the "ins" on election day.[8] In May, 1953, the Federal Reserve Board accordingly took steps to make it easier for banks to make loans and the Treasury Department handled its financing of governmental obligations with the same end in view. In the autumn of 1953, the Secretary of the Treasury publicly took a position in favor of cuts both in the corporation excess profits tax and in personal income taxes; these tax reductions, plus some decreases in excise taxes, went into effect in the middle of 1954.

By the final months of 1954 it was clear that these policies were having a marked effect, with personal income up sharply, a steep upturn in corporate earnings, and a rapid rise in residential construction. The responsiveness of the economy to monetary and fiscal controls in both directions in 1953 and 1954 seemed to lend great weight to the view that governmental policy could indeed regulate economic activity, an issue that had been widely and intensely de-

---

[8] There is ground for the fear, though the link between unemployment and partisan voting is complicated and not wholly understood. For a discussion of the issue see Angus Campbell *et al., The American Voter* (New York: John Wiley, 1960), pp. 381-401.

bated since the thirties. The Council of Economic Advisers took pains to underline the point in its 1955 Economic Report:

What gave them [these public policies] a special character was their promptness and heavy reliance on monetary policies and tax reductions. The shift from credit restraint to credit ease before an economic decline had begun, the announcement of sizeable tax reductions before it was generally appreciated that an economic decline was actually under way, the submission to the Congress of a comprehensive program for encouraging the growth of the economy through private enterprise — these early measures to build confidence were by far the most important. For they strengthened confidence when it was needed, and they thereby rendered unnecessary any later resort to drastic governmental programs in an atmosphere of emergency.[9]

It is also worth noting, however, that it was the indirect forms of control through monetary and fiscal policy, and not direct wage and price regulations, that proved effective.

The same lesson appears to be implicit in attempts to control the economy in more recent years. Because of concern over rising prices and a widespread belief that union wage demands were the chief reason for them, the Council of Economic Advisers in its 1962 Annual Report announced a policy of "wage guideposts," an effort to control inflation through public pressure upon unions and management to restrict wage demands and concessions to the current average increase in "productivity," i.e., the increase in the value of goods and services produced by a unit of labor, such as a man-hour. In principle, a wage increase no larger than the increase in what the average worker can produce does not increase the employer's costs and so gives him no reason to raise prices. Notice that to tie wage increases strictly to productivity assumes that the relative share of the national income allocated to workers and to those receiving income from ownership of capital should be kept the same, a value assumption workers often do not accept. Notice also that labor productivity typically has little to do with the worker's own efforts; the chief influence upon productivity is the use of machinery. Obviously a garment worker can produce much more if he spends his day operating a complex sewing machine than if he spends his day sewing by hand. The productivity formula therefore raises some fundamental ethical and value questions, and this fact may help explain why wage "guideposts" based upon productivity levels proved quite ineffective in holding down both wages and prices.

Though the computations of productivity increases rest upon some uncertainties and some arbitrary assumptions, the Council continued for some five years to suggest that productivity increases justified wage increases of 3.2 percent annually; although it was also careful to state that it recognized the need for modification of this figure in particular industries with special problems (such as difficulty in attracting labor) and that it urged businesses whose productivity had

[9] Economic Report of the President (January, 1955), p. 20.

increased by a larger amount to cut prices as their contribution toward economic stabilization.

The guidepost policy received a great deal of publicity and was widely discussed in labor and management circles; but in the negotiation of wage agreements it was widely ignored. Relying as it did upon voluntary compliance by unions, which had the bargaining power to demand and receive more than the guideposts would allow, and by managements with considerable incentive to pay more in order to assure a supply of needed labor skills, the policy could not have been expected to work in a period in which there was no real pressure from the public to pay attention to it.

To a political scientist its chief function can be seen as political and not economic. By issuing the guidepost policy and periodically publicizing it, the federal administration proclaimed to the voters that it was trying to protect the consumer, a widely sought and welcome message. At the same time, its voluntary character reassured union and management officials that the final price and wage decisions continued to be theirs, also a welcome message. The wage guideposts therefore stand as particularly neat examples of the political wisdom of reassuring anxious groups about complex technical areas in which there is no possibility for the general public to check and to learn that the reassurance may be misleading. In some industries the guidepost policy did undoubtedly have an effect, though it is difficult to say how much. Where the employer could not easily pass on increased costs to consumers in higher prices, or where there was no productivity increase, it had the effect of keeping wages down. It had no similar dampening impact upon profits. We do not suggest, of course, that the guidepost policy was deliberately put forward to deceive. It clearly was not. The very complexity of the issue and the temptations to confuse economic and political functions made it easy for the policymakers to share the assumptions of the general public that the policy would indeed curtail inflationary trends.

During 1968, to take a final example, indirect controls through fiscal and monetary policy again became the chief resort of national economic policy. They did so in part because the guidepost policy was no longer taken seriously by a high proportion of the business and labor community and in part because economists became more concerned about the growing buildup of inflationary pressures than was the general public. Indirect controls, not requiring public cooperation, therefore seemed appropriate.

Despite strong urging by the President that taxes be increased as an anti-inflation weapon, traditional congressional reluctance to raise taxes, especially in an election year, prevailed until dramatic events spread economists' fears of inflation to a wider public.

An international financial crisis in March, 1968 gave rise to fears about the soundness and purchasing power of the dollar. Interest rates rose to new highs. Other prices, meanwhile, had also continued to advance month by month. Congress now passed a Revenue and Expenditures Control Act which imposed a 10 percent surcharge on income taxes. The Federal Reserve Board, meanwhile, resorted to increases in the discount rate to tighten credit. In the spring of 1969, the cost of credit was the highest in the nation's history, and interest rates remained high in 1970. At the same time, the very high levels of federal spending, chiefly for the war in Southeast Asia and other military purposes, continued to work in the opposite direction — providing a continuous spur toward higher prices. The result by mid-1970 was an uncertain and unhappy combination of economic trends involving increased unemployment and a continuing rise in prices.

CONCLUSIONS AND PROJECTIONS

Economic growth is not so much the name of a clear political goal that benefits everyone as it is a set of alternative economic policies that are usually controversial and whose impact on various groups of the population cannot be fully predicted given the present state of economic knowledge. The public policies the United States government has adopted in this area have influenced people's beliefs, expectations, and states of mind as well as their pocketbooks and the quantity and range of goods and services available for them to buy. The fact, nonetheless, that government actions can predetermine the rate of economic growth within rough limits means that the future is certain to see continuing efforts to affect that rate, just as it is certain to see political opposition based upon various affected interests. The well-being of particular groups of Americans is involved in the most direct way, as are highly technical and complex economic calculations and highly simplistic political myths.

One clear lesson to be drawn from recent economic policy is that the goals of policymakers are frequently not successfully attained, in spite of our increased knowledge of economic processes and our sophisticated mathematical models of how the economy works. In 1970, governmental efforts to curtail investment and production as a way of fighting inflation contributed to increasing unemployment while price rises continued. The mass public therefore suffered the adverse effects of two different conditions without enjoying the promised benefits of the restraining measures; and no one was sure how long this state of affairs would continue. Governments have little choice but to continue to try to influence economic trends, and this policy area will remain a major battleground of conflicting interests.

A more general conclusion about public economic policy is that it chiefly serves the interests of those who are economically powerful and affluent. It does so through taxing policies that are regressive in their total impact and through governmental spending that functions, directly and indirectly, to subsidize those who already have the most of what there is to get. The evidence for these conclusions appears less specifically in the present chapter than it did in Chapter 5 on poverty and racism, and as it will in the chapters to come on elite-mass relationships. While they deal with different phases of the *political* process, these chapters, taken together, present an integrated picture of the links among the procedures for formulating economic policy and its impact upon economically diverse people.

Addendum: Economists Launch Inflation Cycle

ART BUCHWALD

WASHINGTON — Today we're going to have our quiz on inflation. You've had enough time to read up on it so you should do very well. All right, let's begin:

QUESTION: Where does the word "inflation" come from?

ANSWER: In 1887 there was a bar and grill owner in San Francisco named George Inflation. One day he failed to receive a shipment of booze from the East. Since the demand for booze was great, George Inflation decided to charge 15 cents for a shot of whiskey, instead of the standard 10 cents. He also made the shot glass smaller.

This did not stop his customers from buying booze, so he raised the price to 20 cents, then 25 cents. The other bars in San Francisco raised their prices accordingly, and when their customers complained the other bar and grill owners would say "Blame it on Inflation."

Thus, inflation soon became part of the English language.

QUESTION: Why is everyone so fascinated by inflation?

ANSWER: Because there are so many things that you can do with it. You can hold it; you can turn it around; you can spiral it; you can send it skyhigh; you can let it get out of hand; you can try to curb it; restrain it; stop it; and during feeding hours you can go to the bank and watch it eat up your savings.

QUESTION: What causes inflation?

ANSWER: Economists. They're always talking about it. The trouble with inflation is that the more you talk about it, the more inflated things become. When the government says it's worried about inflation, business gets worried, too, and so it raises its prices to protect itself against the inflation the government is worried about — which, of course, brings on more inflation.

QUESTION: Then why doesn't the government shut up about inflation?

ANSWER: Because it wants Congress to extend the 10 per cent surtax, and it has warned that, unless there is a surtax, inflation will run rampant.

QUESTION: What's the difference between inflation running rampant and inflation spiraling out of sight?

ANSWER: There isn't much, providing you can put a brake on the economy.

QUESTION: Is that the best way to stop inflation in its tracks?

ANSWER: Not necessarily. You can cool off the economy when it overheats and you can dampen investment in economic expansion or you can try to reverse the wage-price upward cycle. But they're only temporary solutions. The key word, of course, is "restraint" on the part of business and labor, which, of course, is out of the question.

QUESTION: Can you live with inflation?

ANSWER: You can if the bank doesn't take away your house.

QUESTION: What about a little inflation?

ANSWER: Some economists say that a little inflation is a good thing because you have full employment. Other experts say it's better to have unemployment than inflation.

QUESTION: Why do the latter say that?

ANSWER: Because they're working. Whether or not you have inflation, you're still going to need economists to tell you what you've got.

QUESTION: What can the little guy do about inflation?

ANSWER: Write to his congressman and tell him if he doesn't do anything about it he's going to see that he's unemployed in 1971, which will be his contribution to fighting inflation.

Reprinted from the Madison *Capital Times*, July 17, 1968.

United States Foreign Policy and the Third World 7

In the aftermath of the Vietnam experience, searching questions have been raised about the premises, character, and future directions of American policy with respect to the Third World. Few observers were content with the consequences of the policies of the 1960's, but their prescriptions covered a wide range of alternatives. The truculent view of some military and private sources was that we should have stood fast behind what they understood to be past principles and used greater force earlier to prevent the spread of communism into yet another outpost of the "free world." Others saw contemporary conditions as foreclosing such options. But in this view, since hapless policymakers were then left with a set of several equally unpalatable choices, they were subject to criticism for their mistakes of judgment (however serious) merely on the grounds of hindsight. Perhaps the most fundamental critique of American policy, however, asserted that the United States was now the world's leading imperialist nation, acting in its private interest to hold back social change and economic development throughout its free-world colonial empire. Vietnams were just a continuing part of the price of such a role.

169

We cannot reach definitive judgments about so many issues in a single brief chapter. Instead, we shall sketch the problem, both for the United States and for the Third World countries; briefly review American policies, their rationale, and their consequences; and then concentrate our efforts on identifying the analytical questions that would lead to sound judgment. Some of the implications and possibilities discussed may seem harsh to Americans used to viewing the world through the complacent screen of our oft-stated benevolent intentions. In this case, however, many of the consequences of American policy are felt exclusively by Third World governments and people, so we cannot ignore their perspective in our analysis.

THE PROBLEM: THE CIRCUMSTANCES OF THE THIRD WORLD

The broad term Third World is not intended to suggest unity or similarity among member nations. Rather, it distinguishes those ninety-odd nations, most of them newly independent former colonies but some of them with longer histories, which are low in industrialization and in income, and which are not incorporated within either the First World of the United States and Western Europe or the Second World of the Sino-Soviet bloc nations.[1] Sharp regional differences in traditions, history, social structure, economies, and political styles exist within the Third World, and indeed from nation to nation within some regions. Because our analysis is directed at the general outlines of American policy, however, rather than at relations with any one country, we shall employ the term when we mean to emphasize those characteristics (non-industrial economies, generalized poverty, non-alignment) that such nations do have in common. As we shall see, the use of the inclusive term is increasingly justified by member nations' growing self-consciousness of their shared interests and common status in the world. This is fostered both by their experiences as a bloc in the United Nations and through their mutual opposition to some American policies.

Third World nations have before them the clear image of American and other industrial nations' economic prosperity, which contrasts dramatically with the reality of their own grinding poverty. The thrust toward "catching up" or "developing" so as to be able to provide food, shelter, and clothing for their increasing numbers of people is thus crucial. The transition to industrialization may not be an inevitable choice, and perhaps it is neither a practical nor a desirable one, but it seems to be at present the goal of nearly all of the "underdeveloped" nations.

Despite the apparent polar alternatives of capitalist and socialist routes to development demonstrated by the industrialized nations, Third World economic strategies have ranged greatly. Most countries

[1] This characterization of the Third World, and the concept of three worlds of development, is drawn from Irving Louis Horowitz, *Three Worlds of Development: The Theory and Practice of International Stratification* (New York: Oxford University Press, 1966). Horowitz is chairman of the Department of Sociology at Livingston College, Rutgers — The State University, New Brunswick, New Jersey.

have adopted mixed economies reflecting their pasts and their present external influences. India and Brazil, for example, have been more capitalist than nationalist, while Egypt and Algeria have been the reverse. But all four have significant fractions of their productive capacity under the socialist form of ownership. The one thing that all such nations do have in common, of course, is the constant need for careful centralized planning in order to make maximum use of their limited resources. The luxury of a "pure" *laissez faire* capitalist route is historically foreclosed to them, despite the extent to which it is preferred and imposed by Americans.

No matter what economic route is used to try to move the nation from "traditional" to "modern" economic status, large accumulations of capital are needed to build the power plants, transportation systems, and factories that will ultimately mean industrialization and growth. Such capital might be amassed from a favorable balance of trade, expropriation, taxation, external sources such as grants, loans, or foreign investment, or some combination of these. Each "source," however, presents serious limitations. Most of the Third World nations start from subsistence-level agricultural or primary commodity economies. This means that they must export raw materials to earn the money to import basic capital goods and finished products, a position historically assuring an unfavorable balance of trade. (See Table 1.) In many cases, ownership or control of the industry producing the exported commodity is in the hands of foreign investors, and the

TABLE 1
Leading Export Commodities of Underdeveloped Nations
(based on 1967 trade data)

Country	Number of leading export commodities	Export of leading commodities as percent of total exports	Leading export commodities
Argentina	4	61	Meat, Wheat, Corn, Wool
Bolivia	1	63	Tin
Brazil	4	58	Coffee, Iron Ore, Cotton, Cocoa
Cameroon*	3	65	Cocoa, Coffee, Aluminum
Cent. African Rep.	3	90	Diamonds, Coffee, Cotton
Ceylon	3	89	Tea, Rubber, Coconut
Chile	3	85	Copper, Iron Ore, Nitrates
Colombia	2	69	Coffee, Oil
Congo, Dem. Rep.*	4	74	Copper, Tin, Diamonds, Coffee
Congo (Brazzaville)	2	76	Wood, Diamonds
Costa Rica*	2	60	Coffee, Bananas
Dominican Repub.	5	91	Sugar, Coffee, Cocoa, Bauxite, Tobacco
Ecuador*	3	84	Bananas, Coffee, Cocoa

Country	Number of leading export commodities	Export of leading commodities as percent of total exports	Leading export commodities
Ethiopia	4	84	Coffee, Hides and Skins, Cereals, Oil seeds
Gabon	4	86	Wood, Manganese, Oil, Uranium
Ghana	4	78	Cocoa, Diamonds, Wood, Manganese
Guatemala*	4	69	Coffee, Cotton, Bananas, Sugar
Guiana	4	83	Sugar, Bauxite, Alumina, Rice
Haiti*	3	68	Coffee, Sugar, Sisal
Honduras*	3	67	Bananas, Coffee, Wood
Iran	1	91	Oil
Iraq	1	92	Oil
Ivory Coast	3	81	Coffee, Cocoa, Wood
Jamaica*	4	75	Alumina, Bauxite, Sugar, Bananas
Libya	1	99	Oil
Malaysia	4	73	Rubber, Tin, Wood, Iron Ore
Mauritania*	1	91	Iron Ore
Nicaragua	5	69	Cotton, Coffee, Meat, Cottonseed, Sugar
Nigeria	3	69	Oil, Peanuts, Coffee
Paraguay	6	77	Meat, Wood, Cotton, Quebracho, Tobacco, Oil seeds
Peru	6	78	Copper, Fishmeal, Cotton, Silver, Lead, Sugar
Philippines	3	70	Coconut, Sugar, Wood
Sierra Leone*	3	78	Diamonds, Iron Ore, Palm Kernels
Uganda*	3	83	Coffee, Cotton, Rubber
Uruguay	3	84	Wool, Meat, Hides
Venezuela	2	98	Oil, Iron Ore
Vietnam, South	2	90	Rubber, Rice

*Data for 1966 or latest year for which reports are available.

Note: Since these data are based on one year's experience, they should not be used as a final description for any one country. In any one year, the composition of products may shift due to market conditions or internal production difficulties. The purpose of this tabulation is to show the general pattern of dependency on a limited number of products going into the export trade.

Source: Calculated from International Monetary Fund, International Financial Statistics, July, 1968.

"developing" nation enjoys comparatively little return from sale of the product. (Some would add that accumulation of capital in this way would take too long in any event; the enormous pressures for raising the standard of living in the present would not allow its use.)

Expropriation (nationalizing of industries owned by foreign interests) is possible, particularly where the nation has a crucial resource such as oil. But it can be a less than satisfactory answer, as several nations have learned. While it does mean that the developing nation will realize all of the income derived from the sale of such commodities, the market for raw materials is dominated by a few wealthy purchasers who can exert strong pressure to keep prices down. This assures continuation of an unfavorable balance of trade because the developing nation must still import finished products and basic goods needed for industrialization, and these it must buy in world markets. Furthermore, expropriation removes the prospect of future investment of foreign capital and frequently brings retribution from the foreign owners' governments. In the case of the United States, it has meant anything from elimination of economic assistance (Peru, Bolivia) to the landing of Marines (Dominican Republic) or assistance to contending governmental factions (Guatemala, British Guiana). Taxation is also an impractical route to capital accumulation, almost by definition. Within a developing country, not only are there scarce resources and very limited income on which taxes might be levied, but those few people who do have such wealth are either in control of the government or so powerful that any effort to tap their assets could result in the overthrow of the government.

The difficulties involved in using external sources of capital for development are several. Not least among these are the political strings likely to be attached, whether the funds come from First World or Second World governments. Because their political conflict means that neither of the competing industrial-nation blocs is willing to channel its funds through multilateral organizations such as the United Nations, Third World nations must simply bargain for the best terms they can get from one or another of the Cold War antagonists. In either case, they may be forced to yield some of their independence and flexibility in exchange for the assistance. Use of *private* foreign capital for development means that a comparatively large share of the returns will go to the foreign investors instead of the developing nation, and it frequently implies political penetration (sooner or later) by the investors' government in support of its nationals' investments.

Use of any one or more of these routes to capital accumulation involves hard choices, risks, and probable reduction of recently-won independence. But this is not all. Other pressing economic and political factors further complicate the process of development for Third World nations. Traditional methods of agricultural production, limited availability of usable land, and a rapidly increasing population mean that the process must take place amidst severe food shortages. Table 2 shows the impact of population increase on growth

TABLE 2
Less Developed Countries: Annual Growth Rate of GNP, Population, and Per Capita GNP

(1957-58 average to 1963-64 average)

Countries	Annual GNP growth rate[a] (percent)	Annual population growth rate[b] (percent)	Annual per capita GNP growth rate (percent)
Latin America:			
Argentina	0.6	1.7	−1.1
Bolivia	3.5	2.3	1.2
Brazil	5.3	3.1	2.2
Chile	3.3	2.3	1.0
Colombia	4.6	2.8	1.8
Costa Rica	4.1	4.0	.1
Ecuador	4.3	3.2	1.1
El Salvador	5.7	2.9	2.8
Guatemala	4.5	3.0	1.5
Honduras	3.6	3.1	.5
Jamaica	3.9	2.0	1.9
Mexico	5.3	3.1	2.2
Nicaragua	5.3	2.9	2.4
Panama	4.9	3.0	1.9
Paraguay	2.2	2.2	0
Peru	6.4	2.3	4.1
Trinidad and Tobago	6.0	3.0	3.0
Venezuela	4.5	3.8	.7
Far East:			
China (Taiwan)	7.1	3.1	4.0
Korea	4.7	2.9	1.8
Malaya, States of	3.9	3.1	2.8
Philippines	4.9	3.2	1.7
Thailand	7.4	3.0	4.4
Vietnam	3.5	2.8	.7
Near East:			
Cyprus	3.6	1.2	2.4
Greece	6.2	.7	5.7
Iran	4.7	2.4	2.3
Israel	10.5	3.6	6.9
Jordan	9.5	2.9	6.6
Turkey	4.0	2.9	1.1
South Asia:			
Ceylon	3.5	2.5	1.0
India	4.4	2.3	2.1
Pakistan	4.5	2.5	2.0
Africa:			
Ethiopia	4.5	1.4	3.1
Ghana	5.1	2.5	2.6
Kenya	3.5	2.9	.6

Malawi	2.1	3.0	− .9
Morocco	2.0	3.1	−1.1
Nigeria	3.3	2.0	1.3
Southern Rhodesia	3.6	3.3	.3
Sudan	4.5	2.9	1.6
Tunisia	4.7	2.6	2.1
Uganda	3.4	2.5	.9
Zambia	4.7	2.9	1.8

[a] GNP growth rates are AID estimates based largely on official national statistics.

[b] Population growth rates are based on "AID" country, U.N., and other source data.

Source: U.S. Senate, Committee on Foreign Relations, *Hearings, Foreign Assistance 1965,* 89th Cong., 1st sess., 1965, p. 113.

rates. Frequently, short-term food needs become so pressing that technical resources and money must be redirected toward resolving crises and developing an agricultural base sufficient to provide subsistence in the future. Further, instead of advancing toward the vision of affluence which the developed nations hold for them, the people of Third World nations must be asked to make even greater sacrifices, in order that their nation's limited resources can be directed into building an industrial base. The price of industrialization has historically been very high — in England, in the United States, and in the Soviet Union — and its impact on Third World peoples now can seriously threaten the stability of their governments.

The political setting of the Third World creates a unique convergence of pressures. Internally, lack of experience, foreign intrigue, and severe economic pressures have led to high political volatility. Time and historical circumstances alone permitted the growth of deliberative parliamentary governments elsewhere. Such luxury has not been granted to the developing nations. Instead, semi-authoritarian forms have emerged as the means of efficiently converting mass needs and demands into governmental action. Significant roles are played by the military in many nations, either through a series of "palace revolutions" or coups or by serving as the vanguard of revolutionary mass action. Charismatic leaders emerging from military ranks have struggled with the dilemmas of development for a while only to be in some cases replaced by military-generated coups or engaged in international conflicts which consume resources and attention.

The external environment of Third World nations is of course dominated by the continuing Cold War. Third World policymakers must constantly seek to avoid entanglement in what to them is an essentially irrelevant conflict. But the developed world is the only available source of outside financial assistance, and the only market for their products. Further, both major antagonists constantly seek to use Third World nations for their own purposes — if not actually for territory on which to establish military bases, then for espionage, "showcases," or acquiring votes in the United Nations. Some strategically favored developing nations may on occasion find the Cold

War to their own advantage, for it may mean that loans, grants, technical assistance, or military weapons are readily available from one or both of the great powers. But for most of the Third World, the Cold War involves danger, internal interference, and both limitations and political strings on financial assistance for their development.

Nor have we more than begun to characterize the problem. Development presents social as well as economic and political problems. Widespread illiteracy, rapid urbanization, low social mobility, and racial or religious conflicts impede growth in many nations. Sharply skewed class structures — with a very few people of enormous wealth, no middle class, and nearly the entire population at or below the subsistence level — present formidable obstacles to prompt, peaceful change. Entrenched elites frequently resist the measures needed to assure progress for the masses, and revolutionary action may be the only way in which more equitable distributions can be achieved. Hoping for drastic change to be brought about by currently dominant elites in behalf of the masses — in short, asking for the powerful to share their power — may be quite unreasonable. In any event, the fact is that nearly two-thirds of the world's population do not have the most basic necessities to support life adequately. The vision of the developed world is before them — "poverty-level" income in the United States is from five to 10 times the average income of most of the Third World nations — and one can hardly expect anything short of the most determined efforts to move toward that goal.

THE NATURE OF THE UNITED STATES' INTEREST IN THE THIRD WORLD

A nation's foreign policy normally reflects that definition of its national interest — its goals, needs, and aspirations — which is dominant among its policymakers. When a nation has the power which leads it to try to realize at least a large share of its national interest *vis-a-vis* other states, as the United States did in the post-World War II years, this definition becomes a shaping force for the rest of the world. For the first two decades of the Cold War, the United States was principally concerned about its own national security. The doctrine of containment led to a nearly exclusive emphasis on the military defense of nations along the Soviet border against anticipated Soviet aggression. Initially, the emerging nations of the Third World became subjects of concern in this Cold War context as sites for military bases, as tracts of land that were either "ours" or "theirs," and as the arenas of major postwar crises — such as Iran, Korea, Suez, and the Congo. They were also serviceable in nonmilitary ways: as impartial spectators whose votes in the United Nations would serve to record the (presumably favorable) balance of world opinion, or as sources of raw materials (particularly oil and certain crucial metals).

Even in these years of overriding concern about possible military confrontation with the Soviet Union, there was conflict between long-range and short-range definitions of the American national interest.[2] Most policymakers realized that in the long run, the United States' security would be enhanced by having stable, popularly-supported governments elsewhere in the world which were able to undertake their own defense. Economic development, more equitable distribution of wealth, and dramatic social and political progress — even upheaval — would be necessary before most Third World nations could reach this point. But short-range security demands seemed to make it imperative that the United States acquire bases and allies from whatever governments happened to be in power at the time. Having negotiated alliances, leased facilities, or obtained influence through providing military assistance, the American national interest tended to be served by stability and continuation of the status quo in such nations — at whatever cost to the longer-range interests.

By the latter half of the 1950's, as more former colonies acquired their independence, they began to be viewed less as terrain of relevance to armed conflict and more as the ultimate prize to be won in Cold War competition. Two changes helped to shift the definition of the American national interest away from an exclusively military-strategy view of the Third World. First, the Cold War seemed to be settling down to a long-term, non-nuclear conflict in which the ultimate victory might go to the side which captured and held the loyalty (and trade) of independent Third World nations. Second, the multiplication of Third World nations and indigenous revolutionary movements caused the old concept of a single containment boundary around the Soviet bloc nations to be replaced with the prospect of a world-wide contest involving subversion or other influencing of Third World governments. The detente between the two superpowers was also accompanied by a loosening of alliances with their associated nations, so that on many issues there appeared to be several centers of power, more widespread competition, and consequently more opportunities for independent smaller nations to act as they saw fit.

The result of these changes was to secure somewhat greater emphasis for the longer-range aspects of the definition of American national interest. Economic development and technical assistance became a larger part of American goals for the Third World, but they were still seen as important chiefly for the purpose of maintaining a stronger resistance to communism. And the American image of the world and U.S. security needs was now global in character.[3] This meant that the outbreak of violence anywhere in the world would

---

[2] The conflict between long-run and short-run aspects of national security is well brought out in Max Millikan, "The United States and the Low Income Countries," in Kermit Gordon, ed., *Agenda for the Nation* (Washington, D. C.: Brookings Institution, 1968). Millikan is professor of economics and Director of the Center for International Studies at MIT. He is a member of the Advisory Committee on Economic Development of the Agency for International Development.

[3] The concept of "globalism" as a problem in American foreign policy is discussed by many sources. One comprehensive consideration by analysts essentially friendly to the official goals of U.S. policy is Edmund Stillman and William Pfaff, *Power and Impotence: The Failure of American Foreign Policy* (New York: Random House, 1966). Both Stillman and Pfaff are staff members of the Hudson Institute, an independent research organization with close relationship to the Defense Department.

be a source of concern, regardless of the merits of its origins or the strategic nature of the nation's location or resources, because it might lead to the acquisition of new Soviet influence. To combat this, an American presence would be necessary. The limited funds which the United States was prepared to devote to foreign assistance were therefore divided among the many nations of the Third World in accordance with a priority system favoring military and economic aid to those nations most threatened by some form of upheaval. In effect, the United States began to see its national interest as involved in the internal tensions and developmental problems of much of the world. Again, however, there was conflict between long-range and short-range definitions; and when this conflict occurred, the short-range security interest normally won out. Thus, concern for economic development was often manifested by contingents of military advisers, shipments of weapons, and very limited unrestricted capital grants.

The American national interest also had a further economic dimension of mixed public and private character: continued growth and prosperity in the United States seemed to require access to critical raw materials, opportunities for profitable investments, and sales to foreign markets. Policymakers could not be unconcerned with the success of American overseas investments and trade activities. Indeed, there was nothing new about government support for businessmen abroad; ample precedent for it existed — from the "Open Door" policies of the nineteenth century to the "Dollar Diplomacy" days of the twentieth century. The only new circumstances were a multiplication of markets and an awakened recognition among major corporations (some of whose leaders had seen only waste in American foreign aid grants) that there were substantial profits to be made from an international approach to business. Thus, a kind of supplemental dimension to definitions of the national interest developed, one that emphasized the maintenance and furtherance of opportunities for American businessmen within developing nations.

By the end of the 1960's, the "national interest" that the United States saw as related to the Third World still consisted chiefly of national security needs, with (their) long-term economic development and (our) continued business opportunities as compatible but subordinate goals. The definition was fluid and shifting, however — at least in theory — as new conditions were perceived by new policymakers.[4] But the momentum generated by decades of commitment to the paramount security emphasis inherent in the militant anti-communist ideology of the early Cold War would not be overcome easily. American policy would have to be shaped against the background of the experience of Vietnam. Worse, it would be received by the aspiring peoples of the Third World in exactly the same

---

[4] For a discussion of the importance of definitions of the national interest, and the needs for revision in such definitions, see Henry Kissinger, "Central Issues of American Foreign Policy," in Gordon, *op. cit.*, note 2 above. Kissinger is Professor of Political Science at Harvard University, currently serving as Foreign Policy Adviser to President Nixon.

context. In this way, the United States' definition of its national interest becomes part of the problem of Third World development — as well as part of the explanation for the direction of American policies.

AMERICAN POLICIES TOWARD THE THIRD WORLD

We shall consider the nature of U.S. policies, their rationale, and their consequences, by a closer look at three categories: national security, economic development, and promotion of American business opportunities. These policy areas are not really separable, of course. Military power is used to enhance economic interests as well as on behalf of national security, economic goals are seen as related to security, and so forth. Categorization will facilitate analysis, however, and the various types of policy will be reintegrated for an overall analysis at the end of the section.

In March, 1947, President Harry Truman announced what has come to be known as the "Truman Doctrine": "We cannot allow changes in the status quo by such methods as coercion, or by such subterfuges as political infiltration." This declaration came in the context of the Greek civil war, in which a highly authoritarian government sought to put down a revolution which enjoyed considerable popular support but included strong local communist components. For more than two years, British troops had fought on the side of the Greek government they had set up, finally achieving a measure of stability despite continued corruption in the government and severe inflation in the economy. The British, however, were unable to keep up their efforts; their own financial situation was so desperate that they had no alternative but to withdraw their troops. The United States proceeded to take over the support of the Greek government campaign through supplying weapons, military advisers, and substantial amounts of money. The decision to intervene was perceived by the President as essential to American security given the context of a global struggle between contrasting ways of life, and it has come to be understood in these terms ever since.

The commitment in Greece was a major turning point in American foreign policy. It effectively marked the beginning of the period when national security concerns led to the use of Third World nations, particularly those on the perimeter of the Soviet bloc, as buffer states, with prevention of the spread of communism seen as more important than the nature of the government or long-term economic development. Ultimately, Greece as well as Turkey were incorporated into the North American Treaty Organization; but despite massive amounts of military and economic assistance, their financial conditions and general economic levels remained low. In the 1960's, continued dissatisfaction led to several changes in the makeup of the government in Greece. Apparently still acting to promote national security, American policymakers tended to support the more conservative factions in each case.

The Korean War of 1950-1953 provides an Asian illustration of this early stage of American policy. South Korea was considered crucial as another testing ground of what was assumed to be Soviet expansionism. Experts now differ about the extent to which the two crises were instigated or encouraged by the Soviet Union. In the case of Greece at least, it seems clear that the Soviet Union had declined to help because it considered the revolution a hopeless cause.[5] And it is also apparent that the belligerent threats of the South Korean government to invade the North may have contributed to the North's decision to send its armies south. In any event, this aggressive act triggered American involvement. When the American army appeared to be pushing toward the Chinese border, the Chinese too became involved. The war then settled into a longterm stalemate. Nearly two decades after the end of the war, South Korea had received economic assistance so massive in character that it was becoming a showcase of economic growth. The government, however, showed little progress toward more democratic organization or operation.

As the perceived communist threat became global, the Eisenhower administration set about to tie as many Third World nations as possible to the United States through alliance treaties. Acting on the model of the NATO pact, alliances were formed with Turkey, Iran, Iraq, and Pakistan (CENTO) and, together with Britain and France, with Thailand and Pakistan directly and Laos, Cambodia, and South Vietnam by informal extension (SEATO). Bilateral defense treaties were undertaken with the Philippines and Taiwan. Pursuant to these various treaties, considerable military assistance was extended. Similar help was made available when the key neutralist nation in the world, India, was engaged in border skirmishes with the Chinese. Ironically, the major use of American military assistance occurred not in defense against communist attack but in small wars between nations allied with the United States, such as Pakistan and India.

When the containment policy was rendered obsolete in the late 1950's due to the development of indigenous popular movements all over the world, the United States faced new difficulties in serving its security interests. Any independence movement in an African or Asian colony, or any revolutionary movement in Latin America, might serve as a route to power for communists. Almost without considering the limits of propriety or capability, the global approach to security was extended once again to cover such possibilities (the "Eisenhower Doctrine"). The United States in effect served notice that it might see its security involved, and act accordingly, not only in internal conflicts in nations with which we had alliances, but also where violence was threatened or occurred elsewhere in the world.

One illustration of the meaning of this commitment occurred in Lebanon in 1958, when Marines landed and occupied the country for four months. The cause of the disorder was an effort by Lebanon's

---

[5] Based on a quotation from Joseph Stalin, reported in Milovan Djilas *Conversations with Stalin* (New York: Praeger, 1962), p. 164.

incumbent anticommunist president to change the country's constitution in order to have another term in office. Arab nationalists, supported by aspiring Lebanese politicians, had formed a powerful coalition in opposition. Calls for the violent overthrow of the government came from Egypt and Syria, but U.N. observation groups could find no major foreign sources of arms or men behind the opposition. There was undeniable fighting, however, and it seemed to be part of a trend toward revolutionary disorder throughout the nations of the Middle East. At the height of the fighting, the president abandoned his efforts to succeed himself, but nevertheless called for American assistance. The Marines had been alerted for months and landed the next day. Soon U.S. forces armed with atomic howitzers increased in size to a total of seven thousand men. President Eisenhower told Americans in a television address that the situation was like the Greek civil war and various communist conquests of the early 1950's, and that American troops were required to defend Lebanese sovereignty and integrity. They did so by acceding to the election of a new president, whereupon the fighting died away. But a precedent had been set for the involvement of U.S. troops in the internal affairs of Third World nations, even in cases where the opposition to the local government came not from communists but from indigenous nationalist forces. This precedent was much recalled in 1965, when American Marines again landed in the Dominican Republic. In this instance, there was no solid evidence of communist involvement in the revolution, but the American Embassy thought there was, and President Johnson acted accordingly. The consensus of experts now, however, is that the Embassy was either hysterical or acting as the agent of the conservative military forces who were ultimately installed in power through U.S. help. In any event, the United States commitment to a global view of its security needs, reaching into the internal affairs of Third World nations, began to appear more like a determination to use force to prop up any government that could be induced to request U.S. intervention.

The leading example of American policy under this global definition was of course the Vietnam War. Escalating slowly but steadily from the dispatch of the first U.S. advisers in the early days of the Cold War, the American commitment finally became one of maintaining an unpopular government against an indigenous revolutionary movement which enjoyed not only widespread popular support but also the active assistance of a neighboring communist country. To make matters worse for the United States, the site of this insurrection was dense jungle on the Asian mainland, 10,000 miles from the United States. Neither a half million U.S. troops, nor bomb tonnages exceeding those dropped by all sides during the entire second World War, succeeded in halting the progress of the revolutionary movement.

These examples of American national security policies with reference to the Third World are less isolated than they may at first appear. For the sake of brevity, we have not taken up Cuba, the Congo, Guatemala, or other incidents where the American actions were perhaps less visible but no less concerted efforts to aid one faction against another, or to help win an election for one side rather than another. All of these interventions stem from a single unifying motivation: concern that unless the United States acted decisively, communist penetration would succeed in gaining control of the government and produce a new ally for the Soviet Union or China. Another factor runs through all of these recent bold assertions of American power, and that is the importance of domestic politics in the formulation of foreign policy. Few policymakers have been willing to give their opponents any ground for charging them with being too weak in "standing up to the communists." The dynamics of domestic politics seem to be such as to lead decisionmakers to take the strongest of possible stances against even remotely possible contingencies which might lead to communist gains. The chagrin at "losing" Cuba is no doubt partly responsible for this bellicosity, but so is an undifferentiated conviction that the security interest of the United States is intimately involved in the domestic difficulties of small nations anywhere in the world.

Economic Development Policies

It seems accurate to say that the economic growth of the Third World has always been a goal of American foreign policy, but it has usually been obscured by the urgency or turned to the service of short-range security needs. Nevertheless, increasing importance has come to be attached to economic development. Efforts to promote economic growth may take several forms.[6] Reliance may be placed on the domestic effort (such as saving or taxation) made by the developing nation itself, and perhaps aided by lowering trade barriers. Or policies may be designed to spur the investment of private capital in certain countries, such as pressuring a recipient country in order to improve the investment climate, or providing tax incentives for investors. A third means of promoting growth is through governmental transfer of capital to the developing nation. "Public" capital may be channeled through bilateral means in the form of direct grants, loans repayable in dollars at conventional interest rates ("hard" loans), or loans repayable in local currency only at interest rates well below market levels ("soft" loans). Or such capital may be channeled through multilateral organizations such as the World Bank or United Nations facilities on any of the same terms. Only the United Nations can be considered truly multilateral in the sense of not being controlled by the major source of funds, the United States; American voting strength in the World Bank gives the U.S. effective control over the policies and key personnel of that organization.

In the early years of the Cold War, America concentrated its economic aid on the reconstruction of Europe. There was recognition

---

[6] An excellent source on the evolution of U.S. economic development policies from 1943 through 1962 is David A. Baldwin, *Economic Development and American Foreign Policy* (Chicago: University of Chicago Press, 1966). This account draws freely on that source. Baldwin was at the time a Research Fellow of the Brookings Institution in Washington, D. C.

of the development needs of the newly emerging nations, although their proliferation, population expansion, and substantial capital needs were not fully appreciated. Success with the Marshall Plan in Europe and the widening of the Cold War struggle shifted attention to the Third World as early as President Truman's Inaugural Address in January, 1949. This was the famous "Point Four" program (so-called because it was the fourth point in the President's program for peace), which pledged United States financial aid and technical assistance for economic development. Long-term security and prosperity interests were emphasized, along with the economic benefits the United States could realize from the emergence of prosperous trading partners, and the need for access to crucial raw materials held by the Third World nations.

The specific policies employed by the United States in the first years after the announcement of the Point Four program were not much different from before. Essentially, they consisted of emphasizing the need for greater effort on the part of the developing nations themselves, and particularly the need to attract private investment. This was a period of selling private enterprise as a doctrine and supporting it with a refusal to make other funds available if private capital could be used for the task. The extension of loans by the United States was governed by standard principles of business risk and prospects of profit. In the words of one of the leading authorities on U.S. economic policies, "American provision of public capital was based on three guiding principles: keep it small; keep it under American control; and minimize the competition with private investment." [7]

Proposals were put forward in the United Nations even in this early period for the establishment of "no-strings" multilateral funding of economic development through various U.N. organs. The United States resisted all forms of support by U.N. agencies for the extension of multilateral loans, arguing in effect that the underdeveloped nations had overestimated their need for capital or that they were not doing enough to attract private investment. U.S. cooperation was of course essential, because for practical purposes the U.S. was always the chief funding source. American policymakers preferred that major funding be through the World Bank, or through more obviously bilateral sources (such as our Export-Import Bank or direct arrangements for loans or grants with the United States government) from which maximum political mileage could be secured. The still-potent resistance of business leaders to any form of foreign aid helped to keep economic assistance on a strictly "businesslike" basis — not tied to military defense needs. Where loans were extended, terms were ordinarily the same as one would obtain in any commercial loans transaction, i.e., repayable in dollars at competitive interest rates within a relatively short and fixed term of years. Only extraordinary circumstances resulted in outright grants of U.S. funds to developing nations.

The World Bank came in for severe criticism from the under-

---

[7] *Ibid.,* pp. 22, 81.

developed nations in the late stages of the Truman administration. It was alleged that the World Bank extended loans only on the same conventional basis as other private lenders, and that it withheld funds where it thought that governments should look to private investors for capital. The World Bank had been established to provide funds for international development in the aftermath of World War II, in part on the assumption that the judgment of "hard-headed" bankers and businessmen would create a viable international market without regard for the political pressures of self-interested governments. In practice, however, the directorate of the bank was controlled by the United States — or rather, by the New York financial community. The Bank normally functioned in concert with U.S. policy, not necessarily because of prior agreement between it and the U.S. government, but because of shared assumptions and criteria for judgment between U.S. government and Bank officials. At the time the bank was created, however, it was better prepared to take risks on behalf of such political purposes as long-term development than either private businesses or the United States government. In this way, it ultimately began to set precedents for U.S. government policies, and to inspire business support for such actions. In part, the Bank was provoked by the U.N. criticism, but it also saw an unfulfilled need and opportunity in the Third World. As a consequence, it began to make "soft" loans, which involved no commitments to export trade in order to secure the funds with which to repay the loans.

By the mid-1950's, it began to be clear that the previous decade's policies to aid Third World nations in their economic development had not been successful. Domestic efforts on the part of the developing nations could not be increased because the rich did not identify with nationalistic goals and did not wish to risk their wealth in such endeavors; and the poor could barely achieve subsistence, let alone contribute to saving and growth. Private investment was discouraged by unrelenting American trade barriers which prevented underdeveloped nations from earning the foreign exchange necessary to repay such investments. The nationalism, degree of government planning of the economy, and anticolonialism of the Third World nations also discouraged private investment. Nor did the conventional loan appear attractive to developing states.

These circumstances led to a modest change in American policy in the late 1950's. Major emphasis continued to be on lending through the World Bank, and the United States government doggedly resisted all multilateral funding arrangements through the United Nations. The Special United Nations Fund for Economic Development (SUNFED), much favored by the underdeveloped nations, was still strongly opposed by the United States, on the grounds that it would be both wasteful and duplicative. But, while continuing to insist upon the need for private investment (and indeed greatly expanding the practice of U.S. government guarantees of the security of such investments), American policy began to shift toward acquiescence in "soft" loans. These were extended on an experimental basis only, following the lead of the World Bank. The significance of such loans was that the recipient nation was under less pressure to export in order to repay in American dollars, and the costs of paying the interest would be substantially less in any event. The local currency in which the loan would be repaid could only be spent within that country itself, which meant the certainty of some future spending or investment by the United States government and further spurring of the local economy. The breakthrough to soft loans was originally due almost as much to the desire on the part of the U.S. government to dispose of agricultural surpluses as to any altruistic goal; but the precedent, once established (like so many others in government), began to expand and legitimate other types of loans as well. In subsequent years, the principle of the soft loan became so well established as to be the primary means of transfer of public capital. But its effects were considerably reduced, though by no means eliminated, by the requirement that loans be spent for (more expensive) U.S.-produced goods and shipped in (more costly) U.S. merchant vessels.

But in the last years of the 1960's, the pressures of the Vietnam War and a growing general disillusionment with foreign aid led to sharp reductions in all American efforts to assist Third World nations. The shift toward greater emphasis on economic rather than military assistance during the early 1960's had been accompanied by a steadily reducing total expenditure on foreign aid.[8] The United States had been investing nearly two percent of its gross national product in foreign aid during the early years of the Cold War, and the proportion was 1.5 percent even in the mid-1950's. By the mid-1960's, however, even though the GNP had doubled since post-War days, foreign aid was down to one percent. By the late 1960's, it was down to below 0.5 percent; for countries other than Vietnam, aid resources were very sharply reduced if not eliminated altogether. In 1967, the U.S. had been tenth among the noncommunist developed nations in proportion of GNP devoted to public and private development assistance, ranking behind France, the Netherlands, Portugal, West Germany, Great Britain, Belgium, Switzerland, Japan, and Australia in that order. In strictly public capital transfers, it ranked somewhat higher, but still below many European nations. Real per capita income in the United States is about double that of the other developed nations, and it seems obvious that the United States did not carry a proportionate share of development assistance even before the sharp reductions of 1968 and 1969.

Private Investment Policies

In order for private investment to contribute to the flow of capital to the underdeveloped world, several conditions must be met. Private investors must have confidence in the intention and capacity of the recipient nation to repay. This means that the recipient nation must have political stability and a government committed to maintaining an economy in which such contracts are honored. It also means that

[8] This discussion rests on Millikan, *op. cit.,* note 2 above.

the debtors, whether they be governments or private entrepreneurs, must be able to sell in a world market and obtain dollars with which to repay the loan. Stability, determination to repay, and capacity to repay, are thus the features of a good "investment climate."

American policies designed to foster such favorable climates have been roughly the same throughout the postwar decades. The central theme is the efficacy of private enterprise. In the words of one moderate authority on economic policy:

To representatives of the less developed nations, it must seem that the United States never tires of citing the advantages — real and imagined — of an economic system based on private enterprise. The main advantages of private investment cited by American policymakers were: first, private investment is more "flexible," presumably referring to the relative absence of governmental "red tape." Second, private investment is "non-political," presumably referring to a supposed absence of interference in domestic affairs by private investors. And third, private investment often carried with it technical knowledge and managerial skill.[9]

The specific techniques by which American policymakers reinforced the priority given to private investment in the early years of the Cold War included outright refusal to make government grants or loans where private funds might be available; referral of requests for capital to the World Bank (which itself declined to make development funds available where they might be "competing" with private investors); and determined diplomatic efforts to open various nations to "fair" treatment for American private investors.

Ranged against the American commitment to private enterprise and the means adopted to further private investment were Third World nationalism and a need for central planning and control, as well as the apparent instability of many governments and economies. Relatively little private money was actually invested in developing nations. In the mid-1950's, the U.S. government began to supplement its exhortations about private enterprise with provision of "investment guaranty" contracts to American businessmen. These guarantees assured them against certain "nonbusiness" risks in Third World investments, such as exchange problems or expropriation, and resulted in some increases in the flow of private funds. Investment opportunities in Europe and Canada, however, still attracted much more capital than Third World countries. The efficacy of the guaranty program was indisputable, however, for by the mid-1960's more than a billion dollars worth of such insurance for Third World investments had been extended. To some degree, of course, U.S. government willingness to employ military force to maintain stability (and hence a favorable investment climate) in Third World nations must also be counted as a factor relevant to private investment patterns.

The one aspect of investment-relevant policy which was under complete American control — trade and tariff policy — was *not* brought to bear on this problem in any but marginal ways. Third

---

[9] Baldwin, *op. cit.,* p. 19. Extensive quotations from American officials are included on pp. 20 and 195 ff.

World nations could only acquire the dollars with which to repay private loans by selling exports, principally in American markets. The executive branch made strong efforts to get the Congress to reduce at least some trade barriers, but no significant reductions were ever achieved. In particular, protections against agricultural products (the most likely Third World product) remained fixed at prohibitive levels. In effect, the policies of the United States government have centered upon promotion of opportunities for private investment, but the terms, problems, and consequences involved in following that route have not been attractive to Third World nations. The private investor, on the other hand, could earn substantial profits from Third World investments if he kept ownership or control of commodities produced and arranged their sale himself. In addition, of course, he would have his investment insured by the U.S. government. The extent to which this form of circular private capital flow contributed to long-term development of Third World economies, however, is at least questionable. By the end of the 1960's, informed judgment seemed to be that substantial inputs of public capital were needed to get the process of economic development moving to the point where it might make productive use of private investment.[10]

THE CONSEQUENCES OF AMERICAN POLICIES TOWARD THE THIRD WORLD

The Third World Perspective

In many ways, the greatest divergence of perspective and interest in post-World War II years has been between the developed worlds and the Third World, rather than between the United States and the Soviet Union. The two superpowers have been absorbed in their own mutual conflict, but they have acted in quite similar ways with respect to the rest of the world. One analyst describes the process this way:

They [the U.S. and the U.S.S.R.] competed for power and influence in the Third World. Each put great stress on its military might. Each invested more in the symbols of prestige, like the space race, than in projects that might change the face of the Earth.

Each developed military, paramilitary, and diplomatic bureaucracies that were mirror images of the other. Neither was interested in exporting its system to other countries so much as using its system as an ideology around which to rally supporters and clients. The United States was as anxious to create a truly *independent* capitalist economy in the poor countries of Asia, Africa, and Latin America as Russia was to establish *independent* communist regimes there. Indeed, the United States has usually not favored the accumulation of *local* capital and the Soviets have frequently opposed *local* revolutionaries . . . .[11]

[10] Millikan, *op cit.,* p. 538.
[11] Reprinted by permission of the World Publishing Company from *Intervention and Revolution: America's Confrontation with Insurgent Movements Around the World* (p. 24) by Richard Barnet. A New American Library book. Copyright © 1968 by Richard Barnet. Barnet is a former State Department and Arms Control and Disarmament Agency official, and now co-director of the Institute for Policy Studies in Washington, D.C.

The Third World nationalist need not be a revolutionary to hold a totally different view of what needs should be given priority in the world. After two decades of the Cold War, most Third World nations still have one-crop, agriculturally-based economies and average per capita incomes below $300. The gap between the developed nations and the Third World is *widening*, not closing.[12] Private investment means that somebody else reaps the profit from a country's riches rather than that country itself. The reason for this worsening condition, to many Third World nationalists, is the pattern of United States policies just reviewed. Let us examine some of the consequences of American policies as perceived from the perspective of the Third World.

The world's economic situation has improved greatly since World War II.[13] World export more than doubled, and the exports of developing countries rose more than 50 percent (from $19 billion to $29 billion). But the expansion of the Third World nations proceeded much more slowly than that of the developed nations, with the result that their share in world exports dropped from nearly one-third in 1950 to little more than one-fifth in 1962. Table 3 reflects some of these patterns. According to United Nations analyses, the inability of the less developed nations to attain a higher rate of exports led to a slackening in the rate of expansion in world exports in the early 1960's. Because their products were chiefly raw materials, they were faced with inelastic or declining demand. Prices of primary products such as coffee, tin, and cocoa (on which several Third World economies depend) also fell dramatically in the early 1960's. Ghana's 1965 receipts per ton of cocoa, for example, were about one-quarter of what the world market price had been in 1954. In part, this was probably due to the efforts by Third World nations to export more, but some part may also be attributable to the capacity of a few giant purchasers to keep prices down. In any event, the Third World's continued need for capital equipment and manufactured goods led to an increasingly unfavorable balance of trade and draining of their small supply of capital. Technological progress, evidenced chiefly in development of synthetics and inexpensive substitutes for raw materials and in more efficient use of such raw materials as are still needed, is alleged in the same report to have contributed to widening the gap rather than to making more and cheaper products available to less developed nations.

The United States policies which appear to have contributed to these effects (and other undesirable results) in the eyes of Third World spokesmen have been incisively summarized by Professor Irving Louis Horowitz in a major study as follows:[14]

(1) Under various forms and in various degrees, the United States maintains, by the selective manipulation of the international economy, various kinds

---

[12] This is the so-called "Prebisch thesis," named for a very influential book by the Argentinian development economist. See Raul Prebisch, *Towards a New Trade Policy for Development* (New York: United Nations Publication,1964).

[13] Horowitz, *op. cit.,* pp. 167-169 provides the basis for these assertions.

[14] *Ibid.,* p. 120.

TABLE 3A
The Patterns of Export Trade   (1960-1965 annual averages)

Class of products	Exports from developed nations		Exports from underdeveloped nations	
	Billions of dollars	Percent of total	Billions of dollars	Percent of total
Extractive Industries	$29.2	30.0	$24.3	83.8
Food, beverages, tobacco	13.9	14.3	8.4	28.9
Crude materials (excluding mineral fuels)	11.6	11.9	6.8	23.5
Mineral fuels	3.7	3.8	9.1	31.4
Nonextractive Industries	68.0	70.0	4.7	16.2
Chemicals	7.7	8.0	0.4	1.3
Machinery and transport equipment	28.5	29.3	0.3	0.9
Other manufactured goods	30.6	31.5	3.9	13.6
Miscellaneous	1.2	1.2	0.1	0.4
Total	$97.1	100.0	$29.0	100.0

Note: Developed countries: United States, Canada, West Europe, Australia, New Zealand, South Africa, and Japan.
 Underdeveloped countries: all countries other than developed and Communist countries.
 Source: United Nations, *Statistical Yearbook 1966,* New York, 1967.

TABLE 3B
Patterns of Export Growth: Developed vs. Underdeveloped Countries

	Value of exports (billions of $)		Annual rate of growth
	1950	1965	1950-1965
World exports			
Total	53.5	156.3	7.4%
Exports of developed countries			
Total	35.9	122.5	8.5%
To each other	25.0	95.5	9.4%
To underdeveloped countries	10.9	27.0	6.2%
Exports of underdeveloped countries			
Total	17.6	333.8	4.5%
To developed countries	12.4	26.2	5.2%
To each other	5.2	7.6	2.5%
Exports of underdeveloped countries (excluding major petroleum products)			
Total	14.2	23.7	3.6%
To developed countries	10.0	18.5	4.2%
To each other	4.1	5.2	1.7%

Source: Hal B. Lary, *Imports of Manufactures from Less Developed Countries* (New York: Columbia University Press, 1968), p. 2.

of military, political, and cultural privileges which encroach upon the sovereignty and independence of Third World countries. (2) Although Third World industries are nominally free, American business firms often control the major branches of production and technology, which means they can influence the political structure and the internal social life of each nation. (3) The United States controls the international trade market and, not the least significant, the money market. In this way it manipulates world prices and arbitrarily lowers the values of primary products or the kinds of products manufactured in the Third World. With equal arbitrariness it manipulates the prices of finished manufactured goods, thus creating a constant drainage on the developing nation. (4) The United States is able to raise interest charges at will; and even when it does not do so, its credit position provides it with a constant economic edge, since, given the unequal starting point of the Third World, its member nations can barely repay the interest, let alone the principal on loans issued. (5) The United States controls and monopolizes a considerable portion of the communications and transportation industries and by so doing controls a good deal of what can and cannot be traded and between whom. For example, it uses its maritime shipping as a political weapon against opponents.

The Third World challenge to American economic policies came to a head at the United Nations Conference on World Trade and Development in 1964. Seventy-seven less developed nations formed a bloc which attempted to persuade the developed worlds to treat them as equals rather than as clients or subordinates. Their basic premise was the thesis of the widening gap set forth above. Their concern was fed by the United Nations estimate that in the 1970's the annual gap between what the undeveloped nations will require merely to feed their expanding populations, and what they can expect to earn from selling their products on the world market, will start at $20 billion and get larger. Specifically, the Third World nations sought to encourage the developed worlds to reduce trade barriers and permit expansion of Third World exports in order that capital accumulation could proceed.

Voting on the resolutions at the conference revealed that the United States stood alone, though sometimes with the support of Britain and France, against practically all proposals. Two representative illustrations drawn from a total of 28 major resolutions will show the extent of American isolation on these issues: General Principle One stated: "Economic relations between countries, including trade relations, shall be based on respect for the principle of sovereign equality of states, self-determination of peoples, and non-interference in the internal affairs of other countries." The United States cast the only negative vote, against 113 affirmative and two abstentions, on this question. General Principle Three stated, "Every country has the sovereign right freely to trade with other countries, and freely to dispose of its natural resources in the interest of the economic development and well-being of its own people." The United States voted against this also. In every instance where the resolution called for or emphasized Third World independence, sovereignty, economic diversification, trade adjustment or expansion, the United States voted in the negative, either alone or with a tiny minority of other nations.[15] The official United States explanation appended to the report of the conference was that the measures called for were not really going to provide efficient assistance to the underdeveloped nations, and that the resolutions prejudged the results of a study that had also been proposed. It is worth noting also that the forthcoming presidential election may have influenced some American votes toward purity on the side of private enterprise. Whatever the cause, of course, such voting behavior had the effect of confirming the impressions of many Third World nationalists that the United States did not create the consequences they experienced out of misplaced benevolence or lack of understanding, but rather out of conscious intention.

The American Perspective

It goes without saying that America's own image of the consequences of its policies toward the Third World is more optimistic. Again, of course, it tends to emphasize the short-run and security aspects of the American national interest. From the point of view of national security, there are achievements to be noted: no Third World nation has slipped into the communist camps since Cuba, and some (Indonesia is the prime example) appear to have withdrawn substantially from such influences. Economic achievements may also be identified. Even with their population increases, the average rate of growth of the less developed nations for which statistics are available has been about two percent per year, which is higher than the developed nations attained at comparable periods in their development.[16] Much of this is due to the success (rates above five percent per year) of such nations as South Korea, Taiwan, Thailand, Mexico, Israel, and Peru — most of which have been special recipients of American assistance because of U.S. security objectives. Even prior to the reductions of fiscal 1968 and 1969, American aid had been concentrated, and its effects therefore likely to be more visible. Eight countries received 80 percent of U.S. development loan funds in the early 1960's — Pakistan, India, South Korea, Indonesia, Turkey, Brazil, Chile, and Colombia. (Even for these countries, however, informed American judgment was that the input of capital was too low for it to be used with maximum efficiency.[17]

One's outlook does not need to be very optimistic to contrast sharply with the pessimism and discouragement of Third World nationalists. In absolute terms, American decisionmakers also tended to see the consequences of their Third World policies as disappointing. Where Third World aspirations and expectations had far exceeded the capacity or willingness of industrialized nations to help, American policymakers had apparently underestimated the Third World's problems or relegated them to low priority among the goals of American

---

[15] *Ibid.*, pp. 175-185 summarize the voting.
[16] Optimistic interpretations may be found in Millikan, *op. cit.*, particularly p. 523.
[17] *Ibid.*, p. 537.

foreign policy. Some American officials considered the problem of Third World inability to make effective use of new capital as a major obstacle to development. Others frankly viewed the Third World as having few real prospects except as either a raw material supplier or a field for quick-return extractive investments. Such divergence of thinking about the proper goals and expectations to hold about the Third World at least has the merit of raising the right question: What place *should* the goal of Third World development have among the priorities that make up the American national interest? And what *kind* of development should be sought? Although such concerns were effectively muted by the continuation of the Vietnam War, nothing in the way of new policy from the Nixon administration suggested that there would be significant change from the short-range, security-oriented policies of the previous decades. Nor was there likely to be a reduction of the emphasis on private investment, or tariff barriers to Third World exports, that had exacerbated relations at the United Nations Conference of 1964.

AMERICAN POLICIES TOWARD THE THIRD WORLD: SOME ANALYTICAL QUESTIONS

The circumstances of the Third World present very serious, perhaps insoluble, problems. The difficulties of development may be too great even for the most generous, selfless, and well-conceived policies of the industrialized nations. But the history of the first two decades after World War II suggests that a substantial cause of the "problem" originates within the borders of the industrialized nations themselves, certainly including the United States. Not only have American foreign policies not aided Third World development as much as they might have, but in several instances they have retarded or prevented it — at least in the eyes of Third World nationalists, and perhaps in a more objective view as well. What obstacles within the domestic political process of the United States, or its value system, have prevented the development of foreign policies more in keeping with Third World definitions of needs and goals?

Let us make two bold assumptions which will have the effect of bringing this analytical question into sharper focus. Neither is a foregone conclusion, and perhaps not even persuasive or probable. But they will permit us to illustrate some analytical needs. First, we assume that a "better" view of the long-range American national interest would be *closer to*, not further from, the Third World's own view of its needs and goals. We acknowledge the "realist" view, holding that the United States must assure its security and prosperity first and employ all its resources exclusively and consistently in behalf of these goals.[18] But there has also been a strong current of thought

[18] For an unusual statement of this point of view in stark form, see the report of a speech by President Johnson to troops in Vietnam reported in the *New York Times* of November 2, 1966. ("There are three billion people in the world, and we are only 200 million of them. We are outnumbered 15 to 1. If might did make right, they would sweep over the United States and take what we have. We have what they want.")

holding that Third World development *is* in the long-range security and economic interest of the United States. Further, we doubt that, even with severe domestic problems, Americans will be willing to ignore the plight of the Third World — or that the Third World will permit us to do so. Thus, we shall assume for present purposes that the "real" national interest lies in doing more that is consistent with Third World definitions of needs (i.e., channeling of development capital through multilateral organizations instead of private investment, reduction of trade barriers, or elimination of "buy American" restrictions).

Second, we assume that the current character of American policy toward the Third World is neither coincidental nor the product of policymakers' casual reactions to crises or opportunities. The argument is sometimes made that no clear rationale, or deliberate purpose, but only mistakes of judgment, happenstance, hasty reaction, or bureaucratic inertia, lies behind government decisions.[19] Such a view simply fails to see the value premises or implicit assumptions involved in the decision, perhaps because it shares them so fully. Professor Louis Halle illustrates this point from his State Department experience: [20]

In 1948 the government had for some years been conducting programs of technical assistance in Latin America, and only there. It seemed reasonable that this novel way of conducting international relations might have its uses elsewhere in the world as well, and I recall one occasion especially, a late evening at the end of the day's work, when the Deputy Director of American Republic Affairs and I talked casually about this possibility.

Then, sometime in November, a routine message from the President's speech-writing assistant in the White House requested the Department to send over, in due course, any proposals it had for the contents of the Inaugural Address that the President was to deliver in January. Following established procedure in these matters, the Director of the Office of Public Affairs called a meeting of the interested divisions, to which my friend the Deputy Director went in representation of American Republic Affairs. A Mr. Ben Hardy, pad on knee, took down the various proposals put forward at the meeting as they were accepted. The first proposal advanced and accepted was a statement of support for the United Nations; second was an assurance that the European Recovery Program would be continued; third, the announcement of an intention to organize a common defense among the free nations of the Atlantic area.

Any more?

There was a pause while everyone searched his mind. The Deputy Director, recalling our evening conversation, ended the pause by asking: how about technical assistance for undeveloped countries (the word "underdeveloped" had not yet been coined), like what we're doing in Latin America?

[19] For an illustration of a major analysis which takes current policies to be inappropriate but no more than mistakes on the part of policymakers, see Stillman and Pfaff, *op. cit.*

[20] From pp. 21-23, 29-30 in *The Society of Man* by Louis J. Halle (New York: Harper & Row, 1965).

That's a good idea, said the Director of Public Affairs, put it down, Ben.
So "Point Four" was set down without further discussion, and there the
meeting adjourned.

When the four points proposed for inclusion in the President's address
went up through the Department's clearance-machinery, the fourth was
discarded. Here I do not have the details, but I have no difficulty in
surmising. Any responsible officer was bound to ask what thought and
analysis had entered into the proposal of a program for giving technical
assistance to countries all over the world. What countries specifically? What
kinds of technical assistance, specifically? On what scale? How much would
it cost? Until at least rough answers to these questions were available, until
at least the feasibility of such a program had been determined, it would
be irresponsible to have the President announce it. So the first three points,
without the fourth, were sent on to the White House.

A few days later, the Director of Public Affairs received a phone-call from
the presidential assistant, who complained that, while the three points
were OK in themselves, they were mere "boiler-plate" (government slang
for the cant statements that are always thrown into speeches). I think, he
said, the President would like to have something in this speech that's just a
bit original.

At this juncture, without proper time for reflection, the Director of Public
Affairs found himself standing on the shore of his own Rubicon. He took
a deep breath, and crossed over.

There had been a fourth point, he said, but it had been thrown out.

What was it?

The Director told what it was.

That's great, said the voice from the White House, and "Point Four" went
back in again.

If anyone gave the matter a further thought, from that moment until the
delivery of the Address on January 20, I find no indication of it. "Point
Four" was a public-relations gimmick, thrown in by a professional speech-
writer to give the speech more life.

When the newspapers dramatized it in their principal headlines on the
morning of January 21, the White House and the State Department were
taken completely by surprise. No one — not the President, not the Secretary
of State, not the presidential assistant or the Director of Public Affairs —
knew any more about "Point Four" than what they could read for themselves
in the meager and rather rhetorical language of the speech. No one could
answer the pressing questions of the newspaper-reporters, of the
Congressmen concerned with appropriations, of the foreign diplomats. It
was only now, after the Inaugural Address had been delivered and the
"bold new program" acclaimed all over the world, that machinery was set
up in the government to look into the possibilities of such a program and
make plans. The inauguration of an actual program was not to come until
twenty-one months later — twenty-one months of hard-packed confusion in
which the careers of good men were broken and ulcers proliferated. . . .

At President Truman's press-conference, six days after the Inaugural
Address in which he electrified the world with his announcement of the
"Point Four" program, he was asked: "Mr. President, can you give us any
background on the origin of Point Four?"

"The origin of Point Four (he replied) has been in my mind, and in the
minds of the government, for the past two or three years, ever since the
Marshall Plan was inaugurated. It originated with the Greece and Turkey
propositions. Been studying it ever since. I spend most of my time going

over to that globe over there trying to figure out ways to make peace in the world."

I have emphasized the role of accident in what actually happens. Its role, however, is dominant only in the close-up view. . . .

I cannot believe, however, that this close-up view is right. As someone afterwards said, "Point Four" was "in the air" at the time, as Darwin's theory of evolution had been "in the air" when he published his *Origin of Species*. . . . If the series of accidents that produced "Point Four" had not occurred, another series of accidents would have produced it in another way, under another name.

In our case, we have two decades of experience in which the same basic policies were employed and a consistent set of priorities followed. We believe that analysis should therefore search for deeper, more fundamental explanations than inadvertence or reaction. We do not mean that who holds key policymaking positions is insignificant. The growth of business support for foreign economic assistance and the expansion of private investment overseas, for example, are closely related to the dramatic increase in the number of businessmen in State Department policy positions and to the institution of the investment guaranty program.[21] But *all* administrations have been highly responsive to business needs and values. The chorus of praise for private enterprise which has been directed at the Third World continues without regard to which political party controls the U.S. government. The question is why such values are pressed with such single-mindedness by Democrats and Republicans alike in the face of local resistance and contextual inapplicability. What we mean is simply that comprehensive explanation for consistent basic policy actions over extended periods of time probably must transcend the particular individuals in power and be found instead in deeper sources within the political system, economy, or society.

Adopting these two assumptions brings us to the focus of our analytical question: what obstacles have prevented policies closer to Third World-defined needs? Two major lines of argument were vigorously put forward in the late 1960's. One found the explanation in the ideology held by men in power, the other in the economic imperatives of American capitalism. We shall briefly review each.

The ideological explanation sees American decisionmakers imbued with a "we/they" view of the world, in which the threat of communism is everywhere and only the United States has the responsibility and power to hold back this thrust on behalf of decency, civilization, and freedom. The United States must therefore become a world policeman, serving the cause of orderly progress by preventing violent upheavals and insisting upon law and order. An example of analysis along these lines is Richard Barnet's *Intervention and Revolution*.[22] Barnet sees the "National Security Managers" of the

---

[21] For interesting evidence on these points, see David S. McClellan and Charles E. Woodhouse, "Businessmen in Foreign Policy," *Southwestern Social Science Quarterly*, vol. 39 (March, 1959), pp. 283-90, and, by the same authors, "The Business Elite and Foreign Policy," *Western Political Quarterly*, vol. 13 (March, 1960), pp. 172-90.

[22] Barnet, *op. cit.*

1960's as men whose ideas and attitudes were formed by the events occurring during the time when they first acquired their understanding of international politics, i.e., Munich and World War II. What causes aggression, in their eyes, is weakness and instability; the United States must therefore assert its power in every situation where violence is threatened. Here is how Barnet argues his case:

The National Security Manager still tends to look at the "Underdeveloped World" as a vast Gray Area in international politics. No part of it is of intrinsic interest, unless, of course, it supplies some vital commodity. Otherwise it can capture the official attention in Washington only if it symbolizes some struggle which transcends the minor turmoil of native politics. To the man of the West, Paris and Berlin are important places in their own right, for they symbolize his own historical heritage. But Danang, Santo Domingo, and Kinshasha penetrate his consciousness, if at all, only as battlefields, and then only if the fight is about something sufficiently important. He has almost no knowledge about such places, their people, or their politics, and little personal commitment to them. They represent either sources of strength, strategic or economic, or points of vulnerability. "Vietnam is not the issue," National Security Managers have frequently confided to critics who question whether systematic bombardment is the best way to secure freedom for the Vietnamese people; "it is the testing ground for the Communist strategy of Wars of National Liberation. If they win here, they will strike elsewhere. If they lose, they will not be so ready to start another."

The National Security Manager is a global thinker. In themselves, local problems of other countries are not worthy of his attention; it is the transcendent importance of local revolutionary struggles that warrants intervention. Interference in purely domestic matters is still unjustified as a matter of law and sound policy. Unfortunately, he hastens to add, the line between domestic and foreign matters has blurred. When political factions struggle with one another in far-off places, their conflict is an expression of a single worldwide struggle. The real contestants remain the same. Only the battlefield shifts. The battle, which takes the form of a series of guerrilla wars, is not about Vietnam or Greece or the Dominican Republic any more than World War II was about Iwo Jima or Sicily. Wherever men struggle for power, one can always find International Communism, the ubiquitous political scavenger, ready to use genuine local grievances as ammunition in a global holy war. Global strategy, more than local conditions, dictates the site of the next engagement between International Communism and the Free World.

At this point let us try to look more closely at the mental set of the National Security Manager as it bears on the U.S. commitment against revolution. The ultimate bureaucratic dream is the perfect freedom of unlimited power. It is the ability to push a button, make a phone call, dispatch a cable, and know that the world will conform to your vision. The capacity to control, or, as he might put it, to have options, is a much clearer objective for the professional statesman than the purposes to which he would put such power. The guiding stars of the working bureaucrat are not cosmic goals. One can find a few expressions of an official eschatology in flowery speeches on National Purpose, or in the negotiated generalities of the Basic National Security Policy papers representing the collective wisdom of the foreign-policy bureaucracy. Usually, however, the National Security Manager prides himself on avoiding theological and "nonpragmatic" speculation. He has faith in his intuitive grasp of the art of *ad hoc* politics.

Yet, in developing official policy on U.S. intervention, he is not quite so free as he thinks. Just as he casts his adversary, the Revolutionary — Castro, Mao, Ho — in the inevitable role of foreign agent, so he has picked out a well-worn part for himself. It is the role of the imperial peacekeeper.[23]

The good intentions of the United States thus serve to legitimate actions which in the case of other nations might appear imperialistic and self-serving. Forgetting that the law enshrines a particular status quo that may be intolerable to some, the National Security Manager enforces the American view of law and the status quo as humanitarian obligation. Drawing on assumptions about the American experience, the National Security Manager believes it impossible to speed up the process of Third World development without undergoing intolerable dangers of communism.

This bare-bones sketch of the ideological explanation for the current structure of American foreign policy with regard to the Third World at least highlights its major thesis: that policy actions stem from *ideas* in the minds of the relatively small group of men who make such decisions. As we shall see later, this group of men is quite small indeed, and in many respects self-perpetuating, so that it is not impossible that many quite specific ideas could be shared among them. It is also possible that these ideas are by now widely shared, at least among those relatively elite persons who are likely to come to positions of power in foreign affairs at all. If ideological explanations such as Barnet's are correct, changes in foreign policies might occur when such ideology was moderated by new evidence, changing conditions, or unmistakable events; or when men with a different ideology came to power.

But what if the explanation of foreign policy behavior lies not in ideas but in even deeper sources? Are some other factors responsible for such ideology in the first place, perhaps rendering it a facade for more selfish purposes? Or is the ideology simply irrelevant, and the cause of action the compelling force of basic economic needs? The economic imperatives argument holds that the real causes are to be found only at this level. Harry Magdoff's *The Age of Imperialism*[24] may serve as an example. Magdoff presents evidence to show that the United States, as the preponderant capitalist nation, does and must engage in systematic exploitation of the Third World as a means of maintaining its own prosperity. The motivations for this exploitation consist of the need for raw materials, the profits to be made from foreign investment (which have risen, he alleges, from 10 percent of domestic profits to nearly 25 percent, between 1950 and 1965), and the need to sell export goods in the world. His table and accompanying text indicate the nature of his argument concerning the need for raw materials.

[23] Reprinted by permission of the World Publishing Company from *Intervention and Revolution* (pp. 28-29) by Richard Barnet. A New American Library book. Copyright © 1968 by Richard Barnet.

[24] Harry Magdoff, *The Age of Imperialism: The Economics of U.S. Foreign Policy* (New York: Monthly Review Press, 1969). Copyright © 1969 by Harry Magdoff. Copyright © 1966, 1968 by Monthly Review Press. The following excerpt from pages 52-53 and 198 of this work is reprinted by permission of Monthly Review Press. Magdoff is an independent economic scholar and an editor of *Monthly Review*, a socialist journal.

TABLE 4
Critical Materials Used for Jet Engine

	Pounds used in jet engine[a]	Imports as percent of consumption[b]	Where this material is produced[c]
Tungsten	80-100	24%	U.S. (30%) South Korea (19%) Canada (12%) Australia (8%) Bolivia (8%) Portugal (7%)
Columbium	10-12	100%	Brazil (54%) Canada (21%) Mozambique (18%)
Nickel	1,300-1,600	75%	Canada (71%) New Caledonia (20%)
Chromium	2,500-2,800	100%	South Africa (31%) Turkey (19%) Southern Rhodesia (19%) Philippines (18%) Iran (5%)
Molybdenum	90-100	0	U.S. (79%) Canada (10%) Chile (9%)
Cobalt	30-40	100%	Congo (Leopoldville) (60%) Morocco (13%) Canada (12%) Zambia (11%)

[a] From Percy W. Bidwell, *Raw Materials* (New York: Harper and Bros., 1958), p. 12.
[b] Calculated from data in U.S. Department of Interior, *Minerals Yearbook, 1966,* Washington, D. C., 1967.
[c] Major producers of the material in the noncommunist world. The percentages in parentheses represent the amount produced in the country in 1966 as a percent of total production in noncommunist countries. The source for this information is the same as note b.

The facts presented here are of course no mystery to business or to the government planners and coordinators of policy. President Truman established in 1951 the Materials Policy Commission cited above, to study the materials problem of the United States and its relation to other non-communist countries. The resulting five-volume report was issued with much publicity in the midst of the Korean War. The theme of raw materials sources as an ingredient of foreign policy crops up not only with respect to direct United States requirements but also as it concerns United States responsibility as the leader of the "free world" to see to it that Western Europe's and Japan's supplies of raw materials are assured. Consider, for example, this frank statement by former President Eisenhower:

One of Japan's greatest opportunities for increased trade lies in a free and developing Southeast Asia. . . . The great need in one country is for raw materials, in the other country for manufactured goods. The two regions complement each other markedly. By strengthening of Vietnam and helping insure the safety of the South Pacific and Southeast Asia, we gradually develop the great trade potential between this region . . . and highly industrialized Japan to the benefit of both. In this way freedom in the Western Pacific will be greatly strengthened.

Magdoff also argues that the techniques by which this neo-colonialist relationship is maintained include (a) control of the international monetary and banking structure, (b) trade restrictions, (c) political and military pressures to maintain friendly governments and permit American private enterprise to dominate local economies, and (d) economic assistance to keep Third World nations in peonage situations. This phase of Magdoff's argument may be illustrated from the following excerpt:

The chains of dependence may be manipulated by the political, financial, and military arms of the centers of empire, with the help of the Marines, military bases, bribery, CIA operations, financial maneuvers, and the like. But the material basis of this dependence is an industrial and financial structure which through the so-called normal operations of the marketplace reproduces the conditions of economic dependence.

A critical element of the market patterns which helps perpetuate the underdeveloped countries as dependable suppliers of raw materials is the financial tribute to the foreign owners who extract not only natural resources but handsome profits as well. The following comparison for the years 1950-1965 is a clear illustration of the process and refers to only one kind of financial drain, the income from direct investments which is transferred to the United States:

| | (billions of dollars) | | | |
	Europe	Canada	Latin America	All other areas
Flow of direct investments from U.S.	$8.1	$6.8	$3.8	$5.2
Income on this capital transferred to U.S.	5.5	5.9	11.3	14.3
Net	+$2.6	+$ .9	−$7.5	−$9.1

In the underdeveloped regions almost three times as much money was taken out as was put in. And note well that besides drawing out almost three times as much as they put in, investors were able to increase the value of the assets owned in these regions manifold: in Latin America, direct investments owned by United States business during this period increased from $4.5 to $10.3 billion; in Asia and Africa, from $1.3 to $4.7 billion.

Magdoff further argues that a mature capitalist economy no longer has choices about such policies. In his words, "Imperialism is not a matter of choice for a capitalist society; it is the way of life of such a society." [25]

If Magdoff is right, there is little prospect of change in American foreign policy short of drastic modification of the American economic system itself, which would probably have to involve substantial change in power distribution within the society and polity. No modification of ideology, and no change of policymakers, which was not accompanied by such economic restructuring, could hope to institute

[25] *Ibid.* p. 26.

foreign policies of the type we have been hypothesizing. It is of course crucial that we attempt to ascertain which of the two types of argument is correct. In reality, this may mean *how much* (if any) of each is accurate and therefore should be made part of the citizen's own judgment about the roots of foreign policy. To reach such judgment, we must know much more about the values and ideology, the power sources and distribution, and the decisionmaking process, of American politics. It is time to start on that inquiry.

INSTITUTIONS
AND PROCESSES III

The four policy areas just reviewed may now seem more closely related than they did at first. Although they were selected only for their contemporary social importance, each set of policies and consequences appears to reflect similar values and priorities. In every case, the American values of individualism, property rights, and material prosperity are paramount. Government policies and their actual consequences, in other words, appear to reflect precedence of these values over such others as economic, social, or racial equality. We shall return to a more detailed discussion of this pattern in Chapter 16.

But in this Part, our focus shifts to the ways in which these policies are produced. We have not yet asked how or why policies take the form they do, nor have we seen evidence about the relative parts played by elites and masses in shaping policies. By exploring these subjects, the eight chapters of this Part attempt to shed some light

VOTE IN THE STREETS
I'M A BUM FOR PEACE
I'M A BUM FOR PEACE
I'M A BUM FOR PEACE

on our central question concerning the structure of power in the United States. We begin by setting up the problem: what is it that we must know about elites, masses, and their interaction? Chapter 8 does this, and sketches the character of elites briefly. Chapter 9 then examines the legal setting — the distribution of power accomplished by the Constitution and its contemporary significance. Chapter 10 looks more analytically at elite behavior within the institutions of the national government, focusing principally on the key positions of power within them. Chapter 11 probes intra-elite relationships, and Chapter 12 the opportunities that elites have to develop influence over masses. The last three chapters reverse this approach, taking a mass perspective and asking how and when masses can influence elites.

Elites and Masses: 8
Who Governs?

Who governs? This crucial question, central to democracy as well as to resolving the dispute between competing American political ideologies, may well be unanswerable in any final and authoritative way. Elaborate methodologies have been developed and applied by a wide variety of social scientists, but the multiplicity of key definitions, the elusiveness of "power" as an objective quality, and the tenacity of conflicting ideological perspectives have prevented agreement from being reached. But there is no reason why precise definitions and careful analysis cannot drastically narrow the range of possible interpretations and focus the alternatives for citizens' judgment. This chapter sets up and begins an inquiry that will accomplish this task. By Chapter 15, many components will have been assembled, and in Chapter 16 we shall hazard a tentative choice among two alternative characterizations.

In our review of the basic disputes between the dominant American political belief system and its contemporary challengers, we said that the former held a "pluralist" image of power in the United States. This meant that power is seen as diffused among many groups, whose competition for support and advantage takes place in a context of fair procedures, subject to the general control of the electorate acting through public officials who responsively arrange the necessary compromises among the many legitimate interests. Group memberships teach democratic and leadership skills, and prevent extremism. The political system itself is seen as producing policies in the public interest, manifesting the widely shared political values, and therefore being democratic. The contemporary challengers, on the other hand, saw power as tightly concentrated among a power elite or ruling class, with resultant policies reflecting that group's interests and values and not those of the mass public. The political system not only operated with the wrong values and priorities, but denied realization of the different values and aspirations held by the lower classes. Thus, it was far from a democracy. The gap between the pluralist and the ruling class or power elite images is very great, and, as we noted earlier, shaped in part by ideological assumptions. Our problem now is to design an inquiry that will enable us to resolve some or most of the issues in dispute concerning the structure of power in the United States, while avoiding the effects of ideology.

IMAGES OF POWER: THE OPEN QUESTIONS

Images of power range from the relatively democratic pluralist view (which asserts mass control of major policy directions through elections, and specific issue-representation through membership in competing interest groups) to the economic ruling class interpretation which sees centralized power wielded manipulatively by a few corporate oligarchs.[1] The vital questions, answers to which would add up to a clear characterization of the actual structure of power, may be organized into three major categories: (1) the composition, origins, attitudes, and cohesion of elites; (2) the nature and sources of mass attitudes and unfulfilled aspirations, and the extent and character of mass participation in politics; and (3) the balance of initiative and constraints actually existing in the elite-mass relationship; for example, if elites generate most policy initiatives themselves and are not actually subject to mass constraints, an elite-based structure of power is indicated — and vice versa. We shall consider each set of questions separately.

(1) Elites

Elites are those people who hold more of the resources of power than others. Where the cut-off line is drawn between elites and non-elites (or masses) is not crucial. Everybody has *some* power, of course,

[1] It may be worth noting that no analysts seriously argue the validity of the classic or New England Town Meeting model of democracy, in which informed citizens act on all matters of policy and direct their agents in government to carry out their will. "Democratic" pluralism is the *most* democratic interpretation asserted by empirical political scientists, and its "democratic" nature is disputed even by those who accept most of its empirical findings. See Peter Bachrach, *The Theory of Democratic Elitism* (Boston: Little, Brown, 1967).

but at some point the disparity between a Congressman, corporation president, or newspaper editor and a steelworker, welfare mother, or student becomes very clear. Elite status, in our eyes, is determined by the ability to affect the action of others. It is enough that a person *can* affect government action, not necessarily that he *does* in every case. (Whether he does or not is a matter of great interest in regard to any specific policy area, but it does not determine whether or not he belongs in the *general* category of elite. The concept of elite cannot be limited to those who can actually be shown to have affected a particular decision, for that would make elite status contingent upon the evidence-collecting skills of the analyst rather than the characteristics of the person himself.)

Elite status may flow from the mere possession of disproportionate wealth, status, knowledge or other power-yielding resource, held as *a personal attribute*. Persons in this general category are more capable of exercising influence over public policy than the ordinary citizen, if they choose to so apply their resources. Or elite status may flow from holding an *institutional position* within the society which gives rise to the capacity to directly control or affect the lives of others, such as an officer or director of a major corporation or an official of government. In the latter case, both the voluntary compliance granted to legitimate authority and the availability of means of coercion greatly add to the potential power held.

It is this second category of elite status in which we are most interested, and on which our analysis will focus. First, we need to know who such people are — their age, race, education, income, occupation, and other background characteristics. In particular, we shall be interested in the extent to which they represent a cross-section of the American population, or, on the other hand, are more like those in the first, or personally-based, elite category. If the latter is the case, and those with the greater wealth and status are also the occupants of the major economic and governmental institutions, we have inferential evidence of general elite domination. Socioeconomic background characteristics, it may be inferred, usually give rise to class-based values and priorities, economic interests, and overall perceptions of the world. A government staffed by wealthy professionals and businessmen would probably not be as understanding of the conditions, needs, and desires of workers, housewives, or blacks as they would be themselves. But socioeconomic background evidence is only inferential. It is possible that upper class decision-makers understand lower class needs and act in accordance with them, or even that their values and interests are substantially similar, so that when they act for themselves they in effect act for all. Common sense and experience must determine the conclusiveness to be accorded to inferences drawn from particular configurations of socioeconomic evidence of this kind.

The careful analyst, of course, will seek corroboration wherever possible. Thus, second, we should seek to learn how the occupants of the major power positions in the key economic and governmental institutions acquired their positions. The underlying issue is whether elite status is open broadly to many people, or whether there are some specific criteria which generally determine who can become a major powerholder. If a man was elected, how did he acquire his nomination and his initial public visibility? In other words, to what set of interests and priorities did people have to be acceptable before they could have a chance to acquire elite status? This will tell us much about the kind of policy orientation they are likely to have while holding their institutional position. If they were appointed to their offices, by whom and subject to what standards? Again, we seek insight into the probable values and interests that will animate them while in office. A poor youth, for example, might well attend an Ivy League college and law school on scholarships and rise through a great banking corporation to substantial wealth and membership on the Federal Reserve Board; such a career line, however, would suggest upper class values and interests rather than those associated with his socioeconomic origins.

Third, we could improve on these bases for inference by acquiring direct evidence about the political values and attitudes of such elites. Some studies of the attitudes of elites at various levels have been made, although their comprehensiveness and depth of analysis are not very satisfactory. It is difficult to get comprehensive and accurate responses from men in major positions of power, in part because they are rarely available and reluctant to take firm stands on key issues. Where such evidence is obtainable, of course, we have a clear basis for comparing elite values and attitudes with those of masses. This avoids all the problems of inference and assumption which prevent complete confidence in the apparent implications of socioeconomic background data.

Finally, the most conclusive evidence of all is that pertaining to actual elite behavior. Socioeconomic background, origins, and general values and attitudes alike may lead in one direction, while the decisionmaker actually acts in the opposite direction. If possible, we should seek to learn to what extent men in power consciously act together, as a single unit with agreed purposes, and how much they just happen to generate specific policies out of their ongoing conflicts. But it is even more difficult to acquire comprehensive and accurate evidence about actual elite behavior than about their values and attitudes. Men in power do not act in public, and their public speeches (or private accounts to interviewers) may be totally at odds with their real behavior; or they (or others) may quite sincerely understand their behavior to have been based on one rationale when they were in fact responding to other motivations. It is because of these evidential difficulties that we have spent so much time in defining what men in government have done in the way of public policymaking in our four policy areas. In effect, we *have* a solid characterization of actual elite behavior, waiting to be combined with this analysis as soon as it is completed.

We shall begin to answer these questions about elites in this chapter, with the examination of data about their socioeconomic backgrounds and attitudes, and some consideration of the implications of these data. Evidence about past careers and rise to current positions will be presented here and in the next three chapters, along with some further evidence about attitudes and behavior.

(2) Masses

Perhaps the most important evidence needed is that pertaining to mass values and attitudes. In particular, we want to know how mass values and attitudes compare with those of elites and with the policies that are actually carried out by government. If they are substantially the same, we need to ask next about the sources of such mass values and attitudes. As best we can tell from admittedly sparse evidence, are they genuinely self-generated by masses themselves, or are they the product of elite action or indoctrination? If mass values and attitudes are truly self-generated, *and* similar to elites' and government policies, we have good grounds for inferring at least that the political system does not deny mass goals.

But if mass desires are *not* similar to those of elites, *or* are not expressed in public policies, *or* are essentially the product of elite manipulation of some kind, then we must infer that the system is elite dominated. If elites in effect produce the mass values and attitudes to which they later generously respond, of course initiative rests with elites. If they fail to enact mass values and attitudes into effective policy, the same conclusion is even clearer. If elites hold dissimilar values and *do* act according to masses' preferences, an unlikely combination, we have a system whose official management at least is in the exclusive hands of elites.

A second means of gaining insight into the nature of mass-elite relationships and the real locus of power within the system is to examine the extent and character of mass political participation. By exploring the electoral process, from the presentation of issues and programs by candidates and parties to the bases on which people decide whether and how to vote, we may see something of the extent of mass influence over government officials and policies. There are also many other forms of mass political participation, such as protests, riots, and lobbying — and there is a large number of Americans who avoid all contact with politics. We need to know the reasons for each of these forms of behavior, and particularly the extent to which they are either reactions to elites or responses to masses' life situations. Then we need to know what effect any and all of these forms of political participation have on the subsequent behavior of elites. To the extent that mass actions do lead to effective policy changes, we have evidence of widely-spread power within the system — and vice versa.

In all probability we shall find that mass values and attitudes are segmented according to race, age, religion, income, or other characteristics. Our problem then becomes the slightly more complex one of seeking to ascertain how often the goals of various subgroups are expressed in public policies, which if any group more often achieves its goals, and to what extent policies reflect elite rather than *any* mass subgroup's goals. Regardless of whether or not there are important divisions within masses, a further question is the extent of mass support for the political system itself as distinguished from any particular policies or practices it may be following. Strong generalized support may be taken as inferential evidence that, on the whole, other values and attitudes are being served — or that masses are strongly caught up in established ideology.

We shall begin the presentation of mass values and attitudes, the analysis of their origins, and the consideration of mass political participation, in Chapters 13 and 14. In Chapter 15, we shall move to a more specific examination of the character of mass impact on policy.

(3) Elite-Mass Linkage

Power involves a kind of transaction between two or more people, in which the greater resources of one cause the other(s) to act in certain ways. Similarly, leadership implies followership; one cannot be a leader unless there are those who more or less willlingly follow. Institutional elites and masses are thus in a reciprocal relationship; initiatives and constraints flow back and forth between them. The actions of elites, taken with a view to probable mass reactions, are perceived by masses, whose responses in turn either suggest new actions to elites or cause them to recognize new limits on their action. Or mass demands, conceived in a context of perceived limits, are acknowledged by elites, who act to contain or promote them as their own interests and understanding of probable mass responses suggest.

The problem for analysis is identification of the relative balance of initiative and constraints between elites and masses. Clearly, if nearly all real capacity to initiate policy changes were coupled with nearly complete capacity to impose constraints, on one or the other side of this continuing power equation, that side would be dominant and we would have an additional component of evidence concerning the true structure of power. We must seek to understand when and how elites initiate policy changes, and the extent to which masses are able to impose constraints on them. Conversely, we must also try to find occasions and means of mass initiation of policy changes, and assess the way in which elites are able to impose constraints on *them*.

Several different approaches are required to deal with this complex problem in the shifting dynamics of elite-mass interaction. In the next two chapters, we shall discuss the structural setting and the distribution of power and decisionmaking capacity within the institutions of the national government. Then we shall look at the interlocking relationships between elites in and out of government and seek to assess the influence this linkage generates. In our last chapter addressed primarily to elites, we shall examine the opportunities which elites have to shape mass understanding and response through both private and governmental means. Chapters 13 and 14 attempt similar analyses from the perspective of masses.

Let us reiterate what is at stake in this inquiry. Neither masses nor elites are powerless. We know that each can initiate change, and each can constrain the other, under particular circumstances. Our question presses further: how much power of initiative and constraint characteristically lies on each side, and under what conditions is the normal balance disrupted? When and how can elites impose their preferences on unwilling masses? When and how can masses force elites to change their policies or institute new ones? Even this phrasing of the question lacks sophistication and subtlety, but it will serve to start us on the path toward greater understanding of the real structure of power in the United States.

GOVERNING ELITES: COMPOSITION AND ORIGINS

(a) The General Category of Elites

In broad social and economic terms, the United States is a distinctly stratified society. In other words, some people have much more wealth and status — important resources of power — than others. The unequal stratification of such resources (which is the basis of our first or general category of "elite") may be briefly characterized by reference to long-established and continuing patterns of distribution of income, wealth, and status in the United States.

The basic pattern of distribution of annual personal *income* is a sharp pyramid, with many people at the base and a relative few at the top. The income of the top 10 percent of the people, for example, is roughly equal to that of the entire lower 50 percent. Income distribution has fluctuated very slightly in the twentieth century, despite wars, depression and inflation, and five decades of the "progressive" income tax. Figure 1 shows that the proportion of national personal income received by each income-tenth has remained roughly constant since 1910. The highest tenth receives almost as much in the most recent years as it did in the first three decades of the century. Only slight changes have occurred; there has been a slight increase in the share received by each of the four next highest income-tenths, but this has been countered by a reduction in the aggregate share received by the lower half of all income recipients. More recent evidence indicates that, despite a steady rise in real income (which has now at least temporarily been reversed by the post-1968 inflation), the proportionate shares of income received remain constant. The top five percent of families and unrelated individuals in 1966, for example, received 20 percent of all income, or considerably more than the lower 40 percent put together.[2] It is this fact, given its apparent permanence as a feature of American socioeconomic life, which requires recognizing some people as "elite" and others as nonelite.

[2] U.S. Department of Health, Education, and Welfare, *Toward a Social Report* (Washington, D.C.: U.S. Government Printing Office, 1969), p. 44.

FIGURE 1

Percentage of National Personal Income, Before Taxes, Received by Each Income-Tenth*

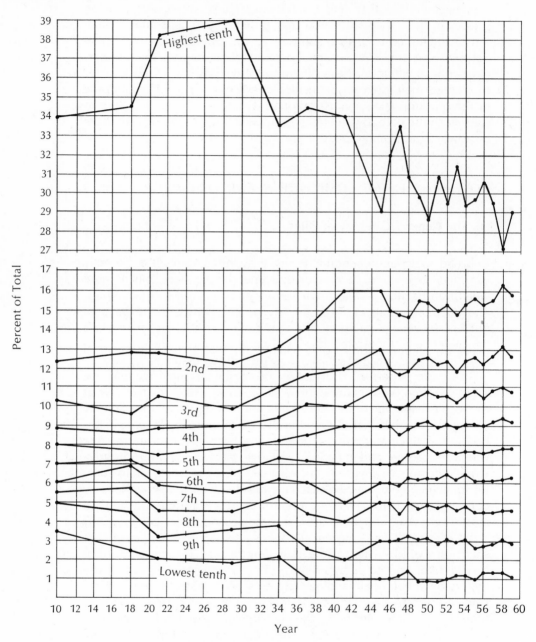

* In terms of "recipients" for 1910–37 and "spending units" for 1941–59.

Source: Data for 1910–37 are from National Industrial Conference Board, *Studies in Enterprise and Social Progress* (New York: National Industrial Conference Board, 1939), p. 125. Data for 1941–59 were calculated by the Survey Research Center. Figures for 1941–46 are available in rounded form only. Previously unpublished data for 1947–58 are reproduced by permission of the Board of Governors of the Federal Reserve System, and data for 1959 by permission of the Survey Research Center. Figure adapted from table appearing in Gabriel Kolko, *Wealth and Power in America* (New York: Frederick A. Praeger, 1962), p. 14.

But annual personal income is not the only effective measure of economic inequality. Another approach is to focus on the distribution of *wealth* — the total of accumulated assets (property, bank accounts, stocks, etc.) held by people. The leading study of wealth distribution in the United States examined the holdings of the top one percent of the population in comprehensive detail, using federal estate tax data as the principal basis of calculation.[3] It concluded that in 1956 (the latest year for which data could be assembled), the top one percent of all adults held 26 percent of the total wealth in the United States. In 1922, the top one percent had held 32 percent of the wealth, but their share had dropped to 28 percent by 1933 and 21 percent in 1949. By the early 1950's, however, the trend had reversed and the top one percent were steadily increasing their share of wealth. It was 24 percent in 1953, and, as we just noted, 26 percent in 1956; other less comprehensive studies suggest that this trend has continued up to the end of the 1960's.

The nature of the wealth distribution pyramid is graphically portrayed in a study which drew on the same analysis. In *Power and Privilege*,[4] Gerhard Lenski calculated wealth distribution in terms of the proportions of the adult population holding various amounts. Table 1 presents his results. It shows that less than five percent of the people hold almost 40 percent of national wealth, while the lowest 50 percent of the population has only eight percent. Moreover, the accumulation of only $30,000 (in 1950 dollars) in personal net worth is sufficient to place one among the top five percent of American wealthholders.

TABLE 1
Estimated Distribution of Wealth in the United States, 1953

Assets	Percentage of adult population	Percentage of wealth
Less than $3,500	50.0	8.3
$3,500 to $10,000	18.4	10.2
$10,000 to $20,000	21.2	29.3
$20,000 to $30,000	5.8	13.4
$30,000 to $50,000	2.7	9.5
$50,000 to $100,000	1.0	6.2
$100,000 to $1,000,000	0.9	16.6
$1,000,000 to $10,000,000	0.04	5.2
$10,000,000 and over	0.0006	1.3
	100.0	100.0

Source: Calculated from Robert J. Lampman, *The Share of Top Wealth-holders in National Wealth: 1922-1956* (Princeton, N. J.: Princeton University Press, 1962), Tables 34 and 99.

From *Power and Privilege* (p. 339) by Gerhard E. Lenski. Copyright © 1966 by McGraw-Hill Book Company. Used with permission of McGraw-Hill Book Company.

[3] Robert J. Lampman, *The Share of Top Wealth-Holders in National Wealth* (Princeton, N. J.: Princeton University Press, 1962). The data in this paragraph are drawn from p. 24.

[4] Gerhard Lenski, *Power and Privilege* (New York: McGraw-Hill, 1966).

In regard to both income and wealth, the evidence shows that the pattern of sharp inequality is a *permanent* one. Little change occurred in the shares of national income received or wealth held over several decades. The implication is that only marginal redistribution, and then only to the next highest echelons, has occurred in the twentieth century. This is confirmed by Gabriel Kolko's analysis of the impact of the federal income tax on national income distribution, the results of which are shown in Table 2. Using U.S. Census Bureau

TABLE 2
Percentage of National Personal Income Received by
Each Income-Tenth after Federal Income Taxes

Year	Highest	2nd	3rd	4th	5th	6th	7th	8th	9th	Lowest
1947	31(−2)*	15	12	10	9	8(+1)	6	5(+1)	3	1
1949	28(−2)	15	13(+1)	11	9	8	7(+1)	5	3	1
1950	27(−2)	15	13	11	10(+1)	8	7(+1)	5	3	1
1951	28(−3)	15	13(+1)	11(+1)	9	8	7(+1)	5	3	1
1952	27(−3)	15	13(+1)	11	10(+1)	8	7(+1)	5	3	1
1953	28(−3)	15	12	11(+1)	9	8	7(+1)	5	4(+1)	1
1954	27(−2)	15	13	11	9	8	7(+1)	5	4(+1)	1
1955	27(−2)	16	13	11	10(+1)	8	6	5(+1)	3	1

* Numbers in parentheses indicate change in percentage points from before-tax income.

Source: Bureau of the Census, *Statistical Abstract of the United States — 1957* (Washington, D.C.: Government Printing Office, 1957), p. 309. These data, collected by the Survey Research Center, include capital gains but exclude income-in-kind.

Reprinted from Gabriel Kolko, *Wealth and Power in America* (New York: Praeger, 1962), p. 34.

reports as his source, Kolko found that, during the period 1947-1955, the highest income-tenth lost from two to three percent of national income through income taxation, but that it still emerged with more than the lowest 50 percent put together.

These findings, taken together, show clearly that the "progressive" income tax has not altered the basic pattern of distribution of income and wealth, and that this pattern is one of sharp and permanent inequality. By "permanent," of course, we do not mean that no individuals ever rise from a low income group into the top five percent, or that all members of the top five percent remain at that level forever. But very wealthy persons are much more likely to add to their holdings than to lose them; even in periods of recession, they continue to add to their relative standing because of the greater depth and resilience of their financial resources. The entry of a few new members into the upper echelons, therefore, does not alter the basic pattern of continuity in the elongated American economic pyramid. And where income and wealth are so unequally distributed on a permanent basis, we may begin to infer the existence of distinctive and shared values and interests among at least the upper echelons. (To be sure, the distribution pyramid in the United States is not as sharply unequal as it is in some other nations; but our question here is the existence of a distinctive American elite, not the relative disparities between the United States and other nations.)

The distribution of *status* within the society occurs through a number of complicated processes, some of them reaching back through centuries. Race, religion, national origin, time of arrival on the American continent (except for the American Indian), ancestral achievements, family wealth, and individual aspirations all contribute to one's status position today. Status is in part assigned by societal norms, cultural values, and popular expectations, and in part acquired by an individual's own actions. Over time, certain occupations and societal roles come to acquire general prestige rankings in the public mind, and a rough hierarchy of status can be constructed. This is what is attempted in the North-Hatt Occupational Prestige Scale, shown in Table 3. Relatively slight modifications in these rankings

TABLE 3
North-Hatt Occupational Prestige Scale

Rank	Occupation	Prestige score
1	U.S. Supreme Court Justice	96
2	Physician	93
3	State governor	93
4	Cabinet member in the federal government	92
5	Diplomat in the U.S. Foreign Service	92
6	Mayor of a large city	90
7	College professor	89
8	Scientist	89
9	United States Representative in Congress	89
10	Banker	88
11	Government scientist	88
12	County judge	87
13	Head of a department in a state government	87
14	Minister	87
15	Architect	86

Reprinted from Leonard Reissman, *Class in American Society* (New York: Free Press, 1959), p. 153.

occur over time, in response to particular attitudinal trends or events, but the general pattern again remains constant. Certain occupations (physician, college professor, scientist, banker) carry high prestige, but the list is dominated by specific institutional positions in government (five of the six with prestige scores of 90 or more, for example.)

Particular rankings are less important than the fact that there exists a generally shared perception of prestige associated with certain occupations and governmental positions. The practitioners of these occupations and holders of these positions thus acquire a status, and perhaps accompanying credibility, well in excess of that enjoyed by the ordinary citizen. In terms of status, such occupations place some people in the general category of elite; they have important resources of power which they may develop into political impact. The holders of the prestigious government positions, of course, acquire an additional resource enabling them to persuade people that their views and actions are correct and should be followed. The occupation of lawyer, so dominant in American politics, ranks nearly as high as those listed in Table 3, and is in any event almost a prerequisite for many of the governmental positions listed.

Although status and prestige rankings are not usually compiled with such factors in mind, it is clear that they reflect educational attainments, and thus the pre-existing family wealth, of the people who hold the positions involved. Practically all of the occupations and government positions listed require at least a college education and most require some post-graduate work or even a specific graduate degree. Educational attainment is partly a mark of individual aspiration, ability, and application, of course, but the major condition precedent is that one come from a family background which provides the motivation and the financial support necessary for going to college and graduate school. Although about 42 percent of all high school graduates now enter college, evidence shows that this group is still quite disproportionately drawn from the upper income groups. In the 1960 census, of those aged 16 to 24 in families with less than $5,000 income per year, only 19 percent reported attending college. In families with income between $5,000 and $7,500 per year, the comparable figure was 33 percent; and in families with more than $10,000 income, it rose to 49 percent.

Even more graphic confirmation of this relationship emerges from *Project Talent,* a study by the U.S. Department of Health, Education, and Welfare. The study examined the activity during the first year after their graduation of those high school students who had ranked in the *highest* fifth in academic ability.[5] If their parents were in the top quarter of Americans in socioeconomic terms, 82 percent went to college; but if their parents were in the bottom quarter, only 37 percent did. Nor is this compensated for in later years through any form of self-help, scholarships, or government assistance such as the G.I. Bill. Overall, 95 percent of the high-status people eventually started college and only 50 percent of the low-status people, despite the similar high rankings in terms of academic ability. By the time of graduate or professional schools, the gap is even wider. Five years after high school graduation, those high school graduates in the top fifth by ability are five times more likely to be in a graduate or professional school if their parents were in the top socioeconomic quartile than if their parents were in the bottom socioeconomic quartile.

These data show that an individual's status, because of its close link to education, depends in important ways on his family's income while he was growing up. Family income in the past shapes the life

[5] The data in this paragraph are drawn from U.S. Department of Health, Education, and Welfare, *Toward A Social Report, op. cit.,* p. 20.

situation of an individual not only in terms of status but also in terms of future income. The status-income linkage is thus very close, and it sets enduring patterns which are only marginally affected across generations. Table 4, which should be read in conjunction

TABLE 4
Occupations Ranked by Income-Tenth[a], 1929-52

Occupational Groups	1929	1935-36	1949	1951	1952
Lawyers	1	1	1	1	
Physicians	1	1	1	1	
Dentists	2+	1	1	1	
Full professors (large state university)	2+	1			2+
Associate professors (large state university)	2−	2+			2−
High-school principals[b]	1	1	1	1	
High-school teachers[b]	3+	1	2−	3+	
Elementary-school teachers[b]	4	2−	3	4	
Social workers	5	3	5−		
Ministers	4	3−	6		
Nurses	6−	6−	6		
Engineers	1	1	2		
Skilled and semiskilled workers (by industry)[c]					
Automobile	6	5+	5		
Chemical	7+	5−	5		
Machine and machine tools	6−	5	5		
Furniture	7	6+	7−		
Iron and steel	5−	6+	5−		
Paper and pulp	6	6+	5−		
Unskilled workers (by industry)					
Automobile	7	6+	6+		
Chemical	7	7+	6		
Machine and machine tools	8	7	6−		
Furniture	8−	8	8		
Iron and steel	7	8	6−		
Paper and pulp	8	8+	6−		

[a] Income is based on average annual income. Income-tenths are ranked in descending order: 1 equals the highest tenth, 10 the lowest tenth, etc. A plus or minus sign indicates the highest or lowest third within the income-tenth.

[b] Cities of more than 500,000.

[c] Average of combined incomes.

Reprinted from Gabriel Kolko, *Wealth and Power in America* (New York: Praeger, 1962), p. 84.

with Table 3, shows how occupation relates to income. The high-education, high-status occupations (lawyer, physician, professor, etc.) rank in the highest income-tenths, while unskilled workers are in the lowest. This was true in the 1920's, 1930's, 1940's, and 1950's.

This evidence shows that status, occupation, and income are closely associated with each other, and that the same basic distribution patterns continue across the decades and generations. Of course, we know from experience that some individuals from poor families acquire education and/or high status and income, thus merging with the established upper echelons. But the general pattern is as we have described it here; reality for most people is repeating cycles within the same general status and income level. And we have not even touched upon the special barriers that have for many generations held blacks at the lowest levels of American society.

What we have sketched briefly here is the basic class structure of the United States. The permanence of quite sharp income, wealth, and status differentials within the American population is a fact of life with potentially profound political significance. It is clear that, at least in the general terms which we are employing in this first category, there is a distinct elite which enjoys the preponderance of these key resources of power. Within this elite, of course, there are further gradations. The income and wealth of a relative handful greatly overshadow those of people in the next higher echelons. This is probably meaningful in terms of further increments of power. In 1953, the top one percent of adults in terms of wealth, for example, held 76 percent of all corporate stock, 100 percent of all state and local government bonds, and 78 percent of all other bonds.[6]

The principal point of this analysis is not to conjure up images of robber barons or economic royalists, however, but to quite simply establish that there is a pool of individuals whose disproportionate share of power resources mark them as an identifiable elite in the general sense. How many people make up this pool? The top five percent of adults, a proportion we have seen as meaningful regarding income and wealth, would be about 6,000,000 people. All the practitioners of the high-status occupations of lawyer, physician, professor, scientist, banker, and top business executive would together constitute a slightly larger number of persons, most of whom would probably be included within the first group as well. Many other people, perhaps an equal number, are so closely associated with this uppermost echelon through family, social, or business ties as to be for all practical purposes includable within it. The difference between five and ten or even fifteen percent of the population is not important; a relatively small group holds a very large share of the key resources that can lead to power. The next questions are whether institutional elites are drawn from this general pool, and how each set of elites compares with the less favored majority in terms of values and interests.

(b) Institutional Elites

The social backgrounds of men in major governmental positions have always been highly unrepresentative of the population as a whole.[7] Despite notable exceptions, the historical pattern has been for key

---

[6] Lampman, op. cit., p. 209.

[7] The major source, from which the data in this paragraph were drawn, is Donald Matthews, The Social Background of Political Decision-Makers (New York: Random House, 1955).

government positions to be filled from the pool that we have just described. This is confirmed by a variety of empirical studies. They show that political decisionmakers are quite disproportionately white anglo-saxon Protestants with high incomes, many of whose families have been active in politics for generations. Their occupations are almost entirely the upper-status ones, principally the law. Although they make up less than one percent of the adult population, lawyers usually constitute about 60 percent of the two houses of the Congress and all of the justices of the Supreme Court; lawyers constituted 70 percent of all Presidents, Vice-Presidents, and Cabinet members between 1877 and 1934. Such lawyers are far from a cross-section even of their own profession: in most cases, wealth, family political involvement, or a large corporate law practice (or some combination of these) also lies behind high political position. The education of nearly half of all decisionmakers took place in Ivy League schools — chiefly Harvard, Yale, and Princeton — or in the elite eastern small colleges modeled on them. What emerges from this body of research, despite contrasting definitions, time periods, and offices covered, is a composite picture of government conducted by a narrow slice of the population — and one reflecting the very characteristics of income, status, and education that we have just described as "elite."

A particularly good analysis which illustrates these general propositions is Donald Matthews' study of members of the U.S. Senate during the period 1947-1957.[8] Matthews found that 84 percent of the 180 senators involved had gone to college (at a time when only 14 percent of the white population over 25 had done so) and that 53 percent had been to law school. Sixty-three percent of the Democrats were lawyers, 45 percent of the Republicans; 17 percent of the Democrats were businessmen and 45 percent of the Republicans. The other occupations represented were those of farmer, professor, and other professionals such as minister or physician. There were no representatives of any blue collar occupation, only one woman, and no blacks. The senators came from families of the upper and middle class, as measured by their fathers' occupations; Matthews notes that "the children of low-salaried workers, wage-earners, servants, and farm laborers, which together comprised 66 percent of the gainfully employed in 1900, contributed only seven percent of the postwar Senators."[9]

The implications which such a pattern of origins and occupations carry for the operation of the Senate as an institution may be seen from Table 5, which shows the occupational makeup of Senate committees. All proposals for constitutional amendments and all nominations for the Supreme Court, for example, must pass the scrutiny of the Judiciary Committee, 81 percent of whom were lawyers. Businessmen made up more than half of the membership of the Banking

[8] Donald Matthews, *U.S. Senators and Their World* (Chapel Hill, N. C.: University of North Carolina Press, 1960). Page citations are from the Vintage Books edition (New York: Random House). The educational and occupational data are from pages 26-36.

[9] *Ibid.*, p. 19.

TABLE 5
Occupational Distribution of Members of Senate Committees

Committees	Law-yers	Busi-ness-men	Farm-ers	Pro-fes-sors	Other profes-sionals
			Occupations		
Foreign Relations	59%	16%	6%	16%	4% = 100% (38)
Appropriations	55%	27%	12%	0%	5% = 100% (31)
Finance	46%	36%	11%	4%	4% = 100% (28)
Armed Services	55%	32%	6%	3%	3% = 100% (31)
Agriculture & Forestry	50%	19%	27%	4%	0% = 100% (26)
Judiciary	81%	6%	6%	6%	0% = 100% (31)
Interstate & Foreign Commerce	60%	29%	6%	0%	6% = 100% (35)
Banking & Currency	28%	55%	3%	10%	3% = 100% (29)
Interior	52%	27%	14%	0%	7% = 100% (29)
Public Works	50%	35%	6%	3%	6% = 100% (34)
Labor & Public Welfare	50%	25%	4%	14%	7% = 100% (28)
Government Operations	53%	26%	8%	3%	10% = 100% (38)
Rules & Administration	51%	29%	8%	3%	8% = 100% (38)
Post Office & Civil Service	56%	20%	13%	4%	7% = 100% (45)
District of Columbia	62%	27%	4%	2%	4% = 100% (48)
All Senators	54%	27%	7%	5%	7% = 100% (167)

Note: Data represents 80th through 84th Congresses. Committee assignments of less than one year's duration omitted.

Reprinted from Donald Matthews, *U.S. Senators and Their World* (New York: Vintage Books, 1960), Appendix E, p. 290. Copyright © 1960 by the University of North Carolina Press.

and Currency Committee, even though they constituted only about a quarter of all senators. What emerges is a pattern whereby each occupational grouping asserts control over government action in the areas of special concern to it. We shall see further implications about this in a later chapter.

The Senate, of course, is only one institution of government. Its counterpart, the House of Representatives, is somewhat — but only somewhat — less aristocratic in origins and occupations. Although it normally includes a few low-status occupations, it frequently has a higher proportion of lawyers. In general, it displays essentially the same income, status, and occupational characteristics as the Senate. The Supreme Court reflects a greater preponderance of high status backgrounds, in part because it has been made up of the upper echelons of the legal profession.

The executive branch, which most analysts see as now holding the important initiative and decisionmaking capacity within the federal government, displays some variations of the same basic characteristics. A major study covering 1,041 individuals who held 1,567 executive appointments from March 1933 through April 1965 was published in 1967 by the Brookings Institution.[10] The study reports that 39 per-

[10] David T. Stanley, Dean E. Mann, and Jameson W. Doig, *Men Who Govern* (Washington, D.C.: Brookings Institution, 1966).

cent of these leaders had gone to private school; the total for the Department of State was 60 percent. Upper-status origins are indicated also by the fact that 26 percent of all appointees were lawyers and 24 percent were businessmen at the time of appointment. Sixty-three percent of all Cabinet secretaries (86 percent of the military secretaries), 66 percent of all under secretaries, and 50 percent of all assistant secretaries were either businessmen or lawyers at the time of appointment.[11]

Other studies, focusing on smaller numbers of strategically-located decisionmakers, have produced findings which shed further light on the social backgrounds of executive officials. For one thing, a pattern of circulation appears to be developing, in which decisionmakers are neither men with lifelong careers in government service nor the close associates of the man who is elected to the presidency. Instead, they are men who move back and forth between the upper echelons of business or law and government. Historian Gabriel Kolko studied the backgrounds and career lines of 234 major decisionmakers in the foreign policy field during 1944 through 1960.[12] He found that men whose career origins were in big business, investment banking, or law held 60 percent of the positions involved in the study. Table 6, drawn from this study, shows that men with such origins held many more foreign policy positions than men who rose through the ranks of government service. The implication which Kolko draws is that an overlap of attitudes and interests can hardly fail to arise under such circumstances of circulation back and forth between business, law, and government.

Nor is the convergence of upper echelon personnel between government, business, banking, and law at any point a product of electoral decisions. In another study of top political decisionmakers, it was found that only 28 percent of the higher politicians in 1933-1953 rose largely because of elective offices; 62 percent were *appointed* to all or most of their political jobs before reaching top positions.[13] What is implied in these findings is that the executive branch represents an even higher status echelon than does the Congress, and one that is even further detached and insulated from popular electoral control. In part, this may be due to the increasing need for expert knowledge in the generation and implementation of government programs. But the apparent circulation of decisionmakers between government and the high-status, specialized occupations in the corporate, legal, and financial worlds occurs under both political parties, and seems to imply at least an opportunity for certain "private" preferences to exert significant influence.

What have we gleaned from this analysis of the social background characteristics of our two kinds of elites? The existence of a relatively small group of people who are specially favored with key resources

[11] These are apparently recalculations by Gabriel Kolko, in *The Roots of American Foreign Policy* (Boston: Beacon Press, 1969), note 6, p. 141.

[12] Kolko, *op. cit.*

[13] C. Wright Mills, *The Power Elite* (New York: Oxford University Press, 1956), p. 230.

TABLE 6
Occupational Origin of Individuals, by Number of Government Posts Held, 1944-60

Occupational origin	Individuals with four or more posts				Individuals with less than four posts			
	No. of individuals	% of all individuals	No. of posts held	% of all posts studied	No. of individuals	% of all individuals	No. of posts held	% of all posts studied
Law firms	12	5.1	55	8.1	33	14.1	72	10.6
Banking and investment firms	18	7.7	94	13.9	24	10.3	24	3.5
Industrial corporations	8	3.4	39	5.8	31	13.2	49	7.2
Public utilities and transportation companies	0	.0	0	.0	4	1.7	4	.6
Miscellaneous business and commercial firms	7	3.0	32	4.7	17	7.3	35	5.2
Nonprofit corporations, public service, universities, etc.	7	3.0	37	5.5	7	3.0	12	1.8
Career government officials (no subsequent non-government post)	15	6.4	85	12.5	11	4.7	19	2.8
Career government officials (subsequent non-government post)	8	3.4	38	5.6	12	5.1	13	1.9
Career government officials (subsequent non-government post and return to government post)	8	3.4	45	6.6	6	2.6	15	2.2
Unidentified	1	.4	5	.7	5	2.1	5	.7
Totals	84	35.8	430	63.4	150	64.1	248	36.5

Reprinted by permission of the Beacon Press, copyright © 1969 by Gabriel Kolko. From Gabriel Kolko, *The Roots of American Foreign Policy* (Boston: Beacon Press, 1969), p. 18.

of power seems established, as does the fact that men in the major positions of government are drawn chiefly from this group. We may infer, though it has by no means been established, that people in the general category of elite share some values and interests that are distinct from those of the majority of the people, and that governmental elites may also hold such commitments or unconscious perceptions. Sharing a high level of income, wealth, and status — and, most likely, coming from families with histories of similar standing — does not necessarily mean that even governmental elites will hold similar views on all matters. Indeed, at times their economic interests or their conceptions of the public interest may be diametrically opposed. The occasions and nature of the conflicts that result constitute one of the crucial issues of political analysis.

The pluralist view holds that conflicts among institutional elites are frequent, with resolution of major questions dealing with the basic directions of public policy awaiting electoral determination by the people. Supporting this view is evidence of the distinctive social backgrounds among subgroups of elites. For example, Andrew Hacker surveyed the backgrounds of the presidents (as of 1959) of the 100 largest industrial corporations, and compared them with the back-grounds of the 100 senators in 1959.[14] Presidents were somewhat more likely to have gone to private school (28 percent to 15 percent) and an Ivy League college (29 percent to 15 percent) than senators, and to have exchanged their town and state of origin for metropolitan resi-dence and national mobility. Hacker concluded that these and other similar findings helped to explain the existence of significant tensions between the major economic and political institutions. Without denying that conflicts do arise, the contrary view holds that such differences in origins and life experience, and in current institutional responsibilities, do not give rise to perceptions or preferences that are in conflict over fundamental questions. Both groups of men, for ex-ample, would be strongly defensive of orthodox political values, the present distribution of wealth, and the basic structure of the eco-nomic system. In this context, their differences would be over the particular shares to be distributed among established claimants, or over the means of more effectively serving such agreed ends.

The extent to which values and interests are in fact shared among elites, and if so, the extent to which such values and interests differ from those of the masses of nonelite people, are empirical questions. Inference from the existence of similar and distinctive social back-ground characteristics, while suggestive, is not conclusive. Similarly, the existence of internal conflicts between subgroups of elites can only be inferred from social background distinctions. On larger ques-tions, their essential homogeneity and difference from the mass pub-lic may be more determinative. In the next section, we shall make a start on analysis of potentially more conclusive attitudinal and be-havioral evidence.

THE PROBLEM OF ELITE VALUES AND ATTITUDES

The utility of socioeconomic background analysis lies in the gross comparison of the characteristics of one group of people with another (here, elites vs. nonelites). Sharp differences in backgrounds may lead to situations where the kinds of values and attitudes that devel-op also may differ consistently between the groups — as aggregates, at least. But, within such general confines, many other factors also contribute to shaping values and attitudes. For example, specialized family or personal experience, loyalties to political parties, occupa-tional role orientations, individual personality or ideology, or the characteristics of particular issues, may lead to a wide variety of specific priorities and preferences within each group. There may thus be many different configurations of political values and atti-tudes of members of even a relatively small group such as our general category of elites. The distinctiveness of resources and life style may even in some cases be overcome by such factors, so that an individual's political perceptions and orientations may resemble

[14] Andrew Hacker, "The Elected and the Anointed: Two American Elites," *The American Political Science Review*, vol. 55 (1961).

those of subgroups of the general population more than those of objectively "elite" persons. Unfortunately, little is known about the extent to which these apparently reasonable possibilities are actually borne out in practice.

Understanding of elite values and attitudes is inhibited by two types of problems. One is the inherent complexity of human belief systems and cognitive and perceptual processes. The subjective impact of apparently clear objective circumstances is apparently very different for different people; for some, it is direct and consistent, while for others it may seem to be completely reversed. The concept of socioeconomic status — class — illustrates this lack of "fit" between objective and subjective "reality." Subjective class identification is probably more relevant to attitudes and behavior than such objective factors as income, education, or status. But Americans are celebrated for holding subjective class identifications which contrast with the apparent implications of their actual socioeconomic circumstances. Before their values and attitudes can be understood, the presence and relative importance of such factors must be sorted out and characterized, along with the effects of other factors (political party loyalties, occupation, ideology) in regard to different subject areas and specific issues. Though we have barely begun to illustrate it, the complexity of the problem seems obvious.

The second problem has to do with the kinds of analytical tools and efforts that have been directed at the task. It may seem surprising, but very little survey analysis has been directed at elite values and attitudes; we know much more about mass sociopsychological processes than we do about that of elites, perhaps partly because of access problems. Values — the commitments of people to abstract but fundamental principles such as individualism or equality — are hard to explore in brief questionnaire surveys. For such information, there are only impressionistic accounts by the chroniclers of the upper class.[15] Survey-oriented social scientists tend to concentrate on more easily pin-pointed attitudes toward specific issues. But even in this area, information is very scarce. Surveys of national cross-sections of the population do turn up a proportionate number of people with high income, education, and status, and to an extent such data can be used to describe the attitudes of our general category of elites. But our category is relatively limited, and its members would be a very small number of even the highest income, education, and status group of national survey respondents. Better survey evidence is available at the community level, where researchers have more deliberately sought out the relatively wealthy; here also, however, the number of those high enough to fit into our general category of elite is very few.

[15] See, for example, Ferdinand Lundberg, *The Rich and The Super-Rich* (New York: Lyle Stuart, 1968) or E. Digby Baltzell, *Philadelphia Gentlemen: The Making of a National Upper Class* (Glencoe, Ill.: The Free Press, 1958).

In regard to institutional elites, the lack of reliable quantitative data is no less acute. Again, the best sources are the more or less impressionistic accounts of informed observers of particular institutions, processes, or individuals.[16] There are some careful survey studies of the attitudes (and, to some extent, the values) of specialized subgroups of elites, such as delegates to national presidential nominating conventions, corporation presidents, or community officials and leaders. Except for the corporation presidents, however, these institutional elites are at subordinate, rather than decisive national, levels of decisionmaking. For the values and attitudes of major national government elites, the best sources are the many case studies, memoirs, and biographies accumulated over the years. The product of their views and actions — the public policies followed by the government — may also shed some light on their values and attitudes; but, for many reasons that we shall explore in later chapters, it is a very gross and uncertain means of characterization.

In the paragraphs that follow, we shall use what evidence is available to sketch briefly the pattern of values and attitudes of both our general category of elites and that of institutional elites. In the final section, we shall fall back on the great body of qualitative research and journalistic observation, and extract some frankly speculative interpretations about elite orientations and style.

(a) The General Category of Elites

Drawing on a large body of national attitude research and studies of voting behavior, high socioeconomic status people may be broadly characterized as more informed, more ideologically oriented, and more involved in politics than others.[17] They are also distinguished by greater orientation to issues, greater support for the political system, and a higher sense of capability to affect action in politics. In general, they tend to hold conservative views on both domestic and international issues, although an identifiable minority is decisively liberal in regard to government services and civil rights.

To what extent do they conceive of themselves as a class distinct from others? In a national study made through the facilities of the American Institute of Public Opinion (Gallup Poll) in 1964, Lloyd Free and Hadley Cantril sought to explore class identifications.[18] They asked a cross-section of the population, "In the field of politics and government, do you feel that your own interests are similar to the

[16] The biographical and case study literature is vast; a particularly good example of perceptive revelation of values is Alpheus T. Mason, *Harlan Fiske Stone, Pillar of the Law* (New York: Viking Press, 1956).

[17] Unless otherwise noted, characterizations are drawn from Angus Campbell, Philip Converse, Donald Stokes, and Warren E. Miller, *The American Voter* (New York: John Wiley, 1960).

[18] Lloyd A. Free and Hadley Cantril, *The Political Beliefs of Americans: A Study of Public Opinion* (New York: Simon and Schuster, 1968), p. 18.

interests of the propertied class, the middle class, or the working class?" The responses were:

Propertied class	5%
Middle class	37%
Working class	53%
Don't know	5%
	100%

But this self-identification was not consistent with the respondents' other characteristics. The authors note:

... more than one-fourth of those with incomes of $10,000 a year or more identified their interests with the "working class," as they defined the term, while more than one-fifth of those with incomes under $3,000 associated themselves with the "middle class." Similarly, three out of ten of the professional and business group identified with the "working class," while more than one-third of the blue-collar workers saw themselves as members of the "middle class." [19]

The question nevertheless reveals some matters of importance. Very few people associate themselves with a "propertied class," but those who do display some distinctive characteristics. For example, the people who saw themselves in the propertied class were only 40 percent "liberal" on the authors' scale of support for various types of government assistance to ordinary people, while middle class people were 57 percent liberal and working class people were 74 percent liberal. Of the propertied class, 57 percent characterized themselves as either moderately conservative or very conservative, as compared to 35 percent of the middle class and 31 percent of the working class. Table 7 shows attitudes toward the use of government power and

TABLE 7
Class Identification, Attitudes Toward Government Power,
and Political Party Identification

	Propertied class	Middle class	Working class
Government power:			
Has too much	53%	33%	18%
About right as is	30	39	39
Should use more	16	25	34
Don't know	1	3	9
Political party:			
Republican	54%	33%	16%
Democratic	22	38	62
Independent	23	26	21
Other, don't know	1	3	1

Source: Free and Cantril, *The Political Beliefs of Americans* (New York: Simon and Schuster, 1968), pp. 218 and 234.

[19] *Ibid.*, pp. 17-18.

political party identification of the various self-described class levels. Given the thorough blurring of subjective class identification in the United States, and the enduring but frequently cross-cutting pull of long-established political party loyalties, these distinctions are fairly sharp. When we recall that this national survey could include only a small sprinkling of those actually high enough in income and status to be in our general category of elites, the implication is that class-based and distinctive policy orientations do in fact exist.

Some greater insight can be generated from focusing on special subgroups of elites, even though there is considerable risk in generalizing from small and possibly unique populations. One of the few studies which deliberately sought to include a large enough number of very wealthy people to be able to analyze their attitudes responsibly was conducted by two sociologists in a medium-sized (100,000) Michigan city.[20] Together with a random sample of the community, they included a special group of people whose income in 1960 placed them in the top one percent of wage earners (over $25,000) and, for comparison, a special group of poor people with incomes ranging from less than $2,000 upward, depending on the number of dependents involved. Among other queries, they asked all respondents to say which interest groups in the country ought to be most powerful in shaping government policy. Many people (44 percent of all respondents) volunteered that all should be equal. But 64 percent of poor blacks said that all should be equal, while 14 percent nominated labor unions and eight percent suggested some other group. Only 39 percent of rich whites, however, endorsed equal status for all groups, while 30 percent nominated big business for supremacy and 27 percent favored some other group. No poor black suggested priority for big business and no rich white endorsed priority for labor unions. The authors concluded tentatively that rich people are less egalitarian than the lower classes, preferring instead government by their own kind.

A more specific and tangible comparison is provided by answers to three questions about government assistance to poor and black citizens. Table 8 shows these results. The first question had to do with providing temporary incomes for poor people who would take job training, the second was a general one about all forms of assistance to the poor, and the last concerned the open housing provisions of recently enacted civil rights legislation. In each case, opposition rose with income. The rich whites were decisively more opposed to all three forms of government assistance, standing in stark contrast to black attitudes and substantially distinct even from middle income whites. It is possible to attribute too much significance to one study of a single city, of course, but the implication of distinctiveness again seems clear.

[20] William H. Form and Joan Rytina, "Ideological Beliefs on the Distribution of Power in the United States," *American Sociological Review,* vol. 34 (1969), pp. 19-31. The data in this paragraph are from p. 26.

TABLE 8
Opposition to Federal Help for Disadvantaged Strata (in percents)

Income	Race	Government should not pay poor to go to school (a)	Government has done too much for poor (b)	Government should stay out of open occupancy (c)
Poor	Negro	30	8	8
	White	46	23	62
Middle	Negro	17	15	8
	White	64	32	73
Rich	White	78	72	96
Total, analytic	%	52	31	57
sample	(N)	(350)	(351)	(344)

Reprinted from William H. Form and Joan Rytina, "Ideological Beliefs on the Distribution of Power in the United States," *American Sociological Review*, vol. 34 (1969), p. 28.

Other studies based on national surveys show distinctive attitudinal characteristics among the best-educated echelons. Because education generally correlates with pre-existing family income, these results are suggestive of at least the general direction of elite orientations (though not of the specific causal origins of particular attitudes). Higher education usually leads people to have greater confidence in and support for government action, possibly due to faith in the capabilities of technical experts or simply in the acts of people like themselves — or perhaps because educated people are more likely to read or hear about and absorb the explanations of government officials. At the same time, events or new pronouncements by government officials tend to have greater effect on highly educated people. An example of both parts of this apparent phenomenon may be seen in the trend of opinion regarding whether or not it was a mistake for the United States to become involved in the Vietnam War. Figure 2 presents the findings of the Gallup Poll as to the proportions of people of varying educational levels who, over a crucial three and a half year period, said that U.S. involvement was a mistake. Less educated people were more dubious at the start, while college people denied that an error had been made. As time went on, however, college people responded much more drastically, and by 1969 they believed that a mistake had been made in larger proportions than did less educated people. Many other issue areas display the same sequence of opinion change, and it is usually the most educated people who are both highly supportive of government action and most ready to change with shifts in government policy or new events.

FIGURE 2
Agreement That U.S. Involvement in Vietnam Was a Mistake, by Education Levels

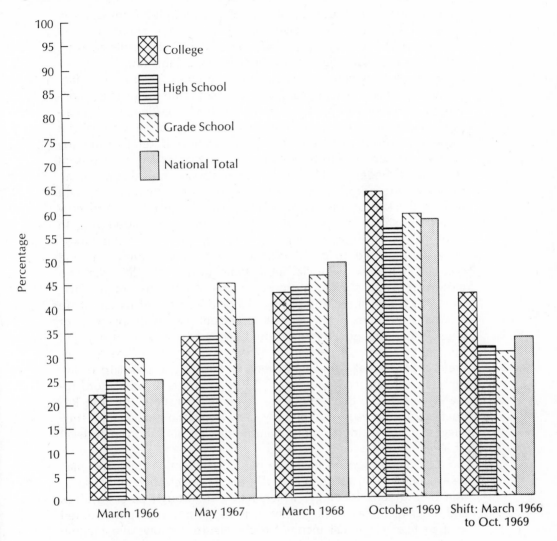

Source: *Gallup Opinion Weekly* (October, 1969), p. 15.

These general findings again imply a set of shared (conservative) values and attitudes among our general category of elites, but they are neither conclusive nor comprehensive. Nor do they imply that institutional elites, who (although usually drawn from this group) are by comparison a relatively small number of probably quite individualistic people, hold similar values and attitudes. Even if they did, of course, the institutional setting and responsibilities of the latter elites would introduce a potentially new set of factors between such attitudes and their behavior. Let us examine some of the limited evidence that focuses directly on such elites.

(b) Institutional Elites

Understandably, institutional elites are distinctly well-informed, issue-oriented, ideological, and self-confident about their ability to influence political outcomes. Although most of the survey evidence available deals with subgroups of institutional elites, this finding is characteristic of practically all research on such elites. Their basic values are also explored in some subgroup analyses. One major study contrasted the responses of delegates to the 1956 presidential nominating conventions of both the Democratic and Republican parties with those of a national cross-section of Democratic and Republican party voters.[21] As part of an effort to probe to what extent both sets of respondents understood and were committed to the value of equality, they were asked to agree or disagree with statements thought to be indicative of aspects of political, social and ethnic, and economic equality. The political equality statements turned out to measure chiefly political cynicism, and the political "influentials" (delegates) proved to be considerably less disenchanted than the voters. On matters of social and ethnic (racial) equality, the two groups were very similar. But on economic issues, the "influentials" were much less likely to feel that "labor does not get its fair share of what it produces" (21 percent agreement, versus 45 percent for voters); that "the government should give a person work if he can't find another job" (24 percent to 47 percent); and that "the government ought to make sure that everyone has a good standard of living" (34 percent to 56 percent.)[22] These contrasts are the more remarkable because they reflect the combined consensus of both Republican and (presumably more liberal) Democratic delegates. They suggest strong economic conservatism among this subordinate level of elites.

Economic conservatism on the part of convention delegates may be explained in part by their high degree of politicization and absorption of orthodox ideology, which may cut through party loyalties and otherwise relevant liberalism. It is also, we may assume, rooted in their highly atypical income levels. Figure 3 shows the income distribution of convention delegates in 1964, as reported by political scientists McKeough and Bibby. Almost 39 percent of the Republicans and 30 percent of the Democrats had incomes over $25,000, and thus they were among the top ten percent of American wage earners. The nominating conventions, moreover, are usually seen as one of the areas of political decisionmaking where lesser elites predominate. If this is true, it suggests that the higher elites may be even further removed as far as any form of representativeness in background or attitudes is concerned.

[21] Herbert McClosky, "Consensus and Ideology in American Politics," *The American Political Science Review*, vol. 58 (1964).
[22] *Ibid.*, Table 5.

FIGURE 3
Income Distribution of Convention Delegates, 1964

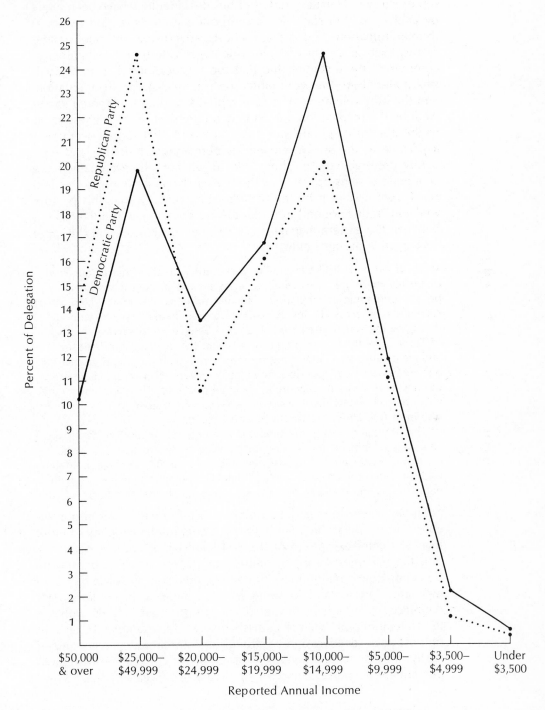

Source: Kevin L. McKeough and John Bilby, "The Costs of Political Participation" (Princeton, N.J.: Citizens Research Foundation, 1966), p. 84.

Another group of institutional elites for which attitudinal data are available is the upper echelon of businessmen, bankers, and other top executives. Detailed studies of business ideology have been made by analysis of the speeches of corporate presidents, and by long-term examinations of corporate reports, advertising, and public statements. Even in an era of large-scale organization and technological complexity, these studies find that top businessmen laud individualism, materialism, the work ethic, the free market, profit-orientation, and the other elements of classic capitalism. This is tempered somewhat by the recognition, particularly on the part of the highest levels of the eastern corporate and financial world, that some government assistance to the less advantaged is permanent, desirable, and eminently preferable as an alternative to what might eventuate if the economic system operated without such backup support. One excerpt from a speech by the president of I.B.M. typifies this posture well, illustrating not only attitudes toward government but the tension between the eastern managers of the larger businesses and the more conservative business elite:

Much as we may dislike it, I think we've got to realize that in our kind of society there are times when government has to step in and help people with some of their more difficult problems. Programs which assist Americans by reducing the hazards of a free market system without damaging the system itself are necessary, I believe, to its survival. . . .

To be sure, the rights and guarantees that the average man believes in and insists upon may interfere, to some degree, with our ability to manage our enterprises with complete freedom of action. As a result, there are businessmen who either ignore or deny these claims. They then justify their views by contending that if we were to recognize or grant them, the whole system of free enterprise would be endangered.

This, it would seem to me, amounts to an open invitation to exactly the kind of government intervention that businessmen are trying to avoid. For if we businessmen insist that free enterprise permits us to be indifferent to those things on which people put high value, then the people will quite naturally assume that free enterprise has too much freedom.[23]

Survey evidence regarding the same institutional elite is also available. *Fortune* magazine's 500 survey is a continuous sampling of more than 300 chief executives of the 500 largest industrial corporations, plus the 50 largest banks, insurance companies, retailers, transportation companies, and utilities.[24] It demonstrates that such top businessmen are alert to, and to some extent concur with, contemporary definitions of problems in the society. Confronted in 1969 with the flat statement that "we are a racist society," for example, 15 percent of these key executives agreed strongly and another 31 percent agreed partly; the comparable figures for a sample of college youth were 38 percent and 40 percent, and for all youths 18-24 years of age, 28 per-

[23] Thomas B. Watson, cited in Robert Heilbroner, *The Limits of Capitalism* (New York: Harper and Row, 1966), p. 34.

[24] *Fortune*, vol. 80, (September, 1969), contains a description of the sampling procedure and all the data reported here, with the exception of that comparing attitudes with youth, which are from the October, 1969 issue.

cent and 46 percent. When the issues turn to economic matters, however, the gap is much greater. Two-thirds of top businessmen saw fears of the military-industrial complex as greatly exaggerated and opposed shifting funds to domestic uses, at exactly the same time as 52 percent of a national Gallup Poll said that too much was being spent on defense and only eight percent said that such expenses were too low. The general pattern of similarity and difference between corporation presidents and national cross-sections may be seen from a comparison of their respective definitions of the greatest problems facing the United States in 1969, presented in Figure 4. The presidents were asked what were the "most pressing and critical problems" and the national sample was asked for the "most important problems." Despite some problems of comparability in categories and in respondents' propensity to give multiple responses, it seems clear that the top businessmen take a broader and more governmental overview, in which economic problems receive special attention. And their orientations toward solutions are distinctive also. When asked what level of unemployment they regarded as unacceptable under today's social and economic conditions, more than half of the responding executives gave answers of five percent and up. By contrast, national samples regularly rank economic security-insecurity as crucial hopes and fears. These differences in viewpoint are exactly what we would expect, given the institutional responsibility of the top executives. But this is just the point. Decisionmakers can only act on their perceptions — on what they understand to exist and require solution. If government actions are shaped by the circulation of elites from top levels of business to government, or by government officials who take their cues from businessmen's definitions, then such government actions will be in tune with public concerns on some issues but not on others. Whether they *should* be on any given issue, of course, is another question entirely.

The top businessmen also appear to be distinctively concerned about communism. Asked in 1969 whether the communist threat were greater or less than a decade earlier, 31 percent said it had increased, 41 percent said it was the same, and 26 percent said it had decreased.[25] Those who saw it as having decreased based their views chiefly on the decline of Soviet hostility and relative power on the international scene. Those who saw it as increasing, however, were thinking chiefly in terms of an internal threat; two-thirds of such respondents traced the rising danger to communist involvement in student and black protest movements.

Confirmation that institutional elites tend to be more fearful of the dangers of communism emerges also from the major study of American attitudes toward communism and tolerance for unorthodox political behavior, Samuel Stouffer's *Communism, Conformity, and Civil Liberties*.[26] Conducted at the height of Senator Joseph McCarthy's

---

[25] *Ibid.*

[26] Samuel A. Stouffer, *Communism, Conformity, and Civil Liberties* (New York: Doubleday, 1955). Page citations from the Science Editions paperback, (New York: John Wiley, 1966).

FIGURE 4
Definitions of Greatest Problem Facing U.S.
(Corporation Presidents and National Cross-Section, 1969)

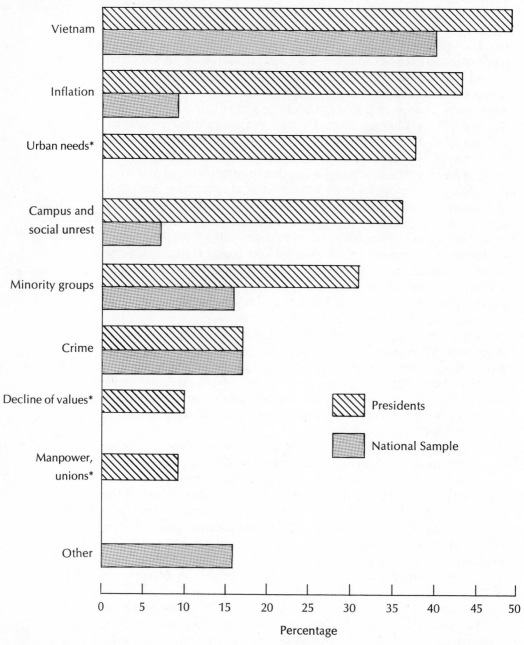

Source: Corporation presidents, *Fortune* 500 survey, September, 1969. National sample, Gallup Opinion Weekly, March, 1969.

*Not asked of national sample .

anticommunist activity in the 1950's, this study sampled a national cross-section and selected community leaders in small cities across the country. The community leaders, local rather than national institutional elites, nevertheless saw communism as a more pressing problem and a greater threat than did ordinary citizens, very few of whom saw it as a threat at all. By a nearly two-to-one majority, they expected communism to be rooted in the lower classes and the less educated. And they were much more likely than average citizens to view communists as "crackpots," "queer people," or "warped personalities." [27]

But the most salient finding of the latter study, and one that is repeated wherever the investigation has been made, is that institutional elites appear more tolerant of unorthodoxy and more supportive of the democratic liberties of free speech and assembly than do ordinary citizens.[28] It may be attributable merely to a quicker recognition of the relation of hypothetical situations to standards of civil liberty, more elaborate ideology, greater confidence in capacity to manage events, or a sense of responsibility as public officials. Or it may be that education and socialization in the life of politics have promoted genuine respect for the rules of the game of democratic politics. In any event, elites uniformly display greater endorsement of the traditional civil liberties than do nonelites; what they *do* in particular circumstances, of course, is another question.

These findings about the values and attitudes of institutional elites substantially exhaust the available evidence. The themes they suggest include a generally conservative class-shared attitudinal posture which emphasizes economic problems and priorities but encompasses such civil liberties as racial equality and established procedures as well. We may have what one political scientist called an "activist subculture," [29] in which wealth and status is high, ideology well developed, and both interest and confidence in managing government are marked. This does not suggest insensitivity to what others in the society want, but rather the rudiments of consensus on how, when, and to what extent such desires should be served. We shall expand on these scattered impressions in the next section.

THE NATURE AND IMPLICATIONS OF THE AMERICAN "ESTABLISHMENT"

What follows is a frankly speculative extraction from patterns in the foregoing evidence, many exhaustive case studies and biographies, and our own political experience and intuition. We think that the character of leadership in the American political system may fairly be characterized as an "establishment," if the proper definitions are used, and that this situation carries profound implications for both the structure of power and the process of change in the United States.

[27] *Ibid.,* pp. 172-175.
[28] *Ibid.,* Chap. 2. See also McClosky, *op. cit.*
[29] V. O. Key, Jr., *Public Opinion and American Democracy* (New York: Alfred A. Knopf, 1961), Chap. 21.

The concept of an "establishment," though vague and subject on occasion to images of conspiracy, has an expressiveness which justifies its use. For us the term encompasses that large proportion of men holding positions of power (in government *and* in private affairs) who have come to share roughly the same values, interests, political ideology, and sense of priorities about what government should be doing. Most of all, "establishment" denotes the sense of shared proprietary concern for the continued success of the enterprise — meaning the American system, in its familiar social, economic, and political dimensions. Admission to the "establishment" is not easy, and it is never automatic. Instead, it is contingent first upon possession of some distinct power resource, such as institutional position (in politics, business, education, etc.), talent, money, family status, and so forth. Among the many with such resources, some are distinguished by their concern for the success of the enterprise (the American political order in all essential outlines), their willingness to play by the familiar rules, and their talent for finding and articulating the compromise or making the sacrifice that insures conflict reduction. These are the crucial attributes. It is such men to whom established leaders will reach out and invite into membership in the loose and highly informal "establishment." Members recognize each other not by labels or lapel pins, but by the orthodoxy they share; for example, the readiness with which they can negotiate with each other, even across class lines or occupational boundaries. Establishment types are "regular guys" who try to understand the other fellow's problems, avoid "rocking the boat" publicly, and instead do what they can to reach accommodations in which all end up better off than when they started. Mutual trust, mutual support, and mutual advantage knit the establishment together; but it is never so self-conscious and coherent as when challenges arise to the very system which has made possible this relaxed and congenial arrangement.

The establishment recognizes its antagonists on both left and right, uses their complaints to demonstrate its own middle-road propriety, but acts against them only when they "go too far." In part, this is because the establishment has loose margins at either side, with some useful part-time members moving back and forth, and it prefers to act only at such late stages that practically all its members and identifiers will concur that "something must be done." (This was true, for example, when conservatives took the lead in the late stages of undermining Senator Joseph McCarthy in the 1950's, and it was true again when liberals formed the cutting edge of prosecution of radicals and peace movement leaders in the 1960's.) Within the establishment itself, consensus is highly valued. But men may disagree on occasion, particularly over the *best* route by which to preserve the system in times of crisis, without risking their membership unless their convictions lead them to take anti-system instead of system-preserving actions.

Thus our concept of "establishment" envisions no unified upper social class dominating the nation's political structure, though great wealth and upper class connections give many the beginning platform from which they can achieve such a status. Nor do we envision economic imperatives as the sole or even prime determinants of establishment actions, though in the absence of compelling reasons to the contrary they will often be the "natural" principles of behavior. We do not even envision much explicit consultation among establishment members about positions to take on forthcoming issues, though this is partly because none is necessary. Our concept of an establishment is, therefore, not the tight ruling group of some elite theories, but neither is it the benevolent representative theory of some democratic pluralists. Our establishment ranges between the two, depending on the type of issue involved. On most everyday, routine issues and decisions, it may function much as the latter view would expect. But on fundamental questions, or when the system itself is threatened, it acts in ways characteritic of the former.

Nor is our model of an "establishment" here intended as our final characterization of the American structure of power. It is no more than a working hypothesis, grounded in a substantial but not conclusive body of evidence. But it carries vital implications concerning the process of political change in the United States.

We do not imply that there is necessarily anything sinister about this "establishment." We do not even suggest that this group is doing anything conspiratorially, or even contrary to the public interest. But the clear evidence of government decisionmaking dominated by a small and circulating elite consisting chiefly of the upper echelons of big business, banking and investment, and the law, most of whom share many social and economic background characteristics, lends credibility to the hypothesis. We asserted our belief that men in government shared certain orthodox values and ideology also held by men at the top in private affairs, and that such values and ideology led them to mutual support for the established rules of the game of politics and particularly to a shared concern for the preservation of the basic outlines of the economic and political systems. We have not "proved" this assertion, nor can we from the evidence which is available. But the similarity of background and interest, together with the opportunity and access available, implies strongly that shared ideology and shared concern for defense of the system is likely to exist at this level. On fundamental questions, in other words, we expect nearly all members of the establishment to be of one mind — i.e., that the American system as it now operates should be preserved in all its essential characteristics.

But social background and shared responsibility for the management of public affairs are not the only factors operating to cause decisionmakers at this level to see issues from a single perspective. Most men in key positions are of roughly the same generation, and they thus became politically "aware" at the same period in American history. All of us tend to be structured permanently by what was happening in politics at the time we happened to tune in to such matters. For one generation, Vietnam has meant opposition to a callous and wasteful foreign policy. For many of their teachers, however, political socialization occurred during the early days of the Cold War or the late years of World War II, when one did not question the need to defend the "free world" and resist the spread of communism. For those who made up the establishment in the 1960's, the structuring experiences dated back to the pre-World War II failures at containing Hitler, and they showed that they remembered those lessons. The analogy to Munich and the inevitable failure of appeasement was offered again and again as a rationale for policy in Vietnam. The image of international communism as a unified, monolithic force was shared by most decisionmakers. Thus, wherever trouble broke out in the world, including the United States, the guiding hand of Moscow was discerned. An oft-cited classic example is the allegation of Dean Rusk, made two years after the Chinese Revolution while he was in charge of Far Eastern operations for the State Department, that Mao Tse Tung was a Russian agent. Mao's regime, he asserted, was "a colonial Russian government — a Slavic Manchukuo on a large scale — it is not the government of China. It does not pass the first test. It is not Chinese." [30] The point is not that any man can be wrong on occasion. It is that each generation shares a basic image of what is going on in politics, and what is likely to happen, which is largely produced by the lessons they perceive to be drawn from experiences at the outset of their careers. As such, the establishment of the 1960's and 1970's shares an understanding of the world which comes from the 1940's and before.

The convergence and rigidification of beliefs and principles of action among the top echelon of decisionmakers is further aided by some characteristic features of large-scale organizations. Once a position has been taken and the organization has become committed to it in terms of allocation of resources and the career investments of personnel at various ranks, it is very difficult to modify its methods, purposes, or actions. Many large agencies of the national government, such as the FBI or the State Department, are now committed to a view of the world, a set of procedures, and an understanding of how things should work, that reflect and support the establishment's principles. They see, and report to their superiors, that which is consistent with their expectations and career aspirations. One classic example of the triumph of organizational commitments over evidence is the experience of strategic bombing during World War II.[31] The Air Force and its supporters had insisted for years that bombing could by itself destroy German war production, cripple the armed forces, and eliminate the German people's will to fight. The U.S. Air Force accordingly had been designed and trained for strategic bombing, which was carried out with high optimism and massive loads of explosives. But, according to the careful post-war Strategic Bombing Survey undertaken by the Air Force itself, strategic bombing never seriously affected war production, had little or no effect on the capacity of

---

[30] Dean Rusk; as quoted in Ronald Steel, *Pax Americana* (New York, Viking, 1967), p. 129. In 1961, Rusk became Secretary of State, serving in that capacity until 1969.

[31] This account is drawn from Herbert Wilensky, *Organizational Intelligence: Knowledge and Policy in Government and Industry* (New York: Basic Books, 1967), pp. 24-34.

the armed forces or the will of the population, and incurred heavy losses into the bargain. Intelligence failures, equipment failures, and faulty analyses of the German economy and society were also involved, but the chief conclusion was simply the incapacity of bombing to accomplish the goals set for it. The same conclusion was arrived at from a similar official study in Japan after the end of hostilities there. But the Vietnamese experience suggests that lessons about the limited capabilities of air power have still not been learned.

An establishment of relatively small size thus experiences many self-confirming and supporting messages from its environment. Its approach to politics and its view of the world are validated from almost every trusted source — in bureaucratic memoranda, in the communications media, and at the country club. Attitudes and practices may, under such circumstances, become hardened. Supported by the belief in the rightness of their actions, and even in the sacred nature of their responsibility to defend the system against those who would undermine it, members of the establishment may become highly resistant to basic change.

But this does not mean that they are insensitive or inflexible. Indeed, long-term stability is promoted by short-term flexibility (within limits) and adroit channeling of thrusts toward change — in part through judicious use of available coercive power. Although one major characteristic of the establishment is its shared basic beliefs and principles of political action, it would be a gross misinterpretation to see such agreement extending to rigidity of *membership* or of *specific policies*. Indeed, one of the most stability-producing features of American ideology and practice — of the American system, in other words — is its flexibility. By opening itself to new members, to new ideas, and to new policies, the American system incorporates thrusts toward change into its upper-level consensus. *Such new members, ideas, and policies must, however, accept the basic framework of political values, ideology, structure, and style on which that system is based.* To the extent that they do, of course, extra-systemic movements for change are effectively blunted. Popular movements lose their leaders and their platforms. New government policies include enough of their proposals so that progress seems evident and reasons for unusual political activity no longer exist.

The process by which rising leaders with new ideas or programs are drawn into the establishment is known as *cooptation.* Many aspiring young men seek leadership positions and try to display their ideas and talents in order to put themselves in a position where they can become candidates for cooptation. Others find that their efforts on behalf of a particular constituency gain attention and produce opportunities to take on governmental responsibility and carry out some of the programs they have been urging. In both cases, establishment-arranged appointments to offices or aid in electoral advancement leads to rise in stature and responsibility. The sobering consequences of responsibility then combine with the real difficulties of achieving goals through the many labyrinths of this complex political process, and the candidate is induced to practice the skills of accommodation and mutual support that are the hallmark of the establishment. If he shows these skills and his concern for the maintenance of the essential outlines of the system, he will rise further; if he does not, he will soon decide to leave government, thereby losing his prospective establishment status. Cooptation does not mean that the new leader gives up his independence, ideas, or program entirely. He retains substantial proportions of each, but learns to adapt them into the framework of the established system so that they are compatible with it. He frequently does succeed in changing things, if he is a skillful advocate of his causes, but not as much as he might originally have wished (and for reasons which he — and we — might rightly consider fully persuasive). The directions of public policy may shift in response to such initiatives after strenuous efforts by the new leader, his supporters, and the new allies his establishment status has opened up for him. When the process has run its course, some new policies have been instituted; the basic complaints against the system have been reduced; the establishment has absorbed new members and the system has acquired new defenders. The basic outlines of the system have again survived. Flexibility in the short run, in other words, means permanence in the long run.

Other types of flexibility also contribute to the stability of the American political system. Many layers of government mean many possible alternative ways to achieve particular goals, and those who seek ends not acceptable to men in power may be directed from one government to another, from one type of approach to another, or from one branch, committee, or department to another. Demands which at first seem indigestible or extreme may be converted into another form and thereby rendered satisfiable. A minority group's claim for status and recognition may be salved by appointment of a prominent leader to a visible position, or by the naming of a public monument or park in their honor. Or, if not quieted by such costless tactics, they may be diverted by displacing their claims into aggression against another minority religious or racial group. Some claims can be converted into economic demands, or largely settled in such terms. The materialistic orientation of the people and the abundance of the economy have made this a recurring tactic throughout American history. By merely increasing the size of the total economic product and directing the new surplus toward the demanding group, their claims could be satisfied without depriving those who were already advantaged of any of their possessions or expectations. In the history of labor-management conflicts, for example, an increase in total production and therefore total profits (or an increase in price to the consumer) made it possible to grant higher wages without reducing owners' returns. Workers, for their part, tended to be satisfied by higher wages and to abandon any other goals such as control over the means of production themselves.

Flexibility is thus a means of absorbing, blunting, and deflecting thrusts toward change. But flexibility does not operate alone as a system characteristic which promotes stability. It operates in tandem with other factors which induce or compel behavior into the established channels which invoke it. American political ideology emphasizes procedural regularity, and insists upon working through the means provided for the attainment of political goals. The "law and order" ethic legitimates action against those who do not follow such prescribed procedures. And, under conditions of the late twentieth century, the official agencies of law enforcement have a vast monopoly of the power that is necessary to compel obedience. Thus there is a considerable array of inducements at work to direct political activity into forms which can be dealt with by the established order without serious threat.

In effect, the political system offers many routes by which to seek one's goals, most of which lead to conversion of those goals into forms compatible with the basic outlines of the system. Its flexibility tends to absorb both leaders and goals, and to result in incrementally modified elites and policies. Many pressures channel political action into these approved forms, and when they fail there are both accepted grounds for legal compulsion and the requisite power to authoritatively prevent disobedience. Against this resourceful complex of containing forces and the broad support they apparently invoke from wide segments of the population, it is very difficult to generate fundamental change.

Over the years, these factors have helped to render the American system stable — not in itself an undesirable characteristic for a political system to enjoy. Most people probably would assess the costs of this stability (in terms of lost opportunities, unfulfilled aspirations, poverty for some, etc.) as entirely tolerable. To many, stability is the highest priority in politics. Whether stability continues to be equally desirable today, when measured against perhaps greater costs and more challenging conditions, is a more acute and more controversial question. After an extended period of stability, unabsorbed pressures for change may build to explosive potential. Or issues may arise which even the most flexible system finds difficulty in containing.

9 The Constitution: Structure, Symbol, and Resultant Political Style

Very few of the present effects of constitutional provisions are necessarily inherent in the words of the document itself. Some parts of it are strictly followed, but some are outrageously tortured to authorize the doing of acts not only unimagined by, but anathema to, the original Framers. In nearly 200 years of spirited goal-seeking by individuals, groups, and other entities with influence in politics, the original values and preferences of the Framers have interacted with shifting balances of power to produce a Constitution which is more an accumulation of traditions and styles of behavior than a written document.

The present Constitution is a partly-enabling, partly-legitimating construct in the minds of political elites, with some echoes filtering through into the general public. From time to time, the Constitution takes a tangible form, as when a Supreme Court decision operates to change relationships among political actors, or when a third-party presidential candidate appears likely to gain enough votes to force an election into the House of Representatives. In each case, other actors who are sufficiently motivated and powerful may exercise their

242

influence to revise the effects of the original manifestation of the Constitution in their favor. Congress may modify the Supreme Court's decision, or the two major parties may make an agreement to cast some of their votes to the other so as to foreclose the third party's chances of gaining leverage. Provisions of the document only set the initial stage on which the interplay of power among political actors takes place. Some actors are enabled to get what they wanted by means of those provisions, or through the initial interpretation of them, while others have an action which they have already taken legitimated by the same process. Thus, the real determinants of what is to happen are found in the relative power of participants, and the Constitution is only one of several tools for political actors to use in search of their ends.

But this is not to say that the Constitution is meaningless with respect to who gets what and how in American politics. The express provisions of the document and authoritative interpretations by Congress, Court, President, and other institutions are persuasive and sometimes conclusive devices in shaping political action. Men in government as well as the general public may be persuaded of the necessity or desirability of an action if it is associated with the Constitution, and they frequently seek to conform their behavior to constitutional norms when the latter do not conflict with their goals and preferred methods. Let us look at several illustrations of the effects of constitutional provisions on the practice of politics today, as a means of establishing the range of consequences which the Constitution has on both politics and public policies in the contemporary context.

CONTEMPORARY EFFECTS OF CONSTITUTIONAL PROVISIONS

The Inability to Act

Perhaps most readily demonstrated of all consequences is the Constitution-caused incapacity on the part of the national government to perform various types of actions normally associated with governments in the modern world. In the early years of the United Nations, for example, many of its members considered that a proper goal of a purportedly civilized international community would be to assure that such barbaric acts as Hitler's systematic extermination of more than 6,000,000 Jews did not recur. In this first flush of post-World War II idealism, a multination treaty known as the Genocide Convention was drawn up. It provided in relevant part:

In the present convention, genocide means any of the following acts committed with intent to destroy, in whole or in part, a national or religious, ethnic or religious group, as such:
(a) Killing members of the group;
(b) Causing serious bodily or mental harm to members of the group;
(c) Deliberately inflicting on the group conditions of life calculated to bring about its physical destruction in whole or in part; . . .[1]

[1] Article II, Convention of the Prevention and Punishment of the Crime of Genocide (Resolution 260 of December 9, 1948, U.N. doc. A/810, p. 174).

If the signatory nation failed to prosecute the officials, individuals, or groups engaging in the act of genocide, an international tribunal would be empowered to do so; there would thus be no problem of legitimacy as occurred with the Nuremburg Trials in 1946. Forty-odd nations of the world ratified the convention in fairly short order, and some saw it as a step toward acknowledgment of community responsibility for raising the moral standards of nations' behavior. When the treaty was presented to the United States Senate for approval, however, it was referred to the Judiciary Committee and never again heard of. No hearings were held, nor was it the subject of serious consideration at any time. This was not just the work of recalcitrant Southerners: few others were willing to come out for the treaty, despite its clear purposes, because it might have been construed to cover attacks on Negroes. In such a case, attempts to apply it in the United States would run afoul of several constitutional incapacities. For example, the Sixth Amendment provides for a trial in the district where the alleged crime was committed, and by a jury of one's peers. International tribunals would hardly qualify under those limits. Further, the national government has no constitutional power to define acts as crimes unless they come within the scope of some other granted power. In other words, the national government cannot make murder a federal crime generally, though it can make murder of a federal official engaged in the pursuit of his duty a crime because it has power to carry out the tasks assigned to it and that particular murder would be an interference with its assigned task. Thus, the treaty provided a means whereby the national government and not the states would be defining crimes, and this too ran contrary to established constitutional limitations. For these reasons, the United States declined to entertain the Genocide Convention, despite the urging of other nations.

Nor is this type of incapacity an isolated episode. For many years in the 1960's, civil rights workers attempting to register black voters in the South were harrassed and intimidated by local whites, sometimes to the extent of beatings and murder. Appeals to state law enforcement authorities were unavailing, on occasion because these were the very persons engaged in the intimidation. Appeals to the federal government, however, were equally unavailing. In the absence of federal power to make such local acts a crime, the only constitutional power of the national government extended to such specific acts as preventing a citizen from voting or having his vote counted, and did not include murder or beatings of those who sought to encourage citizens to vote. In several cases, FBI agents stood powerlessly by while (state) crimes were committed; the extent of the FBI agent's capacity was to conduct investigations to see if any federal laws had been broken. In effect, individual citizens were left entirely on their own in a hostile environment.

Instances of this kind might be multiplied indefinitely, but the point has been made. Perhaps it is also clear that the lack of constitutional power was not the *only* cause of these patterns of national government inaction: the preferences of some political actors strongly supported inaction, and there was apparently not enough motivation or strength in those who favored action to reverse the trend. Constitutional incapacity was a convenient and persuasive means to prevent an act which many actors opposed. That this need not always be the result, or at least not when there is general agreement about the desirability of the end, may be seen from the next illustration.

Auxiliary Means to Agreed Ends

Where a sufficient number of relevant political actors care enough, it is usually possible to achieve desired goals despite apparent constitutional incapacities. One of the conclusions emerging from the celebrated crime investigations of the early 1950's was that the individual states were unable or sometimes unwilling to cope with organized local betting rings, and that federal support would encourage or embarrass them into action. But as we have seen, there is no federal power to make local acts crimes, and of course the FBI can only investigate those matters so as to discover if there are some related aspects over which the national government has jurisdiction. In this instance, however, there was a will to act, and so a way was found; the constitutional authority to raise revenue was drawn upon, and a $50 tax laid on all bookmakers in the country. Those who paid the tax and filed an address to which the revenue stamp would be sent were promptly reported to the local police, and a follow-up could be made to see whether the local police had acted or not. If a bookmaker elected not to pay the tax, of course, he was in default of a legal obligation to the federal government and could legitimately be made the subject of direct FBI investigation, and ultimately prosecuted not for bookmaking but for failure to pay the tax and obtain the stamp.[2] National government capacity to gain agreed ends was in this case limited only by the priority given to the prosecution of cases and the financial investment (in bookmaker-investigation personnel) which the Congress was willing to make.

Although the means are somewhat awkward, the national government gains capacity to do many things through this or similar types of rationalization. In the early years of the twentieth century, for example, one of the major goals of social welfare advocates was the elimination of child labor. Efforts to obtain prohibitory laws from the states, which had clear constitutional power to legislate such statutes, were generally unavailing. This was sometimes because state legislatures were under the influence of the very industries over which regulation was sought. Or they were reluctant to put the industries in their particular state under a competitive disadvantage by forcing them to pay higher wages than companies in other states. The movement therefore turned to the national government, but found that the only available federal power was that regulating interstate commerce. Under then-current Supreme Court definitions of "interstate commerce" (the Framers having failed to provide any

[2] *United States* v. *Kahriger*, 345 US 22 (1952), is the Supreme Court decision which upheld this arrangement.

clues to the meaning of the term), the mere act of production in a factory did *not* make it "in commerce" and was therefore outside the scope of federal power. But a resourceful Congress nevertheless enacted a law which forbade the *shipment across state lines* of any goods which had been made with child labor, thereby achieving nearly the same ends as if it had possessed the power to eradicate child labor in the first place. An equally resourceful Supreme Court, however, held that the statute was too palpable in its intent and was therefore void as being in excess of Congressional powers.[3] And so the matter rested [4] — the political system being powerless to legally eliminate the practice of child labor — until a new and bolder Congress enacted an analogous statute which sought to regulate labor relations in factories. A newly chastened Supreme Court then reversed past precedent and upheld such regulations as a legitimate aspect of the commerce power.[5] Since then, the congressional imagination and the Supreme Court's acquiescence have pushed the definition of commerce to the point where Congress can now constitutionally require little luncheonettes in the backwoods of Georgia to serve blacks, even if the luncheonette never sees a person who is traveling in interstate commerce and never buys supplies from another state. The theory which sustains constitutional power is that even though the luncheonette itself is not "in commerce," it has an "effect" on commerce because people who eat in the luncheonette do not go to eat in restaurants which *are* in commerce.[6] If this sounds like an elaborate way to say that the Supreme Court is currently unwilling to limit congressional power to regulate commerce, consider the case which provided the basis for the decision just described. A farmer who was growing his full quota of grain under crop limitations (an exercise of the commerce power) decided to grow more, solely for his own use in feeding his chickens and not for sale anywhere. He was held to be in violation of the limitations on growing nevertheless, because the grain he grew himself he would not buy in commerce, and he thereby had "an effect" on commerce and came within the congressional power.[7]

In these instances, constitutional incapacities were overcome, though at the cost of some awkwardness of means and administration, and at the cost of some rational credulity as far as the Supreme Court is concerned. The support of enough sufficiently influential and strategically located interests committed to the goals of the policies involved was what enabled a different result to be obtained than in the former series of illustrations. Both strength and location of supporters is critical, for the Supreme Court (or other institutions

---

[3] The case was *Hammer* v. *Dagenhart,* 247 US 251 (1918).

[4] A constitutional amendment to authorize child labor laws was passed by the Congress, but it did not receive ratification by a sufficient number of states to become effective.

[5] *National Labor Relations Board* v. *Jones & Laughlin Steel Corporation,* 301 US 1 (1937).

[6] *Heart of Atlanta Motel* v. *Maddox,* 379 US 241 (1964).

[7] *Wickard* v. *Filburn,* 317 US 111 (1942).

on occasion) can block attainment of some ends for considerable periods of time (though clearly not permanently).

The States and the Nation

The Constitution makes broad allocations between the states and the national government of the power to tax various types of goods and activities. A brief tracing of the consequences of these allocations suggests another dimension of impact of constitutional provisions on contemporary politics. Since the states retained power to tax all objects within their jurisdictions except imports, the national government was effectively foreclosed from tapping the most lucrative source of income — property, including both land and personal property. But as the need for governmental revenue grew, and the states encountered severe resistance from property-taxed citizens, the national government's end of the bargain began to look better. The income tax provided a means for acquiring revenue which was sufficiently removed from the taxpayer as to be relatively immune to resistance. Further, the national government ran none of the risks that a state did when it sought to reach taxable resources within its boundaries. States, on the other hand, were constantly faced with a competitive situation in which other states would offer tax benefits to encourage industries to move from one state to another. Many states, therefore, were naturally reluctant to take full advantage of the resources which were available lest the company become aggrieved and move elsewhere. Thus, a provision originally designed to prevent the garnering of enough revenue to overawe the states ultimately had the reverse effect, due to changed economic conditions.

By the mid-twentieth century, the federal revenue-raising capacity was so much greater and more efficient than that of the states that some form of centralization was practically necessitated. Even with grants-in-aid to the states and other more drastic revenue-sharing proposals, it was clear that revenue-raising capacity alone would mandate federal involvement in (if not control over) the activities of governments in the country for the foreseeable future. What had begun as a deliberate scheme to promote a decentralized-government purpose had ended as a powerful inducement to centralization. In this and other ways, economic developments have out-dated and reversed precise constitutional provisions. The provisions themselves are well observed, but the consequences are far from what the Framers intended.

The Constitution as a Determinant of the Character of Party Politics

Observers of American politics are fond of characterizing the two major political parties as decentralized, locally-oriented coalitions of divergent elements which coalesce only in the few months before a presidential election. Because of this, the American party system is capable of promoting intraparty compromise and moderation, but less effective in providing coherent linkage between the wishes of majorities and government action in that image. These characteristics of party politics are caused in important ways by some very basic structural provisions of the Constitution: federalism, separation of powers, and the electoral college.

Federalism refers to the division of powers between constituent units (the states) and a single central unit (the national government) such that each has defined powers and is supreme in its own allotted sphere. It implies a balance and a certain amount of tension between the two, with the deliberate purpose of permitting local majorities or other interests not dominant in the central government a base of power from which to seek their own ends. Although the Constitution does not expressly provide for federalism as such, it does confirm it as a fact of life (indeed, the Framers had no choice, given the independence and power of the states in 1787) and does specify the powers and obligations of each level of government to the other. That is all it needs to do, however, for several natural effects immediately follow: the presence of real power to do important things at the state level means that political actors who seek the benefits of government action, as well as men who seek power, must focus on the states. Those who are successful in controlling or influencing the actions of a state government for their own ends have a strong vested interest in maintaining and defending that control, and therefore the political parties in each state may well become more concerned about state affairs than national affairs. State elections and the subsequent uses of state patronage (both jobs and contracts) are frequently more vital to political party activists than are national issues, candidates, or policies. Because each state party contains a distinctive set of interests and particular priorities about its needs, the national party is reduced to not much more than a very loose coalition of 50 state parties, each with a divergent view of what the national party should do and why it should do it. Party activists, used to a local struggle for control of their major source of rewards and benefits, retain their localism and private-interest attitudes even when they enter the national political arena. The fact of federalism almost by itself mandates internal divisions and conflict within the major political parties, and it assures a decentralized and locally-oriented ethos as well.

Separation of powers refers to the division of specific national government powers among the institutions of the national government. A more accurate description of the actual distribution of powers in the American system would be "separated institutions sharing powers." [8] This is because the separation is not accomplished precisely according to the nature of the power, but rather each type of power (legislative, executive, judicial) is scattered among the major institutions. The President, for example, has the (legislative) power of veto, and the Senate has the (executive) power of confirming ap-

[8] This apt phrase was coined by Richard Neustadt in his *Presidential Power: The Politics of Leadership* (New York: John Wiley, 1960).

pointments of ambassadors and department heads. Most of the legislative powers of the national government, of course, are located in the Congress, most of the judicial in the Supreme Court, and so on. What the separation of powers does is to assure that the power of government is placed in several hands, each of which is linked to a distinctive constituency. The probability is high that the several constituencies represented will not share the same values nor the same priorities about what government ought to be doing, and conflict will inevitably result over all but the most innocuous questions. Although many men in government may belong to the same political party, the fact that they are located in different institutions and responding to distinctive constituencies leads them to disagree with each other. Thus, the party is divided again, and not even its national officeholders share a clear position on its programs. Instead, each fragment of the party claims that its views are representative of the entire party, and then proceeds to seek allies from within the other party who may share the particular views of that fragment on a given issue. Separation of powers in effect assures internal conflict among the officeholders of both the majority and the minority in the national government, and encourages attempts at temporary alliances between like-minded elements across party lines.

The electoral college is one of the Framers' peculiar compromises, a device which allots ballots for President and Vice-President among the states according to the size of the state's total congressional delegation (two for each, representing the two senators, plus an additional number equivalent to the number of representatives from that state in the House of Representatives). In order to maximize its weight in national party circles, each state has provided that all of its ballots will go to the winner of the popular vote for President in that state. This means that the heavily populated states (the urban and industrial states such as New York and California) represent very critical prizes in the eyes of any presidential candidate. The gain or loss of a few votes in those states could mean the difference between gaining or losing large blocs of electoral ballots, while the smaller states represent much lower risks and opportunities. Consequently, presidential candidates become specially tuned to the needs and goals (and ethnic minorities) of the urban states, with important effects on both the character of the political parties and the government itself. For example, both political parties become split between the urban-(and liberal-) oriented presidential candidates and their supporters on the one hand, and the more rural (and conservative) orientation of the party's congressional officeholders and small state members on the other. Within the government, the split continues — with a President forced to contend with reluctance and opposition from his own party colleagues in his efforts to obtain the kinds of programs which are sought by his special urban constituencies. For the political parties, the electoral college means an inevitable source of internal divisions.

But there are some compensating returns from the electoral college structure, at least for the two major parties. Just because the electoral college works on a winner-take-all basis in each state, it makes it difficult for a new third party to compete successfully for the single most important prize in politics, the presidency. To have a chance to win the presidency, a party must seek to gain a majority of votes in the electoral college for its candidate. This means that the new party must try to build a base in *all* the states, not just a particular region in which its candidates might be very popular, because no one region can produce enough electoral votes to make up a majority of the electoral college ballots. In trying to compete in all the states, however, the new party runs into difficulties in getting on the ballot, great financial burdens, and the prospect that one or the other of the two established parties will have a majority support in most states anyhow. Thus the electoral college, by shifting the actual decision in the presidential election from total popular vote to a winner-take-all, state by state system, preserves the established two-party structure and discourages the development of third parties.

However sketchy, these illustrations serve to point up some important consequences which the provisions of the Constitution have on American politics and public policy. We have seen that the words of the Constitution in and of themselves contain few imperatives and do not normally determine the outcome of specific issues. Instead, constitutional provisions are a kind of a fundamental starting point which political actors use as their values and interests and relative influence dictate. The lack of constitutional power to perform a paricular act may be decisive, if enough strategically located men do not want the act to take place and others, who do support it, are not willing to make a special effort to see it succeed. But a similar lack of power in other circumstances may be successfully (though awkwardly and perhaps inconsistently) circumvented, if enough individuals and other interests strongly desire particular goals. This is not to say that the provisions of the Constitution are *merely* instruments, to be used by various political actors as they see fit. There are traditions and expectations surrounding many specific provisions; and these traditions and expectations are felt very strongly by political elites, whose careers and prospects are deeply committed to the need for consistent and predictable behavior on the part of other men in government. As a result, many provisions take on an independent status and meaning which *in the absence of compelling reasons to the contrary* will probably control the outcome in any given case. When determined and powerful men or groups seek particular goals, however, constitutional words are not likely to prevent them from attaining their ends. In time (if they are successful), their preferences will become the new and accepted interpretation of the Constitution's meaning, and new generations will begin their political goal-seeking from this new departure point.

We have also seen that extragovernmental forces may over time (1) totally reverse the intent and original effects of constitutional provisions, and (2) create almost irreversible necessity for federal government involvement in the affairs of other governments in the nation. The taxing powers of state and national governments, originally allocated to preserve the most lucrative and easily reached source of revenue for the states, have been totally reversed in effect by the new conditions of a nationalized, mobile economy. At present, practical economic realities establish the national government as the only efficient vehicle of revenue-raising, and thereby it is placed at the focus of all governmental effort to cope with societal problems which require the expenditure of money. Finally, we have seen that the broad strokes of constitutional structure have their echoes in the characteristics of political parties, and in the relationships between men in government, which shape the nature of the output that emerges. Perhaps the present character of the American party system would have evolved under any circumstances, but it has surely been fostered and is presently supported by the provisions of the Constitution.

The most vital single point to be made when considering the implications of the American Constitution is thus implicit in these illustrations: there is simply no mechanical inevitability about American politics which is inherent in the Constitution. Nothing *necessarily* follows because of the wording of the document, and *everything* depends to a greater or lesser degree on the preferences and priorities of the more powerful political actors of the particular time period. This realization lends crucial significance to the process by which the Constitution is interpreted and rendered into contemporary applications in politics. Whoever manages to affix his preferred interpretation on what the Constitution shall mean gathers to his support all the latent and generalized aura of legitimacy and traditionalism which the Constitution evokes from others in government and in the general public. *Who interprets* the Constitution is therefore a more important issue for practical purposes than *what the document says.* Nor is it clear in any given instance which institution or other participant will win the battle for establishing the authoritative constitutional interpretation. There are many participants in the grim but sometimes invisible struggle within the national government for the power to determine what the Constitution "requires" on any particular issue, and much is at stake in each of these contests. As we examine this struggle and the stakes involved in it in more detail, it will become clear that the Supreme Court is an intensely politicized organ of government — and by no means the only voice in interpretation of the Constitution.

WHO SHALL SAY WHAT THE CONSTITUTION SAYS?

Most Americans, if pressed, would probably say that the Supreme Court is the proper vehicle for interpretation of the Constitution. Moreover, it would be difficult for them to comprehend the basis for challenging the right and power of the Court to do so. Such is the triumph of Alexander Hamilton's argument, written into constitutional doctrine by the adroit opportunism of Chief Justice John Marshall. The complete acceptance of Hamilton's argument today, however, should not obscure the bitter clash of values and competing philosophies between Hamilton and Jefferson over the question of who was to interpret the Constitution. Hamilton's total victory brought with it mixed costs and benefits, and has had fundamental consequences for the nature of the American system of government. We shall first review the stakes in the conflict and then examine the effects of Hamilton's victory.

Hamilton had argued for a limited monarchy at the Constitutional Convention, but supported the final product as being acceptable for the economy-developing purposes which he had in mind. Together with John Jay and James Madison, he authored several essays designed to promote ratification of the Constitution in New York and known under the collective title of *The Federalist Papers*. For the most part, Hamilton stressed the utility of union and the need for a strong central government as reasons for accepting the document, but he saved his special enthusiasm for two innovations included in the Constitution which improved upon the old Articles of Confederation. These were a strong and vigorous executive to carry the laws into effect with force where necessary, and an independent judiciary with the power of judicial review (the power to declare acts of the Congress unconstitutional).

In arguing for judicial power to declare acts of the other branches unconstitutional and therefore void, Hamilton employed the legal analogy of the relationship between principal and agent.[9] The people (the principal) having granted the agent (the national government) only certain powers and not others, Hamilton argued, any act in excess of those granted powers would be void. But this left the problem of how the invalidity was to be determined: how does anybody know when an act of a legislature is in excess of the powers granted to it? Certainly sincere and knowledgeable legislators had decided that the act *was* within their powers, or they would have chosen another means of attaining the end they had in mind. Hamilton argued that these determinations were questions of law (and the Constitution conveniently *declares* that it is the law of the land) and as such ought to be decided by the Court. Jefferson insisted that the question of whether the principal had delegated a particular power to the agent ought to be decided by the principal himself, and certainly not by the agent. In other words, he wanted the people to determine in every instance whether the act of the legislature was authorized or not. The Constitution itself does not specify by what means its provisions are to be interpreted, and so the issue devolved into a test of logic, persuasiveness, and power between the two positions. Analysis of the debate suggests that two major disagreements divided the parties, and that both of these disagreements were rooted in the same conflict of values.

First, Hamilton and Jefferson had quite different views as to the nature of a constitution. To Jefferson, it was a fundamental allocation of the people's powers and superior to the ongoing acts of government. For these reasons, it was not law in the ordinary sense of

[9] See essay number 78 of the *Federalist Papers*.

a statute or code, but rather the people's instructions to their government about the goals and purposes which it should pursue. These goals and purposes would be changeable through time, of course, as circumstances changed, and Jefferson insisted upon the right of the people to be able to change their Constitution regularly. Hamilton, on the other hand, saw the Constitution as a technical legal document with more or less fixed meaning, requiring legal expertise for interpretation. He argued that the Court was more likely to possess the expertise and wisdom necessary to divine the meaning of the document's words. Although he acknowledged that the Constitution flowed from the people, he insisted that their ratification had carried with it authorization to the Court to act as interpreter.

Second, the two men disagreed over the nature of the act of interpretation which was involved. Since Jefferson viewed interpretation as requiring the making of value-based choices, it then followed that the choice should be made by the people themselves; but if that were not feasible, then by that institution closest to the people — normally their recently elected representatives in either state or national legislatures. He was particularly unwilling to be subjected to the value choices of a body of men not elected but appointed (and for life terms), by members of the very national government whose exercise of powers was being questioned. Hamilton blandly declared that there was no act of choice involved in interpretation of the Constitution, and that it was simply a matter of comparing the statute with the words of the Constitution and registering the mechanical judgment that would be apparent from the comparison. He expressed confidence that the independence and life terms of judges would enable them to rise above the petty strifes of the day and render decisions that were true to the basic intent of the document.

What really divides the antagonists in this debate is a wide gulf between their respective value premises and priorities. Jefferson feared the self-serving tendencies of the financiers and businessmen represented by Hamilton and the Federalist Party, and he sought to prevent them from staffing and using the Supreme Court to legitimate their aggrandizing schemes. His trust in the people was by no means complete, but he preferred their judgments to those of any self-selected elite. Hamilton feared the property-redistributing tendencies of the masses, and so sought to keep control over the scope of legislative powers in the hands of a trustworthy body sympathetic to property rights. Lawyers, already accustomed to reverence for the traditions and practices of the past, would be — particularly if well selected — another bulwark in defense of the Constitution's protections for the established order.

In principle, Jefferson's position appears the more logical and the more democratic. If, as seems evident, the act of interpretation is one involving value choices, then choice by the people or their recently elected representatives seems more democratic than choice by an appointed body which is not accountable to the people in any way. But Hamilton's view was made into authoritative doctrine by Chief Justice John Marshall in the case of *Marbury* v. *Madison* in

1803.[10] To add insult to injury, Marshall accomplished his feat while Jefferson was President, with a Republican majority behind him in the House of Representatives. He did it by declaring unconstitutional an act of Congress which (he said, though others doubted) was contrary to the Constitution. The institution restrained by the declaration of unconstitutionality was the Court itself, so Marshall faced no problem of failure to comply. Despite some wavering in the face of Jefferson's pressures, Marshall stuck to the principle of the Court's power of judicial review throughout the remaining thirty years of his term on the Court. He had the political sophistication not to actually exercise the power, however, and it was not until 1857 and the *Dred Scott* case [11] that the second test of judicial review occurred. This too met with strong political reaction, and the principle of judicial review did not become firmly established in practice until after the Civil War. By then, the Court proved to be an effective defense against the experiments of several states with social legislation, but the acceptance of the Hamiltonian position was widespread.

Why did Hamilton win the argument so fully that by now it is difficult to recapture the enormity of the choice which was unconsciously made? Surely the American penchant for legalism and the law is both cause and effect here. Americans were a receptive audience for Hamilton's legalistic approach to political problems. Further, the group to which Hamilton first appealed was made up chiefly of the upper and upper middle classes of propertied people. They may have perceived the same advantages in the prospective role of the Court as he did. Special support for the Court's power of judicial review came from the business and wealthier interests right up through the famous Court-packing conflicts of the New Deal period. The latter event suggests another reason why the Hamilton argument may have succeeded in the long run. There is nothing inevitable about what the Court will do in any given situation, for the real determinant of decisionmaking is not the power of the Court so much as it is the particular preferences of the judges who happen to be sitting on the Court at the time. The presence of liberal judges leads to liberal decisions, as the Warren Court era demonstrated; and thus the Court may become a Hamiltonian instrument which acts in behalf of Jefferson's ideals. This realization may lead to acceptance of the Court's power of judicial review by *all* political actors, each of whom hopes to control the presidency and thus the channel of appointment to the Court. Careful choice of appointees to the Court — and longevity on their part — may permit greater impact on the directions of public policy than some Presidents generate in four years in the White House.

There seems little doubt, however, that the location of the power of judicial review in the Supreme Court adds an important dimension to the character of American politics. For one thing, it tends to depoliticize some issues and convert them into a form in which only

---

[10] *Marbury v. Madison,* 1 branch. 137 (1803).
[11] *Dred Scott v. Sanford,* 19 Howard 393 (1857).

some men — lawyers and their clients — rather than the entire citizenry, are the relevant decisionmakers. Taking some of the great
value conflicts of the society into the Supreme Court for resolution
probably siphons off some of the tensions and bitterness from our
politics and perhaps renders them more stable. But this can be a
mixed blessing, for sometimes people probably *ought* to become
engaged in vital questions affecting their future. The Supreme Court
is not the final authority on any question about which a large number of people care strongly, of course, for there are many ways to
combat or circumvent a single decision. It is nevertheless, even as a
contingent decisionmaker, able to structure public understanding
of some issues and to resolve many others without much public attention. Again, evaluation of the desirability of this would depend on
one's attitude toward popular participation and the need for a preliminary decisionmaker in a large society with many public issues
of considerable complexity.

In any event, the Supreme Court is not left to do the job of constitutional interpretation by itself. Many other institutions and political
actors take part in shaping the meaning of the Constitution in any
particular situation. The Court is, after all, an essentially passive institution, requiring several prior decisions by a variety of political actors before it even gets a case to decide. Why and under what circumstances do some people or other interests decide to sue another?
Litigation is not the most direct and sure way of gaining one's political ends, and therefore it must be utilized because other routes
appear blocked or unpromising. The courts thus become a kind of
supplementary political lever — a means of moving other institutions
to action, or occasionally a route to gaining some limited specific
ends. Other choices within the legal arena include decisions as to
whether or not to appeal, decisions by the Department of Justice
as to the position it wishes to take on cases which are appealed to
the Supreme Court, and all the decisions of trial and lower appellate
court judges on aspects of a case both before and after the Supreme
Court decides it.

Nor are the many participants in the legal process allowed to
decide important questions through interaction alone. Neither the
Congress nor the President has been supine before the Supreme Court
in American history. Both have instead reacted strongly to decisions
which they considered inappropriate or undesirable. Congress can
pass new statutes only marginally different from one ruled unconstitutional, it can initiate constitutional amendments to overrule decisions, or it can and does express its displeasure by modifying the
Court's jurisdiction or severely challenging and perhaps rejecting
confirmation of newly appointed justices. The President's cooperation is usually necessary to enforce Court decisions, so he is often in
an even stronger immediate position to prevent the Court's interpretation of the Constitution from becoming definitive or final. Presidents
have ignored the Court, flatly refused to obey its decisions, or simply
nominated judges with totally different views from those previously
prevailing. Thus, even when the Court does receive and decide a case

which puts forward a particular interpretation of the Constitution, the other institutions may reverse, modify, or ignore its determination. Much of the time, questions of the Constitution's meaning are resolved without the involvement of the Court at all, as when the President, the Congress, the political parties, and others establish precedents and traditions which are unchallenged or unchallengeable in courts. For example, the President is solely responsible for determining when the Constitution's guarantee to the states against domestic insurrection should be invoked. The political parties decide through their accumulated years of practice how the electoral college shall work, and so forth. Thousands of lower court opinions generate a wide variety of constitutional interpretations. In addition, statutes and regulations specify the jurisdictional boundaries of courts and agencies, particularize the generalities of the Constitution in infinite numbers of ways, and authorize or preclude the bringing of claims to enforce constitutional "rights."

The history of interactions among the many participants in American politics suggests that the interpretation of the Constitution is considered too important an act to be left to the Supreme Court. Even if it were capable in practice of hearing cases on all the disputed aspects of the Constitution, the other political actors are too vitally concerned about gaining their ends to defer to the preferences of the judges. The contest over who shall affix his preferences as the established meaning of the Constitution is one which involves great stakes — perhaps the winning or losing of major prizes of politics — and so it is on occasion bitterly fought. The final, authoritative meaning of the Constitution (assuming one ever finally emerges) is thus more a product of relative political power than of legalistic analysis.

But the Constitution itself is not a mere cipher in the eternal struggle to gain benefits and avoid burdens which constitutes the stuff of politics. The document is the product of the Framers' very distinct value premises and priorities, and it embodies many of the political values described in the previous section. Indeed, perhaps it is best characterized in those terms.

THE ORIGINAL CONSTITUTION: LIMITED GOVERNMENT, PROPERTY RIGHTS, AND ANTIMAJORITARIANISM

(1) Limited Government

The underlying theory of the American Constitution fully embodies the commitments to the values of limited government and contract. The national government, even today, is a government of delegated powers, and it can perform no acts not authorized somewhere in the text of the Constitution or "necessary and proper" to their effectuation. In addition, several types of actions are expressly prohibited. The document represents the entire body of powers and limitations of government, and as such is the complete contract between the collectivity of individuals making up the society and the governmental agent. The political value of legalism is inherent in the so-called "supremacy clause" in which the Constitution declares itself to be the supreme law of the land, binding upon all governmental officials at all levels.

Against this general background of shared political values, several compromises between divergent interests reflect the nature of the political conflict which did exist among the Framers. Men from small states resisted representation in the legislature that was exclusively population-based and managed to secure equal status in the Senate. Southerners extracted a prohibition against interference with the importation of slaves for a fixed period of time. And the electoral college was constructed to balance the weights of the small and large states in selecting the President. Because of these and other differences between some of the Framers, the document does not reflect logical consistency or precise symmetry, and it has often been called a "bundle of compromises." But it is easy to over-estimate the extent of conflict and the scope and difficulty of necessary compromise at the Constitutional Convention. Much was shared in the way of political values, and the Framers had very definite convictions about certain critical principles of government — all of which made compromise on the limited differences of interest among them more attainable.

Generations of historians have battled over the proper interpretation to be placed on the nature of the Constitutional Convention and the goals and purposes of the men who attended. To some, it was a conservative counterrevolution in reaction to the excesses of liberalism inherent in the Declaration of Independence. To others, it was a far-sighted, bold experiment in expanding the frontiers of democracy. Politicians disagreed from the very moment that the veil of secrecy was lifted from the proceedings of the Convention, Patrick Henry, for example, declaring that he had "smelled a rat." James Madison, the chief note-taker at the Convention, did not publish his records for more than fifty years after the Convention was over, and he has been accused of polishing them to assure that they would lend support to his changing views.[12] Nineteenth-century historians, perhaps sympathetic to Federalist principles, tended to be specially struck by the Framers' accomplishments, occasionally implying that they were touched by divine inspiration. In reaction to this school of Constitution-worship, Charles Beard lent support to Progressive Movement realism in 1913 with the publication of his *An Economic Interpretation of the Constitution.*[13] Beard very nearly turned American history upside down by arguing first that the Framers were men who had acquired vast holdings of bonds and scrip (issued by the Continental Congress during the Revolutionary War) at the low values to which they had fallen because of the inability of the Congress to pay its debts. He implied that they had then constructed

[12] For a thoroughly revisionist view which is very hard on both Madison and Marshall, see William Crosskey, *Politics and the Constitution in the History of the United States* (Chicago: University of Chicago Press, 1953).

[13] Charles Beard, *An Economic Interpretation of the Constitution* (New York: Macmillan, 1913).

a powerful government which could raise revenue and pay off the bonds at full value — to their great personal profit. This debunking was viewed by some as in very bad taste, but it helped others to find it possible to look at the Constitution as a value-laden document with quite human strengths and weaknesses. Not for four decades did scholars seek to verify Beard's allegations, and when they did it appeared that he had at the very least overstated his argument.[14] But few now deny that there was at least a shared upper-class ethos among the Framers and that economic interests played some part in shaping the Constitution. Thus, although we can make no attempt to reach a final interpretation about the Framers' purposes, it is possible to analyze what they wrote into the document and to point to two very broadly shared principles of government which are evident in the Constitution. The two themes which apparently united most of the men present at the Convention of 1787 were the need to protect property rights and a concern to prevent rampant majoritarianism.

(2) Protection for Property Rights

Much of the motivation for the Annapolis Convention which proceeded the call for revising the Articles of Confederation, and for the latter as well, came from dissatisfaction on the part of businessmen with the protectionism of the states and the tendency of some state and lower units of government to promote both inflation and the avoidance of debts. For financial and creditor interests, the Constitution was a triumph. They gained (1) prohibitions against state import restrictions and taxation, (2) prohibition against state impairment of the obligations of contracts, (3) a single central source of coining money and regulating its value, (4) prohibition against state use of paper money or other legal tender, (5) a system of courts operated by the central government so that they did not have to take chances with locally-run state courts in states to which their debtors had removed, (6) a guarantee of full faith and credit in one state to the acts and judgments of another, so that they could pursue their debtors more effectively, and (7) a guarantee of a republican form of government for the states, as well as provisions for putting down domestic insurrections, so that they need fear no further incidents such as the celebrated Shays' Rebellion of 1787-1788 in western Massachusetts. In all of these respects, the Framers acted consistently to promote the enforcement of contracts, the collection of debts, the maintenance of stable valuation for money, and the promotion of a national economy. These are surely economy-building goals, at least under the conditions of the times, but their implementation through the new Constitution came at the expense of many small farmers and artisans. In that respect the Constitution favored one class's interest over another's. Nor was the desire of some of the

---

[14] The leading counter to Beard is Robert Brown, *Charles Beard and The Constitution* (Princeton, N. J.: Princeton University Press, 1956).

small farmers to promote inflation or avoid debts or protect their local industries merely an ungrateful rejection of contractual obligation. At least in their eyes, and perhaps objectively, the eastern financiers and businessmen were profiting unconscionably from usurious interest rates and other forms of economic exploitation which they imposed upon the hapless and frequently indigent farmers and artisans. Shays' Rebellion, and other west-east tensions such as the Whiskey Rebellion of later years, grew out of the perception by western workingmen that they were being exploited by urban financiers. In the latters' eyes, the Constitution was another means for furthering this continuing exploitation.

(3) Antimajoritarianism

Consistent with the desire to protect property rights, but drawing more specifically on the anticipation of redistribution of property by the masses, the Framers built into the document layer upon layer of obstacles against simple majority rule. It may be instructive to see how fully almost every one of these restrictions has been moderated in the subsequent years. If it had not been possible to find ways around these limitations, it seems probable that the Constitution would have enjoyed less widespread and/or more critical reception in recent decades. The major limitations on majority rule, and the means found to circumvent them, include the following: (a) Amendment to the Constitution is very difficult, requiring two-thirds votes of both houses of Congress and ratification by three-quarters of the states. But informal means of amendment have been developed, such as by the shifting interpretations of the Supreme Court. (b) The electoral college is a device designed to give discretionary power to the elected delegates and keep the people from direct choice of the President. But delegates to the electoral college run on a pledged basis, only rarely violating their pledges; ballots list the names of the presidential candidates and most voters do not realize that an intermediate step is involved at all. (c) Separation of powers prevents the people (supposedly represented in the Congress) from working their will in the government as a whole. But the President and the Court both have taken on a kind of virtual representation of majority will, as the House has fallen into the hands of its senior members from chiefly rural, safe districts. And the party system cuts across the separation to induce some degree of cooperation between the branches. (d) Senators were originally selected by the state legislatures. But direct election of Senators was accomplished by constitutional amendment in 1917, and for decades before that state legislators had run for election on the basis of pledges to vote for one or another Senatorial candidate. (e) Judicial review offers a means of applying restraints to the legislature, supposedly the representatives of the people. But Congress and President together have shown imagination in pressuring the Court or avoiding the implications of its decisions. (f) The division of the legislature into two houses was an attempt to introduce institutional jealousies and constituency rivalries into the popular branch and thereby reduce coherent action. But the party system and Presidential leadership have promoted some degree of unity between the two houses.

The catalogue might be expanded, but the point should be clear: this impressive list of conscious efforts to fragment, divide, and neutralize the will of the people cannot be coincidental, nor is it likely that a government thus paralyzed in practice could have long endured. What has sustained the American political system is perhaps not so much the quality of its Constitution as it is the capacity of political elites to generate a style of political behavior that satisfies the different demands of both the major economic and social interests *and* the masses of average citizens.

What has transpired over the years in the United States is more or less of a commentary on *both* the Framers and the flexibility of the American politician. Somehow, amidst this complex process, political actors have apparently found it convenient and practical to perpetuate reverence for the Constitution as the embodiment of wisdom and justice in government. Perhaps we should examine the other side of this vital equation — perceptions about the Constitution in the minds of the American people.

THE CONSTITUTION: IDEOLOGY AND SYMBOL

As an instrument of government, the Constitution appears to have immediate behavior-conditioning effects upon political elites and to serve a more general legitimating function for the general public. Men in government internalize the past precedents and traditions surrounding particular provisions and so enable each other to understand and predict official behavior. Men outside of government revere and apparently desire the sense of continuity and propriety which the Constitution radiates, and so they seek assurance that new actions are consistent with the Constitution. On occasion, this leads men in government to compete with each other for the power to interpret the Constitution as favoring their position in a political controversy and thereby gain the acquiescence of the less involved. To all political actors, apparently, there is potential payoff in promoting and sustaining the idea that the Constitution contains all necessary answers to public problems if we will but follow its principles.

In one important respect, the Constitution itself promotes this continuity-symbolizing role. In some provisions, the document is eminently precise, leaving little to chance; but in other respects it is almost unconscionably vague and indeterminate ("the President shall take care that the laws be faithfully executed . . . ."). Careful analysis indicates that the *precise* provisions have to do principally with the manner in which elections are to be conducted, or, essentially, with the question of who is to hold office. The *vague and ambiguous* provisions, for the most part, have to do with the powers of officeholders, or, in other words, with what the incumbents are to do with their powers once they are in office. Political elites, therefore, should be enabled to have confidence that officials are indeed the duly elected ones, for there is very little uncertainty about such matters. But the directions in which the officeholders may take the nation are very marginally circumscribed (except for a few specific prohibitions), and they are practically free to do whatever they are able to justify out of their political mandate and circumstances.

Continuity and symbolic reassurance are furthered also by the fact that contention over the meaning of particular phrases in the Constitution translates political controversies into the less heated arena of legal debate. It also simultaneously reminds both participants and people of what it is that they share — acceptance of the same Constitution and the accumulated political association which it represents. Stifling of political controversy in this fashion has not led to later upheavals, perhaps because differences were more over divisions of the economic product than they were over such fundamental matters as how the political or economic systems should be organized. Indeed, past reductions of tensions by translating them into the form of legalistic debates has probably added to a tradition of nonfundamental political debates which is now part of the American political style. Let us look more systematically at the ways in which constitutional provisions merge with established values and ideology to create a distinctive American political style.

IDEOLOGY, CONSTITUTION, AND POLITICAL STYLE

The Constitution, as we have seen, scatters official power across a wide spectrum of positions within the governments of the United States. First, it divides power in important ways between the national government and the various state governments, and then it further fragments the power of the national government among the three major branches. Subsequent developments have carried this fragmentation well beyond the Framers' intentions, so that significant portions of the capacity to govern are today located (through a combination of tradition, necessity, and aggrandizement) in, for example, the committees of the Congress, the Joint Chiefs of Staff, or the middle ranges of the bureaucracy throughout the executive branch. What this pattern of power distribution means, as has often been noted, is a multitude of pressure points (sometimes less neutrally characterized as veto points) located across the map of American government. Not surprisingly, what results is a political system which is highly sensitive to the status quo — one that does not readily produce new policies which would tend to destroy established relationships. Usually, it takes a wide-ranging and determined effort to reach all of these veto points and neutralize them, or reach some form of accommodation with their preferences, so that a broadly supported new policy can be instituted.

There is nothing casual about the status quo enforcing consequences of the Constitution's scattering of power. It is entirely consistent with the Framers' antigovernment biases. It conforms completely to their (and their successors') views about the need for freedom of action for private power: the only way that individuals can be sure of complete freedom to serve their own ends as they see fit is through the reduction of government action to a "lowest common denominator." Moreover, it follows the more fully articulated political principles of James Madison, often termed the "father of the Constitution," in every basic feature. Madison, perhaps the most scholarly of the Framers and at the same time completely in tune with their concern for the threat of majoritarian redistribution of property, provided an intellectual framework for the simpler value preferences of his Constitutional Convention colleagues. He argued that the dangers anticipated from a rampant popular majority could be checked effectively by enlarging the scope of the republic so that there would be so many different special interests within the potential "majority" that no single, coherent majority could form and stay united long enough to do real damage to the status quo. By giving each component interest within the potential "majority" a selection of possible power points within the governmental structure at which to aim, their cross-pressuring and mutually-containing potential would be realized.

The Constitution thus not only facilitates the realization of the pluralist (many groups, many veto points) image of how government does and should work; it is itself based on a conviction about the desirability of such a process. It should be clear that the creation of substantial and necessary units of power at a multitude of places within the political system invites (if it does not impel) various groups to seek to control those component elements of the total capacity of government which may happen to be most available or vulnerable to them. But this inducement to group activity is not coincidental. It is instead the fruition of Madison's hopes for institutionalizing the social process which he believed would be the means of permitting the people to take part in their government but at the same time assuring that the government would still be able to do the right thing (i.e., what the better informed and generally wealthier people thought was best). Madison's thesis is sometimes known as the principle of "natural limits to numerical majorities." This means that when majorities in favor of an action reach a size sufficient to have a chance of achieving their goals, their internal diversities would be so great as to fragment them. This prospect is made more likely by districting systems which require a very large (and nation-wide) majority and which result in election of their most moderate representatives, multiple power points within the governmental structure so that each divergent interest can effectuate its opposition, and, just for good measure, division of the national government into branches so that a further level of opportunity for opposition and disabling internal tensions will be provided. In this manner, argued Madison, ill-intentioned majorities would be held in check. Of course, so would "well-intentioned" majorities, but Madison was arguing to and on behalf of the propertied upper classes of his day. His readers were not democrats, but aristocrats (or plutocrats) who favored more direct and explicit limitations on popular influence over government policies. Madison carried the day because he convinced some of them that he had devised a subtler and less provocative means to their preferred ends than they had thought possible.

The pluralist characterization of how politics and government operate in the United States thus has a long and respectable intellectual history. It begins with the intentions and achievements of the Framers of the Constitution, and it is carried into effect today by the provisions of the governing document they produced. It is little wonder that this image should have such ideological power by now, or that it should be effective in shaping the American political style. Madison's thesis, and the Framers' intentions as they constructed the new government, sought to preserve the capacity of the wealthy, propertied aristocracy to shape the nation's policies. These purposes lay behind the origin of the pluralist interpretation, though of course they may not still hold true today. But it is not unreasonable to think that some portion of the consequences they sought may still inhere in their combined ideological and constitutional achievement. These underlying assumptions, for example, lead to some distinctive characteristics of politics in the United States.

For one thing, American politicians tend to engage in a balancing act, in which they measure the weight, determination, and potential governmental access of interests which seek something from government, and act according to this calculus instead of on the basis of the merits of the claim involved. Officeholders assume the posture of referees, despite the fact that they are products of the system's power equations themselves. As referees, they uphold the "rules of the game," which amount to the specified ways in which groups seeking influence are supposed to go about their efforts. Theoretically at least, fairness, hearings, due process, and tolerance of opposing positions constitute part of these rules of the game.

The concentration on the rules of the game, however, may obscure two crucial aspects of the process of politics. The nature of the rules is to allow certain kinds of competition among certain established players, and also to foreclose and label illegitimate some other kinds of conflicts. Bargaining, negotiation, compromising — which are the leading characteristics of the American political style — are possible only when the "antagonists" share certain assumptions about what the game is about and how it should be played. Management and labor can agree to submit issues to arbitration only when the issues at stake are sufficiently confined within shared value premises that they are soluble by factual analysis or compromises which do not deprive either side of its essential holdings. Wages or specific assembly-line grievances offer this potential, but not questions of the nationalization of the factory or the workers' right to hire the company president. Similarly, the rules of the game of politics allow only those types of disagreements which acknowledge shared value premises. These are disagreements within the basic framework of the status quo — disagreements about who gets how much of a particular economic product, for example, or over the application of an accepted rule. To play by these rules, in other words, is to acknowledge the premises and continuity of the basic economic and political structure of the American social order.

Not only is the validity of all that lies behind the rules accepted by playing under their management, but the kinds of results that can be obtained are also shaped by the rules. Behind the rules lies a particular status quo, not an ideal form of political order. When the rules limit the scope of challenge or possible change, they therefore eliminate much of the possible range of alternatives and specify that the status quo can only be changed by a certain amount. Thus, if only limited changes are possible, the rules become part of the means of maintaining the status quo, and to defend the rules as if they were neutral is really to defend the substance of the status quo. This gives new significance to the American penchant for concentration on procedure — how things are done — rather than the *substance* of what government is doing. It is as if it were more important whether all the established procedures were followed than whether the right thing were done or not. Countless tragedies have been constructed around this dilemma, from classic drama to the present, but the issue has not yet surfaced for widespread recognition in regard to American political principles.

The inducements to engage in politics under the essentially pluralist rules of the game are very strong. Constitutional structure, original intentions, and present political styles all militate in this direction. Just as there are strong attractions, however, so are there strong auxiliary coercions for those who do not comply. The widely shared popular commitment to the established rules — which usually overlooks the fact that such rules shape what can be done — first applies a social support behind such behavior. Next, reputation for breaking the rules may lead to social or economic sanctions — ostracism from established society, exclusion from economic opportunities, loss of a job. If deviant behavior persists, legal reprisals are likely to be followed (or perhaps paralleled) by physical coercions such as jail or other injuries. Those who seek substantial change in the policies produced by government may thus appear to be nothing but rule-breakers, and may well suffer serious punishments into the bargain.

It should be clear that this discussion of the rules of the game and the American political style provides only superficial confirmation for the pluralist characterization of the American political process. That the rules promote, and the style endorses, such an image of the political process does not take it out of the realm of hypothesis and/or ideology. The function of ideology, after all, is to explain, rationalize, and promote behavior in accordance with an established structure. Such group conflict as does occur may be over marginal matters such as who gets how much of the economic rewards of a plentiful economy, and not over fundamental questions of any kind. In the latter case, all groups may concur and hew to a single line; or other sources of power superior to them may channel their actions so fully that the result is the same. Thus, the chief consequence of their interaction for our purposes may be that they serve as an effective barrier to efforts toward change which are generated by new groups or segments of the general public.

We cannot conclude this discussion without commenting on the label that the rules and the American political style have put on conflict as a social process. We have seen how the rules and the style combine to discourage behavior not consistent with the premises behind the rules. Action at odds with the rules — in short, provocation of serious conflicts of values or behavioral norms — is deplored as being violative of "the American way." But there is nothing inherently immoral or socially reprehensible about conflict as such. Conflict of a fundamental kind (i.e., conflict over ends and not just over means) may be essential under some conditions in order to release constructive forces in a society and remove restraints that simply will not eliminate themselves. Nor is the distinction between nonviolent and violent types of conflict sufficient to permit moral or historical judgments. To take a very obvious example, slavery would not have been eliminated in the United States without violent conflict — unless one wishes to argue that blacks should have been willing to wait another two centuries until white plantation owners were persuaded of their own immorality so strongly as to overcome their economic interests. Conflict, in short, must be judged not on the basis of its existence, and not on the basis of its nonviolent or violent nature, but in terms of the entire context in which it takes place. If, on balance, it serves to further social and humanitarian progress, and other means toward these ends are blocked by dominant forces within the society, then the disapproval directed toward conflict is essentially a vote on behalf of one's private interest in maintaining the status quo. Widespread consensus within a society may be similarly good or bad, depending on what the consensus supports and how general the interests that profit from it. Where the consensus maintains conditions or policies that are in the special interest of a few and not in the general interest, consensus surely is undesirable. A broadly shared consensus on either goals or methods which most of the society conceived to be in its interest would be valuable.

This is not intended as an unequivocal call for conflict instead of consensus. It is simply intended to point up the fact that political systems can find both functional at different stages in their development, and that too much of either is likely to be destructive. In the American case, at least for the past decades, both the rules of the game and the general political style have strongly insisted upon consensus and denigrated or repressed conflict. We may, and perhaps should, be en route to redressing that balance in the 1970's. Soon, perhaps, the validity in the argument for *avoidance* of issues may again be visible. The American style of not facing issues, of insistence upon following the rules and letting the results fall where they may, has the merit of reducing conflict. Some conflicts may be potentially disastrous: they may be of such a fundamental nature as to be quite insoluble without mass violence. Where this is the case, the prospect of seriously self-destructive mass violence may suggest that avoidance of issues and deflection of attention elsewhere is morally and politically preferable. The crucial variable is the nature of the context: neither conflict nor consensus has meaning except in terms of goals sought and conditions existing, and what is useful and desirable in one setting may be disastrous in another. For the present, of course, we operate with the political style and the rules which we have been describing.

Power and Decisionmaking in National Government Institutions 10

As any newspaper reader quickly learns, the authoritative institutions of American government — the two Houses of Congress, the Supreme Court, and the executive branch — do not make up a single-minded, homogeneous instrument of policymaking. Each is responsive to a distinctive set of external pressures, each has its own rules and procedures, and each has evolved a unique internal distribution of power. At the same time, the power of the United States government (in the sense of the capacity to act on a matter) is spread broadly among these several institutions. Little coherent government action can emerge without some form of affirmative cooperation from most or all of them. Thus, what *does* emerge must succeed in winning the support of, or at least neutralizing opposition from, the interests which are dominant in each institution.

But this is only the beginning. The interests and priorities which shape government policies are far from representative even of the distinctive constituencies which support the particular institutions. Instead, they reflect first, the special internal distribution of power achieved by the nature, rules, and procedures of the institution; and second, the preferences of the men who hold the key positions of power. Further, these men use the power of their strategic positions in ways that are conditioned by tradition and perceived as political necessity. They identify with the institution through which they wield their power, and they seek to represent that institution in transactions with similar power centers in other institutions. They also recognize the investment they share with the other governmental powerholders in maintaining the political structures that support them. What results is a style of mutual accommodation and bargaining among the various institutional power centers in which both self- and mutual preservation play an important part.

Government policies, therefore, reflect the preferences, interaction, and style of the men who occupy the relatively few power centers that dominate each major institution. Instead of describing each institution in comprehensive detail, we shall concentrate on identifying the key positions in each from which policies are determined. After analyzing the factors which contribute to the power of such strategic positions, we shall show in a general way what political priorities are paramount among the men who hold them. Finally, we shall examine the interactions among such power centers and what they mean.

THE HOUSE OF REPRESENTATIVES

There are 435 members of the House of Representatives. This fact, straight from sixth-grade civics, has profound significance for the distribution of power and the operating procedures within the House. The 435 representatives face a bewildering array of complex problems, a vast national budget, and a sprawling federal bureaucracy. Few of them come to Congress with any special expertise or experience that would enable them to cope effectively with such problems. Their time to acquire such knowledge is limited, both by the demands of service to their constituents and by the imminence of the next election. What little staff they have must devote most of its time to mail, errands, and, again, the forthcoming election.

Even, or perhaps particularly, for representatives with the sincerest intentions of translating constituents' wishes into governmental action, the task is extremely difficult, if not impossible. They must develop two types of capabilities: a subject area expertise in order to know what should be done, and an administrative sophistication enabling them to recognize whether or not executive branch employees are acting (and spending authorized funds) to carry out congressional policies in the manner prescribed. In both areas, they can act as independent policymakers only if they are able to acquire knowledge on their own, not if their knowledge depends upon inevitably self-serving voluntary disclosures by the executive branch or from private power centers.

For all these reasons, they have little choice but to divide their governmental responsibilities among individuals or committees formed out of the House membership. Through specialization, at least some of the members will have a chance to develop the expertise and the managerial oversight to make independent policymaking possible. Presumably, members will exercise such capabilities in accordance with the will of the majority of the House. But when there is a division of labor, a stratification of power results. Special knowledge or responsibility in a subject area gives the possessor the tools and the prestige to cause others to go along with his views of what should be done. Formation of a task group implies leadership within it, and the chairman of a committee may come to exercise disproportionate influence over its work. To a considerable extent, these are the inevitable costs of a necessary division of labor.

It is a mistake, however, to take it for granted that the congressmen with the greatest knowledge of an area necessarily have the greatest influence upon policy. Values play at least as great a part as facts; indeed, the two are not really separable. If a particular set of values or a particular ideology dominates a committee or a house of Congress, that fact is likely to be a more important shaper of policy than is expertise.

Over the years, the House of Representatives has evolved a unique form of dividing its labor, such that most of its capacity to act lies in the hands of about 25 men occupying its key positions. Moreover, such men are chosen solely by virtue of their "seniority" (length of service). Although this may appear a mechanical, and therefore politically neutral, means of selection, in fact it places power in the hands of older, usually more conservative men. This is because longevity in the House depends on having a relatively "safe" electoral district. Many such districts are found in the rural South or the Midwest, usually the more conservative parts of the nation. Some districts in the more liberal large cities regularly return candidates of the same political party, but the availability of alternative political careers and the volatility of city districts tends to eliminate any given representative before he reaches the higher levels of seniority.

The overall effect of this House system is to create a highly structured game. In this "game," only the oldest members actually hold power, the next level of members have invested many years in moving up the ladder and are more or less patiently awaiting the death or retirement of their elders, and the newest and youngest members are close to impotent. The house has roughly co-equal echelons of leadership positions, both reflecting this principle clearly. The first type of position is that on committees, each of which carries responsibility for the actions of the House in a major policy area; the major position is that of chairman, with secondary status for the ranking member of the minority party. The second type of position is that of leadership in the management of the House itself; these include the Speaker of the House, the political party positions such as majority and minority leaders (and secondarily their "whips" or assistants), and the Rules Committee. Let us briefly examine the powers of these offices and the characteristics of their holders.

(1) Policy Area Committees

There are 21 standing committees in the House, ranging in importance, and prestige, from Civil Service and Post Office to Armed Services, Ways and Means, and Appropriations. Most committees have 20-25 members (Appropriations has 50), appointed from each party roughly according to the partisan ratio then prevailing in the House. Each representative usually serves on two committees. Although he naturally seeks assignment to a committee whose work will be of concern to his district, he has no means of appeal from the decision of the party leadership. With seniority, however, he may move to a more prestigious committee when openings arise. It is no coincidence that the two most prestigious policy area committees in the House are those dealing with money matters — Ways and Means with tax bills (including the separately-financed social welfare legislation such as Social Security and Medicare) and Appropriations with expenditures. Raising and spending money is absolutely crucial to the operation of the government; it is the area in which the Congress wields its greatest influence over policy and the surest route to maximum influence for any individual representative.

The chairman of each committee decides when, and if, the committee shall meet, sets the agenda, and controls all hearings and executive sessions. From the perhaps hundreds of bills submitted to his committee each year, he chooses which, if any, will be considered by the full committee. He can shape the list of witnesses at public hearings, control the detailed drafting of the legislation in executive sessions, manage the bill when it is debated on the floor of the House, and represent the House in any later negotiations with the Senate over differences in bills passed by the two houses. In all of these activities, of course, his personal preferences regarding the form and desirability of the legislation play a crucial role.

The chairman is not completely autonomous, of course. The President, or the House or party leadership, may bring pressure on him, and the members of his committee may seek to force him to act as they prefer. But the chairman has powerful defenses at his command. Neither the President nor the leadership wants to incur his opposition, for they know that the chairman can cause delay, drastic revision, or even destruction of legislation that he dislikes. Nor do the members of his committee wish to lose either the opportunities to obtain special provisions in legislation that the chairman can grant them, or the public visibility that his good will makes possible for them. At all times, the chairman also has on his side the traditions of the House that call for action only in accordance with duly established procedures — in this case, with the recommendations of the standing committee having jurisdiction over the subject area of the bill. The House almost never considers, and even more rarely enacts, legislation which is completely opposed by the chairman of the applicable committee. In part, this is because an alert chairman knows when to join a majority position; but even when he does so, he leaves the clear mark of his preferences on the final product.

The ranking member of the minority party on a committee gains some leverage from representing his party and mobilizing other party members on behalf of specific positions. He becomes the chairman of the committee when his party wins majority control of the House. Frequently, this prospect gains him a friendly *modus vivendi* with the chairman, for both men have served on the committee for a long time and know that they may be destined to rotate with each other for the rest of their political careers. Having served together for some time, the two men probably also share a strong concern for the "proper" working of the House itself, and for the efficient discharge of the responsibilities of their committee to the House. In many ways, therefore, the two positions complement each other, rather than serving as opposing correctives.

(2) House Leadership Positions

The major leadership positions within the House itself are filled by the majority political party, usually through application of the seniority principle. The key position is that of Speaker of the House. The Speaker presides over House debates on bills, recognizing to speak those whom by pre-arrangement or preference he considers appropriate. He shapes the House agenda, deciding what bills will receive priority. He designates the members of the "conference committees" who will represent the House in negotiations with the Senate. He controls the referral of bills to committees, sending them to friendly or unfriendly receptions in accordance with his preferences. He makes public visibility possible for, or ignores, members as he chooses. Not least, he is privy to the President's preferences and intentions regarding the legislative program for that session of Congress, and can (if he wishes) work in harmony with the President to schedule and obtain passage of desired legislation.

The majority and minority leader positions within the House are more strictly political party leadership positions. In both cases, seniority is a major factor, but policy views representative of the mainstream of the party are also influential in determining election by the party's caucus. The duties of these leaders, assisted by their elected "whips," are to mobilize party members behind legislative positions that the leadership has decided to be in the party's interest. Members of the House are often under pressure to support the position of the President when he is of their party or to join with other members of their party in opposition to a President of the other party. (Many measures before the House are not made matters of party discipline, of course, and in such cases members are free of all pressures to vote with the leadership.)

Another group of positions of crucial importance to the management of the business of the House is that of membership on the Rules Committee. These are perhaps the most coveted committee positions in the House, and are filled, predictably, with its most senior members. All proposed legislation must go through the Rules Committee en route to the floor of the House. The function of the Rules Committee is to set specific rules for debate and voting on each piece of business in order to conserve the time and order the transactions of that unwieldy body. In practice, this means that the Rules Committee exercises an important influence over the form in which that legislation will be presented and the real prospects for its passage. Particularly at the close of Congressional sessions, the Rules Committee (frequently in the person of its chairman) may prevent legislation from reaching the floor. Or it may attach such rules for debate and voting as are calculated to assure its defeat, such as permitting unlimited amendments to a tax bill which represents a number of delicate compromises. At other times, the Rules Committee may content itself with making clear to the chairman of a policy area committee that certain provisions must not be included in prospective legislation.

Certain other powers inhere in the leadership of the two political parties in the House. Principal among these is the power to fill committee assignments by selecting among new and returning members of the House; the member who receives a coveted, prestigious assignment is likely to be one who has previously demonstrated party regularity, and he is expected to be properly appreciative in the future. If he is not, he may be overlooked in future assignments. Serious application to developing the expertise necessary to make the House function more effectively is rewarded equally with party loyalty, and the representative who applies himself diligently often finds that he is appointed to more and more visible and rewarding positions of responsibility within the House. The party leadership is also one of the major sources of information for ordinary members, most of whom would otherwise have no better sources than the daily newspapers. Party leaders provide knowledge about the President's plans and make arrangements for joint action by all party members in response to those intentions. No representative can be successful by himself; he must have the support of many other representatives, and the political party machinery is the most promising way to secure it. Thus, the party leadership gains an important kind of leverage within the institution.

Why do the other members acquiesce in the dominance of these two types of leadership positions? The simple answer is that, as a practical matter, there is very little that they can do about it. Communication among the balance of the 435 members is very difficult, and it is inhibited by party and ideological differences. Even if they could agree on measures to redirect or unseat the leadership, the total control of the parliamentary machinery by the established leaders would make such action very complicated, requiring a degree of perception, trust, skill, and discipline not likely to exist in any large body. If they did replace the leadership, moreover, the new leaders might be even less desirable than the old ones.

A more sophisticated answer would point out that most members do not even want to extract themselves from the web of seniority-based leadership management. A representative depends for re-election on being able to achieve certain visibility in his home district, preferably through being able to accomplish some tangible benefit for his constituents. He can do so in his early terms in the House, when his need is greatest, only through the assistance of established members — such as the chairman of his committee or the party leadership. Almost before he realizes it, he has incurred debts to his senior colleagues. Further, he soon acquires a degree of seniority himself — a kind of investment in perpetuating the established "move-up" system — and he becomes socialized into the House tradition: "to get along, go along." In other words, he begins to find that the established procedures not only contain payoffs for him if he votes with his chairman and his party leadership,,but he too begins to identify with the House and the accommodating, bargaining system to which it is committed. He becomes sympathetic to the constituency problems of other members, giving higher priority to the harmony of relationships between members and the reduction of conflict within the House than to the solution of the great problems of national public policy.

What types of men hold the key positions in the House? Table 1 shows some basic data about the incumbents of major positions in the 1969-1971 House of Representatives. The mere fact that a chairman or House leader came to Congress in the 1920's and is over 70 years old does not necessarily mean that he is either conservative or out of touch with the intervening five decades of rapid changes in American society. But neither is it a reason to be encouraged about the probable responsiveness of the people's legislators.

Many congressmen are much more aware of problems in the management of the House than observers, of course. But acting to install new leadership would not only provoke drastic conflicts; it would constitute an antitraditional act. And so members wait politely for senile leaders to die or retire, in the interim seeking to cover up for their incapacities. In this deep commitment to following the hallowed traditions of the House, no matter the cost in the adequacy with which public problems are dealt with, we find one of the aspects most completely characteristic of its institutional and social life. Only the most demanding emergencies can wrench members out of traditional behavior, because all of the rewards and penalties of their political lives are based on acting in accordance with that predictable standard. Their capacity to do things for their constituents, and their progress up the political ladder, depend on following tradition. Not to do so, no matter what the issue at stake, normally means severe damage to their effectiveness within the House and perhaps the end of their careers.

THE SENATE

The Senate contains only 100 members, and it prides itself on dispensing with the many formal rules and procedures that characterize the House. In contrast to what it views as "the lower house," the Senate tries to operate with a minimum of organization and a maximum of gentlemanly agreement in which the objection of one senator can prevent or delay the transaction of crucial business. But in fact,

TABLE 1
Biographical Survey of Political Leaders and
Committee Chairmen of the House of Representatives,
(91st Congress, 1969-1971)

Position	Name	Age (as of 4/1/70)	Business occupation or profession	Religion	Year entered Congress	District (including type of area); percentage of vote in 1968
Political Leadership						
1. Speaker	McCormack, John W.	78	Lawyer	Roman Catholic	1928	9th Massachusetts (urban-Boston) 62%
2. Majority Floor Leader	Albert, Carl Bert	61	Lawyer	Methodist	1946	3rd Oklahoma (8 rural counties) 68%
3. Majority Whip	Boggs, Hale	56	Lawyer	Roman Catholic	1947	2nd Louisiana (urban-New Orleans) Not available
4. Minority Leader	Ford, Gerald R.	56	Lawyer	Episcopalian	1949	5th Michigan (urban-Suburban: Grand Rapids) 63%
5. Minority Whip	Arends, Leslie C.	74	Banking and farming	Methodist	1935	17th Illinois (7 rural counties) 65%

Committee Chairmen

Committee	Name	Age	Occupation	Religion	Year	District
6. Agriculture	Poage, William Robert	70	Lawyer	Universalist	1937	11th Texas (11 rural counties) 97%
7. Appropriations	Mahon, George H.	69	Lawyer	Methodist	1935	19th Texas (17 rural counties) 100%-unopposed
8. Armed Services	Rivers, L. Mendel	64	Lawyer	Episcopalian	1941	1st South Carolina (9 rural counties) 100%-unopposed
9. Banking and Currency	Patman, Wright	66	Lawyer	Baptist	1929	1st Texas (18 rural counties) 100%-unopposed
10. District of Columbia	McMillan, John L.	Not available	Lawyer	Baptist	1939	6th South Carolina (9 rural counties) 58%
11. Education & Labor	Perkins, Carl D.	54	Lawyer	Baptist	1949	7th Kentucky (22 rural counties) 62%
12. Foreign Affairs	Morgan, Thomas E.	63	Medical doctor	Methodist	1945	26th Pennsylvania (24 rural counties) 64%
13. Governmental Operations	Dawson, William L.	83	Lawyer	Christian Scientist	1943	1st Illinois (urban-Chicago) 85%
14. House Administration	Friedel, Samuel N.	71	Businessman	Jewish	1953	7th Maryland (urban-Baltimore) 80%

Committee Chairmen (cont.)

Position	Name	Age (as of 4/1/70)	Business occupation or profession	Religion	Year entered Congress	District (including type of area); percentage of vote in 1968
15. Interior and Insular Affairs	Aspinall, Wayne N.	73	Lawyer, teacher, and farmer	Methodist	1949	4th Colorado (35 rural counties) 55%
16. Internal Security	Ichord, Richard H.	43	Lawyer	Baptist	1961	8th Missouri (15 rural counties) 58%
17. Interstate & Foreign Commerce	Staggers, Harley O.	62	Teacher and sheriff	Methodist	1949	2nd West Virginia (20 rural counties) 62%
18. Judiciary	Celler, Emanuel	81	Lawyer	Jewish	1923	10th New York (urban-New York City) 71%
19. Merchant Marine and Fisheries	Garmatz, Edward A.	67	Businessman	United Church of Christ	1947	3rd Maryland (urban-Baltimore) 81%
20. Post Office & Civil Service	Dulski, Thaddeus J.	54	Accountant	Roman Catholic	1959	41st New York (urban-Buffalo) (78%)
21. Public Works	Fallon, George H.	67	Advertising	Roman Catholic	1945	4th Maryland (urban-Baltimore) 66%
22. Rules	Colmer, William Meyers	80	Lawyer	Methodist	1933	5th Mississippi (16 rural counties) 100%-unopposed

23. Science and Astronautics	Miller, George P.	79	Civil engineer	Roman Catholic	1945	8th California (urban-Oakland) 64%
24. Standards of Official Conduct	Price, Charles Melvin	65	Journalist	Roman Catholic	1945	24th Illinois (urban-East St. Louis) 71%
25. Veterans' Affairs	Teague, Olin E.	59	Military	Baptist	1946	6th Texas (12 rural counties) 100%-unopposed
26. Ways and Means	Mills, Wilbur D.	60	Lawyer	Methodist	1939	2nd Arkansas (15 rural counties) Not available

Major Appropriations Subcommittees

27. Defense	Mahon, George H.	See #7				
28. Foreign Operations	Passman, Otto E.	69	Businessman	Baptist	1947	5th Louisiana (17 rural parishes) 100%-unopposed
29. Military Construction	Sikes, Robert L. F.	63	Newspaper publisher	Methodist	1945	1st Florida (9 rural counties) 85%
30. Public Works	Kirwan, Michael J.	83	Businessman	Roman Catholic	1937	19th Ohio (urban-Youngstown) 70%

Source: Official Congressional Directory: 91st Congress, 1st Session (Washington, D. C.: U.S. Government Printing Office, 1969).

the Senate has evolved an elaborate set of rules and traditions governing the behavior of members. These standards are presided over by an institutional establishment — an informal group of usually senior senators distinguished principally by their commitment to the Senate as an institution. This group asserts authority not only over internal procedures but also on occasion over the policy positions assumed by the Senate as a body. Membership in the inner circle of the Senate is personal rather than institutionally based. Supplementing this form of leadership is a division of labor which carries many of the same benefits and costs as in the case of the House of Representatives. Again, the types of positions may be divided between policy areas and Senate leadership.

(1) Policy Area Committees

The differences between House and Senate committee structure and operation are minor, reflecting chiefly the difference in size of membership in the respective Houses. The Senate has fewer, smaller committees, with a somewhat different prestige ranking. Finance and Appropriations, which deal respectively with revenue and expenditures, are (despite the Senate's secondary role in House-initiated money matters) probably the most important committees. Foreign Relations, because of the Senate's special powers in that field, is a more visible committee and one that attracts many senators, but its impact on policy is not great. Judiciary, because of its power to confirm or reject Supreme Court nominees and the Senate's special concern for proposed constitutional amendments, is also a high status committee. Armed Services and Agriculture follow, and the remainder are reserved for specialists and newcomers.

The formal powers of the chairman of a Senate committee are much the same as those of a House chairman, but in practice they fall short of the autocracy of the House model. Operating with smaller numbers and a more relaxed, gentlemanly ethos — perhaps aided by the fact of having six-year terms — the Senate chairmen tend to consult more with their members, grant them more visibility and influence within the committee, and proceed on the basis of a general consensus. The chairman is clearly the leader, and no junior senator would be unaware or dare to ignore that fact; but the operation of the committee is normally more harmonious.

The Senate's traditions of elaborate courtesy among members extends to the manner in which pressure is applied to induce chairmen to bring legislation forward, and to the relationship between the ranking minority member of a committee and its chairman. Rising to the chairmanship of a Senate committee implies not only substantial seniority, but also deep commitment to the Senate as an institution and to its "proper" functioning within the system. No President and no party leader would insult the dignity of the Senate by brash or blatant attempts to coerce a committee chairman. And party differences would ordinarily play a small part in the deliberations of senior members of a committee. In short, in the Senate there is at least the appearance of a greater role for consideration of the merits of issues, and a smaller organizing role for the political party.

(2) Senate Leadership Positions

Although the position of President Pro Tem of the Senate corresponds in form to that of Speaker of the House, in practice it is no more than an honorific title bestowed on a very senior member. The actual managerial functions performed by the Speaker in the House are in the hands of the Senate Majority Leader. This officer is elected by the senators of the majority party at the outset of each session; once chosen, of course, a senator usually retains his position as Majority Leader until he dies, retires, or is defeated for re-election. The choice is influenced, but not controlled, by the relative seniority among senators of the majority party. But more important is the reputation of a Senator for commitment to the protection and furtherance of the Senate as an institution, his mainstream position within the party on major issues, his adherence to the traditional rules and procedures, his sense of fair play, and his parliamentary skills. Choice of the Minority Leader by the minority party is based on similar criteria.

Both Majority and Minority Leaders serve informing, scheduling, and unifying roles for their respective parties, in effect combining the duties of Speaker, party leaders, and Rules Committee in the House. The Majority Leader coordinates the activities of Senate committees, seeking to bring bills to the floor in accordance with his view of the proper priorities for that session. He selects members of the conference committees which will seek to negotiate differences between House and Senate versions of legislation enacted. He is the chief source of information for other senators, as well as the means toward public visibility, additional institutional responsibilities, or improved committee status for them. He consults regularly with the Minority Leader so that most of the Senate's business can go forward with the support of a broad consensus. Both Leaders are normally consulted and kept informed of major developments by the President, although matters of party strategy or program are reserved for the Leader of the President's party.

Behind the two Leaders of the Senate is the inner "establishment" or club of generally senior senators. This group has no precise boundaries, but some senators are clearly inside and some others just as clearly outside. Membership is personal, based in part on acceptance of the Senate's traditional ways and in part on the senator's political skills and style. The senator who works hard and effectively on committees and at other tasks assigned him by the leadership, thereby contributing to the work of the Senate, is soon marked as a potential member. If he continues to show tolerance and respect for other senators, demonstrates a strong concern for the harmonious transaction of the Senate's business and the preservation of its reputation, and is not too "far out" on issues, he may be consulted more and more often about important matters of Senate policy. In time, he will be fully socialized and eventually integrated into the social grouping within which most of the major decisions of the Senate are made.

The individual senator, whether a member of the inner group or not, is somewhat more capable of making himself felt within the institution than is a member of the House. He is no more likely to be able to redirect or unseat the leadership, nor, again, is he likely to really want to try. But he can count on being able to gain the floor and address the Senate, which a representative may not be able to do. Further, the Senate's tradition of operating on the basis of unanimous consent means that the objection of a single senator can delay or, in some cases, prevent action on particular matters to which one Senator is opposed. The Senate's famous filibuster rule, for example, permits any Senator or group of senators to talk for as long as they are physically capable, and some have held the floor in excess of twenty-four hours. Toward the close of a legislative session, a filibuster or even the threat of one by one or more senators can result in a leadership decision to abandon proposed legislation. Thus, the individual recourses of a senator are substantial, though it is questionable whether he can develop any greater ultimate impact on the policies produced than his counterpart in the House. In both cases, the leadership's grip on the machinery of the institution is very strong.

The Senate leadership during 1969-1971 is shown in Table 2. The key senators are roughly the same age as the key representatives, but they are distributed somewhat more broadly across the nation — and across the ideological spectrum. As a result, the Senate, though clearly the stronghold of Southern defense against civil rights legislation by virtue of the filibuster rule and Southern dominance of the Judiciary Committee, is somewhat more liberal in its basic orientation than is the House.

What do these characteristics of power distribution and incumbency mean for the overall operation of the Congress? Clearly, the men of power are far from representative of the national population. They are much older, probably much more conservative, and they are motivated by long-established traditions which set additional boundaries to what they can seriously consider or hope to accomplish in the way of legislation. Because such men are rarely challenged effectively in elections, they do not feel the pressures for change within the society except as the interests and people with whom they have close contact happen to present such problems to them. Under these conditions, the Congress is normally likely to be responsive to developments in the economy or society chiefly in arbitrary, unpredictable, and conservative ways. Further, what appear to be challenges to the system itself are likely to be met with lack of understanding and severe reaction. On such matters, nearly all men of power are likely to be of a single mind.

A second major consequence of the existing pattern of power in the Congress is its great dependency on effective leadership. Unless the President and the party leaders within the two houses establish clear and agreed priorities, and work effectively to coordinate committee actions and floor debates, very little legislation will be pro-

TABLE 2
Biographical Survey of Political Leaders and Committee Chairmen of the Senate
(91st Congress, 1969–1971)

Position	Name	Age (as of 4/1/70)	Business occupation or profession	Religion	Year entered Congress and/or year entered Senate	State (including pop. in 1960); percentage of vote in most recent applicable election
Political Leadership						
1. Majority Leader	Mansfield, Michael J.	67	Professor of History and Political Science	Roman Catholic	1943 & 1953	Montana 674,767 65%
2. Majority Whip	Kennedy, Edward M.	38	Lawyer	Roman Catholic	1962	Massachusetts 5,148,578 75%
3. Minority Leader	Scott, Hugh	69	Lawyer	Episcopalian	1941 & 1959	Pennsylvania 11,319,366 51%
4. Minority Whip	Griffin, Robert P.	46	Lawyer	Congregational Christian	1947 & 1966	Michigan 7,823,194 56%
Committee Chairmen						
5. Aeronautical and Space Sciences	Anderson, Clinton P.	74	Insurance	Presbyterian	1941 & 1949	New Mexico 951,023 53%
6. Agriculture and Forestry	Ellender, Allen Jos.	79	Lawyer and farmer	Presbyterian	1937	Louisiana 3,257,022 unopposed

Committee Chairmen (cont.)

Position	Name	Age (as of 4/1/70)	Business occupation or profession	Religion	Year entered Congress and/or year entered Senate	State (including pop. in 1960); percentage of vote in most recent applicable election
7. Appropriations	Russell, Richard Brevard	72	Lawyer	Methodist	1933	Georgia 3,943,116 unopposed
8. Armed Services	Stennis, John Cornelius	68	Lawyer and farmer	Presbyterian	1947	Mississippi 2,178,141 unopposed
9. Banking & Currency	Sparkman, John J.	70	Lawyer	Methodist	1937 & 1946	Alabama 3,266,740 61%
10. Commerce	Magnuson, Warren G.	64	Lawyer	Lutheran	1937 & 1944	Washington 2,853,214 65%
11. District of Columbia	Tydings, Joseph Davies	41	Lawyer	Episcopalian	1965	Maryland 3,100,689 63%
12. Finance	Long, Russell B.	51	Lawyer	Methodist	1948	Louisiana 3,257,022 unopposed
13. Foreign Relations	Fulbright, J. William	64	Lawyer	Disciples of Christ	1943 & 1945	Arkansas 1,786,272 59%
14. Government Operations	McClellan, John L.	74	Lawyer	Baptist	1935 & 1943	Arkansas 1,786,272 Not available

15. Interior and Insular Affairs	Jackson, Henry M.	57	Lawyer	Presbyterian	1941 & 1953	Washington 2,853,214 72%
16. Judiciary	Eastland, James Oliver	65	Lawyer and farmer	Methodist	1943	Mississippi 2,178,141 71%
17. Labor and Public Welfare	Yarborough, Ralph Webster	66	Lawyer	Baptist	1957	Texas 9,579,677 56%
18. Post Office and Civil Service	McGee, Gale William	55	Professor (History)	Presbyterian	1959	Wyoming 330,066 54%
19. Public Works	Randolph, Jennings	68	Professor and journalist	Seventh Day Baptist	1933 & 1958	West Virginia 1,860,421 60%
20. Rules and Administration	Jordan, B. Everett	73	Textile manufacturer	Methodist	1958	North Carolina 4,556,155 56%

Major Senate Appropriations Subcommittee Chairmen

21. Department of Defense	Russell, Richard B.	see #7				
22. Deficiencies & Supplementals	Byrd, Robert C.	52	Lawyer	Baptist	1952 & 1959	West Virginia 1,860,421 68%
23. Military Construction	Mansfield, Michael J.	see #1				
24. Public Works	Ellender, Allen J.	see #6				

duced. At best, the Congress is an institution that operates on a fits and starts basis; the number of powerful men who must be convinced of the necessity of a particular action, and the difficulty of persuading them, together with the multitude of public problems on which action of some kind must be taken, mean that a given subject comes before the Congress for serious consideration only once every few years. Unless the leadership does its job well, the chance for action will pass with only a half-way measure enacted, or a patchwork product that makes conditions worse instead of better.

Finally, this decentralization of power into the hands of a relatively few congressmen means that many veto points are created from which the positions and prerogatives of well-established groups can be defended even against the wishes of a large majority. Because it is so easy for one or two key congressmen to block legislative action, and so difficult for the leadership to mobilize support at all the necessary points of the legislative process, inaction (and advantage to those favored by the status quo) is a frequent result. The other likely result is legislation of the "lowest common denominator" kind — legislation which offends few, usually because it has no serious effect on the status quo. One may well ask, of course, whether such legislation is capable of solving problems.

THE SUPREME COURT

After two decades in which the Supreme Court has had major impact on a wide range of public matters — segregation, political freedoms, defendants' rights in criminal cases, state legislative and congressional districting, to mention only a few areas — it hardly seems necessary to stress that it plays a major policymaking role within the national government. Although it can make decisions only on cases which are brought before it, the Court's powers to interpret the Constitution and judge the acts of other branches render it an integral part of the political process. In order to decide what a statute or an executive regulation means, whether an act by a government official is consistent with authorizing legislation, or whether either is consistent with the Constitution, the justices must make choices. These choices are inevitably based, at least in part, on their personal values, preferences, and goals. Nor is it a coincidence that the same issues which have been before the Congress or the executive branch are also brought before the Supreme Court. Thus, the Court is different from the other institutions in form, but not in political character or in impact on the society.

The Supreme Court consists of only nine men, each of whose votes is of equal weight. It has no committees, and (with rare exceptions) all of the justices personally hear arguments on, discuss, and vote on every case. Nevertheless, there are ways in which influence becomes concentrated within the Court. Not all justices are equally determinative in shaping the Court's policy positions. Official status, the division of labor among the justices, and their reputations, personalities, and style as individuals are the chief reasons for sometimes sharp differences in their real power.

The position of Chief Justice offers the principal opportunity within the Court to affect the nature of its decisionmaking. In nearly two centuries under the present Constitution, there have been only 15 Chief Justices, as compared with 38 Presidents. A politically astute Chief Justice who assumes his position at a relatively early age and enjoys a long life may leave a more lasting imprint on the public policies of the nation than some Presidents. Chief Justice John Marshall (1801-1835), for example, probably had considerably more effect on the development of the United States than several of the Presidents who held office during the nineteenth century. Not all Chief Justices have left the mark of a Marshall, a Hughes, or a Warren; some have found the tasks of the office, the strongmindedness of other justices, or the issues of the times to be more than they could manage. To be effective, a Chief Justice must employ the political skills of bargaining and accommodation. He must develop and use the formal powers of his office in harmony with the more personal techniques of small group leadership in order to bring a majority of the Justices into agreement with the policy positions he favors.

The formal powers of the Chief Justice are few. But tradition and practice have combined with an increasing caseload to make them important sources of leverage within the Court. For example, the Chief Justice presides at the conferences where the justices select the cases on which they will hear arguments and write opinions expressing new or clarified rules of law. Of the many thousands of cases appealed every year, the Court must of necessity decline to hear the great majority and allocate its time to the 150-200 cases presenting what the justices see as the most important issues. Although all of the justices have the right to review all of these potential cases, the Chief Justice has a larger staff and therefore makes it his responsibility to see that all appeals are reviewed; he suggests which cases should be selected for further hearings and which should be rejected. Discussion at these conferences thus proceeds under an agenda and a preliminary selection set by the Chief Justice. If he has done his work carefully, the cases actually chosen for the Court's subsequent calendars will look very much like his original list.

The Court's practice is to hear oral arguments on cases for two-week periods and then to take the next two weeks for research, decisions, and opinion-writing. Decisions on cases are made at regular conferences of all Justices, again presided over by the Chief Justice. At these conferences, the Chief Justice normally structures the issues for resolution in each case, and then opens the floor for discussion among the Justices. Voting on the case, however, proceeds from the most junior justice (the most recent appointee) up to the Chief Justice. Because he votes last, the Chief Justice holds the decisive vote in closely-divided cases. Although each vote in a 5-4 majority is of equal importance to the outcome, the final vote cast gains something of a trump card status by virtue of its conclusive effect.

Perhaps more important than casting the last vote is the Chief Justice's power (when he is in the majority) to select who will write the majority opinion in the case. If the Chief Justice wants to state the rule of law applicable to the case in terms consistent with his own policy preferences, he may write the opinion himself. Or he may assign it to another justice of like views. In some cases where the outcome of the case has been decided before the Chief Justice's turn to vote, he may decide to vote with the majority even if he does not wholly agree with them; this will give him control over the writing of the opinion and thus prevents an extreme statement which he would oppose.

The writing of the majority opinion is a crucial stage of the Court's work. Through this opinion, other political actors and the public will learn of the Court's position and its reasoning, and a new bit of substance will be added to the body of law and precedent which supposedly guides or controls behavior in the nation. The scope and nature of the rule laid down by the Court in an opinion is normally more important than who wins or loses the case itself. The opinion exercises the Justices' broad discretion as to whether their decision will be grounded in a new, perhaps drastic, interpretation of the Constitution, or whether it will rest on a narrow interpretation of a statute or a minor omission by one of the figures in the case. Further, the author of the opinion can write it in such a way that the reasoning behind the decision appears to apply to many similar or analogous situations, or he can confine it so sharply that no other cases or behavior need ever be affected.

The justice who is chosen to write the opinion in a crucial case thus acquires substantial influence within the Court, at least in that subject area. (It also means public and professional visibility and the satisfaction of judicial egos, a fact which gives the politically astute Chief Justice a kind of patronage to bestow on associate justices who vote with him.) There are limits to this power, of course; if an opinion writer seriously misrepresents the views of the other justices who voted with the majority, any one or more of them may decline to join in the opinion. In some cases, this may mean the loss of the necessary vote(s) to make up a majority. The opinions are circulated within the Court in draft form for comments by the other justices, and the process of negotiation and compromise over the wording of it may take weeks. In some instances, the majority-uniting solution is an opinion in which conflicting or ambiguous positions are taken — in effect, postponing precise formulation of new rules of law to some future time or another institution.

The Chief Justice has some other powers, mostly of a housekeeping nature, which he can use to make the daily routines of the other justices relatively more pleasant. He also serves as head of various bodies having administrative responsibilities over the lower federal courts, thus giving him opportunity to influence the opinions of lower federal court judges in a number of issue areas. Within the Supreme Court, however, he must rely for further influence on the personal support and regard which he generates from the other justices.

The only other institutional positions of importance within the Court emerge from seniority relationships among the associate justices. When the Chief Justice votes with the minority in a case, the senior associate justice in the majority chooses the writer of the opinion. The justice with the longest tenure on the Court may also acquire some added prestige particularly because he is most likely to be selecting opinion-writers when the Chief Justice votes in the minority, but he rises above his fellows only slightly by virtue of such prerogatives.

This analysis is not intended to suggest that the other Supreme Court justices are without means of developing significant influence as individuals. Instead, we stress that power within the nine-member Supreme Court is very much the product of individual reputation, effort, personality, and style. There are many ways in which justices can maximize their influence. By developing expertise in difficult subject areas, for example, or through earning a reputation for hard and effective work on the Court, a justice may end up writing far more than his share of opinions. Or by combining with other justices through pre-conference "caucuses" or simple log-rolling, a justice may help form coalitions that establish Court policy positions of great significance. Four votes are required to select a case to be heard on appeal, for example; justices convinced that particular aspects of existing law should be changed may simply vote to hear any cases raising such issues, regardless of the Chief Justice's suggestions. The experience of the Court's decisionmaking throughout history shows that justices have frequently coalesced to form blocs for or against certain national policy developments. During some such periods, one or two "independent" justices have shifted back and forth between the blocs, casting the deciding votes on first one side and then the other.

The extra-Court prestige of a justice, such as his intimacy with a President, may contribute to his capacity to exercise influence on the Court. More often, his real power depends on the persuasiveness with which he argues cases among his fellows and the personal esteem in which they hold him. If he is almost always accurate, incisive, and unabrasive in intellectual discourse, if he is tolerant of the views and mistakes of others, if he is able to combine policy disagreement with personal friendship, and if he understands the range of the possible and practical for the Court and does not seek decisions that are inconsistent with the underlying nature of the system, then he may become highly influential. In short, the Court operates with a premium on an accepted political style in much the same way as do the two houses of Congress. Though here it is much influenced by the language and techniques of legal scholarship, it is as well formed and as institutionally defensive as elsewhere in government. The maverick who challenges the long-established operating procedures of the Court, who fails to do his share of the work of the institution, or who advocates actions that are "far out" in the eyes of his fellows is not likely to be effective.

Because of the relatively small number of men who have served as

Chief Justice, or even as justices of the Supreme Court, it is difficult to generalize about the types of men and political preferences that have been dominant. All of the justices have had legal training, and most have been either prominent in the law or in political life. The President consistently nominates men who would be likely to follow his policy preferences, and senators just as consistently resist confirmation when a nominee holds views contrary to *their* preferences. Republican Presidents tend to nominate men from the ranks of the federal or state judiciary or from large private law firms, while Democrats are more likely to nominate from political life, such as the Congress or the Cabinet. Presidents have occasionally guessed wrong about a nominee's probable actions on the Court, or have paid political debts instead of seeking policy support. Eisenhower's nomination of former Chief Justice Warren and Kennedy's appointment of Justice Byron White are only the latest in a series of such examples. But by and large, the best cues to the political preferences of the Chief Justice and the other members of the Court are the goals of the President who appointed them. Since Roosevelt appointees gained full control of the Court in 1941, it has been generally liberal, with the exception of a short period of Truman-appointee dominance in the late 1940's and early 1950's. The prospect of several Nixon administration appointees, however, suggests that the next decades will see a much more conservative Court.

THE EXECUTIVE

To most Americans, congressmen and judges are chiefly important because they are members of important governmental institutions, but the President of the United States is viewed to be important as an individual: the most powerful in the world, it is often said, yet responsive to the will of the people.

The serious student of politics soon comes to realize that this reassuring if puzzling picture of the President is too blurred to be very helpful in understanding his role in the American political scene. The President is as much a part of an institution as are less conspicuous and less prestigious public officials. In much of what he does he is highly dependent on others and on what others will accept — far from "most powerful" if that phrase is taken to imply that he is free to embark on any course of action he likes. Under some conditions, on the other hand, he can be close to omnipotent, not because of any powers granted to him in the Constitution and laws, but because of his influence over public opinion and therefore over what people think and what they demand of government. We will first examine the constraints on the President and then the conditions under which those constraints are weakened or eliminated.

Limits on the President's Maneuverability

That the President is chosen by election and has an interest in his own re-election or in keeping his political party in power is the most conspicuous formal constraint upon him, but it is unquestionably a minor one compared to the others. As Chapter 14 makes clear, the policies a President and his party pursue are not the only reasons people support or oppose him on election day. Party identification, the candidates' personalities, and the advantage an incumbent enjoys over a challenger are all important factors.

Nor is the electoral college method of selecting him a major constraint on what he does, though it undoubtedly sometimes has an influence. Under this system, each state is allotted electoral votes roughly in proportion to its population; a candidate normally gets all the electoral votes in each state in which he has won a majority of the popular votes. Since it is therefore especially to his advantage to carry the most populous states — those with large cities in them — he has some incentive to appeal to the large city voters. Remember that rural over-representation in both houses of Congress gives those bodies the opposite bias, making them less sensitive to the interests of urban residents. The electoral college system, however, is at most a minor constraint upon the President. Only three times in our whole history has it produced an outcome different from what would have been the case under direct popular election, though the possibility of that happening constantly keeps alive an interest in changing the electoral system. Probably more important, the Nixon election in 1968 showed that it is possible, even under the electoral college system, for a candidate to win an election by making little effort to carry the large cities and by appealing chiefly to rural and small town voters of the South and Middle West. Presidential candidates have to put together some kind of a coalition of supporting groups to win, but they have considerable leeway in deciding to which demands they will be responsive and which they will play down or ignore.

The most potent constraint on the President is his need to rely upon the information and advice of his subordinates for most of the decisions he makes. The President is one man, charged by the Constitution with the duty to "take care that the laws be faithfully executed." To do so, of course, he needs help. At present, there are more than 2,000,000 executive branch employees (not including the armed forces, though they too are clearly important means at his disposal) engaged in this effort. Not surprisingly, the effect of thus parceling out the power and responsibility of the presidency is to create the same kind of division of labor and resulting dispersal and stratification of power that occurs in the other institutions.

The modern President spends much of his time trying to learn what executive branch employees are doing in his name and trying to persuade or coerce them into doing things the way he wants them done. He is usually aware of how badly he needs capable, independent (and therefore strong-minded) people in positions of responsibility, even at the risk of finding that they have different ideas and programs from his own.

In trying to set up a staff organization that can make discharging these responsibilities possible for a human being, Presidents tend to delegate powers in a highly personal manner. To some extent, allocations of power are implied in the creation of permanent departments and bureaus of the executive branch, but their role may vary according to Presidential preference and his confidence in their top management. Three broad classes of people in the executive branch influence presidential decisions and policy. The first consists of incumbents of those positions which are most personal in nature — where the powerholders are intended to serve the President's need to know what is going on and to mobilize and apply his power on his personal behalf. Examples of such positions include the major White House assistants, the Director of the Bureau of the Budget, and the office of Attorney General. The second class consists of positions created by statute which have specific and continuing responsibilities, where the powerholders owe their status to their offices rather than to their special relationship to the President. Individuals among the secretaries of Cabinet-level departments may be close friends of the President and enjoy considerable special influence for that reason, but they also have outside or public responsibilities fixed by law which force them to play an independent role at times. Examples of major positions of this sort are the Secretary of Defense, the Secretary of State, the Director of the FBI, the Chairman of the Federal Reserve Board, and members of the independent regulatory commissions such as the Interstate Commerce Commission. The third class consists of staff members at lower levels of all these types of executive agencies: people who gather and screen the information upon which top officials act and who often themselves make decisions which go far toward shaping the course of future policy.

To a degree that often surprises newly elected Presidents themselves, all these subordinates limit and influence what he can do. Beset with hundreds of other pressing matters, a President cannot often re-examine in detail a recommendation his special adviser on welfare policy may make to him about an income maintenance program or independently change his attorney general's recommendation that a particular person be nominated for a Supreme Court vacancy. He may, of course, do this sort of thing occasionally on a matter on which he feels especially strongly or in response to still other pressures on the President — such as those from powerful elements in his political party, in Congress, or in pressure groups.

Whenever a President tries to put into effect a policy that lacks support among those who have to carry it out, he faces a formidable obstacle. In these circumstances, his formal authority to issue directives may do him little good. Long-term staff members in any large bureaucratic organization learn many devices to delay, reinterpret, or ignore directives they do not like, and it is all the easier because responsibility for any course of action or lack of action is difficult or impossible to pinpoint. Both Dwight Eisenhower in the fifties and Franklin Roosevelt during World War II formally ordered federal officials to be sure that any company awarded government contracts did not discriminate against blacks in hiring or promoting their work forces, and both established commissions to carry out the directive. In both cases, the order was ignored far more than observed.

In an important sense, the basic power of the President is the power to persuade, the implication being that when he cannot persuade his subordinates that they favor what he favors, his power is minimal. This is a crucial point, though there are areas of policymaking discussed below in which it has little applicability.

The constraints civil servants place upon the power of the President are not wholly random or dependent on the whims of subordinates with a variety of values or ideologies. To a significant degree, this form of constraint functions to minimize policy change. Any change disrupts established routines, relationships, and statuses in an agency and so evokes resistance among at least part of the staff. This tendency is enhanced by the psychological and organizational ties a long-established agency develops to particular clientele groups. The Visa Division of the Department of State, for example, has attracted and kept staff members who share the view that the nation's security is in their hands and that a significant relaxation of standards for granting visas for entry into the United States is a disservice to the nation. Veterans groups and other patriotic organizations reinforce this view and help win appropriations and support for staff members who put it into practice. In the face of bureaucratic anchoring of this sort, even an act of Congress, let alone a presidential directive, has at times brought little change in the actual award of visas.

Because executive organizations operating in controversial areas do develop links to specific interest groups, a President who wants to maintain some maneuverability for himself sometimes must deliberately create agencies with overlapping jurisdictions and diverse clientele ties. An examination of this ploy and of its implications for elite and presidential influence appears in Chapter 12.

Plainly, the structural pattern of the executive branch has a strong impact upon presidential behavior and presidential power. Anyone wishing fully to understand that impact must analyze in detail the organization, jurisdiction, and interest group ties of every agency. Figure 1 lists the major organizational units with which such an analysis would deal. It makes it clear that a modern President formally controls policy in an extremely wide range of important concerns, necessarily delegates most of the decisionmaking to others, and acts chiefly on information and recommendations supplied by others even in the small proportion of decisions he ultimately makes himself.

A group of administrative agencies in the Executive Office of the President helps the Chief Executive coordinate recommendations from the vast executive branch and acts upon many of them without his personal intervention. The Bureau of the Budget is particularly concerned with fitting appropriations requests from the agencies into an overall executive budget, screening recommendations for new substantive legislation, and overseeing administrative procedures. The National Security Council serves to accommodate the sometimes disparate interests of the armed forces, the State Department, the intelligence services, and domestic agencies in the field of foreign policy. The make-up of the Executive Office of the President changes from time to time, but these two agencies, together with the White

FIGURE 1
The Government of the United States

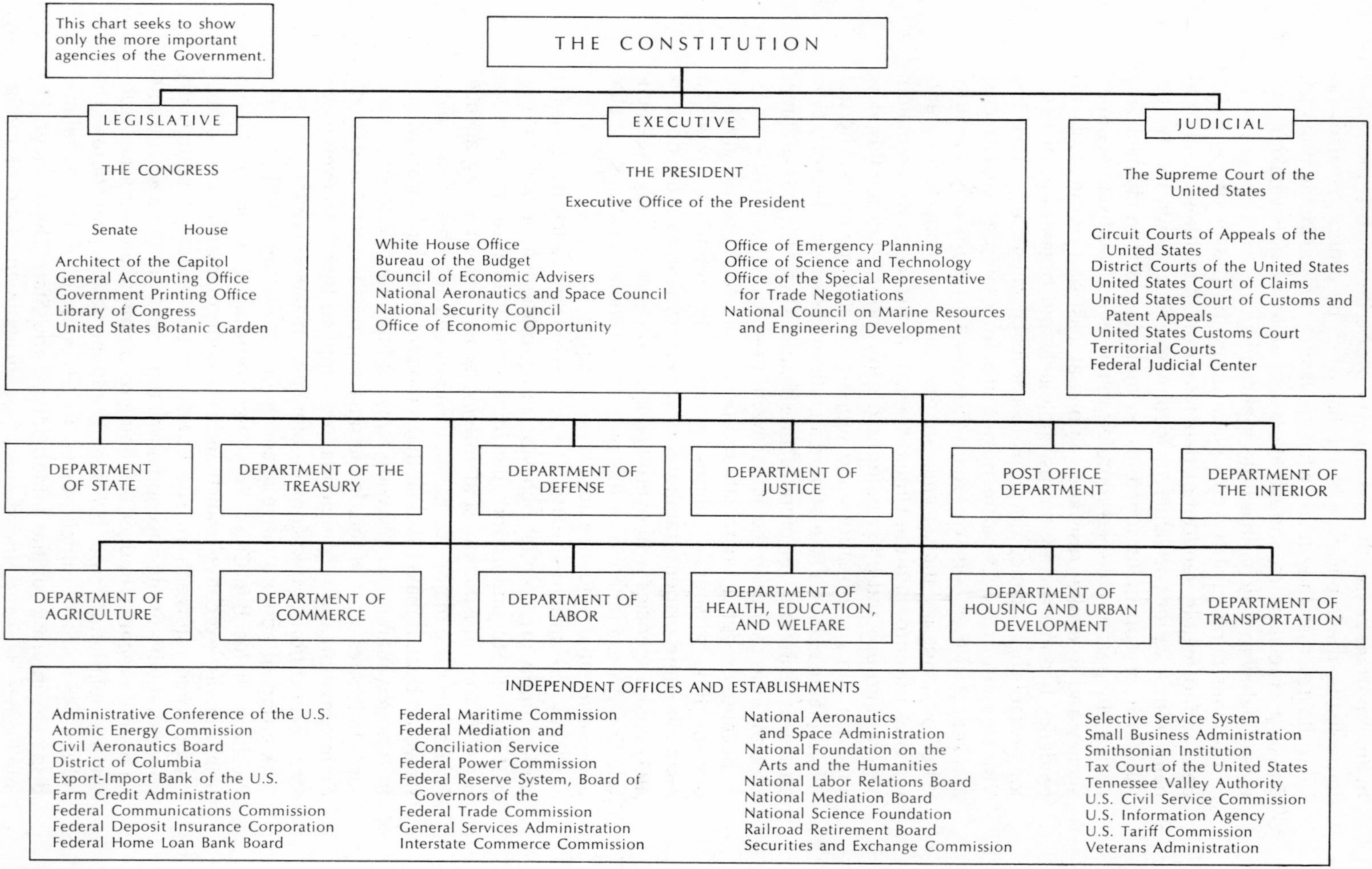

This chart seeks to show only the more important agencies of the Government.

THE CONSTITUTION

LEGISLATIVE

THE CONGRESS

Senate   House

Architect of the Capitol
General Accounting Office
Government Printing Office
Library of Congress
United States Botanic Garden

EXECUTIVE

THE PRESIDENT

Executive Office of the President

White House Office
Bureau of the Budget
Council of Economic Advisers
National Aeronautics and Space Council
National Security Council
Office of Economic Opportunity
Office of Emergency Planning
Office of Science and Technology
Office of the Special Representative for Trade Negotiations
National Council on Marine Resources and Engineering Development

JUDICIAL

The Supreme Court of the United States

Circuit Courts of Appeals of the United States
District Courts of the United States
United States Court of Claims
United States Court of Customs and Patent Appeals
United States Customs Court
Territorial Courts
Federal Judicial Center

DEPARTMENT OF STATE

DEPARTMENT OF THE TREASURY

DEPARTMENT OF DEFENSE

DEPARTMENT OF JUSTICE

POST OFFICE DEPARTMENT

DEPARTMENT OF THE INTERIOR

DEPARTMENT OF AGRICULTURE

DEPARTMENT OF COMMERCE

DEPARTMENT OF LABOR

DEPARTMENT OF HEALTH, EDUCATION, AND WELFARE

DEPARTMENT OF HOUSING AND URBAN DEVELOPMENT

DEPARTMENT OF TRANSPORTATION

INDEPENDENT OFFICES AND ESTABLISHMENTS

Administrative Conference of the U.S.
Atomic Energy Commission
Civil Aeronautics Board
District of Columbia
Export-Import Bank of the U.S.
Farm Credit Administration
Federal Communications Commission
Federal Deposit Insurance Corporation
Federal Home Loan Bank Board

Federal Maritime Commission
Federal Mediation and Conciliation Service
Federal Power Commission
Federal Reserve System, Board of Governors of the
Federal Trade Commission
General Services Administration
Interstate Commerce Commission

National Aeronautics and Space Administration
National Foundation on the Arts and the Humanities
National Labor Relations Board
National Mediation Board
National Science Foundation
Railroad Retirement Board
Securities and Exchange Commission

Selective Service System
Small Business Administration
Smithsonian Institution
Tax Court of the United States
Tennessee Valley Authority
U.S. Civil Service Commission
U.S. Information Agency
U.S. Tariff Commission
Veterans Administration

Source: U.S. Government Organization Manual, p. 628.

House staff, are its major components. Increasingly, burdened Presidents are adding to the White House staff individuals who advise them on specialized and controversial policy areas such as foreign policy, welfare policy, and pollution of the environment. This development amounts to still another form of overlap among agencies concerned with specific policy areas, for the State Department and the C.I.A. also deal with foreign policy, at least four cabinet departments and the Office of Economic Opportunity with welfare policy, and the Interior Department, the Commerce Department, and others with pollution.

The other serious limitation on presidential power is the need to win congressional cooperation for major policies. The President must constantly try to induce the Congress to enact his legislative program and provide the appropriations necessary to carry it out. On domestic policy matters, he frequently does not succeed, even when his own political party controls both houses of Congress and he vigorously pushes his program. Both Harry Truman and John Kennedy found it impossible to induce the Congress to go along with the major domestic policies they strenuously advocated, even though both were Democratic Presidents dealing with Congresses dominated by Democrats. When the opposition party dominates even one House, the likelihood of deadlock is of course greater, for both the President and the congressmen then have an incentive to create the impression that their efforts to promote the public interest are being blocked by a recalcitrant, partisan opposition party.

When such conflict occurs, either the President or the Congress may espouse the more liberal position. The fairly consistent pattern taken by a long series of more or less liberal twentieth-century Presidents left the impression for a time that the Congress could be counted on to take more conservative postures than the President in such areas as labor, welfare, conservation, and civil rights. In the Nixon administration after 1968, however, the reverse pattern prevailed. Congress still severely limited the President's maneuverability, but now it did so by approving more liberal programs than he wanted on a wide variety of issues: pollution control, welfare benefits, social security benefits, federal aid to education, and desegregation of the public schools, among others.

Buttresses of Presidential Power

On some of the most important policies, these constraints on the President become weak or insignificant. They fail to operate because he is able to bring into play his most important source of power: his influence over mass public opinion. When public opinion is powerful and united enough, it carries the Congress and the officials of the various executive agencies with it.

Presidential sway over public opinion is greatest on issues that create serious anxiety without pitting clearly defined or organized groups against each other. A threat from a foreign power or a serious and lengthy economic depression make virtually everyone anxious and at the same time make people eager for resolute leadership without clear demands for particular lines of action or policy directions. On such matters, it is generally assumed that the President has information and expert advice not available to the mass public and that he should be supported and followed. Not so when he recommends restrictions on labor union activity or higher benefits to welfare recipients — policy proposals that predictably pit workers and employers or liberals and conservatives against each other.

When President Kennedy told the country that Russian missile emplacements in Cuba threatened this country, he created a level of anxiety conducive to promoting general support for his ultimatum to the Russian Premier demanding that they be removed, even though that policy carried considerable risk of nuclear war. In such a crisis situation, the President was able to structure opinion rather than merely respond to it; and in doing so he carried Congress with him and destroyed any possibility of serious footdragging or resistance on the part of the State or Defense Departments. The same was true of the Tonkin Gulf incident. It was also true of the economic crisis presented by the Great Depression of the 1930's, which produced anxiety in the entire population, including the business community, and gave President Franklin Roosevelt a ready and manipulable audience for the resolute actions which, he confidently told a frightened country, would put us back on the road to recovery.

The conditions for this kind of overriding presidential power are sometimes created by events outside his control; but at other times he can create them himself. It was certainly not conscious government policy to create the Great Depression, even though ignorance of economic principles may have encouraged public policies that contributed to it. Nor was the Japanese attack on Pearl Harbor in 1941 an effort by the President to give himself crisis powers. The Cuban missile crisis and the Tonkin Gulf incident are not such clear cases in this regard; many do see them as deliberate efforts to create strong public support for presidential policy. President James Polk's action in sending United States troops into disputed border territory, thus starting the Mexican War, is another example of a presidential action which left little room for an opposition to function.

The conclusion would seem to be that it is overly simple to generalize about presidential power without specifying the kind of issue involved. On most issues, of the sort that regularly involve conflicting interests based upon economic position, occupation, and socioeconomic status, the President reflects established interest patterns more than he changes them. On the occasional issue that is of deep concern to virtually everyone and that evokes strong anxiety and uncertainty (rather than clear, but differing, ideas) about what should be done, the President's power to shape opinion and policy is very great. In these situations, the formal and legal checks upon him become formalities and not real constraints, for a majority of congressmen and of bureaucrats are likely to be swept along with the dominant tide of opinion. That the President is sometimes subjected to overriding constraints and sometimes largely free of them does not necessarily add up to a balanced situation or a "happy medium" so far as the power of the Chief Executive is concerned. For this kind of variation in presidential power, averages are meaningless. A virtually free hand in a major crisis can come close to destroying the checks that operate in normal times. This is an especially telling consideration when the President can himself create a sense of crisis.

Formal Powers and Real Powers

This analysis of the conditions that constrain or augment the influence of the President of the United States reveals something important about the relationship between the legal powers of a public official and his actual ability to shape public policy. Article II of the United States Constitution and various statutes grant to the President a number of important legal powers. He is supposed to "take care that the laws be faithfully executed," recommend legislation to Congress, act as Commander-in-Chief of the armed forces, and appoint a large number of civilian and military officers to their posts. He may remove some government officials for any reason he likes or for no reason, and he may remove others if he can show that they have been guilty of malfeasance or other grounds for removal specified in the laws creating their offices. He may pardon persons convicted of federal crimes. He may propose treaties to the Senate for ratification, may enter into "executive agreements" with foreign countries without any need for Senate ratification, and may recognize foreign countries or break diplomatic relations with them on his own initiative.

This is an imposing list of formal powers, especially so because some, especially the first three, are extremely broad in character. To recite such a list, however, is to understand almost nothing about the true powers and influence of the President. If, in taking "care that the laws be faithfully executed," appointing, and so on, he acts only or chiefly in conformity with the information and recommendations provided by top civil servants, a group of congressional leaders, or some combination of these, his formal powers are largely ritualistic and empty ones. If he arouses wide and intense public concern by creating a sense of crisis and widespread anxiety, the list of formal powers is also largely meaningless because he can then shape the policies of governmental organs that are supposed to check him. To learn what the formal powers of a public official are is only to begin to understand his place in the political system. How he uses those powers depends upon patterns of support and opposition from political actors with resources for influence at their disposal, not upon the legal words or constitutional provisions.

CONCLUSIONS

What part do these organs of government play in shaping policy outputs? We have already seen that the Congress is conservative, operates by fits and starts, and depends heavily on presidential leadership. The Court is usually a passive but not ineffective extension of the views of the President who appointed the Chief Justice and a majority of the other justices. And the President, on whom all action really depends, seeks with an *ad hoc* arrangement of personal aides to acquire the knowledge and the leverage necessary to make the whole eighteenth-century mechanism operable in the modern world. We can express these findings somewhat more elaborately in two major interpretations.

First, the distribution of power and the pattern of incumbency in the institutions of the national government are such as to give each a specific role to play. The President is often the initiator of new policies because only he has the information-gathering capabilities of the executive branch at his disposal. He is the major source of leadership, coordination, and priority-setting for the other institutions, although he may anticipate their demands and values to avoid deadlock. By considering the diverse assessments of the problems and needs of the nation which are produced within the departments of the executive branch, and comparing these with the analysis of resources needed and available as seen by the Bureau of the Budget, the President formulates a program for action. Because he is the highest official of the government, he can command public attention for his program. Through forceful articulation of such priorities and the drafting of proposed legislation, he can set in motion a process which may result in the desired action.

In this process, the Congress becomes a kind of accommodator and conservator of established features of the status quo. Those interests which were unrepresented or ineffective in shaping the President's program are likely to have access to one or more of the many veto points in the House or Senate. And because nearly all interests with a major investment in the status quo have some form of representation in the Congress, the chances are that nothing truly destructive of their status will be enacted. The Congress therefore performs a kind of adjusting and accommodating function by which the proposed legislation is fitted to the preferences and perceived needs of established groups. With provisions for the most far-reaching kind of change thus removed from legislation, the Congress makes it acceptable to the great bulk of the interests which are powerful enough to count. That this is not an unpopular legislative function may be seen from public opinion studies, which regularly show higher proportions of public trust in the Congress than in the President or the Court.

The Supreme Court plays the role of legitimator in this involved process of institutional interaction. Those interests which are defeated, or not fully victorious, in struggles within the other institutional arenas may seek to challenge acts they oppose in the courts. The Supreme Court may in such instances become their last line of defense, and its upholding of a statute or executive act becomes the official act of legitimation. After that moment, there is no appeal but to the people, and that, in the face of the unanimity of the major institutions of government, is a very poor prospect. This is a general interpretation, of course, and not every instance of institutional interaction will fit this mold; but most do, and the reason is that the dominant power centers in each of the various institutions have come to behave in consistent ways over time and to play expected roles.

Two levels of interaction are noticeable among the branches of government. The usual posture is one of wary bargaining among equals, in which each organ is concerned about advantaging its own special policy interests and protecting its institutional prerogatives. But constant engagement in this process leads to familiarity, predictability, and a shared commitment to following the established style. This bargaining, accommodating experience serves as a uniting bond among all power centers. When the legitimacy of the system itself is challenged in some way, therefore, nearly all power centers react as one and seek to remove or repress the challenge as quickly and as ruthlessly as possible. Such a challenge is not one to be met with partial measures or promises of future study, as are demands for increased rewards on the part of regular participants in the legislative process. Instead, because the challenge is directed at the existence, shared policy preferences, and practices of the power centers themselves, it appears to the conservative men whose lives have been invested in gaining such positions to be wholly illegitimate if not revolutionary. And nothing in the established rules of political style and procedure requires that any tolerance be given to those who voluntarily place themselves outside the boundaries of legitimacy and propriety. Further, effective elimination of such challenges will help induce others to operate within the framework that has given rise to the agreeable distribution of power now in effect among the various organs of government.

11

Relationships Between "Public" and "Private" Centers of Power

The American pattern of formal allocation of power to various levels and branches of government, it would seem, is paralleled by a more or less informal concentration of power in a few key points within the major institutions of government. When analyzed carefully, a convergence of attitudes and interests among major powerholders becomes manifest, at least with regard to the most fundamental questions of public policy. A similar phenomenon occurs when the supposedly clear distinction between "governmental" and "private" spheres is examined carefully. Not only do the men who manage various governmental and "private" institutions move back and forth from one form of responsibility to the other, but the two types of institutions cooperate closely, perform functions for each other, and act interchangeably to promote mutually shared purposes.

The blurring of the public-private demarcation line is a perfectly natural consequence of the growth of extragovernmental sources of power and the interdependence of modern economic and social relationships. Those who seek goals involving major allocations of benefits and burdens must use or neutralize the leading vehicle applicable to such purposes — the federal government. In time, there develops an interpenetration between different levels of government and between centers of "private" power and all levels of government. The relevant questions then become: Who does what to or for whom at this powerholder's level? What is thereby implied for the locus of power within elites, and for the size of the power gap between elites and nonelites?

In short, this chapter examines transactions among elites, and their implications. We shall first sketch some representative types of "private" power centers, and then examine the nature of the linkage between them and units of government, illustrating some of the results of this pattern. In a final section, we shall show the continuing relevance of evolving patterns of federal-state-city relationships. At stake in this inquiry is a substantial component of the pluralist image of power distribution in American politics. To what extent is there intraelite conflict over important questions? Do public officials mediate such conflicts or are they otherwise resolved by compromises which reflect the preferences of interested nonelites? Pluralism assumes that there is both conflict and compromise of this kind. Or, on the other hand, is there a kind of power plateau in which elite agreement transcends differences, and nonelites are able to exercise only comparatively minimal influence? Findings which point in the latter direction would suggest a gap in the pluralist image.

TYPES OF "PRIVATE" POWER CENTERS

In an effort to use the term "power center" in a clear and precise way and also mean what intelligent people usually assume it means, we will define as a "power center" any organization that is able to build up very large economic resources or political resources or both. Economic resources are fairly easily measured, in principle at least, in terms of capital at the disposal of the organization: money, real estate, machinery, and inventories of goods. The term "political resources" refers to the organization's ability to win the support, loyalty, and compliance of people. By these tests the following American organizations are leading examples of power centers: General Motors, the American Iron and Steel Institute (a trade association of iron and steel manufacturers), the National Council of Churches, American Farm Bureau Federation, the AFL-CIO, the American Medical Association, and the Association of Land Grant Colleges. Some of these, like General Motors, owe their power basically to their economic resources, which, in turn, enable them to secure the loyalty, in varying degrees, of large numbers of stockholders, suppliers, dealers, customers, and employees, as well as other people impressed by the corporation's status and institutional advertising. Others, like the churches and the universities, owe their power to the attachment of large numbers of people to religious and educational values, and this support in turn helps them build up economic resources.

Let us explore the nature of economic power centers somewhat further, for they are perhaps the clearest example of the growth of units of power which can no longer be seen as "private" in character or consequences. The General Motors Corporation may serve as a convenient example. In economic, political, and social terms, it is comparable only to the more important nations of the world. Its annual sales receipts are larger than the *combined* general revenues of the eleven quite populous states of the northeastern United States: New York, New Jersey, Pennsylvania, Ohio, Delaware, Massachusetts, and the other five New England states.[1] It has 1,300,000 stockholders and more than 700,000 employees in 46 countries of the world. Although it is the largest of the great American corporations, it is not distinctively different from several others. Here is a government lawyer's characterization of Standard Oil of New Jersey.

With more than a hundred thousand employees around the world (it has three times as many people overseas as the U.S. State Department), a six-million-ton tanker fleet (half again bigger than Russia's), and $17 billion in assets (nearly equal to the combined assessed valuation of Chicago and Los Angeles), it can more easily be thought of as a nation-state than a commercial enterprise.[2]

These two companies, and a handful of others like them, dominate the American economy in sales, assets, and profitability. In part, this is because two, three, or four giants so dominate key markets that competition is replaced by tacit cooperation. For example, the aluminum market is shared entirely by Alcoa, Reynolds, and Kaiser; more than 95 percent of automobiles by General Motors, Ford and Chrysler; more than 90 percent of telephone equipment by Western Electric; more than 75 percent of steel by U.S. Steel, Bethlehem, and Republic; and 90 percent of copper by Anaconda, Kennecott, Phelps Dodge, and American Smelting. Given this stature and market dominance, many such companies are able to simply set prices at the levels required to produce predetermined percentages of profit. In this and other respects, the decisions of their officers have broad public consequences; the slightest adjustments in the uses to which such aggregates of assets and productivity are put cannot help but reverberate throughout the business, financial, governmental, and consumer worlds.

Nor should the international scope of American corporations be overlooked in this analysis. Table 1 shows the *world's* twenty largest corporations, ranked according to their sales in 1968. Eighteen of these are American-based corporations, many of them larger in economic resources than most of the nations of the world. These and other American corporations carry on trade all over the world and have investments abroad which in 1967 totalled over $59 billion. The greatest share of their investments were in Canada (nearly one-third) and Europe (almost the same proportion); but a substantial fraction was in Latin America (over 16 percent) and some in Asia (seven per-

---

[1] Richard J. Barber, *The American Corporation* (New York: E. P. Dutton, 1970), pp. 19-20. Unless otherwise indicated, all data in this and the next two paragraphs are drawn from this source.

[2] *Ibid.*, p. 20.

TABLE 1
World's Twenty Biggest Industrial Corporations, 1968
(ranked by sales; $ in millions)

Rank	Corporation	Country of principal affiliation	Sales	Assets	Net Income (after-tax)	Employees
1	General Motors	U.S.A.	$22,755	$14,010	$1,732	757,231
2	Standard Oil (NJ)	U.S.A.	14,091	16,786	1,277	151,000
3	Ford Motor	U.S.A.	14,075	8,953	627	415,000
4	Royal Dutch/Shell	U.K./Netherlands	9,216	14,303	935	171,000
5	General Electric	U.S.A.	8,382	5,744	357	400,000
6	Chrysler	U.S.A.	7,445	4,398	291	231,089
7	IBM	U.S.A.	6,889	6,743	871	241,974
8	Mobil Oil	U.S.A.	6,221	6,872	428	78,300
9	Unilever	U.K.	5,534	3,432	206	312,000
10	Texaco	U.S.A.	5,460	8,687	836	78,475
11	Gulf Oil	U.S.A.	4,559	7,498	626	60,300
12	U.S. Steel	U.S.A.	4,537	6,391	254	201,017
13	ITT	U.S.A.	4,067	4,022	192	293,000
14	Western Electric	U.S.A.	4,031	2,722	192	176,970
15	Standard Oil (Calif.)	U.S.A.	3,635	5,770	452	47,885
16	McDonnell Douglas	U.S.A.	3,609	1,335	95	124,740
17	Du Pont	U.S.A.	3,481	3,289	372	114,100
18	Shell Oil	U.S.A.	3,317	4,230	312	39,080
19	Westinghouse	U.S.A.	3,296	2,271	135	138,000
20	Boeing	U.S.A.	3,274	2,186	83	142,400

Source of Data: *Fortune's* 1969 surveys.

From p. 258 of the book *The American Corporation* by Richard J. Barber. Copyright © 1970 by Richard J. Barber. Published by E. P. Dutton & Co., Inc. and reprinted with their permission and the permission of the author.

cent) and Africa (three percent). In addition to the sheer size and volume of business carried on by these aggregates of economic resources, their international activities impose further imperatives upon governmental policymakers. Any significant interference with the continued profitable conduct of these enterprises, at home or abroad, is likely to send severe shock waves rolling through the American economic and political scene. Unemployment, loss of profits, and general economic decline are only part of the prospect; political repercussions, including calls for military action, are likely to result as well. Thus, the needs and priorities of major corporations become very much a part of governing elites' perceptions of *their* needs and priorities. And this occurs even for individual policymakers who might be relatively less enthusiastic about the profit-seeking activities of American business; the present context is such that a great deal is at stake in even the most marginal troubles which business might experience.

The presence of such power centers forces a convergence of interest upon governmental elites, whether they welcome it or not, but it is not usually seen as such beyond the elite level. The normal image is more often that of government as the antagonist or regulator of business. Throughout American history, concern about the undue influence of various "private" power centers has been a prominent political theme, a source of widespread concern, and a form of political appeal that has repeatedly garnered wide and strong public support. Some of the more prominent examples of this phenomenon have been Andrew Jackson's battle against the United States Bank in the 1820's, the Know Nothing movement built upon opposition to the Catholic Church in the 1840's, concern about trusts and oligopolistic corporations since the 1880's, anxiety about the anarchists and communists in the first half of the twentieth century, and fear of the power of labor unions in the 1940's.

Each of these issues dominated American politics for a time. The recurrence of each theme, coupled with its consistently strong appeal to a wide swathe of the public fearful of a threat to its economic security or its way of life from an organization or movement perceived as powerful, testify to the political utility of power centers for their opponents, whether or not those centers are winning important benefits for themselves. Sometimes, of course, these power centers or others have indeed been highly influential and in a position to hurt large numbers of people. Sometimes they have been far less powerful than their opponents perceived them to be. In either case, they have become a focus for political pressures and demands for governmental regulation of their activities.

The reactions of power centers to this pattern of pressures have varied. For those groups which clearly did have important powers to hurt others, the most conspicuous form of reaction has been acceptance of governmental controls over some of their behavior as a means of allaying widespread fears of their power. Beginning with the Interstate Commerce Act of 1887, Congress imposed controls on a wide range of business groups and activities, thus responding to the rapidly increasing concentration of financial and industrial power that followed the coming of the industrial revolution to the United States. The political pressure to restrain corporations or "trusts" was intense in the late nineteenth and early twentieth centuries. Populist Party candidates had won enough elections with this issue as their main appeal to encourage both major parties to take it up.

There is no question that the potential powers of the business organizations these laws sought to regulate were impressive or that in practice their powers had repeatedly been used to the disadvantage of various groups — for the most part unorganized mass publics. Corporations cut prices to drive competitors out of business and then charged customers unable to turn elsewhere "what the traffic would bear." Some companies bought votes in legislative bodies and favorable action from other public officials through outright bribery or favors that did not fall far short of it. Through "yellow dog" contracts obligating workers not to join a union and other repressive measures, employees were frequently kept in a state of economic dependence or intimidation. Power over pricing practices was further concentrated through trade associations such as the American Iron and Steel Institute, the Sugar Institute, the Association of Railway Executives, and the American Truckers Association. The National Association of Manufacturers, organized in 1895, served chiefly to coordinate and encourage employers' efforts to curb the growth and activities of labor unions.

As wide segments of the public grew concerned with restraining one or another of these forms of business power, the national government enacted regulatory laws; and in some cases, state governments did so as well. With only a few periods of retreat, notably the 1920's, the years between the late 1880's and the entry of the United States into the Second World War in 1941 were marked by a succession of laws purporting to assure that business groups would be restrained in their power to take advantage of customers, competitors, workers, and stockholders: antitrust laws, statutes curbing unfair advertising, restrictions on public utility rates and services, regulations of labor practices, restraints on securities sales and stock exchange practices, and many others.

Such legislation and the administrative arrangements they established created a kind of link between government and private business which throws a revealing light on the tie between economic power and political power. It is a relationship both subtle and complex; one that has become fairly clear only after many years of analysis by economists and political scientists, who have had to resort to social psychology as well as their own disciplines to unravel its character. Two points may be made.

First, it is in the eyes of most men in government and business simply impossible to imagine applying the antitrust laws to today's giant corporations. The economic and political consequences of such a disturbance seem so great that no one takes the prospect seriously. In the late stages of the Johnson administration, a presidential Commission's secret recommendations for new antitrust laws were first suppressed, then denied, then ignored. The same fate befell a Nixon administration task force on antitrust priorities; its very existence was denied, then its report treated as confidential, and ultimately its recommendations were ignored. Antitrust legislation is, for practical purposes, no longer relevant to the concentration of economic power, regardless of which political party is in power in the White House.

Second, in one field of governmental regulation of business after another, the "regulation" has served to quiet public doubts and anxieties far more effectively than it has altered the behavior of powerful business groups. The law and the administrative activity purporting to carry it out have effectively dampened fears of exploitation by power centers. They have, that is to say, influenced people's state of mind and served the political purpose of allaying actual and potential restiveness. At the same time pricing, wage, and other economic policies have continued to be determined by essentially economic and organizational considerations stemming from demand-supply relationships and from the feasibility of collusive agreements among sellers, of other deliberate restrictions on the supply of goods, services, or labor, and of "administered pricing" by firms enjoying a monopolistic or oligopolistic position. Widespread political arousal and conflict based upon fear of business power has thus been replaced by essentially ritualistic administrative procedures to determine "fair" pricing and other practices, while relative economic resources have still determined who gets what in profits and in wages. Among the more conspicuous examples of this form of development have been regulations of radio and television services; air, railroad, and public utility rates; pure food laws; closed shops; antitrust laws; and income tax laws.

Economists and political scientists who have studied public regulations of business have uniformly concluded that the regulators typically become instruments of the private groups they are ostensibly controlling. This conclusion, however, is not obvious either to businessmen or to consumers. If it were generally evident, the psychological impact of the governmental regulatory procedures would of course quickly disappear.

Another type of extragovernmental power center is produced by the accumulation of political resources around a person or movement. Frequently, such movements have been built out of appeals to public fears and perceptions of threat from some relatively intangible source, or when the public has been polarized by contrasting images of danger. Builders of such movements normally characterize themselves as responding to mass pressures, but the extent of genuine mass support is always at least a relevant question. Examples of this political phenomenon are the Know Nothing movement against the Catholic Church before the Civil War, concern about internal anarchist subversion in the early twentieth century, and concern about communist subversion following each of the world wars, as expressed in the Palmer Raids of the 1920's and the McCarthyism of the 1950's. Neither at the time they occurred nor at a later time has it been clear or readily verifiable to what extent the targets these movements attacked were in fact able to dominate other groups or to control their behavior — to what extent they were in fact powerful or only figments of the imagination. As a general rule, contemporary fears of them have come to be regarded in later times as exaggerated.

Nonetheless, they serve to *create* important power centers among their attackers and opponents. Power in these cases has rested upon the ability of leaders of antisubversive movements to rally apparently fervent and enthusiastic support for their stance of opposition to an allegedly evil ideology. In each instance a political position formerly regarded as deviant and not very respectable has attracted large followings and enabled its leaders to attack incumbent public officials and "mainstream" policies with some success. Public officials, public employees, and private citizens who could be pictured as "soft" on communism, anarchism, or the alleged machinations of the Pope became highly vulnerable, with the result that both dissent and tolerance of dissent were suspect and penalized. In this way, a wide range of public opinion was either eliminated from the public forum or substantially weakened. In such instances, power is created by securing strong influence over public beliefs and perceptions rather than by winning a high degree of control over widely sought goods or services.

The linkage of this kind of power center to official governmental agencies is rather different than is the case with *economically* powerful organizations. Toward the latter there is merely a posture of regulation and control, while the organizations are in fact left relatively free to use their economic resources to augment their income. The posture of regulation serves to win political support or neutrality, which is necessary and critical to any form of stable and continuing governmental action. Power centers based directly upon political support, however, are bound to exert a more direct and substantial effect upon public policies as long as their political support continues. McCarthyism generated severe restrictions upon civil liberties, and sharply limited foreign policy initiatives. It intensified the strains of the Cold War, threw a cloud over the careers of many federal employees, changed the prevailing norms and objectives in many public agencies, and produced such important new policies as more severe curbs on immigration, widespread security checks, and changed curricula in the public schools.[3] The movements based upon popular anxieties about anarchism, communism, and the New Left in the first six decades of the twentieth century had many of the same results. The populist movement of the late nineteenth and early twentieth centuries generated such electoral changes as rather widespread resort to the direct primary, the referendum and the recall election. It also initiated the outlawing of such railroad practices as rebates to favored customers, controls over railroad and public utility rates that were effective as long as widespread public concern with these matters continued, and even the establishment of cooperatively owned banks in some midwestern states in which the movement was strongest.

Power centers, then, never stand wholly apart from government and public officials. They are analytically distinct from official public agencies in the sense that their power derives directly from private concentrations of wealth or from widespread citizen support for an ideological position. At the same time, the examples just cited make it clear that public agencies and officials themselves become absorbed into the power centers in one or another way, functioning as their instruments in at least part of their official roles. For the *economically* powerful centers public officials help create a broad base of public support through governmental reassurance that the harmful potentialities of these concentrations have been checkmated by regulatory public policies. For the centers created by wide and intense support for an ideology or a leader, officials themselves identify in some measure with the ideology, translating ideological demands

[3] The extent to which McCarthyism was truly a mass-based movement has been severely challenged in a careful study by Michael Rogin. See *McCarthy and the Intellectuals* (Cambridge, Mass.: MIT Press, 1966), which argues persuasively that conservatives used the McCarthy facade to accomplish a variety of goals — and that anticommunism was only partly a motivating force even for them.

into official policy, legitimizing them, and weakening opposition groups both through exhortation and physical or bureaucratic repression.

FORMS OF LINKAGE BETWEEN "PUBLIC" AND "PRIVATE" POWER CENTERS

The metaphor of mutual penetration of one another, or partial absorption into each other — of governmental agencies on the one hand and power centers on the other — is far more apt and revealing than the more customary metaphor of *pressure* upon government by "outside" organizations. It is more apt because it points more accurately to the tactics that ordinarily account for substantial influence upon public policies by powerful political actors.

Both the pressure metaphor and conventional wisdom suggest that personal friendships, buttonholing officials at cocktail parties, judicious (or injudicious) use of campaign contributions, hard sell persuasion, and occasional outright bribery are leading examples of tactics that prove effective in winning pressure groups what they want from legislators, from administrators, and sometimes even from judges. These and similar strategies are of course employed, but the evidence is clear that they cannot normally be counted on to work unless the official is already receptive to the people trying to influence him, either because he is somewhat sympathetic to their cause or because he suspects that those who support it are able and willing to back it with votes or other significant sanctions. A study of how lobbyists and members of the United States Senate and House of Representatives felt about the effectiveness of various forms of lobbying reinforces this conclusion.[4] In this study, the author concluded from his research that solid facts, cogent arguments, and evidence of the power of the lobbying group were the really effective ploys in making public officials receptive. Personal presentation of arguments, contacts by constituents, and collaboration among interest groups and help to congressmen in lining up reinforcements in policy battles are likely to bring results. Entertaining and parties were rated very low as lobbying techniques and bribery as virtually unknown (though it is more common in state legislatures and has been employed occasionally in dealing with administrative officials).

The general import of this study and of other analyses of the methods and effectiveness of placing pressures upon public officials is clear enough. Personal friendships and appeals unquestionably win petty favors, but in themselves they do not bring long run and substantial influence. That comes only when there is evidence that a group of people with some kind of power at their disposal will be significantly helped or hurt by the public policy under consideration. A legislator or administrative official is likely to pay respectful attention to any spokesman for an interest group who can give him

---

[4] Lester A. Milbrath, "Lobbying as a Communication Process," *Public Opinion Quarterly*, vol. 24 (Spring, 1960), pp. 32-53.

solid information about either the effects of a policy proposal upon his group or about the degree of their concern. Technical information about the possible harmful effects of an underground atomic bomb detonation or convincing evidence of anxiety about it among residents of the region will not be ignored, though it may, of course, be outweighed by evidence of the military, industrial, or scientific usefulness of the blast or evidence that a different powerful group strongly favors it. A major weapon in the hands of a lobbyist for a power center, then, is knowing what he is talking about.

This is not to say that the most meritorious course of action is bound to prevail. Convincing evidence that a large group of people strongly wants something because they are moved by illusory fears can be very effective, as can evidence that a small but economically powerful group is aroused about an issue. A public official may define "merit" in terms of the ability or willingness of those who espouse or oppose a course of action to help or to hurt; he will pay the greatest attention to spokesmen who can give him sound information about the actual problems faced by an important group of people, and on the effects proposed policies will have on those problems.

Alliances among groups of people are often especially influential. Unorganized workers in the thirties at first had little political impact of their own, but they gained a great deal in the depths of the Great Depression when a large part of the middle class espoused some of their interests, thus giving them sufficient strength to win guarantees of their right to join unions and bargain collectively and to secure the protections of the Social Security Act, the Fair Labor Standards Act, and other prolabor policies at the federal and state levels. The antipoverty programs of the sixties similarly reflected the sanctions available to those members of the middle class who sympathized with the poor rather than the influence of the poor themselves. Restrictive labor legislation and many other probusiness policies derive a major part of their support from the American Farm Bureau Federation, which benefits from rural overrepresentation in state legislatures and the national Congress. A policymaking official is well served by a lobbyist if the latter provides him with sound and persuasive information about the bases of such political alliances.

The mere expression of opinion or the urging of a position, no matter how eloquent, logical, or friendly, will have little lasting effect on a public official so long as he has no evidence that it is widely shared by people with some sanction they can wield or when there is an indication that the policy urged upon him is widely opposed. Spokesmen for the League of Women Voters and labor union officers supporting policies on such nonlabor issues as civil rights carry little weight with legislators and administrators, who are quite aware that these persons represent small constituencies.[5] When a labor union official supports or opposes a policy on wages or the right to organize, he carries far more weight, for it can be taken for

---

[5] Cf. Robert E. Lane, *Political Life* (New York: Free Press, 1959), pp. 66-67.

granted that on these matters most rank and file union members, many nonunion workers, and many liberals sympathetic to labor will support him.

Whether a pressure group tactic is effective depends, then, upon what it tells a public official about the extent, the intensity, the stability, and the ability to wield sanctions of supporters and opponents. There is nothing magical or necessarily potent about organization in itself. The National Association of Manufacturers, the American Medical Association, and other wealthy organized groups have lost public policy battles when their far less tightly organized opponents gained sufficiently wide-ranging support. As already noted, the very spectacle of a conspicuous, large organization sometimes arouses fears and effective opposition. Tacticians for pressure groups and power centers must accordingly plan carefully, avoiding actions that may appear arrogant, concentrating on solid information, and playing where possible upon the active or latent sympathy of public officials for the causes they espouse. They can benefit as well from most of the means through which elites garner influence over masses, which are discussed in Chapter 12.

EXCHANGES BETWEEN THE NATIONAL GOVERNMENT AND PRIVATE POWER CENTERS

An important facet of our political socialization, and an important basis of regime legitimacy, is inculcation of the belief that government can be counted on to keep the reins on private power centers and so assure that they operate in the public interest. We have noted that this belief is valid in some respects and that it needs serious qualification in others. Perhaps the major respect in which it is misleading is its complete failure to recognize that government itself is typically a major source of the power held by "private" power centers and a major contributor to their financial resources and political support.

Government expenditures and other support which results in the creation of new and ultimately powerful centers of power have been illustrated at length in our earlier analysis of the military-industrial complex. A less readily visible example of the same general process, but with potentially even broader consequences, may be found in the area of developing new knowledge and techniques for industrial and social applications. Technological advancement and multiplying social problems have inspired a large ($25 billion per year) new (400 percent rise in the last 15 years) research and development sector of the economy. Nearly all of the multiple profit-making opportunities generated by research findings and newly developed products and techniques will accrue to private enterprise, through production and sale of the new equipment (frequently to the government) or through use of new labor-saving techniques or other cost-saving equipment. But, as Table 2 shows, the federal government provides more than 60 percent of the funds used for research and development, frequently employing profit-making private enterprises to do the actual work. In effect, the vast expenses of research and

TABLE 2
Who Puts Up the Money, Who Does the Work ($ in millions)

			Performers				
			Universities and colleges				
Sources	Federal government	Industry	proper	federal contract research centers	Other nonprofit institutions	Total	Percent distribution: Sources
Federal government	$3,500	$ 9,100	$1,600	$700	$660	$15,560	62%
Industry	—	8,200	60	—	70	8,330	33%
Universities and colleges	—	—	840	—	—	840	3%
Other nonprofit institutions	—	—	100	—	170	270	1%
Total	$3,500	$17,300	$2,600	$700	$900	$25,000	100%
Percent distribution: Performers	14%	69%	10%	3%	4%	100%	

development in the technological age, most of it destined to generate multiple new opportunities for private profit-making, are socialized. The federal government puts up 62 percent of the money used for these purposes in the United States, private industry only 33 percent; but private industry does 69 percent of the work, and eventually winds up with the profit-making opportunities from all of the work. The federal government is thus the provider of future opportunities for business and the chief supporter of the major "think-tank" firms that hold the keys to the character of the future economic and social order. Of the more than half a million professional scientists and engineers engaged in research work in the United States, 82 percent are federally supported.

This is far from the only form of government financial support for private industries, of course. But it is an especially useful example of how an entire industry can be quickly generated by government investment. And, perhaps more important, it shows how new ties of mutual dependence are rapidly constructed. The government's need for space and defense research and development was a major part of the thrust behind this development, but by no means the sole reason. Other burgeoning problems produced similar needs, which the universities and a new sector of private industry were glad to serve. But government is now heavily dependent on university and industry performance of this research, and in turn the university and private researchers depend almost entirely on government support for their livelihood and existence. There can scarcely fail to develop a convergence of interest between such interdependent partners, to say nothing of the private producers who stand to profit from the findings of research.

Perhaps the identification of specific convergences of interest and other forms of interdependence between agencies of government and units of private industry is an overly crude way of sketching the government-private relationship. But it is clear and tangible. Other tangible links include, as we have seen, the growing interchange of personnel. Less tangible, but perhaps equally potent, is the fact that elites in government and in private economic power centers perceive and are affected by the same domestic social problems. They both recognize the depth of the problems and the necessity for government to take some drastic steps to solve them, such as instituting vast job training programs, supporting urban transportation system developments, or rebuilding the decaying cities of the nation. Where government must invest, private industry stands to profit from carrying out the tasks. Several major corporations have begun to take part in designing construction or reconstruction of entire cities, in terms of their physical settings, the organization of their economic life, and their governing mechanisms. Others have entered the field of education, not only providing books and equipment, but also wholly packaged multidisciplinary curricula and automated means of presentation. Many others have taken on a variety of other governmental functions within the cities, overseeing or performing activities formerly associated only with politically responsible units of government. Again, mutuality of perspective and interest between public and private power centers seems clear.

But let us not overlook the long-established forms of government assistance to private economic power centers. The large American corporations vary greatly in the degree to which their power is dependent upon government, but it would be impossible to find even one really large one to which government does not contribute in a significant degree through tax benefits, subsidies, contracts, and the mobilization of political goodwill by identifying the corporations with widely approved national purposes such as defense and space exploration.

From the very beginning of the nation's history, federal and state governments have subsidized private business enterprises, and this pattern has had far more significant tangible effects than *regulation* of business, which commonly receives greater attention and publicity. Benefits to business have taken the form of outright money payments, but more often occur indirectly through services rendered without charge or for much less than they are worth, through exemption from taxes imposed upon others, and by shielding some business enterprises from competition.[6] In the last instance people pay the subsidy in the role of consumers; in the other instances they pay in the role of taxpayers.

---

[6] The material on governmental subsidies to private business is based in part upon the discussion of that topic in Clair Wilcox, *Public Policies Toward Business* (Homewood, Illinois: Richard D. Irwin, 1968), pp. 429-452.

In hundreds of ways governmental agencies serve as laboratories and research agencies for a wide range of business enterprises, the taxpayers providing services the businesses would otherwise have to provide for themselves. Economic statistics giving employers information on wage levels, costs, and other matters in specific markets; census data that guide product choice and marketing strategies; maps and other navigational aids published by the Coast and Geodetic Survey; crop estimates by the Crop Reporting Service, and weather information for airlines and shippers are examples. The National Bureau of Standards tests materials for industry. The TVA gives the formulas for new chemical fertilizers to the fertilizer industry. The list of free governmental services could easily be extended.

Subsidies in money are almost as widespread. In the nineteenth century, railroads received extensive grants both of valuable public lands and of money, but they are not significantly subsidized today. Other common and private carriers benefit enormously from public grants, however. This is especially true of trucks, which use the public highways for which passenger cars pay more, and heavy trucks far less, than their proportionate shares. The interstate highway system constructed largely in the sixties has greatly increased a form of subsidy well established in earlier years.

Both inland and transoceanic shipping have benefitted substantially from public subsidies: by the improvement of harbors, rivers, and canals, by the grant of cargo preferences to American vessels, by a requirement since 1954 that at least half of all tonnage procured by the government or supplied by it to other governments be carried in American ships. The government has sold ships to private operators for a few cents on the dollar. Construction subsidies for new commercial ships sometimes exceed half the cost. The liner "United States" cost $76,800,000, of which $43,900,000 was paid by the taxpayers — and the remainder by the United States Lines.

For commercial airlines, the taxpayers provide the capital costs of airports and airways at public expense, as well as traffic control and weather reporting facilities. Some airlines also receive operating subsidies. In the late 1960's the President recommended that the federal government bear about 90 percent of the cost of developing supersonic transport planes which would permit the commercial airlines to offer very rapid service on transoceanic and transcontinental flights. Under this procedure the government assumes the risks which make commercial profits possible.

Through various devices the federal government similarly heavily subsidizes power companies using atomic energy to generate power, American exports, and newspaper and magazine publishers. Billions of dollars of subsidization to the silver mining industry have taken the form of required purchases of silver by the United States Treasury at a fixed price well above the market price. As a result, the entire domestic output has been diverted to the government, which simply buries at West Point, New York, the silver excavated in the mountain states.

Special tax benefits permit many types of business enterprises to retain large amounts of money and place the burden on other taxpayers, chiefly wage and salary earners. When corporations build facilities designated as essential to defense production, they can deduct a large part of the cost from their taxable incomes. Special tax benefits to the mining, oil, and gas industries have cut their taxes about in half, depriving the Treasury of hundreds of millions of dollars and making many large stockholders in these industries wealthy men.

Another form of benefit to the same industries bans or drastically curtails the importation of foreign coal and oil, requiring American consumers of these products to pay higher prices than they would for the foreign fuels. The Export-Import Bank makes loans to American businesses, and to their foreign customers to stimulate export sales of American goods. These government loans, together with foreign aid grants, furnish the money that has maintained American exports at high levels since World War II.

Public services are often made available to private business at much less than their actual cost: research and education, fire protection, technical assistance to the lumber industry, permission for sheep and cattle to graze on public lands for smaller fees than are charged on private ranges, delivery of newspapers and magazines at a loss. As one writer has put it, "In the postman's bag, as he staggers up the street, are pounds of periodicals that denounce the government for doing many things, but not (it may be safely assumed) for cutting the costs and contributing to the profits of publishers." [7]

Since the middle of the nineteenth century, the federal government has helped farmers; in the last 35 years agricultural aid has increased and predominantly gone to large and commercial farms. Virtually all the methods already mentioned are used, including loans and purchases, restrictions on competitive imports, subsidizing exports, curbing the supply available for sale, providing free land and services, and making it easy and inexpensive for farmers to secure credit, electrification, and crop insurance.

It is unthinkable that a government would grant a major financial benefit to a business or other affluent group unless it can be justified as contributing to some objective that is widely and strongly supported. Each one of the subsidies that gives money, status, and influence to private business groups is bolstered by such a justification, which, in turn, provides the popular support or acquiescence that must underlie the benefits. To encourage exploration for oil (and the construction of defense plants) is to contribute to the national defense; to subsidize newspapers and magazines is to promote education and culture; to subsidize agriculture is to safeguard the vitality of both our food supply and the virtues of rural America; and so on.

Whether a particular subsidy does in fact contribute to these widely supported objectives is often debatable and difficult or impossible to determine. Some argue that because the subsidies are in general

[7] *Ibid.*, p. 437.

paid when losses are incurred rather than when a business operates efficiently, they reward incompetence. Sometimes they do unquestionably contribute to the establishment or augmentation of an important national resource, though it is usually impossible to say how much, or what the balance of general gains against windfall profits to a business is. The very ambiguity about this crucial point is what makes these policies politically viable and feasible. It is probably a safe assumption that those who benefit most from them are also most impressed with their contributions to the national welfare. Those people who do not benefit financially from them, however, are also likely to be only dimly or not at all aware of their existence and to be not easily aroused to protest against them because of the availability of a justification in terms of the national interest.

Regardless of the justification, however, the larger subsidies help create a concentration of political and economic power in which the distinction between the private organization and the governmental entity becomes clouded. In an odd way, there is a "symbiosis" between government and subsidized industries, just as there is one between government and regulated industries. In the one instance, governmental rhetoric and ceremony help legitimate the use of the economic bargaining weapons of private groups. In the other instance, government money or power legitimates and augments private money and power. The first process is labelled regulation and thereby publicly justified. The second process is labelled promotion of some honored national goal and thereby also publicly justified.

EXCHANGES BETWEEN STATE GOVERNMENTS AND PRIVATE POWER CENTERS

If the national government and private power centers systematically buttress each other, the state governments are also important components in the same power system. An appreciation of the specific functions the states serve in the system is necessary to a realistic understanding of the distribution of political influence in the United States.

As one element in the power structure, legal doctrine about the constitutional position of the states is pertinent here. Chapter 9 noted that the Constitution serves to legitimize the position of the interest groups with ready access to the courts. In legal theory, the Tenth Amendment of the United States Constitution gives the states "reserved powers": all powers not delegated to the national government or prohibited to the states. Some powers, such as taxation, are exercised concurrently by the national and the state governments. Others, such as power over foreign policy, are forbidden to the states. Each of the fifty state constitutions further restricts the permissible range of state action. That, at least, is the legal function of the state constitutions. Many of them carry it to highly detailed proscriptions, chiefly against various types of regulation of corporations and forms of taxation and spending. These legal provisions must be recognized as making available a powerful channel of access for those interest groups to which judges, state executives, and legislative officials are sensitive and responsive. They have often served as justifications for striking down proposed restrictions on powerful groups, especially business groups, and for striking down proposed benefits to workers, consumers, and the poor. Sometimes they have protected the civil rights of relatively powerless groups. In these respects, the records of the various states are highly uneven; the legal weapon is available, but it is not necessarily used.

Both the legal and the political resources of the state governments have bolstered private power centers most effectively in those states that are most homogeneous with respect to their economic base or their ideological complexion. In the states of the deep South, the dominance of the white supremacy ideology has turned the state governments into effective buttresses of the Ku Klux Klan, the white citizens' councils, and the employers, landlords, and labor unions that benefit economically from exploitation of blacks as workers, as tenants, and as consumers. These various political actors have facilitated the continued incumbency in public office of officials who serve their private interests. The state governments are therefore part of a complex of public and private interests whose economic, ideological, and status needs benefit in common from cooperative, overlapping courses of action. Until very recently there was little black or liberal challenge in these states to this power complex.

Similarly, the state government of Texas has long facilitated the aggrandizement of power in the hands of oil and grazing interests by avoiding significant restrictions upon their operations in the interest of consumers or employees and by minimizing their taxes. In Colorado, the copper mining industry so dominates the state's economy that the state legislature is highly sensitive and responsive to its interests.

Such exchanges of benefits between a state government and an economically or ideologically dominant power complex are less feasible in the degree that a state is economically and ideologically heterogeneous. Heterogeneity goes furthest in the more populous states which include both large urban complexes and rural areas marked by some diversity in crops and in rural industries. In such states there is inevitably a wide range of political opinion and a multitude of overlapping interests and organized interest groups that prevent any one of them from dominating the others over long time periods. Clothing manufacturers and Consolidated Edison in New York, steel and coal mining in Illinois, and right wing ideologues and organizations in southern California are all conspicuous and powerful interests; but none of them can count on the kind of continuing and relatively unchallenged influence in their respective state legislatures that goes to oil and grazing in Texas or to the beneficiaries of the white supremacy ideology in Mississippi.

Even in the heterogeneous states, dominant power in limited policy areas is sometimes created and perpetuated through a complex exchange of symbolic restrictions and tangible benefits between government and private industrial groups. This pattern has already been described and illustrated as it occurs in federal politics, and its dynamics are the same at the state level. Here too, it is especially likely where there is concern among unorganized consumers about exploitation by industry but no clear way for consumers to tell when rates or services are reasonable. Accordingly, state public service commissions serve in practice to legitimize the charges and quality of service of gas, oil, telephone, and other public utilities; highway departments provide vital benefits for trucking interests; and so on.

Because most states are naturally less heterogeneous than the country as a whole, and because some states are dominated by one or a few interest groups, the net effect decentralization of policymaking has upon the states is evident. It enhances the influence of particular interest groups in the degree that they have greater power in a particular state than in the national government. Because of business-agriculture coalitions and log rolling, labor policy made at the state level reflects management interests more than national labor policy does, except for a few states with large populations of industrial workers, such as New York and Michigan. Even more clearly, policies determining the civil rights of blacks are chiefly responsive to white supremist groups in the Southern and border states in which access to policymaking positions is largely closed to all who dissent from the white supremacy ideology. At the same time, national civil rights policies must be more responsive, symbolically or instrumentally, to the range of heterogeneous opinions on civil rights.

The issue of national or state control of these and other controversial matters is not an academic one; it frequently becomes intense and heated. In the labor field, we have had, and continue to have, lively debate over whether nationally defined rules regarding the right to picket should preempt the right of the states to enforce their own rules, which in most states are more restrictive of union picketing.

Similarly, the federalizing of all social security and welfare programs, and federal control over civil rights legislation is favored by some and opposed by others because both proponents and opponents recognize that interest group influence over these matters is vitally affected by the level at which policy is formulated. The implications of the slogan "states rights" for interest group influence are therefore clear. Symbolically, "states rights" evokes an idyll of local self-rule and democracy. In practice, it rationalizes far greater power for already powerful groups than they otherwise enjoy: greater power for white supremacy in the South, for industrial employers in largely rural states, for the aircraft manufacturing industry in California, and so on.

THE FEDERAL – STATE – CITY – PRIVATE POWER COMPLEX

The language of the Tenth Amendment might lead one to expect neat and clear distinctions between the functions performed by the national government on the one hand and those carried on by the states, the cities, and other subdivisions of the states on the other. Throughout American history these distinctions have in fact been indistinct and fuzzy, with the various levels of government helping each other in carrying out many functions and competing with each other in some.

During approximately the past fifteen years, the American federal system has changed its character in a far-reaching fashion. Through the nineteenth century and the first decades of the twentieth, the federal government shared some functions with the states. Federal and state law enforcement officers often cooperated with each other, for example, and both federal and state courts grant citizenship to naturalized immigrants. More important was a fast growing trend in the twentieth century for the federal government to encourage the states to undertake various activities by granting them money to do so. Such grants-in-aid programs were established to promote highway construction, vocational education, employment exchanges, municipal airports, and many other functions. In some cases the federal government provides all the money; more often the states have to match federal money in some proportion. Usually, the states have to accept minimal federal standards and surveillance as the price they pay for federal grants. In each of these cases supporters of a policy who are more powerful in Washington than in some of the states have succeeded in using the grant-in-aid device to accomplish their objectives, even in those states in which they have little influence.

On occasion, even more direct federal pressure than the lure of additional revenue has been employed. The Social Security Act of 1935, for example, imposed a three percent payroll tax on all covered employers, but provided that any state which passed an unemployment insurance law would receive this money back, to be used in paying insurance benefits under the law and in its administration. In 1935, only one state, Wisconsin, had an unemployment insurance law; two years later all 48 states did. They were virtually forced to enact them by this "tax offset" device, even in the agricultural states in which enthusiasm for supporting the largely urban unemployed was minimal.

A section of the Taft-Hartley Act of 1947 illustrates still a different form of power deployment based on the federal-state link. Section 14b permits employers and unions to enter into "union shop" agreements, under which employees are required to join a union within a stated period of time; but any state is permitted to outlaw the union shop within its own borders by passing a so-called "right-to-work" law. Not surprisingly, most Southern states did pass right-to-work laws, but they are rare elsewhere (and generally ignored in traditionally unionized industries such as printing, even where the laws exist). This example from the field of labor relations makes it even clearer that any federal-state or federal-local relationship amounts to a determination of which pressure groups will be most influential. What looks at first like a legal question of inter*governmental* relations turns out to be a question of politics, influence, and power.

Influence and power for the federal government, it appears, depend heavily upon (1) its far greater ability to raise money through taxes than is true of state and local governments; and (2) the extent to which federal policymakers use their money and their legal supremacy to promote particular policies at the state and local levels. In the last fifteen years there have been far-reaching changes in the deployment of both these determinants of power.[8] Federal grants to the states and to local governments more than tripled in the decade of the sixties. Some of the money went to activities traditionally looked upon as an exclusive preserve of state and local governments: education and local law enforcement. Some of it, as noted in Chapter 5, went to fighting poverty and to creating new political demands and new political conflicts in the cities.

In legal theory, an American city (or county) is a subdivision of the state government and subject to its authority, as defined in the state constitution and laws. The major impact of the vast recent spurt in federal grants, however, has been the establishment of direct federal-city links, often bypassing the state government, often giving the cities considerable political autonomy from the states through their acquisition of federal funds, often creating political cleavages between established political regimes in the cities and the federal policymakers dangling money with strings attached before them. Let us look at the patterns the federal-city links have taken.

Underpinning federal grants are political benefits which elites and the masses in the cities can extend to, or withold from, the incumbent regime in Washington. Big city mayors can influence the vote in federal elections. While this normally means that the predominantly Democratic city organizations support Democratic candidates for national office, that support cannot be taken for granted; it can be unenthusiastic and ineffective. In 1968, Mayor Richard Daley of Chicago did little or nothing to support the Democratic candidate for Senator from Illinois, assuring the reelection of the Republican incumbent, Everett Dirksen. Businessmen in a city may fail to dig into their pockets for campaign contributions to national government officials who have not helped promote the economic prosperity of the city. The poor and otherwise deprived may seriously embarrass and hurt the federal government through civil disobedience and riots. All these actual and potential political concerns have helped motivate the increased federal largesse to the municipalities, regardless of which political party is in power. They have made the national government far more responsive to demands from the cities than the state governments have been, for state officials are more often sensitive to the interests of rural areas and are constrained by legal and political obstacles both to raising revenues and to spending money to solve urban problems.

With the spurt in federal money available for spending in the localities, both state and city governments have stepped up their lobbying in Washington and must now be counted among the major

[8] This discussion of recent changes in the federal structure is based in part upon James L. Sundquist and David W. Davis, *Making Federalism Work* (Washington, D. C.: Brookings Institution, 1969), and upon *Legislators and Lobbyists* (Washington, D. C.: Congressional Quarterly Service, 1968), pp. 63-64.

pressure groups on the national government. By 1967, at least 11 states and eight large cities had established Washington offices or representatives, most of them set up since 1961. Officials of other states and every city of any size must make frequent trips to the national capital to solicit money from many different federal agencies and departments for hundreds of local needs and purposes.

By the mid-1960's, one consequence of this increased dependence upon Washington was considerable protest by officials at all three levels of government against the confusion in, and often complete absence of, coordination in the administration of federal grants. Different coordinators established by various federal agencies for their own programs were themselves badly in need of coordination. Programs to train the poor for jobs, for example, were administered and financed in various ways by the Office of Economic Opportunity, the Department of Labor, and the Department of Housing and Urban Development. Purely from the point of view of administration, cities had become battlegrounds for federal agencies.

Federal defense, war, and space expenditures have done far more to bring jobs and profits to many communities than the urban development, poverty, and welfare programs explicitly designed to improve economic and social conditions. This is true, obviously, because Congress appropriates many times more money for national security and space. Competitive lobbying for these contracts is brisk, and in some measure the outcomes reflect the influence of key figures on the congressional committees overseeing defense and space programs. They also reflect administration political strategy. A revealing, if extreme example of the ability of an influential congressman to buttress the prosperity of his district is the case of Representative L. Mendel Rivers, Chairman of the House Armed Services Committee. By 1970, the South Carolina district Rivers represents had an estimated federal payroll and federal contracts of more than three billion dollars a year. In the district were an air force base, a Polaris missile facility, a submarine training base, a navy supply center, a naval weapons station, a naval hospital, an army depot, a marine corps air station, and a marine corps recruiting depot. Corporations which established branch plants in the district after Rivers became Committee Chairman in 1965 were Lockheed, McDonnell Douglas, Avco, and General Electric.[9]

Some federal programs to help nonelites in the cities posed a serious challenge to the local political organization and sometimes to old line federal agencies as well. The most dramatic examples of such a development have been the community action agencies and, later, the model cities programs. By playing the role of organizer and advocate of the poor, the former seemed to many local politicians and elites to be a potential disturber of the political status quo and a rival claimant for federal money. Even though model cities, unlike community action, is administered by city hall itself, the program encouraged neighborhood residents to organize and take an interest

[9] *The Nation*, vol. 210 (January 19, 1970), p. 41.

in local programs and thereby also aroused political tension and conflict. The tension stems basically from the sometimes contrary pulls of pressing urban problems and of the political and status interests of powerful groups in the large cities. The model cities structure, nonetheless, offers a viable basic scheme for planning and executing programs in urban slums which involve the joint partici- pation of federal, state, and local governments and of representative neighborhood resident organizations.

A great many federal agencies have developed programs to deal with economic and social decay in nonmetropolitan areas, and these too suffer from lack of effective coordination. Economic develop- ment districts sponsored by the Department of Commerce, resource conservation and development projects under the aegis of the De- partment of Agriculture, and nonmetropolitan planning bodies of the Department of Housing and Urban Development were the most important of some ten types of coordinating structures for multi- county areas functioning in 1969. Here also a new and more unified pattern of federal-local relationship was required to deal with prob- lems more profound and more complex than the old *ad hoc* grant- in-aid programs ever contemplated. It was clear at the beginning of the decade of the seventies that experimentation and a far-reaching restructuring of our federal system was under way, but the pattern of the new structure was still far from clear.

The new ferment over the character of American federalism has focused most clearly in recent years in political conflict over the amount of autonomy state officials should have in administering federal grant money. Although city governments have not been as responsive to the needs of the poor as the latter would like, they are inevitably far more responsive to those needs than state legislatures and executives, whose continuation in office depends largely upon support from rural areas and from business organizations. On a num- ber of fronts, the Nixon administration has favored the routing of fed- eral grants through state officials. This policy amounts to a formula for minimizing the influence of cities, and especially of the urban poor, in the administration of federal grants.

One acute and revealing example occurred early in 1970 in a battle over whether federal funds to improve law enforcement should be allocated directly to cities or whether all such money should be routed through the state capitals. Although it is the middle class that is most aroused over crime and the importance of law and order, the residents of the urban slums suffer most from crime. Clearly, the place to attack crime effectively is primarily in the city slums, and direct grants to cities for law enforcement would place much of the federal money there. To allocate it to the states would mean that a relatively small portion of the money would go to the areas in which crime was most serious and most of it to suburban and rural police forces, who would use it largely to buy equipment to sup- press demonstrations and riots; for in these localities political pres- sure for such use is intense and police forces eager to respond to it. State autonomy in dispensing the grants would therefore assure their use for quite different purposes than direct allocations to the cities. This example illustrates the sense in which the national government's grant-in-aid policies strongly influence the outcome of conflicts between city and state governments over particular issues. The policy of returning some part of federal tax monies to the states in unrestricted grants through "revenue sharing," also a battleground in the emergence of a new pattern of federalism, involves the same basic issue.

CONCLUSIONS

If in retrospect this chapter seems a bit of a blur, the reader should take heart. Our point has gotten across to him. Power and influence intertwine intimately within the various levels of government and within the elites who manage the national institutions which carry such misleading labels as "private" and "public." No clear-cut divisions exist; interpenetration and mutuality of interest sew national elites together and unite them with their lesser partners in the states and cities. Occasionally, idiosyncratic constituency pressures or competition over profitable opportunities cause tensions or even brief eruptions. The general pattern, however, is one of the transactions of the business of government and of business within the channels of accommodation and mutual interest here described. Where initiative lies in this situation — whether private elites press government into service to gain their ends, or vice versa — may not even be really crucial. The purposes to be served, it appears, are so similar that it makes very little difference on which side the balance of initiative actually lies. But what of the vast majority of persons, who are not engaged in these day-to-day transactions? They are, in effect, spectators, and what they see may be only a small portion of what takes place. The national government's relationships to private power centers and to state and city governments are usually justified in such terms as the encouragement of private or local enterprise; "partnership" with outside groups or with state governments; the accomplishment of such widely supported objectives as national security or effective law enforcement; and administrative feasibility and simplicity. How this justification is accomplished is the subject of the next chapter.

Linkage: Elites and Masses 12

To this point, we have described who elites are, what they appear to believe, and the general legal and institutional setting in which they operate. Their resources and their special status in government, we noted in the last chapter, made it possible and necessary for them to develop means of mutual accommodation and assistance. But elites neither operate exclusively according to their own preferences, nor in invisible isolation. By some means, the wants of the vast majority of the population must be satisfied or deflected, and the necessary consent secured for the continued transaction of national and international affairs.

There are many possible ways in which this can be achieved. Elites may contribute to shaping mass wants along lines which they find it convenient or practical to serve. They may act through government to create or promote mass demands, together with the confidence that such demands are indeed being served. Or they may interpret any and all government actions as necessary and proper, under the circumstances, for the benefit of masses. We do not mean to suggest that masses are infinitely manipulable, nor that all citizens are equally supine before the blandishments of elites. It does not require an example as salient as the Vietnam War to establish these points. But it is clear that elites have many opportunities to develop influence over what nonelites understand about politics and how they respond to government actions. They act with perceptions of mass wants and probable responses in mind, but they may often find it easier to justify what they choose to do for reasons of their own, than to seek to learn or follow possibly different mass preferences.

This chapter considers some of the means which elites employ, examining first the opportunities available to institutional elites, and second those available to the more general category of elites. To some extent, the opportunities of institutional elites involve some classic elements of leader-follower relationships, and we shall sketch some of these premises at the outset of our discussion. It will become evident that the distinction between the opportunities for generating influence over masses are not crisply divided between institutional or governmental elites and private elites. As was true elsewhere, each supplements and extends the other in a cooperative effort to promote mass concurrence with government policies.

Men in positions of power are leaders in the sense that others, faced with the choice of whether or not to follow them, normally see no alternative but to do so. Some members of institutional elites have acquired their power in part through convincing numbers of people that it is in their interest to support them, and in such cases the transactional nature of the leader-follower relationship is more obvious. In all cases, however, refusal on the part of numbers of people to follow their leaders' directions or appeals means the breakdown of smooth governmental functioning. Elites, therefore, have a large stake in maintaining the voluntary support of mass publics, and they may be expected to adapt their actions where necessary to do so. The context for thus maintaining support or acquiescence seems distinctly favorable under modern circumstances.

Underlying the ability of political leaders to influence what the mass public wants and expects is the incapacity and lack of opportunity of most people to know in detail either the facts of controversial public issues or the causes of developments. As already noted, everybody is constantly susceptible to military, economic, physical, and other dangers over which government has major control; and everybody can, potentially, be helped enormously in his economic affairs and in his social status through governmental actions. Though this much is clear enough, it is often quite unclear whether specific public policies are bringing benefits or sacrifices to particular groups. Do heavy armaments expenditures and preparedness in such forms as airborne planes constantly carrying hydrogen bombs and spy ships near hostile territories bring protection from attack or do they make attack more likely by inducing potential enemy countries to engage in counterthreats? Are they shields or signals of aggressive intent? Is foreign country X friendly or hostile? Will prices be moving upward quickly during the next year and is a tax increase a way to prevent it? On questions like these, what people come to believe depends heavily upon the cues government itself provides. A foreign government can be portrayed by political leaders and political gestures as friendly or as hostile; and its actions and intentions can even be influenced in one or the other direction by these same leaders' own acts. In this way, political leaders become a major influence upon what their own followings believe. Similarly, price increases, perhaps stimulated in part by the government's own monetary and fiscal policies, can be offered as a reason a tax increase is needed; and leaders themselves build up public support for such a tax increase. It is obvious that the publicized policies of governments thus help create public wants, expectations, and beliefs. This is bound to be true for the two reasons already suggested: the central role government plays in providing people with the facts upon which their beliefs and wants are based; and the great uncertainty about which governmental acts will produce which results.

When people are anxious and have no way to be sure what will help and what will hurt, they are especially willing, and even eager, to receive and to believe cues from authoritative political leaders that will alleviate their doubts and their fears. It is evident that this is exactly the situation that usually prevails in many fields of public policymaking. The typical citizen who sees a great deal of unemployment around him and fears it will increase has no basis for knowing how to restore prosperity. He is therefore eager to believe that the President of the United States and the economists upon whom the President depends for advice do know. It is relatively easy in such a situation for a President to win popular support and acquiescence for spending, credit, or public employment policies that he says will solve the problem.

Similarly, the typical citizen must rely very heavily for his beliefs upon what the government tells him about the friendly or hostile intentions of foreign governments. The creation of a North Atlantic Treaty Organization in 1949 for the declared purpose of preventing Russia from overrunning Western Europe militarily was the most direct reason and the most persuasive evidence the majority of people had for believing that Russia desired to overrun Western Europe and might do so unless prevented by superior military might. As already suggested in other connections, the establishment and daily functioning of regulatory commissions to protect consumers against unfair prices or other unfair business or labor practices serves to reassure people that they are in fact protected, for they have no direct way of learning or knowing what prices or rates are fair and whether the business firms with which they must deal are making excessive profits or exploiting them in other ways. Unclear benchmarks and ambiguity about what is fact and what is fair are characteristic of the complicated issues with which government deals; therefore, the susceptibility of mass publics to the influence of leaders regarding what they believe is all the greater.

On some issues, the empirical benchmarks *are* relatively clear, and so this form of influence is less potent. The passage of several civil rights laws in the early 1960's ostensibly guaranteeing blacks the right to vote and to enjoy equality and fair dealing in other respects was not likely to convince many who were living in urban slums that they were really better off, for the evidence of political and economic discrimination and deprivation was clear, constant, and unmistakable in the ghetto. In this case, the new civil rights laws very likely did have the effect of raising the blacks' aspirations and of making them believe they had a *right* to better conditions than they were manifestly experiencing. It is likely that the increased disparity between such expectations and actual conditions was an important underlying cause for the numerous riots in American urban ghettos in the sixties. To most whites, on the other hand, the enactment of the new civil rights laws apparently did signal rapid progress for the blacks. Several survey research studies point to an impressive difference among ghetto residents, other blacks, and whites in beliefs about whether blacks have made significant progress since World War II. In a nationwide poll conducted for *Newsweek* in 1966, 57 percent of blacks from the ghettos said they believed that they have failed to share in progress, but only 28 percent of all blacks said so.[1] Another study, made in 1964, showed that 76 percent of the whites said they believed there had been either "a lot" or "some" improvement in the position of the black man in this country "in the past few years."[2] While the studies of white and black responses were made in different years and are not perfectly comparable, they do suggest a general belief in black progress which, however, is not widely shared by ghetto residents. Several polls in particular cities corroborate this conclusion.[3]

Here we have a striking instance of the differential influence of public policies upon political demands and expectations. To most whites and to blacks not themselves living in the ghettos, the laws signalled real progress; in the ghettos they signalled unfulfilled promises and deception. The former had no clear benchmarks for judging progress and so were strongly influenced by the laws as symbols; the latter had benchmarks that were all too clear and all too discouraging.

INSTITUTIONAL ELITES AND THE MASS PUBLIC

We shall consider the means of generating influence through each major branch of government separately, for the opportunities and consequences are distinctive. At the end of this section, we shall again engage in some speculative extractions, this time on the manner in which the American penchant for orderly legal processes and standards contributes to the social control capabilities of elites.

[1] *Newsweek*, August 22, 1966.
[2] Data from Survey Research Center, University of Michigan.
[3] "Six-City Study; A Survey of Racial Attitudes in Six Northern Cities: Preliminary Findings" (Waltham, Massachusetts: Lemberg Center for the Study of Violence, June 1967, mimeo).

Elite Influence Through the Executive Branch

To a considerable extent, policymakers are dependent upon others
for information on which to act, and subordinates thus acquire a
lever, and a potent one, for influencing top-level policy. A President's
decision to commit funds to a new weapon system is based on information from subordinates about the ways in which existing defenses are weak, what potential threats enemies pose, what the effects
of various policy alternatives will be on his and his party's chances
of re-election, what the decision will mean in the way of jobs and
unemployment in various sections of the country, and so on. He cannot possibly know or learn all these things by himself in the hundreds
of areas in which he must make decisions. Subordinates are therefore in a position to influence his decisions very powerfully through
their own decisions about which data are pertinent and which are not,
what is to be stressed and what is to be ignored. They do this every
day, often not consciously trying to influence top decisions, but
nevertheless doing so.

To a large degree, a staff member in an administrative agency is
limited and guided in his choices and judgment by the role assigned
to him and to the unit for which he works. He is not free, if he wants
to keep his job and win promotion and the favor of his colleagues
and superiors, to put anything he wishes into the reports he writes. If
he works for the Extension Service of the Department of Agriculture,
he is not expected to develop or emphasize data suggesting that the
agricultural price support program chiefly subsidizes wealthy and
commercial farmers and fails to benefit small and marginal farmers.
People inclined to do so are not likely to accept a position in the
Service in the first place or to survive there long if they do accept one.
A staff member in a state conservation department is not normally
expected to devote his energies to trying to demonstrate that the
economic interests of paper factories that pollute the rivers are more
important than conservation interests; but an employee of a state
agency to promote industrial development may well be expected to
do exactly that. To a considerable extent, then, the very establishment
of an administrative unit and the assignment to it of responsibility
for a particular job is a way of making sure that certain kinds of
information will be gathered and emphasized and that they will come
to the attention of decisionmaking authorities.

This last fact offers to the resourceful policymaker a way to maximize his own influence over policy directions even though he is
dependent upon others for information and guidance. He can exercise control over the range and the jurisdictions of administrative
units under him. If, in a controversial policy area, information is
channeled through a single agency dominated by a particular interest
or clientele, the top decisionmaker is in a very real sense the prisoner
of that agency and of the interests it reflects. He knows only or largely
what it tells him; and what it tells him will predictably further the
interests of the groups that dominate it, and ignore or soft pedal

information harmful to that group. To some extent this kind of selective attention to information is deliberate, but for the most part it is subconscious, since people are tempted to perceive what they want to see and what serves their interests.

An executive who receives data from two or more agencies with overlapping jurisdictions, dominated by different interests, enjoys far more freedom. He will get a wider range of information upon which to act; and he will be in the position of umpire among contending groups rather than the captive of one of them. As already suggested, to be able to influence the *organizational pattern* for making policy in a controversial area is to be able to win such freedom and maneuverability and therefore to gain influence over which publics will win, what they will gain, and how much. This is a key mechanism through which elites can influence what mass publics get.

President Franklin Roosevelt made especially telling use of this kind of strategy and maneuverability. He liked to set up agencies with conflicting and overlapping jurisdictions. This made for confusing organization charts; but it guaranteed that when different groups of people had conflicting interests, a top level coordinating agency like the Budget Bureau or the President himself would be made aware of the problem rather than letting it be settled by some subordinate agency sensitive to only one interest. In his umpiring of such disputes, the President could consider not only the data and arguments of the contending administrative agencies under him but also the probable loss or gain of votes for his party in the next election from each possible course of action.

This same principle, relating influence to organizational pattern, has an important application below the level of the chief executive. An economic elite group which can win continuing influence over the policy directions of an administrative agency is in a strong strategic position to win mass acquiescence in the favors it achieves. A government agency at the federal or state level that is established to control the relationship between an organized business group and an unorganized consumer group is bound to come to see itself as responsible for the continuing survival and success of the businesses under its charge. It will become sensitive to the importance of maintaining a profitable operation and will therefore be sympathetic to petitions for increases in charges. It is bound to receive from the organized businesses a stream of messages that have the effect of making the governmental administrators see business problems from that group's point of view. At the same time, the consumers, being unorganized, can exert no such subtle but powerful psychological embrace around the administrative agency. On the contrary, the very existence and functioning of the agency are taken as signals that the consumer is being protected, for that is the reason the agency was established. The net effect, therefore, is that the business groups get much of what they want and at the same time remain relatively protected from public resistance or protest. We have noted this phenomenon elsewhere in this book; but it can be seen here as a mechanism through which particular economic elites gain both political maneuverability and mass acceptance for that maneuverability.

Elite Influence Through the Legislative Branch

In the legislative branch of the government, as in the executive, channels of influence run both from mass publics to elites and from elites to mass publics. In this chapter, we are concerned with the latter. Basic to legislative policymaking are the allied processes of logrolling and coalition building; and these are also fundamental in explaining elite influence. It is the rare issue, such as a declaration of war or a strong civil rights bill, that arouses a fairly strong interest, pro or con, in virtually all members of the legislative body. When this happens, it is because there is widespread concern or controversy over the issue in the country at large. On most issues that come before a legislative body, only a relatively small proportion of the legislators take an active interest and most have only a mild concern or none at all, largely reflecting the interests or lack of interest among their constituents. A proposal to raise the tariff on foreign coal imports will certainly evoke strong interest in the coal-producing areas of Pennsylvania, West Virginia, and Illinois and thus among legislators representing these areas; but most other congressmen are not likely to be strongly aroused even though some of their constituents use coal to heat their homes or factories. A proposal to appropriate federal funds to change the flow of the Colorado River will certainly awaken hopes or anxieties in legislators from the states bordering the river, but probably will not deeply stir legislators from Georgia, Alaska, or New Jersey.

Where this combination of strong interest among a few legislators and apathy among most prevails, conditions are ripe for bargaining: for logrolling and coalition building. The congressman from Pennsylvania who very much wants support for a higher tariff on coal knows he can probably get supporting votes from colleagues from states without coal mines in return for his good will and the resulting expectation that he will support those colleagues in the future on some issue on which *they* badly need support. He may have an understanding with congressmen from cotton growing states that he will vote for higher price supports for cotton: an issue in which he and his Pennsylvania constituents have relatively little interest. More likely there will not be an explicit understanding about vote trading at all, but rather a gentlemen's recognition that a favor rendered today deserves a return favor in the future.

This process serves to identify the representatives of unaware or apathetic masses with the interests of relatively small economic groups that have a lot to gain from a public policy. It makes it possible for a group that is strongly interested to put together a coalition composed largely of the uninterested or the mildly interested. One of the most common forms of coalition in American legislatures allies urban business groups with legislators from rural areas, which are heavily over-represented in both houses of Congress and in the legislatures of those states that have large urban areas. This form of logrolling has frequently given business groups substantial support on labor and welfare issues, where business interests frequently clash with those of urban workers, low income groups, and the poor. In return, it has helped Southern rural legislators to win support from Northern conservatives for weakening civil rights bills and for legislation to help large farming and commercial farming interests. As this last example suggests, the division of American states into districts for electing members of state legislatures and national congressmen has often made it easier for the interests of mass publics to be subordinated to those of elites.

A second, and related, feature of legislative bargaining that wins mass support for economic and political elites is the frequent translation of concrete demands into emotionally appealing "style" issues. If support for fair employment practices for blacks or open housing ordinances comes to be perceived as part of a radical or communist plot to overthrow American institutions, opposition to these reforms becomes widespread and intense, even among people who might otherwise see them as elementary justice for an unfairly deprived group of Americans. For many years social security legislation, and later compulsory medical insurance for the aged, were widely regarded as forms of socialism; and so they were heatedly resisted by people who feared an alien form of government. In this way a relatively small elite of organized doctors, insurance companies, and politicians gained strong political support for a position that was detrimental to the economic interests of most of those who supported it. Proposals to fluoridate water in order to protect children's teeth are frequently resisted with great emotion as an insidious effort to force ingestion of medicine, or even a plot to poison the population organized by alien or radical conspirators.

In each of these examples and others that might be cited, the political debate tends to center around ominous rumors and deep anxieties regarding unverifiable allegations, rather than around the demonstrable advantages and disadvantages of the policies in question. The frequent possibility of translating a concrete legislative proposal into a style issue of this kind, with its consequent intense and widespread arousal of irrational mass concern, is clearly a mechanism through which elites can gain mass support for specific policies. It is more feasible in legislative policymaking than in administrative agencies or in the courts because it depends directly upon publicizing issues and evoking widespread public response.

Elite Influence Through the Courts

In the courts as well, a number of distinct factors assure that elite interests will be accorded great weight in decisionmaking. The nation's judges and lawyers are drawn disproportionately from the prosperous and from groups with high social status. Law school education, like public education generally, consists in part at least of the inculcation of elite values. Accused persons with money and social status are far more likely than those without these advantages to benefit from competent legal advice and defense. Finally, the elaborate legal code and the established processes for interpreting and enforcing it work in the interests of the advantaged. Each of these points needs to be considered more fully.

The last of these factors is both more subtle and more potent than the others, and it underlies and bolsters them. Americans have always been proud to say that we have "a government of laws, not men." That belief stems from our development of an elaborate code of legal rules that are relied upon to settle conflicts and to determine guilt or innocence, theoretically with a minimum of human arbitrariness and with a maximum of impersonal "equality before the law." Justice is portrayed as blind: blind, it is alleged, to differences among litigants in income, color, race, education, social position, and so on.

In a crucial sense, this very blindness to real differences means that the legal code repeatedly offers justifications for dealing harshly with the disadvantaged and leniently with the elite. We have already alluded to Anatole France's trenchantly-made point: "The law in its splendid impartiality prosecutes both the rich and the poor for stealing a loaf of bread or sleeping under bridges." In an essay that has had a wide influence upon contemporary social science, the German sociologist Max Weber analyzed the phenomenon more precisely if less pointedly than Anatole France's epigram does. He suggested that any system of justice depending upon formal legal definitions and classifications and upon precedent becomes a ready instrument for "rationalizing" the interests of the elite — that is, for finding acceptable reasons to serve the interests of the elite. This is the case because the judges' attention is turned away from the concrete situation and problems of the litigants and their ethical implications and toward the unclear, formal categories which can be used to justify any action and are likely to be used in practice to justify the judge's predispositions and prejudices. The man who steals a loaf of bread to feed his hungry family is fitted into a formal, abstract classification — larceny. And the legal code prescribes penalties for larceny, not for a particular person driven to desperate action by his desperate situation. Law makes the concrete abstract and thereby justifies the overlooking of concrete differences. Weber therefore concludes that, "The property-less masses especially are not served by a formal 'equality before the law'...."[4]

This effect of a legal code is not to be understood as a plot against the mass public or a deliberate deception. It is typically unplanned, unintended, and unrecognized; and it is therefore the business of a social scientist to understand it, as Weber has tried to do. Though it is a significant tendency and all the more widespread because it is unintended and unrecognized, it is countered in some measure by other tendencies, such as those considered in the next chapters, which confer influence upon mass publics.

[4] H.H. Gerth and C. Wright Mills, eds., *From Max Weber: Essays in Sociology* (New York: Oxford University Press, 1958), p. 221.

It is evident that this subtle function of legal codes reinforces other advantages elites enjoy in the judicial process. A person from an upper middle class background, accustomed to high status and to some measure of influence, is likely to accept this happy state of affairs as in the public interest. And he would probably view challenges to this bias on the part of the disadvantaged as violating the legal codes whose formal and ambiguous propositions rationalize the affluence of his peers. Not all judicial behavior reflects this tendency, of course, and the next chapter calls attention to some influences that work in the opposite direction.

The high cost of legal protection and its unequal availability is another potent factor in fostering the influence of elites in judicial policymaking. The fact that it is largely the fairly affluent and the corporations that employ legal talent reinforces the tendency for lawyers to shape legal codes into rationalizations of elite interests. Very likely, however, the sheer inability of a large proportion of the population to buy legal counsel and assistance is an even more telling fact. Many of the individuals charged with crime confess on the spot or in the police station without a lawyer's advice; and this has remained true even since the Miranda decision requiring that an accused be advised of his legal rights and his right to counsel.

The unequal availability of legal talent is also a central influence upon the formulation of broader public policy. Corporations often provide legislative committees with drafts of proposed bills on topics of interest to them. An early draft of the Taft-Hartley Act, for example, was prepared by lawyers employed by the National Association of Manufacturers. In the formulation of administrative policies of direct concern to consumers and to businessmen, corporations also enjoy an advantage. A government agency representing the interests of consumers can typically hire too few attorneys, and those are poorly paid and inexperienced compared to the lawyers representing a large corporation charged with violating a proconsumer law. In three antitrust cases on which one study reports, the lawyers representing the Antitrust Division of the Department of Justice were outnumbered by lawyers for the defendants 5-30, 10-50, and 5-103 respectively. Counsel for the defense receive salaries that may be 10 times as high as those of the government lawyers; and turnover among lawyers for government agencies is typically high.[5] Partly because salaries are low, law school graduates often see jobs in government agencies as ideal training grounds for subsequent lucrative employment by the companies the agencies are supposed to regulate. This expectation in itself may condition the behavior of counsel.

The fundamental conditioning factors, however, are consumer interest, adequate appropriations, and strong political support. This form of public spending is always regarded with some suspicion by conservatives and is a readily available object of appropriations cuts, which can be justified to the general public as serving the interests

---

[5] Clair Wilcox, *Public Policies Toward Business* (Homewood, Ill.: Richard D. Irwin, 1960), p. 103.

of governmental economy and tax saving. The sums involved are typically very small compared to the total budget; and so the major impact of such "economies" is in weakening enforcement of pro-consumer and prolabor policies rather than in significant tax savings. This procedure is all the more feasible politically because it is usually possible for legislators to carry it out while retaining the advantage of having publicly defended the *principle* of government support for the consumer, the disadvantaged, and the low income groups. The net effect is frequently a weakening of a political challenge to elites through a largely symbolic concession to mass publics.

The Managerial Uses of "the Law"

The value systems of all societies support obedience to constituted authorities, but the American emphasis on the character and role of the law seems distinctive. American thinkers have assiduously developed the notion that the solutions to problems are to be found within the body of the law, perhaps partly to impose some distance between elites and masses. The unstated assertion behind such a notion is that the quality of being "law" somehow lifted a statute or regulation out of its inevitable character of being merely the expression of the preferences and interests of those men who happened to be successful in shaping its ultimate form. When aggrieved, the average American is likely to say, "There ought to be a law . . . ." And when he seeks goals through the political process, his opponents or his leaders are likely to explain that the law requires that he conform to a particular standard, or that he must obey "because it is the law." In both cases moral imperatives have been inserted into the concept of law, suggesting that once the value preferences of men have been written into statute they acquire some higher stature than what they had before and must now be obeyed without regard to their specific content or the justice of their provisions. Some men who are more powerful than others exercise their values and create a statute to their liking; other men, also winners in the game of power-seeking, interpret these statutes as their value preferences suggest. In what respect then does it make sense to say that "this is a government of laws *and not of men?*" Clearly, only in the sense that the speaker believes (or wishes his audience to believe) that law is not applied arbitrarily in this system, and that certain standards of fairness and consideration for others may be anticipated. These are empirical (factual) questions, however, on which we might gather data and reach conclusions. But as a preliminary, we must get free of the notion that there is some mystical validity to whatever majority or elite preferences find their way into the words of a statute, court decision, or regulation.

The effects of the generally accepted assumptions about the sanctity and importance of the law are many. For one thing, they operate to shift considerations of the merits of issues to specialized arenas and persons. If a statute once enacted acquires special status and must not be questioned, then the only occasion for real choicemaking in regard to its content occurs in the late stages of drafting, amendment, and passage in the legislature. In some cases, courts will be able to make critical choices in the process of affixing an authorative interpretation upon the statute. In both cases, lawyers — those with special skills in the drafting and interpretation of words and phrases — will exercise considerable influence over the exact provisions and the precise applications of the statute. The precedent-oriented training and cautious background which lawyers bring to their tasks operate to limit the change (in any direction) from the status quo which can be made through a statute or decision. In neither case will the matter be thrown open for broad public consideration of the value choices or questions of priority which are involved. Thus, a need for expertise is experienced by a society which transacts its public business through the provisions of statutes and regulations, and the particular skill group with the greatest claim to such expertise — lawyers — becomes in effect the brokers of public policy. Issues are issues insofar as they can be phrased as such as a result of the understanding and conceptualization of those who deal in the law, and only such decisions as can be articulated by the traditional language of the law can be made by the polity. Instead of a public consideration of preferences and goals for present or future, there can be only a technical and professional dialogue on the question of the precise manner in which things are to be done. To an extent, a politics of means gains precedence over a potential politics of ends.

Uncritical adoption of the established provisions of the law in regard to the procedures of politics has the further effect of institutionalizing the status quo. Every set of rules must be based on certain premises about the right way to do things in politics, and when those rules acquire independent validity as "the law," other kinds of political behavior are foreclosed. But no rules can be neutral: they either support or prevent interference with a present order of things, a present distribution of power and influence within the society. They set a range within which change must take place, and tip the scales in behalf of those who currently (under the existing rules) have been most successful and are most powerful.

Let us take an example, admittedly oversimplified, from outside the American context, where these implications may be more immediately visible. The substance of "international law" was created and developed mostly in Western Europe and the United States. It reached its fullest flower in the late nineteenth and early twentieth centuries when the Western countries were not only dominant internationally but also colonizers of most of the rest of the world. International law recognized the power of nations to expropriate the property or investments of foreign nationals within their boundaries, but provided that such action required compensation at full value to the original owners. This would mean that a former colony which gained its independence would not be able to take over the mines, plantations, or oil wells which foreign corporations had developed within it, unless it was prepared to pay them full value for their holdings. A country which had few other resources and a low standard of living would probably be unable to do so, and would be faced with the prospect of watching the foreign investors extract its mineral resources and reap great profits from their sale, while its own people bordered on starvation. Believing that the mother countries had merely exploited their resources in order to build up their own economies, many newly-independent former colonies believed themselves justified in acquiring such properties anyway. They either refused to pay any compensation at all or offered token payments over extended periods of time and in their own currency, terms which investors were not likely to find satisfactory. To them, the "international law" which required payment for what was originally and in their eyes rightfully their own property was merely a convenient construct of colonial profiteers, never consented to by them, and therefore not binding upon them. To some Americans, however, it was an illegal and unconscionable interference with property rights deserving of reprisal in any feasible manner. The point is that the fairness and justice of a procedure established by law depends on the perspective from which it is viewed, and however neutral it may appear to some, it may quite reasonably appear to others that it preserves and protects an unjust status quo.

Laws limiting dissent, controlling elections, regulating police powers, or prescribing the manner of student participation in universities, all may carry the same implications, at least in the eyes of some beholders. Reflecting the satisfaction of those who currently dominate with the status quo, they provide channels for action and attempted change which are basically consistent with that status quo, and they outlaw actions which are seriously at odds with it. In other words, they establish a range of results that are tolerable to the dominant and which can be achieved by action in conformance with the rules. Adherence to those rules can mean acquiescence in that limited range of potential results. Those who seek other results, of course, must face the question of whether to change their goals or seek them outside of and probably in violation of the existing rules. This is the point at which the uncritical devotion to "the law" as an abstract entity, divorced from its specific provisions or consideration of whose ends it serves, becomes so important to the nature of American politics. The political value of law and procedural regularity is an effective aid to social control — perhaps a necessary one, depending on one's particular perspective and whether or not he feels represented by the currently dominant groups. But it is not an aid to clear thinking about the real nature of politics in the United States.

"PRIVATE" ELITES AND THE MASS PUBLIC

Institutional elites' actions normally enjoy the support of a wide variety of nongovernmental elites, many of whom are strategically located so as to develop the impression of wide public approval and support for such policies. For many people who are on the peripheries of the establishment or who hope eventually to gain admission, promotion of support for government action is automatic. But some "private" institutions are more capable of generating comprehensive or long-term support than others. We shall consider the part played by private elites in terms of four illustrative types of institutions they control: the universities, the communications media, interest groups, and political parties. Afterwards, we shall assess the overall social control capabilities of elites.

Elite Influence Through Higher Education

There are more than 2,200 institutions of higher education in the United States, ranging from junior colleges to institutions with 30 to 40 thousand students and an equal number of faculty, staff, and administrators, which offer a variety of Ph.D. and other professional degrees. They are not usually seen as part of ongoing political processes, except as recipients of large proportions of state budgets or the site of student outbursts. But they are an integral part of the configuration of power in the United States and serve some vital functions. Any analysis which seeks to locate sources of elite influence or to trace uses of power must make a point of analyzing the political role of institutions of higher education. We shall sketch the outlines of this political role briefly, using the major universities as our principal source of illustration. In general, our thesis is that elites dominate these institutions more fully than most others within the society, and use them to serve their needs and to influence both rising near-elites and the mass public toward support of established structures, policies, and practices.

The parameters of the university's functions are set by four factors: the people who govern it, the sources of its financial support, the purposes which these and other forces encourage it to serve, and the people who execute these tasks — i.e., the faculty. A recent study by the Educational Testing Service, the well-known and authoritative testing arm of American higher education, sheds comprehensive light on who trustees and regents of colleges and universities are, and what they think about higher education. Table 1 highlights some major aspects of the socioeconomic backgrounds of these trustees, omitting breakdowns of all but the two categories of selective private universities (selective in regard to admissions, such as the Ivy League and similar schools) and public universities. It suggests quite simply that the governance of universities, more than any other institutional area we have examined, is in the hands of persons in our general category of elite. Nearly two-thirds of all college and university trustees in the nation are in the top one percent in income level; in the case of the selective private universities, 43 percent earn over $100,000 per year. The occupations of trustees are nearly all the highest-status ones, with business executives making up 35 percent of the total. The prevalence of businessmen helps to explain the fact that 20 percent of all trustees, including all the trustees or regents of junior colleges, community colleges, and small private colleges, are members of the board of directors of one or more corporations whose stock is traded on a stock exchange. A total of 46 percent of the

TABLE 1
Socioeconomic Backgrounds of Members of College
and University Governing Boards, 1967 (in percents)

	Total, Trustees of all U.S. colleges and univ.	Trustees of selective private univ.	Trustees of public univ.
Age			
under 40 yrs.	5	1	3
40-49 yrs.	21	11	20
50-59 yrs.	37	42	34
over 60 yrs.	36	46	40
Income			
below $10,000 per yr.	8	2	2
$10-$19,999 per yr.	18	3	13
$20-$29,999 per yr.	15	6	15
$30-$49,999 per yr.	19	18	27
$50-$99,999 per yr.	20	26	24
over $100,000 per yr.	16	43	16
Occupation			
Lawyer	10	13	20
Merchandising executive	7	3	7
Manufacturing executive	17	27	18
Bank or insurance executive	11	14	12
Professional	32	21	19
All other	23	22	24
Number of corporations, traded on a stock exchange, for which served on board of directors:			
None	78	53	76
One	10	15	11
Two	5	13	5
Three or more	5	18	6

Source: Rodney T. Hartnett, *College and University Trustees: Their Backgrounds, Roles, and Educational Attitudes* (Princeton, N. J.: Educational Testing Service, 1969), pp. 57-59.

trustees of the selective private universities overlap with boards of directors of these major corporations, and 18 percent serve on three or more such corporate boards. In general, the selective private universities tend to have the wealthiest, highest-status trustees, perhaps partly because board positions are filled chiefly by the boards themselves on a kind of self-perpetuating basis. The typical board member of a public university is most often a lawyer, perhaps because open positions are filled chiefly by appointment by the governor, who may tend to pay political debts thereby.

Trustees' political attitudes may be estimated in part from their political party identifications and self-described ideological orientations. Of all trustees, 58 percent were Republicans and 33 percent

Democrats; 21 percent described themselves as conservative, 15 percent as liberal, and the remainder as "moderate." [6] The proportion of each remained roughly constant among the various types of institutions. But perhaps of more immediate relevance are their attitudes toward issues which are likely to arise in the university context. Responses to several such issues, posed in the form of statements, are highlighted in Table 2. It is clear that the trustees believe higher education is a privilege and not a right, and that one of the functions of the university is to train faculties and students in accordance with established standards and procedures. In response to other questions, the trustees made clear their determination to maintain control over all major decisions within their universities. Beyond doubt, the structure of university governance indicates firm guidance and charting of basic directions by elites.

TABLE 2
Trustees' Attitudes on University Issues
(percent agreeing or agreeing strongly)

	Total, Trustees of all U.S. colleges and univ.	Trustees of selective private univ.	Trustees of public univ.
Attendance at this institution is a privilege, not a right	92	98	80
All campus speakers should be subject to some official screening process	69	45	68
Students who actively disrupt the function of a college by demonstrating, sitting-in, or otherwise refusing to obey the rules should be expelled or suspended	81	71	83
Students involved in civil disobedience off the campus should be subject to discipline by the college as well as by the local authorities	49	29	46
The requirement that a professor sign a loyalty oath is reasonable	53	33	52

Source: Hartnett, *College and University Trustees, op. cit.,* p. 60.

[6] Rodney T. Hartnett, *College and University Trustees: Their Backgrounds, Roles, and Educational Attitudes* (Princeton, N. J.: Educational Testing Service, 1969), p. 65.

The pattern of financing most institutions of higher education provides a major link to the more formal governing structures of both federal and state governments — and, presumably, to those dominant in such circles. Public institutions, of course, receive most of their financial support from state (or, in some cases, local) governments. They characteristically charge relatively low tuition, with the deficit made up from public tax revenues. (A provocative and carefully detailed analysis of the sources of revenue and actual recipients points out that, overall, this amounts to working-class financing of low-cost educations for middle-class youth.)[7] The dependence of these institutions on the largesse of state legislatures makes them especially anxious to serve the needs and preferences held by individual state congressmen and the interests dominant in the state generally. Thus, there is a strong desire to be "useful," as defined by key businesses and industries, and to avoid the taint of unorthodox political ideas or behavior that might antagonize established powers in the state. Despite these pressures, of course, tensions between the larger state universities and their legislatures are frequently high.

Both public and private universities also rely heavily on financial assistance in various forms from the federal government. This is true of public universities as well as private. Public universities such as the University of Michigan and the University of California receive about 50 percent and 40 percent respectively of their annual budgets from the federal government; at private universities such as the University of Chicago and Harvard, the totals are roughly 65 percent and 40 percent respectively. Federal assistance takes many forms, from loans and grants to students, buildings, and equipment to performance of research and teaching functions (ROTC, for example) on the campus, or providing contract services. In the latter case, the university in effect acts as a direct arm of the United States government, whether in experimental programs of crime control or poverty amelioration in the United States or in developing agriculture or training police and bureaucrats in developing countries. In every case, these funds are valued by universities, and a major university must place and keep itself in a position to compete successfully for such grants if it is to retain its status. Not only does the capacity to hire and provide research opportunities for well-reputed faculty members depend on funds of this type, but a substantial share of the operating budget of the university is also contributed in this way. Some university administrators have seen this as a welcome chance which will be of service to the society; others are less enthusiastic, but none deny the reality of the pressure.

The purposes of the university are much less concretely demonstrated than the last two parameters, but we can begin to see the kinds of pressures that contribute to defining them. Three basic purposes may be identified, though how most universities rank them in terms of priority may be disputed. First is the purpose of providing

---

[7] Lee Hansen and Burton A. Weisbrod, *Benefits, Costs, and Finance of Public Higher Education* (Chicago: Markham, 1969).

social mobility for students and well-trained functionaries for the economy and society. These goals are complementary: students and their parents visualize college education principally as a means of getting a good job, and the economy and society require alert, aspiring, adaptable men and women to perform a multitude of tasks. The result is a vocationally-oriented program of instruction whose chief criterion of success is the student's acquisition of a job offering prospects of income and status. To prepare students for such jobs, the current structure of the economic and social order must be taken as a given, their needs assessed and extended into the future, and students shown how to adapt to and fulfill those needs.

Second is the purpose of providing knowledge that will help solve problems facing the society. To be of assistance, the definitions of such problems must be similar to the manner in which they are defined by the relevant policymakers; otherwise the results of the research will not be used and the purpose will not be served. The result is that much research effort is devoted to finding ways for those who are currently dominant to better carry out their policies. In seeking to solve problems of social disharmony, this perspective may lead to defining those who for one reason or another do not accept the orthodox and established behavior standards and life styles as "maladjusted" or "criminal," and to developing techniques for better controlling such "deviants." In the case of problems perceived by private industry, university efforts amount to socializing the sometimes high costs of research and development, while benefits accrue chiefly to the user industries.

Third is the intellectual purpose of the university — to transmit the culture and wisdom of the past, to adapt it to the needs of the present and the future, and to help students develop the capacity of critical and independent thinking about themselves, their society, and their world. This is the most difficult, least accepted, and least accomplished of the university's purposes. To think critically and evaluatively about oneself and one's surroundings requires severe effort, self-discipline, and the destruction of a lifetime's complacent assumptions. It provokes sharp reaction from an insecure but financially vital outside world. And so it does not often occur, and if it does, it is not often sustained for long.

The faculty must operate within the context fixed by the various factors just reviewed. Men and women who teach seek advancement and security, let us assume, with much the same natural ratio as others in their society. To be well regarded in one's own institution and in one's profession, to do the research that makes for visibility and mobility, and to avoid the controversies that spell an end to advancement, faculty members must accept the basic standards which trustees, financial sources, and accepted university purposes have set for them. The real deviant soon becomes uncomfortably visible, pressures focus on him, and he either returns to his accepted role or loses his university status. Nor is this established role uncongenial to many university faculty. Their class origins, identification with a prestigious profession, need for access to men of knowledge, money, and power, and their current position of authority lead them to adopt the perspective of the "is." Their task is to explain, rationalize, and project the present into the future.

What is the impact of these various forces upon the students who pass through American institutions of higher education? In general, survey evidence suggests that the long-term effect has been to induce them to trust and support the acts of government more fully than ordinary citizens. College graduates are better informed, take part in politics more, and are more fully imbued with orthodox ideology, than those of comparable age and life experience who do not attend college. To some extent, the effects of college education may be mistakenly attributed to the effects of either youth (the proportion of college educated is higher with each new generation and age group) or to economic status (college students come from wealthier families and earn more income after college.) The autonomous influences of these separate factors is seldom made distinct. College education has repeatedly been shown to have an independent effect, aside from the fact that it usually coincides with both youth and wealth. Taken by itself, it correlates with greater confidence in the established political system and its current policies. Nor is the reaction to the Vietnam War really an exception to these general propositions. As we saw in Chapter 8 (Figure 2), college graduates at first supported the war more strongly than others and only shifted to greater conviction that the U.S. had made a mistake *after* President Nixon began to withdraw troops. The campus-based dissent against the war began as a very small movement; its escalation took several years and repeated provocations, and even then in many cases seemed to be limited exclusively to opposition to the single policy of war in Southeast Asia.

It is clear, therefore, that the universities offer elites a major means of developing long-term influence, both by shaping vocational orientations and skills and by instilling the political ideology and broad behavioral cues that will lead to later support. Nevertheless, some universities, some faculty, and some students do not fit these general descriptions. How and why some do not, and how normally impotent students generated such undeniable political impact in the late 1960's and 1970, will be examined in a later chapter.

Elite Influence Through the Communications Media

Underlying these institutional, psychological, and political channels through which elites gain and retain advantages in the policymaking process are some basic supports for elites deriving from the flow of information, news, and opinion about public affairs.

The obvious and most widely accepted view of the link between communications media and policy formation emphasizes the opposite effect: the importance of news media as channels through which citizens are kept informed and so able to exercise influence over public policies. "Know ye the truth and the truth shall make you free." There is, of course, an important sense in which this view holds true. Without information readily available through newspapers, magazines, radio, and television, most people would have little chance of exercising influence upon government at all or even of knowing when an issue of concern to them arises.

At the same time, a great deal of our recently acquired knowledge about opinion formation and opinion change points unmistakably to a number of mechanisms through which mass publics are placed at a disadvantage and subjected to both deliberate and unconscious influence from elites. Some of these have already been mentioned in other connections. There is, first, the basic fact that a substantial proportion of the people have relatively little interest in news of public affairs and do not especially try to expose themselves to it. One form of evidence for this fact appears in Converse's findings that only a relatively small proportion of the population, the elite, have clear and logically consistent political beliefs and interpretations about public issues.[8] One study which questioned people both about what they knew and whether they had an opinion on eight different public issues found that from 22 percent to 55 percent of the population, depending on the issue, either had no opinion or had one but did not know what the government was doing.[9] Also in point is the finding that much political information is "retailed" by opinion leaders to larger audiences. Such a two-step flow of messages in the media gives elites, who are somewhat better educated and have somewhat higher status than the recipients of the messages, a disproportionate influence.[10]

Among the opinion leaders who help control the two-step flow are editors and reporters themselves, who are in an especially strategic position to decide which news is emphasized, which soft-pedaled, and which ignored. More than that, those who shape the media regularly "create" news in an important sense by choosing the questions they ask public figures and by themselves suggesting the answers. A politician or political celebrity frequently agrees with a reporter's "Do you believe that . . ." question and thereby finds himself publicly taking a position that is widely reported and that may not have entered his head until the reporter asked the question. His responses, therefore, are greatly influenced by suggested answers.

From these two basic facts, a relatively large measure of indifference from the mass public and control over the flow of messages by opinion leaders, a number of other pertinent influences on mass opinions emerge. We have noticed earlier that some kinds of political issues, usually labeled "style" issues, do consistently arouse deep and widespread concern. Public figures seeking mass support therefore have a political stake, news media an economic stake, and many political spectators a psychological stake in translating ordinary issues into style issues. In subtle ways this process goes on all the time. For

[8] Philip E. Converse, "The Nature of Belief Systems in Mass Publics," in *Ideology and Discontent,* ed. David Apter (New York: Free Press, 1964), pp. 206-61; see also Robert E. Lane and David O. Sears, *Public Opinion* (Englewood Cliffs, N. J.: Prentice-Hall, 1964), pp. 57-71.

[9] *Ibid.,* pp. 59-60.

[10] Elihu Katz and Paul Lazarsfeld, *Personal Influence* (New York: Free Press, 1955).

at least a part of the public, economic, social, and welfare policy in the city ghettos is seen in the context of a black plot to attack or degrade whites. Part of the sympathizers with each side of labor-management issues see the other side as dupes of an antisocial or alien conspiracy. A business regulation policy that serves in practice to give the regulated industry most of what it wants is translated into a picture of a benevolent government agency safeguarding the consumer and the public interest. To some degree, everyone seeks out in the news the particular facts or interpretations that fit his preconceptions and ignores facts and interpretations that do not. When news reports refer to style issues of the kinds illustrated, a large number of people eager to find such interpretations will predictably concentrate on these and ignore counterevidence. In this way, a combination of economic, political, and psychological factors tends to divert a part of the mass public from clear-eyed weighing of the news and its implications for their own interests and to render them manipulable to influence, though the manipulation is probably as often unintended as planned.

Newspapers and television and radio stations are themselves big business, and to a considerable degree they are merged into commonly owned chains and business complexes. Television stations are frequently affiliated with newspaper publishers. With few exceptions, such as the noncommercial educational stations, they rely chiefly on advertising by other businesses for their profits. These considerations do not preclude the possibility that reporters and editors will sometimes hold and express competing and liberal views, but the great majority of publishers and editors share the interests of the economic elite and the protection of these interests is typically presented as the acceptable and patriotic view, while contrary views are sometimes presented as characteristic of an outside or at least vaguely unAmerican influence.

The predilection to expose ourselves to facts and interpretations that fit our preconceptions and to ignore those that challenge them finds expression in another way as well. People seek out the papers, the news stories, and the editorial points of view that reinforce their beliefs rather than those that challenge them. In the measure that newspapers, columnists, and radio commentators present public issues in terms of style issues and myths that fit people's fears, suspicions, and anxieties, their appeal and their circulation is increased, for the evidence is clear that a relatively small part of the public concerns itself with the details of complex public issues and news developments. In this way, a large part of the public is reinforced in its fears and becomes more easily manipulable.

Contrary views are available in the United States, of course, in the liberal and leftist press as well as in the conservative newspapers and broadcasting media that offer relatively comprehensive news coverage and analysis. As already indicated, however, the audiences for these media are comparatively small; and they are also largely self-selected to reinforce prior views. For the most part, it is a particular group of intellectuals, not the mass public, that reads either serious liberal journals like *The Nation* or serious conservative ones like *The National Review*. Therefore, such media do not serve in practice as a leavening influence upon the mass public. It is not as though every citizen were subjected to the wide range of political analysis and political ideology and philosophy available on the American journalistic scene. To a very large degree, what we have are relatively small groups of elites who subject themselves to congenial points of view by selecting their sources of information and opinion. And at the same time the great mass of the people subject themselves largely to highly simplified versions of the dominant political issues. This basic fact makes it possible for politicians and other elites to cast issues into forms that will often produce the responses they want in mass publics. Typically such recasting is not conscious manipulation or deception. More often opinion leaders are influenced by their own economic, social, or other interests to perceive issues in these forms. The student of public opinion and communication must recognize that the dissemination of information and of benefits is a complicated and often quite subtle process.

The influence of political elites over the content of the media of mass communication is a powerful adjunct of other devices through which they influence the beliefs and political demands and support of mass publics. What the President of the United States says and does is automatically news. His office lends drama to his pronouncements and actions. The same is true in lesser degree of other conspicuous public officeholders and activists: cabinet members, senators, governors, political party leaders. Because people are curious, anxious, and interested in what such figures have said and done, the newspapers, television stations, and popular magazines have strong economic and psychological reasons to keep them in the limelight. It is evident, therefore, that these officials can far more easily convey information, impressions, and arguments to a mass public than can people whose names and influence are not well known to the journalists and to the public. The chief effect of this fact is that the influence of elites can be intensified and multiplied. An administration that thinks it will benefit from a liberal civil rights policy can easily convey to a very large public the impression that the enactment of a new civil rights law represents dramatic progress. Publicizing of particular cases strongly shapes the view the public has of all developments in that area. Human interest stories about a few striking black advances in employment or housing shape people's thinking even if the cases are not typical.

Because controversial public issues are typically highly complex, and it is hard or impossible to know what causes what, people have to simplify them in their own minds in order to think about them at all. They come to be perceived in terms of some metaphor or simple model. Urban riots may be viewed as the result of outside agitators stirring up basically satisfied blacks in the ghettos. Or they may be viewed in terms of aggrieved poor people finally demanding through militance and violence what they deserved to get long before. Political speeches and public policies help shape the particular simplified view that people adopt, and so do newspaper and television reports. Once a particular metaphor of this kind comes to define a complex situation for a person, he tends to fit later news about it into the same mold and to see all developments as offering further support for the view already adopted. People have to make some sense of complicated and threatening situations, and so they perceive selectively in order to bolster the view that serves some function for themselves and reassures them. Some people are far more rigid and blind in their selective perception than others, of course; but selective perception is a temptation for everybody and a mechanism which political analysts have to take into account. The opposite of selective perception is reality testing — checking one's tentative beliefs against verifiable conditions and observations and changing the beliefs when the facts call for it. In scientific research, reality testing is fundamental and crucial. In reacting to politics it is often difficult, and people manage to engage in it to different degrees.

Elite Influence Through Interest Groups

Interest groups are frequently thought of as devices through which the interests of mass publics are effectively communicated to decisionmakers; but they also serve the opposite function in the American political system, becoming largely a channel through which particular elites win the support of wider publics. To see how this is done involves an understanding of some subtle and nonobvious political processes, some of which have already been mentioned in other connections.

A key fact is the tendency of people engaged in making or selling the same product or service to form an organization to promote and protect their interests. Steel manufacturers, broadcast station licensees, trucking companies, physicians, stockbrokers, real estate brokers, cotton farmers, all these and hundreds of other groupings of people with the same production or sales interests have organized into associations to win favorable governmental policies for themselves and sometimes to influence private economic policies as well.

Notice that such interest groups typically represent economic or social elites. Usually, though not invariably, the people who ultimately *buy* their goods or services do not find it natural or easy or even possible to organize themselves into interest groups. The consumers of manufactured or grown products, the patients who pay physicians' bills, the viewers of television programs and commercials rarely organize to promote their interests politically or economically. They find it hard or impossible to do so for some obvious reasons — their large numbers, their lack of face-to-face contacts or facilities for communicating with each other, and above all, the fact that people do not often think of themselves in the role of consumers. They find themselves politically divided on the basis of other crisscrossing interests: economic, ethnic, regional, religious, ideological, and so on. All of this can be summed up in the generalization that people's interests as producers, for which they are paid, are typically seen as primary and are intensely pursued. People's interests as consumers are typically perceived as secondary and are hard to pursue in an organized and effective way.

There are some exceptional groups of consumers who do organize effectively; but these groups are themselves elites rather than part of the mass public. Companies that ship their products by truck or rail are organized into interest groups, and the consequence is that their interests, like those of the truck and railroad carriers, are politically protected. But the ultimate buyers of these products, who do not form interest groups, pay for the protections accorded to these elites both in higher prices and in taxes, which often go into government subsidies to various businesses. Similarly, management groups, which are consumers of labor, are organized into effective interest groups. Here again the outcome often is that organized labor and management groups are able, through political and economic agreements, to pass the costs of their price and wage gains onto a mass public of consumers that is not organized — at least not in the role of consumer.

The difficulty of organizing interest groups made up of consumers is especially burdensome on the poor — that large part of the mass public least likely to be represented and helped by any kind of interest group of producers or sellers, including labor unions. Fewer poor people vote than do the more affluent, and they do not vote as a bloc in any case. Their main economic resource is their labor, and because they are largely unskilled, intermittently employed or unemployed, and not attached to the mass production industries, they are, for the most part, not organized into labor unions. What political power they do have derives chiefly from the support they get from sympathetic liberals and others who do have political resources. For reasons already considered, however, such support frequently produces largely symbolic benefits for the poor and the disadvantaged: laws declaring their right to vote in a social setting that makes it unlikely they will use the right massively and effectively; laws purporting to protect them from economic exploitation when the agencies administering the laws are influenced chiefly by the economically powerful; civil rights laws that reassure liberals that their values are being advanced but which have only token effect in actually making housing, credit, jobs, and social status available to those who suffer from widespread social discrimination.

Interest groups, therefore, serve chiefly to institutionalize and formalize the exercise of political resources deriving from wealth, social status, and the ability to organize effectively — that is, they operate for the benefit of the elite. They are not generally and widely efficacious as a resource for the mass public.

Elite Influence Through Political Parties

To some extent, though not as clearly or consistently, the same must be said of political parties. The three central characteristics of the major American political parties all make it easier than it would otherwise be for elite groups to use the parties as vehicles for mobilizing support for their interests. The parties are "catch-all" and opportunistic in their rhetoric and their appeals; party discipline is minimal or nonexistent; and the locus of power in both major parties is local and decentralized. The implications of each of these characteristics for elite maneuverability is worth attention.

Both the Republicans and the Democrats appeal in each election campaign to a range of groups with different, and sometimes conflicting, political interests. In both parties leading figures and governmental officials can be found all along a spectrum running from moderately liberal to staunchly conservative, with occasional deviants even farther "out" on both ends of the spectrum.

In any two-party system, there is bound to be a tendency for both parties to be both wide-ranging and generally centrist in their public appeals, for only through that strategy can a party hope to elicit enough votes to win elections. A party that becomes clearly identified with a particular ideological position, and especially one that appeals to an atypical minority of the population, obviously alienates more voters than it wins over. The American major parties rarely behave in this way, though the Republican Party came close to it in its right-wing rhetoric during the 1964 Presidential campaign; consequently, it lost the election by an unprecedented majority.

It is usually possible as well to identify some economic, ethnic, or other social groups as more or less solidly aligned with one or the other major party for relatively long time periods. From the Civil War until at least the middle 1960's, the overwhelming majority of large business executives were Republican in their affiliations, as were blacks and farmers from the Civil War until the middle thirties. After World War II, the party ties of farmers become more complicated, those farmers most clearly benefiting from price support programs identifying with the Democrats, and others, such as corn and hog farmers and those in the Northeast and along the West Coast, reverting to their traditional Republican affiliation. Fairly stable in their Democratic ties until recently have been Southern whites, and, since the thirties, labor groups, the ethnic groups of the large cities, and the intellectuals. Each of these groups began to split away from the Democrats during the sixties.

The absence of party discipline in the major American parties means that a Republican or Democrat who achieves a public office is usually entirely free to support or oppose particular policies regardless of his party's stand on the issues. In disciplined parties, such as those in England, a party member who fails to support the party position on a major issue can expect to be disciplined; sometimes he is even expelled from the party. In the United States discipline is extremely rare, and Republican and Democratic legislators at all levels of government constantly cast votes inconsistent with their parties' platforms or caucus decisions.

One effect of this state of affairs is that the values of those who command political resources are reflected in legislators' votes even when they conflict with the party's formal positions or rhetorical appeals. Southern Democrats consistently vote against civil rights laws even when their party's platform has endorsed them. A congress-man from Pittsburgh is likely to vote for a high protective tariff to keep out foreign steel even if his party favors fewer restrictions on foreign trade.

The net effect of such lack of discipline is that an American voter has no assurance that the party he supports will in fact work for the policies or principles it has promised to support in order to attract his vote. On the contrary, he can be quite certain that, as a party, it will do nothing of the kind. More than that, the lack of party dis-cipline leaves every candidate and officeholder more vulnerable to pressure from powerful interests in his constituency. In a disciplined party system, pressure groups have to concentrate on influencing the party's platform, for that is what determines the subsequent be-havior of party members in supporting or opposing policies. In an undisciplined system, the platform becomes largely symbolic, as already noted; and the individual candidate or officeholder himself becomes the focus of pressures. It is not surprising, therefore, that there may exist a "senator from Boeing Aircraft Corporation" or that many candidates and legislators from diverse areas should be offered large campaign contributions by conservative Texas oil interests. Where there are undisciplined parties, elites can take advantage of the loose parties to maximize their impact upon individual policymakers.

It is apparent that the third characteristic of the major parties, decentralization of power to the state and local level, makes the kind of pressure and bargaining just described even easier and more effective. There has never been in the United States a national party organization or a national party boss capable of laying down policies that the state and local party leaders have to follow. On the con-trary, the effectiveness of the major parties' national committees and the success of aspirants for presidential nominations (the only elective office with a national constituency) hinge upon how many local party leaders and organizations they can induce to support them — finan-cially, with votes at the national nominating conventions, and by mobilizing the local constituencies on election day. From the point of view of a county or state chairman, moreover, the chief function of a presidential nominee is to help carry local and state candidates into office with him.

The local party organization cannot afford to be unresponsive to local interest groups that can help finance campaigns or influence voters. The more diverse and conflicting local interests are, the more leeway the party organization has, for it can then play them off against each other and gain some maneuverability for itself. A na-tional party organization with real power would, of course, represent the ultimate in such maneuverability and freedom from pressure by particular elite groups, while the extreme cases of susceptibility to domination by a local interest occur in those constituencies in which one industry significantly surpasses all others in wealth and control over economic conditions. Party organizations in large cities typically fall somewhere between these two extremes.

The Management of Party Decisions

The major agencies for decisionmaking in the Republican and Democratic parties are the quadrennial national party conventions that nominate presidential candidates and party committees at local, state, and national levels. In both these kinds of organizations, there is a high degree of oligarchic control and assurance of strong representation for elite interests.

Delegates to the presidential nominating conventions are chosen by a variety of methods, which change frequently. Most common are local conventions, typically tightly controlled by local party activists; direct selection by local or state party officials; and direct primaries. In 1968, the governors of Georgia and Louisiana appointed the entire delegations to the Democratic Convention from those states.

A Commission on Party Structure and Delegate Selection that studied Democratic Party delegate selection in 1968 uncovered an impressive list of abuses and irregularities, most of them characteristic of selection procedures in both major parties. Decisions about how delegates are selected are frequently left to the discretion of elected or appointed party officials, sometimes with no written rules to guide them. Proxy voting in effect delivers the votes of large numbers of delegates to state and local party conventions into the hands of the leadership, to be cast as the latter wish. Secret precinct caucuses are common in some states. Other devices have assured tight control by local and state party leaders.

Once the national nominating conventions begin, other traditional practices keep control largely in the hands of the established leadership. An incumbent President is especially potent at the convention of his own party. He may have renomination for the asking or handpick his successor; may dictate the platform; designate the officers of the convention, and, through his influence in various states, select many of the delegates. White House aides are on hand to oversee every significant phase of convention activity, including platform drafting, challenges to delegates' credentials, physical arrangements, and program.

Even at the convention of the opposition party, the very size of the gathering, running to several thousand people (some of them with fractional votes), assures a high measure of oligarchic control over these same decisions. Control over access to the loudspeaker system and the ability of the convention chairman to recognize or to refuse recognition to particular delegates is an especially important power. These advantages of the party officials have been countered to some extent in recent conventions by the ability of dissident delegates to make their case on the television networks.

Delegates to the national conventions do not mirror the makeup of the nation's population very closely. They overrepresent the middle aged, whites, males, Protestants, the well-educated, and people with relatively high incomes. At the 1968 Democratic Convention, 16 state delegations had no voting members under 30 and another 13 had only one delegate under 30. In the Republican Convention that year, only one percent of the delegates were under 30; 42 delegations had no voting member under 30. Women composed 13 percent of the Democratic delegates and 17 percent of the Republican delegates.[11] In the same year, 1.9 percent of the voting delegates to the Republican convention were black, and 5.5 percent of the Democratic delegates.[12]

Figure 3 in Chapter 8 depicted the income distribution of convention delegates in 1964. Though mean income for all households that year was $6569, only 14.7 percent of the Democratic delegates and 13.2 percent of the Republicans had incomes under $10,000.[13] The poor and people with low incomes could not ordinarily afford to become a delegate in any case. It costs substantial sums to campaign to become a delegate, as well as to travel to the convention. In addition, many state parties assess the delegates for contributions in amounts that ranged, in 1964, from $200 in Connecticut to $15 for South Carolina Republicans. The barriers to influence within the political parties are thus many — some obvious, some subtle, but all effective in promoting control by long-term participants with the economic resources to achieve it.

CONCLUSIONS

The opportunities open to elites are indeed substantial. That they are not more successful in manipulating consent for their preferred uses of government may be a testimony to their internal differences, failure to mobilize their capabilities behind a coherent program, sharing of basic wants with masses, or their sense of self-restraint and deference to mass preferences — or to the strength of mass assertiveness. What is truly impressive, however, is the scope and subtlety of the social control mechanisms open to elites. Not only do they set the parameters for operation and manage the basic policies of schools and colleges, media of communication, and vehicles of representation, but they also shape the dominant ideology and even the societal definitions of orthodoxy and deviance. Consider so basic a matter as the definition of what is a crime, or what constitutes psychological maladjustment. A "crime" is an act punishable by the full weight of the law enforcement mechanisms. But, with the possible exception of such personal violence as domestic homicides, "crimes" are such because the dominant forces in the society have asserted their values and their standards over other sectors of the population and defined them as such. Consider one who, without political or economic philosophies in mind, nevertheless loots a ghetto warehouse in order that his family may have clothes and conveniences. He may be understood by some as having made a silent complaint against racism and

[11] Democratic National Committee, "Report of the Commission on Party Structure and Delegate Selection" (unpublished and unnumbered).
[12] *Ibid.*
[13] Kevin L. McKeough and John F. Bibby, "The Costs of Political Participation: A Study of National Convention Delegates" (Princeton, N. J.: Citizens' Research Foundation, 1966), p. 84.

unequal distribution in the existing economic and social order — an order he had no part in creating, to which he has never consented, but whose laws he must obey or face the most severe punishment. The power to define his act as a crime is not a neutral power, but one which has the effect of preserving the economic and social order established for the convenience of those who benefit from it.

"Psychological maladjustment" is behavior of an antisocial or deviant kind. It creates disharmony and does not "fit" with what others have accepted as routine or tolerable in life. But because such behavior has been so labeled by an authoritative source, drastic consequences follow. The individual will be ignored, dismissed or derided; he may even be incarcerated for "treatment" or "rehabilitation." The definition of what is normal and what is deviant, of course, is a definition reflecting the assumptions and preferences of the existing social and economic order. Those who reject socialization into the motivations and life styles which support that order are thus cast aside. Whoever is able to define "deviance" belongs, together with those who succeed in defining "crimes" to their liking, at the seat of the social control mechanism of the society. Patently, their acts are not neutral.

Finally, we must return briefly to the role of the university. The institutions of higher education, it should be clear, are not only sources of ideology and means of implementing policymakers' goals, but they are also major means of authoritatively defining what is and is not acceptable behavior. By producing knowledge, they facilitate the better functioning of the status quo. Thus, by virtue of their basic activities, they cannot be neutral either; they too must serve whatever priorities animate their society.

These considerations may make mere political machinations seem like polite games. To an extent, these opportunities are unavoidable and inevitable accompaniments of organized society. That they have not been marshalled more coherently by elites to serve their purposes is remarkable. But it may be due to the fact that masses are either impervious or resistant to such ultimate forms of management.

13 Nonelites: Political Context and Basic Attitudes

Masses are neither dupes nor pawns. Ordinarily, their social and economic circumstances make other activities of higher priority than the conduct of government, and elites do what they can to assure them that their needs and wants are being served adequately without close political involvement. If the need is perceived and conditions are right, however, masses are capable of generating strong and purposeful political power. But let us proceed more systematically.

The term "mass" itself can be misleading, because it may suggest an undifferentiated aggregate of equally powerless persons. Though infelicitous and awkward, "nonelites" more accurately reflects the empirical distinction that we have been working with — that between those having resources or position of great power and all others. But the "all others" have a very large range of resources and positions among them. Some have relatively many of the resources of power; some have none. The capabilities of leadership, power mobilization, withdrawal of legitimacy, and generation of insistent new demands, however, are clearly present within this vast majority of people. By contrast with elites, any individual or group among nonelites is markedly inferior in the capacity to influence government or gain their ends. But their potential power, when and if they mobilize it, is very significant. Elites know this, and act accordingly.

In this chapter, we shall first examine the social setting of nonelites — the life situation of middle and lower classes as it is revealed by the basic characteristics of income, opportunity, and living conditions. We shall then explore the ways in which political values and attitudes are formed, looking particularly at the source of attitudes and their permanence. Finally, we shall sketch the basic substance of political beliefs held by Americans, and the major outlines of differences among subgroups of the population. In later chapters, we will examine political participation and its impact on government policy.

THE SOCIAL SETTING OF NONELITES

To an extent, the social setting of nonelites has already been described. Several features of poverty were presented in Chapter 5, and the basic class structure of the United States was characterized in Chapter 8. But our purpose here is to create a context for understanding the political attitudes and behavior of nonelites generally, and so we must add some further relevant dimensions of the life situation of both working class (including blacks) and middle class Americans. "Nonelites" include a wide variety of races, religions, income and educational levels, and life experiences, so that our characterization must of necessity be generalized. Nevertheless, it is an instructive point from which to begin our analysis.

American affluence is both celebrated and real. Per capita gross national product and real income are the highest in the world; per capita personal income in constant dollars in 1966 was about four times as high as it was in 1900.[1] The problems with these achievements lie in the *actual distribution* of income and in the *permanence* of such patterns. Since World War II, the share of total national income received by families and unrelated individuals in the lower 40 percent of the population has remained virtually constant at about 14 percent. For the lower 60 percent, well over a majority of the population, it totalled about 30 percent in 1966. In specific terms, the median income of *all* white males in that year was $5,364. (The term "median" means that half of all income-earning white men earned *less,* and half earned *more,* than that amount.) Black men had a median income in the same year of only $2,961. White and black women earned significantly lower amounts than men of the same race, although in many cases they were performing the same work.

Thus, the affluence of Americans does not reach to all levels of the population. For at least the lower 40 percent or so of families — those which are within the shifting definitions of "poverty" and those just above that line — economic hardship is the form that reality

---

[1] U. S. Department of Health, Education, and Welfare, *Toward A Social Report* (Washington, D. C.: U. S. Government Printing Office, 1969), pp. 42-44. All data in this paragraph are drawn from this source.

takes. Even the next highest 20 percent of families, whose income is nearly proportionate to their share of the population, lives with the threat that a major illness or sudden economic downturn can drop them back to the poverty level.

For the working classes and perhaps the lower half of the middle class, therefore, economic insecurity is a major fact of life. For example, the low wage-earner, possessing less education and fewer skills, is the last to be hired and the first to be laid off. Blacks in particular experience this effect, and have greater difficulty in gaining entrance to unions which might provide protections against such results. Economic growth and recessions thus have exaggerated effects at the lowest wage-earning levels. Much of the apparent reduction in numbers of poverty-level families in the mid-1960's was due to a booming economy's absorption of these workers; the inflation-control measures and recession of the post-1968 years have meant rapidly rising unemployment and a drop in the real wages of most workers.

The working class wage-earner, moreover, is subject to other kinds of economic insecurity besides the cyclical fluctuation of the economy. In many cases, technological changes make his skills obsolete, and an entire industry normally introduces labor-saving devices simultaneously, so that he has no alternative sources of employment. Jobs may also depend on the employer's financial status, and on the ups and downs experienced by the company for reasons wholly beyond the workers' control; workers are hired as contracts are secured, and laid off again when they are completed or the company experiences other reverses. Illness or injury to the wage-earner, a major sickness in his family, or a lingering terminal illness by one of his parents, may mean lost wages and ruinous hospital and medical bills. An occasional strike raises many of the same risks.

The conditions of work among the working or lower middle classes are also distinctive. In many cases, employment means hard and exhausting physical labor. For some, work is on an assembly line, where speed is essential and the number of units produced is the measure of income or the criterion of further employment. Constant loud noise and danger may be present. For others, safer and more comfortable settings may imply highly routinized, tedious work requiring intense concentration. Nor are white collar workers insulated against undesirable work-place conditions: routine work, highly bureaucratized rules and requirements (and, for women, menial and subservient roles) are characteristic of many lower-paid positions. For most working class persons, travel conditions also contribute to insecurity and frustration: public transportation systems are crowded, inconvenient, expensive, and time-consuming; but the alternative of cost and upkeep of a car may be a serious drag on family income.

The general health conditions of Americans are not commensurate with national affluence, and hardships focus on the lower socioeconomic levels. The United States has a lower life expectancy at birth than 15 other nations of the world, higher infant mortality rates than 14 countries, and higher rates of death from a variety of diseases than several other countries.[2] Lower classes, and particularly blacks, experience higher incidence of infant mortality and higher death rates from infectious disease than the middle and upper classes. For example, for employed males aged 45-64, those with incomes of less than $2,000 have three and a half times as many disability days as those over $7,000. People at lower income levels do not make use of preventive services or visit doctors for medical care, no doubt chiefly because of their cost. More than 20 percent of people in families with income under $3,000 have *never* visited a dentist, as compared to seven percent of those in families with incomes over $10,000. Fifty-four percent of children under 17 in families with more than $10,000 income had physical checkups, in contrast to 16 percent for those in families of less than $2,000. Medical care prices have risen at a 50 percent higher rate than the cost of living in the last decade, and the costs of hospital services even faster. Medicare covers only about 35 percent of total medical expenses, and then only for those over 65. Nearly half of the remaining population is covered by some form of private health care insurance plan, but these pay, on the average, less than half the costs of the care extended. Health conditions and their costs, it seems clear, constitute an acute portion of lower classes' economic and social circumstances.

The living conditions of the working and lower classes are also distinctive from those enjoyed by the more affluent. The most drastically substandard housing in the country is found in rural settings inhabited chiefly by the poor — and, again, principally the black poor. Large city neighborhoods are normally crowded, and cost per square foot of living space is frequently higher than in the suburbs. Blacks in particular have little choice over where they will live, however, as the nation's sharply (and in many cities, increasingly) segregated city ghettos attest. Moreover, the incidence of crime is far higher in lower class areas, and particularly in black areas, than elsewhere. Despite all the concern about crime expressed by middle class suburbanites, it is the poor — and again the black poor — who experience most of the nation's personal crimes. Table 1 compares the incidence of crime by race and income. Except for the theft of property, which naturally occurs more often to those who have it to start with, the lower income levels experience more incidents of every kind of crime than do the higher levels. Whether due to the surroundings in which they live or the lack of effective police protection, crime is a condition which they must live with to a degree unknown to the middle and upper classes.

We may well ask to what extent there is real opportunity for individual members of the lower classes to escape from these circumstances. We have already seen the effects of income levels on educational opportunity in the extended analysis in Chapter 8; the continued clamor over public school educational issues in the nation's cities suggests that this general situation reaches down to the ele-

[2] *Ibid.,* pp. 6-10. The data apply to the mid-1960's.

TABLE 1
Victimization by Race and Income
(rates per 100,000 population)*

	White			
Offenses	$0-$2,999	$3,000-$5,999	$6,000-$9,999	Above $10,000
Total	2,124	2,267	1,685	2,170
Homicide	0	0	0	0
Forcible rape	58	46	0	17
Robbery	116	91	42	34
Aggravated assault	146	289	147	220
Burglary	1,310	958	764	763
Larceny ($50+)	378	700	565	916
Auto theft	116	183	167	220

	Nonwhite		
Offenses	$0-$2,999	$3,000-$5,999	$6,000+
Total	2,894	2,581	3,387
Homicide	56	0	0
Forcible rape	111	60	121
Robbery	278	240	121
Aggravated assault	389	420	121
Burglary	1,336	1,261	2,056
Larceny ($50+)	501	300	363
Auto theft	223	300	605

* Rate per 100,000 population of each specific race and income group.

Source: 1965 Survey by the National Opinion Research Center for the President's Commission on Law Enforcement and Administration of Justice.

Reprinted from U.S. Department of Health, Education, and Welfare, *Toward A Social Report* (Washington, D. C.: U.S. Government Printing Office, 1969), p. 59.

mentary and secondary schools as well. But Table 2 presents an important overall summary of the character of social mobility opportunities in the United States. It compares respondents to a U.S. Census Bureau survey according to their *fathers'* occupations and *their own* current occupation, as a means of measuring relative improvement or decline in status. The column at the left shows fathers' race and occupations, and the horizontal rows are the respondents' present occupations. In general, white children tend to remain in the same occupation and status level as their fathers. Today's higher white collar jobs are filled by people whose fathers had similar jobs. For whites, however, there is some net upward mobility. For example, 36 percent of whites whose fathers were in the "lower manual" occupations are themselves in the same category; but 23 percent have moved up to the "higher manual" level, and 21.3 percent of such children have gone as far as the high white collar status. But for blacks, there is

TABLE 2
**Mobility from Father's Occupation by Race for Civilian Men 25 to
64 Years Old, March 1962** (percentage distribution)

Race and father's occupation	1962 Occupation*						Total	
	High white collar	Lower white collar	Higher manual	Lower manual	Farm	Not in experienced civilian labor force	Percent	Number (000)
Negro								
Higher white collar	10.4	9.7	19.4	53.0	0.0	7.5	100.0	134
Lower white collar	14.5	9.1	6.0	69.1	0.0	7.3	100.0	55
Higher manual	8.8	6.8	11.2	64.1	2.8	6.4	100.0	251
Lower manual	8.0	7.0	11.5	63.2	1.8	8.4	100.4	973
Farm	3.1	3.0	6.4	59.8	16.2	11.6	100.0	1,389
Not reported	2.4	6.5	11.1	65.9	3.1	11.1	100.0	712
Total, percent	5.2	5.4	9.5	62.2	7.7	10.0	100.0	—
Total, number	182	190	334	2,184	272	352	—	3,514
Non-Negro								
Higher white collar	54.3	15.3	11.5	11.9	1.3	5.6	100.0	5,836
Lower white collar	45.1	18.3	13.5	14.6	1.5	7.1	100.0	2,652
Higher manual	28.1	11.8	27.9	24.0	1.0	7.3	100.0	6,512
Lower manual	21.3	11.5	22.5	36.0	1.7	6.9	100.0	8,798
Farm	16.5	7.0	19.8	28.8	20.4	7.5	100.0	9,991
Not reported	26.0	10.3	21.0	32.5	3.9	6.4	100.0	2,666
Total, percent	28.6	11.3	20.2	26.2	6.8	6.9	100.0	—
Total, number	10,414	4,130	7,359	9,560	2,475	2,517	—	36,455

* Combinations of census major occupation groups. *Higher white collar:* professional and kindred workers, and managers, officials, and proprietors, except farm. *Lower white collar:* sales, clerical, and kindred workers. *Higher manual:* craftsmen, foremen, and kindred workers. *Lower manual:* operatives and kindred workers, service workers, and laborers, except farm. *Farm:* farmers and farm managers, farm laborers and foremen. Classification by "father's occupation" includes some men reporting on the occupation of a family head other than the father.

Source: Unpublished tables, survey of "Occupational Changes in a Generation."
Reprinted from U.S. Department of HEW, *Toward a Social Report, op. cit.,* p. 24.

much heavier concentration in the lower occupations to start with, less mobility, and little retention of higher status once gained. Children of lower manual fathers move up at much lower rates than whites; children of higher white collar fathers drop *back* into the lower manual category! In analyzing these mobility data, of course, we must keep in mind that the general structure of employment in the country has shifted toward white collar jobs and away from those classified here as lower manual or farm. Thus, some share of apparent "mobility" is due to broad structural changes and not to the relative striving and achievement of individuals. This realization leads to the sobering conclusion that the mobility experience for lower status people has been modest at best, and for blacks practically non-existent.

These conditions of the socioeconomic setting of the great majority of American working and lower middle class people establish the context for their political behavior. Economic hardships and insecurity are constant; it takes very substantial effort to maintain existing levels of income and status, and prodigious effort or good fortune to move ahead. There is substantial lack of health and medical services, educational opportunities, neighborhood and work-place amenities, and protection against crime. What is taken for granted at middle class levels does not exist for near-majorities of the population.

The implications for politics are several. Unfulfilled needs exist, and might be served by elite action or by nonelite mobilization and demand. But there is very little time readily available for the latter investment; the demands that daily living impose on working and lower middle classes tend to exhaust both time and psychic and physical resources. And a number of external barriers, some already examined and more to be discussed shortly, operate to discourage or deflect mass assertion of group demands. Finally, there is no way of knowing that mass goals would be attainable even if a concerted effort were made, and good reason for predicting that they might well be denied. Let us see to what extent these factors are operative.

HOW ATTITUDES ARE FORMED

In examining how people can influence the government, it is common and tempting to think of each individual as a free, autonomous unit expressing his desires about what government should do and should be. Is a person really all that free and independent as an adult? Or have his ideas been molded early in his life to encourage him to have particular political and party loyalties, to see established political regimes and officials as benevolent or as threats, to believe that he should obey laws or feel free to resist those he does not like, to hold particular values or ideologies about politics and government?

Clearly, these questions deal with a fundamental issue that political scientists cannot ignore. If people's attitudes and beliefs about governmental officials and political institutions are largely or completely shaped and stabilized by the time they are adults, then governmental responsiveness to the "will of the people" or to mass publics really means responsiveness to what was inculcated into people when they were children. In that case, the only hope for social change lies in changing what children are taught. Such a political system seems largely closed and resistant to forces for change: for the adults from whom children learn are themselves resistant to change. This would be a "system" in a tight and depressingly complete sense of the word.

There is good reason to doubt that people's political beliefs and values are that completely determined by their early experiences. At the same time, the evidence is strong that the family, the school, and other early influences upon the child do a great deal to shape his views of the political world and that these initial molding agencies have a lasting impact. The "developmental process through which the citizen matures politically"[3] is called "political socialization." Political scientists and sociologists have only recently begun to do systematic research on the socialization process. What we have learned about it is intriguing and important, but most of what we would like to know is still undiscovered.

If a person clings to particular beliefs, loyalties, and attachments, even in the face of developments that might reasonably give him cause to question them, it may be because those beliefs and loyalties are necessary to his own self-conception. A man who has been socialized as a child to take pride in being a citizen of a democratic country may refuse later to accept evidence that his country's domestic or foreign policies serve the interests of a narrow elite or are not benevolent in the broadest sense of the word. To believe such evidence would hurt his pride and his self conception. Some of the writers on political socialization have relied upon such a notion of the "political self" to help explain the inclination to cherish and hold fast to early political loyalties, to feelings of attachment or hostility toward political institutions, and even to opinions about particular public issues and officials.[4]

For some people induction into the political culture is not a source of pride, but rather a painful, embarrassing or demeaning experience which they have good reason to resist. A middle class white child finds it a source of gratification to be told by his family and his teacher that he is a citizen of the most democratic and most powerful nation on earth, that his country's chief magistrate is a benevolent President, and that he or one of his friends may legitimately aspire to that office. A black child is probably taught the same thing in school, but his other experiences, and probably his family, also teach him that blacks can expect to do low paid and demeaning work and that the likelihood of a black becoming President is virtually nil. Many blacks in the past, given no choice, have had to rationalize this lowly political role and have developed a deep loyalty to the country and its political institutions. Others, especially in recent years, responded readily as they grew older to cues inviting them to refuse to accept this traditional view of the state, its officials, and themselves; as a result, they have developed resistant political beliefs.

Unfortunately, we cannot generalize with much confidence about the crucial issue of to what extent early political beliefs, feelings, and opinions persist into adult life. Clearly some people do change in some or all these respects while others change very little. Many middle class Americans who were children in the relatively prosperous and relatively peaceful 1950's developed highly favorable views of the American government and of such officials as the Presi-

---

[3] The definition is from Richard E. Dawson and Kenneth Prewitt, *Political Socialization* (Boston: Little, Brown, 1969), p. 17.
[4] *Ibid.*, p. 19.

dent and the policeman. Some of these people changed these views drastically in the troubled sixties in response to a Vietnam War they thought unjustified, as well as to severe social problems and disturbances in the cities. Others apparently held fast to their earlier views.

People do change with changed conditions, though some change more readily than others. The person whose political self does not need the reassurance of old ties is free to learn and to change his cognitions and attachments accordingly. Another reason for new patterns of political socialization over time lies in the new sources of information and of learning to which a person is exposed as he grows older. In place of the family and the school, his political observations come largely from the communications media and from his associates. These generalizations tell us nothing about specific people or groups; nor do they tell us about the specific conditions under which socialization, as children or as adults, takes place. For the answers to questions about these matters we must turn to empirical studies.

It is from his family, from his school, and from his friends that a child acquires his first ideas about the state and politics. These "agents of political socialization" have their effect both through direct teaching and in indirect and subtle ways that probably produce more powerful and more lasting impacts upon the child's political beliefs than does direct teaching. The child hears political views and political party attachments stated by his parents and his friends and takes them as a model to emulate. Impressions from family, school, and peer group experiences about authoritarian or democratic ways of making decisions are generalized to political objects. Because most families and virtually all schools try to teach the child to believe and to behave in ways that will be widely approved in the culture, their influence is essentially conservative: to inculcate feelings of loyalty to the established regime and to justify prevailing values. The family is most influential when it supports widely held attitudes, not when it inculcates deviant or idiosyncratic ones.[5] Some important exceptions to this effect of early socializing agents will be considered shortly.

In addition, we have more specific findings about the effects of the family upon the political beliefs of children. Children are especially likely to adopt the party affiliation of their parents. One study found that 76 percent of a group of high school students shared their parents' party loyalty when the two parents were in agreement on the point.[6] As we might expect, family influence on a voter's preference is greatest when the party outlooks of the members of the family are the same, interest in politics is high, and the same family preference has been retained for considerable time.[7] Republican voters seem to conform somewhat more strongly to family influence than Democrats do. American parents have strikingly more influence

---

[5] Robert D. Hess and Judith V. Torney, *The Political Development of Attitudes in Children* (Garden City, N. Y.: Anchor Books, 1967), p. 113.

[6] Kenneth P. Langton, *Political Socialization* (New York: Oxford University Press, 1969), p. 59.

[7] Herbert McClosky and Harold E. Dahlgren, "Primary Group Influence on Party Loyalty," *American Political Science Review*, vol. 53 (September, 1959), pp. 757-776.

upon their children's party affiliations than is true in France. Only 29 percent of French voters can even name their father's political orientation, while 91 percent of American voters can do so.[8]

There has been little research on family impact upon attitudes toward specific political issues. One study that compares parents' and children's views on school integration and prayers, allowing communists and atheists to speak, political cynicism, and religious affiliation found only a moderate degree of influence: considerably less than for party identification. Children are much less cynical than their parents. Longer exposure to politics evidently makes people less trusting. In general, the family seems to have the strongest influence upon quite specific and concrete political beliefs and the least impact upon vague and abstract beliefs.[9]

The School as a Socializing Agent

Schools chiefly serve to reinforce the child's attachment to the country. It is therefore not too surprising that a study of a national sample of high school seniors found that whether or not they had taken a course in civics made little difference in their political knowledge, interest, belief that they could influence political events, cynicism about politics, tolerance, or inclination to participate in politics. Only for a black subsample was there a noticeable difference between those who had and those who had not taken the course. Blacks who took the course showed greater knowledge, greater sense of political efficacy, greater tolerance, and an image of the good citizen as loyal rather than participative. It may well be, however, that black students with these attitudes were disproportionately selected, or selected themselves, to take the course; the authors of the study suspect this was the case. If they are right, the course makes little difference in attitudes either for blacks or for whites.[10] Another study found that the civics curriculum in the Boston area had little effect upon students' participation in politics, but did make them more chauvinistic and firmer supporters of the democratic creed.[11] While the curriculum brought little change in attitudes, it apparently reinforced existing social class differences in beliefs about the proper role of the citizen. A study of civics textbooks used in these middle class, lower middle, and working class communities of Boston suggests that children are trained to play different political roles depending upon their parents' income level and social status. Only in the upper middle class com-

[8] Phillip E. Converse and Georges Dupreux, "Politicization of the Electorate in France and the United States," *Public Opinion Quarterly*, vol. 26 (Spring, 1962), pp. 1-24, 13.

[9] M. Kent Jennings and Richard G. Niemi, "Transmission of Political Values from Parent to Child," *American Political Science Review*, vol. 62 (June, 1968), pp. 175-180.

[10] Kenneth P. Langton and M. Kent Jennings, "Political Socialization and the High School Civics Curriculum in the United States," *American Political Science Review*, vol. 62 (September, 1968), pp. 862-867.

[11] Edgar Litt, "Civic Education, Community Norms, and Political Indoctrination," *American Sociological Review*, vol. 28 (February, 1963), pp. 69-75.

munity were the children given education or insight into the value, utility, and desirability of citizen participation in policymaking or exposed to the idea of conflict and disagreement as inherent in politics. In the working class community, where political involvement was already low, civic training stressed the view that formal governmental institutions and procedures work in harmony for the benefit of citizens. In the lower middle class community there was training in the elements of democratic government supplemented by an emphasis upon the responsibilities of citizenship, but not on the dynamics of the political process. A supplementary study of the children in the three neighborhoods found that 70 percent of the upper middle class children, 55 percent of the lower middle class children, and 32 percent of the working class children had a "most favorable" view of participation. At higher income levels, children are taught to be participants in policymaking; at low levels they are taught to accept the outcomes of the political process as legitimate.[12] A study of Oregon high school teachers found that the political values which get into the classroom foster uncritical acceptance of the system.[13] All these findings are consistent with the conclusion that school courses do little to change students' political attitudes, serving chiefly to reinforce attitudes inculcated earlier.

Fellow students can modify the pattern of political beliefs and attitudes inculcated by the family and the school. Students who develop close ties with peers gravitate toward the dominant political views in their peer groups even if these are different from those they learned as children.[14] One study of working class students found that they move toward the adoption of middle class political norms when they make friends with other students from both middle class and working class backgrounds; but, as might be expected, those who spent their time chiefly with other working class students had their earlier attitudes reinforced.[15]

Students of political socialization have tried to explain differences in people's confidence that they can have an influence upon what the government does — a personal characteristic commonly labeled "sense of political efficacy" by social scientists. Some people are convinced that nothing they do will matter in shaping public policy, while others believe they are influential in this respect. The point is important because a person with a low sense of efficacy is likely to be alienated and doubtful that the government serves the interests of people like himself. Research on the relative influence of the various agents of socialization upon one's sense of political efficacy shows that the family has almost four times as much impact in this regard as either the peer group or the school. The family affects the sense of political efficacy of all students, and serves chiefly to increase it. The school functions almost exclusively to raise the sense of

---

[12] *Ibid.*, pp. 72-74.
[13] Harmon Zeigler, *The Political Life of American Teachers* (Englewood Cliffs, N. J.: Prentice-Hall, 1967), chap. 4.
[14] Dawson and Prewitt, *op. cit.*, p. 142.
[15] Langton, *op. cit.*, pp. 131, 135, 137.

efficacy of those students who rank low scholastically. Children with higher I.Q.'s also have a higher sense of efficacy, though this may simply mean that they learn better what their teachers tell them about politics.[16] The face-to-face peer group chiefly serves to move students with a medium sense of efficacy to a high sense of efficacy.[17] The most significant conclusion to be drawn from findings like these is that the most important influences upon children operate largely to increase their belief that government is responsive to their wants and therefore to buttress their trust in government.

What Children Learn through Political Socialization

The most persistent finding of the socialization research done so far is that children see the government and public officials as benevolent, have great trust in them, and think they are almost never wrong. The first officials of whom the American child becomes aware are the President and the policeman. Children feel a personal attachment to the President, seeing him as benevolent, dependable, powerful, and possessing leadership skills. They regard the policeman as slightly lower but still see him as benevolent and dependable.[18] As the child grows older he learns to differentiate the private from the public sector of society and he also moves from a highly personalized image of government in terms of a few authority figures to a more institutionalized view. Lawmaking and the Congress take on a more significant role in his eyes.[19]

The concept of political parties develops rather late. One study found that not until the eighth grade could 50 percent of sampled children think of a single difference between the parties.[20] At all grade levels, the most common view was that both parties do about the same things and contribute equally to national and personal welfare.[21] Children generally think adults should belong to parties, but do not believe people should vote a straight ticket.[22]

The strong emphasis upon a favorable view of government and public officials which prevails in the most widely known socialization studies may well seriously overstate this optimistic conclusion because these studies have dealt almost exclusively with middle class children and most of them were done in the early 1960's, at a time when there was relatively little popular unrest and civil disturbance. The late sixties saw the appearance of a "credibility gap," another label for distrust in government, and that in itself raises a serious question about the stability of early political attitudes. This question

[16] David Easton and Jack Dennis, "The Child's Acquisition of Regime Norms: Political Efficacy," *American Political Science Review*, vol. 61 (March, 1967), pp. 25-33, 34.

[17] Langton, *op. cit.*, p. 174.

[18] David Easton and Jack Dennis, *Children in the Political System*, (New York: McGraw-Hill, 1969), pp. 147, 231; Fred I. Greenstein, *Children and Politics* (New Haven, Conn.: Yale University Press, 1965), p. 32.

[19] Easton and Dennis, *Children in the Political System*, pp. 115-123.

[20] Greenstein, *op. cit.*, p. 67.

[21] Hess and Torney, *op. cit.*, p. 92.

[22] *Ibid.*, p. 96.

is especially in point because the most distrustful group in the late sixties consisted largely of adolescents and young adults from upper middle class families. We have little data that directly bear on this vital issue, however.

There is other evidence that the early socialization studies may have dealt with a special set of conditions not valid for other times or for other groups not part of the middle class. The few available studies of poor children and black children found some significantly different socialization patterns among these people. A study of children in the poverty stricken Appalachian region of eastern Kentucky found them dramatically less favorable to political authority than the middle class children who were respondents in earlier studies. In their greater cynicism, these children reflected the views of their families, and especially their fathers. Indeed, Appalachian children in families without a father in the home are significantly *more* favorable to political authority than others.[23]

Blacks expect unequal treatment from public officials, especially local officials, far more than whites in comparable socio-economic circumstances. Young and northern blacks expect better treatment than older and southern blacks do. These expectations, one can assume, make younger and northern blacks more likely to resent unfair treatment when it occurs and more likely to support protests against it.[24]

It should be no surprise, in view of the research findings already reviewed, that upper class children exceed those with less status in their capacity and motivation for political participation.[25] The working class child expresses more emotional attachment to the President and sees government in more personal terms and less in terms of issues. He also sees laws as more rigid than does the child from an upper income family, and he has a lower sense of political efficacy.

Political socialization refers to a particular way of thinking about and explaining the development of mass attitudes and demands, just as systems theory, group theory, and functional theory represent particular ways of asking questions and organizing data. As we suggested in discussing those approaches, such theoretical models have the advantage of encouraging certain forms of inquiry, but they also divert attention from others. The focus upon political socialization ignores or underplays controversy, dissent, and those attitudes critical of governmental regimes which adults acquire in reaction to official acts that violate their norms and their expectations. To be maced while watching or participating in a demonstration, to be denied necessary food and clothing amid loud publicity about a war on poverty, to be drafted to fight in a war that seems unnecessary and

---

[23] Dean Jaros, Herbert Hirsch, and Frederic J. Fleron, Jr., "The Malevolent Leader: Political Socialization in an American Subculture," *American Political Science Review,* vol. 62 (June, 1968), pp. 564-575.

[24] Dwaine Marvick, "The Political Socialization of the American Negro," *The Annals of the American Academy of Political and Social Science,* vol. 361 (September, 1964), pp. 112-127, 119.

[25] Greenstein, *op. cit.,* p. 94.

unjust also inculcate beliefs about the political order. But the resentful and alienated attitudes that such experiences teach are likely to be interpreted as evidence of inadequate political socialization in childhood by those who begin with the assumption that the socialization process serves the function for the political system of building support for its persistence. The socialization studies have taught us some important things about how and what children learn about the political order; but they emphasize only one phase of the process by which mass publics come to have particular beliefs and perceptions regarding the political world.

Beliefs inculcated early in a person's life have a continuing influence upon his perceptions of the world. To sort out political leaders, institutions, parties, and ideologies as benevolent or malign, trustworthy or erring, is to give meaning to the world and to define one's own role in the political system. Disturbances in such a pattern involve some redefinition of one's own identity, a difficult and often painful process. Early beliefs therefore influence later perceptions and interpretations of political events. It is tempting, and reassuring, to see and interpret them as confirming what one deeply wants to believe. Early socialization in the belief that the Democratic Party is usually right may, for example, lead people to reject allegations that it is the "war party" — either by denying that the Democrats get the country into wars more often than do the Republicans or by perceiving wars waged by Democratic administrations as necessary to protect the national interest.

Sometimes it seems that a belief system based upon recent events is simply superimposed upon an earlier one, the two then coexisting. In this case, the individual may inconsistently turn to one or the other, depending on what kinds of cues have recently impressed him. When concerned with evidence of atrocities by American troops in Vietnam, he may denounce the war and be strongly "dovish." When talking about worldwide ideological tension, he may be impressed with the importance of stopping communism far from American shores. This kind of theoretical model of cognitive development helps account for the absence of "constraints" or consistency in people's beliefs.

The last chapter noted a number of mechanisms through which elites influence mass beliefs deliberately or unintentionally. Central to many of these was the disposition of masses to take cues about political threats and reassurances from the acts and speeches of political leaders and other elites, including the communications media. In the measure that this occurs, early beliefs change.

A second reason for change is strong factual evidence that the old beliefs are poor interpreters of a new situation. Not all perception is selective, and therefore it does not always serve to reinforce prior beliefs. Continuing, clear evidence gradually makes an impact. A generation taught in the twenties and thirties that munitions makers are a major cause of wars was slowly persuaded in the late thirties and early forties that Hitler, Nazi Germany, and fascism were real threats. Many members of a later generation impressed by Hitler and

World War II with the hazards of appeasing real enemies slowly came nonetheless to believe in the late 1960's that a war in Vietnam labeled as defense against aggression was really unjustified American intervention in the internal civil turmoil of a small Southeast Asian country. In both these instances, early beliefs were strongly resistant to inconsistent cues. In both, some people never changed their prior beliefs, continuing to see Hitler as an excuse for munitions makers to start a war or, later, continuing to see critics of the Vietnam War as latter day appeasers of a new Hitler. But among many people, it is evident that early cognitions did change, that both factual evidence and governmental cues played substantial roles in determining the character and the pace of the change, and that some parts of the population were more susceptible to the governmental cues while others were more influenced by reports from such nongovernmental sources as news stories depicting the undemocratic acts of the South Vietnamese government, the ineffectiveness of the war as a device to fight communist ideology, and the killing of civilians in the Vietnamese countryside.

RELATIVE GRATIFICATION AND RELATIVE DEPRIVATION

Some people are basically satisfied with the political system, though not always with particular policies. They see the system as a "legitimate" structure of power to which they are subject, and they utilize its normal election processes and their indirect access to legislatures, executive agencies, and courts to try to achieve their wants. Though it is not possible to define the threshold between relative gratification and relative deprivation precisely or quantitatively, these people, normally the great bulk of the population, are relatively satisfied with what the system offers them. This does not necessarily mean that they get the most of what there is to get. People with small incomes and little political power are satisfied with that state of affairs if they have been socialized to believe that there is no great disparity between the benefits they receive and those they are legally and morally entitled to receive. Such a condition of "relative gratification" is especially likely if they are reassured that the system itself will correct occasional disparities. For many, the political socialization process effectively furnishes such a belief and such reassurance.

It is this kind of mass posture toward the political system that David Easton has labeled "supports" in his frequently cited work on political systems. The term "supports" does not refer to demands for particular public policies, but rather to a general sense that the system and the regime that heads it are legitimate and can be counted on to be responsive to the demands of *any* significant group. Such support confers considerable policy maneuverability upon governmental policymakers.

NONELITES' BASIC POLITICAL VALUES AND ATTITUDES

What political beliefs are actually held by Americans today? What do they *want*, and what do they *expect*, from their government? We shall look first at the kinds of general priorities and concerns that people have, then at some specific characteristics of opinion, and finally at how Americans compare with other countries in regard to views toward their government. Some of the major current issues, however, such as race relations, Southeast Asia, and military and space expenditures, will be reserved for more detailed analysis when we focus on nonelites' impact on policy in Chapter 15.

In analyzing the political attitudes of such a large aggregate of people, we must be sensitive to several principles of interpretation. Although opinion polling is a sound social science tool, users must exercise some care. The form of the question is important, for it may shape answers in several ways. For example, a long check-list of possible answers may result in the impression that people have many strong opinions; a "free-answer" question, in which the respondent must himself think up his answer, may come closer to measuring his real knowledge and concern. Behind this caution lie some even more important facts about the distribution of opinion in a heterogeneous society. People differ greatly in the subjects about which they are concerned, the information they possess, and the intensity with which they hold preferences about particular subjects or issues. In many cases these differentials reflect the nearness of the subject or issue to matters of great personal or economic interest to the respondent. This is another way of saying that attitudes are often related to respondents' class status, race, religion, occupation, place of residence, ideology, or political party identification. Some issues appear to touch people primarily in terms of their class status (which may be measured through its basic components: income, occupation, and education); others seem to activate loyalties or perceptions along racial or religious lines. Sometimes the same issue strikes different people differently, some seeing it as a simple matter of group economic benefit while others understand it as a major question of religious or ideological principle.

On any given subject, therefore, there may be wide variations of interest, information, and preferences — with conflicts of opinion existing not only between groups but also within the same individuals. Further, opinion may shift over time, sometimes steadily as events or campaigns bring new facts or interpretations into focus, sometimes sharply after a single dramatic event or government action. Understanding complex and fluid public opinion in detail at any given moment may be very difficult or even impossible. But it is not difficult at all to identify and describe the major contours of enduring values and attitudes that form the basic structure of nonelite political beliefs. The semipermanent assumptions and preferences are what we examine here. Similarly, we shall point out some consistent features of subgroup attitudes (such as the higher levels of information and support for government among the more educated) as occasions arise.

It should not be surprising that, when the general public is asked to say in their own words what their principal personal aspirations and fears are, the answers are cast chiefly in terms of economic security

TABLE 3A
Personal Aspirations (Specified by 10% or more of sample)

Improved or decent standard of living	40%
Children — adequate opportunities for them (particularly education); children themselves do well, be happy, successful	35
Own health	29
Health of family	25
Happy family life	18
Peace; no war or threat of war	17
Have own house or get better one	12
Maintain status quo	12

TABLE 3B
Personal Fears (Specified by 10% or more of sample)

War	29%
Health of family	27
Own health	25
Deterioration in or inadequate standard of living	19
Unemployment	14
Children — inadequate opportunities for them (particularly education); children themselves do poorly, be unhappy, unsuccessful	10
Can't think of any fears or worries	10

Source: Lloyd A. Free and Hadley Cantril, *The Political Beliefs of Americans*, p. 97. Copyright 1968 by Simon and Schuster, Inc. Reprinted by permission of Simon and Schuster.

and health. Tables 3A and 3B present the responses given by a national cross-section in 1964. War and peace issues enter the picture in important ways, but no other strictly political matters are included among the aspirations and fears voiced by 10 percent or more of the respondents. Communism was listed as a fear by only eight percent of the sample. When all responses were taken into account, personal economic or living conditions and employment matters were mentioned by 75 percent of the sample, childrens' opportunities by 38 percent, international matters by 41 percent, and domestic political subjects by 22 percent.[26]

These basic concerns seem to lie behind broad support for government action in the social welfare field. From the time that responsible public opinion surveying began in the 1930's, large majorities have favored the basic social security and social assistance programs that were ultimately enacted. Often, public support preceded enactment by several years or even decades, as in the case of medical care. The federal social welfare programs of the 1960's enjoyed no less support, with two-thirds majorities favoring most aspects of the poverty program, aid to education, housing, the reduction of unemployment,

[26] Lloyd A. Free and Hadley Cantril, *The Political Beliefs of Americans*, (New York: Simon and Schuster, 1968), p. 99.

and so forth. There can be little doubt about the strength of public demand and support for these "welfare state" types of policies.

But this desire for government to be of service in regard to the problems of daily living in an industrial society does not take precedence over some basic practical and ideological limits. Nearly equal majorities say that taxes are too high, and the lower income levels are usually most resistant to taxation. The latter fact is sometimes cited as an inconsistency on the part of those who are the probable beneficiaries of much of the social legislation to be funded by such taxes; but it may be no more than insistence that those who can better afford the burden of taxation should carry a larger share. An interesting example of the enduring strength of the work ethic, a continuing element of the American value structure, may be seen in attitudes toward government's role in assuring income for people. When talk of income maintenance plans, negative income taxes, and guaranteed annual wages became prevalent in early 1969, a national sample was asked their views on a specific version — a government guarantee of at least $3,200 per family per year. In the same survey, they were asked their reactions to the idea that government should guarantee enough *work* so that a family would be assured of at least $3,200 a year. The questions were not posed alternatively, but consecutively, so that respondents did not have to choose between them. Nevertheless, their answers show clearly that people seek only government assistance to enable them to do what they feel they should do, i.e., work. Table 4 presents these totals, which range from nearly two-

TABLE 4
Attitudes Toward Guaranteed Income and Work, 1969
(in percents)

	Income			*Work*		
	Favor	Oppose	No opinion	Favor	Oppose	No opinion
National	32	62	6	79	16	5
Education						
College	26	71	3	75	23	2
High sch.	31	64	5	77	18	5
Grade sch.	40	50	10	83	9	8
Occupation						
Prof. and bus.	26	68	4	75	20	5
White collar	26	66	8	80	17	3
Farmers	21	74	5	73	23	4
Manual	36	58	6	82	14	4
Income						
Over $10,000	24	72	4	76	16	8
Over $7000	27	69	4	78	15	7
$5-6,999	33	62	5	81	14	5
$3-4,999	40	54	6	77	17	6
Under $3,000	43	44	13	77	11	12

Source: *Gallup Opinion Weekly*, January, 1969, pp. 20-21.

thirds majority rejection of the guaranteed income plan to nearly four-fifths majority support for the idea of guaranteed work. If previous experience holds true in this case, however, support for guaranteed income plans should rise as their desirability is argued and people become more familiar with their workings. Assuming government support for and eventual enactment of such a program, public support would probably reach majority levels by the time it went into effect and would continue climbing thereafter.

The distribution of support for these two different types of programs is also significant. Divisions which arose were centered on aspects of class, rather than race, region, religion, age, or sex. Lower status persons tended to be more supportive of both, which is understandable (and consistent with regard to almost every question of social legislation that arises). But not even manual workers, or those earning under $3,000 per year at the time of answering the survey questions, developed majority support for the guaranteed income. Even those who stood to gain immediate economic benefits preferred to work instead of being assured of income without work. It seems clear that the work ethic aspect of traditional American ideology is still viable, and even at the lowest levels of the economic order.

When the general public's attention is turned to their aspirations and fears for the United States as a nation, a more strictly politicized listing emerges. Tables 5A and 5B show these results, again based on

TABLE 5A
National Aspirations (Specified by 10% or more of sample)

Peace	51%
Improved or decent standard of living, greater national prosperity	28
Employment — jobs for everyone	15
Education — more and/or better schools	11
Settlement of racial or integration problems	10
Public morality	10

TABLE 5B
National Fears (Specified by 10% or more of sample)

War	50%
Communism	22
Economic instability, inflation, depression	13

Source: Free and Cantril, *The Political Beliefs of Americans*, pp. 104-105. Copyright 1968 by Simon and Schuster, Inc. Reprinted by permission of Simon and Schuster.

a national survey conducted in 1964. International matters dominate the list of answers volunteered, followed by the ingredients of economic security and opportunity. In general, these are extensions of personal hopes and fears, with serious concern for government's role in international affairs added. The Vietnam War was underway but had not risen to the level of concern of the later 1960's at the time of this survey. Racial matters were mentioned as a fear by nine percent of the sample; they tend to rise and fall with such incidents as riots. In recent years, international concerns have remained dominant among public concerns, crime has occasionally exceeded racial matters, and inflation has followed well behind.

The identification of the problems that are perceived by the public and the broad outlines of preferences about the role of government may serve as a prelude to a more subtle search for the way in which people organize their thinking and their preferences to form a more or less coherent orientation toward politics. In some studies of American opinion patterns, the principal distinctions made are between attitudes toward international affairs and those toward domestic affairs. This is not a very satisfying approach, at least under recent circumstances, because it suggests a sharp dichotomy between the two spheres and the role of government in each. Higher-status people tended to be antigovernment economic conservatives in domestic affairs and progovernment "internationalists" in regard to foreign affairs. Conversely, lower-status people were progovernment welfare state liberals domestically while opposing involvement overseas. No really satisfying way of integrating opinion toward both national and international affairs in a manner similar to their actual interdependence has yet been developed, however, and most analysts continue to talk separately about the two areas.

One approach which seems particularly successful in revealing important dimensions of opinion regarding domestic affairs at least is that put forward by Lloyd Free and Hadley Cantril, well-known professional students of American opinion, in a major book entitled *The Political Beliefs of Americans.*[27] Using responses given by a national cross-section to a series of questions in 1964, they constructed two "spectrums" of opinion. One was called the "operational" spectrum, and was composed of answers given to questions regarding specific government actions or proposals in the areas of medicare, poverty, housing, and aid to education. The other was labeled the "ideological" spectrum, and made up of answers to more abstract, less tangible questions about how problems ought to be solved or whether the government is interfering too much in private and economic affairs. Those who consistently favored government assistance in the concrete matters were either strong liberals or predominantly liberal, depending on the number of affirmative responses they gave. The reverse responses led to classification as predominantly conservative or completely conservative. The same approach was followed in regard to the ideological spectrum, with endorsement of government solutions and denial that it was interfering too much marking the liberal category.

When the two spectrums were compared, some very interesting and revealing findings emerged. In *operational* terms, 65 percent of respondents were completely or predominantly liberal. But in *ideo-*

---

[27] *Ibid.* The analysis in the following paragraphs is drawn from Chap. 3.

logical terms, only 16 percent were. Fully 50 percent of respondents were *ideologically* conservative, compared to only 14 percent who were *operationally* conservative. This suggests that when it comes down to a question of what government should do in a specific situation, people want action to solve problems. But when issues are cast in the form of abstract philosophies or basic values, they endorse the conservative and more traditional assumptions. Or, in other words, the grip of ideology remains strong even in the face of specific needs and actions to the contrary. The questions that gained such support for the conservative side of the ideological spectrum were very standard American nostrums: the federal government is interfering too much, it is regulating business and interfering with the free enterprise system, social problems could be solved if government would keep hands off and let people handle them themselves, anybody who wants work can find it, and we should rely more on individual initiative and not so much on welfare programs. No doubt some people can cheerfully voice such beliefs and then move for government action to solve problems; 46 percent of ideological conservatives were operational liberals. But conservative ideology meant only half as much support for liberal measures as did liberal ideology. And those who were conservative ideologically made up almost the entire group of those who were conservative operationally. Thus, the conservative nature of the ideology, and its continuing strength, appear to be important factors making for resistance, even among the general public, to government social legislation.

What implications do these findings carry? For one thing, they suggest a bifurcation between rhetoric and performance. For another, they suggest that the way in which people focus on politics, and what they see as important, may follow such distinctly different dimensions. Those who think and perceive in ideological terms may care most about the abstract principles and the rhetoric surrounding government. Those who are operationally oriented may be more concerned with what is being done about more concrete problems. This implication finds confirmation in Free and Cantril's analysis of their respondents' ranking of public concerns. Ideological conservatives ranked such intangibles as preserving economic liberties and states' rights at the top of their list of concerns, while liberals gave first place to specific actions such as aid to education and ending unemployment. Thus, in addition to the standard divisions among people on class, racial, religious, and other such grounds, we must add another distinction on the basis of perceptual orientations. It is related to the class position, but not identical with it.

We should not leave the subject of how people organize their thoughts about politics without considering the extent of real concern about communism and socialism. In general, when people are asked to give free answers about their hopes and fears for the nation or their personal worries, communism ranks quite low. One of the most salient findings of the Stouffer study of national opinion in 1954, at the height of the McCarthy era, was that only one percent of the population voluntarily listed communism as a concern. But

22 percent of those shown in Table 3B listed it as a national fear, and the proportion of persons ranking it high as a concern in check-list or yes-no type questions is usually fairly high. In 1964, in response to Free and Cantril's twenty-three question check-list, for example, "combatting world communism" emerged second only to "keeping the country out of war" as a national concern. And, asked how much danger they thought communists were here in the United States, 62 percent of the same respondents answered "a very great deal" or "a good deal." [28] The uncertainty and conflicting interpretations to which these findings give rise is due in part to the difference between free-answer and check-list type questions, and in part to the analytical difference between the threat of war from international conflict with communist countries and the threat of subversion from internal deviants.

The several findings about communism and attitudes toward it may be combined tentatively and speculatively as follows. First, antipathies toward communism as both international threat and internal menace are stronger among the higher class levels and, as we saw in Chapter 8, particularly among top businessmen. The general public fears war, and identifies international communism with that prospect. All retain at least some vestiges of the American ideological commitment to private property and the superiority of American institutions, but ideological conservatives are particularly moved by these factors and are especially strident against both manifestations of communism. There are, therefore, continuing forces within the country, localized chiefly in the upper class levels and the ideological conservatives, which feel threatened and agitate against communism. From time to time, the general public responds to such elite appeals, or segments of nonelites associate problems which they perceive with such an ultimate source. Thus, if there are student disruptions or civil rights demonstrations, and they are annoying or hard to understand, it may be because of this menace which has been much talked about in other connections. No doubt this argument overstates the matter somewhat, but it is intended to make the point that the basic seat of anticommunism in the United States does not lie in the general mass of the people. There is support there, but the evidence indicates that there is much stronger support and concern among those in the higher levels of class status who are ideologically conservative.

Let us turn now to an attempt to gain some perspective on the nature of American orientations toward politics and government through comparison with the views other populations have toward their governments. Such a comparison was made in the mid-1960's in a five-nation study by Gabriel Almond and Sidney Verba, entitled *The Civic Culture.*[29] This analysis explores the orientations of samples of the general population in the United States, the United Kingdom,

[28] *Ibid.,* p. 119.
[29] Gabriel Almond and Sidney Verba, *The Civic Culture,* (Princeton, N. J.: Princeton University Press, 1963).

West Germany, Italy, and Mexico. The extent to which Americans are distinctive in their conviction that their political institutions are right and good can be seen from Table 4. Whether as a consequence of political ideology or not, Americans gave answers listing the Constitution, political freedom, democracy, or similar items much more often than did respondents in other nations. Although Americans were proud of their economic system also, Germans did outdo them in this respect. On the other hand, Americans were distinctively low in volunteering answers having to do with the arts, sciences, or attributes of the country's environment.

Americans also felt more engaged in the continuing political processes of their country, and drew more satisfaction out of voting. Given the criteria employed for measuring the "democraticness" of the political values and expectations of the population, the United States emerged ahead of the other four nations. Great Britain did frequently equal or exceed the United States in some categories. In one area, where respondents were asked a more specific question probably not encompassed within orthodox political ideology, not only Great Britain but also Germany surpassed Americans in images of democratic conditions. Table 5 compares the five nations' population samples in regard to their expectations of "serious consideration for your point of view" when dealing with either administrative officials or police. Americans, it is clear, are less confident of such treatment than either Englishmen or Germans; the differences in respect

TABLE 4
Aspects of Nation in Which People Take Pride

Percentage who say they are proud of:	U.S.	U.K.	Germany	Italy	Mexico
Governmental, political in- stitutions	85	46	7	3	30
Social legislation	13	18	6	1	2
Position in international affairs	5	11	5	2	3
Economic system	23	10	33	3	24
Characteristics of people	7	18	36	11	15
Spiritual virtues and religion	3	1	3	6	8
Contributions to the arts	1	6	11	16	9
Contributions to science	3	7	12	3	1
Physical attributes of country	5	10	17	25	22
Nothing or don't know	4	10	15	27	16
Other	9	11	3	21	14
Total % of responses*	158	148	148	118	144
Total % of respondents	100	100	100	100	100
Total number of cases	970	963	955	995	1,007

* Percentages exceed one hundred because of multiple responses.

Reprinted from Gabriel Almond and Sidney Verba, *The Civic Culture* (Princeton, N. J.: Princeton University Press, 1963), p. 64.

TABLE 5
Consideration Expected from Bureaucrats and Police, by Nation

"If you explained your point of view to the officials (police), what effect do you think it would have? Would they give your point of view serious consideration, would they pay only a little attention, or would they ignore what you had to say?"

Percentage who expect:	U.S.		U.K.		Germany		Italy		Mexico	
	bureauc.	pol.	bureauc.	pol.	bureauc.	pol.	bureauc.	pol.	bureauc.	pol.
Serious consideration for point of view	48	56	59	74	53	59	35	35	14	12
A little attention	31	22	22	13	18	11	15	13	48	46
To be ignored	6	11	5	5	5	4	11	12	27	29
Depends	11	9	10	6	15	13	21	20	6	7
Other	0	—	—	—	1	2	6	6	—	1
Don't know	4	2	2	1	8	11	12	14	3	4
Total percentage	100	100	98	99	100	100	100	100	98	99
Total number	970	970	963	963	955	955	995	995	1,007	1,007

Reprinted from Gabriel Almond and Sidney Verba, *The Civic Culture* (Princeton, N. J.: Princeton University Press, 1963), p. 72.

to Great Britain are particularly sharp. Of interest also is the fact that, for Americans, there is a class-based drop in expectations of consideration for one's point of view. Those with some university education have more confidence in receiving consideration than do those with less education. In Britain, by contrast, higher proportions of the lowest educated respondents expected consideration from the police than did people with university educations.[30]

The sketch that we have drawn of American beliefs and orientations toward government thus reflects some of our earlier hypotheses about the strength and importance of ideology. It also shows that general public attitudes toward what should receive priority and what government should be doing reflect many of the actual circumstances of people's lives that we reviewed in the early part of this chapter. Further, the divisions between attitudes which follow such social distinctions as class, education, etc. are real. Let us see how all of these factors are reflected in the political behavior of nonelites.

[30] *Ibid.*, p. 73.

14 Political Participation by Nonelites

There are many forms of political participation. A substantial proportion of these forms are monopolized by elites, such as personal contact with decisionmakers, large contributions to political parties, lobbying, bringing test cases before the Supreme Court, or instituting extensive campaigns for or against contemplated legislation. Nonelite participation may take these forms, but it is for practical purposes limited to those kinds of activities in which a citizen may engage near his home and with limited resources and time. Even under these realistic standards, nonelite participation is nevertheless distinctly low, whether measured by the resources brought to bear by individuals or groups, by the proportion of the people who actually take part in the officially authorized channels, or by the proportion who engage in other types of participation. In the established channels, such as political parties and elections or interest groups, the incidence of participation rises sharply with class status; it varies directly with all three factors of income, occupation, and education. Both political parties and interest groups tend to be hierarchically organized, bureaucratic, and long-enduring forms of organization in which, not surprisingly, stable and self-perpetuating leadership elements develop a tacit modus operandi for the conduct of interorganizational transactions. Alternative forms of participation such as demonstration, petitions, or ad hoc campaigns for particular goals, do arise from time to time, sporadically venting demands for change and revealing needs that have gone unheeded within the established channels. But even in these informal processes, participation is low and often reflects the same class biases as do the official channels.

The reasons why nonelite political participation is both low and class-related have caused much speculation over the years since survey evidence first made them analytically clear. It may be that the lower classes are simply satisfied with the higher classes' management of the political system, that they have more economically productive uses for their time, or that they are simply uninformed or too apathetic to care about public affairs. Or it may be that they have been inculcated with the belief that their role is to accept what their betters achieve for them and that all works automatically for the best in this ingenious system. Or perhaps they are too busy trying to make ends meet amidst economic hardships, or else they know from past experience or intuition that it will do no good to press for their goals through the established system because it is designed to permit elites to deflect, delay, and ultimately deny them. It is worth trying to resolve some of these issues. In this chapter, we shall first explore the orthodox channels, looking particularly at the incidence and nature of participation and its meaning for the system as a whole. Then we shall examine the alternative forms of participation, and their implications.

THE ELECTORAL PROCESS

Who Votes, and How?

In general, about 60 percent to 65 percent of adult Americans vote in a presidential election, despite (a cynic would surely add, "or, perhaps, because of") all the publicity, campaigning, and public urging that is directed toward participation. This proportion is lower than in any other major industrialized nation, and many small, rural, and otherwise "developing" nations. In the normal off-year congressional election, the proportion drops to about 50 percent, and in many state, city, and local elections it falls still further. Only about 10 percent of the adult population ever performs any more strenuous electorally-related act than voting, such as going to rallies, campaigning, contributing, or taking part in primaries.

If we look at the entire span of American history, legal ineligibility to vote has been a far more important limitation than lack of desire to vote. In the eighteenth and early nineteenth centuries, the right to vote was limited chiefly to male, white, Protestant property-owners. Religious and property restrictions ended with the Jacksonian reforms of the 1830's. The enfranchisement of blacks and of women is largely a twentieth century development. Since World War II, there has been a great deal of emphasis upon eliminating both legal and informal restrictions upon black voting: primaries in the Southern states in which only whites could vote, literacy tests arbitrarily interpreted so that blacks would not pass them, refusal of registration, residency requirements that discriminated against the mobile, and poll taxes that discouraged poor whites as well as blacks. One result of the elimination of many of these limitations has been the election of black mayors in Cleveland and Gary, Indiana, as well as mayors and sheriffs in a few localities in the deep South. The extension of voting rights has not brought a drastic, or even a significant, change in the pattern of economic or political discrimination on the basis of color. Indeed, the laws publicized as "civil rights laws" have chiefly dealt with the right to vote.

In the early 1970's, strong support was developing among both conservatives and liberals for a constitutional amendment that would give eighteen-year-olds the right to vote. The history of the extension of voting rights to blacks helps us understand why this proposal should be so widely favored. The right to vote helps tie people to the polity and legitimizes established policies. In itself it does not bring significant change in policy directions.

"Turnout," as the act of voting on election day is known to political analysts, is closely related to intensity of preference for one or another candidate or party, and in turn to class level and membership in active political groups. Nearly 90 percent of college-educated persons vote in a presidential election, nearly 80 percent of high school graduates, but only a little over half of those with only a grade school education. The gradation is constant all the way down the status ladder; skilled workers, for example, vote with greater regularity than unskilled workers. Union members vote with distinctly greater consistency than similarly situated workers who do not belong to unions; the same is true of other organized groups.

Other demographic characteristics also are associated with the disposition to vote. Men are more likely to vote than women, a fact which almost certainly reflects widely held beliefs about the proper role of women in society; this is true in almost all countries. The young are less likely to vote than older people, due partly to residency requirements that discriminate against the mobile and partly to the greater integration of older people into the political system. Blacks are much less likely to vote than whites even when they are not legally barred or informally intimidated from doing so. People who live in urban areas vote more frequently than rural residents, probably because political life in the cities is more stimulating and there are more social pressures to vote. Voting participation rates are far lower in the South than in other regions, chiefly because of the high proportion of the Southern population that is poor, black, and relatively less educated.

The turnout of voters depends not only upon these socio-economic characteristics but also upon people's interest and involvement in party politics. That high status voters go to the polls more often chiefly reflects their greater belief that it matters how they vote and who wins. Anyone who strongly feels that it makes a difference is obviously more likely to vote than those who do not.

For some, nonvoting is an expression of their rejection of that belief — of their assumption that the major parties present no real choice and that the voters have little influence upon what government does. The proportion of nonvoters who consciously reject the electoral system in this way has probably always been small, but it very likely increased with the widespread belief among "doves" in the late 1960's that neither party was responsive to the sentiment in favor of withdrawing from Vietnam.

Turnout and participation patterns are clearly fundamental to the outcome of the political process. The sharp disparities in levels of participation that we have seen contribute to extending the influence of the upper classes. One leading scholar suggests conceiving of political participation in terms of three types of people: "apathetics" (persons who are uninvolved in any way), "spectators" (people who seek information, vote, talk about politics, etc., but are not themselves active), and "gladiators" (people who go to meetings, become active in a party, etc.).[1] If we then imagine the gladiators (perhaps 3 percent or 4 percent of the population) battling before a stadium half full of spectators (about 60 percent of the people), while a third or more of the population (the apathetics) simply stay home and ignore the battle, we have a rough characterization of the American electoral process in operation. It might be desirable to add to this characterization that in some cases the spectators are prevented from becoming gladiators, and that the "apathetics" may include some who tried to take part and lost. Thus modified, the characterization is not inapt at all.

The Decision to Vote for a Particular Political Party

How a voter casts his ballot when he does vote depends upon his orientation toward the political parties, the issues, and the candidates. Most Americans identify with either the Republican or the Democratic Party and feel attached to that party, even though they may occasionally vote for a candidate of another party. Such "party identification" typically develops early in life, is fairly stable over time for most people, and is the best single predictor of how they will vote.

In terms of democratic theory, people's views on policy issues should be the crucial influence upon voting, but the studies of voting behavior for the most part show the opposite: that the American public is remarkably uninformed about public issues and about which party stands for what position. Those who are informed, on the other hand, apparently do base their choice of which party to support largely upon the issues.[2] The voters vary greatly in how sophisticated

---

[1] Lester Milbrath, *Political Participation* (Chicago: Rand McNally, 1963), p. 20.
[2] V. O. Key, *Public Opinion and American Democracy* (New York: Alfred A. Knopf, 1967), p. 461, Table 18.1.

they are about issues, ranging from a relatively small proportion (about 12 percent) who have a clear political ideology to about 22 percent for whom politics has no issue content at all. Between these groups are many who see politics as helpful or harmful to labor, farm, or other groups important to them, and some who simply relate Republicans or Democrats to good times or bad times.[3]

Because relatively few people are attuned to issues, and perhaps also because political parties do not try very hard to take clear and distinct issue positions, long-standing loyalties to the parties acquire even greater importance in shaping voting behavior. Once identification with a particular party has been established, it tends to continue throughout a voter's lifetime. In effect, the voter comes to make use of his political party as a "reference group" — that is, he takes his cues as to where he stands on issues from the party and its leaders rather than the other way around. It is just too time-consuming for the average man to try to form independent opinions about every issue. Besides, each political party might be on his side on five issues and against him on five, with no distinction between them on another ten. How can he know which are going to be more important in the next four years or which a given party or candidate is going to deliver on? Thus, it is both more efficient and quite rational for him to simply commit himself to the party whose general approach, style, composition, or rhetoric is more to his liking. For most people, this means that the party of their parents and friends is their party.

Two groups of people, however, are more free of these generationally-transmitted political party loyalties than others. One group is made up of well-informed people who do make choices between parties and candidates on the basis of their positions on one or two basic issues, or who are dissatisfied with both parties for one reason or another. This group is relatively small, perhaps not more than 5 percent of eligible voters, but it includes many people who are in positions to influence others through writing, speaking, and campaigning. The other group is at the opposite pole of knowledge about issues, and is particularly responsive to characteristics of the candidates involved. Voters who have strong party loyalties tend to see the major candidates accordingly; their party's man is strong, sincere, competent, and humane, while his opponent is the opposite. But people in this latter group, having no strong party ties, are more likely to react — and vote — according to their personal feelings about the candidates. These feelings are generated by how he looks on television, what he seemed to be like in a photograph published in a magazine or newspaper, or from scraps of rumor and conversation. Election studies show that candidates are perceived in widely differing ways. Eisenhower, for example, was seen as a sincere, decent man with great leadership qualities, thereby drawing an unusual outpouring of support from all levels of voters. Goldwater, on the other hand, was perceived negatively, as a "radical," and Johnson

[3] Angus Campbell, Philip Converse, Warren Miller, and Donald Stokes, *The American Voter* (New York: John Wiley, 1960), p. 249.

thus acquired many votes that normally would have gone to the Republican candidate.[4]

The importance of the personal image communicated to potential voters leads candidates to take elaborate steps to project themselves favorably. Through careful planning, down to the level of gestures, dress, mode of speech, and the vagueness or specificity with which issues are discussed, a particular impression of the candidate is engendered. Professional public relations consultants have played an increasingly important role in shaping campaign plans and campaign advertising. In the view of many critics this new emphasis in electoral campaigning tries less to help the voters learn what the candidate is like and what he believes than to build a synthetic figure that fits current popular hopes and that may be quite misleading.

National elections in the United States, therefore, represent a contest between essentially permanent basic social groupings, in which a substantial minority of people shift back and forth between the parties on the basis of particular issues or beliefs about the candidates. The decades since the 1930's have seen the South, urban residents, blue collar workers, and minority groups disproportionately identified with the Democratic Party, and the wealthier, rural, Protestant, and better educated people with the Republican Party. The events and conflicts of the 1960's have apparently begun to fragment these coalitions and set in motion at least some readjustment, but we shall first characterize the established patterns and then move on to consider recent changes.

Table 1 summarizes some important evidence about the participation rates and relative support for the two major parties among the basic social groupings in the United States. It documents the low participation rates of the least educated and lower classes, particularly blacks, 64 percent of whom did not vote prior to 1960. Notice also the differential rates of participation in different years: 1948 was a year of low voting turnout for all groups, and many more people voted in both 1956 and 1960, suggesting that interest and/or concern rose in the interim. Some groups support one party much more often than the other, as we have suggested, and some also move back and forth between the parties with more volatility than others. The Eisenhower candidacy in 1956, for example, pulled usually Democratic workers into the Republican column, but the Kennedy candidacy of 1960 brought them back to the Democratic Party. College educated people, however, delivered nearly constant majorities to the Republican candidates in both years.

The Meaning of Elections

What significance do elections have in the American political system? The answer depends in important ways on whether we are talking about the system itself (in the sense of stability, or national integra-

---

[4] Angus Campbell, "Interpreting the Presidential Victory," in *The National Election of 1964*, ed. Milton Cummings (Washington, D.C.: Brookings Institution, 1966), p. 259.

TABLE 1
The Voting of Major American Social Groups, 1948, 1956, and 1960 Elections

Group characteristics	Vote republican	Vote democratic	Other	Not voting
Education				
1948				
Grade school	16	35	4	45
High school	29	34	4	33
College	54	17	8	21
1956				
Grade school	35	24	1	40
High school	41	34	1	26
College	62	28	—	10
1960				
Grade school	29	37	1	33
High school	38	42	1	19
College	57	32	1	10
Occupation of head of family				
1948				
Professional and managerial	58	14	3	25
Other white collar	38	38	5	19
Skilled and semiskilled	15	52	4	29
Unskilled	12	33	5	50
Farm operators	13	25	4	58
1956				
Professional and managerial	57	27	1	15
Other white collar	48	30	1	21
Skilled and semiskilled	39	32	1	28
Unskilled	24	29	—	47
Farm operators	40	34	—	26
1960				
Professional and managerial	46	39	3	12
Other white collar	46	37	1	16
Skilled and semiskilled	31	44	3	22
Unskilled	27	41	—	32
Farm operators	50	25	2	23
Race				
1948				
White	29	33	4	34
Negro	10	18	8	64
1956				
White	46	29	1	24
Negro	12	23	1	64
1960				
White	42	38	1	19
Negro	15	36	3	46

Source: National surveys conducted by the University of Michigan Survey Research Center. The 1948 and 1956 data are reported in Austin Ranney, *The Governing of Men* (New York: Holt, 1958), pp. 291-293. The 1960 data were furnished by Philip Converse.

From Fred I. Greenstein, *The American Party System and the American People*, p. 13. Copyright © 1963. Reprinted by permission of Prentice-Hall, Inc.

tion, as they are achieved in part by political parties and elections), about the impact elections have on mass beliefs about politics, or about their actual consequences for the policies followed by government and the character of mass influence in shaping those policies. A brief exploration of the potential meanings of elections will establish some perspective for our analysis of contemporary changes in voting and party identification.

The history of American political parties, and particularly the permanence of the two-party system, tends to suggest that they have on the whole accurately reflected mass preferences. For nearly 150 years, the United States has maintained the same basic party system. This means that, for practical purposes, with rare and temporary exceptions, only two parties have had any serious chance of winning the presidency or even a substantial minority in the Congress.

A great many "third" parties have existed over the course of American history, and one of these, the Republican Party, even managed to become a major party; but it did so only by displacing the Whig Party as one of the two major ones during the 1860 election of Abraham Lincoln to the presidency. Most American third parties (Know Nothing, Prohibition, Populist, Greenback, Socialist, Communist, Progressive, Liberal, American Labor, Peace and Freedom, and others) have had relatively short lives. They have chiefly espoused policy positions regarded in their times as more or less deviant or "extreme," though many of these gained broad popular support and so began to look quite conventional. The chief function of these parties for the political system has been to introduce policy innovations: to make it clear that a course of action earlier thought deviant was in fact widely supported and so induce one or both the major parties to espouse that position itself. Universal, compulsory education for children, the progressive income tax, prohibition of the sale or use of intoxicating beverages, the Tennessee Valley Authority, governmental guarantees of the right of workers to organize labor unions, and many other policies first became live issues because a third party made them their campaign issues.

Though third parties have occasionally elected their candidates to public offices at every level of government except the presidency, the two party system has remained intact throughout American history. That it has done so tells us something fundamental about mass political belief patterns. It indicates that the American people have never been divided for a long period of time into two well defined groups that basically and intensely differed with each other on the whole range of public issues regarded as most critical. In Italy and in France since World War II, there has been such a division of the mass public into those with a rightist-center ideology and those with a leftist orientation. People in these two ideological camps have quite consistently differed with one another on foreign policy, economic policy, church-state relations, and educational policy. Within each camp, there are additional differences on one or more of these matters, and so seven or eight distinct political parties have sprung up to compete for the various shadings of the right, the center, and the leftist vote.

One can readily understand from these examples that a multi-party system is likely wherever such a "bi-modal" pattern of mass political beliefs exist — that is, wherever the voters form two distinct ideological coalitions that take contrasting positions on the range of basic political issues.

In the United States, and in other countries with two party systems, mass political beliefs, by contrast, are "uni-modal." While people of course differ on particular issues, they have not formed clearly defined ideological blocs which stand for basic differences on all the central policy directions of the state and continue to do so over long time periods. Because people who differ on one issue are likely to agree with each other on some others, politics is made less intense emotionally. Given this pattern of mass political beliefs, a political party that wants to win elections is well advised to take a stand near the center of the belief spectrum on the major issues and to remain vague regarding those matters on which public opinion is seriously divided. This is precisely the strategy major parties do pursue in countries with uni-modal patternings of mass beliefs. In such a system, parties that take a clear ideological position different from the centrist one obviously limit their appeal to a minority, often a rather small minority, of the voters. On ethical grounds such a stand may be the only tenable one for supporters of these parties; but it has the effect of limiting third parties to an experimental and educational role. Because parties chiefly interested in winning elections must adopt a center position, the major parties do not often differ significantly on issues. They each want to elect their own leaders to public office. Sometimes, when it is unclear what most of the public wants, the major parties do differ on specific issues. But often they differ more in their rhetorical tone and style than in the policies they actually put into effect. Both major parties in the United States embrace within their ranks a gamut of policy positions ranging from far right to moderate left — a fact that further illustrates the relative unimportance of issues as a determinant of party membership or support. With two parties competing for the center track where the votes are, still another party trying the same strategy would have little chance of success; it is bound to be absorbed by the major parties in their efforts to broaden their support. Hence, a uni-modal pattern of mass beliefs encourages a two-party system.

The strong impact of party identification, the attachment of particular social groups to a political party, and the relatively minor effect of issues all suggest that many people take it for granted that either the Republican or the Democratic Party can be counted on to stand for whatever they value most of the time, and they vote on that assumption, with little attention to the specifics of particular campaigns. In view of the difficulty any voter might have in sorting out all the pertinent issues and the stands on them, this posture is understandable, and it minimizes the effort and time the voter has to expend in making up his mind. The wide range of policy positions and ideologies in both major parties and their lack of party discipline leave some question, however, about the accuracy of judgments reached in this fashion.

The American political party and election system thus contributes to stability and moderation, and apparently to national integration. Whether it is equally effective in promoting public satisfaction (in more than superficial ideological terms) or having an impact on policy matters, however, is a more difficult question.

For most people, voting is the most potent of all symbols of popular rule and therefore a powerful influence upon the legitimacy of a regime which holds public office. Whether a group of political actors wins or loses in an election, the fact that it has supposedly been consulted evokes its support for the government. It may not like some policies the government pursues, but it is far less likely to challenge its right to pursue them than would be the case if the government had not been elected. In this critical sense, elections moderate social tensions and inhibit potential civil strife. Frequently, perhaps usually, this is the chief function they serve for the political system, though that hypothesis is a debatable one and not easily susceptible to rigorous testing. Provisions for compulsory voting in some countries as well as social pressures to vote in order to prove one is a "good citizen" doubtless reflect an awareness that people who vote are psychologically inoculated against fundamental resistance to the state. Even more clearly, the use of elections in nondemocratic states reflects the same awareness. Some forms of election do not even offer the *possibility* of defeating unpopular candidates or policies, for they amount only to an opportunity to ratify actions already taken, as in the plebescites of totalitarian countries. It is precisely in such rigged elections, nonetheless, that legal and social pressure to vote has been strongest. The citizen who fails to vote is suspect as a potentially disloyal person and can expect the kind of ostracism that would await a member of a primitive tribe who refused to participate in a communal fertility rite or war dance. Sometimes elections are rigged so as to eliminate candidates who stand for a genuine alternative on controversial issues, as in many elections in the deep South, some in the North, and virtually all elections in one party states. The results are nevertheless publicized as mandates to the government and fervently accepted by many as exactly that.

Apart from their uses in promoting and symbolizing social solidarity, in what degree do elections provide policy guidelines for public officials to follow? On the occasional major issue on which the two major parties disagree they apparently do furnish a clear mandate, though historical examples warn against making this logical assumption without empirical checking. In 1928, the Democratic platform favored repeal of the Eighteenth (prohibition) Amendment and the Republicans were "dry." A Republican victory did indeed delay repeal for four years even though public sentiment increasingly favored repeal and in 1932 both parties' platforms reflected that sentiment. In 1964 escalation of the Vietnam War, certainly a major issue, was favored by Barry Goldwater, the Republican candidate, and opposed by Lyndon Johnson, his Democratic opponent. Though Johnson won by a wide margin, he moved quickly after election day to escalate the war. Though this is not by any means the only instance in which a major party disregarded what appeared to be a clear popular mandate, elections do in such instances provide a benchmark for evaluating the performance of a regime. This can be an important factor in the following election, as it evidently was in 1968; but there is no guarantee that it will be one.

Even when elections do offer a real choice, however, they are not a sufficient condition of democracy. Election mandates are almost always unclear, and it is always possible to justify departures from them on the ground that conditions have changed since election day. Even when there is every intention on the part of elected officials to heed the voice of the people as they understand it, election mandates typically furnish only the vaguest kind of guide to administrative officials and judges who have to make decisions in particular cases. Does the fact that the winning political party promised to hold down prices mean that it should put a program of wage and price ceilings into effect when some economists forecast rising prices and others disagree? Should officials elected on such a plank institute price controls after prices have risen two percent? Four percent? Ten percent? What difference should it make if the winning political party also promised to avoid governmental intervention in the economy as much as possible?

Dilemmas like these face modern governments all the time. The decisions taken to resolve them are bound to reflect a complex set of group interests and guesses about the future political and economic effects of one or another course of action. They cannot be predetermined, or even guided very far, by the votes people cast in election campaigns.

Because of the American parties' lack of clear issue stands, the tendency of candidates (once elected) to act as they consider necessary under the circumstances, and the non-issue-based characteristics of American voting behavior, it is very difficult to say precisely what elections mean in the United States. We have no doubt that it makes a difference which party or candidate wins an election, at least in the sense of the general approach to problems of governing, if not in the specific policies followed. But the permanence of the basic social coalitions underlying the parties, and the arbitrariness of both parties' internal processes preceding nominations, preclude exact definition of the role of elections. Events can split the basic social coalitions; indeed, such a process may now be underway. But in the past, only the Civil War and the Depression of the 1930's were of sufficient magnitude to realign the major social blocs and redirect the party system. After the Civil War, the Republicans were dominant for nearly seventy years, with only two Democratic intrusions (Cleveland and Wilson). After the Depression, the Democrats took over and remained in office, with the exception of the Eisenhower years, until 1968.

Exhaustive electoral analysis has led the leading experts, at the University of Michigan Survey Research Center, to categorize American elections into three very broad types.[5] The first and most frequent type of election is the "maintaining" election, in which the party with the numerically larger basic social coalition is returned to office. The second and least frequent type of election is the "realigning" election or "realigning era" of elections, in which events of cataclysmic proportions have succeeded in rending the majority coalition and installing a new coalition in power through the vehicle of the other party. Third is the dual category of "deviating" and then "reinstating" elections, in which for some reason the minority party wins a particular election without altering the basic underlying social coalitions and is subsequently replaced by the permanent majority party again. The Wilson and Eisenhower years are cited as the kinds of aberrations that constitute deviating years, and the elections of Harding and Kennedy represent the return of the same dominant social coalition. This is a quite low-level estimate of the quality of popular impact on government policy directions, of course. It implies that policymakers can count on support for practically anything they wish to do, at least as far as elections are concerned. Mass impact, however, may simply be more subtle than the very gross outlines of policy preference that are possible through the instrument of elections. Or more recent elections and contemporary changes may suggest that these characterizations are obsolete. We shall keep these possibilities in mind as we examine recent events.

Electoral Changes in the Late 1960's and Early 1970's

The election of 1964 provides a good point from which to begin, because it shows the enduring "New Deal coalition" of voters in exaggerated form, plus the beginnings of race-grounded cracks in that governing social grouping.[6] The Goldwater candidacy provided an unusual event in American party politics, a presidential election based chiefly on sharp ideological differences between the parties. With Goldwater deliberately appealing to conservatives and the South, Johnson was allowed to preempt the middle ground. The result was massive defection from the ranks of traditional Republican voters, particularly college graduates and professionals, and an unprecedented 16 million vote margin of victory for Johnson. Although ideological conservatives and hard-core Republicans supported him, Goldwater won only the segregationist states of the deep South. Perhaps the long-range significance of this election, however, lies in the latter fact: several Southern states had been drifting away from the national Democratic Party over racial issues for years, but this was the first time they had been brought into the Republican column on election day. For many Southerners, the Republican Party thus be-

---

[5] Angus Campbell, Philip Converse, Donald Stokes, and Warren Miller, *The American Voter* (New York: John Wiley, 1960).

[6] This analysis is drawn from Philip Converse, Aage Clausen, and Warren Miller, "Electoral Myth and Reality: The 1964 Election," *The American Political Science Review*, vol. 59 (1965), pp. 321-336.

came the new vehicle of segregationist sentiment, and the South acquired greater influence in Republican Party internal decision-making.

The shifts that occurred from 1964 to 1968 offer lessons in several areas of American politics. They demonstrate unequivocally that neither of the major parties is ever permanently down and out. Events can always restore it, at least as far as winning the next election is concerned, because the party out of power is the only means the electorate has of replacing the people who have been in power and presumably are responsible for the events that have occurred. They also show that the apparent popular choice of policy directions may not be effectuated through any given presidential election: elected on the basis of a less aggressive policy in Vietnam, Johnson thereafter escalated the war. Of course, he also accomplished many social welfare programs to which his supporters gave equal priority.

The events that intervened between the elections of 1964 and 1968 were many, but their relative importance for the election of 1968 can be sorted out.[7] The Vietnam War was a major factor, of course. A long-established image among the electorate in the 1950's and early 1960's was that the Republicans were the party of peace, but also of economic hardship; the Democrats were the war party, but also the party of economic prosperity. The Goldwater candidacy apparently temporarily reversed the war-peace aspects of this image, but it returned with a vengeance as 1968 approached. A second and nearly commensurate sequence of events was the series of urban riots occurring between 1965 and 1968. Racial matters have always held the potential of splitting the Democratic coalition, and this result seems to have at least started to occur as a result of the riots and of stiffening white resistance to black efforts to attain full citizenship. A third factor was the increasing public attention to crime and "law and order," perhaps as a means of expressing resentments against blacks that commitments to the abstract principle of racial equality made it difficult to voice directly. Resentment against peace demonstrations also contributed to the momentum of this movement away from the Democratic Party. Even those most opposed to the Vietnam War strongly disapproved of violent outbreaks and peace demonstrators in general. Those opposed to the war and sympathetic to war protestors made up only three percent of the electorate. There was such a wide sense of breakdown in authority and discipline, feeding on militant political dissent as well as on racial outbreaks, that "law and order" ranked with Vietnam and race problems as major factors in influencing the outcome. The candidacy of George Wallace, of course, gave special focus to these latter complaints.

The results on election day were the most dramatic shifts that have, in all probability, ever occurred in the United States. The Democratic

[7] This analysis draws on Philip Converse, Warren Miller, Jerrold G. Rusk, and Arthur C. Wolfe, "Continuity and Change in American Politics: Parties and Issues in the 1968 Election," *The American Political Science Review*, vol. 63 (1969), pp. 1083-1105.

total dropped from more than 61 percent of the two-party vote in 1964 to less than 43 percent in 1968. Nearly 40 percent of Nixon's votes came from people who had voted for Johnson in 1964, and other Johnson votes (as well as many Goldwater votes) went to Wallace. The detailed analysis conducted by the University of Michigan Survey Research Center led to the conclusion that the Wallace candidacy probably did not change the outcome. Wallace drew as much or more from sources that would otherwise have gone to the Democratic candidate as from the Republican potential; this may be due, in part, to the deliberate efforts to cultivate Southern support that were made by the Nixon ticket. Disgruntled Democrats, who had previously used the McCarthy candidacy to express their dissatisfaction with the Johnson adminstration, departed from their usual party, refused to vote for the office of President, or simply stayed home. Only black voters, among all normal Democratic supporters, voted and supported their party more than in previous elections. Ninety-seven percent of all black voters in the country voted for Humphrey, while less than 35 percent of white voters did.

Do these dramatic events and shifts in familiar voting patterns indicate that major changes are underway? Much-publicized Republican arguments say that the South and the relatively well-off lower middle class are ready to join with traditional Republican supporters — chiefly on racial and "law and order" grounds, but also for economic self-defense reasons — to constitute a new governing coalition for the next decades. Against this are the established patterns of semipermanent party loyalties and the traditional attractiveness of the Democratic Party during times of economic hardship. The usual indicia of electoral behavior would seem to indicate that it is much too soon to envision the end of the "New Deal coalition" and Democratic Party dominance, particularly if economic issues become salient. Table 2 shows the political party identifications of adults as of July, 1969, perhaps one of the early high points of the Nixon administration. Although Democratic identification is down 5 percent from 1960, Republican is also down 2 percent. The gain is among independents, a rise of 7 percent since 1960, which might indicate people in transition from one party to another, or people turning away from both parties. But the table shows clearly that the Democrats maintain a substantial margin; they have only to hold their party identifiers and add a few more people from among the ranks of independents in order to win the ordinary national election. This has been the case ever since the New Deal days, and it is the mark of a still-dominant social coalition. Among the lower classes, for example, Democratic strength remains high; among professionals and the best educated, furthermore, the drift seems to be toward independent status rather than toward the Republican Party. Another major indicator of continuity in the Democratic coalition is found in the pattern of congressional voting in 1968. There was very little change in the proportion of seats held by Democrats at this or lower levels, despite the sharp changes in presidential voting that went on.

TABLE 2
Adult Political Party Identification, July 1969 (in percent)

	Republican	Democrat	Independent
National	28	42	30
Sex			
Men	28	39	33
Women	28	44	28
Race			
White	30	39	31
Nonwhite	X	X	X
Education			
College	35	28	37
High School	27	42	31
Grade School	24	52	24
Occupation			
Professional and business	31	32	37
White collar	30	38	32
Farmers	35	40	25
Manual	23	46	31
Age			
21-29 years	23	35	42
30-49 years	28	41	31
50 and over	31	45	24
Religion			
Protestant	33	39	28
Catholic	20	50	30
Jewish	X	X	X
Region			
East	29	43	28
Midwest	33	37	30
South	19	47	34
West	33	39	28
Income			
$10,000 and over	31	34	35
$ 7,000 and over	30	36	34
$ 5,000-$6,999	23	44	33
$ 3,000-$4,999	30	45	25
Under $3,000	26	53	21
Community size			
1,000,000 and over	26	42	32
500,000 and over	25	42	33
50,000-499,999	19	48	33
2,500-49,999	33	40	27
Under 2,500, rural	34	36	30

Source: *Gallup Opinion Weekly,* August, 1969.

But, as we have seen, events can work substantial changes in voting alignments. At this point, we must characterize the 1968 election as indicating no more than short-term changes, with the probability of reinstating the Democratic coalition, particularly if economic issues become paramount. But the direction of events seems to be along lines that have already, and may well continue to, realign voting blocs on a continuing basis. Polarization between blacks and whites, if they continue, can split the Democratic Party; the Republican Party has no such problem. The eighteen-year-old vote will, according to most studies, make very little difference in outcomes. The youngest age groups vote with the least regularity of all groups, and their preferences appear to be (overall) not much different from the party preferences of their elders.

College students, probably the most likely younger group to constitute a force for change in electoral politics, do not display strong indications of doing so. The breakdown of political party identifications among college students in January, 1970, was 27 percent Democratic (down eight percent in three years), 21 percent Republican (down 5 percent in three years), and 52 percent independent (up 13 percent in three years.)[8] The drift to independent status is substantial, but the disaffection from the major parties may be temporary. At least, when asked in other surveys whether new parties should be created, or whether the existing system can be made to work, college students overwhelmingly opt for the moderate, system-confirming alternatives.

Thus, the indications of wide-scale change through the political party system and elections do not appear strong. In the absence of truly rending social conflicts, the existing party support patterns appear likely to continue. The discontented groups, principally blacks and some college students, have the electoral effect of polarizing great majorities against them; until they pick up substantial numbers of allies, their electoral effect will be the reverse of their preferences. This is not to say that they will be without influence, of course, but simply that such influence as they muster will not be generated through the electoral route. This makes it all the more important to examine the other ways in which nonelites generate impact on policy and policymakers.

THE INTEREST GROUP PROCESS

Almost equally well established among means of influencing decision-makers in the United States is the practice of forming groups to press shared claims, or joining existing groups for the same purpose. Once again, however, it appears to be the relatively higher levels of people in terms of class or sense of political efficacy who actually do join such groups. The incidence of group membership in the United States is considerably higher among the middle and upper middle classes than it is among the lower echelons. Moreover, the manage-

[8] *Gallup Opinion Weekly,* January, 1970.

ment of groups requires long-term investment of time and other resources, and is thus more open to the upper levels. Continuing involvement in group leadership also leads to an enduring commitment to the general structure of relationships among groups and their leaders — i.e., to a familiar status quo, in preference to a possibly unpredictable future. Day-to-day interaction among groups has the effect of rigidifying their relationships and limiting the extent to which they can serve as instruments of mass participation.

There is constant bargaining and opportunistic maneuvering for advantage over wage and price policies, zoning ordinances, changes in social security laws, subsidies to shipbuilders, contracts for airplanes and space research, tax laws, and so on. Such matters are likely to become public issues and objects of political attention whenever a group sees a way to benefit from new legislative, administrative, or judicial policies dealing with one of them. A Defense Department contract for a new type of supersonic plane obviously does not become a political issue until it is technically feasible to build such a plane. Nor does it become a political issue if everybody involved assumes that only one manufacturer can build it. But because such a contract involves benefits running to millions of dollars for plant managers, stockholders, scientists, employees, and subcontractors it is sure to become a public issue if there is competition for the award of the contract. Similarly, proposals for governmental restrictions on the kinds of buildings that can be erected in a new subdivision of a city are not likely to appear or to become a public issue until somebody has begun to make plans to develop the subdivision and until some of the people concerned (developers, prospective homeowners, businessmen) have reasons to believe they can get more of what they want through the city government's procedures for formulating zoning laws than through private negotiation with each other.

Involved in the emergence of any issue as a *political* issue, then, is a technological or environmental change of some kind and also a belief by some group affected by that change that it can get more of what it wants through politics than through alternative channels for dealing with the problem. These two conditions do not always occur at the same time; the second may appear a long time after the first. Protection for child labor did not become an important political concern in the United States until long after children were employed and exploited in factories. But when it seemed possible that state legislatures could be induced to pass child labor laws, in the late nineteenth and early twentieth centuries, this issue became a widely and hotly fought one. In the light of earlier discussions in this book, it will be clear to the reader that a belief that a group can get what it wants through political action is really the same thing as a belief that it can get additional support for its position from a wider public with political sanctions at its disposal.

Involvement in political maneuvers for immediate tangible benefits is a kind of game playing. To win larger tax exemptions or avoid a traffic fine or participate in a local political fight over zoning regulations for business arouses the interest of those affected, often quite intensely; and for the most active and adept at this kind of politics it carries a zest for winning against obstacles. It is a test of personal and group resourcefulness as well as of flexibility in meeting challenges and in finding a workable solution. This kind of politics necessarily involves a willingness to recognize the rights of opponents to exist and to play the political game, a willingness to compromise, and a sharing of some underlying values with opponents, even while contending with them over particular issues. Its keynotes are flexibility, opportunism, compromise, and a search for the potentialities in the political situation — for the combination of tactics and resources that will maximize tangible political gains. The maneuvering is necessarily carried on by relatively small cadres of activists, though one of the major resources at their disposal is the support in votes, money, moral approval, or fighting ability of a mass following. Another resource is the understanding of other activists concerned with the issue. The adept political tactician is able to put himself in his opponent's place sufficiently well to understand his needs and wants and the limits of his ability to make concessions. Effective political bargaining within the established rules for political action presupposes as great a bond of empathy with one's opponents as with one's allies. In the measure that a man is flexible enough and free enough of constraining anxiety to be able to see the world from his adversary's perspective, he will be able to devise effective political tactics. Indeed, the very act of responding to another group in this way reassures both sides that their respective interests are being protected. What emotion is involved in such politics springs from the zest of analyzing strategic potentialities as well as from the gratification or disappointment of a tangible payoff or loss.

Group membership is thus the preserve of relatively higher status persons to start with, and, by the characteristics of group interaction, the process is converted from a representing one to more of a mass-managing one. Furthermore, it is easy to overestimate the numbers of Americans who are included within one or more voluntary associations. Much as Americans may be known as "joiners," just a little more than half actually belong to a group. Figure 1 compares the United States with other countries in this respect, and Table 3 shows what kinds of organizations people belong to in these countries. The United States, it appears, leads other countries in the proportion of its population (57 percent) which belongs to some voluntary association. But examination of the types of organizations to which people in the various countries belong reveals that Americans are uniquely high in membership in religious organizations, and in fraternal organizations such as the Elks, Masons, Moose, Rotary, Kiwanis, etc. In the case of the more political and potentially mass-based organizations, such as unions, the United States is not notably high in membership proportions, trailing both of the other advanced industrial nations in the comparison. Other data reported in the same study show that nearly half of those reporting membership in a group belonged to

FIGURE 1
Membership in Voluntary Associations, by Nation

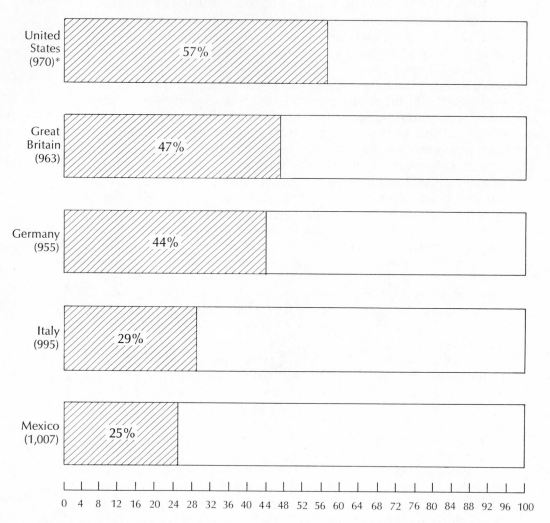

Numbers in parentheses refer to the bases upon which percentages are calculated.

Source: Gabriel Almond and Sidney Verba, *The Civic Culture* (Princeton, N.J.: Princeton University Press, 963), p. 264.

only one such group.[9] Thus, in terms of inclusiveness as well as class level of participants, the structure of voluntary associations in the United States is not a very direct means of transmitting the needs and demands of segments of the lower echelons of nonelites to the higher levels.

[9] Gabriel Almond and Sidney Verba, *The Civic Culture* (Princeton, N. J.: Princeton University Press, 1963), p. 264.

TABLE 3
Membership in Various Types of Organizations, by Nation

Organization	U.S.	U.K.	Germany	Italy	Mexico
Trade unions	14	22	15	6	11
Business	4	4	2	5	2
Professional	4	3	6	3	5
Farm	3	0	4	2	0
Social	13	14	10	3	4
Charitable	3	3	2	9	6
Religious[a]	19	4	3	6	5
Civic-political	11	3	3	8	3
Cooperative	6	3	2	2	0
Veterans'	6	5	1	4	0
Fraternal[b]	13				
Other	6	3	9	6	0
Total percentage of members	57	47	44	30	24
Total number of respondents	970	963	955	995	1,007

[a] This refers to church-related organizations, not to church affiliation itself.
[b] U.S. only.

Reprinted from Gabriel Almond and Sidney Verba, *The Civic Culture* (Princeton, N. J.: Princeton University Press, 1963), p. 246-247.

ALTERNATIVE FORMS OF POLITICAL PARTICIPATION

The alternative forms of participation span a wide range of activities. Some of them are as authorized and accepted, though less formalized, as elections or interest group actions. Others are discouraged or forcefully repressed, but nevertheless amount to major means by which segments of nonelites participate in politics and may generate impact on policy. In the latter case, of course, many consequences may ensue, some quite different from those sought by the participants themselves. In general, however, although the alternative forms are frequently efforts to reach around the established channels, many of the same class biases are visible in them as appear in parties, elections, and interest group activity.

One of the most obvious and well accepted routes of communication and "pressure" from nonelites to decisionmaking elites is the simple act of writing a letter, or signing a petition, to be sent to an official or a newspaper. Congressmen are sometimes said to "wait for the mail" before making up their minds how to vote on an issue. There are several problems with this assumption, however. One is that people tend to write or petition to those whom they have reason to believe are on their side to start with or who are at least on the fence. This means that letter-writers favoring a proposal write to those decisionmakers who favor it, and those against write to those who oppose it. The net result, even if the decisionmakers take their mail seriously, is no change in positions. Another problem is that decisionmakers become inured to pressure campaigns organized by perhaps very small interest groups. But even more important is the fact that the act of writing letters, and to a lesser extent carrying and signing petitions, is more likely to be undertaken by people who are better-educated and of a higher class level. Moreover, even within class and education levels, it is an act more likely to be undertaken by conservatives than by liberals. In an effort to find out why the 1964 Republican strategists thought there was a "hidden" conservative vote, the Michigan Survey Research Center compared those who wrote letters to officials or newspapers with those who did not in terms of their political preferences.[10] The researchers found, first, that only about 15 percent of the population had *ever* written a letter to a public official, and that two-thirds of *all* letters were written by a total of three percent of the population. This three percent was distinctly conservative in every ideological dimension; by "vote" of letter-writers, Goldwater would have been elected by a comfortable majority. Thus, if decisionmakers took guidance, or if officials sought to measure the mood of the country, from the views expressed in the mail to officials and newspapers, they would gain a very skewed image.

Some alternative forms of participation are built in to the process of administering and implementing laws. Juries, for instance, are intended as a means of placing a significant function in the hands of citizens, and might well serve as means of communicating to higher levels citizens' dissatisfaction with law and/or their circumstances. But juries are constituted from lists of voters or of propertyowners (or, in the case of grand juries, from "blue-ribbon" panels), and thus reflect class orientations. Despite this, juries in many cases involving political figures and issues (Black Panthers, draft resisters, the Chicago 8 trial, etc.) have refused to convict or have been relatively lenient, suggesting that some potential future prosecutions may have been discouraged by these results. In many areas of government activity, there are requirements for advisory boards of citizens. Urban renewal, Selective Service, and other agencies deliberately engage citizens in the implementation of their programs. But relatively little impact is developed on behalf of the preferences of ordinary citizens, because the participants in these programs have been drawn from the higher echelons of nonelites. Businessmen, local leaders, and higher status people generally have dominated these positions. Only in the Community Action Agencies of the poverty program has there been a real contest over who is to shape a government program. In this area, lower class citizens did begin to take part, and the result was first an amendment to the law which gave local governments control over the local aspects of the programs, and then such controversy that the funding for many local units was sharply cut back or eliminated.

A much less institutionalized form of participation that has arisen

[10] These data are drawn from Converse et al., "Electoral Myth and Reality," *op. cit.*, p. 333.

from time to time in American history, and particularly in the decade of the 1960's, is the protest demonstration, sit-in, disruption, or deliberate refusal to obey rules. Those who have been unable to make themselves heard through the established channels have resorted to these tactics, often with great success, when their claims were consistent with generally shared values and not too much at odds with the basic features of the political system. But where they have been unable to find allies after a period of time, or when they were perceived as dangerously outside of established values or the familiar political practices, the weight of rejection and repression have come down hard on them. Successful protest-type activity requires allies, or at the very least the inaction of those who might oppose the protestors. It creates risks of a personal kind for the participants, and is difficult to sustain for a long period of time without a supportive environment. It depends on achieving some tangible goal, usually from an existing political structure.

Another even less institutionalized alternative form of participation is the spontaneous riot. Although clearly grounded in the circumstances of ghetto existence, the riots of the 1960's were spontaneous, by contrast to deliberate obstructive sit-ins or other protest tactics. Touched off by one or another form of provocation, they often engaged thousands of participants for days at a time. The immediate consequences were destruction of millions of dollars worth of property and the deaths of many ghetto residents at the hands of police and National Guard forces. Subsequently, there were increased government programs of assistance to ghetto and other poor people, but also strong popular support for future repressive measures and political candidates who stood for such action.

Patterns of participation in both riots and student demonstrations offer some insight into these alternative forms of participation. In the case of the ghetto riots of 1967, for example, it is clear that substantial proportions of each community were involved. Supplemental studies undertaken for the National Commission on Civil Disorders estimates that participants numbered from 11 to 35 percent of the residents of the riot areas in the major cities (Detroit, Newark, New Haven) where riots occurred.[11] The composition of the rioters was roughly representative of the occupational makeup of the ghetto population, with a slight emphasis downward, toward the less skilled and the unemployed. Nearly all of those arrested during the riots were residents of the neighborhood involved.[12] The riots thus were fairly broad-based actions by cross-sections of the area populations. They were not caused by the "criminal element," or by "outside agitators," or by any tiny minority of militants. They were, it seems fair to say, genuine expressions of community protest of an essentially political kind. Certainly they were perceived as such by most blacks; and several surveys have shown that, while most blacks do not ap-

[11] Robert M. Fogelson and Robert B. Hill, "Who Riots? A Study of Participation in the 1967 Riots," *Supplemental Studies for the National Advisory Commission on Civil Disorders* (Washington: U. S. Government Printing Office, 1968), p. 231.
[12] *Ibid.*, p. 236, 237.

prove of rioting, they see it in many cases as being necessary and helpful toward achieving black goals.[13] Younger blacks in particular tend to believe that violence will be necessary before such objectives are attained.

But the same riots were perceived quite differently by whites. We have already seen the electoral consequences that came about in major part because of these riots and other race problems. National elites, with some limited exceptions, tended to emphasize theories that outside agitators, a few militants, or habitual troublemakers in the communities had caused the riots. The Kerner Report, with its emphasis on "white racism," stood alone and largely unheard as an explanation. Table 4 shows the causes seen by six key groups within

TABLE 4
"Theories" of Riot Causation Among Six Occupations (in percent)

Proportions rating "theory" as "main reason" or "largely true"

"Theory"	Po-lice	Educa-tors	Social workers	Political workers	Mer-chants	Em-ployers
A. Unheard Negro complaints	31	70	72	72	48	47
B. Criminal elements	69	33	27	27	65	42
C. Nationalists and militants	77	46	38	39	65	62
D. Riots as Political acts	27	26	25	20	23	24
E. Police brutality	9	33	37	53	21	7
F. Negroes basically violent	28	8	4	8	23	11

Reprinted from Angus Campbell and Howard Schuman, "Racial Attitudes in Fifteen American Cities," in *Supplemental Studies For the National Advisory Commission on Civil Disorders* (Washington, D.C.: U.S. Government Printing Office, 1968), p. 96.

fifteen major cities of the country in 1968. Merchants, employers, and the police saw the riots as primarily the work of criminal elements and nationalists or militants; educators, social workers, and political workers came closer to the image held by blacks themselves. Only small minorities in any category saw the riots as political acts. Consistent with these impressions on the part of local elites, white residents of the same cities perceived the riots in opposite ways from their black neighbors. Table 5 presents these contrasts very clearly. It is as if the two groups of people had seen totally different events, which of course they did. Most whites in these surveys saw the riots as opportunities for looting, and a substantial minority said that even orderly marches to protest against racial discrimination were unjustified; two-thirds believed that sit-ins were unjustified. In the after-

[13] Opinion data in this section are drawn from Angus Campbell and Howard Schuman, "Racial Attitudes in Fifteen American Cities," in *Supplemental Studies, op. cit.*, pp. 48-52.

TABLE 5
Have Riots Helped or Hurt the Negro Cause? (in percent)

"On the whole, do you think the disturbances have helped or hurt the cause of Negro rights, or would you say they haven't made much difference?"

	Negro		White	
	Men	Women	Men	Women
Helped	37	30	13	14
Hurt	22	24	69	59
Helped and hurt equally	12	11	7	7
Made no difference	21	28	9	17
Don't know	8	7	2	3
	100	100	100	100

"Why do you feel that way?"

First reason given	Negro		White	
	Men	Women	Men	Women
Helped:				
Tangible gains (e.g., more jobs)	19	20	8	8
Whites understand Negroes' problems better	14	10	8	8
Show of Negro power	9	5	2	1
Hurt:				
Destruction, injury	8	8	2	3
Increased anti-Negro sentiments	16	19	64	54
Made no difference:				
No tangible gain	19	23	5	12
Negroes are still not satisfied	0	1	7	10
Don't know	15	14	4	4
	100	100	100	100

Reprinted from Campbell, *op. cit.*, p. 49.

math of the riots, there can be little doubt that white opinion hardened firmly against further advance by blacks. By comparison, the actions of (essentially white) national elites may well seem generous.

The pattern of participation in student demonstrations shows that very few members of even this relatively activist group had actually taken part in demonstrations. A CBS-sponsored survey was completed in late 1968, after three years of campus demonstrations, by which time one might expect a pattern of participation to have become fairly well established.[14] Only 12 percent had ever participated

[14] Columbia Broadcasting System, "Generations Apart: A Study of the Generation Gap conducted for CBS News" (New York: CBS, Inc., 1969). Participation data may be found on p. 29, breakdowns by ideology on p. 39.

in a sit-in, however, six percent in a riot, and only 24 percent in a march, despite the peaceful and legitimate character of the latter. Moreover, the 13 percent of students who were by their attitudes classified as "revolutionaries" or "radical reformers" made up the overwhelming share of those who had undertaken the more militant actions. Most students were only moderate reformers, confident that the system could be made to work, and opposed to militant tactics. There were nearly as many conservatives as revolutionaries and radicals put together. The principal implication that can be drawn from these data, therefore, is that campus demonstrations, like many other forms of participation, are indeed the province of a relative few. Many others may share their views, of course, at least on the issue of war in Southeast Asia, but they make little use of any means of making such views known.

CONCLUSIONS

It is hard to find a way of interpreting nonelite participation in politics except as a lesser version of the basic elite-mass relationship. Those nonelites who are relatively higher in class status take part much more regularly, and probably are more likely to find their interest convergent with national elites. As we descend the social ladder, we encounter more and more people with less and less participation and (in all probability) impact on policy. We do not mean to suggest that the lower classes are without impact, nor to permit the implication that elections are incapable of setting basic policy directions. There are times when elections make a great deal of difference; and by and large, many majority wishes find their way into expression through them — if we view elections over the long sweep of history and in very gross terms. But there is much initiative in the hands of the upper echelon of decisionmakers, and great need for special leadership acts and helpful structuring by events to frame the issues so that majorities can express themselves in a timely fashion. Between elections, the channels of influence are so arbitrary and uncertain that no comprehensive impact can be developed, and only occasional, probably unrepresentative demands come through and are carried out in policy. In the next chapter, we shall see how such demands have an impact on decisions and how the between-elections means of influence operate.

The Impact of Nonelites on Public Policy 15

Elections are an uncertain vehicle of political participation. Interest groups are highly specialized. The alternative forms of participation are erratic and even counterproductive. And yet needs, claims, and demands *are* injected into the visible political arena by the actions of segments of nonelites. At least to some extent, elites feel obliged, or are forced, to respond. Their response may be merely symbolic, or negative, or marginal in comparison with the demands made; but there nevertheless is often *some* response, and sometimes one consistent with nonelite demands.

Frequently, a fully satisfactory "solution" may be impossible because of perceived conditions, because of opposition from other segments of nonelites, or because of elites' other priorities and preferences. These determinations are made by elites, of course. Their strategic location and preponderance of power, status, and legitimacy enables them to decide how to fit demands that are strongly pressed and supported by established values into the ongoing mix of policy and practice that characterize the political system. Other demands can normally be deflected or dismissed. In this process, elites are aided by the screening effect of the greater participation and efficacy of the better educated and higher status persons among nonelites. The latter operate to cushion or even absorb much of the thrust of deviant, minority, or lower class demands before they emerge into the national political arena and begin to induce elite response.

In this chapter, we shall explore the processes by which elites or some of them respond to needs felt or demands expressed by segments of nonelites. Our focus is on elite behavior of either an anticipatory or preventative kind, perhaps role-induced by the perceived obligations of public office or the responsibility of power, perhaps induced by the simple threat of loss of power or domestic chaos that would otherwise occur. In particular, we are concerned with the extent to which segments of nonelites can oblige elites to act in ways that they would not otherwise have done. We are searching for the limits to which nonelite movements of varying character can press elites into action to serve their goals. A sense of how far elites can be pushed under varying circumstances will help us to get a more subtle sense of the relative balance of initiative between elites and masses. We shall first survey the sometimes deflecting, sometimes facilitating effects of the organization and operation of government structures themselves. Then we shall look briefly at some examples of efforts by segments of nonelites to bring about new policies under different circumstances: blacks and racial equality, college students and the war in Southeast Asia, and the growing effort to contain military and space expenditures. In a final section, we shall reach some tentative conclusions.

WHEN AND HOW ESTABLISHED AUTHORITIES RESPOND

In many instances, at least some portion of elites *wants* to respond; they may even have been waiting for a chance to do so. Elites may support mass demands because they expect to benefit themselves from doing so. Free universal public education is a case in point. Before the industrial revolution came to the United States, free public education was an issue that divided Americans along economic class lines. It was a major plank in the platform of one of our earliest third parties, the Workingmen's Party, which gained considerable support among wage earners in Philadelphia between 1828 and 1832. The issue grew less and less controversial as industrial technologies required that a larger proportion of the work force be literate and possess elementary skills in arithmetic and in what were then called the "agricultural, industrial, and mechanic arts." Indeed, many states began establishing normal schools, state colleges, and universities around the middle of the nineteenth century, and in the Morrill Act of 1862 the federal government helped them to do so. As industry and agriculture have required work forces with increasingly complex skills, elite support for education at all levels also increased. To some degree, this trend has been further bolstered by the fact that methods of financing state universities provide a direct subsidy to the largely middle class students who attend them.

Sometimes elites have even more pressing and immediate economic reasons to support mass demands. In the early years of the twentieth century, a growing number of states enacted minimum wage laws. It was widely accepted that if workers were unable to live on their earnings, they should be entitled to a wage that would at least support their families at a subsistence level. This policy was supported both on a moral basis and because it was recognized that men could not even work efficiently when undernourished. A chief reason for the enactment of the first federal minimum wage law in 1938 was its support by some powerful industrial groups, especially New England textile manufacturers. Forced by unions of their workers to pay higher wages than their unorganized Southern competitors, the New England mill owners saw in the minimum wage a device to increase their competitors' labor costs to the level of their own, thereby improving their competitive position.

Social security legislation, certainly a significant benefit to a large part of the public, has also enjoyed substantial elite support, partly for economic reasons, partly for other reasons. With growing worker demands for industrial pension plans, backed by the right to strike, employers were under strong pressure to make some concessions. Governmental old age benefits financed by regressive pay roll taxes paid chiefly by the workers and by consumers represented an economical solution. In consequence, frequent improvements in benefits and coverage of American social security legislation have been relatively uncontroversial since the basic federal law was enacted in 1935.

But there is an even more compelling reason for the success of mass demands for elementary social security protections: anxiety about widespread public restiveness and militancy if large groups of people are being denied what they have come to believe every human being deserves. All industrialized countries, including those that have not pretended to be democracies or responsive to mass demands, have therefore instituted social security systems, virtually all of them established earlier and extending wider protections than the American system does. In Germany, for example, the highly elitist and authoritarian government of Bismarck provided extensive social security protections as early as the 1880's. Fear of mass restiveness or violence has unquestionably been a major impetus for the enactment of other governmental programs benefitting nonelites. In Chapter 5, we noted that widespread civil disobedience and urban riots mobilized support for voting rights laws and for some concessions, real or symbolic, to black demands for an end to economic discrimination and other affronts. Conspicuous restiveness and civil disobedience must therefore be recognized as another, often potent tactic through which masses can exert an influence upon public policy.

This discussion has deliberately moved from a consideration of such routine channels of influence as voting and legislative bargaining to those some regard as illegitimate, such as civil disobedience. The analysis and the illustrations should make it clear that there is no clear dividing line between legitimate and illegitimate tactics. Similarly, there is no clear empirical distinction, but only an analytically useful one, between people who feel relatively gratified and those who feel relatively deprived. It is the relatively deprived who are most likely to support political strikes, boycotts, riots, civil disobedience, or civil war as channels of influence.

It is tempting, but misleading, to classify people neatly as content or dissatisfied, as exhibiting a sense of gratification or a sense of deprivation, as perceiving the political system as legitimate or illegitimate, as believing they are efficacious or politically powerless. Test results do of course categorize people in these ways; but there is also clear evidence, some of it already cited in this book, that people may vary in these related aspects over time, by issue, and according to the social context in which the question is presented to them. How stable and how consistent any individual or social group is in these respects is an empirical question, to be answered by observation and research. To take stability and consistency for granted is to underestimate the complexity of the human being and to guarantee that some of the most significant political phenomena will not be investigated or fully understood.

People who feel undeservedly deprived in some respect that is important to them are likely to resort to civil disobedience or violence as a way of influencing the political system. Occasionally an individual acts alone in a violent manner, as in the case of the lone political assassin or terrorist or the person who tries by self-immolation to galvanize others into opposition to public policies he regards as immoral. Far more frequent and far more significant politically are the cases in which a substantial group of people feel a strong sense of deprivation with respect to the same issue, such as social, economic, and political equality, the military draft, or the Vietnam War. In such instances violent or nonviolent demonstration is likely; and if it is widely enough publicized and supported, it does win some degree of influence for the demonstrators. Economic boycotts, defiance of official restrictions upon mass demonstrations, and riots are all fairly common forms of this tactic. Whether or not they are defined as legal at a particular time or place, they must be regarded by the realistic analyst of political processes as forms of mass action that will predictably occur under the conditions described here. Chapter 5 traces the story of how these tactics have won some gains for the poor and for those deprived of voting rights. We have already noted how the possibility of their occurrence has made elites willing to make concessions in such policy areas as social security and protective labor legislation. In its extreme form this tactic for achieving mass influence becomes sustained violent resistance or revolution, as in the American Revolution of 1775 to 1781 and in the Civil War.

The efficacy of civil disobedience and militance in winning benefits for masses depends ultimately upon how much popular support these tactics rally for their cause. When they serve dramatically to call attention to deprivations widely regarded as shocking and unfair, they are effective in rallying such support. Until the civil disobedience campaigns of the early sixties and the riots of the middle sixties, a large part of the American people were blissfully unaware of the "other America" living in poverty or denied basic civil rights. The increasingly militant demonstrations against the Vietnam War awakened many Americans to an awareness of the dubious grounds under which the Johnson administration had justified escalation of the war, to its high toll in civilian and military casualties, and to the corruption and unpopularity of the Saigon regime.

Civil disobedience and violence do, as we have seen, create a "backlash" and so damage the political position of those who engage in them. Militance unquestionably does antagonize some people and evoke repression. The historical record leaves no doubt, however, that it also wins support for righting genuine wrongs. Where such real deprivations can be dramatically brought to attention, these militant tactics are the most potent political device in the scanty arsenal of tactics available to nonelites.

Administrative Responsiveness to Mass Publics

Administrative agencies operating in controversial areas of public policy are always responsive to particular constituencies and clienteles, as noted in Chapter 12. Usually an agency's constituency is some elite, organized group; the Civil Aeronautics Board, for example, is chiefly responsive to the interests of the major commercial airlines. Occasionally an administrative agency, or the sub-division of an agency, is chiefly responsive to the interests of a nonelite group, of some substantial mass public with a problem over which the agency has jurisdiction. In the relatively infrequent instances in which this happens, the explanation is basically the same as the explanation for mass influence generally. Elite groups have come to support the nonelite group, at least ambivalently, either because the elites themselves will benefit economically from such support or because the elites are insecure and fearful of widespread resistance to the system from which they draw their privileges and their favored status. Let us consider briefly several administrative agencies responsive to the interests of the poor — chiefly blacks — one which served the interests of poor farmers for a time, and one which promoted the interests of unorganized workers.

The Community Action Agencies established in many communities under the Economic Opportunity Act of 1963 are a pertinent example, but will only be mentioned here as they have already been discussed in Chapter 5. Recall that though they have reflected the interests of the poor in their efforts and policy directions, they have been severely handicapped by inadequate funds, opposition, and harassment from established municipal political organizations.

Another agency actively working to support the demands of urban blacks was the Community Relations Service of the Department of Justice in 1967 and 1968, while Ramsey Clark was Attorney General. Staffed largely by black militants working in the ghettos and headed by a black man, the Community Relations Service tried seriously to ascertain the grievances and needs of the ghetto residents at a time when virtually no whites or governmental officials really knew anything about daily life in the ghettos. The Service began to reach the black population and to arrange negotiations with city officials and business men that might have avoided further polarization, racial tension, and riots. With the accession to office of the Nixon administration in 1969, its already meager appropriation was further cut and its support in the upper reaches of the Department ended. It is revealing, nonetheless, that at the very time J. Edgar Hoover, Director of the FBI (also in the Justice Department) was strongly advocating forceful repression of black militants and charging them with subversive ties, a different unit of the Department should have been able, even feebly, to pursue a position sympathetic to the blacks and based upon the assumptions that the militants could in some sense represent the needs of ghetto residents and that only by developing some awareness of their grievances and demands could a violent racial conflict be avoided. The divergent organizational emphases reflected the divergent inclinations of many whites; and the far greater financial support for the FBI probably also reflected fairly well the greater strength in public sentiment for the repressive approach. Under Attorney General John Mitchell, the Department was even more sensitive to this repressive sentiment.

The experience of the Fair Employment Practices Commission created by Presidential Order during World War II supplements the lesson taught by the Community Relations Service about administrative responsiveness to black mass publics. Early in 1941, A. Philip Randolph, President of the Sleeping Car Porters Union and a widely known black leader, organized a March on Washington Movement to protest discrimination against blacks in hiring, promotion, and firing practices. President Franklin Roosevelt was seriously concerned both about the divisive effects of the threatened march upon a country just becoming involved in World War II and also about the grave diplomatic blow the march would represent in a nation he had recently described to the world as the "arsenal of democracy" and the protagonist of "the Four Freedoms." Accordingly, Roosevelt agreed to establish a federal Fair Employment Practices Commission authorized "to receive and investigate complaints of discrimination" both in government and in private industry and to take "appropriate steps to redress valid grievances." In return, Randolph canceled the march. The Commission and its staff spent the war years trying valiantly, and usually vainly, to end racial discrimination in hiring in some of the areas in which it was most blatant. Although there was a minor success with the Capitol Transit Company in Washington, D. C., Commission actions in its major cases were consistently negated at higher echelons, and in 1945 the Commission's appropriation was cut off. In this case, both the wartime manpower shortage and such egalitarian sentiment as existed explained the establishment and maintenance of the agency; but it could boast few policy victories and could not even survive the end of the war and the easing of the labor market it brought.

Some more effective agencies have served the interests of more specialized segments of the mass public for limited periods of time. Between 1936 and 1941 the newly-established National Labor Relations Board unquestionably promoted the economic interests of workers, especially those in the mass production industries: steel, automobiles, rubber, textiles, mining, and some others. The Board vigorously enforced the Wagner Act provisions requiring employers to recognize unions of their employees and to bargain with them in good faith; and it defined "appropriate bargaining units" in such a way as to facilitate the growth of industrial unions catering to semi-skilled and unskilled workers. The shock of the great depression and accounts of employer intimidation and terrorism of their employees elicited wide sympathy for workers in those years and also shook public confidence in the ability and good faith of management — an opinion pattern sufficient to support the policy directions of the NLRB in its first five years. With the striking growth in union membership, the decline in unemployment, and the onset of World War II this supportive climate changed, with the consequence that the NLRB began about 1941 to anticipate in its administrative policies many of the restrictions upon workers and unions later to be incorporated in the Taft-Hartley Act of 1947.

The thirties also saw the emergence of agencies serving the interests of poor farmers. The Resettlement Administration, later incorporated into the Farm Security Administration, promoted experiments in co-operation, especially among Southern tenant farmers, that for a time gave the latter serious governmental support and encouragement. However, these agencies also evoked severe anxieties that they were fostering basic changes in land ownership patterns, and so were demolished in the forties, largely under the onslaught of a bitter campaign against them by the American Farm Bureau Federation. The change in the climate of sympathy for victims of the depression and of interest in social experimentation already noted in the labor field had consequences in farm policy as well. This range of examples illustrates the close link between insecurity among elites and administrative support for mass demands and needs.

CONTEMPORARY PROBLEMS: SOME CASE STUDIES IN ATTEMPTED CHANGE

(1) Blacks and Racial Equality

Aspects of the socioeconomic situation of blacks have been reviewed extensively in Chapters 5, 8, and 13. We shall concentrate here on the attempts by blacks to bring about policy changes that would achieve greater equality with whites, and on both elite and nonelite responses to those efforts.

The civil rights movement emerged from the courtroom in the mid-1950's under the leadership of Martin Luther King, the Southern Christian Leadership Conference, and the Student Non-violent Co-ordinating Committee. With some limited but highly visible white support, Southern blacks began a series of chiefly legal and almost always nonviolent activities. Bus boycotts, freedom rides, lunch counter sit-ins, marches, and other forms of dramatic protest supplemented continuing efforts to exhaust legal barriers and integrate schools and other facilities. The presence of the major news media and the frequently violent reactions of Southern officials and citizens helped to build new awareness and support in the general public outside the South. It also kept steady pressure on the federal government. Congress was finally induced to respond with two voting rights acts in 1957 and 1960. They were loose, minimally funded, and difficult to enforce; but they were the first such acts since Reconstruction days. The Eisenhower administration established the precedent of committing federal troops to the enforcement of court-ordered school integration in Arkansas in 1957, a precedent which made it possible for the only slightly bolder Kennedy administration to secure similar victories in Alabama and Mississippi.

By 1963, the black population of the country, by normal standards of political participation, was deeply engaged in the effort to bring about greater equality of opportunity. According to one national survey, 33 percent of all blacks had participated in an economic boycott, 12 percent had marched in a demonstration, and nine percent had picketed a store.[1] Middle and upper income blacks had led the way, with 63 percent nationally (79 percent in the South) joining in a boycott, 44 percent participating in marches, and 23 percent in picketing. Participation in such activities on the part of leaders was even higher, and more than one-fifth of all leaders had already gone to jail at least once for their activities. Moreover, 49 percent of *all* blacks throughout the nation declared their willingness to take part in sit-ins, and 47 percent (63 percent of middle and upper income blacks) were willing to go to jail if necessary.

This is a dramatic mobilization of political effort. It was fueled not only by exasperation at continuing deprivation, but also by the conviction that white attitudes were improving and would continue to improve if only whites could be made to see the needs and the humanity of blacks. In the same 1963 survey, half of all blacks and nearly 90 percent of black leaders said that white attitudes were better than they had been five years before.[2] Black leaders in particular were persuaded that whites wanted a "better break for Negroes" rather than "to keep Negroes down," by better than five to one majorities.[3] Blacks generally saw local businesses and public facilities as determined to discriminate, but had great confidence in the capacity of the federal government, and particularly the executive branch, to help with these problems.

At this time, white majorities were generally sympathetic to the black cause, although their appreciation of what blacks were like and

[1] William Brink and Louis Harris, *The Negro Revolution in America* (New York: Simon and Schuster, 1964). All data in this paragraph are drawn from the tables on p. 203.

[2] *Ibid.*, p. 130.

[3] *Ibid.*, p. 126.

what they wanted tended to be stereotyped and formalistic.[4] Large majorities approved, at least in the abstract, of black peoples' rights to vote, to unrestricted use of buses and trains, job opportunities, and decent housing. Smaller majorities approved of further federal civil rights legislation to enforce these rights, and of the use of troops to back up court orders for school integration. Majorities recognized the fact of discrimination, but probably not the depth of the causes. "Equal treatment" seemed to be the way whites understood black goals. In retrospect, this probably meant equality of opportunity rather than the kind of equality of conditions or results that blacks had in mind. And there were visible signs of limits to the reality of equality that whites were prepared to grant blacks; more than half of all whites nationally were unwilling to have a black family living next door.

The change began in 1965. Another civil rights act had been accomplished in 1964, certainly the most sweeping of the mid-twentieth century sequence; it provided federal sanctions against discrimination in housing, jobs, public accommodations, and to an extent in schools as well. And a major voting rights act was enacted in 1965. But conditions of life for the ordinary black citizen were little if any better than a decade earlier, when this extraordinary effort began. All the talk, effort, public eloquence, legislation, and personal sacrifices delivered very little in the way of tangible change. All that was different was the form, not the fact, of discrimination and deprivation. In the Watts section of Los Angeles, for example, the five years prior to 1965 had seen rising rents, deterioration in housing conditions, and only the most marginal improvement in income levels. In other cities, unemployment in the slum areas where blacks lived was three times the national rate, and in several cities more than a third of such residents were either unemployed or underemployed (working part-time or at low-wage jobs while qualified and looking for adequate employment.)[5] The Watts riot of August, 1965, was triggered out of this smoldering situation.

Nearly simultaneously, younger black leaders began to resent whites' condescension and unconscious assertion of the superiority of their values, standards, and capabilities. Whites seemed to be saying through their attitudes and actions that blacks should emulate whites more, play the limited tactical game of familiar white politics, and thereby become integrated with white society on essentially white terms. Many of the younger blacks saw new depths to white racism in this set of attitudes. One of their responses was to insist upon black leadership in the fight for freedom, and upon the validity of black values and practices. Integration upon white terms, representing an act of condescension by whites, was rejected, and the "black power" slogan was coined. The reaction of the news media and eventually of the general white public to this concept, at that time neither known to nor accepted by blacks generally, was sharply

[4] *Ibid.,* p. 142. All data in this paragraph are from this source.
[5] U.S. Department of Labor survey, 1966.

negative. The idea of black power seemed to spark fears well beyond the intentions or capabilities of any of its limited tenets. In 1964, the proportion of whites saying that "Negroes have tried to move too fast" stood at 34 percent, with 32 percent saying "not fast enough." One year later, in November 1965, the comparable figures were 49 percent and 19 percent. In October 1966, they stood at 85 percent and three percent respectively.[6]

Urban ghetto disturbances, militant marches and demonstrations, and increasing pressure from blacks on schools and employment marked 1966, and 1967 saw an unprecedented wave of riots in city after city across the country. To some extent, the black struggle for equality had finally been carried to the cities of the North instead of localized in the South. Black leaders were also increasingly militant in their rhetoric, and much of the nation's press and other news media began to see "reverse racism" in Black Power or nationalist rhetoric. In any event, white resistance began to stiffen. The first groups of Northern whites to show determined resistance to further black gains were, perhaps understandably, those most likely to suffer as a result. In 1966 national surveys, Italian and Polish Catholics, generally residents of the class-level neighborhoods to which blacks were most likely to move and the people whose jobs would be made more competitive by black advancement, revealed serious concern and antipathy to blacks. More than twice as many members of these subgroups of the white population reported being uneasy about racial violence as did other, less threatened groups; they were also much more strongly opposed to the prospect of blacks moving into their neighborhoods than the others.[7]

The gap between black and white perceptions also began to widen at this time. Table 1 compares black and white perceptions of the causes of the riots of 1967, as determined by the Louis Harris polling organization. Whites saw outside agitation, where blacks saw social conditions (poverty, prejudice, lack of jobs, etc.) as the principal causes. Moreover, blacks understood that there were pre-existing grievances against storekeepers, where whites saw no more than a desire to loot. In response to the question of whether they thought demonstrations (*not* riots) had helped or hurt the black cause, whites moved from 51 percent saying they had helped in 1963, to 31 percent in June 1966, and only 15 percent in October 1966.[8] In other words, as early as 1966 practically all whites saw black militancy when reaching the level of a demonstration as counterproductive. In 1967, whites saw the riots as having been harmful to blacks' goals by the ratio of 22 to 1.[9]

But at the same time blacks, while not approving of rioting, nevertheless saw the riots as producing net beneficial results for blacks,

[6] *Public Opinion Quarterly,* vol. 32 (Fall, 1968), p. 522, citing Louis Harris survey.
[7] William Brink and Louis Harris, *Black and White* (New York: Simon and Schuster, 1967), p. 109.
[8] *Public Opinion Quarterly,* vol. 31 (Winter, 1967-1968), p. 659, citing Louis Harris survey.
[9] *Ibid.,* p. 662.

TABLE 1
Reasons for the Riots, 1967

Now I want to read you some statements about looting of stores during riots.
For each tell me if you agree or disagree.

1967: August 9	Agree	Disagree	Not Sure
The stores looted have charged Negroes exorbitant prices.			
National total	16%	47%	37%
By race:			
Whites	13	50	37
Negroes	50	14	36
White shopkeepers in Negro neighborhoods have gouged Negro customers.			
National total	18	43	39
By race:			
Whites	14	47	39
Negroes	58	11	31

What do you think are the two or three main reasons riots have broken out
in this country? Any other reasons?

1967: August 9	Nationwide	Whites	Negroes
Outside agitation	40%	45%	10%
Prejudice, promises not kept, bad treatment	19	16	36
Poverty, slums, ghetto conditions	16	14	28
Lack of jobs, unfair employment	12	10	29
Negroes are too lazy to work for their rights	11	13	5
Uneducated people, don't know what they are doing	11	11	9
Teenagers looking for trouble	7	7	7

Source: *Public Opinion Quarterly*, Winter, 1967-1968.

and were sympathetic to the rioters. Table 2 shows how blacks felt about the riots as of 1966. It seems clear that there is a realism born of understanding of conditions here, and that blacks have a far more optimistic view of the ultimate productivity of riots. A *Fortune* magazine survey of a sample of blacks in thirteen major U.S. cities not long after this provided further confirmation of black disapproval of, but also recognition of the probable utility of the riots. A total of 40 percent of blacks under 25 said that violence would be necessary to achieve black goals; one interesting feature of this survey was that more blacks currently earning over $100 per week agreed with this statement than did blacks earning less than $100 per week.[10]

[10] *Fortune* (January, 1968).

TABLE 2
Black Reaction to 1966 Disturbances

	Total rank and file	Non-South	South	Under 35 years	Leadership group
Riots have helped	34	32	35	38	41
Have hurt	20	26	15	21	19
Made no difference	17	23	16	15	18
Would join riot	15	13	18	19	1
Would not join	61	62	59	57	75
Think there will be more riots	61	62	61	66	79
Will not be	8	7	8	7	2

Source: William Brink and Louis Harris, *Black and White* (New York: Simon and Schuster, 1967). Copyright © 1966, 1967 by Newsweek, Inc. Reprinted by permission of Simon and Schuster.

This grim black realism about the efficacy of the riots was matched by an analogous white attitude. Asked in 1967 by the Gallup organization what should be done about *preventing* riots in black areas, as many whites chose one or another repressive measure as could think of an approach to improving the social conditions under which blacks lived. Forty-one percent of whites surveyed said that the police should use more force, while a similar number wanted to improve living or working conditions for blacks.[11] At the same time, 62 percent of another national sample of whites said that they favored shooting looters during a riot while only 28 percent disapproved.[12]

In 1968, the law and order movement came into full development. Majorities of whites continued to support economic opportunity for blacks, but to be strongly resentful of unorthodox ways of showing dissent or demands. Both Martin Luther King, the major black leader, and Robert Kennedy, the white politician on whom most blacks had pinned their hopes, were assassinated in the Spring of 1968. More riots ensued, but the great bulk of the white population had apparently turned against any form of disruption, regardless of the provocation. In the Michigan Survey Research Center's election study of 1968, less than 20 percent of all respondents supported the right of people to take part even in demonstrations "that are permitted by the local authorities."[13] Support for the black cause, though still legitimate in the abstract equal economic opportunity sense, had apparently been greatly eroded by a wave of resentment against the means of effectuating equality for blacks and the tactics associated with that cause.

By 1969, according to a national survey conducted by *Newsweek* magazine, large majorities of whites saw the United States as changing

[11] *Public Opinion Quarterly*, vol. 31 (Winter, 1967-1968), p. 675.
[12] *Ibid.*, p. 674, citing Louis Harris survey.
[13] Philip Converse, Warren Miller, Jerrold Rusk, and Arthur C. Wolfe, "Continuity and Change in American Politics: Parties and Issues in the 1968 Election," *American Political Science Review*, vol. 63 (1969), p. 1105, footnote 27.

for the worse, facing more racial violence, being too lenient with black militants, and failing to give sufficient power and discretion to the local police. Better than ten to one majorities called for stronger handling of black militants.[14] Whites had always refused to see police brutality as a factor in the riots, at a time when more blacks identified this as a cause than any other single factor;[15] in 1969, whites took even stronger positions in favor of repression. The *Newsweek* survey emphasized the feeling of resentment on the part of working class whites, whose earning power was shrinking, but who saw blacks as the recipients of special governmental favors.

Although there had been a civil rights act enacted in 1968, it had encompassed antiriot provisions as well. The election of 1968 ended executive branch emphasis on continued desegregation efforts, as well as any further prospect of legislation. By mid-1969, it was clear that the Nixon administration would not give black causes a significant priority. Soon the investigation and prosecution of black militants became of greater concern to the national administration, and police raids were initiated on several Black Panther headquarters. In one, according to the Grand Jury report, the police had first conducted essentially a vigilante raid — in effect murdering two sleeping blacks and wounding several others in a surprise attack — and then deliberately covered up with false reports to the press and public. Other instances of official violence against blacks, in Augusta, Georgia, and at Jackson State College in Mississippi, made it appear that the forces of "law and order" had declared open war on blacks. The federal administration took no action, in sharp contrast to its behavior in the 1960's.

What is to be learned about elite-mass relationships and the process of change from this sequence of events? No doubt this is a very special situation, with a very small minority (approximately 11 percent of the population) asserting demands that at least a substantial proportion of the remaining population does not understand or strongly opposes. The first series of pressures by blacks succeeded in moving the official makers of public policy into action. There was support from the great bulk of the public for such action; the existing value system offered considerable support for the black claim to equality, at least in legal and formal or opportunity terms. But elite responsiveness, never great, was soon slowed by growing white disapproval of the tactics used by blacks. In all probability, elites did less than they might have to further the black causes; in retrospect, however, there is little evidence to validate the idea that mass support would have been forthcoming for those elites who had ventured further in behalf of black goals. If there is fault to be assigned in this respect, it probably lies more with elite failure to have acted long before the 1960's to advance the idea and practice of equality.

Responding opportunistically, or realistically if one prefers, after 1967, elites for practical purposes dropped the black causes. Forceful

---

[14] *Newsweek*, October 6, 1969, p. 35.
[15] *Public Opinion Quarterly*, vol. 32 (Fall, 1968), p. 524, citing Louis Harris survey.

efforts might have succeeded against even the then-existing opposition; desirable or not, elites can usually institute their preferences if they are determined enough. But in this case they were not; the opposition was clear, and the movement was effectively reversed by 1969. Not only was specific assistance to blacks essentially terminated, but tacit encouragement was given to reactionary tendencies among both Southern and other law and order elements. Thus, even the underlying value change toward recognition of blacks as people with a history and deserving of citizenship, which was apparently underway from 1964 forward, may have been slowed or stopped.

It is difficult to say whether it was black resort to violence or inherent white racism that was the primary cause of the demise of the civil rights-black justice movement. But it is clear that racism is a real and enduring factor among whites of all status levels, and that animosities against minority use of violent tactics are deeply grounded. Racism is one of the major factors dividing elements of the lower classes and preventing them from coalescing around economic claims. Without the kind of fundamental value change that takes many years, the prospect of blacks reaching something approaching their goals seems very limited. Nor does it seem likely that, having once seen what might have been possible and been denied it, blacks will resume their former relatively quiescent role. The only likely alternative under these circumstances is continuing escalation of violence, with resulting polarization on both sides.

(2) College Students and the War in Southeast Asia

In many ways, the experience of those who sought to reverse the course of American policy in Southeast Asia duplicates that of the black movement, although of course the life situations and level of deprivation of the latter have never been experienced by white Americans. But the rise to some degree of popular acceptance, the failure to obtain any tangible results, and the subsequent degeneration into violent protest and swift negative reaction, is much the same. Both blacks and the antiwar movement had significant effects on policy; they achieved these effects, however, by a kind of inside route in which they affected elites, and not through the mobilization of broad mass support. Let us review the process chronologically.

In some important respects, of course, the political setting of the war in Southeast Asia presents a distinctive set of characteristics. As a matter of foreign policy, in which the armed forces were involved, it fell within that range of presidential discretion and initiative in which the Congress has not sought to assert itself. Given this traditional deference to the President, in part suggested by the Constitution's conferring of substantial power on the President as Commander-in-Chief, there were few ways to enforce limits on his actions. Moreover, neither Congress nor the general public had any reliable way of knowing for sure what the situation was like in Vietnam. In the context of uncertainty, the natural tendency is to accept what the supposed experts decide is necessary to be done; once the commitments were made and the necessity for them repeatedly portrayed to the public, the entire development of policy and events was seen in these terms. Not to trust one's elected leaders in an ambiguous situation would be a drastic departure from traditional patterns of behavior. Finally, the subject of Vietnam raised issues of patriotism, national prestige, and anticommunism. Once national honor was committed and troops deployed, many of these symbols became engaged. The presentation of the issues by the Johnson administration, of course, emphasized these aspects strongly, as a means of mobilizing support for administration policies.

Dissent from these policies began on the campuses as early as 1963, but was still relatively small in 1964. During that election campaign, the aggressive language of the Republican Goldwater made Johnson's policy and assurances about not sending troops to Vietnam sound moderate indeed. The war was not highly salient for the general public, with more than a third of the voters unable to answer survey questions about policy preferences for U.S. action in Vietnam. Of those who had preferences, nearly four times as many preferred "taking a stronger stand, even if it means invading North Vietnam" as wanted to "pull out of Vietnam entirely." [16]

In February, 1965, the United States began the bombing of North Vietnam. This was to be the first in a series of acts which campus dissenters perceived as escalations of the war and by which they were thus provoked into greater activity. The "teach-in" stage of antiwar activity then ensued, with many debates staged on campuses between administration members or supporters and prominent dissenters. It is even possible that the Johnson administration sought to give legitimacy to dissent in this fashion as a means of defending itself against what it expected to be the major pressure in the country — toward greater (and more dangerous) military action in the war.

As the commitment of American forces grew throughout 1965, and the draft began to cut more heavily into American life, the war became much more salient to the general public. In the fall of 1965, it was strongly supported, however, particularly by the better educated and higher status people. [17] The first major round of campus outbursts occurred in 1966, with disruptions of speeches given by administration members, and demonstrations and sit-ins directed at the draft. The dissenters were still a tiny minority, and the troop commitment in Vietnam was growing.

By mid-1967, there were half a million American troops in Southeast Asia, a series of urban riots had swept the country, repeated campus outbreaks were occurring, a balance of payments problem was developing, and mounting budget deficits indicated growing inflation ahead. Not all of these were related to the Vietnam War, of course, but they joined to create a context of turmoil and tension. Most of the campus dissent was directed at the war and the draft,

[16] Converse, *op. cit.*, p. 1086.
[17] See Figure 1 following.

and public opposition to the war was rising. Nearly half of the population now said that U.S. involvement in Vietnam had been a mistake, but college graduates continued to show support for the administration, and self-characterized "hawks" outnumbered "doves" by five to three ratios.[18]

A chiefly student-sponsored movement that sought to reach adult voters and affect the course of the war was generated in 1967 as a move to "dump Johnson," and in early 1968 it evolved into the campaign to win the Democratic nomination for Senator Eugene McCarthy, a prominent dissenter. In February, 1968, the so-called "Tet offensive" by the VietCong shocked Americans into the realization that military matters were proceeding less satisfactorily than most official accounts had indicated; the proportions of voters declaring that Vietnam had been a mistake rose to equal the number who still supported the administration's rationale.[19] In the first Democratic primary, in New Hampshire in early March, Senator McCarthy's student campaigners succeeded in getting 42 percent of the Democratic vote for their man, while President Johnson's write-in campaign secured 48 percent. The result was interpreted as indicating great antiwar sentiment among Democrats, and it set in motion a train of events that had immeasurable impact on the election in November. First, President Johnson announced that he would not seek renomination, declaring that this had been his intention all along. Peace talks with the North Vietnamese were started in Paris. Senator Robert Kennedy entered the campaign for the Democratic nomination, after much hesitation.

Subsequent analysis shows that the McCarthy victory in New Hampshire was only partially due to "dove"-style antiwar sentiment. The Michigan Survey Research Center found that New Hampshire McCarthy voters were indeed unhappy with the Johnson administration, but that a whole range of problems were on their minds. On the issue of Vietnam itself, those who wanted a *stronger* prosecution of the war outnumbered those who wanted to end it by nearly a three to two margin.[20] Among all Democrats who were interviewed in the national phase of the Center's surveying before the Democratic Convention, more McCarthy supporters eventually favored Wallace than any other candidate considered in 1968.[21] Thus it seems clear that many observers overestimated the extent of antiwar feeling within the electorate at that time in 1968. Well over half now agreed that involvement in Vietnam had been a mistake, but these totals must have included many who were simply frustrated at not being able to win the war faster.

The Democratic Convention of August 1968 represents the next major event in the expanding student-based movement against the war. Those who went to Chicago probably represented only a relatively small proportion of all students at that time, but the result of the

---

[18] See Figure 2 following.
[19] See Figure 1 following.
[20] Converse, *op. cit.*, p. 1092.
[21] *Ibid.*, p. 1093.

events in Chicago again had powerful effects on the nature of public opinion and the election itself. Public reaction against the demonstrators and in favor of the police was very strong, as we suggested earlier. Not even those who took "dove" positions on Vietnam itself showed significant support for the demonstrators.[22] Only one in six or seven whites felt that the United States made a mistake in getting involved in Vietnam and that the best course would be to pull out entirely. But even within this group, almost 70 percent denied that "too much force" had been used by the Chicago police, and the main body of opinion was that "not enough force" had been used against the peace demonstrators. Those who were against the war and sympathetic to demonstrations were a tiny minority of the population, about 3 percent. Most other people were adamantly opposed to the demonstrations. It is impossible to tell whether the violence that occurred in Chicago actually gained or lost support for the antiwar cause, but it is clear that it promoted much support for "law and order" candidates.

By the time of the 1968 election, much of the indecision of 1964 had of course been eliminated, and the voters had clear preferences on Vietnam. Table 3 shows, however, that there had not been a great

TABLE 3
Attitudes on Vietnam Policy, 1964 and 1968, Whites Only

"Which of the following do you think we should do now in Vietnam?
1. Pull out of Vietnam entirely.
2. Keep our soldiers in Vietnam but try to end the fighting.
3. Take a stronger stand even if it means invading North Vietnam."

	Pull out	Status quo	Stronger stand	Don't know, other	Total
Northern Democrats					
1964	8%	25	29	38	100%
1968	20%	39	35	6	100%
Northern Republicans					
1964	8%	19	38	35	100%
1968	20%	39	36	5	100%
Southern Democrats					
1964	8%	25	28	39	100%
1968	17%	36	38	9	100%
Southern Republicans					
1964	10%	18	42	30	100%
1968	15%	29	48	8	100%

Source: Philip Converse, Warren Miller, Jerrold Rusk, and Arthur C. Wolfe, "Continuity and Change in American Politics: Parties and Issues in the 1968 Election," *American Political Science Review*, vol. 63 (1969), p. 1086.

[22] Data in this paragraph are all drawn from *ibid.*, pp. 1087-1088.

reduction in the proportion of people who wanted a stronger stand. In three of the four categories, the proportion even went up. There were higher proportions favoring pulling out entirely, but they were still only about half as large overall as those wanting stronger action. The electorate, in short, did not turn against the war, and certainly not through the action of campus-based dissenters. The signs of revulsion against violent actions, and of trust in the established officials and practices, suggest instead the opposite conclusion.

Nevertheless, the proportions of the adult population who said that the Vietnam War had been a mistake continued to rise. As we now realize, this group is composed of both "doves" and "hawks," the latter presumably feeling that it would be better not to be involved in wars that we were not prepared to do everything possible to win. Figure 1 shows the trend in attitudes toward American involvement. It demonstrates that by late 1968 there was strong agreement that it had been a mistake, and that this sentiment continued into the first year of the Nixon administration. Nixon's own ratings remained high for the first year he was in office, showing particular strength after his November, 1969 announcement of slow but apparently assured troop withdrawals. His expressed commitment toward this end actually came earlier in the year, and may have accounted for the rise in proportions believing the war was a mistake. In mid-1969, 29 percent of the adult population favored immediate withdrawal from Vietnam, but this went down to 21 percent after Nixon's November speech, and back up to 35 percent in February 1970.[23]

The overall trend, apparently set in motion by the Tet offensive, the abdication of Johnson, and the McCarthy successes, saw the majority shifting to antiwar preferences in early to mid-1968. Figure 2 shows the trend in self-characterization of "hawks" and "doves," according to the Gallup Poll. But this pattern of nonelite preferences did not substantially alter support for existing institutions and officials in what were apparently perceived as their efforts to extricate the United States from the war. And it provided only the broadest kind of limits on the kinds of actions that the President and other policymakers might take; the latter remained essentially free to act as they saw fit under the circumstances, but to interpret their actions in terms of the prevailing opinion context. The Cambodian excursion, despite all the reaction it inspired on campuses, by itself did little to change this pattern.

In conclusion, it seems clear that most members of the general public continue to trust the established officials of government, and particularly the President, in this type of situation. They are strongly opposed to dissent and particularly strongly disapproving of violent dissent even where not initiated by the dissenters themselves; and they are subject to appeals based on patriotism, nationalism, and anticommunism. But these facts do not mean that the campus-based dissent of the 1960's was without consequence for the character of government policy. Quite the contrary; students had major effects,

[23] *Gallup Opinion Weekly*, March, 1970, p 9.

FIGURE 1
Proportion of Adult Population Saying U.S. Involvement in Vietnam Was a Mistake, 1965-69

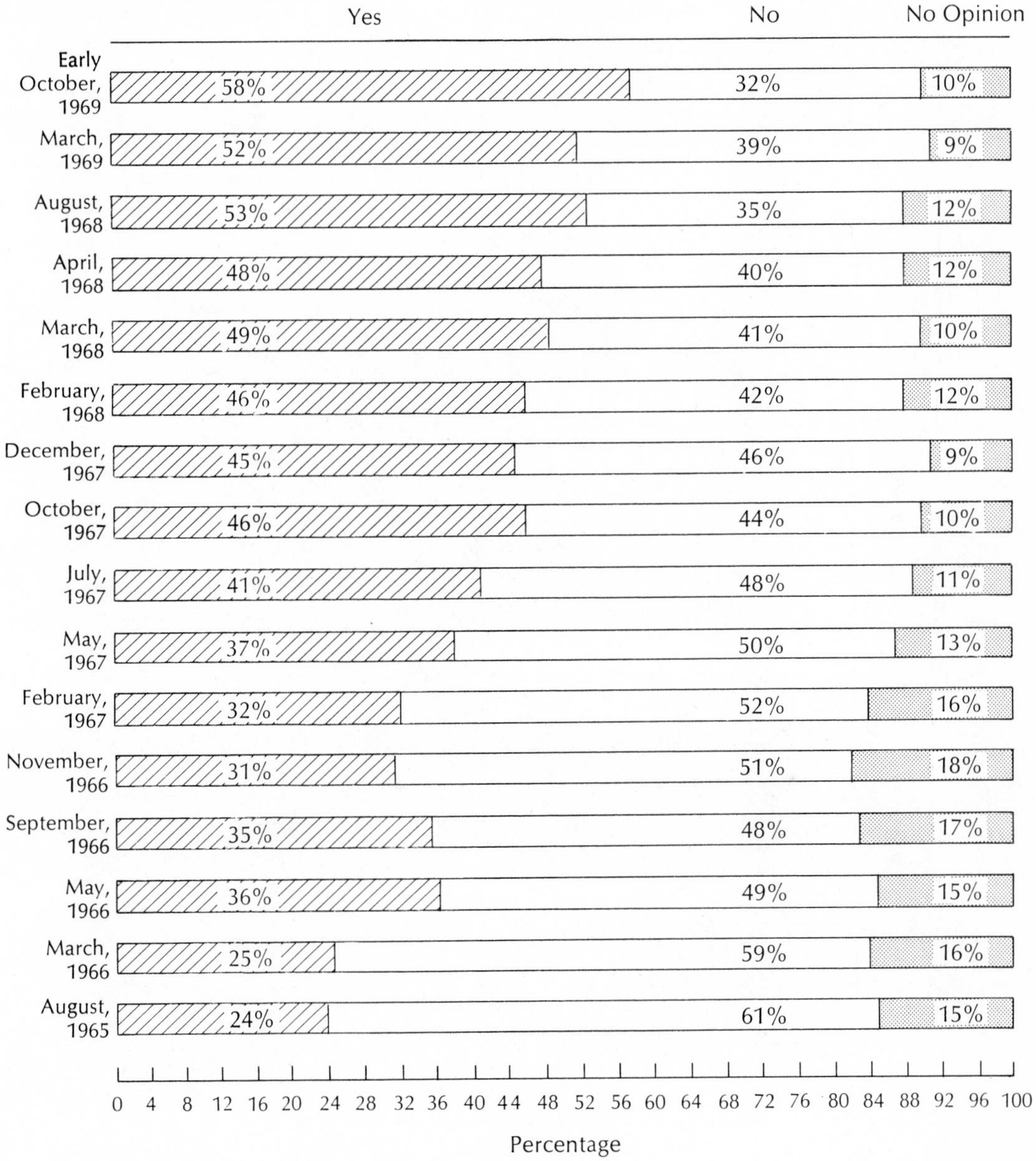

	Yes	No	No Opinion
Early October, 1969	58%	32%	10%
March, 1969	52%	39%	9%
August, 1968	53%	35%	12%
April, 1968	48%	40%	12%
March, 1968	49%	41%	10%
February, 1968	46%	42%	12%
December, 1967	45%	46%	9%
October, 1967	46%	44%	10%
July, 1967	41%	48%	11%
May, 1967	37%	50%	13%
February, 1967	32%	52%	16%
November, 1966	31%	51%	18%
September, 1966	35%	48%	17%
May, 1966	36%	49%	15%
March, 1966	25%	59%	16%
August, 1965	24%	61%	15%

0 4 8 12 16 20 24 28 32 36 40 44 48 52 56 60 64 68 72 76 80 84 88 92 96 100

Percentage

Source: *Gallup Opinion Weekly*, October, 1969, p. 14.

but on elites and opinion-makers, not on the general public. College students are at least near-elites, and men in power seek the approbation of rising generations and their prospective leaders. It is embarrassing, if nothing else, for government officials to have highly visible and continuing dissent in the citadels of culture and learning in the nation. The issue of Vietnam might never have been seen in the same

Figure 2
Pro and Con War Sentiment, 1967-1969

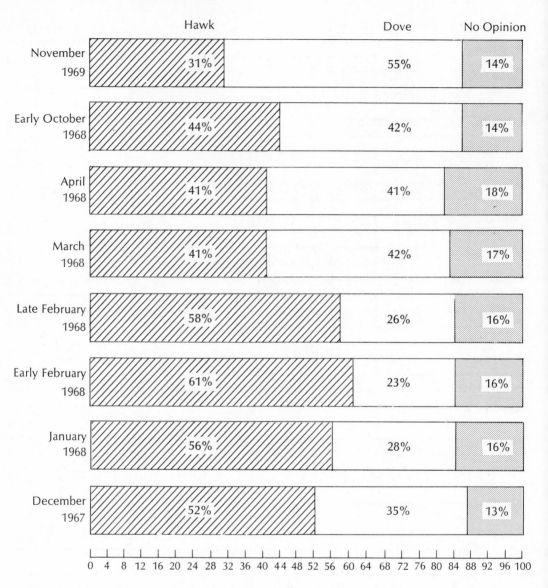

Source: *Gallup Opinion Weekly*, December, 1969, p. 8.

moral and ethical terms if these had not been emphasized from the campus, and government policymakers would have found it much easier to gain support for escalation of the war if it had not been for this student movement. The McCarthy candidacy, the Johnson withdrawal, and even the relatively moderate public posture assumed by President Nixon, are traceable in important ways to the movement. Its failure to sway most political spectators should not obscure its significant intra-elite effects. So too, the mere fact that some segment of the population is actually engaging in violent actions assumes the stature of a serious threat in the eyes of national elites both in and out of government. The danger they see is not in the capacity of the dissenters to bring about their goals, but in the fact of social chaos, and the prospect that other groups will respond similarly, thus endangering the structure of order and civility which they consider it crucial to maintain. Even if they care little about the Vietnam issue, therefore, it may be better to have the war ended than to have business endangered, inflation rampant, and repeated violence in the streets.

(3) Efforts to Control Military and Space Expenditures

This subject area presents another distinctive set of characteristics. No segment of nonelites is actively seeking to build support from other nonelites or to cause elites to change their policies. What active opposition there is to military expenditures comes from some liberal officials and a larger number of intellectuals — academics, writers, and political analysts. And yet, among the general public, there is substantial disapproval of military and space spending levels and strong opposition to the present mix of spending priorities. Lacking vehicles to bring about such policy changes, and experiencing substantial deprivation and other pressures, many working class and lower middle class people apparently are led to vent their resentments against the visible proponents of change in other government policies — blacks and college students.

Both military expenditures and space exploration funds benefit from the effects of national pride, patriotism, and anticommunism. The urge to be first, to be most powerful — and to beat the communists — is felt at all levels of the general public. But there is widespread agreement, shared among all class levels, that military spending is too high. In mid-1969, 52 percent of a national sample said that too much money was being spent for military purposes, 31 percent that military spending levels were about right, and only eight percent that they were too low.[24] Rich and poor, people with college and grade school educations, and all ages and races expressed similar views in almost the same proportions.

In the case of space expenditures, there is much the same basic position. Three times as many people wanted to reduce such expenditures as wanted to increase them in 1969, and a majority opposed attempts to land a man on Mars. On this issue, however, there were substantial differences between class levels. College educated and higher income people apparently believed that there were uses to the exploration of space, or simply were more interested in scientific adventures than lower classes. Table 4 shows the breakdown by income and education levels of support for increasing or reducing space expenditures. Lower income people clearly oppose even the present levels of space spending, in all probability because they see many higher priorities for the use of such money.

[24] *Gallup Opinion Weekly,* July, 1969, p. 11.

TABLE 4
Attitudes Toward Space Expenditures, February, 1969

"The U.S. is now spending many billions of dollars on space research. Do you think we should increase these funds, keep them the same, or reduce these funds?"

	Increase	Keep same	Reduce	No opinion
	%	%	%	%
National	14	41	40	5
Education				
College	19	51	28	2
High School	15	43	37	5
Grade School	9	29	56	6
Income				
$10,000 & over	22	48	27	3
$ 7,000 & over	19	49	30	2
$ 5,000-$6,999	15	37	42	6
$ 3,000-$4,999	7	33	55	5
Under $3,000	8	32	53	7

Source: *Gallup Opinion Weekly,* March, 1969, p. 17.

Confirmation that lower-income opposition stems from a strong sense that there are other higher priorities for government spending comes from an important national survey conducted in 1969 under the sponsorship of *Newsweek* magazine.[25] This survey questioned a large number of people in order to obtain a representative sample of all Americans earning between $5,000 and $10,000 per year, the so-called "middle Americans." The answers obtained regarding several alternative government spending priorities that this large majority of the population would like to see set, provide a context for some vital understanding of contemporary politics. These answers are shown in Figure 3. First, we may note that domestic economic matters, and then the "law and order" principle, dominate the list for which more government money should be spent. Defense, space, and foreign assistance are goals for which it was believed less money should be spent — and there is little question that these respondents ranked such expenditures very low indeed. A contrast of actual government priorities (Chapter 6) with those preferred by this large majority of people suggests a very large gap between elite and mass preferences, or at least between elite action and mass preferences.

But the level of "middle-American" dissatisfaction with current government spending priorities, and the resentments evidenced elsewhere toward violent dissent, should be seen together. They are both reflections of a severe and worsening economic squeeze, plus some

[25] *Newsweek, op. cit.,* pp. 35, 45.

FIGURE 3
Spending Priorities of "Middle Americans", 1969

"On which problems do you think the government should be spending more money—and on which should it be spending less money?"

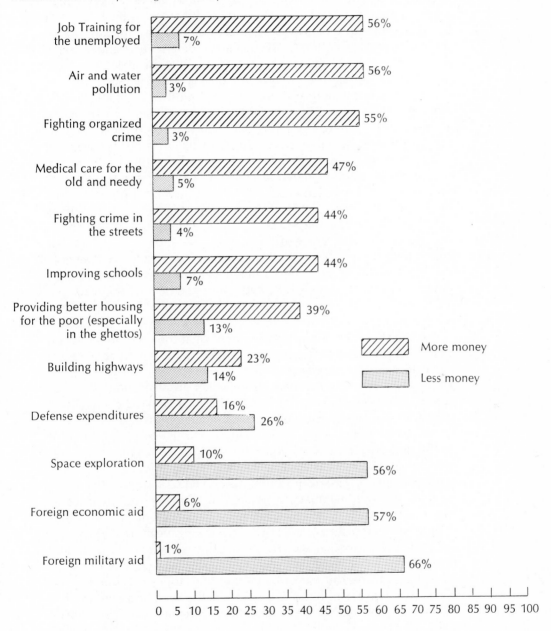

Source: *Newsweek*, October 6, 1969, p. 46.

other social pressures that focus particularly powerfully upon this large segment of the population. Inflation and rising unemployment have created just the conditions of economic insecurity that we projected in the first section of Chapter 13. The continuing war in Southeast Asia, in which neither victory nor withdrawal seem within reach, is a special burden, for it is within these income levels that the draft hits most heavily; the upper middle class makes use of student deferments, ROTC, occupational deferments, and Reserve deferments to avoid military service completely, or at least combat duty, but the children of "middle Americans" have no such options. It is the "middle Americans" too who are most directly affected by the rise of blacks, and by the pressure of government on behalf of blacks. It is their neighborhoods to which blacks are most likely to move, and it is their jobs which are most likely to be displaced by blacks. In this context, perhaps it is remarkable that support for economic opportunity measures remains high. This is particularly true, given the prejudices that still exist against blacks, and the assumptions that blacks could do something about ghetto conditions or lack of jobs if they really wanted to. Suspicions of "welfare cheaters" endure despite repeated findings that recipients are willing but unable to find work or physically incapable of it. Finally, we may note that the 1960's and 1970's *are* a time of at least *some* value change, though this may be more visible and publicized than widespread. The life-styles of "hippies" and other youth, particularly college youth, receive much media attention; so does violent dissent on campus and in the streets. Those who know only what they see on television or read in the newspapers may perceive the movement as a severe threat to existing values.

There appear to be no channels by which dissatisfaction with economic circumstances and the continuing war could be effectively translated into policy changes. Such channels as exist are dominated by the upper status levels, whose views are generally supportive of established government priorities and policies. The grip of the traditional values, orthodox procedures, and basic ideology concerning the superiority of American institutions, is still very strong. The status of elites and the legitimacy associated with their positions leads to trust in the system, if not satisfaction with its present policies. Anticommunism's appeals are still powerful. Lacking means of carrying out the policy changes that would improve the situation, many middle Americans instead focus their disapproval on the most visible groups who appear to be causing or benefiting from today's troubles — the black, the young, and the dissenter generally. Social class establishes distinctive perspectives, and economic circumstances exacerbate tensions; believing in the validity of the American system, the response is to take out frustrations on available symbols of the new age. As yet, these responses are only inchoate tendencies, actually acted upon by only a few. And yet they help to explain why nonelites generally experience such difficulty in generating impact on policy; quite simply, more time is spent on the subjects that divide than on the goals that might unite and provide greater benefits for all.

SOME TENTATIVE CONCLUSIONS

The three case studies of distinctive types of nonelite-elite interaction and opinion contexts suggest some preliminary implications. Several of these have already been touched upon in the closing paragraphs above and in the earlier sections. Elites are preponderant but not absolute; they can influence popular reactions, shape opinion fairly readily through particular types of appeals, and in some cases proceed in spite of popular preferences to the contrary. But they maintain their predominance through degrees of responsiveness, particularly in the face of popular mobilization in behalf of desired goals. Where events do not deflect popular demands and diversions do not fully absorb them, elites may undertake policies that would not otherwise have been pursued, or acknowledge constraints that they would not have accepted before.

But nonelites experience severe difficulty in disseminating information and mobilizing numbers of people in behalf of shared goals. Few people have much time, and fewer have the resources, for such activity; most people are economically insecure, vulnerable to a variety of symbolic appeals, and habituated to trust in the actions of others. It is difficult to perceive alternatives, harder still to overcome probable past rejections of efforts to affect policy. Real tensions and divisions exist between major segments of nonelites. Dominant political ideology insists that all works for the best, and that the American government embodies the legitimacy and traditions that justify obedience and support. And elites use their resources of legitimacy and coercive power to draw support for their policies and isolate and discredit their opponents.

These reflections suggest that significant nonelite impact on policy has several prerequisites. It requires a particular configuration of conditions so that (1) near-chaos is experienced by many people, but they are at the same time (2) detached from their commitments to the established system and (3) insulated against the effects of the natural divisions within their ranks. This set of conditions does not occur often, if at all. Chaos is most likely to come from severe recession or depression, accompanied by other pressures such as war or deep social conflicts. Detachment from the established system requires either profound failure or some other extended series of events that discredit officials and institutions alike and eliminate the sense of deference that most people have toward them. Elites can and must help with this process: repeated revelation of fraud or misconduct violative of widely shared values must be demonstrated. But elites must first make such mistakes. Repeated vigilante attacks on minority groups, if exposed by authoritative sources (e.g., the Chicago Grand Jury report on the Chicago police raid on Black Panthers in December, 1969), could succeed in undermining respect for authority and the credibility of the police. Insulation against the tensions borne of prejudice and conflict between subgroups of nonelites can only come about if there is some higher shared value, goal, or commitment that binds people together despite their differences. In our final chapter, we shall try to project the kinds of circumstances that might converge in such ways so as to make such conditions possible. But first, we must reach some integrated conclusions about the general structure of power in the United States.

POLITICAL CHANGE IN THE UNITED STATES IV

By this point, we have nearly completed the analytical phase of our investigation. From our survey of government policies and their consequences in four illustrative problem areas, we moved to an examination of the decisionmaking institutions and processes of the American political system. Working backward from the reality of what government is doing, we have sought explanation of why it has done such things.

But orderly description of first one aspect of American politics and then another, although essential to systematic understanding, does not by itself fulfill our needs and purposes. We must now seek to integrate our findings into consistent, comprehensive interpretations about how this system works, for whose benefit, and why. And then we must use such interpretations and conclusions as background for an assessment of the directions which this political system may and should take in the future.

427

In reaching these interpretations and projections, we shall be moving from analysis to evaluation. In the process, of course, the authors' own evaluative judgments and preferences will be intimately involved. Although we shall present plausible major interpretations and projections alternatively, our selection of alternatives and the manner in which we present them inevitably reflect our value judgments. For the record, therefore, we have explicitly noted our personal judgments at the close of each chapter. By this time, readers should be competent to select from, accept, or reject the views of textbook authors in the same critical manner as they would the views of others. If our readers are not yet alert to their own needs, and capable of being independent thinkers, then we have failed in our purposes in this book — and no doubt we would fail to persuade them of the validity of our own judgments as well. The two chapters that follow, therefore, though not polemics, are frankly value-infused interpretations of all that so far has been presented. They attempt to come as close as possible to reaching conclusions about the central questions of this book: Who rules, and how? How does change occur? What difference does it all make to the people and problems of the 1970's?

Patterns of Power 16

Before we can assess the prospects for various forms of political change in the future, we must reach some integrated interpretation of where power now resides and how it is wielded. The task of this chapter is to synthesize the separate analyses of problems, policies, ideology, structure, and decisional processes that have been developed in earlier chapters. Do they "add up," so that one or two consistent themes of power and its usage may be formulated? If so, what are these themes? Or are policies, values, and processes so disconnected, even unrelated, that the American political system responds unpredictably and unsystematically to shifting, *ad hoc* coalitions of officials, interests, and forces? Each of the many potential answers to these questions implies a particular spectrum of possibilities for the future; each suggests a distinctive set of prospects and tactics for political change. To omit (or to err in) such basic judgments is to risk irrelevance, the eternal danger of idealism in politics.

In broad historical perspective, events and actions may sustain a variety of very general overall characterizations. But we require a more concrete — and yet conceptually unconfined — interpretive base. We shall begin by retreating for a moment to reconsider the concept of power and the indicators by which we may recognize it in action. Then we shall examine some alternative judgments about the distribution of power in American politics which seem supportable from the evidence we have examined. Of course, some important questions remain open, because they have not been asked, or evidence is not available, or they involve evaluative premises about which observers are bound to disagree. We shall try to identify and illustrate some of these open questions, so that readers may begin to fit their own experience and observation into one or another of the alternative interpretations. Finally, we shall state our reasons for the judgments we now hold about our political system.

POWER AS APPLIED IN THE UNITED STATES: SUMMARY AND SYNTHESIS

The concepts of power and of politics used in this book are broad and inclusive. We first defined power as the use of resources in such a manner that others were induced to conform their behavior to that which the holder of the resources perceived to be desirable. This meant that we saw power as a *relation* between two or more people. There are always some people who are able to shape the behavior of others, sometimes even without deliberate intent; social life is a web of power relationships. For purposes of manageability, however, we did cut back our definition of politics to include only those uses of power having to do with whether and how government was to be employed in regard to any given subject.

The intent of thus casting our analytical net so broadly was to guard against developing excessively narrow or formalistic images of politics. The institutional framework of government, the authorized processes for filling positions within it, and the formal acts of public officials, though vital objects for study, are only a very small part of political activity. Accompanying them are deep and conflicting currents of value commitments, economic interests, and social aspirations. These and other continuing struggles mean that power is in constant use throughout the society. Occasionally, powerholders gain and hold their ends exclusively in private transactions, but frequently their power flows through government — shaping its policies and using government as another means toward their goals.

Power is a complex concept, open to almost infinite qualifying and categorizing refinement. Many such efforts result in distinctions which, if effective at all, serve only to channel attention away from the central question: which people hold the resources that enable them to achieve their goals and shape the behavior of others within the society? We did not draw any such distinctions earlier (such as between "power" and "influence," or between "power" and "authority") because they were unnecessary to our broadly inclusive purposes and use of the concept. From our focus on public policies and their consequences — on power in its applied form — "power" included *all* the various uses of resources, outside and inside of government, that culminated in government action or inaction. Because we are now about to take up various interpretations of the actual distribution of power among political actors in the United States, however, we should make two clarifying observations about the concept.

First, forms of power differ in character. In its most fundamental form, power involves physical coercion — immediate capacity to cause death or injury, imprisonment, or destruction of property. The much-quoted slogan, "power grows out of the barrel of a gun," is no more than a succinctly stated truism, albeit one sometimes forgotten. But coercion comes in many forms — economic pressures, social ostracism, legal harassment — which fall short of that ultimate stage. We may imagine a continuum of increasingly subtle forms of coercion, starting with physical force and culminating in the gentle types of social control practiced in some modern societies by means of ideological indoctrination and media management. The form, however, is less important than the fact of power. Whether the carrot or the stick is in use at any particular moment, it is still power that is involved; and if the activity has to do with whether or how government shall be employed, it is political.

Second, power may be distinguished as to its location within the society. In most modern societies, private persons and entities have or can develop power resources which enable them to accomplish many of their goals. But some resources are almost exclusively available to government officials. One of these is the entitlement, according to the established constitutional system, to take certain actions — such as to raise taxes, or prohibit strikes, or to do other things commonly associated with governments. This type of power is sometimes called "authority," and the acceptance by the people of an existing government's right to do such things is termed "legitimacy." The terms employed are not important, but the idea of certain resources and types of power being located only in one established government is. It means that the institutions and officials of government hold certain essential components of the total capacity for social control within the society. These components may be bestowed or withdrawn by the people, according to their judgments about how well the system is working, so that they do not exert a constant weight on the power scale.

Drawing these distinctions in this manner should emphasize the importance and the *nature* of the part played by government in men's struggles for their goals. A moment's reflection regarding each distinction shows that those who would achieve their ends have no choice but to merge themselves with government and use it as an agency for extending and increasing their privately-developed powers. In the larger contest for wealth and status, power is a tool, and government's power is a necessary tool. In the first distinction, we saw that the really vital type of power is that of physical coercion: the power to kill, injure, jail, or destroy the property of another man. *Legitimate* power to do this, as well as the physical means, rests with government officials. All other such uses of power, and all competing armed forces, are prohibited, defined, and punished as crimes. Government is thus the sole possessor of the most fundamental form of power — not to mention its unique capacity in regard to the lesser forms of coercion. Our second distinction, between private and governmental power, pointed up the fact that some powers are held only by governments. This means that private aggregates of power must often make use of government's independent power resources in order to secure goals unattainable exclusively through private action. But it also means that they must control government, if only to prevent it from being used by others to take away their gains. Where the means of applying power in its most fundamental form (i.e., the police and other military forces) are monopolized by government, it is imperative for those who aspire to wealth and status to control the uses of that power. Others too may seek to share in determining how government's power shall be used, and the struggle broadens. Thus again, government becomes the focal point of power usage in the society.

This discussion implies, again, that government cannot be neutral. It acts in response to the interests of those with the greatest power resources in the society. These powerholders experience strong inducement to merge themselves with government and use its coercive powers to serve their combined private and public ends. Who are these likely rulers? There is ample evidence about who holds the largest private power resources in any society, and this evidence could be used to show that they run the government. From readily available proof of sharp disparities in economic possessions and social status between classes, one might infer government by an upper class elite. Many studies do just this.[1]

But there are some important intervening questions to be asked, questions to which answers satisfactory to those who are most determined to view the United States as an operating democracy have not yet been given: (a) What proof is there that upper class elites, despite their comparatively vast power resources, actually *can* and *do* apply that power to control the government? (b) *Even if they do* (even assuming, for example, that their members or agents hold most of the key positions in government and dominate its policymaking), how do we know that their actions are not entirely consistent with the preferences of the people? In other words, these analysts would argue, there need be no inconsistency between elite governance and democracy.[2] The people may freely choose these leaders in elections, or the leaders (however chosen) do in fact accomplish what the people want, or should want, or both. These are demanding questions, perhaps born of ideological resistance to the idea that the United States might be controlled by an upper class oligarchy. It is extremely difficult to find the evidence necessary to prove elite motivation one way or another. But these questions do point to the fact

[1] G. William Domhoff, *Who Rules America?* (Englewood Cliffs, N. J.: Prentice-Hall, 1967).

[2] For a full discussion of these problems, see Peter Bachrach, *The Theory of Democratic Elitism* (Boston: Little, Brown, 1966). See also Jack L. Walker, "A Critique of the Elitist Theory of Democracy," *American Political Science Review*, vol. 60 (1966), pp. 285-295, and Robert A. Dahl, "Further Reflections on the Elitist Theory of Democracy," *ibid.*, pp. 296-305.

that those who reach the latter conclusion are making a substantial inference, i.e., that social background characteristics and economic interests control behavior. The inference seems plausible and likely to many scholars, but totally unjustifiable to others. The conflict has raged for decades, sometimes politely, but sometimes with real emotion, as befits a fundamental question of power and its implications.

We have tried to circumvent this scholarly controversy, and the real evidential problem it highlights, by the approach we have taken in this book. We did not try to identify power in the private sphere and then trace it toward possible merger with, control of, or pressure on, the institutions of government. Instead, we reversed the process entirely. We started with actual governmental policies and their consequences, and then reached back into the characteristics of the political system in search of explanations of these consequences. With sufficiently precise description of who benefits and who loses by the action of government over time, of the priorities actually operative in shaping these patterns, and of the manner in which values, ideology, structure and decisionmaking processes cause or reinforce them, we thought we might emerge with a viable characterization of how power is used and for whose benefit. If this characterization shows that power is used for the principal benefit, and consistently in the exclusive interest of the upper class whose members occupy most government offices, *then we are close to resolving the crucial questions of whether or not they use their power in accordance with their own needs and preferences.* In other words, we have characterized their *actions,* from which we can much more safely infer their motivations. Comparison with popular needs and preferences is then the only remaining step, and one presenting relatively little difficulty.

Our purpose is thus to identify the power structure of the United States through linking a description of the consequences of government actions to the interests and power of a definable segment of the society. To try to do this accurately and without becoming overwhelmed with insignificant or diversionary details, we shall concentrate on those dimensions of government policy which are most fundamental. Just as some types of power are more basic than others, so are some issues of politics more crucial than others. These are issues of the nature of, and control over, the major sources of power in the society — the basic framework of the economy or the police and military forces — and issues concerning the distribution of the major social and economic rewards available — wealth, racial equality, and so on. We have examined a total of four policy areas — military expenditures, poverty and racism, economic stability and growth, and U.S. policies toward the Third World. Our question thus becomes: what is there in the policies of the U.S. government in these areas which bears on these fundamental questions of politics?

Patterns of Policies and Their Consequences

We shall briefly review the substance of these policies, and then their respective consequences. In the earlier analyses, we saw that military expenditures far outdistanced appropriations for domestic social purposes, and that it is apparently much more feasible politically to reduce the latter during periods of budgetary pressure. Policies dealing with poverty and racism at first promoted some advances in both these areas, were then officially ignored, and only recently began to shift toward reduction of the deprivations which have evolved. But actual appropriations for these purposes have been small, the conditions of assistance many, and the path of action strewn with procedural obstacles. Efforts to maintain economic stability and promote growth are constant, but within a context of primacy for private initiative. Support for the corporate economy takes many forms: price supports, subsidies, loans, limitations on competition, tariffs, overseas assistance, management of the financial system. Policies toward the Third World are designed to build military barriers against communist countries, either through acquiring bases or by assuring that well-armed anticommunist governments are in power. Development policies insist upon opportunities for American businesses, either as investors or as trading partners, and thus implicitly urge capitalist economies upon those countries.

The outcome of military expenditure policies has been a vast military establishment, with strategic capacity for nuclear annihilation of the world several times over and domestic concern for preserving its status and resources. Research and development needs have forged a strong link between the military and scientific community, and social turmoil has recently led to development of domestic counter-insurgency capability and political police. The economic consequences of these policies have included development of a new and highly dependent aerospace industry, with contracts, employment, and profits concentrated in a relatively few companies and localities of the nation. The space program, closely allied to similar military, technological, and industrial interests, deepens this pattern of consequences.

Policies dealing with poverty and racism have made little headway against the problems which they seek to alleviate. The very modest levels of funding are responsible in major part for this ineffectiveness, though perhaps other reasons are to be found in the reluctance or resistance encountered from state and local governments. Substantial proportions of funds appropriated for improvement of urban slums, transportation, and other facilities ultimately have been found to benefit landlords, real estate developers, and contractors more than the "target populations." Many blacks are newly registered to vote, but segregation and discrimination in schools, jobs, and housing continue nearly unchanged. For one period in the 1960's, the income gap between whites and blacks actually widened. Anti-inflation policies, resulting in layoffs for the last-hired, least-skilled, and most expendable employees (usually blacks), threatened to counteract or wipe out all the limited gains that had been achieved. Indeed, the argument was made that the principal effect of national policies in the related areas of poverty and racism has been to lead supporters (and opponents as well) to the impression that much had been done for the black and the poor of the nation, and that others should now have their turn.

Economic stability and growth policies were highly successful in the 1960's (in terms of their premises and intentions), until expenditures for the Vietnam War generated a new wave of inflation. The income tax cut of 1963 in particular demonstrated that the economy could be sharply spurred by deliberate manipulation of incentives and of the ratio of government expenditures to revenue. The principal beneficiaries of growth-inducing policies naturally were the larger corporations and investors who were best able to take advantage of the incentives offered; in time, increased economic activity was felt in the form of rising demand for labor and consequent reduction in unemployment. The rise in real wages, however, did not keep pace with war-induced inflation. Efforts to control inflation through tight money policies, increased taxes, and reduced government expenditure began by 1969 to reverse the employment trend. With Vietnam War expenditures continuing, and with no government controls on wages or prices, inflation-limiting policies had the effect of inducing layoffs and unemployment again. Business activity of various kinds began to slow, and in 1970 government economists began to define the economic problem as a recession.

American Third World policies appear to have delayed nationalist social reform movements as well as an indeterminate number of actual or potential communist-supported movements which might have culminated in communist governments. Military assistance programs have been extensive — and apparently successful in their own terms — in a few countries close to the borders of major communist nations (e.g., Greece, Korea, Taiwan, Thailand, Turkey). Airfields, missile bases, and other military installations have been maintained throughout the world, with, no doubt, inhibiting (or, possibly provocative) effects on the behavior of other nations. Economic policies have helped U.S. investors and corporations to penetrate the markets of Western Europe and to enjoy favorable competitive terms and profit margins in less developed countries. In the eyes of at least some Third World nations, American economic policies have caused a widening of the gap in productivity and wealth between the developed and undeveloped worlds. And occasional military interventions in support of economic goals or in defense against perceived communist thrusts have led some such nations to see the United States as the major counter-revolutionary, status quo-preserving force in the world.

Patterns of Policy Goals and Priorities

What priorities and goals are visible in these patterns of applied power concerning fundamental dimensions of politics? In the military and economic dimensions, we noted that some policies could be seen as successful *in terms of their fundamental premises*. The success or failure of policies have importance chiefly as descriptions of their consequences; what concerns us now is the nature of the

premises upon which policies are based — a subject often left un-
examined. When analyzed, these unstated premises show some remarkable concurrence upon key principles, which in turn have
profound implications for the nature of the underlying power structure. *At all times, government policies assume that the existing organization, operations, motivations, and perceived needs of the American economic system must be preserved and furthered in every practical way.* No other premises or motivations evident in U.S. public
policies effectively displace this basic assumption. Nor can any goal,
however desirable in the abstract, be implemented effectively if it
conflicts with it. Recognizing this basic premise, government actions
and their consequences may be *understood* as a coherent, integrated,
and purposeful package. Without such recognition, they can only be
described with puzzlement at apparent contradictions and chagrin at
the mixture of successes and failures, hopes and frustrations.

The needs of the economic order are expressly applied in the area
of economic stability and growth. They are evident in development
policies, and again in military expenditures. The military establishment and the space program are also vital to such foreign policy goals
as limiting communist expansion and inducing developing nations to
adapt their economies to ours and reach more harmonious long-term
relationships. Anticommunism itself rests heavily on the desire to
protect the existing economic order and the values surrounding it.
Policies to combat poverty encounter resistance because they conflict
with other values associated with the economic system (self-reliance,
rewards according to effort and talent, etc.) and because they threaten
the distribution of wealth and power which that system creates. Racism lingers in part because stronger measures to enforce desegregation and equal opportunity would also run counter to economic
values (such as freedom to sell property or hire workers) and perhaps
disrupt current operations within that system. In short, although our
policy areas were chosen only because of their diversity and continuing social importance, actual government policies in each area seem
to flow from the same economic premises. What appeared to be
isolated, independent problem areas, each with a distinctive set of
problem characteristics and relevant political forces, now appear to
be overlapping, integrated extensions of a single unified set of policy
priorities and limitations.

Can we formulate a rough priority ranking of the values and goals
which dominate policymaking in these areas and perhaps in other
apparently "independent" areas as well? Clearly, economic values
and property rights are central among them. The right to a return
on invested capital, to be protected in the achievement of such return
by armed forces if necessary, and to the unrestricted use and secure
enjoyment of one's property, converge to impose imperatives for
government action overseas and to create imperatives for, and erect
barriers against, government action in domestic affairs. The United
States must stand firm against communism and in favor of an open
door in developing nations; it must maximize economic growth but
at the same time tread lightly in combatting poverty and racism be-

cause of these strong commitments. Associated with property rights are the allied economic values of materialism, profit-maximization, and the exaltation of productivity as a sufficient measure of societal achievement. Below this upper echelon of high-priority values are some reflections of them which have more general applications, such as anticommunism and the tendency to resort to military force if the dominant economic values are not being adequately served by other means. Still lower on the scale, and subject to a strong general commitment to the existing distribution of wealth and racial status, is the value of equality. Centuries of much rhetoric and some action have led to the achievement of real stature for equality, though it remains subject to the higher priority of other values.

Links to Underlying Values, Structure, and Decisionmaking Processes

In our earlier analysis of American political values, we identified several as historical contenders for ascendancy: property, equality, legalism, limited government, and so forth. In the extrapolation of values from patterns of policy consequences just concluded, we fashioned a rough ordering which may by extension lead to an operational (or *applied,* as distinguished from historically received, rhetorical, or symbolic) ranking of *all* American political values and goals. The central economic values which we identified and ranked as paramount need not have been explicit in the minds of policymakers at the time of enacting policy. Nor have we yet asked whether they are characteristic of any other group or segments of the population. But they are evident in several apparently independent policy areas and across lengthy time periods; whether implicit or explicit in the minds of policymakers, they seem to have been prime movers in the shaping of policies.

These chiefly economic values and goals, thus identified, may serve as a beginning framework for understanding the relative weights attached to other political values. The latter must be assigned lesser status in the hierarchy, and, most appropriately, according to the extent to which they are in harmony with and serve to further the paramount values and goals. Ultimately, we emerge with a serviceable and historically-grounded image of the priority ranking of political values which currently animates the American political system. In brief, it amounts to the protection and promotion of the American economic system and the distribution patterns it has established by various means culminating in military force; within this context, equality, humanistic justice, and majoritarianism contend with racism, materialism, and fixed procedures.

Just as patterns of policy consequences lead to an identifiable hierarchy of political values, so do both of these show consistent links with characteristics of political structure and processes. The constitutional structure and institutional arrangement of American government, for example, place limitations on the legal capacity of national, state, and local governments and disperse the total governing power across a wide landscape of levels and branches. The effects of this are to assure primacy for the private sphere on most questions. Those who are able to generate the greatest power out of private sources are able to shape the basic patterns of thought and behavior, because government is unable to act coherently in majoritarian interests. Instead, government is open to penetration by major private interests, which then use its many veto points to establish redoubts against the threat of change in the privately-established reality of economic and social life. Majorities of people are delayed if not prevented from achieving their common goals by their internal divisions and by the complex of procedures and limitations that must be transcended. For decisive government action to occur, it must either be entirely consistent with the limits and goals established by external powerholders, or there must be some highly unusual organizing force (such as an extreme emergency or a charismatic leader, or perhaps both) operating to unify the dispersed powers into purposeful applications.

Similarly, decisionmaking persons and processes operate with a set of imperatives and constraints that add up to reinforcement of the economic priorities. To begin with, many offices are filled by persons who had previously risen to high positions within the legal, banking, or business communities. Their orthodoxy seems assured. Even persons who achieve high official status from extra-establishment positions experience powerful inducements to adhere to accepted priorities. They are normally appointed to governmental responsibilities only because they have acted out their commitment to established values in some way. After doing so for some time, they may find that it is a natural and congenial set of standards with which to operate, and that it is also a way to avoid a rash of complaints from others in high places. More important, nearly every officeholder shrinks from the prospect of national unemployment or depression, and thus he finds himself committed almost by default to maintaining the growth and prosperity of the existing economy as a (if not *the*) major priority of government.

Many officeholders are thoroughly familiar with the need for good relations with major sources of wealth. Both political parties, and nearly all candidates for nominations within them, are able to compete effectively only through the support of large contributors. Major senatorial nomination or election campaigns now involve sums approaching $5,000,000 per candidate, and Presidential nomination-and-election sequences require hundreds of millions of dollars. Access to the mass media, if not the official support of those who own them, is essential to winning office. Officeholders thus learn the importance of economics early, and in a multitude of ways. Under these circumstances, their decisionmaking cannot help but reflect priorities that are essentially those of the established economic system. In short, neither structures nor processes are neutral in the sense of giving rise equally to any number of different patterns of policy. Instead, they contribute to reinforcement of the standards that yield this particular set of results.

In every major stage of analysis, this review suggests that the policy consequences we have examined are not the product of accident or coincidence. They reflect a consistent relationship between policies, values, institutional structures, and the officials and processes by which decisions are made. Each of these political factors independently contributes to, and in effect, reinforces, the primacy of property rights and the protection and promotion of the economic system as the basis of policymaking. But there is still a causal question remaining. Our evidence does not establish whether it is the politicoeconomic institutions themselves which dictate these results, the men who happen to hold power within them, or some external force such as extragovernmental elites (or, conceivably, the general public) which actually brings about the patterns we have seen. In other words, we have defined the consequences and apparent standards of power usage, but we have not yet reached the point of identifying the holders of dominant power who make these policies as they are. That is the task of the next section.

ALTERNATIVE INTERPRETATIONS OF POWER DISTRIBUTION

The pattern of consequences and of operative values may flow from quite different structures of power. We shall pose, and critically examine, three alternative interpretations: (1) power located chiefly in official government positions, whose incumbents respond to a mix of constituency and interest group pressures; (2) power extracted from both public and private resources by an establishment which seeks to shape popular preferences into forms which can be used to support its own basic goals and the system itself; and (3) power derived from private economic resources by a relatively few persons who influence government in their interest, using it to promote popular acquiescence, discourage resistance, or both.

Each of these interpretations seems to us capable of explaining the pattern of consequences described, if certain other conditions are taken to be true and other specific assumptions are made. None of them, of course, is likely to be entirely accurate. They are merely abstractions (not caricatures, we trust) drawn illustratively out of successive stages of a continuum of (a) increasing *concentration* of power in "private" hands, and (b) concurrently decreasing genuine *popular impact* on public policy. But they serve to suggest the directions which interpretations may take and the nature of the questions that must be resolved before final conclusions can be reached.

(1) Power as the Prize:
Competitive Pressures in the Governmental Arena

This interpretation denies that there is either a conscious, deliberate purpose *or* a unified power structure behind the making of national policy — except for those instances where practically the entire population is of a single mind on an issue. It holds that each area of public policy involves distinctive problems and separate sets of political actors and forces, such that each policy produced by government is the result of a unique and complicated process of interaction. Accordingly, each product can only be understood through an independent analysis focusing on the particular circumstances and the idiosyncratic features of the policymaking processes and people that were involved. In other words, policies vary unpredictably in substance, depending on what the men in office perceived, sought, and did, and on the complex of forces and circumstances that happened to exist at that time. By implication, if the public had strong preferences otherwise, or if the officeholders were different, or if the institutional mechanisms of government were different, the end results would also be different. This interpretation is essentially the image of power discussed earlier as "pluralism." It contains at least six major elements, each of which makes some necessary assumptions about the economic and social setting in which American politics take place.

(a) The political system is sufficiently separable from the economic and social systems in the United States that it may be understood chiefly through analysis of the behavior of men in the institutions of government and in the electoral processes by which they acquire such offices. This is partly due to an especially narrow definition of politics, holding that the latter is nothing more than activity in and around governmental institutions. Further, politics is self-contained, in the sense that practically all important factors influencing such behavior are included within those immediate surroundings. Analysts need never look beyond decisionmaking processes and elections, for nearly everything else is either irrelevant, not amenable to scientific study, or the province of some other social science.

But this restrictive definition itself flows from an image of *boundaries* around distinct systems of relationships — "economy," "society," "polity" — each of which is largely independent of what goes on in the other. It is this sense of detachment and separation which leads to images of "politics" as no more than the internal machinations of government and the official channels immediately surrounding it. Moreover, this same sense of boundaries leads to analysis of politics exclusively in its own terms. For example, it becomes difficult to distinguish major issues from minor issues except in "political" dimensions. Either all decisions appear equally significant, or the "important" ones are those on which the voters most often express themselves or on which the Congress had the longest debate. Those decisions which allocate the things most desired by people or most fundamental to the maintenance of the established economic and political order are not viewed as being any greater in importance.

(b) Government's independent power resources give it the decisive balance of power within the society and enable it to serve as the mechanism through which all other spheres of activity may be managed. Government responds principally to general popular preferences expressed in elections, and secondarily to the pressures of organized interests. Thus, it can become an arbiter between conflicting interests, or an agent of the general will, essentially in accordance with the people's wishes. This is partly because of the prominence and efficacy of the electoral process, where all men have equal power in the sense of one vote. But it is also because the equal power principle spreads further: the American economic and social systems either do not produce serious inequalities of power between individuals or groups, or those inequalities are not translated into effects upon governmental decisionmaking. In short, relevant private power is distributed roughly equally throughout the society. All groups have about the same capacity and opportunity to shape governmental action, and politics becomes a contest (nearly always decided by votes) for the right to shape the direction of government policies.

(c) The power of government is parceled out into so many component branches, agencies, committees, and offices that every significant interest within the society is able to gain access and affect the course of government action. Each locus of power within the framework of government is capable of delaying or preventing action. Government becomes in effect a much-elaborated system of checks and balances in which opportunities to veto action are broadly distributed, and affirmative action can be taken only when practically everybody concurs in the form it should take and its necessity. The society, instead of being a vast aggregation of individuals, is actually organized into a large number of distinct interests, most of which are represented by groups or associations. All of these have or can gain access to one or more of the many "veto points" among the institutions of government. Thus, there develops a harmonious linkage between governmental and societal structures, with the divisions in one paralleling divisions in the other.

(d) Government provides an arena within which the various interests in the society contend with each other for the often conflicting goals they seek. Public officials, because they control the use of decisive (governmental) power, must be at the center of these conflicts. They serve as brokers, mediating the differences between competing interests and helping them to find the necessary compromises. This is a broadly representative process because practically every citizen is or can be represented by one or more groups and thereby have his interests weighed in the process of policymaking. Conflicting pressures are applied to officials in roughly the same proportions that they are felt within the society. Divisions within the society are in effect translated into negotiable claims and adjusted; officials certify the accommodations through their authoritative support for one or another public policy.

(e) These accommodations are reached through a set of well-established procedures which assure fairness and opportunity to all; all groups share a commitment to making such a process a continuing reality. Compromises which are just and acceptable to all do not emerge by accident: they develop because of strict adherence to principles of procedural due process. These procedures call for full and fair hearings, consideration for others' points of view, and self-limitations where the larger system otherwise might be endangered. Each interest has an investment in preserving a setting where it can be confident of always receiving fair treatment; therefore all act to protect the fairness and openness of the procedures by which decisions are made.

(f) The brokerage role played by public officials in reaching accommodations, and the residual discretion which the conflicting-pressures situation permits them, means that the general public exercises meaningful control over the general direction of public policy through elections. Further, the system as a whole amounts to a stable, satisfied equilibrium of groups and individuals. The officials who serve as mediators of conflicting claims are either elected or directly responsible to those who are. The wide availability and equal weighting of the vote therefore allows the people to choose at least the broad priorities which will dominate in the government. The entire political system, though with some acknowledged imperfections and time lags, is thus tuned to popular preferences. And it is certainly controllable by the people if they care enough to exert themselves to do so. If they do not, it must be because they are satisfied with its operations. Support for the latter conclusion comes also from the fact that the many conflicting pressures within the society (both between opposed interest groups, and within an individual who belongs to two or more perhaps opposed groups) apparently operate to hold the entire society to the middle of the road. Extremes are avoided in this way, as the great majority of people insist successfully upon continued compromise and accommodation. In such a setting, faith in the workings of the established political system is likely to be and remain high.

These six components of the competitive pressures model make up a familiar and in many ways persuasive image of power in the United States. We all can point to many areas in which there is conflict between interest groups and others, and where government power is wielded by public officials to mediate and thereby further the public interest. Policy outcomes frequently do favor first one group and then another, and elections indeed often do set policy directions for the future.

But there are several barriers to acceptance of this interpretation. Some have already been suggested explicitly: it employs a very narrow, tunnel-vision kind of definition of politics, by virtue of which much of the usage of power in the world is omitted (particularly that which determines what can become a political issue, and in what form), and difficulty in distinguishing more important from less important issues is fostered. Others are implicit in our presentation: it rests on the extra-empirical conviction that the United States is an open, democratic political system in which all citizens play roughly equal parts in shaping government policy, and it strains to fit interpretation to this optimistic assumption. It never asks, for example, to what extent the American political parties actually present the electorate with the full range of possible policy choices at elections, nor to what extent both parties are controlled by factors other than popular preferences.

We shall consider two major criticisms of this interpretation. First is the charge that nearly every major assumption about the associated economic and social structures in the United States is wrong. And second, it is argued that this view fails to explain why a consistent pattern of policy consequences and operative values exists — unless one makes some very agile intellectual leaps or some very unlikely assumptions about the society we live in. It is the latter criticism that interests us most, for the former has been made often and with little effect on those who choose to adhere to this interpretation. But let us consider each in turn.

First, there seem to be solid grounds for challenging almost every assumption about the American social and economic structure which is essential to sustaining this interpretation of the structure of power. The social and economic systems are not separate from, but intimately integrated with, the political system. We saw earlier in this chapter, for example, that one could not rise to the top in the former without both acquiring the capacity to, and experiencing the necessity of, exerting power in the latter.[3] Inequalities of social status and economic possessions (and hence of the major resources of power) in the United States are too obvious and too widely documented to require much elaboration. Wealth, whether measured by income or by property holdings, is heavily concentrated in the upper twentieth of the population, with severe deprivation in the lowest third. Vast accumulations of economic power in the form of the great corporations are under the control of a relative handful of owners and managers. The social structure clearly represents these facts of economic life: a small upper class dominates the major institutions and controls the corporate economy, while a large middle class takes its cues from them. More than half of the population, however, consists of blue-collar workers, low-salaried office personnel (particularly women), and the unemployed and unemployable. This large proportion of the society is divided against itself, with whites resisting the progress of blacks and men defending their "prerogatives" against women, so that the upper echelons' preponderance of effective power is even greater than its share of wealth and official positions would suggest. Although each system — economic, social, and political — is "open," in the sense that some members of each rising generation are able to penetrate or be coopted into the upper reaches, the general patterns are *continuity* (those on top stay there) and *concentration and overlap* (those on top of one merge with those on top of the others). "One-man, one-vote" thus evokes a democratic illusion: power flows from many sources other than votes, and concentrations of power of various kinds regularly move into government and work their will through it.

[3] In part, this is a matter of definition of what constitutes "power" and what activities are "political." The reader should recognize by now that we are committed to broad definitions of both, and he should choose the definitions that strike him as most reasonable under the circumstances. But we do not stand solely on our definition for this point: the empirical verification is also extensive, and we think persuasive.

The critique responds specifically to each element of the model. (a) The disparity in power among elements of the society means that government is open and vulnerable to *some* special interests but not to others. (b,c,d) Not everyone is involved in or represented by an organized interest group. The interplay of such groups thus may be a contest, but only among the relatively more powerful segments of the society; it is particularly *un*representative of the powerless lower echelons. (e) The procedures are neither consistently applied nor productive of citizen satisfaction. Instead, they are selectively employed to advance the interests dominant in government, prevent significant change in the status quo, and legitimate coercion when considered necessary. (f) The general public is offered effective choices only between candidates and policies put forward by two political parties which are themselves subject to the entrenched power of the upper social and economic structure. Participation in such elections is very low, perhaps not only because of legal and cultural exclusions, but also because of recognition of the futility of seeking to affect action under these conditions.

This readily documentable characterization of the social and economic realities underlying the American political system suggests much less benign and self-congratulatory *value judgments* about its operation than those put forward by the pluralistic interpretation. At the very least, there are substantial grounds to doubt the propriety of terming this system "democratic." More important for our analysis, the crucial assumptions of the competitive pressures model concerning the surrounding social and economic structure seem to seriously lack *empirical accuracy*. And if it is *factually* invalid in these important respects, as well as dubious in its accompanying value judgments, the model itself appears to be undermined.

The second criticism of a pluralistic interpretation is that the consistent pattern of policy consequences and operative values which we have identified is left completely unexplained. This is a crucial point with profound implications for the validity of the competitive pressures model. The first criticism, examined above, has been made regularly, exhaustively, and with considerable evidential support. But it has not been accepted by some political scientists, because the linkage between social and economic inequalities of power and the actions of government have not been demonstrated to their satisfaction. It is not enough, in the eyes of those who subscribe to the competitive pressures model, to show that inequalities result in concentrations of power in the upper echelons of the population, and that these same people hold a very high proportion of the key positions in government. It must also be shown that such people (a) *actually use their power* to cause government to act in ways that are (b) *not only in accordance with their own interest, but also opposed to the public interest*. This is a high standard of proof, perhaps sought because of the deep desire to believe in the relatively democratic competitive pressures interpretation of power. It is not an illogical standard, only a very difficult one to meet amidst the understandable limitations on acquiring accurate evidence about the motivations of decisionmakers.

The evidence we have developed, however, permits this difficulty to be circumvented, and it responds to the issue of whether government action is shaped according to the preferences of private power-holders. Admittedly, our evidence is neither exhaustive nor even comprehensive, but the tentative inferences it permits stand in direct contrast to the interpretation of the structure of power which the competitive pressures model offers. We have seen the consequences produced by government policies, and we have extrapolated the value priorities which actually dominate government action. The central theme emerging was one of action in behalf of the preservation and promotion of the economic order, frequently at the cost of personal deprivations for many millions of citizens as well as denial of other values which are at least rhetorically exalted. Such actions were, however, entirely consistent with the interests and power of the upper echelons of the overlapping social and economic structures of the United States.

In the light of such evidence, it seems fair to draw the inference that the patterns discerned were brought about by *some* consistent and purposeful force operating through the government. We may then demand of alternative interpretations of the structure of power that they attempt to explain *how* this consistent pattern may have been produced. The competitive pressures model offers only happenstance, coincidence, or a deterministic explanation that somehow men's decisions, group pressures, and popular preferences all converged to produce this particular pattern. We think there must be more plausible explanations. It seems to us much more likely that there is some harmonizing principle or force behind consistent and regularly recurring patterns of policy outcomes that favor one powerful group in the population. Accordingly, we shall reject the competitive pressures model *except with regard to minor decisions,* and concentrate on the search for more plausible interpretations of the structure of power as it applies to the fundamental issues of politics.

Suppose that we accept the inference that *some* consistent and purposeful force is shaping government policies, and that there is unequal power inherent in the existing economic and class structure which overlaps into politics. What interpretations of the structure of power then follow? We think there are two major ones, which we shall evaluate after presenting each briefly.

(2) Power as Social Process: Establishment Orchestration of Econo-Political Life

This interpretation accepts the competitive pressures model with regard to minor decisions, though with less optimistic conclusions about government refereeing group conflict in the public interest and more emphasis on special interests' success in achieving their selfish goals. For major issues, however, such as the nature of the basic structure of the economic and political order and the permanence of the established patterns of distribution of wealth and social status, a more unified power structure comes into being. Various units and holders of power coalesce to form a coherent and nearly singleminded force capable of managing major sources of private power, the government, and the general public alike.

The "glue" that holds this coalition together and enables it to work so effectively in defense of the status quo comes from two primary sources. One is the class-originated shared values and interests of the establishment, itself consisting of a circulating group of men moving freely among the upper echelons of the overlapping economic, social, and political systems. These men are accustomed to holding and exercising power developed out of their "command post" positions. Their life experiences and current interests have led them to a strong commitment to orthodoxy and defense of the integrated economic and political structure. They see these values as synonymous with the public interest, not as self-serving.

The other source is the willingness of the general public, or at least the majority of the visible, audible, and active members of it, to endorse and support the actions of the major officials of their government. This acquiescence is built from many sources: faith in the institutions established by the Constitution, lack of alternatives, apathy, political party loyalties, hopelessness, fear of coercion. One of the major sources of this acquiescence, however, is the wide dissemination and effective inculcation of the familiar American political values and ideology — itself one of the major achievements of the establishment. From twelve or more years of schooling, to patriotic rituals, to media messages, the citizen lives in a context of symbolic assurances, materialism, racism, and benevolent rationalizations about how his government does and should operate. Embedded in this body of myth are the clear grounds of establishment dominance. At least some fragments of this belief system become implanted in the citizen's mind, available to be drawn upon in times of stress by the status- and legitimacy-exuding establishment.

Under ordinary circumstances, few major issues arise. Most public policies and private practices fit snugly within the approved contours of the established economic, social, and political systems, and special interests are free to seek their narrow ends within this context. When conditions change, and more basic questions are forced to the fore, the establishment begins to rally to the defense of the systems that have served it so well. Despite some disagreements about the best way to preserve the basic framework of the status quo (e.g., by yielding some further substance in the direction of greater equality versus "standing firm"), a consensus usually emerges with little direct consultation. Action then occurs simultaneously on many fronts to mobilize public support for particular forms of government action as the means to meet and "solve" the crisis. Taking their cues from the actions of the uppermost echelons, many lesser officials and associated elites (mayors, policemen, Chambers of Commerce, etc.) institute similar (or more drastic) policies and manifest their support for the general system-preserving program undertaken.

What looks like a consciously synchronized and coordinated movement may be no more than an elaborate follow-the-leader game. And what appears to be slavishly ideological mass support may be no more than silence amidst a failure of perceived alternatives. But the establishment seems to have managed the situation, and by so doing it improves its chances of succeeding again the next time — unless the social situation has reached a point where open opposition destroys the harmonious image. Then the issue comes down to the capacity to apply physical coercion to some without losing the public acquiescence and cooperation necessary to make the system operable.

(3) Power as a Tool: Economic Dominants Manage the System

This interpretation represents the end of the continuum at which power is most tightly concentrated in private hands and public impact on policy is least. It holds that economic resources are the paramount sources of power, and that those relatively few persons who own or control the uses of them are in a virtually unchallengeable position of power in the system. They set the operative values and priorities in their own private interest. They can direct the actions of men in government or, through control of the foundations, universities, and mass media, shape the attitudes of the general public. Normally, they provide only general direction, but when necessary they can and do assert specific control over areas of government action. A principal tool for thus managing the society (and in some respects, the world) for their own benefit is resort to physical coercion. Although efforts are made to publicly present this resort to the basic forms of power as necessary and desirable, the lower classes in particular are kept aware of the ready availability of government's police and other military forces because these are frequently used against them.

There is in this view a distinct structure of power — a more or less definable and self-conscious group of individuals, sometimes labeled "the ruling class." This group uses its extragovernmental resources to control nominations, elections, and governmental decisionmaking, not necessarily in specific terms but in the sense of maintaining general boundaries within which action may go on unrestricted, but beyond which rejection is swift and drastic. The motivations of this group are almost exclusively economic: maximization of the profits of the corporate economy. All areas of government activity are subjected to that overwhelming purpose. Nor is the need for government support limited to a desire to defend domestic prerogatives already established. Because of the pressing need of the current economy for new opportunities to invest surplus capital, there is special need for this economic class to exert control of government so as to use it to assure profitable opportunities in the developing nations of the world.

SELECTING AMONG ALTERNATIVES: QUESTIONS AND IMPLICATIONS

In at least one important respect, these two interpretations are in complete agreement: on all fundamental questions, a unified power structure is ready and determined to defend the status quo in drastic and effective ways. But in most other respects, they are quite distinctive. The economic dominants model in effect abstracts one dimension — the economic — out of the establishment orchestration model and erects it into a simpler, harsher characterization of the structure of power. The economic dimension is surely central to the establishment orchestration model, and the proper one to build upon if only one theme is to dominate. But the effects of doing so are to construct not only a different basis of power today but an associated distinctive set of implications for the prospects and tactics of change.

The economic dominants model sees power arising from economic holdings and tightly concentrated in private hands, with government as tool. The establishment orchestration model sees power flowing from several resources (of which economic strength is a major one), and thus spread more broadly within the upper echelons of the society. Decisive power in any situation may rest with an *ad hoc* coalition of establishment members, depending on the subject area, the dynamics produced by specific events and social conditions, the skills of strategically-located individuals, and the particular configuration of popular attitudes toward the government and the issue. Private power merges subtly with government's independent powers after an exchange in which men at the top act and draw symbol- and ideology-induced support for that action from key segments of the general public. Again, the result may be the same, but the process is different. The establishment orchestration model envisions a somewhat more open process, with interchangeable roles for a larger number of top figures, greater mutual dependence between men in and out of government, and greater reliance upon popular support more or less "voluntarily" extended.

The economic dominants model emphasizes economic sources of power and economic motivations on the part of the ruling elite, with capitalism as the source of the values and ideology that facilitate their management of the system. The establishment orchestration model is not only multicausal, but it sees an independently-generated set of values as more important than economic interests on at least some decisionmaking occasions. This belief system, perhaps originally influenced quite strongly by the nature of the economic system, is seen as now self-perpetuating apart from the specific needs of the contemporary economic order. Although it has a strong economic component, it is made up also of the heritage of Anglo-American legal thought, Judaeo-Christian religious postulates, and such elements as nationalism, patriotism, and equality. When the establishment acts, it does so on the basis of one or a combination of these various received values and beliefs. There is thus more room for uncertainty on its part, and greater need for confidence that key segments of the population concur and support it. To state the point from the perspective of nonelites, the establishment is more vulnerable to popular demands.

The economic dominants model assumes fuller recognition of the divergence of interests between upper and lower classes and a more distinctive set of values and ideology among those lower classes. Accordingly, although it too sees ideology-based manipulation as a convenient means of managing the masses, physical coercion plays a greater part in maintaining elite governance. In part because coercion is employed so regularly, the lower classes are kept aware of their different interests. Of course, the middle and upper classes are not normally cognizant of such violence and would probably assume it to be necessary and justified if they were. The establishment orchestration model tends to see lower classes as more fully captured by the values and ideology promulgated by the establishment, so that they do not clearly recognize the divergence of their interests from the middle and upper levels. Thus, management of popular preferences is easier. The underlying value system is a real contributor to the stability of the economic and political order because it teaches the population to "genuinely" want, accept — and defend — essentially what is in the establishment's interest. Physical coercion, though necessary at times, is a last resort. Further, indiscriminate use of physical coercion involves the risk of reducing support (and bestowed "legitimacy") from a people acculturated to revere due process.

The economic dominants model has the virtue of zeroing in on the central theme of power and presenting a clear and coherent interpretation of the American power structure. It permits clearer assignment of motivation and much greater apparent predictability of future elite behavior. The establishment orchestration model, although it posits the same results in crisis situations, envisions those results as flowing from a distinctively more complex structure and process. The differences are not insignificant, in the light of our concern for the prospects of change. Stated briefly, the most crucial issues are: (1) the relative solidarity and singlemindedness of decisive elites and the extent to which they are able to command, as opposed to being obliged to seek to acquire and develop, the power resources of government; and (2) the extent to which their management of the polity is accomplished through consent or quiescence manipulated or coerced from the lower classes, as opposed to drawing more upon apparently "voluntary" popular support. These are the vital open questions, for which conclusive evidence is still lacking. And much is at stake in the answers tentatively chosen.

The implications for change may already be obvious. If the economic dominants model is correct, elites are largely impenetrable by nonelites; nor is government a significant means of nonelite access to a share of power. But, at the same time, there is greater consciousness of divergence of interest and deprivation among the lowest classes. Under these conditions, there may be a continuing tension between the desire for change below and the rigid structure of power above. For change to occur, however, drastic reconstruction of the social order from below — by forceful means — may be the only route. However unlikely to come about, and perhaps unattractive to contemplate, no other method of change seems possible under this interpretation.

If the establishment orchestration model is correct, elites' incomplete domination of government, and their need for its legitimating power, opens an aperture for nonelite penetration. If representatives of such nonelites are successful in acquiring key offices and resisting cooptation as establishment agents, they may succeed in short-circuiting accepted practices or even in introducing new priorities. Because the underlying values generate broad and "voluntary" support for the existing economic and political order, and the establishment is genuinely dependent on this support for effective management of the system, two paradoxical results follow. The establishment becomes sensitive to the need to at least appear to satisfy changing demands among the major segments of the population, and may even be led to new policies by such changes. But changes at the level of values and ideology require long periods of education and demonstration, among the principal devices for which is the behavior of leading establishment figures themselves. One implication of this mutually reinforcing situation is that power relationships may remain apparently stable for some time, while shifts in underlying values are actually steadily eroding the bases of that power. When a dramatic event or condition sparks bold action by some establishment figure, he may encounter widespread approval and acceptance of his initiative, much to the surprise of all who remain steeped in the conventional wisdom.

Thus, under the establishment orchestration model, relatively peaceful change seems somewhat more possible. It does require a special convergence of men, events, and conditions, and even then it is likely to proceed only to modest lengths before enough popular demands are satisfied to reduce the situation to a manageable level again. Further, it requires a period of value change to bring broad segments of the people to the point where their desires induce some establishment members to act boldly in unprecedented directions. The few truly change-oriented representatives of nonelites who penetrate the establishment and remain uncoopted are not able to do more than raise the issue. Although this is a major means through which segments of the public can reach new priorities, it is only the latter's determined insistence upon doing so that will cause the rest of the establishment to agree to the wholesale modification of government policies.

Which of these two interpretations of the structure of power is the more accurate? Although we felt able to dismiss the competitive pressures model (except for minor decisions) as conceptually confined and evidentially unsupported, we noted earlier that available evidence left two major open questions between the latter two models. Readers may draw upon their own observations and experience, and perhaps succeed in filling these gaps to their own satisfaction. As may be clear from our analysis, we tentatively accept the more complex establishment orchestration interpretation. We acknowledge the revealing thrust of the economic dominants version, and view it as an often accurate portrait; and we are aware of the utility of clear and direct answers to the fundamental "who rules?" question. But there seem to us to be more currents of power at work, greater uncertainty in the ways in which power is mobilized and applied, and more (though by no means direct) effects of popular attitudes. For these reasons, our image of the American power structure — pending further evidence — is essentially that of the establishment orchestration model. Perhaps we are also affected by the contrasting implications for the nature and prospects of change; discouraging as it is, the establishment orchestration model nevertheless holds out some hope for a process of change which falls short of full-scale revolution. The latter, as we shall see, remains a possibility. In the next chapter, we shall look more systematically at forms of change and the conditions associated with each, accepting as our premise that the basic structure of power in the United States is that described here as the establishment orchestration model.

17 Political Change

This chapter addresses the crucial questions about the future of the American political system. Some are merely analytical-descriptive: Will there be change? What kind? Others are evaluative-prescriptive: What kind of change *should* there be? How may such change come about? These questions force us to develop some very crude theory of how political change does and can occur, given the political power structure and associated social and economic order now extant in the United States. Applying this general framework to circumstances as they develop, we can then generate some sense of what types of change are most likely and how to bring about changes which we may consider desirable.

We shall first construct our crude theory of when and how change occurs, and of what determines the form such change will take. In practical terms, our theory will be little more than a set of analytical categories which facilitate thinking about change; in some respects, however, we shall be specifying what factors and relationships among factors make change of various kinds *more*, or *less*, likely. Then we shall apply this framework to contemporary events in the United

States, in an effort to assess the probable end result of the forces now in motion in this country. Finally, we shall suggest what seem to us to be some imperatives about the process of change in the United States. Once again, readers are reminded that our analyses are necessarily infused with our own increasingly concerned value perspective, and that they should evaluate our work with their own critical judgment.

THE ANALYSIS OF POLITICAL CHANGE: A FRAMEWORK

When is change likely to occur in the structure or policies of the American political system? What circumstances determine what form it will take? Our approach is based on the premise that certain preconditions cause pressure to build up on the fundamental aspects of the political system. If they are strong enough, modifications of both mass and elite behavior follow, and — depending on the particular configuration of factors, forces, behavior, and events — political change of various kinds and directions then occurs. We shall take up three areas where the preconditions of change are likely to be generated and then identify some of the major questions which determine how much and what kind of effect such conditions will have on the political system. We shall then consider four alternative types of political change possible in the United States, and the prerequisites and processes that are associated with each of them.

(1) The Preconditions of Change

In one sense, political change is continuous. Governing elites regularly make adjustments in established policies, or undertake major policy departures, in response to changing conditions. Such changes may and often do result in alterations in domestic economic or social relationships or in international affairs. One example is the emergence of the Cold War foreign policy and the related evolution of massive defense and space programs — a segment of the economy being almost totally dependent on such expenditures. Another is the decision to institute a "war on poverty." But these are changes which we wish to term *marginal* because their essential effect is to defend and promote the established economic and political structures *and* the traditional outlines of existing patterns of distribution of wealth and status within the society. We shall reserve the term *fundamental* for those instances where there is substantial alteration in the economic or political power structures or in the key governmental policies which bear upon distribution of wealth and status. Fundamental change is change that is drastic in character; it may come about, however, through both violent and relatively peaceful means.

Our approach to the analysis of political change should permit us to distinguish between these two types of change, but be especially sensitive to the relative probabilities of the more fundamental type. *Marginal* change is frequent, requiring little in the way of preconditions. But *fundamental* change is infrequent and unlikely to occur without severe pressures which focus on the central concerns of politics and which are widely perceived and acted upon by masses and elites alike. Following our earlier analyses of the key issues of politics, we would expect fundamental change only when the preconditions begin to disrupt or seriously threaten the basic organization and operation of the economy, the class structure, existing control over the uses of government's coercive powers, or the established patterns of distribution of wealth and status within the society. The more the various preconditions generate such effects, the more probable are changes in the structure and uses of political power, the character of political institutions, and the key policies of government. In short, the severity of dislocations in closely related policy areas determines the probability of fundamental *political* change; we shall consider three such areas in order of their importance for political change.

(a) Changes in the level and distribution of economic prosperity

The most powerful source of pressure on the political system is the state of the economic system, for the obvious reason that it has to do first with the very survival, and then with other avidly sought goals of men in social settings. Despite images of stability, American politics has always been highly sensitive to fluctuations and dislocations in the economy; integration between the two systems is so intimate that political causes are alleged, and political remedies sought, for most perceived deprivations. When the economy is stable and unemployment limited, the political system is normally free of strain even though distribution of economic rewards is very unequal. But if either inflation or recession occurs, pressures begin to build up and distribution differences become salient and provocative; if a depression develops, pressures may become truly explosive.

Much conventional wisdom now holds that economy-managing tools are sufficiently available to government, and their uses well enough understood and accepted, to assure that rational manipulation can maintain a relatively stable and steadily growing economy. The implication is that fluctuations and dislocations are no longer inevitable, or even necessary. Thus, only miscalculation or deliberate obtuseness, perhaps for the advantage of some limited sector of the economy, can lie behind sustained periods of stagnation, inflation, or recession. Miscalculation is possible, of course. When war-induced inflation is countered chiefly by raising interest rates and reducing domestic investment, for example, the result may be continued impetus toward inflation on one level and simultaneously induced domestic cutbacks and recession on another. This seems to have occurred in 1969-1970. The effect was to raise the unemployment rate and create discontent among those blue-collar workers who bore the brunt of this squeeze.

But miscalculation is not the only route to severe economic dislocations in the late twentieth century. At least two other possibilities deserve mention as sources of the pressures that would promote fundamental political change. One is the "technological unfreedom" analysis, which holds that the economy can indeed be managed so as to produce a vast over-supply of consumer goods and technological comfort, but that this will, nevertheless, generate a substantial level of discontent. This discontent flows from the failure to produce the public goods — hospitals, recreation facilities, environmental amenities — which are necessary to human health, safety, and welfare. Consumer goods, material comfort, and leisure time may signify little if the air and water are too polluted, the roads and cities too crowded, and the conditions of life generally too unsatisfying for human enjoyment. Or discontent may derive more simply from the assumption that with all the long-sought material goods finally within reach one should feel satisfaction, but instead people experience frustration and unfulfillment. In either case, a severe reaction might set in. It could take the form of dissatisfaction with the standards and priorities of an economic order which could produce vast quantities of soon-obsolete consumer goods but not the public goods and human amenities that people increasingly seek. Or it could take the less rational form of a prolonged and system-changing assault upon those people generally perceived as presenting obstacles to the "good life" — under present circumstances, probably students, blacks, and the militant poor.

The other possible source of economic dislocation is serious depression. The economic system appears much more mechanistic in the interpretations and theories of economists than is actually the case. Not the proverbial unseen hand of Adam Smith, nor even the manageable equilibriums of John Maynard Keynes, but the human judgments of many more or less "rational" men and women, shape the workings of the economic system. Their wants and desires and expectations, and particularly their judgments about the shape of the future, are the forces which animate this system. If their sense of unfulfillment, or their perception of external events, or their pessimistic image of the future, should draw them away from profit-maximizing behavior, or from confidence in future profit-making opportunities, or from a high level of buying, the whole elaborate but fragile and interdependent structure of the economic system could come crashing down. This is why boosterism is such a vital element of American business ideology, and the gambling, risk-taking entrepreneur such a heroic figure in our folk myths, in spite of the fact that real entrepreneurs take great care to act only when their risks are minimal. The great danger is that savings will exceed investments, and large money surpluses find no job-creating outlets. Stagnation and joblessness, and then depression, might well follow soon after. Thus, continued prosperity and growth rest heavily on human factors, and more specifically, on optimistic assumptions about the future. In the absence of such faith (or the presence of pessimistic judgments), the result could still be a depression — despite all government efforts. And a depression creates an entirely new and highly unstable political situation.

It does so by seriously depriving very large numbers of people of things they want and need. At the same time, a social scientist must be wary of assuming that severe deprivation *inevitably* produces serious social instability, protest, or rebellion. As we have noted in several sections of this book, government not only influences what people get, but also what they expect to receive. It is one of the most awesome powers of modern governments that they have often been able to keep severely deprived people quiescent by creating in them a belief that their sufferings are in a noble cause or that they are only temporary: that even during a major depression, prosperity is "just around the corner."

(b) Social tensions and underlying value changes

A second — and potentially quite independent — major source of pressure on the political system is the rise of tensions and open conflict between major segments of the society. Such conflict is often associated with, and normally exacerbated by, rapid changes in the level and distribution of economic prosperity or other major technological changes. But it can also be generated by noneconomic factors and culminate in deep and widely felt animosities even during periods of economic affluence.

The tensions most likely to lead to the heaviest pressure on the political system are those which link current perceptions of deprivation to long-standing differences between segments of the population. If several such grievances overlap, so that the same people view themselves as constant losers despite being entitled to (and capable of achieving) their goals, the potential for serious conflict is high. For such people, the legitimacy of the established economic and political order may be called into question. They may feel released from normal obligations to obey and justified in the use of violence to gain their ends. Such action, of course, often promotes increased resistance on the part of their natural antagonists within the society. As polarization progresses, both sides become more ready to employ the most basic forms of power against the other.

Deep social divisions exist within the United States, rhetorical calls for solidarity and assertions of consensus notwithstanding. The most visible, long-standing and deeply-rooted of these is that of race. The extent to which racism is entrenched in the psychological makeup, political values, and institutional practices of white America may never be fully understood. But white-black/brown/red tensions escalate with every new assertion of the right to equal status. Should black militancy continue to rise, supported by similar claims from brown and red minorities, and should white intransigence assume ever more peremptory forms, widespread open conflict seems inevitable. The urban ghetto riots of 1965-1968 may be only the beginning. Nor could the political system long endure such outbreaks without moving either to cure the causes or thoroughly suppress the symptoms. In either case, a substantially different political system would emerge.

More productive of the prospect of fundamental change than the tensions created by the demands of relatively small and containable racial minorities are those which find their basis in class conscious-

ness. Suppose most blue-collar workers and other wage-earners —
black and white, men and women — should come to perceive themselves as being jointly exploited for the benefit of a small group of
owners and managers who already hold the vast majority of the
nation's wealth; justice thus entitles them to a much larger share of
the economic product. Their unified numbers alone would assure
great impact, if their power could be organized, led, and applied —
though that is difficult. The idea of such a movement will seem
undesirable or unAmerican to one who has been socialized into
dominant American political ideology. In the past, such class consciousness and assertiveness were discouraged also by legal impedi-
ments, economic sanctions, and physical intimidation or coercion.
Though forced to extreme measures, labor unions finally won the right
to organize and bargain collectively during the Great Depression
of the 1930's. Since then, class consciousness appears to have receded
or been diverted through images of affluence, war, or racial tensions.
If consciousness and militancy were regained, however, the potential
pressure on the political system would be severe.

Other sources of tensions exist, but none compare with race and
class as long-established antagonisms with continuing raw edges.
Religious, regional, and rural-urban conflicts remain real, and could
still contribute to steady pressure on the political system if particular
issues again raise perceptions of deprivation or create frustrations.
But new forms of tension unrooted in old divisions also exist. One
is the general lack of a sense of personal satisfaction that seemed to
pervade the United States at the close of the 1960's. Despite such
achievements as moon landings and the highest standard of living
in the world, many observers saw Americans as lacking contentment,
self-confidence, and a sense of purpose. Work seemed to be providing a less meaningful rationale for life, and to be less of a source
of pride, than previously. Individuals seemed to be sensitive to their
apparent powerlessness to affect the course of events, or even matters that affected their own lives. Their alienation took many forms,
from a concentration upon millions of hours of TV programming
every night in the isolation of their own homes to apathy and cynicism. The hopes of millions were attached emotionally to charismatic
political figures, only to be crushed in a staggering series of assassinations. A steadily rising crime rate, vast urban problems, and environmental decay combined with these developments to create near-
hysteria in many who looked seriously and empathetically at the
problems of the society.

Perhaps the most striking new tension-producing feature of American social life, however, was the new set of values developed by
intelligent and articulate young people during the 1960's. Contrasting
sharply with the materialism, nationalism, conformity, and support
for the economic and political status quo of their elders, the new
value system came to be termed a "counter-culture." Its priorities
were egalitarianism, humanism, participation, and self-fulfillment
through a wide variety of individual activities. These priorities were
acted out in various ways: many college students became heavily

involved first in civil rights and then in anti-Vietnam War activities, some in highly militant forms; others simply dropped out of what they saw as a competitive, materialistic society and adopted communal or hippie life styles. But the most startling form in which the new values were manifested was in the wave of disruptions and riots that struck American colleges and universities and even began to penetrate the high schools during the late 1960's. Viewing their educational institutions as microcosms of the society's hypocrisy, racism, and singleminded self-aggrandizement, many students demanded that their education be made relevant to analyzing the causes of, and solutions for, the social problems around them. They believed that the essentially rationalizing and supporting services the universities supplied to the society should be destroyed. To many in the older generation, for whom education was the route to social mobility and individual attainment under the established structures, the young seemed to be nihilists, anti-intellectuals, or romantic revolutionaries. The lines were sharply drawn, and the conflict often bitter.

These changes began to occur at a time when the society's technological advancement made it both highly competent and highly vulnerable. Capabilities existed for the production and use, for example, of much energy, high-speed transportation, and complex electronic information gathering and processing equipment. But outmoded and overloaded circuitry caused electric power blackouts, and people reacted against being managed by computers. Technology also permitted discontent to be manifested through the manufacture of mind-altering drugs and their potential use in municipal water supply systems, and of small but very destructive explosive devices that could be used against any number of vital targets. The defense of the society seemed to some to require surveillance nets that would provide warning of such actions or anticipatory police investigations that would permit identification of potential troublemakers at an early stage. Technology provided the means for effectuating such social control purposes as well. Thus technology contributes to the creation of conditions in which societal tensions can be readily manifested in drastic ways and becomes an independent source of pressure on the political system. Each new capability carries with it aspects of vulnerability and requires protections; when a society is already experiencing tensions, this process renders the latter especially volatile.

(c) International tensions and events

The obvious interdependence of international and domestic affairs means that events overseas often spark economic and social tensions at home. Such developments may link up with ongoing economic and social trends or they may generate wholly new types of tensions; they may serve either to generate great new pressure on the political system or to deflect already powerful pressures away from it.

The most obvious source of restructured domestic relationships is war, or the immediately perceived threat of war. A relatively small, festering war in a distant place, such as Korea or Vietnam, is likely to create new social divisions or added tension between left and right, at the same time as it promotes first economic well-being and then inflation. A full-scale war, or even a small war close to home, tends to draw wider support and to eclipse all other issues that might otherwise divide people. More complex effects emerge from the threat of armed conflict and from the development of a posture and an ideology that supports constant readiness for nuclear war, such as the Cold War, anticommunism, and the defense expenditures of the 1950's and 1960's. This creates underlying tensions at the same time as it legitimates many actions, and diverts attention from others, in the name of patriotism and national security.

But war and the threat of war are only the most obvious sources of disruptive tensions and the prospect of political change. Of more basic causal significance are the economic circumstances of both developed and undeveloped nations of the world. Depression or severe inflation in industrialized nations have their consequences on the American economy. Further, the availability of investment opportunities, raw materials, and markets in the Third World are of considerable importance to the stability and growth of the American economy. Sharp changes overseas — such as nationalization or severance of trade relations — may reverberate throughout segments of the U.S. economy and induce diplomatic pressure or military intervention to restore American advantage. International developments of a noneconomic nature may also have an impact on American life. The increasing militancy among American blacks during the 1950's and 1960's was due in part to the example of newly independent African and Asian nations, whose nonwhite leaders acquired power and led their countries effectively and with great pride.

This brief analysis of some sources of the intrasocietal tensions and conflicts which are sufficient to raise the possibility of fundamental political change is merely illustrative, and not comprehensive. No doubt there are many other causes of pressure on the political system. But our point is that there must be substantial pressures generated from *some* source before established econopolitical relationships are likely to undergo change of a fundamental kind. If there are several such pressures, and if they converge or overlap in such a way as to be mutually reinforcing (rather than pitting different groups against each other on each issue in a self-canceling and immobilizing fashion), the prospect of such change is greater. Any of the sources we have touched upon may be merely temporary, or one may cancel another, or all of them may be perceived as not having political relevance, and thus not eventuating in change. But without them or their equivalent, we see little prospect of any fundamental change.

(2) The Political Impact of the Preconditions of Change

The preconditions are thus necessary, but not sufficient, causes of fundamental change. What is crucial for our purposes is the manner in which such preconditions become translated into effects on the political system. Multiple sources of tensions clearly exist, some of them deep and others worsening. But there have always been some such tensions, and fundamental political change has not occurred in more than a century. Depressions and severe social tensions have given rise to militant parties and movements seeking fundamental change, but they have failed to achieve their goals. The sources of social tensions must not only produce converging and mutually reinforcing perceptions of deprivation, but these pressures must be translated into politics in particular ways before they are likely to generate fundamental change. We may identify several prerequisites that, if fulfilled, will make change of that order more likely to come about. Again, we see no necessary or inevitable requirement that all of these political effects be present in order for change to take place, but the prospect of change will increase to the extent that each is fulfilled. We shall frame these into three basic questions.

(a) How fully do existing dislocations, tensions, and underlying value changes disrupt established patterns of distribution and detach numbers of people from their previous commitments to the dominant political values, ideology, and behavior? *For fundamental change to occur, there must be shifts in the supportive attitudes of people toward their government; its legitimacy must erode in their eyes, and a vacuum of authority develop.* This is a long-term process, of course, and one which must ordinarily counteract the best efforts of the major socializing and interpreting agents (schools, mass media) of the existing system. It also requires visible, legitimate, leadership; but this is not likely to arise until the trend of popular change is already underway. Thus, the impetus toward change in values must be self-generated. Social and economic conditions, international events, or personal experience must create perceptions of serious personal deprivation which call into question the legitimacy or propriety of established political values and practices. Such perceptions of contradiction, unworkability, or inoperativeness in the present system must be strong enough to survive professed explanations and diversions, such as alleged failure of individuals, racial antagonisms, symbolic appeals, anticommunism, and so forth. Not one or two such perceptions, but an extended and cumulating series of them, will probably be required to bring people to the point of developing new priorities for political action and seriously considering alternatives to the present system. Without widely experienced doubts about established values, at the very least, proposals or movements for change will be ignored, dismissed, or resisted by the very people who constitute an almost irreplaceable component in the process.

(b) How much (and what kind of) power can be mobilized by change-oriented elements within the society, and how does such power relate to elites' power resources? Almost by definition, those who become cognizant of personal deprivation in such a way as to develop commitments to fundamental change do not possess large or immediately effective power resources. A few wealthy, well-connected, or strategically-located persons may identify with the causes of the deprived, and serve as leaders or key supporters. But most persons who currently hold major power resources are probably either already members of the establishment or at least persuaded that the basic structures and values are acceptable and only marginal change is required. *Fundamental change thus normally requires the mobilization of the latent power resources of the currently powerless.* Numbers become crucial; regardless of how slight their individual power, if a substantial segment of the population becomes committed to unified action in support of fundamental change, their joint power is immense. Strategic location within the economy or society is also important; effective strikes in vital service-providing fields (government functions, transportation, etc.) greatly multiply the power of relatively small numbers of people.

But the most crucial factors for mobilizing the powerless into a potentially successful force for fundamental change are *organization* and *communication.* Organization means the emergence of groups of people whose commitment is so complete that they subordinate all economic and other personal goals, and all factional interests of their particular group, to singleminded efforts to awaken numbers of other people to the need for (and prepare them for the action necessary to) achieving fundamental change. Organization-building requires a supportive environment for group members, so that their commitments are regularly reinforced and new members recruited. And it requires substantial agreement on (or at least only limited conflict over) the basic strategy by which change is to be accomplished.

The need for communication has both internal and external dimensions. There must be regular exchanges of information and effective coordination between the geographically (and perhaps in some ways, ideologically) separated units of the growing organization. And there *must* be communication between the organizers and the people whom they seek to mobilize. Unless those on whose numbers the generation of power sufficient to bring about change depends can be brought to the support of the organized movement, or at least detached from their support for established ways and thus neutralized, the movement has little real prospect for success. It will either gradually become aware of its failure and dissipate, or be forced into isolation and resort to indiscriminate terrorism or other desperate and self-destructive measures.

The task of mobilizing numbers of people into a unified, change-seeking force is very difficult. Previously inert individuals must acquire a sense of political efficacy and hope strong enough to project them into action. Various means of attracting attention and reaching people in terms that they can readily identify with and understand are necessary: action, deliberate self-sacrifice, rational persuasion, and blatant propaganda all play parts at various stages. As organization progresses, a series of minor skirmishes in which victories over established institutions or procedures are scored probably contributes to awakening self-confidence and determination. The point is that the bases of solidarity among people must be developed over time and against a background of suspicions, divisions, prejudices, and misunderstandings which have been built up across decades. Without the development of such organization and its promotion of broad support, fundamental change seems unlikely.

(c) How do established elites react to the forces seeking fundamental change? Because they hold the initiative and have responsibility to act in regard to events, existing elites' behavior plays a vital role in the evolving process of change. They may act to promote divisions and hostility within the population, and/or to isolate and discredit groups seeking change, thereby making mobilization difficult or impossible. They may appear to institute, or actually make, marginal changes in policies in order to reduce popular perceptions of deprivation, thereby undercutting (or, in some circumstances, promoting) the thrust toward fundamental change. They may introduce wholly new issues or appeals, such as space exploration, war, or the threat of war, which redirect attention or mobilize support for the existing order. Along with these or other basic responses, they may engage in active repression of change-seeking groups. If done with sophistication and restraint, this may help to solve their problem; but if crudely handled, it can provide the movement with substantial new constituencies.

In each case, it is clear that elite response shapes the opportunities and problems of change-seekers. What determines how elites act? In part it depends on which segment of the establishment is currently dominant within the executive branch. The Eastern upper class, the managers of the great corporations, and welfare-state liberals tend to react with modest policy changes, deflection, and sophisticated repression. Those newer to real power and more steeped in the ideology than in the practice of American government, such as the Southern and Southwestern individualist-conservatives, are more likely to react by exaggerating the threat, appealing to popular fears and prejudices, and escalating open repression.

Neither set of behaviors by itself determines whether the movement for change will *gain* or will *lose* momentum as a result. What it does, essentially, is to shape the degree of polarization in the society. When accompanied by the disaffection, tensions, and loss of legitimacy described earlier, and when there is a cohesive organization ready to act with substantial popular support, a highly polarized situation ripe for fundamental change may be created. What is then required is a spark — the fortuitous event that creates the opportunity for the movement to cross the threshold to real and sweeping impact of some kind. Then, if the existing organization has the skill (or the sheer determination, which often may overcome lack of skill *or* the absence of some important conditions) to apply its power decisively, the whole structure of power may be sharply altered. Again, this need not be through violent revolution, although violence undoubtedly plays a major role in promoting change that is of a fundamental nature. Established elites are quite unlikely to release their grip on governmental power unless convinced that it is necessary or inevitable that they do so. It has often been the escalation of the stakes that comes from serious and repeated mutual violence that has created such conviction. A relatively low level of violence, if sustained amid credible threats of more to follow, has sometimes induced elites to acquiesce in or even institute major changes sought in a relatively peaceful manner. Once the process of change has reached this point, developments are no longer even crudely predictable; the outcome depends on such factors as key individuals' personalities and chance happenings.

We can summarize these general distinctions about the politics of change in terms consistent with our earlier speculations about the difference between top-down and bottom-up processes of change. Thus far, we have been speaking chiefly of fundamental change and its prerequisites. This is because marginal change is almost always possible, at the almost exclusive option of establishment elites. To be sure, there are bounds within which such elites must select their policy options, but these are chiefly of their own making and only partially subject to popular preferences. In a fundamental change situation, however, elites have lost their predominance. They are either fragmented and beginning to contend with each other, or they are struggling to maintain themselves against the demands of a newly powerful antagonist arising from outside their ambit. Clearly, we are dealing with two contrasting levels and processes of change. Change initiated from the top down by established elites occurs because of their perceptions and needs, or perhaps through gradual changes in their membership; such changes are likely to deal with minor policies only, well within the established power systems — or, in short, *incremental* changes. Only when some thrust from outside the establishment (i.e., from below) begins to have an impact on elites' power and status does fundamental change become a possibility. The agency of change must be formed out of the previously powerless, and it must build upon deep social tensions and/or value changes to force its way into the political arena. The more such thrust is generated from below, the more the system itself is the target, and the more fundamental change is likely.

(3) Levels and Directions of Change: Four Scenarios

The summary above says nothing about the *direction* that either marginal or fundamental change may take. Clearly, either may go to the *left,* in the direction of wider sharing of power, wealth, and status within the society, or to the *right,* toward rigid insistence upon the status quo or an even narrower and more restrictive distribution of the same goals. A nearly infinite number of combinations of possible factors in the total political context could give rise to either marginal or fundamental changes in politically left or right directions. We shall reduce this wide range of possibilities to the four most likely types, briefly describe the features of each, and try to specify what determines the direction they may take. In what seems to us their order of probability in the United States today, we shall discuss (a) erratic marginal change — perpetuation of the status

quo with slight changes vacillating left and right but tending ultimately to an integrated and corporate-dominated econopolitical
system; (b) reactionary marginal change culminating relatively
promptly (say, ten to fifteen years) in near-fundamental change to a
system best termed totalitarian electoral fascism; (c) sustained marginal change with a welfare state emphasis, resulting after a longer
time span in something like democratic socialism; (d) revolution,
generated by a left-oriented movement out of certain conditions
associated with these processes, which would result in a more rapid
arrival at *either* fascism *or* socialism, depending upon unforeseeable
circumstances developing as the revolution took place. In each case,
we shall highlight those conditions and processes which our previous
analysis suggests are of key importance.

(a) Erratic marginal change, culminating in a corporate-dominated system

This scenario assumes that no major depression develops; that race
conflict will become even more salient but be more or less effectively suppressed through the isolation and containment of black/brown/
red peoples; that class consciousness remains low and the New Left
proves to be a small and transitory phenomenon, genuinely rejected
by workers and middle class alike and ultimately dissipated or suppressed; and that threats of nuclear war continue but no major land
war is fought beyond the Western hemisphere. In short, basic conditions create no major new dislocations and leave established elites
entrenched in power and with full capacity to orchestrate popular
support for whatever they decide to do.

Under these conditions, the level of perceived deprivation remains
not much higher than at present, the government retains its legitimacy
and authority, and established values are not seriously challenged.
Race tensions continue to be the chief source of social conflict, and
the mass of relatively powerless people is thus divided and dis-
tracted. In this context, the left is again ignored — in part because
disparate factions are engaged in steady conflict over the relative
validity of their diverse doctrines and strategies, and in part because
the left fails to speak to potential constituents in terms they understand. Established elites are relatively unthreatened, and thus able
to respond to what seem to them to be the most important needs
of the nation.

Because elites' concerns center upon continued stability and
growth of the economy, technological and other developments in
that sector provide the principal dynamic of change. More and more,
the continued success of the dominant large corporations (and thus
full employment and continued prosperity for most) depends upon
maintenance of conditions that require the use of government power.
The corporations need, for example, a steady supply of technically
competent bureaucrats and administrators, a predictable set of consumer wants and other conditions so that their long-term planning
is not disrupted, assured profitability of both domestic and foreign

investments, and so forth. Hence, government undertakes promotion of a particular kind of higher education, management of the basic conditions of social life, financing of research and development, underwriting of major risks through subsidies and guarantees, and military protection of overseas activities. And it repels all efforts to change such priorities.

Thus, elites perceive no acceptable alternatives to the growing (and, in the eyes of most, welcome) domination of both the society and the polity by the major corporations. Greater and greater integration between business and government occurs, until the two are nearly indistinguishable. Because established values remain unchanged, economic attainments are the principal measure of progress, and in any event a steadily rising standard of living remains an unchallenged necessity. Existing social problems will also be dealt with, but only when serious incidents occur and then as a second priority and in terms of their symptoms rather than their causes. Occasionally, special efforts will be made to draw popular support for space exploits, threats of nuclear war, or domestic "crusades" against the surface manifestations of problems that may be annoying many people. But the basic line of development will be an extension of the status quo, to the point where a corporate-managed society evolves. Conditions of life will not appear unfree or distasteful to most people, though to a small and permanent minority life will appear intolerably structured by the technological monsters of their own creation.

(b) Reactionary marginal change, culminating in electoral fascism

In this scenario, a sustained serious recession is avoided, perhaps through a new cycle of the arms race, but unemployment remains above the five percent level. This means that the lowest levels of the white working class, and all minority groups, feel the pinch rather seriously, but the middle class remains affluent and unaffected. Race conflict is exacerbated by such conditions, and class consciousness commensurately retarded. The next major source of social tension is some left-oriented political activity, based chiefly in militant black and some white radical enclaves. Because of the isolation of these groups, however, little value change occurs anywhere else in the society. International tensions escalate, partly because of stress upon anticommunism and the communist threat as justifications of expenditures for costly new types of arms and defense systems. The apparent failure to win the Vietnam War also contributes to a special truculence among Americans, many of whom remain convinced that their error was in doing too little, too late. Patriotic self-images and the need for world prestige are also heavily invested in relations with other nations and in space exploration.

Very little value change having occurred for most people, the behavior and expressed attitudes of the militant left appear the more incomprehensible and threatening. One reaction is a return to "fundamentals" for many, a more and more rigid insistence upon conformity to established values and orthodox practices. Claims by racial minorities are firmly rejected as unjustified as well as impractical, and governing elites legitimate such views by declining to support minority claims. Further, they tend to take an increasingly "hard" or "law and order" line with regard to racial outbreaks. Individualist-conservative elites particularly perceive all left groups, black and white, as presenting great threats to revered values. They therefore engage in exaggerated public attacks upon all forms of unorthodoxy, and in a variety of police harassment and prosecutions for every conceivable offense. Organization on the left proceeds very slowly and with great difficulty, as the fears and prejudices of much of the population are successfully mobilized against leftist proposals. The very security of the nation appears to be at stake and thus authorizes almost any measure in the name of patriotism.

The isolation of the left, and the blatant and provocative repression it receives from governing elites, gives rise to a series of guerilla-style terrorist actions. This in turn permits increasingly alarmed elites to initiate infiltration and surveillance on an even broader scale and to engage in even more unrestricted intimidation. The general public, itself alarmed by the previous elite appeals and the apparent reality of their dire predictions, tends to support vigorous repression as necessary and justifiable. Swept along by the hysteria, courts and juries join in finding the means to jail people suspected of unorthodoxy of action or intention. The Supreme Court, staffed by the nominees of the same elites, approves (and thereby legitimates) such uses of the police and judicial systems. The acknowledged vulnerability of the society appears to justify far-reaching supervision and control over behavior to prevent outbreaks.

At the same time, established elites recognize the necessity of promoting economic well-being, by which they mean serving the needs and preferences of various segments of the economy as fully as possible. Accordingly, they proceed much further than under the preceding scenario, actively insisting upon opportunities for American investment and trade in various parts of the world and employing American military power freely in behalf of such ends. Political opposition begins to fade at the same time. Because of their similar perception of conditions in the society, and of the trends among those in authority and among voters, few recognized political leaders seriously dispute the propriety of existing public policy. Elections thus become contests between candidates who all share the same basic commitment to repression of dissent and promotion of the needs of the economy at practically any cost. Regardless of the winning political party, and because of the inability to perceive any alternative to surveillance and repression, such policies once started thus become fixed, and can only intensify. In this manner, by the steady erosion of fixed standards of due process and fair procedures, coupled with rigid insistence upon the status quo, a police state evolves. We have termed the potential American version "electoral fascism" to denote also its grounding in popular support and its focus upon promotion of the present style of a capitalist economic system.

(c) Marginal welfare-state change, culminating in the long run in democratic socialism

This scenario posits some visible and continuing economic dislocation sufficient to bring a sizeable segment of the population — not just intellectuals and left organizers — to the view that something is wrong with the economic order. It could be an awakening to the technological unfreedom analysis, or a concern for conservation of a healthy environment, or a continued recession which reaches more than the lowest levels of workers. What is crucial is that it provide a basis for some degree of class consciousness or other shared consciousness of joint deprivation which is sufficient to overcome the divisiveness of group or racial conflicts. The latter, though hardly likely to mellow in any substantial way, could become somewhat muted in divisiveness if black/brown/red leaders began to interpret their plight in terms of the class or economic system rather than in exclusively racial dimensions. Young people would continue to be the sources of new, more egalitarian and humanistic values; for ever-increasing numbers of them, the older priorities would simply lack validity, and nothing could restore them. Vitally important to the convergence of these conditions in this direction would be the absence of war, for war would inject new obstacles into the path of a growing but fragile coalition which sought to span classes, ages, and races.

Considerable value change, gaining momentum annually as new waves of young people enter the society's mainstream, would make for a temporarily severe "generation gap." Before very long, however, elites themselves would be penetrated by the new standards, and key personnel at middle management levels would begin to see like-minded persons spotted throughout their areas of activity — including politics. Organizations of change-seeking persons would proliferate, venting their impatience with the recalcitrance of the established procedures by repeated outbreaks of violence. Unions in particular would regain their old militancy, as younger workers reinvigorated them, and waves of strikes demanding greater control over the conditions of work (not just higher wages and benefits) would take place. Widening agreement among both elites and the general public in the justice of such causes would inhibit elite repression, although some would occur. Elites would perceive themselves as severely threatened, and they would seek to undercut the new thrust by adjusting policies to yield marginally to the demands. In time, as each adjustment granted new legitimacy to the rationale underlying the demands, and more and more elites were committed to the new values, a major turning point would occur. The most likely of such events would seem to be a sweeping victory for the more progressive political party in an election posing clear-cut alternatives between the new and the old values. After that, major institutional changes (such as the elimination of conservative rules in the Congress) would be possible, and fundamental change could then ensue.

The essential nature of the change would be implementation of the reversal of value priorities: community, human rights, and aesthetic concerns would replace competition, property rights, and materialism. Structural manifestations would include effective political control and direction of the corporate economy, decentralized management of most governmental and productive functions, and widespread participation by ordinary citizens in various stages of policy-making and its implementation. Technological developments would be subordinated to questions about the desirability of their impact. Economic "progress" would be viewed in terms of worldwide, rather than domestic American, circumstances; redistribution of wealth within the United States would be steadily extended to a sharing of resources and productivity with other nations generally.

(d) Revolution, with the ultimate end of either fascism or democratic socialism

Revolution, though hard to contemplate in a heretofore highly stable, advanced industrialized nation where the means of large scale violence are thoroughly monopolized by government, is nevertheless a possibility that must be included. Revolution assumes substantial economic dislocation, at least severe recession, and perhaps depression, which would create wide unrest. Value change is thus not limited to the young, but occurs within a much larger constituency. But the young people must be united and serve as the principal moving force. Social tensions which place militant youth, black and white, in a position where they can join together and with at least some organized workers, are essential. Several factors might contribute to this effect: prolonged war, even a relatively small one; police harassment and blatantly repressive prosecutions; or repeated appeals to popular prejudices against nonconformity among youth. The crucial factors is that there be a continuing source of provocation that overrides racial suspicions and class differences and which brings youth together to serve as the nucleus of the instrument of change.

For such young people, and for those on whom economic, social, or world conditions operate similarly, value shifts are drastic. The government soon loses all legitimacy, and much restraint on behavior drops away. In response to the militant behavior of the young, polarization becomes sharp. Conditions nevertheless make some substantial segment of the population responsive to well-framed appeals by organizations built by the young militants. Major strikes in key industries and occasional victories in local conflicts mark the growing power and capability of the dissenters. Elite repression adds to the organizations' constituencies and causes the young people to seek ways to force more and faster change. At this point the situation is ripe for the final spark which can — if the organizations' leaders are perceptive and determined enough — eventuate in revolution. The spark would have to be so dramatic, and the response of major leaders and groups so indecisive or mutually conflicting, that an impasse would be apparent and police and military forces divided or immobilized. A hopelessly deadlocked Presidential election, repeated waves of bombings or other society-disrupting sabotage, or the imminent prospect of nuclear war, might be capable of providing such a spark.

These circumstances might be reached under either of the processes of change described in (b) or (c) above; the conditions assumed in process (a) appear unlikely to generate revolutionary circumstances. But marginal changes in the desired direction, because they involve similar though less drastic conditions than those that make for revolution, might have a catalytic effect upon militant organizations and induce them to attempt to force the process to its end in one swift movement. And the blatant repression associated with reactionary marginal change, of course, despite less favorable conditions, might persuade such groups that they had nothing to lose and trigger a bold attempt at societal disruption and seizure of power. If a total effort is made, with no reservations of any kind as to means or sacrifice involved, it might succeed. Actions limited to what is perceived as possible rarely exceed such bounds; but actions based on "impractical" aspirations sometimes achieve most of them, much to everyone's surprise. Once the attempt at revolution begins, of course, uncontrollable forces are set in motion. An effort undertaken in the absence of the conditions necessary to success can be totally self-destructive. Whoever mobilizes the means of violence most effectively emerges the winner. Their goals could be the faintly concealed fascism that appeals to many of the powers on the American right, or the democratic socialism that motivates the left. But revolutionary processes assure only that the old order will not survive, and there is no guarantee that what results will be an improvement on it. The result *might* be either fascism or democratic socialism; but there is no way to foresee the outcome until after the revolution has run its course.

These four scenarios are of course very gross characterizations, even abstract caricatures. Many more (and more highly varied) factors would be involved in each process, leading to a great variety of results that would fall between the ends described here. We have presented only a scattered representation of the range of the possible. But these four illustrations do show how some major combinations of conditions and processes might interact to produce particular forms and directions of change. Without *some* such image of what the process of change looks like, and what conditions are requisite to particular types of change, we cannot assess the implications of contemporary events in the United States. With such lines of probability in mind, we may be better able to foresee and affect our future.

PROSPECTS OF CHANGE
IN THE AMERICAN POLITICAL SYSTEM

Analyzing processes of change from a position squarely in their midst requires us to press our sketchy framework very hard and risk the most embarrassing errors. But this is precisely what citizens must do if they are to act in ways that will be timely and effective in shaping their world. We must therefore try to show how the constructs we have developed contribute to citizens' understanding and potential impact on politics. As in the preceding scenarios, we shall do so in terms of preconditions, processes and key contingencies, and probable end results. The question before us is, quite simply, where is the American political system heading in the 1970's? The answer requires not just prescient interpretation of weekly opinion polls and accurate forecasting of world events, but a combination of theory, widely divergent bodies of data, an intuitional sense of the core motivations and rhythms of American life — and remarkable good luck.

Preconditions

At least the early 1970's appear to be marked for greater economic difficulties than were experienced at any time during the 1960's. The Vietnam War continues to promote inflation but government fiscal and monetary controls seem to have generated a recession and rising unemployment in most sectors of the economy. Some of the growing impetus of the ecology-environment movements appears to reject the classic standards of productivity and progress, substituting for them new limits on corporate freedom and demands for public goods and other amenities of life. The Third World is increasingly resistant to high yields on American investments and special trade advantages for American companies. Declining confidence in the future profitability of the economy is evidenced by conservative policies on the part of business and investors. These unsettled conditions appeared likely to persist under an administration committed to both the continuation of the Vietnam War and prevention of inflation exclusively through fiscal and monetary policies.

Social tensions in the United States are at the highest level since at least the depression of the 1930's, and perhaps since the Civil War. Race conflict is deepening, as white resistance gains the tacit (and sometimes explicit) support of the national government, and blacks become more isolated, frustrated, and volatile. Class consciousness is still slight, and frequently barred by racial divisions and other distractions. But it nevertheless seems to be reviving, and could spread if economic conditions worsen sharply. Young people as yet show no signs of reverting to the traditional values nor to the privatized, materialist quiescence of the 1950's. The level of tension is manifest in a variety of incidents too bizarre to be dismissed: repeated bombings, and resultant fortification of police stations in some cities; continuing mass confrontations between militant left or right organizations and established authorities over welfare, segregation, housing, transportation, and other issues; regular assassinations, bombings, and other attacks on prominent figures, usually nonconformists; and open police violence against selected establishment-challenging targets. It does not seem unduly alarmist to say that this might be the first stage of societal disintegration.

Although the Vietnam War appears to be cooling as a source of public unrest, both it and the basic policy it represents remain a potent source of increased tensions. Revival, extension, or repetition of this provocative war could cause redoubled protest. At the same time, withdrawal or the appearance of defeat could lead to a strong reaction from the right. Even if the war merely levels off for the long pull, perhaps with the aid of a switch to a less visible, voluntary army, it will continue to drain resources away from domestic social needs. Tensions will also be spurred by increasing Third World resistance to American penetration; greater reliance on military force and perhaps recurring interventions will be necessary — with all the domestic consequences implied in such action likely to follow — unless the basic principles of United States policy are changed. Further, the need to justify new expenditures for weapons and defense systems by means of exaggerating fears of Soviet and Chinese capabilities will generate the dual consequences of, on the one hand, waves of anticommunism and security-consciousness, and on the other, sharply increased international tensions.

Political Impact

These already serious, and perhaps potentially explosive, conditions are still working their way into the political life of the nation. A substantial segment of young people, but still clearly a minority, appear to have developed distinctive new values and priorities. But they remain essentially surrounded by continuing commitments to established values, practices, and systems of power — or perhaps by total inattention. Though the "silent majority" is in most respects either a meaningless term or a figment of powerholders' imaginations, neither is there any clear manifestation of widespread withdrawal of legitimacy from existing institutions. Malaise, uncertainty, and uneasiness surely exist, but they are not yet strong enough to pull large numbers of people away from habitual patterns.

Nor have the young people yet created the organizations that appear capable of effectively building a unified change-seeking movement. The peace movement remains basically a single-issue, middle class activity. Many of its adherents remain committed to the familiar economic and political systems and see only a single unwise policy which requires correction. The ecology-environment movement is (at the moment, at least) similar; it aims at correcting specific abuses, often without questioning the values or priorities which created them. Both serve to engage people, and perhaps to heighten their political awareness for a time, but only a relatively few become committed to fundamental change in the economic and social order as a result.

The largely middle class (and white) origins of campus-based dissent have also inhibited effective communication with working class people and blacks. The issues that can be the basis of enduring coalitions have not yet been found, though some militant union organizing efforts have been successful. Movements for decentralized local control of government functions, particularly of police, also have the capacity to unite disparate groups and have scored some successes. These efforts have special significance because they begin with real personal grievances and proceed to show new constituencies that the prime causes of their problems lie in the nature of the economic and political power structures. They may also point the way toward resolution of one of the most troubling problems of left-oriented movements: divisiveness and doctrinal quarreling among groups with very similar goals for the society. Bitter conflicts over analyses of political dynamics, strategies for change, and specific tactics often occupy leaders' and intellectuals' energies. Some groups spend much of their resources in self-distinguishing or self-justifying activity rather than in gaining new adherents and building a broad-based movement. The difficulties of bridging the gap between blacks, students, and workers are very great, perhaps insurmountable; continued debates over the best way to do so, however, have the principal effect of postponing the day when serious attempts are mounted.

But by far the most powerful factor inhibiting organization of change-seeking movements is the ferocity and scope of repression which such movements suffer, now and in the past, at the hands of governing elites. The contemporary wave of "conspiracy" prosecutions for widely varying forms of dissent, and the systematic attacks on the Black Panther Party, are only the latest illustration of a recurring cycle that reaches back to the Alien and Sedition Laws of 1798 and the Abolitionist Movement of the early 1800's. Men in government have always used the law, the courts, the police (and other military forces when needed) in concerted fashion to discredit and destroy movements seeking fundamental change. What marks the current official campaign against dissent, however, is the scope of investigative activities and facilities brought to bear: infiltration, surveillance, and anticipatory "preventive" actions are now regularly practiced not only by state and federal agencies, but also by the armed forces and in regard to admittedly lawful political activities. There is very little that cannot be rationalized and accepted as necessary and justifiable for the preservation of the system by people who remain loyal to it and are persuaded that it is endangered. But if government acts in no more consistent and honorable ways than those whom it attacks, it may succeed where change-seekers have not and destroy its own legitimacy in the eyes of the people.

Because repression and appeals to popular fears and prejudices have worked so well before, some elites employ these techniques deliberately and at the first sign of threat. In doing so, they gamble that the polarization produced will be so overwhelmingly supportive that the isolated dissenters will be crushed. But where economic conditions are undeniably unsatisfactory, or the repression crudely conducted, it may produce a reaction by some people in support of the dissenters. Or it may weld quarreling groups of dissenters together in ways they could not have achieved for themselves. The latter effect may now be occurring.

In summary, it seems clear that the left is weak, neither well nor cohesively organized, and subject to growing repression. The right is no better organized; but with substantial influence in government, it has no need to be. The prospects for left-oriented change may be expressed in terms of three contingencies. In question form, they are: Will the American economy resume its stable growth and continue to be satisfying to the needs of most, given the world, domestic, and internal circumstances with which it is now faced? Assuming some degree of economic dislocation, can elites direct the discontent of the lower classes at the militant young and blacks in such a way as to contain them? Assuming that neither the money nor the will to solve the racial crisis can be found under the present (or perhaps any) system, can the resentments of blacks be contained or suppressed without creating system-altering consequences of some kind?

Prospects

As may be apparent from the foregoing, we are pessimistic about the future of the American republic. Tensions are high and climbing, but the signs point to change in directions that we deplore. No amount of unity-seeking rhetoric or patriotic ceremony surrounding the two-hundredth anniversary of the Declaration of Independence can change the realities of deprivation and repression which people can see and feel. If inequality persists (as we expect) and change is sought but prevented (as we expect), only force can — *and will* — maintain the treasured "law and order." We see the United States in the early 1970's as poised somewhere between (a) erratic marginal change eventually culminating in corporate-dominated society, and (b) reactionary marginal change moving steadily toward electoral fascism. The welfare-state process of change is a fading possibility, with revolution rising in its stead — but it is hardly threatening.

What can alter this set of probabilities? Only drastic changes of conditions, we would say: sustained recession or depression, another small war in a Third World location, mounting social disintegration, or other dramatic events. Not even crude elite repression can unify and render potent a movement that has no deep public discontent except racial hatreds on which to build. Americans, gripped by race fixations and with one-tenth of the population semi-legitimately and forcibly confined in a subservient status, may simply be unable to cope with any other major problem. Race conflict, escalating from time to time and likely to continue to do so, both inhibits political coalitions across race boundaries and periodically supplants all other political concerns. The odds are that this factor will prevent all fundamental change except toward greater and greater suppression of blacks and their isolated white supporters. With this dynamic as the central motivator of political change, only one or another form of police state seems likely to evolve.

As analysts, we estimate probabilities. As citizens, we deplore our own estimates. As actors in politics, therefore, we must seek to maximize the chances for some more desirable result. That is why we do what we can to build an independent, active citizenry and to urge it to undertake steady and effective efforts toward change.

Appendixes

The Declaration of Independence

The Unanimous Declaration
of the Thirteen United States of America

When in the Course of human events, it becomes necessary for one people to dissolve the political bands, which have connected them with another, and to assume among the powers of the earth, the separate and equal station to which the Laws of Nature and of Nature's God entitle them, a decent respect to the opinions of mankind requires that they should declare the causes which impel them to the separation. — We hold these truths to be self-evident, that all men are created equal, that they are endowed by their Creator with certain unalienable Rights, that among these are Life, Liberty and the pursuit of Happiness. — That to secure these rights, Governments are instituted among Men, deriving their just powers from the consent of the governed, — That whenever any Form of Government becomes destructive of these ends, it is the Right of the People to alter or to abolish it, and to institute new Government, laying its foundation on such principles and organizing its powers in such form, as to them shall seem most likely to effect their Safety and Happiness. Prudence, indeed, will dictate that Governments long established should not be changed for light and transient causes; and accordingly all experience hath shewn, that mankind are more disposed to suffer, while evils are sufferable, than to right themselves by abolishing the forms to which they are accustomed. But when a long train of abuses and usurpations, pursuing invariably the same Object evinces a design to reduce them under absolute Despotism, it is their right, it is their duty, to throw off such Government, and to provide new Guards for their future security. — Such has been the patient sufferance of these Colonies; and such is now the necessity which constrains them to alter their former Systems of Government. The history of the present King of Great Britain is a history of repeated injuries and usurpations, all having in direct object the establishment of an absolute Tyranny over these States. To prove this, let Facts be submitted to a candid world. — He has refused his Assent to Laws, the most wholesome and necessary for the public good. — He has forbidden his Governors to pass Laws of immediate and pressing importance, unless suspended in their operation till his Assent should be obtained, and when so suspended, he has utterly neglected to attend to them. — He has refused to pass other Laws for the accommodation of large districts of people, unless those people would relinquish the right of Representation in the Legislature, a right inestimable to them and formidable to tyrants only. — He has called together legislative bodies at places unusual, uncomfortable, and distant from the depository of their public Records, for the sole purpose of fatiguing them into compliance with his measures. — He has dissolved Representative Houses repeatedly for opposing with manly firmness his invasions on the rights of the people. — He has refused for a long time, after such dissolutions, to cause others to be elected whereby the Legislative powers, incapable of Annihilation, have returned to the People at large for their exercise; the States remaining in the meantime exposed to all the dangers of invasion from without, and convulsions within. — He has endeavoured to prevent the population of these States; for that purpose obstructing the Laws for Naturalization of Foreigners; refusing to pass others to encourage their migrations hither, and raising the conditions of new Appropriations of Lands. — He has obstructed the Administration of Justice, by refusing his Assent to Laws for establishing Judiciary powers. — He has made Judges dependent on his Will alone, for the tenure of their offices, and the amount and payment of their salaries. — He has erected a multitude of New Offices, and sent hither swarms of Officers to harrass our people, and eat out their substance. — He has kept among us, in times of peace, Standing Armies without the Consent of our legislatures. — He has affected to render the Military independent of and superior to the Civil power. — He has combined with others to subject us to a jurisdiction foreign to our constitution, and unacknowledged by our laws; giving his Assent to their Acts of pretended Legislation. — For quartering large bodies of armed troops among us: — For protecting them, by a mock Trial, from punishment for any Murders which they should commit on the Inhabitants of these States: — For cutting off our Trade with all parts of the world: — For imposing Taxes on us without our Consent: — For depriving us in many cases, of the benefits of Trial by Jury: — For transporting us beyond Seas to be tried for pretended offenses: — For abolishing the free System of English

Laws in a neighboring Province, establishing therein an Arbitrary government, and enlarging its Boundaries so as to render it at once an example and fit instrument for introducing the same absolute rule into these Colonies: — For taking away our Charters, abolishing our most valuable Laws, and altering fundamentally the Forms of our Governments: — For suspending our own Legislatures, and declaring themselves invested with power to legislate for us in all cases whatsoever. — He has abdicated Government here, by declaring us out of his Protection and waging War against us. — He has plundered our seas, ravaged our Coasts, burnt our towns, and destroyed the lives of our people. — He is at this time transporting large Armies of Foreign Mercenaries to compleat the works of death, desolation and tyranny, already begun with circumstances of Cruelty & perfidy, scarcely paralleled in the most barbarous ages, and totally unworthy the Head of a civilized nation. — He has constrained our fellow Citizens taken Captive on the high Seas to bear Arms against their Country, to become the executioners of their friends and Brethren, or to fall themselves by their hands. — He has excited domestic insurrections amongst us, and has endeavoured to bring on the inhabitants of our frontiers, the merciless Indian Savages, whose known rule of warfare, is an undistinguished destruction of all ages, sexes and conditions. In every stage of these Oppressions We have Petitioned for Redress in the most humble terms: Our repeated Petitions have been answered only by repeated injury. A Prince whose character is thus marked by every act which may define a Tyrant, is unfit to be the ruler of a free people. Nor have We been wanting in attentions to our British brethren. We have warned them from time to time of attempts by their legislature to extend an unwarrantable jurisdiction over us. We have reminded them of the circumstances of our emigration and settlement here. We have appealed to their native justice and magnanimity, and we have conjured them by the ties of our common kindred to disavow these usurpations, which would inevitably interrupt our connections and correspondence. They too have been deaf to the voice of justice and of consanguinity. We must, therefore, acquiesce in the necessity, which denounces our Separation, and hold them, as we hold the rest of mankind, Enemies in War, in Peace Friends. —

We, therefore, the Representatives of the united States of America, in General Congress, Assembled, appealing to the Supreme Judge of the world for the rectitude of our intentions do, in the Name, and by the Authority of the good People of these Colonies, solemnly publish and declare, That these United Colonies are, and of Right ought to be Free and Independent States; that they are Absolved from all Allegiance to the British Crown, and that all political connection between them and the State of Great Britain, is and ought to be totally dissolved; and that as Free and Independent States, they have full Power to levy War, conclude Peace, contract Alliances, establish Commerce, and to do all other Acts and Things which Independent States may of right do. — And for the support of this Declaration, with a firm reliance on the protection of divine Providence, we mutually pledge to each other our Lives, our Fortunes and our sacred Honor.

The Constitution
of the United States of America

We the People of the United States, in Order to form a more perfect Union, establish Justice, insure domestic Tranquility, provide for the common defence, promote the general Welfare, and secure the Blessings of Liberty to ourselves and our Posterity, do ordain and establish this Constitution for the United States of America.

Article I

Section. 1. All legislative Powers herein granted shall be vested in a Congress of the United States, which shall consist of a Senate and House of Representatives.

Section. 2. The House of Representatives shall be composed of Members chosen every second Year by the People of the several States, and the Electors in each State shall have the Qualifications requisite for Electors of the most numerous Branch of the State Legislature.

No Person shall be a Representative who shall not have attained to the age of twenty five Years, and been seven Years a Citizen of the United States, and who shall not, when elected, be an Inhabitant of that State in which he shall be chosen.

Representatives and direct Taxes shall be apportioned among the several States which may be included within this Union, according to their respective Numbers, *which shall be determined by adding to* *the whole Number of free Persons, including those bound to Service for a Term of Years,* and excluding Indians not taxed, *three fifths of all other persons.*[1] The actual Enumeration shall be made within three Years after the first Meeting of the Congress of the United States, and within every subsequent Term of ten Years, in such Manner as they shall by Law direct. The Number of Representatives shall not exceed one for every thirty Thousand, but each State shall have at Least one Representative; and until such enumeration shall be made, the State of New Hampshire shall be entitled to chuse three, Massachusetts eight, Rhode-Island and Providence Plantations one, Connecticut five, New-York six, New Jersey four, Pennsylvania eight, Delaware one, Maryland six, Virginia ten, North Carolina five, South Carolina five, and Georgia three.

When vacancies happen in the Repre-

[1] Italics are used throughout to indicate passages that have been altered by subsequent amendments. In this case see Amendment XIV.

sentation from any State, the Executive Authority thereof shall issue Writs of Election to fill such Vacancies.

The House of Representatives shall chuse their Speaker and other Officers; and shall have the sole Power of Impeachment.

Section. 3. The Senate of the United States shall be composed of two Senators from each State, *chosen by the Legislature thereof,*[2] for six Years; and each Senator shall have one Vote.

Immediately after they shall be assembled in Consequence of the first Election, they shall be divided as equally as may be into three Classes. The Seats of the Senators of the first Class shall be vacated at the Expiration of the second Year, of the second Class at the Expiration of the fourth Year, and of the third Class at the Expiration of the sixth Year, so that one third may be chosen every second Year; *and if Vacancies happen by Resignation, or otherwise, during the Recess of the Legislature of any State, the Executive thereof may make temporary Appointments until the next Meeting of the Legislature, which shall then fill such Vacancies.*[3]

No Person shall be a Senator who shall not have attained to the Age of thirty Years, and been nine Years a Citizen of the United States, and who shall not, when elected, be an Inhabitant of that State for which he shall be chosen.

The Vice President of the United States shall be President of the Senate, but shall have no Vote, unless they be equally divided.

The Senate shall chuse their other Officers, and also a President pro tempore, in the Absence of the Vice President, or when he shall exercise the Office of President of the United States.

The Senate shall have the sole Power to try all Impeachments. When sitting for that Purpose, they shall be on Oath or Affirmation. When the President of the United States is tried, the Chief Justice shall preside: And no Person shall be convicted without the Concurrence of two thirds of the Members present.

Judgment in Cases of Impeachment shall not extend further than to removal from Office, and disqualification to hold and enjoy any Office of honor, Trust or Profit under the United States: but the Party convicted shall nevertheless be liable and subject to Indictment, Trial, Judgment and Punishment, according to Law.

Section. 4. The Times, Places and Manner of holding Elections for Senators and Representatives, shall be prescribed in each State by the Legislature thereof; but the Congress may at any time by Law make or alter such Regulations, except as to the Places of chusing Senators.

The Congress shall assemble at least once in every Year, and such Meeting shall be on the first Monday in December, unless they shall by Law appoint a different Day.[4]

Section. 5. Each House shall be the Judge of the Elections, Returns and Qualifications of its own Members, and a Majority of each shall constitute a Quorum to do Business; but a smaller Number may adjourn from day to day, and may be authorized to compel the Attendance of absent Members, in such Manner, and under such Penalties as each House may provide.

Each House may determine the Rules of its Proceedings, punish its Members for disorderly Behaviour, and, with the Concurrence of two thirds, expel a Member.

Each House shall keep a Journal of its Proceedings, and from time to time publish the same, excepting such Parts as may in their Judgment require Secrecy; and the Yeas and Nays of the Members of either House on any question shall, at the Desire of one fifth of those Present, be entered on the Journal.

Neither House, during the Session of Congress, shall, without the Consent of the other, adjourn for more than three days, nor to any other Place than that in which the two Houses shall be sitting.

Section. 6. The Senators and Representatives shall receive a Compensation for their Services, to be ascertained by Law, and paid out of the Treasury of the United States. They shall in all Cases, except Treason,

---

[2] See Amendment XVII.
[3] *Ibid.*

[4] See Amendment XX.

Felony and Breach of the Peace, be privileged from Arrest during their Attendance at the Session of their respective Houses, and in going to and returning from the same; and for any Speech or Debate in either House, they shall not be questioned in any other Place.

No Senator or Representative shall, during the Time for which he was elected, be appointed to any civil Office under the Authority of the United States, which shall have been created, or the Emoluments whereof shall have been encreased during such time; and no Person holding any Office under the United States, shall be a Member of either House during his Continuance in Office.

Section. 7. All Bills for raising Revenue shall originate in the House of Representatives; but the Senate may propose or concur with Amendments as on other Bills.

Every Bill which shall have passed the House of Representatives and the Senate, shall, before it become a Law, be presented to the President of the United States; if he approve he shall sign it, but if not he shall return it, with his Objections to that House in which it shall have originated, who shall enter the Objections at large on their Journal, and proceed to reconsider it. If after such Reconsideration two thirds of that House shall agree to pass the Bill, it shall be sent, together with the Objections, to the other House, by which it shall likewise be reconsidered, and if approved by two thirds of that House, it shall become a Law. But in all such Cases the Votes of both Houses shall be **determined** by Yeas and Nays, and the Names of the Persons voting for and against the Bill shall be entered on the Journal of each House respectively. If any Bill shall not be returned by the President within ten Days (Sundays excepted) after it shall have been presented to him, the Same shall be a Law, in like Manner as if he had signed it, unless Congress by their Adjournment prevent its Return, in which Case it shall not be a Law.

Every Order, Resolution, or Vote to which the Concurrence of the Senate and House of Representatives may be necessary (except on a question of Adjournment)

shall be presented to the President of the United States; and before the Same shall take Effect, shall be approved by him, or being disapproved by him, shall be repassed by two thirds of the Senate and House of Representatives, according to the Rules and Limitations prescribed in the Case of a Bill.

Section. 8. The Congress shall have Power To lay and collect Taxes, Duties, Imposts and Excises, to pay the Debts and provide for the common Defence and general Welfare of the United States; but all Duties, Imposts and Excises shall be uniform throughout the United States;

To borrow Money on the credit of the United States;

To regulate Commerce with foreign Nations, and among the several States, and with the Indian Tribes;

To establish an uniform Rule of Naturalization, and uniform Laws on the subject of Bankruptcies throughout the United States;

To coin Money, regulate the Value thereof, and of foreign Coin, and fix the Standard of Weights and Measures;

To provide for the Punishment of counterfeiting the Securities and Current Coin of the United States;

To establish Post Offices and post Roads;

To promote the Progress of Science and useful Arts, by securing for limited Times to Authors and Inventors the exclusive Right to their respective Writings and Discoveries;

To constitute Tribunals inferior to the Supreme Court;

To define and punish Piracies and Felonies committed on the high Seas, and Offences against the Law of Nations;

To declare War, grant Letters of Marque and Reprisal, and make Rules concerning Captures on Land and Water;

To raise and support Armies, but no Appropriation of Money to that Use shall be for a longer Term than two Years;

To provide and maintain a Navy;

To make Rules for the Government and Regulation of the land and naval Forces;

To provide for calling forth the Militia to execute the Laws of the Union, suppress Insurrections and repel Invasions;

To provide for organizing, arming, and disciplining, the Militia, and for governing such Part of them as may be employed in the Service of the United States, reserving to the States respectively, the Appointment of the Officers, and the Authority of training the Militia according to the discipline prescribed by Congress;

To exercise exclusive Legislation in all Cases whatsoever, over such District (not exceeding ten Miles square) as may, by Cession of particular States, and the Acceptance of Congress, become the Seat of the Government of the United States, and to exercise like Authority over all Places purchased by the Consent of the Legislature of the State in which the Same shall be, for the Erection of Forts, Magazines, Arsenals, dock-Yards, and other needful Buildings;—And

To make all Laws which shall be necessary and proper for carrying into Execution the foregoing Powers, and all other Powers vested by this Constitution in the Government of the United States, or in any Department or Officer thereof.

Section. 9. The Migration or Importation of such Persons as any of the States now existing shall think proper to admit, shall not be prohibited by the Congress prior to the Year one thousand eight hundred and eight, but a Tax or duty may be imposed on such Importation, not exceeding ten dollars for each Person.

The Privilege of the Writ of Habeas Corpus shall not be suspended, unless when in Cases of Rebellion or Invasion the public Safety may require it.

No Bill of Attainder or ex post facto Law shall be passed.

No Capitation, or other direct, Tax shall be laid, unless in Proportion to the Census or Enumeration herein before directed to be taken.

No Tax or Duty shall be laid on Articles exported from any State.

No Preference shall be given by any Regulation of Commerce or Revenue to the Ports of one State over those of another: nor shall Vessels bound to, or from, one State, be obliged to enter, clear, or pay Duties in another.

No Money shall be drawn from the Treasury, but in Consequence of Appropriations made by Law; and a regular Statement and Account of the Receipts and Expenditures of all public Money shall be published from time to time.

No title of Nobility shall be granted by the United States: And no Person holding any Office of Profit or Trust under them, shall, without the Consent of the Congress, accept of any present, Emolument, Office, or Title, of any kind whatever, from any King, Prince, or foreign State.

Section. 10. No State shall enter into any Treaty, Alliance, or Confederation; grant Letters of Marque and Reprisal; coin Money; emit Bills of Credit; make any Thing but gold and silver Coin a Tender in Payment of Debts; pass any Bill of Attainder, ex post facto Law, or Law impairing the Obligation of Contracts, or Grant any Title of Nobility.

No State shall, without the Consent of the Congress, lay any Imposts or Duties on Imports or Exports, except what may be absolutely necessary for executing its inspection Laws: and the net Produce of all Duties and Imposts, laid by any State on Imports or Exports, shall be for the Use of the Treasury of the United States; and all such Laws shall be subject to the Revision and Controul of the Congress.

No State shall, without the Consent of Congress, lay any Duty of Tonnage, keep Troops, or Ships of War in time of Peace, enter into any Agreement or Compact with another State, or with a foreign Power, or engage in War, unless actually invaded, or in such imminent Danger as will not admit of delay.

Article II

Section. 1. The executive Power shall be vested in a President of the United States of America. He shall hold his Office during the Term of four Years, and, together with the Vice President, chosen for the same Term be elected as follows:

Each State shall appoint, in such Manner as the Legislature thereof may direct, a Number of Electors, equal to the whole Number of Senators and Representatives to which the State may be entitled in the

Congress: but no Senator or Representative, or Person holding an Office of Trust or Profit under the United States, shall be appointed an Elector.

The Electors shall meet in their respective States, and vote by Ballot for two Persons, of whom one at least shall not be an Inhabitant of the same State with themselves. And they shall make a List of all the Persons voted for, and of the Number of Votes for each; which List they shall sign and certify, and transmit sealed to the Seat of the Government of the United States, directed to the President of the Senate. The President of the Senate shall, in the Presence of the Senate and House of Representatives, open all the Certificates, and the Votes shall then be counted. The Person having the greatest Number of Votes shall be the President, if such Number be a Majority of the whole Number of Electors appointed; and if there be more than one who have such Majority, and have an equal Number of Votes, then the House of Representatives shall immediately chuse by Ballot one of them for President; and if no Person have a Majority, then from the five highest on the List the said House shall in like **Manner chuse the President. But in chusing the President, the votes shall be taken by States, the Representation from each State** *having one Vote; A quorum for this purpose shall consist of a Member or Members from two thirds of the States, and a Majority of all the States shall be necessary to a Choice. In every Case, after the Choice of the President, the Person having the Greatest Number of Votes of the Electors shall be the Vice President. But if there should remain two or more who have equal Votes, the Senate shall chuse from them by Ballot the Vice President.*[5]

The Congress may determine the Time of chusing the Electors, and the Day on which they shall give their Votes; which Day shall be the same throughout the United States.

No Person except a natural born Citizen, or a Citizen of the United States, at the time of the Adoption of this Constitution, shall be eligible to the Office of President; neither shall any Person be eligible to that

[5] See Amendment XII.

Office who shall not have attained to the Age of thirty five Years, and been fourteen Years a Resident within the United States.

In Case of the Removal of the President from Office, or of his Death, Resignation, or Inability to discharge the Powers and Duties of the said Office, the Same shall devolve on the Vice President, and the Congress may by Law provide for the Case of Removal, Death, Resignation or Inability, both of the President and Vice President, declaring what Officer shall then act as President, and such Officer shall act accordingly, until the Disability be removed, or a President shall be elected.

The President shall, at stated Times, receive for his Services, a Compensation which shall neither be encreased nor diminished during the Period for which he shall have been elected, and he shall not receive within that Period any other Emolument from the United States, or any of them.

Before he enter on the Execution of his Office, he shall take the following Oath or Affirmation:—"I do solemnly swear (or affirm) that I will faithfully execute the Office of President of the United States, and will to the best of my Ability, preserve, protect, and defend the Constitution of the United States."

Section. 2. The President shall be Commander in Chief of the Army and Navy of the United States, and of the Militia of the several States, when called into the actual service of the United States; he may require the Opinion, in writing, of the principal Officer in each of the executive Departments, upon any Subject relating to the Duties of their respective Offices, and he shall have Power to grant Reprieves and Pardons for Offences against the United States, except in Cases of Impeachment.

He shall have Power, by and with the Advice and Consent of the Senate, to make Treaties, provided two thirds of the Senators present concur; and he shall nominate, and by and with the Advice and Consent of the Senate, shall appoint Ambassadors, and other public Ministers and Consuls, Judges of the supreme Court, and all other Officers of the United States, whose Appointments are not herein otherwise provided for, and which shall be established by Law: but the Congress may by Law vest the Appointment of such inferior Officers, as they think proper, in the President alone, in the Courts of Law, or in the Heads of Departments.

The President shall have Power to fill up all Vacancies that may happen during the Recess of the Senate, by granting Commissions which shall expire at the End of their next Session.

Section. 3. He shall from time to time give to the Congress Information of the State of the Union, and recommend to their Consideration such Measures as he shall judge necessary and expedient; he may, on extraordinary Occasions, convene both Houses, or either of them, and in Case of Disagreement between them, with Respect to the Time of Adjournment, he may adjourn them to such Time as he shall think proper; he shall receive Ambassadors and other public Ministers, he shall take Care that the Laws be faithfully executed, and shall Commission all the Officers of the United States.

Section. 4. The President, Vice President, and all civil Officers of the United States, shall be removed from Office on Impeachment for, and Conviction of, Treason, Bribery, or other high Crimes and Misdemeanors.

Article III

Section. 1. The judicial Power of the United States, shall be vested in one supreme Court and in such inferior Courts as the Congress may from time to time ordain and establish. The Judges, both of the supreme and inferior Courts, shall hold their Offices during good Behavior, and shall, at stated Times, receive for their Services, a Compensation, which shall not be diminished during their Continuance in Office.

Section. 2. The Judicial Power shall extend to all Cases, in Law and Equity, arising under this Constitution, the Laws of the United States, and Treaties made, or which shall be made, under their Authority;—to all Cases affecting Ambassadors, other public Ministers and Consuls;—to all Cases of admiralty and maritime Jurisdiction;—to Controversies to which the United States shall be a Party;—to Controversies between two or more States;—*between a State and Citizens of another State;*[6]—between Citizens of different States;—between Citizens of the same State claiming Lands under Grants of different States, *and between a State, or the Citizens thereof, and foreign States, Citizens, or Subjects.*[7]

In all cases affecting Ambassadors, other public Ministers and Consuls, and those in which a State shall be Party, the supreme Court shall have original Jurisdiction. In all the other Cases before mentioned, the supreme Court shall have appellate Jurisdiction, both as to Law and Fact, with such Exceptions, and under such Regulations as the Congress shall make.

The Trial of all Crimes, except in Cases of Impeachment, shall be by Jury; and such Trial shall be held in the State where the said Crimes shall have been committed; but when not committed within any State, the Trial shall be at such Place or Places as the Congress may by Law have directed.

Section. 3. Treason against the United States, shall consist only in levying War against them, or in adhering to their Enemies, giving them Aid and Comfort. No Person shall be convicted of Treason unless on the Testimony of two Witnesses to the same overt Act, or on Confession in open Court.

The Congress shall have Power to declare the Punishment of Treason, but no Attainder of Treason shall work Corruption of Blood, or Forfeiture except during the Life of the Person attainted.

Article IV

Section. 1. Full Faith and Credit shall be given in each State to the public Acts, Records, and judicial Proceedings of every other State. And the Congress may by general Laws prescribe the Manner in which such Acts, Records, and Proceedings shall be proved, and the Effect thereof.

Section. 2. The Citizens of each State shall be entitled to all Privileges and Immunities of Citizens in the several States.

A Person charged in any State with Treason, Felony, or other Crime, who shall

[6] See Amendment XI.
[7] *Ibid.*

flee from Justice, and be found in another State, shall on Demand of the executive Authority of the State from which he fled, be delivered up, to be removed to the State having Jurisdiction of the Crime.

No Person held to Service or Labour in one State, under the Laws thereof, escaping into another, shall, in Consequence of any Law or Regulation therein, be discharged from such Service or Labour, but shall be delivered up on Claim of the Party to whom such Service or Labour may be due.[8]

Section. 3. New States may be admitted by the Congress into this Union; but no new State shall be formed or erected within the Jurisdiction of any other State; nor any State be formed by the Junction of two or more States, or Parts of States, without the Consent of the Legislatures of the States concerned as well as of the Congress.

The Congress shall have Power to dispose of and make all needful Rules and Regulations respecting the Territory or other Property belonging to the United States; and nothing in this Constitution shall be so construed as to Prejudice any claims of the United States, or of any particular State.

Section. 4. The United States shall guarantee to every State in this Union a Republican Form of Government, and shall protect each of them against Invasion; and on Application of the Legislature, or of the Executive (when the Legislature cannot be convened) against domestic Violence.

Article V

The Congress, whenever two thirds of both Houses shall deem it necessary, shall propose Amendments to this Constitution, or, on the Application of the Legislatures of two thirds of the several States, shall call a Convention for proposing Amendments, which, in either Case, shall be valid to all Intents and Purposes, as Part of this Constitution, when ratified by the Legislatures of three fourths of the several States, or by Conventions in three fourths thereof, as the one or the other Mode of Ratification may be proposed by the Congress; Provided that

[8] See Amendment XIII.

no Amendment which may be made prior to the Year One thousand eight hundred and eight shall in any Manner affect the first and fourth Clauses in the Ninth Section of the first Article; and that no State, without its Consent, shall be deprived of its equal Suffrage in the Senate.

Article VI

All Debts contracted and Engagements entered into, before the Adoption of this Constitution, shall be as valid against the United States under this Constitution, as under the Confederation.

This Constitution, and the Laws of the United States which shall be made in Pursuance thereof; and all Treaties made, or which shall be made, under the Authority of the United States, shall be the supreme Law of the Land; and the Judges in every State shall be bound thereby, any Thing in the Constitution or Laws of any State to the Contrary notwithstanding.

The Senators and Representatives before mentioned, and the Members of the several State Legislatures, and all executive and judicial Officers, both of the United States and of the several States, shall be bound by Oath or Affirmation, to support this Constitution; but no religious Test shall ever be required as a Qualification to any Office or public Trust under the United States.

Article VII

The Ratification of the Conventions of nine States, shall be sufficient for the Establishment of this Constitution between the States so ratifying the Same.

Done in Convention by the Unanimous Consent of the States present the Seventeenth Day of September in the Year of our Lord one thousand seven hundred and eighty seven and of the Independence of the United States of America the twelfth. In witness whereof We have hereunto subscribed our Names.

* * *

ARTICLES IN ADDITION TO, AND AMENDMENT OF, THE CONSTITUTION OF THE UNITED STATES OF AMERICA, PROPOSED BY CONGRESS, AND RATIFIED BY THE SEVERAL STATES, PURSUANT TO THE FIFTH ARTICLE OF THE ORIGINAL CONSTITUTION.

Amendment I

[Ratification of the first ten amendments was completed December 15, 1791]

Congress shall make no law respecting an establishment of religion, or prohibiting the free exercise thereof; or abridging the freedom of speech, or of the press; or the right of the people peaceably to assemble, and to petition the Government for a redress of grievances.

Amendment II

A well regulated Militia, being necessary to the security of a free State, the right of the people to keep and bear Arms, shall not be infringed.

Amendment III

No Soldier shall, in time of peace be quartered in any house, without the consent of the Owner, nor in time of war, but in a manner to be prescribed by law.

Amendment IV

The right of the people to be secure in their persons, houses, papers, and effects, against unreasonable searches and seizures, shall not be violated, and no Warrants shall issue, but upon probable cause, supported by Oath or affirmation, and particularly describing the place to be searched, and the persons or things to be seized.

Amendment V

No person shall be held to answer for a capital, or otherwise infamous crime, unless on a presentment or indictment of a Grand Jury, except in cases arising in the land or naval forces, or in the Militia, when in actual service in time of War or public danger; nor shall any person be subject for the same offence to be twice put in jeopardy of life or limb; nor shall be compelled in any criminal case to be a witness against himself, nor be deprived of life, liberty, or property, without due process of law; nor shall private property be taken for public use, without just compensation.

Amendment VI

In all criminal prosecutions, the accused shall enjoy the right to a speedy and public trial, by an impartial jury of the State and district wherein the crime shall have been committed, which district shall have been previously ascertained by law, and to be informed of the nature and cause of the accusation; to be confronted with the witness against him; to have compulsory process for obtaining witness in his favor, and to have the Assistance of Counsel for his defence.

Amendment VII

In Suits at common law, where the value in controversy shall exceed twenty dollars, the right of trial by jury shall be preserved, and no fact tried by a jury, shall be otherwise re-examined in any Court of the United States, than according to the rules of the common law.

Amendment VIII

Excessive bail shall not be required, nor excessive fines imposed, nor cruel and unusual punishments inflicted.

Amendment IX

The enumeration in the Constitution, of certain rights, shall not be construed to deny or disparage others retained by the people.

Amendment X

The powers not delegated to the United States by the Constitution, nor prohibited by it to the States, are reserved to the States respectively, or to the people.

Amendment XI

[January 8, 1798]

The Judicial power of the United States shall not be construed to extend to any suit in law or equity, commenced or prosecuted against one of the United States by Citizens of another State, or by Citizens or Subjects of any Foreign State.

Amendment XII

[September 25, 1804]

The Electors shall meet in their respective states and vote by ballot for President and Vice President, one of whom, at least, shall not be an inhabitant of the same state with themselves; they shall name in their ballots the person voted for as President, and in distinct ballots the person voted for as Vice President, and they shall make distinct lists of all persons voted for as President, and of all persons voted for as Vice President, and of the number of votes for each, which lists they shall sign and certify, and transmit sealed to the seat of the government of the United States, directed to the President of the Senate;—The President of the Senate shall, in the presence of Senate and House of Representatives, open all the certificates and the votes shall then be counted;—The person having the greatest number of votes for President, shall be the President, if such number be a majority of the whole number of Electors appointed; and if no person have such majority, then from the persons having the highest numbers not exceeding three on the list of those voted for as President, the House of Representatives shall choose immediately, by ballot, the President. But in choosing the President, the votes shall be taken by states, the representation from each state having one vote; a quorum for this purpose shall consist of a member or members from two thirds of the states, and a majority of all the states shall be necessary to a choice. And if the House of Representatives shall not choose a President whenever the right of choice shall devolve upon them, *before the fourth day of March next following,*[9] then the Vice President shall act as President as in the case of the death or other constitutional disability of the President.— The person having the greatest number of votes as Vice President, shall be the Vice President, if such number be a majority of the whole number of Electors appointed, and if no person have a majority, then from the two highest numbers on the list, the Senate shall choose the Vice President; a

[9] See Amendment XX.

quorum for the purpose shall consist of two-thirds of the whole number of Senators, and a majority of the whole number shall be necessary to a choice. But no person constitutionally ineligible to the office of President shall be eligible to that of Vice President of the United States.

Amendment XIII

[December 18, 1865]

Section 1. Neither slavery nor involuntary servitude, except as a punishment for crime whereof the party shall have been duly convicted, shall exist within the United States, or any place subject to their jurisdiction.

Section 2. Congress shall have power to enforce this article by appropriate legislation.

Amendment XIV

[July 28, 1868]

Section 1. All persons born or naturalized in the United States, and subject to the jurisdiction thereof, are citizens of the United States and of the State wherein they reside. No State shall make or enforce any law which shall abridge the privileges or immunities of citizens of the United States; nor shall any state deprive any person of life, liberty, or property, without due process of law; nor deny to any person within its jurisdiction the equal protection of the laws.

Section 2. Representatives shall be apportioned among the several States according to their respective numbers, counting the whole number of persons in each State, excluding Indians not taxed. But when the right to vote at any election for the choice of electors for President and Vice President of the United States, Representatives in Congress, the Executive and Judicial officers of a State, or the members of the Legislature thereof, is denied to any of the male inhabitants of such State, being twenty one years of age, and citizens of the United States, or in any way abridged, except for participation in rebellion, or other crime, the basis of representation therein shall be reduced in the proportion which the number of such male citizens shall bear to the whole number of male citizens twenty one years of age in such State.

Section 3. No person shall be a Senator or Representative in Congress, or elector of President and Vice President, or hold any office, civil or military, under the United States, or under any State, who, having previously taken an oath, as a member of Congress, or as an officer of the United States, or as a member of any State legislature, or as an executive or judicial officer of any State, to support the Constitution of the United States, shall have engaged in insurrection or rebellion against the same, or given aid or comfort to the enemies thereof. But Congress may by a vote of two thirds of each House, remove such disability.

Section 4. The validity of the public debt of the United States, authorized by law, including debts incurred for payment of pensions and bounties for services in suppressing insurrection or rebellion, shall not be questioned. But neither the United States nor any State shall assume or pay any debt or obligation incurred in aid of insurrection or rebellion against the United States, or any claim for the loss or emancipation of any slave; but all such debts, obligations, and claims shall be held illegal and void.

Section 5. The Congress shall have power to enforce, by appropriate legislation, the provisions of this article.

Amendment XV

[March 30, 1870]

Section 1. The right of citizens of the United States to vote shall not be denied or abridged by the United States or by any State on account of race, color, or previous condition of servitude.

Section 2. The Congress shall have power to enforce this article by appropriate legislation.

Amendment XVI

[February 25, 1913]

The Congress shall have power to lay and collect taxes on incomes, from what-ever source derived, without apportionment among the several States, and without regard to any census or enumeration.

Amendment XVII

[May 31, 1913]

The Senate of the United States shall be composed of two Senators from each State, elected by the people thereof, for six years; and each Senator shall have one vote. The electors in each State shall have the qualifications requisite for electors of the most numerous branch of the State legislatures.

When vacancies happen in the representation of any State in the Senate, the executive authority of such State shall issue writs of election to fill such vacancies: *Provided,* That the legislature of any State may empower the executive thereof to make temporary appointments until the people fill the vacancies by election as the legislature may direct.

This amendment shall not be so construed as to affect the election or term of any Senator chosen before it becomes valid as part of the Constitution.

Amendment XVIII

[January 29, 1919]

Section 1. *After one year from the ratification of this article the manufacture, sale, or transportation of intoxicating liquors within, the importation thereof into, or the exportation thereof from the United States and all territory subject to the jurisdiction thereof for beverage purposes is hereby prohibited.*

Section 2. *The Congress and the several States shall have concurrent power to enforce this article by appropriate legislation.*

Section 3. *This article shall be inoperative unless it shall have been ratified as an amendment to the Constitution by the legislatures of the several States, as provided in the Constitution, within seven years from the date of the submission hereof to the States by the Congress.*[10]

---

[10] Repealed by Amendment XXI.

Amendment XIX

[August 26, 1920]

The right of citizens of the United States to vote shall not be denied or abridged by the United States or by any State on account of sex.

Congress shall have power to enforce this article by appropriate legislation.

Amendment XX

[February 6, 1933]

Section 1. The terms of the President and Vice President shall end at noon on the 20th day of January, and the terms of Senators and Representatives at noon on the 3rd day of January, of the years in which such terms would have ended if this article had not been ratified; and the terms of their successors shall then begin.

Section 2. The Congress shall assemble at least once in every year, and such meeting shall begin at noon on the 3rd day of January, unless they shall by law appoint a different day.

Section 3. If, at the time fixed for the beginning of the term of the President, the President elect shall have died, the Vice President elect shall become President. If a President shall not have been chosen before the time fixed for the beginning of his term, or if the President elect shall have failed to qualify, then the Vice President elect shall act as President until a President shall have qualified; and the Congress may by law provide for the case wherein neither a President elect nor a Vice President elect shall have qualified, declaring who shall then act as President, or the manner in which one who is to act shall be selected, and such person shall act accordingly until a President or Vice President shall have qualified.

Section 4. The Congress may by law provide for the case of the death of any of the persons from whom the House of Representatives may choose a President whenever the right of choice shall have devolved upon them, and for the case of the death of any of the persons from whom the Senate may choose a Vice President whenever the right of choice shall have devolved upon them.

Section 5. Sections 1 and 2 shall take effect on the 15th day of October following the ratification of this article.

Section 6. This article shall be inoperative unless it shall have been ratified as an amendment to the Constitution by the legislatures of three fourths of the several States within seven years from the date of its submission.

Amendment XXI

[December 5, 1933]

Section 1. The eighteenth article of amendment to the Constitution of the United States is hereby repealed.

Section 2. The transportation or importation into any State, Territory, or possession of the United States for delivery or use therein of intoxicating liquors, in violation of the laws thereof, is hereby prohibited.

Section 3. This article shall be inoperative unless it shall have been ratified as an amendment to the Constitution by conventions in the several States, as provided in the Constitution, within seven years from the date of the submission hereof to the States by the Congress.

Amendment XXII

[February 26, 1951]

Section 1. No person shall be elected to the office of the President more than twice, and no person who has held the office of President, or acted as President, for more than two years of a term to which some other person was elected President shall be elected to the office of President more than once. But this Article shall not apply to any person holding the office of President when this Article was proposed by the Congress, and shall not prevent any person who may be holding the office of President, or acting as President, during the term within which this Article becomes operative from holding the office of President or acting as President during the remainder of such term.

Section 2. This article shall be inoperative unless it shall have been ratified as an amendment to the Constitution by the legislatures of three fourths of the several States within seven years from the date of its submission to the States by the Congress.

Amendment XXIII

[March 29, 1961]

Section 1. The District constituting the seat of Government of the United States shall appoint in such manner as the Congress may direct:

A number of electors of President and Vice President equal to the whole number of Senators and Representatives in Congress to which the District would be entitled if it were a State, but in no event more than the least populous State; they shall be in addition to those appointed by the States, but they shall be considered, for the purposes of the election of President and Vice President, to be electors appointed by a State; and they shall meet in the District and perform such duties as provided by the twelfth article of amendment.

Section 2. The Congress shall have power to enforce this article by appropriate legislation.

Amendment XXIV

[January 23, 1964]

Section 1. The right of citizens of the United States to vote in any primary or other election for President or Vice President, for electors for President or Vice President, or for Senator or Representative in Congress, shall not be denied or abridged by the United States or any state by reason of failure to pay any poll tax or other tax.

Section 2. The Congress shall have the power to enforce this article by appropriate legislation.

Amendment XXV

[February 10, 1967]

Section 1. In case of the removal of the President from office or of his death or resignation, the Vice President shall become President.

Section 2. Whenever there is a vacancy in the office of the Vice President, the President shall nominate a Vice President who shall take office upon confirmation by a majority vote of both Houses of Congress.

Section 3. Whenever the President transmits to the President pro tempore of the Senate and the Speaker of the House of Representatives his written declaration that he is unable to discharge the powers and duties of his office, and until he transmits to them a written declaration to the contrary, such powers and duties shall be discharged by the Vice President as Acting President.

Section 4. Whenever the Vice President and a majority of either the principal officers of the executive departments or of such other body as Congress may by law provide, transmit to the President pro tempore of the Senate and the Speaker of the House of Representatives their written declaration that the President is unable to discharge the powers and duties of his office, the Vice President shall immediately assume the powers and duties of the office as Acting President.

Thereafter, when the President transmits to the President pro tempore of the Senate and the Speaker of the House of Representatives his written declaration that no inability exists, he shall resume the powers and duties of his office unless the Vice President and a majority of either the principal officers of the executive department[s] or of such other body as Congress may by law provide, transmit within four days to the President pro tempore of the Senate and the Speaker of the House of Representatives their written declaration that the President is unable to discharge the powers and duties of his office. Thereupon Congress shall decide the issue, assembling within forty-eight hours for that purpose if not in session. If the Congress, within twenty-one days after receipt of the latter written declaration, or, if Congress is not in session, within twenty-one days after Congress is required to assemble, determines by two-thirds vote of both Houses that the President is unable to discharge the powers and duties of his office, the Vice President shall continue to discharge the same as Acting President; otherwise, the President shall resume the powers and duties of his office.

BIBLIOGRAPHY

The selections that follow have been drawn from the vast and rapidly growing literature on American politics. We have sought to identify additional reading, usually available in paperback, which will fill out each chapter in some important way. Sometimes these selections contrast sharply with the interpretation which we reach; at other times they extend it beyond the point that we consider supported by available evidence; or they represent reflections on approaches or methods worth examining. In no case, of course, can our selections be taken as a comprehensive bibliography. They are beginning, and a highly diversified one.

Chapter 1

Politics as an attempt to describe and explain:

Dahl, Robert A. *Modern Political Analysis.* Englewood Cliffs, N. J., Prentice-Hall, 1963.
Eulau, Heinz. *The Behavioral Persuasion in Politics.* New York: Random House, 1963.
Sorauf, Frank J. *Political Science: An Informal Overview.* Columbus, Ohio: Charles E. Merrill Books, 1963.

Politics as an extension of ethical concerns:

Kaplan, Abraham. *American Ethics and Public Policy.* New York: Oxford University Press, 1963.
Kariel, Henry S. *The Promise of Politics.* Englewood Cliffs, N. J.: Prentice-Hall, 1966.
Pranger, Robert J. *The Eclipse of Citizenship.* New York: Holt, Rinehart and Winston, 1968.

Approaches that mix the two in varying proportions:

Alinsky, Saul. *Reveille for Radicals.* New York: Vintage Books, 1969 (originally published in 1946).
Barber, James David. *Citizen Politics: An Introduction to Political Behavior.* Chicago: Markham Publishing Co., 1968.
Dalfiume, Richard M., ed. *American Politics Since 1945: A New York Times Book.* Chicago: Quadrangle Books, 1969.
Freedman, Leonard, ed. *Issues of the Seventies.* Belmont, Calif.: Wadsworth Publishing Co., 1970.
Gordon, Kermit, ed. *Agenda for the Nation.* Garden City, N. Y.: Doubleday, 1968.
Laing, R. D. *The Politics of Experience.* New York: Ballantine, 1967.
Lipset, Seymour Martin, ed. *Politics and the Social Sciences.* New York: Oxford University Press, 1969.
Myrdal, Gunnar. *Objectivity in the Social Sciences.* New York: Random House, 1969.

Chapter 2

American values and ideology:

Becker, Carl. *Freedom and Responsibility in the American Way of Life.* New York: Vintage Books, 1960.
Boorstin, Daniel. *The Genius of American Politics.* Chicago: University of Chicago Press, 1960.
Girvetz, Harry. *The Evolution of Liberalism.* New York: Collier Books, 1963.
Grimes, Alan P. *American Political Thought.* New York: Holt, Rinehart and Winston, 1966.
Hartz, Louis M. *The Liberal Tradition in America.* New York: Harcourt, Brace and World, 1955.
Lerner, Max. *America as a Civilization.* New York: Simon and Schuster, 1957.
McGiffert, Michael, ed. *The Character of Americans.* Homewood, Ill., Dorsey Press, 1964.

Rossiter, Clinton. *Conservatism in America: The Thankless Persuasion.* New York: Vintage Books, 1955.

The Challenges of the 1970s:

Carmichael, Stokely, and Hamilton, Charles V. *Black Power: The Politics of Liberation in America.* New York: Vintage Books, 1967.
Cowan, Paul. *The Making of an Unamerican.* New York: Viking Press, 1969.
Dolbeare, Kenneth M., and Dolbeare, Patricia. *American Ideologies: The Competing Political Beliefs of the 1970s.* Chicago: Markham Publishing Co., 1971.
Jacobs, Paul, and Landau, Saul, eds. *The New Radicals.* New York: Vintage Books, 1966.
Lowi, Theodore. *The End of Liberalism: Ideology, Policy and the Crisis of Authority.* New York: W. W. Norton, 1969.
Newfield, Jack. *A Prophetic Minority.* New York: Signet Books, 1966.
Seale, Bobby G. *Seize the Time: The Story of the Black Panther Party and Huey P. Newton.* New York: Random House, 1970.

Chapter 3

Bachrach, Peter. *The Theory of Democratic Elitism.* Boston: Little, Brown, 1967.
Coser, Lewis. *The Functions of Social Conflict.* New York: The Free Press, 1964.
Dahl, Robert A. *Pluralist Democracy in the United States: Conflict and Consent.* Chicago: Rand McNally, 1967.
Davies, James C. *Human Nature in Politics.* New York: John Wiley, 1963.
Eulau, Heinz, and March, James G., eds., *Political Science.* Englewood Cliffs, N. J.: Prentice-Hall, 1969.
Gould, James A., and Thursby, Vincent V. *Contemporary Political Thought: Issues in Scope, Value and Direction.* New York: Holt, Rinehart and Winston, 1969.
Lasswell, Harold. *Politics: Who Gets What, When, How.* New York: McGraw-Hill, 1936.
McCoy, Charles A., and Playford, John. *Apolitical Politics: A Critique of Behavioralism.* New York: Crowell, 1967.
McNeil, Elton B. *The Nature of Human Conflict.* Englewood Cliffs, N. J.: Prentice-Hall, 1965.
Merritt, Richard L., and Pyszka, Gloria J. *The Student Political Scientist's Handbook.* Cambridge, Mass.: Schenkman Publishing Co., 1969.
Plano, Jack C., and Greenberg, Milton. *The American Political Dictionary.* New York: Holt, Rinehart and Winston, 1967.

Chapter 4

Barnet, Richard J. *The Economy of Death.* New York: Atheneum, 1969.
Bloomfield, Lincoln P. et al. *Khrushchev and the Arms Race.* Cambridge, Mass.: M.I.T. Press, 1966.
Boulding, Kenneth. *Conflict and Defense: A General Theory.* New York: Harper and Row, 1963.
Clayton, James L. *The Economic Impact of the Cold War.* New York: Harcourt, Brace, 1970.
Hammond, Paul. *Organizing for Defense.* Princeton, N. J.: Princeton University Press, 1961.
Huntington, Samuel. *The Common Defense.* New York: Columbia University Press, 1961.
Kaufmann, William W. *The McNamara Strategy.* New York: Harper and Row, 1964.
Lapp, Ralph E. *The Weapons Culture.* New York: W. W. Norton, 1968.
Melman, Seymour. *Pentagon Capitalism.* New York: McGraw-Hill, 1970.
Neiberg, H. L. *In the Name of Science.* Chicago: Quadrangle Books, 1966.
Peck, Merton J., and Scherer, Frederic H. *The Weapons Acquisition Process.* Cambridge, Mass.: The Harvard Business School, 1962.
Thayer, George. *The War Business.* New York: Simon and Schuster, 1969.

Chapter 5

Carmichael, Stokely, and Hamilton, Charles V. *Black Power: The Politics of Liberation in America.* New York: Vintage Books, 1967.
Clark, Kenneth B. *Dark Ghetto: Dilemmas of Social Power.* New York: Harper and Row, 1965.
Clark, Kenneth B., and Hopkins, Jeannette. *A Relevant War on Poverty.* New York: Harper and Row, 1969.
Cleaver, Eldridge. *Soul on Ice.* New York: McGraw-Hill, 1968.
Coleman, James S. et al. *Equality of Educational Opportunity.* Washington, D. C.: Government Printing Office, 1966.
Coles, Robert. *Children of Crisis.* New York: Dell Publishing Co., 1964.
Deutsch, Martin et al. *The Disadvantaged Child.* New York: Basic Books, 1967.
Donovan, John C. *The Politics of Poverty.* New York: Pegasus, 1967.
Elkins, Stanley. *Slavery.* 2nd ed. Chicago: University of Chicago Press, 1968.
Ferman, Louis A. et al. *Poverty in America.* Ann Arbor, Mich.: University of Michigan Press, 1965.
Friedman, Lawrence M. *Government and Slum Housing.* Chicago: Rand McNally, 1968.
Harrington, Michael. *The Other America.* Baltimore: Penguin Books, 1962.
Knowles, Louis L., and Prewitt, Kenneth, eds. *Institutional Racism in America.* Englewood Cliffs, N. J.: Prentice-Hall, 1969.
Lewis, Oscar. *La Vida.* New York: Random House, 1966.
————. *The Children of Sanchez.* New York: Random House, 1961.
Liebow, Elliot. *Talley's Corner.* Boston: Little, Brown, 1967.
Malcolm X, *Autobiography.* New York: Grove Press, 1964.
Matthews, Donald R., and Prothro, James W. *Negroes and the New Southern Politics.* New York: Harcourt, Brace and World, 1966.
Moynihan, Daniel. *Maximum Feasible Misunderstanding.* New York: The Free Press, 1969.
Parsons, Talcott, and Clark, Kenneth B., eds. *The Negro American.* Boston: Houghton Mifflin, 1966.
Report of the Advisory Commission on Civil Disorders. New York: Bantam Books, 1968.
Sexton, Patricia C. *Education and Income.* New York: Viking Press, 1961.
Valentine, Charles. *Culture and Poverty.* Chicago: University of Chicago Press, 1961.
Van den Bergh, Pierre L. *Race and Racism.* New York: John Wiley, 1967.
Walker, Jack L., and Aberbach, Joel D. "The Meanings of Black Power: A Comparison of White and Black Interpretations of a Political Slogan." *American Political Science Review* 64 (June, 1970): 367–388.
Zinn, Howard. *SNNC: The New Abolitionists.* Boston: Beacon Press, 1964.

Chapter 6

Baran, Paul A., and Sweezey, Paul M. *Monopoly Capital.* New York: Monthly Review Press, 1966.
Edelman, Murray, and Fleming, Roben W. *The Politics of Wage-Price Decisions.* Champaign-Urbana, Ill.: University of Illinois Press, 1968.
Friedman, Milton. *Capitalism and Freedom.* Chicago: University of Chicago Press, 1962.
Galbraith, John K. *American Capitalism — The Concept of Countervailing Power.* Boston: Houghton Mifflin, 1952.
————. *The Affluent Society.* New York: New American Library, 1958.
————. *The New Industrial State.* New York: New American Library, 1968.
Hamilton, Walton. *The Politics of Industry.* Ann Arbor, Mich.: University of Michigan Press, 1957.
Heller, Walter H., ed. *Perspectives on Economic Growth.* New York: John Wiley, 1968.
Mitchell, William C. "The American Polity and the Redistribution of Income." *American Behavioral Scientist* 13 (Nov./Dec. 1969): 201–214.
Musolf, Lloyd D. *Government and Economy.* Chicago: Scott, Foresman, 1965.
Potter, David M. *People of Plenty.* Chicago: Phoenix Books, 1954.
Reagan, Michael. *The Managed Economy.* New York: Oxford University Press, 1963.

Rostow, Walter W. *The Stages of Economic Growth.* Cambridge: Cambridge University Press, 1960.

Samuelson, Paul A. *Economics.* 7th ed. New York: McGraw-Hill, 1967.

Watson, Donald, ed. *Price Theory in Action.* Boston: Houghton Mifflin, 1965.

Wildavsky, Aaron. *The Politics of the Budgetary Process.* Boston: Little, Brown, 1964.

Zeitlin, Maurice, ed. *American Society, Inc.* Chicago: Markham Publishing Co., 1970.

Chapter 7

Abel, Elie. *The Missile Crisis.* New York: Bantam Books, 1966.

Baldwin, David A. *Economic Development and American Foreign Policy.* Chicago: University of Chicago Press, 1966.

Barnet, Richard J. *Intervention and Revolution: American Confrontation with Insurgent Movements Around the World.* New York: New American Library, 1968.

Draper, Theodore. *Abuse of Power.* New York: Viking Press, 1966.

Horowitz, Irving Louis. *Three Worlds of Development: The Theory and Practice of International Stratification.* New York: Oxford University Press, 1966.

Kahin, George, and Lewis, John L. *The United States in Vietnam.* New York: Delta Books, 1967.

Kissinger, Henry L. *The Necessity for Choice: Prospects of American Foreign Policy.* New York: Harper and Row, 1961.

Magdoff, Harry. *The Age of Imperialism: The Economics of United States Foreign Policy.* New York: The Monthly Review Press, 1969.

United States Senate, Committee on Foreign Relations. *Hearings on Vietnam.* New York: Vintage Books, 1966.

Ward, Barbara. *The Rich Nations and the Poor Nations.* New York: W. W. Norton, 1962.

Zeitlin, Maurice, and Scheer, Robert. *Cuba: Tragedy in our Hemisphere.* New York: Grove Press, 1963.

Chapter 8

Bachrach, Peter, and Baratz, Morton. *Power and Poverty.* New York: Oxford University Press, 1970.

Baltzell, E. Digby. *Philadelphia Gentlemen: The Making of a National Upper Class.* Glencoe, Ill.: The Free Press, 1958.

Bottomore, T. B. *Classes in Modern Society.* New York: Vintage Books, 1966.

Dahrendorf, Ralf. *Class and Class Conflict in Industrial Societies.* Stanford, Calif.: Stanford University Press, 1959.

DeGrazia, Sebastian. *The Political Community.* Chicago: University of Chicago Press, 1948.

Free, Lloyd A., and Cantril, Hadley. *The Political Beliefs of Americans.* New York: Simon and Schuster, 1968.

Kolko, Gabriel. *Wealth and Power in America.* New York: Praeger, 1962.

Kornhauser, William. *The Politics of Mass Society.* Glencoe, Ill.: The Free Press, 1959.

Lampman, Robert J. *The Share of Top Wealth-Holders in National Wealth.* Princeton, N. J.: Princeton University Press, 1962.

Lenski, Gerhard. *Power and Privilege.* New York: McGraw-Hill, 1966.

Lundberg, Ferdinand. *The Rich and the Super-Rich.* New York: Lyle Stuart, 1968.

Matthews, Donald. *The Social Background of Political Decision-Makers.* New York: Random House, 1955.

Mills, C. Wright. *The Power Elite.* New York: Oxford University Press, 1956.

Chapter 9

Andrews, William G. *Coordinate Magistrates: Constitutional Law by Congress and President.* New York: Van Nostrand, Reinhold, 1969.

Beard, Charles A. *An Economic Interpretation of the Constitution of the United States with New Introduction.* New York: Macmillan, 1954 (originally published in 1913).

Bickel, Alexander M. *The Least Dangerous Branch.* Indianapolis, Ind.: Bobbs-Merrill, 1962.

Danelski, David J. *A Supreme Court Justice is Appointed.* New York: Random House, 1964.

Krislov, Samuel. *The Supreme Court in the Political Process.* New York: Macmillan, 1965.

McCloskey, Robert G. *The American Supreme Court.* Chicago: University of Chicago Press, 1960.

Miller, Arthur S. *The Supreme Court and American Capitalism.* New York: The Free Press, 1968.

Mitau, G. Theodore. *Decade of Decision: The Supreme Court and the Constitutional Revolution, 1954–1964.* New York: Scribner's, 1967.

Pritchett, C. Herman. *The American Constitutional System.* 2nd ed. New York: McGraw-Hill, 1967.

Shapiro, Martin. *The Supreme Court and the Administrative Agencies.* New York: The Free Press, 1968.

Sutherland, Arthur E. *Constitutionalism in America.* New York: Blaisdell Publishing Co., 1965.

Chapter 10

Bailey, Stephen K. *The New Congress.* New York: St. Martin's Press, 1966.

Berman, Daniel M. *A Bill Becomes a Law: Congress Enacts Civil Rights Legislation.* 2nd ed. New York: Macmillan, 1966.

Bibby, John, and Davidson, Roger. *On Capitol Hill: Studies in the Legislative Process.* New York: Holt, Rinehart and Winston, 1967.

Burns, James MacGregor, *The Deadlock of Democracy.* Englewood Cliffs, N. J.: Prentice-Hall, 1963.

———. *Presidential Government.* Boston: Houghton Mifflin, 1966.

Cornwell, Elmer E. *Presidential Leadership of Public Opinion.* Bloomington: Indiana University Press, 1965.

Corwin, Edward S. *The President: Office and Powers.* 4th ed. New York: New York University Press, 1957.

Fenno, Richard F., Jr. *The Power of the Purse: Appropriations Politics in Congress.* Boston: Little, Brown, 1966.

———. *The President's Cabinet.* Cambridge, Mass.: Harvard University Press, 1959.

Froman, Lewis A., Jr. *Congressmen and the Constituencies.* Chicago: Rand McNally, 1963.

Herring, Pendleton. *Presidential Leadership.* New York: W. W. Norton, 1965.

Koenig, Louis W. *The Chief Executive.* New York: Harcourt, Brace and World, 1964.

———. *Congress and the President.* Chicago: Scott, Foresman, 1965.

McConnell, Grant. *The Modern Presidency.* New York: St. Martin's Press, 1967.

March, James G., and Simon, Herbert A. *Organizations.* New York: John Wiley, 1958.

Mason, Alpheus T. *Harlan Fiske Stone: Pillar of the Law.* New York: Viking Press, 1956.

Matthews, Donald R. *U.S. Senators and Their World.* Chapel Hill, N. C.: University of North Carolina Press, 1960.

Murphy, Walter F. *Elements of Judicial Strategy.* Chicago: University of Chicago Press, 1964.

Neustadt, Richard. *Presidential Power.* New York: John Wiley, 1960.

Polsby, Nelson W. *Congress and the Presidency.* Englewood Cliffs, N. J.: Prentice-Hall, 1964.

Polsby, Nelson W., and Wildavsky, Aaron. *Presidential Elections.* 2nd ed. New York: Scribner's, 1968.

Rossiter, Clinton. *The American Presidency.* New York: Harcourt, Brace, 1956.

Schmidhauser, John R. *The Supreme Court: Its Politics, Personalities, and Procedures.* New York: Holt, Rinehart and Winston, 1961.

Simon, Herbert A. *Administrative Behavior.* New York: Macmillan, 1957.

Sorensen, Theodore C. *Decision-making in the White House.* New York: Columbia University Press, 1963.

White, Theodore H. *The Making of the President — 1960.* New York: Atheneum, 1961.

Wildavsky, Aaron, ed. *The Presidency.* Boston: Little, Brown, 1969.

Chapter 11

Banfield, Edward C., and Wilson, James Q. *City Politics.* New York: Vintage Books, 1963.
Bauer, Raymond; de Sola Pool, Ithiel; and Dexter, Louis Anthony. *American Business and Public Policy.* New York: Atherton Press, 1963.
Cook, Fred J. *The Warfare State.* New York: Collier Books, 1962.
Elazar, Daniel. *American Federalism: A View From the States.* New York: Crowell, 1966.
Engler, Robert. *The Politics of Oil: A Study of Private Power and Political Directions.* Chicago: University of Chicago Press, 1967.
Galbraith, John K. *How to Control the Military.* Garden City, N. Y.: Doubleday, 1969.
Harris, Richard. *A Sacred Trust.* New York: New American Library, 1966.
Kariel, Henry S. *The Decline of American Pluralism.* Stanford, Calif.: Stanford University Press, 1961
Key, V. O. *Southern Politics.* New York: Vintage Books, 1949.
Lens, Sidney. *The Military-Industrial Complex.* Philadelphia: Pilgrim Press, 1970.
McConnell, Grant. *Private Power and American Democracy.* New York: Knopf, 1966.
Milbrath, Lester W. *The Washington Lobbyists.* Chicago: Rand McNally, 1963.
Nieburg, H. L. *In the Name of Science.* Chicago: Quadrangle Books, 1966.
Riker, William H. *Federalism: Origin, Operation, Significance.* Boston: Little, Brown, 1964.
Schattschneider, E. E. *The Semi-Sovereign People.* New York: Holt, Rinehart and Winston, 1960.
Silver, James W. *Mississippi — The Closed Society.* rev. ed. New York: Harcourt, Brace, 1966.
Sundquist, James. *Politics and Policy.* Washington, D. C.: The Brookings Institution, 1968.
―――. *Making Federalism Work.* Washington, D. C.: The Brookings Institution, 1969.
Truman, David. *The Governmental Process.* New York: Knopf, 1951.
Zeigler, Harmon. *Interest Groups in American Society.* Englewood Cliffs, N. J.: Prentice-Hall, 1964.

Chapter 12

Dahl, Robert A. *Who Governs?* New Haven, Conn.: Yale University Press, 1961.
David, Paul et al. *The Politics of National Party Conventions.* Washington, D. C.: The Brookings Institution, 1957.
Domhoff, G. William. *Who Rules America?* Englewood Cliffs, N. J.: Prentice-Hall, 1967.
Duverger, Maurice. *Political Parties.* New York: John Wiley, 1963.
Edelman, Murray. *The Symbolic Uses of Politics.* Champaign-Urbana, Ill.: University of Illinois Press, 1964.
Epstein, Leon. *Political Parties in Western Democracies.* New York: Praeger, 1967.
Hansen, Lee W., and Weisbrod, Burton A. *Benefits, Costs and Finance of Public Higher Education.* Chicago: Markham Publishing Co., 1969.
Hartnett, Rodney T. *College and University Trustees: Their Backgrounds, Roles, and Educational Attitudes.* Princeton, N. J.: Educational Testing Service, 1969.
Katz, Elihu, and Lazarsfeld, Paul F. *Personal Influence.* Glencoe, Ill.: Free Press, 1955.
Kelley, Stanley. *Professional Public Relations and Political Power.* Baltimore: John Hopkins, 1956.
Key, V. O. *Public Opinion and American Democracy.* New York: Knopf, 1961.
Klapp, Orrin. *Symbolic Leaders.* New York: Minerva Press, 1968.
Kolko, Gabriel. *Wealth and Power in the United States.* New York: Praeger, 1962.
Lang, Kurt, and Lang, Gladys. *Politics and Television.* Chicago: Quadrangle Books, 1968.
Lasswell, Harold. *Politics: Who Gets What, When, How.* Cleveland, Ohio: Meridian Books, 1958.
Lowi, Theodore. "American Business, Public Policy, Case-Studies, and Political Theory." *World Politics,* 16 (July, 1964): 677-715.
Lundberg, Ferdinand. *The Rich and the Super Rich.* New York: Bantam Books, 1968.
Matthews, Donald R. *Social Background of Political Decision Makers.* New York: Random House, 1954.
Michels, Robert. *Political Parties: A Sociological Study of the Oligarchical Tendencies of Modern Democracy.* Translated by Eden and Cedar Paul. New York: The Free Press, 1962.

Mills, C. Wright. *The Power Elite.* New York: Oxford University Press, 1959.

Polsby, Nelson W. *Community Power and Political Theory.* New Haven, Conn.: Yale University Press, 1963.

Prewitt, Kenneth. *The Recruitment of Political Leaders.* Indianapolis, Ind.: Bobbs-Merrill, 1970.

Rose, Arnold. *The Power Structure.* New York: Oxford University Press, 1967.

Schattschneider E. E. *The Semi-Sovereign People.* New York: Holt, Rinehart and Winston, 1960.

Ten Broek, Jacobus, ed. *The Law of the Poor.* San Francisco: Chandler Publishing Co., 1966.

Chapter 13

Berelson, Bernard, Lazarsfeld, Paul F.; and McPhee, William N. *Voting.* Chicago: University of Chicago Press, 1954.

Campbell, Angus; Converse, Philip E.; Miller, Warren E.; and Stokes, Donald E. *The American Voter.* New York: John Wiley, 1960.

————. *Elections and the Political Order.* New York: John Wiley, 1966.

Clausen, John A., ed. *Socialization and Society.* Boston: Little, Brown, 1968.

Converse, Philip. "The Nature of Belief Systems in Mass Publics." In *Ideology and Discontent,* ed., David Apter. London: Free Press of Glencoe, 1964.

Converse, Philip, and Dupeux, Georges. "The Politicization of the Electorate in France and the United States," *Public Opinion Quarterly* 26 (Spring, 1962): 1-24.

Converse, Philip et al. "Continuity and Change in American Politics: Parties and Issues in the 1968 Election." *American Political Science Review* 63 (December, 1969): 1083-1105.

Dawson, Richard, and Prewitt, Kenneth. *Political Socialization.* Boston: Little, Brown, 1969.

Downs, Anthony. *An Economic Theory of Democracy.* New York: Harper and Row, 1957.

Easton, David, and Dennis, Jack. *Children in the Political System.* New York: McGraw-Hill, 1969.

Easton, David, and Hess, Robert D. "Youth and the Political System." In *Culture and Social Character,* eds., S. M. Lipset and Leo Lowenthal. London: Free Press of Glencoe, 1962.

Flanigan, William H. *Political Behavior of the American Electorate.* Boston: Allyn and Bacon, 1968.

Greenstein, Fred I. *Children and Politics.* rev. ed. New Haven, Conn.: Yale University Press, 1968.

Hartz, Louis. *The Liberal Tradition in America.* New York: Harcourt, Brace and World, 1955.

Hess, Robert D., and Torney, Judith V. *The Development of Political Attitudes in Children.* Chicago: Aldine Publishing Co., 1967.

Keech, William. *The Impact of Negro Voting.* Chicago: Rand McNally, 1968.

Key, V. O. *The Responsible Electorate.* Cambridge, Mass.: Belknap Press of Harvard University Press, 1966.

Lane, Robert E. *Political Thinking and Consciousness.* Chicago: Markham Publishing Co. 1969.

Lane, Robert E., and Sears, David O. *Public Opinion.* Englewood Cliffs, N. J.: Prentice-Hall, 1964.

Langton, Kenneth. *Political Socialization.* New York: Oxford University Press, 1969.

Marvick, Dwayne. "The Political Socialization of American Negroes." *Annals* 361 (September, 1965): 112–127.

Skolnick, Jerome H. *The Politics of Protest.* New York: Ballantine Books, 1969.

Stokes, Donald S., and Miller, Warren M. "Constituency Influence in Congress." *American Political Science Review* 57 (March, 1963): 45–55.

U.S. Department of Health, Education, and Welfare. *Toward a Social Report.* Washington, D. C.: U.S. Government Printing Office, 1969.

Wolfenstein, Martha, and Kliman, Gilbert, eds. *Children and the Death of the President.* Garden City, N. Y.: Doubleday, 1965.

Chapter 14

Almond, Gabriel, and Verba, Sidney. *The Civic Culture.* Princeton, N. J.: Princeton University Press, 1963.

Campbell, Angus et al. *The American Voter.* New York: John Wiley, 1960.

————. *Elections and the Political Order.* New York: John Wiley, 1966.

Cummings, Milton C., Jr. *Congressmen and the Electorate.* New York: The Free Press, 1966.

Flanigan, William H. *Political Behavior of the American Electorate.* Boston: Allyn and Bacon, 1968.

Graham, Hugh Davis, and Gurr, Ted Robert. *Violence in America.* (Task Force Report to the President's Commission on Violence.) New York: Signet Books, 1969.

Greenstein, Fred I. *The American Party System and the American People.* Englewood Cliffs, N. J.: Prentice-Hall, 1963.

Jennings, M. Kent, and Zeigler, Harmon, eds. *The Electoral Process.* Englewood Cliffs, N. J.: Prentice-Hall, 1966.

Key, V. O. Jr. *The Responsible Electorate.* Cambridge, Mass.: Belknap Press of Harvard University Press, 1966.

Mahood, H. R. *Pressure Groups in American Politics.* New York: Scribner's, 1967.

Sorauf, Frank J. *Political Parties in the American System.* Boston: Little, Brown, 1964.

————. *Party Politics in America.* Boston: Little, Brown, 1968.

Stouffer, Samuel. *Communism, Conformity and Civil Liberties.* New York: John Wiley, 1966 (originally published in 1956).

Chapter 15

Altshuler, Alan A. *Community Control: The Black Demand for Participation in Large American Cities.* New York: Pegasus, 1970.

Clark, Kenneth, and Hopkins, Jeanette. *A Relevant War Against Poverty.* New York: Harper Torchbooks, 1970.

Gurr, Ted Robert. *Why Men Rebel.* Princeton, N. J.: Princeton University Press, 1970.

Kramer, Ralph M. *Participation of the Poor: Comparative Case Studies in the War on Poverty.* Englewood Cliffs, N. J.: Prentice-Hall, 1969.

Moynihan, Daniel P. *Maximum Feasible Misunderstanding.* New York: The Free Press, 1969.

National Advisory Commission On Civil Disorders. *Report.* New York: Bantam Books, 1968.

Roszak, Theodore. *The Making of a Counter Culture.* Garden City, N. Y.: Doubleday, 1969.

Rubinstein, Richard E. Rebels in Eden: *Mass Political Violence in the United States.* Boston: Little, Brown, 1970.

Schoenberger, Robert A. *The American Right Wing: Readings in Political Behavior.* New York: Holt, Rinehart and Winston, 1969.

Spiegel, Hans B. C., ed. *Citizen Participation in Urban Development.* Washington, D. C.: NTL Institute for Applied Behavioral Science, 1968.

Sundquist, James L. *Politics and Policy: The Eisenhower, Kennedy and Johnson Years.* Washington, D. C.: The Brookings Institution, 1968.

Chapter 16

Barber, Richard J. *The American Corporation: Its Power, Its Money, Its Politics.* New York: E. P. Dutton, 1970.

Dahl, Robert A. *A Preface to Democratic Theory.* Chicago: University of Chicago Press, 1956.

————. *Who Governs? Democracy and Power in an American City.* New Haven, Conn.: Yale University Press, 1961.

Domhoff, G. William. *Who Rules America?* Englewood Cliffs, N. J.: Prentice-Hall, 1967.

Domhoff, G. William, and Ballard, Hoyt B. *C. Wright Mills and the Power Elite.* Boston: Beacon Press, 1968.

Kariel, Henry S. *The Decline of American Pluralism.* Stanford, Calif.: Stanford University Press, 1961.

Kaufman, Arnold S. *The Radical Liberal: New Man in American Politics.* New York: Atherton Press, 1968.

Polsby, Nelson W. *Community Power and Political Theory*. New Haven, Conn.: Yale University Press, 1963.
Rose, Arnold M. *The Power Structure: Political Process in American Society*. New York: Oxford University Press, 1967.
Rowen, Hobart. *The Free Enterprisers: Kennedy, Johnson and the Business Establishment*. New York: G. P. Putnam, 1964.
Weinstein, James. *The Corporate Ideal in the Liberal State*. Boston: Beacon Press, 1968.
Zeitlin, Maurice, ed. *American Society, Inc.* Chicago: Markham Publishing Co., 1970.

Chapter 17

Berger, Peter, and Neuhaus, Richard J. *Movement and Revolution*. New York: Doubleday Anchor, 1970.
Cleaver, Eldridge. *On the Ideology of the Black Panther Party*. Mimeographed, circa 1969.
Cruse, Harold. *Rebellion or Revolution?* New York: William Morrow, 1968.
Harrington, Michael. *Toward A Democratic Left*. New York: Macmillan, 1968.
Hayden, Tom. *The Trial*. New York: Holt, Rinehart and Winston, 1970.
Hoffman, Abbie. *Revolution For the Hell of It*. New York: Dial Press, 1968.
Lasch, Christopher. *The Agony of the American Left*. New York: Vintage Books, 1969.
Lockwood, Lee. *Conversation with Eldridge Cleaver, Algiers*. New York: Delta Books, 1970.
Marcuse, Herbert. *Essay On Liberation*. Boston: Beacon Press, 1969.
Oppenheimer, Martin. *The Urban Guerrilla*. Chicago: Quadrangle Books, 1969.
Rubin, Jerry. *Do It! Scenarios of the Revolution*. New York: Simon and Schuster, 1970.
Scheer, Robert, ed. *Eldridge Cleaver: Post-Prison Writings*. New York: Random House, 1967.
Teodori, Massimo, ed. *The New Left: A Documentary History*. Indianapolis, Ind.: Bobbs-Merrill, 1969.

INDEX

Afro-Americans (*see* Racism)

Almond, Gabriel: and comparative political attitudes, 373–374; and functional political theory, 74

Appalachia: and Appalachian Regional Development Act, 136; **poverty, 136**

Armed Services: and Congress, 94, 95, 98; and decisionmaking process, 93, 94; and defense suppliers, 94–95, 101; and scientists, 94

Arms control, 104

Attitudes (*see* Political values)

Banking and Currency Committee, 219–220

Barnet, Richard: and ideological political analysis, 106; and institutional political analysis, 195–196

Beard, Charles, 257

Bentley, Arthur F., 67

Black liberation, 37–43: and Black Panther Party, 42; and Black power, 41; and cultural nationalism, 42; ideology of, 40–43; and New politics, 37–43; political values of, 41–43; and the Third World, 42; and Vietnam, 40

Black militancy (*see* Black liberation; Civil rights; Poverty; Racism)

Black Panther Party (*see also* Black liberation; Cleaver, Eldridge): prosecution of, 413

Black power (*see also* Black liberation): and civil rights, 130, 409–410

Buchwald, Art, 167–169

Business interests, U.S. (*see also* Elites): and communism, 233–235; and the decisionmaking process, 94–95; and defense suppliers, 94–95, 101; and economic growth, 149–50, 166; and education, 334–335; and fiscal policy, 158–159, 164, 165, 166; ideology of, 232; impact on economy of, 162–165, 166; and income, 139; and interest groups, 343; and mass media, 340; and military priorities, 87–90; and political power, 299–304; and poverty, 139–142, 144; priorities of, 233, 301; and profit motive, 150, 232; and regulatory movements, 301–304; and the Third World, 190, 195, 436; and U.S. Foreign Policy, 179, 195; and U.S. Government, 298–304, 308–313; values of, 232–233

Cantril, Hadley: and elite attitudes, 225; and political beliefs, 371

Capitalism (*see also* Class analysis; Economic growth and stability; Political power; Political priorities): and business interests, 232; and political power, 449–451; price and wage stability in, 151; and Students for a Democratic Society, 45; and the Third World, 177–178, 182–187, 190–191, 195, 436; and U.S. Foreign Policy, 99, 107, 177–178, 182–187, 190–191, **195**, 197–199, 436, 437, 438

Carmichael, Stokely, 41

China (*see* Communist nations)

City Governments: and elites, 320; and poor people, 319, 436; and private power, 317; and state governments, 316, 317, 320; and U.S. Government, 317, 319, 320

Civil Rights (*see also* Black liberation): and Black Militancy, 139–140; and poverty, 131–135; and racism, 129–130

Class analysis (*see also* Poverty): and U.S. Constitution, 258–259; and electoral process, 381, 382, 390; and ideology, 50; and materialism, 370; and political analysis, 107–108, 207, 218, 226–228; **and political participation, 395; and** political socialization, 361–362, 364, 375; and political values, 226, 227, 230; and racism, 410, 413, 421

Cleaver, Eldridge: and Black liberation, 42; and Black Panther Party, 42

Cold War (*see also* Military superiority, U.S.; National security, U.S.): and political socialization, 238; and the Third World, 172, 175–177, 182–187; and U.S. Foreign Policy, 99, 179–187

Communications (*see* Mass media)

Communism (*see also* American political values): and anti-communism in U.S., 99, 100, 105, 195, 233–235, 238, 372–3, 438, 439; and business interests, 233–235; and elites, 238; and political priorities of U.S., 438; and the Third World, 179, 182, 436, 437

Communist nations: and ideology in U.S., 99, 100, 105, 195, 415; and military superiority of U.S., 83, 84, 85, 103–104; and national security of U.S., 86, 91, 103–104; and the Third World, 179, 182, 195

Congress, 267–284 (*see also* Economic growth and stability; Poverty; Racism; U.S. Foreign Policy; U.S. Government): and Appropriations Committee, 94, 98; and Armed Services, 94, 95, 98; and civil rights, 408–409; and the decisionmaking process, 93–95, 98, 101, 267–284; **and elites, 327–328; and Executive** Branch, 293–294; and mass publics, 327–328; and political policy, 295, 296; and Supreme Court, 255

Congressional Committees (*see also* House of Representatives; Senate): chairmen of, 270–273

Constitution, U.S., 242–266: class analysis of, 258–259; and democracy, 259–260; elasticity of, 245–247; and Electoral College, 249–250; and extra-governmental forces, 250, 260–261; and federalism, 247, 248, 261; and Hamilton, Alexander, 252–253; ideology of, 260–266; interpretation of, 250; and Jefferson, Thomas, 252–253; and Judicial Review, 252, 253, 254; and limited government, 256–258; limits of, 243–245; and party politics, 247–250, 251; and political legitimacy, 242, 251, 260, 263; and political power, 243, 250; and promptly rights, 258–259; provisions of, 243–251; and public policy, 250; and separation of powers, 248–249, 261; and the Supreme Court, 250; and taxing powers, 247

Cultural nationalism: and Black liberation, 42; and the counter-culture, 45

Decisionmaking process, 93–99, 267–297: and Armed Services, 93, 94; and business interests, 94–95; and Congress, 93–95, 98, 101, 267–284; and the Executive Branch, 93, 101, 288–294; and military priorities, 93–99; and political analysis, 99–108; and political power, 101; and political priorities, 440; and political values, 99, 100, 105, 439; and the Supreme Court, 284–288

Democracy: and Constitution, U.S., 269–270; as evaluative standard, 62–65; and ideology, 32, 34, 62–65; and participation, 44; and pluralism, 35; as political value, 34, 62–65, 439

Democratic Party (see also Political parties): and mass electorate, 389; national convention of 1968, 416–417; and racial policies, 388; and Vietnam, 388

Dominican Republic, 181

Due process (see Legalism)

Easton, David: and political socialization, 366; and systems theory, 73

Economic growth and stability, 145–168 (see also Elites; Mass publics; National security; Poverty; Racism; The Third World; U.S. Foreign Policy): and business interests, 149–150, 162–166; definition of, 147; distribution of, 166; and economic policies, 147–148, 151–166, 436, 437; and employment, 147, 148, 151; and fiscal policy,156, 157–159; and macroeconomic policies, 161–166; and monetary policies, 156–157; and political change, 456–458; and political conflict, 148–149; 155, 166; and political priorities, 436, 437, 438, 439–441; and prices, 151–160; and technology, 146; and U.S. Government, 146, 150, 156; and Vietnam, 158, 437; and wages, 151–160

Economic Opportunity Act, 132–135: and civil rights, 132; provisions of, 133–134; evaluation of, 134

Education: and business interests, 334–335; effects of, 338; and electoral process, 381, 382, 390; and elite influence, 334–337; and ideology, 50, 339, 348; and income, 216–217; and mass publics, 334–339; and political socialization, 361–363; and political values, 228, 335; purpose of, 337–338, 349; and status, 216, 338; and Vietnam, 415

Eisenhower, Dwight David: and civil rights, 408; and Eisenhower Doctrine, 180; and electoral process, 381; and military-industrial complex, 90

Electoral College (see Constitution, U.S.)

Electoral process, 377–390 (see also Democratic Party; Republican Party): and Afro-Americans, 377, 378, 381, 382, 391; and candidates, 379, 381, 386; and class, 381, 382, 390; and education,381, 382, 390; and electoral changes, 387–391; history of, 377–378; and issues, 379, 380, 384, 386; and political legitimacy, 385; and political parties, 379–381, 384, 386; and popular impact, 376, 387; and racism, 377, 378, 381, 382, 391; and voters, 378

Elites: and business interests, 232, 299–304; characteristics of, 204, 207, 218–219, 225; cohesion of, 208, 236–239, 306–308; and communism, 328; and Congress, 266–284, 327–328; and Constitution, U.S., 260; definition of, 206–207; and education, 334–337; effects of, 323, 338, 401–426; and Executive Branch, 288–295, 325–327; and Founding Fathers, 204, 258, 263; and House of Representatives, 220, 269, 270, 271–273; and ideology, 48, 236; and interest groups, 343–344; and intra-elite relationships, 204, 218; and law, 331–333; and mass media, 339–343; and mass publics, 204, 210, 239–241, 333–348, 402–426; origins of, 207, 236; and political analysis, 52, 54; and political change, 464; and political institutions, 204, 207, 218–223, 230–235, 268, 301, 309, 325–331; and political parties, 344–348; and political power, 210, 268, 317, 333–348, 440; and political socialization, 235, 237–238; and political values, 208, 221, 222, 223–225, 229, 236, 328, 348, 371, 372–373; priorities of, 301; resources of, 206, 207, 211–218, 221, 236; responses of, 403–405, 406–407, 407–414; and Senate, 219–220, 273–284; and sources of power, 207, 210, 211–218, 333–348, 396, 440; and Supreme Court, 220, 284–288, 328–331; and the Third World, 176; and U.S. Government, 306–313

Employment (see Unemployment)

Establishment: nature of, 235–241; and political power, 447–449, 450–453

Executive Branch: and Congress, 293–294; and decisionmaking process, 93, 101, 288–294; and elections, 288–289; and elites, 288–295, 325–327; limits of, 288–292; and mass publics, 293, 325–327; and political priorities, 296; powers of, 293–295; and staff organization, 289–292; and Supreme Court, 255; and U.S. Foreign Policy, 294, 414

Fascism, 470–472

Federalism (see Constitution, U.S.; State governments)

Fiscal policy: and economic growth and stability, 156, 157–159; and U.S. Government, 156, 157–159, 164, 165

Founding Fathers (see also Beard, Charles; Hamilton, Alexander; Jefferson, Thomas): as elites, 204, 258, 263; and natural rights, 25–26; political values of, 204, 258, 263

Free, Lloyd: and elite attitudes, 225; and political beliefs, 371

Functional political theory (see also Almond, Gabriel): and political analysis, 73–76

Galbraith, John K., 105, 109

Goldwater, Barry, 387

Gross National Product (see Economic growth and stability)

Group political theory (see also Bentley, Arthur): and political analysis, 67–70

Halle, Louis, 193–195

Hamilton, Alexander (see also Founding Fathers): and Constitution, U.S., 252–253; and judicial review, 252; and mass publics, 253; political priorities of, 253; and Supreme Court, 251–256

Harrington, Michael; and poverty, 128

Hayden, Tom, and military-industrial complex, 107, 109

Health conditions and income, 355

House of Representatives (*see also* Congress; Congressional committees): committees of, 268–270, 271; and elites, 220, 269, 270, 271–273; and ideology, 269; members of, 268; policies of, 273; political values of, 269; rules of, 269–270

Ideological political analysis (*see* Barnet, Richard)
Ideology (*see also* National Security; Poverty; Racism; The Third World): and Black liberation, 40–43; and business, 232; and class analysis, 50; and communist nations, 99, 100, 105, 195, 415; comparative views, 374–375; and Constitution, U.S., 260–266; culture-bound, 16–17; and democracy, 32, 34, 62–65; and dominant American view, 30–37, 48; and education, 50, 339, 348; and electoral process, 380; and elites, 48, 236; and evidence, 17; functions of, 31–35; and House of Representatives, 269; and institutions, 32–33, 374; and mass media, 31, 348; and operationalism, 371; and political analysis, 99–108; and political parties, 348; and political socialization, 30, 348; and political values, 30–45; and private enterprise, 183, 185–187; and Students for a Democratic Society, 43–45; and U.S. Foreign Policy, 99, 106–107, 195–197
Imperialism (*see also* The Third World): and Students for a Democratic Society, 45; and U.S. Foreign Policy, 198–199
Income: and business interests, 139; and education, 216–217; and health, 355; and political parties, 348; and political resources, 211; and political values, 226, 227, 228; and poverty, 119–120; and racism, 123, 353, 436; and status, 217, 356; and U.S. Government, 139; and women, 353
Individualism, 23–24 (*see also* Ideology): and business interests, 232; and competition, 23; and laissez faire, 23, 33; and limited government, 27; and natural rights, 24; as political value, 23, 201
Inflation (*see also* Buchwald, Art): and poverty, 135; and prices, 152; and Vietnam, 135
Institutional political analysis (*see* Barnet, Richard)
Institutions, U.S. (*see also* Congress; Elites; Executive Branch; House of Representatives; Mass publics; Political legitimacy; Senate; Supreme Court; U.S. Government): and ideology, 32–33, 34; and political analysis, 61, 105–107; and political priorities, 439–441; and political values, 33, 34, 439–441
Interest groups: and business interests, 343; and elites, 343–344; and mass publics, 343–344, 391–394
Integration (*see* Racism)

Jefferson, Thomas (*see* Founding Fathers): and Constitution, U.S., 252–3; and judicial review, 252; and mass publics, 253; and political priorities of, 253; political values of, 253; and Supreme Court, 252
Johnson, Lyndon (*see also* Dominican Republic): anti-trust policies of, 303; and defense contracts, 98; and electoral process, 386, 416; and poverty, 11, 132, 140; and Vietnam, 388, 405

Judicial review: and Hamilton, Alexander, 252; and Jefferson, Thomas, 252; and Marshall, John, 254
Judiciary Committee and lawyers, 219–220

Kennedy, John: and civil rights, 408; and electoral process, 381; and poverty, 121
Keynes, John Maynard, and macroeconomic theory, 146, 151
King, Martin Luther, Jr.: and Black liberation, 41; and civil rights, 129, 407, 412
Kolko, Gabriel: and elite characteristics, 221; and wealth distribution, 214
Korea and U. S. Foreign Policy, 180

Labor movement: history of, 114–115; and New Deal, 116–117, 119; and poverty, 114; and racism, 114; and U.S. Government, 114
Laissez faire: and economic power, 33; and individualism, 23, 33; and limited government, 28; and the Third World, 170
Law: and courts, 332; and elites, 332; managerial use of, 331–333; and mass publics, 332; and value preferences of, 331, 332, 333
Lebanon and U.S. Foreign Policy, 180
Legalism (*see also* Law): and political values, 254, 256, 264, 439
Lenski, Gerhard, and distribution of wealth, 213
Lewis, Oscar, and poverty, 126
Limited Government: and Constitution, U.S., 256–258; and individualism, 27; and laissez faire, 28; and majority rule, 27; and natural rights, 27; as political value, 27–28

McCarthy, Eugene, and electoral process, 389, 416
Macroeconomic policies (*see also* Keynes, John Maynard): impact of, 161–166
Madison, James, and Constitution, U.S., 262
Magdoff, Harry, and U.S. Foreign Policy, 197
Marshall, John: decisions of, 285; and judicial review, 254; and Supreme Court, 253
Mass media: and business interests, 340; and elite influence, 339–343; and ideology, 31, 348; and mass publics, 339–343; and political change, 463
Mass publics (*see also* Congress; Executive Branch; National security; Poverty; Racism): aspirations of, 206, 323, 367–368, 422; behavior of, 206, 209, 376–400, 424; composition of, 353; dissatisfactions of, 358, 367–368, 421, 422–424; and education, 334–339; and electoral process, 376–387; and elites, 204, 210, 239–241, 321, 325–333, 333–348, 402–426; health conditions of, 354–355; income of, 353; and institutional elites, 325–333; and interest groups, 343–344, 391–394; intra-mass relationships, 396–400; and law, 332; and mass media, 339–343; and political analysis, 54–55, 99–108; and political parties, 344–348; and political power, 317, 440; and political values, 206, 209, 363–364, 369, 371, 372–373, 374–375; and private elites, 333–348; resources of, 425; and social mobility, 356–357; social setting of, 353–358; and U.S. Foreign Policy, 99; and wage and price controls, 156
Materialism: and business interests, 232; and class analysis, 370; and Constitution, U.S., 258–259; as political value, 28–29, 201, 369–370, 439

Military expenditures, U.S., 81–110 (*see also* Economic growth and stability; Vietnam): and anti-communist ideology, 99, 100; consequences of, 436; and decisionmaking process, 93–99; and domestic needs, 436; and military priorities, 89; and military superiority, 83; and political priorities, 438; public challenge of, 86, 103, 421; and unemployment, 163

Military-industrial complex, 81–110: and business interests, 233; and Eisenhower, Dwight David, 90; and Galbraith, John K., 105, 109; and Hayden, Tom, 107, 109; and military priorities, 90, 92; and Nixon, Richard, 102, 106; and Pilisuk, Mark, 107, 109; and Proxmire, William, 106

Military priorities, U.S., 81–110: and business interests, 87–88, 90; consequences of, 87–92; and decisionmaking process, 93–99; and domestic needs, 91, 103; and federal budget, 89; and geographic mobility, 88; and military-industrial complex, 90, 92; and national security, 92; and nuclear weapons systems, 90, 103; and political analysis, 99–108; and science, 88; and space, 90; and Vietnam, 90, 103

Military superiority, U.S., 81–110: assumptions of, 82; and communist nations, 83, 84, 86; and decisionmaking process, 93–99; and military expenditures, 83; and national security, 82–87; and nuclear weapons systems, 83, 84, 100, 103; and political analysis, 99–108; and Vietnam, 83, 103

Monetary policies (*see* Economic growth and stability; U.S. Government)

National Aeronautics and Space Administration: and military priorities, 90; and political priorities, 438; and space expenditures, 421, 436

National security, 81–110 (*see also* Communist nations; Decisionmaking process; Military superiority): definition of, 92; and the Third World, 179, 181, 182

Natural rights: and Founding Fathers, 25–26; and human rights, 24–27; and individualism, 24; and limited government, 27; as political value, 24, 201; and property rights, 24–27, 438

Negative income tax (*see* Poverty)

New Deal: and labor movement, 116–117, 119; and poverty, 115–119, 126, 140, 143

New politics: and Black liberation, 37–43; and class analysis, 40, 206; and contextual approach to politics, 39; and elites, 223, 237; impact of, 45–47; political values of, 37–40, 48; tactics of, 45–47

Nixon, Richard: anti-trust priorities, 303; and Congress, 293; and desegregation, 413; and the Electoral College, 289; and military-industrial complex, 102, 106; and poverty, 132, 134, 138, 140; and racism, 406; and southerners, 138; and state governments, 319; and the Third World, 192

Nonelites (*see* Mass publics)

Nonviolence: and Black Liberation, 41; and civil rights, 129, 130; and conflict, 265; and new politics, 45–47; and political change, 465; and poverty, 144

Nuclear weapons (*see also* Military superiority): and communist nations, 85, 91, 100, 103–104

Operationalism and ideological spectrum, 371

Participatory democracy and Students for a Democratic Society, 44

Pilisuk, Mark, and military-industrial complex, 107, 109

Pluralism: and Constitution, U.S., 262–263, 264; and democracy, 35; and elites, 222, 237; evaluation of, 444–447; and ideology, 35, 48, 205–206; and political power, 299, 441–444

Political analysis, 52–76, 99–108 (*see also* Economic growth and stability; National security; Racism; The Third World): approaches to, 62–76; and class analysis, 207, 218, 226–228; and decisionmaking process, 99–108; and economic imperatives, 107–108; and elites, 52, 54; and functional theory, 73–76; and group theory, 62–70; and ideology, 99–108; implications of, 55–58; and institutions, 61, 105–107; and mass publics, 54–55, 99–108; and men, 103, 107; and military superiority, 99–108; and political change, 53; and political policies, 52; and political power, 52, 54; and political resources, 54; and political values, 107–108; and poverty program, 139–144; problems of, 58–62, and systems theory, 70–72; and U.S. Foreign Policy, 192–199

Political change, 53–54, 455–476: degree of, 53; direction of, 53, 465–472, 475–476; and economic growth and stability, 456–458; fundamental, 455, 456, 470–472; marginal, 455, 466, 467, 469; origins of, 53; and political analysis, 53, 54; and political impact, 461–465, 473–475; and political power, 431; and political values, 54, 462; and poverty, 115, 139; preconditions of, 455–461, 472–473; types of, 53

Political institutions (*see* Institutions, U.S.)

Political legitimacy, 13, 22 (*see also* Institutions): and commerce clause, 246; and conflict, 297; and Constitution, U.S., 242, 251, 260, 263; and electoral process, 385; and elites, 207; and political power, 13, 433; and political socialization, 308; and state government, 315; and Supreme Court, 296; and U.S. Foreign Policy, 197

Political parties, 344–348, 377–391 (*see also* Democratic Party; Republican Party): composition of, 390; and Constitution, U.S., 247–250, 251; and electoral process, 379–381, 384, 386; and elite influence, 344–348; and income, 348; and localism, 346; and mass publics, 344–348; and national conventions, 347; and party discipline, 345–346; and political socialization, 360; and political values, 345; and racism, 348, 390; as reference group, 380; and third parties, 383–4

Political policies (*see also* Economic growth and stability; National security; Poverty; Racism; The Third World; U.S. Foreign Policy): and decisionmaking process, 93–99; and political analysis, 52, 99–108; and political values, 439

Political power, 431–453 (*see also* Economic growth and stability; National Security; Poverty; Racism; U.S. Foreign Policy): concentration of, 298; concept of, 12; consequences of, 12, 13; and Constitution, U.S., 243, 250; and decisionmaking process 101; definition of, 299, 432; dilemmas of, 10; and economic power centers, 299–304; and elites, 210, 268, 317, 333–348, 440; forms of, 433; and imagery, 304–306; and lobbying, 306, 307; and mass publics, 317, 440; and military security, 92; and political analysis, 52, 54, 99–108; and political change, 431; and political legitimacy, 13, 433; and political priorities, 439–441; and political resources, 7, 12, 299, 432; and poverty, 143; and private power centers, 299–306, 320, 434; purpose of, 48–49; theories of, 441–453; U.S. Government, 10, 11, 12, 325–333, 433, 434

Political priorities, 431–440 (*see also* Economic growth and stability; Military superiority; Racism): and decisionmaking process, 440; and elites, 268, 301; nature of, 438–441; and political analysis, 60, 99–108; and poverty, 139, 140–141, 438, 439; and the Third World, 192, 195, 436, 437, 438

Political resources (*see also* Political policies): and elites, 206, 207, 211–218, 221, 236; and income, 211; and mass publics, 425; and political analysis, 54; and political power, 7, 12, 299, 432; and poverty, 143; and status, 215–218; and wealth, 212–215

Political socialization: and attitude change, 360, 365–366; and class, 361–362, 364, 375; and cold war, 238; definition of, 359; and education, 361–363; and elites, 235, 237–238; and ideology, 30, 348; and legitimacy, 308; and political values, 363–364; and racism, 359, 361, 364; and senators, 279; theory of, 364; and Vietnam, 360, 366

Political system (*see* Institutions, U.S.; U.S. Government)

Political values: of Americans, 23–49; and anticommunism, 99, 100, 105, 195, 223–225, 238, 372–373, 438, 439; and Black liberation, 41–43; and class, 226, 227, 230; and decisionmaking process, 99, 100, 105, 439; definition of, 224; and democracy, 34, 62, 65, 439; and education, 228, 335; and elites, 208, 221, 222, 223–225, 229, 236, 328, 348, 371, 372–373; and founding fathers, 204, 258, 263; hierarchy of, 439; and House of Representatives, 269; and income, 226, 227, 228; and ideology, 30–45; and individualism, 23–24, 201; and institutions, 33, 34, 439–441; and law, 331, 332, 333; and legalism, 254, 256, 264, 439; and limited government, 27–28; and mass publics, 206, 209, 363–364, 369, 371, 372–373, 374–375; and materialism, 28–29, 201, 369–370, 439; and natural rights, 24–27, 201; and new politics, 37–40; and political change, 54, 458–460, 462; and political parties, 345; and political policies, 439; and political socialization, 363–364; and poverty, 128; and private enterprise, 183, 185–187, 188, 195; problems of, 223–225; and racism, 29–30, 38, 39, 112, 227, 230, 232, 439; and Students for a Democratic Society, 43–45;

and Vietnam, 38, 39; and U.S. Foreign Policy, 107–108

Politics, 11–20: analytical perspective of, 11–14; and business interests, 19; definition of, 10–11, 55–58; dilemmas of, 9; and evidence, 17–18; and ideology, 16; importance of, 8; and institutions, 20; and political change, 15; and political power, 7; and political priorities, 15; and political values, 20; and U.S. Government, 10, 11, 12, 19

Poverty, 111–144: and age, 121, 140; and Appalachia, 136; and Black militancy, 139–140; and business interests, 139, 140–141, 142, 144; causes of, 126–127; and city government, 319, 436; and civil rights, 131–135; and class, 115, 142; and Congress, 140; and contemporary policies, 127–144, 436; definition of, 119–120; and Economic Opportunity Act, 132–135; and fiscal policy, 158; history of, 112–115; and income, 119–120; and inflation, 135; and labor, 114; and negative income tax, 137; and New Deal, 115–119, 126, 140, 143; and political power, 143; and political priorities, 139, 140–141, 438, 439; and racism, 111–113, 120–126; scope of, 119; and southerners, 138; and subemployment, 123; and U.S. Government, 112, 139, 144; and Vietnam, 126, 135, 137, 140

Presidency (*see* Executive Branch)

Prices: and economic growth and stability, 151–160; and fiscal policy, 158, 164, 165; and inflation, 152; and wages, 151–160

Private economy (*see* Business interests, U.S.)

Property rights (*see* Materialism; Natural rights)

Proxmire, William: and defense contracts, 95, 102; and military-industrial complex, 106

Racism, 111–144: and Afro-Americans, 30; and age, 121; and Black expectations, 142; and Black militancy, 134–40; and business interests, 232; and civil rights, 129–130; and class, 142, 410, 413, 421; and contemporary policies, 436; and Economic Opportunity Act, 132–135; and education, 123; and electoral process, 377, 378, 381, 382, 391; and elite responses to, 407–414; and health conditions, 355; and income, 123, 353, 436; and integration, 137, 436; and labor, 114; and living conditions, 355; and political parties, 348, 390; and political priorities, 438, 439; and political socialization, 359, 361, 364; and political values, 29–30, 38, 39, 112, 227, 230, 232, 439; and poverty, 111–113, 120–126; and slavery, 112–113; and social mobility, 356, 358; and status, 218, 356, 358; and unemployment, 122–123, 354, 436; and U.S. Government, 112, 128

Republican Party (*see also* Political parties): and class, 389; and electorate, 389; and racial matters, 388; and southerners, 387; and Vietnam, 388

Revolution and political change, 470–472

Schools (*see* Education)

Science: and armed services, 94; and military priorities, 88, 436

Senate (*see also* Congress; Congressional committees): committees of, 278; and elites,

219–220, 279; policies of, 280, 284; rules of, 278, 280

Separation of powers (*see* Constitution, U.S.)

Slavery: and poverty, 112; and racism, 112; and U.S. Government, 112

Soviet Union (*see* Communist nations)

Space (*see* National Aeronautics and Space Administration)

State Governments: and city governments, 316, 317, 320; and elites, 320; and political legitimacy, 315; and poverty, 436; and private power centers, 313–320

Status: and education, 216, 338; and income, 217, 356; and occupation, 215–216; and political resources, 215–218; and racism, 218, 356, 358; and U.S. Government, 316–317

Stouffer, Samuel, and ideology, 233

Students (*see also* Education): and class, 421; and elite relationships, 414–421; and mass publics, 418, 420

Students for a Democratic Society, political values of, 43–45

Supreme Court: Chief Justice of, 285, 286; and Congress, 255; and Constitution, U.S., 250; and decisionmaking process, 284–288; and elites, 220, 288, 328–331; and Executive Branch, 255; and Hamilton, Alexander, 251–256; and Jefferson, Thomas, 252; and law, 331–333; and Marshall, John, 253; and mass publics, 328–331; and political legitimacy, 296; and political policy, 255, 284, 295; and political values, 328; rules of, 285–286; traditions of, 285

Systems political theory and political analysis, 70–72

Technology: and economic growth and stability, 146; and national security, 87

Third World, 165–199: and Black liberation, 42; and business interests, U.S., 190, 195, 436; and capitalism, 177–178, 182–187, 190–191, 195, 436; and cold war, 172, 175–176, 177, 182–187; and communism, 179, 182, 436, 437; definition of, 170; and economic development of, 171–174, 178, 182, 188–190; and imperialism, 187–191; and national security, U.S., 86, 179, 181, 182; and political priorities, U.S., 192, 195, 436, 437, 438; problems of, 170–176; raw materials of, 171–172, 178, 188; and Students for a Democratic Society, 44; and U.S. Foreign Policy, 176–187, 190, 191, 437; and Vietnam, 178

Unemployment: and economic growth and stability, 147, 148, 151; and fiscal policy, 163;

and military expenditures, 163; and poverty, 123; and racism, 122–123, 354, 356; and Vietnam, 126, 135

U.S. Foreign Policy, 165–199: and business interests, U.S., 179, 195; and cold war, 99, 179–187; and communism, 83, 84, 85, 86, 91, 99, 179, 182, 438, 439; and domestic needs, 99; and Dominican Republic, 181; and Executive Branch, 294, 414; and ideology, 99, 106–107, 195–197; and International Trade Market, 190; and Korea, 180; and Lebanon, 180; and mass publics, 99; and political analysis, 192–199; and political values, 107, 108; and the Third World, 176–187, 187–191, 437; and Vietnam, 178, 181, 185; and World Bank, 184, 186

U.S. Government (*see also* Institutions, U.S.; National security; U.S. Foreign Policy): and business interests, 298–304, 308–313; and city government, 317, 319, 320; and economic growth and stability, 146, 150, 166; and fiscal policy, 156, 157–159, 164, 165; and income, 139; and labor, 114; and mass public-elite linkage, 325–331; and monetary policy, 156–157, 164, 165; and political power, 10, 11, 12, 325–333, 433, 434; and political power centers, 305, 306–313, 320; and poverty, 112, 139, 144; and price stability policy, 151–160; and racism, 112, 128; and slavery, 112; and state government, 316–317; and wage stability policy, 151–160

University (*see* Education; Students)

Vietnam: and anti-communism, 415; and Black liberation, 40; and economic growth and stability, 158, 437; and education, 415; and inflation, 135; and military-industrial complex, 105; and military priorities, U.S. 90, 103; and military superiority, U.S., 83, 103; and political change, 461; and political socialization, 360, 366; and political values, 38, 39; and poverty, 126, 135, 137, 140; and Students for a Democratic Society, 43, 44; and the Third World, 178; and unemployment, 126, 135; and U.S. Foreign Policy, 178, 181, 185

Wages and economic growth and stability, 151–160

Wallace, George, and electoral changes, 388

Wealth (*see* political resources)

Women: and income, 353; and political parties, 348, 390

World Bank and U.S. Foreign Policy, 184, 186

Work ethic (*see* Materialism; Political values)